EIGHTH EDITION

FOREIGN POLICY
IN
WORLD POLITICS

Roy C. Macridis, Editor
Brandeis University

Jianwei Wang
Sept. 1992
88th. APSA. Chicago.

PRENTICE HALL, Englewood Cliffs, New Jersey 07632

Library of Congress Cataloging-in-Publication Data

Foreign policy in world politics / Roy C. Macridis, editor. — 8th ed.
    p. cm.
    Includes bibliographical references (p.   ) and index.
    ISBN 0-13-335084-3
    1. International relations.   I. Macridis, Roy C.
JX1391.F65   1992
327–dc20   91-23569

Acquisitions Editor: *Karen Horton*
Editorial/production supervision and interior design: *Joanne Riker*
Cover design: *Patricia Kelly*
Prepress buyer: *Kelly Behr*
Manufacturing buyer: *Mary Ann Gloriande*

Printed in the United States of America

10 9 8 7 6 5 4 3 2

ISBN   0-13-335084-3

Prentice-Hall International (UK) Limited, *London*
Prentice-Hall of Australia Pty. Limited, *Sydney*
Prentice-Hall Canada Inc., *Toronto*
Prentice-Hall Hispanoamericana, S.A., *Mexico*
Prentice-Hall of India Private Limited, *New Delhi*
Prentice-Hall of Japan, Inc., *Tokyo*
Simon & Schuster Asia Pte. Ltd., *Singapore*
Editora Prentice-Hall do Brasil, Ltda., *Rio de Janeiro*

CONTENTS

CONTRIBUTING AUTHORS   ix

PREFACE   xi

1 INTRODUCTORY REMARKS   1
Roy C. Macridis

PATTERNS OF FOREIGN POLICY   2
EVALUATION OF FOREIGN POLICY   3

2 BRITISH FOREIGN POLICY: TRADITION AND CHANGE   7
Brian P. White

GLOBAL INFLUENCE AND THE LIMITS OF POWER: 1945–60   11
    Globalism 11   Atlanticism 13   Europeanism 14
    The Suez Crisis as a Turning Point? 15
TOWARD EUROPE? 1960–80   16
    Globalism 16   Atlanticism 18   Europeanism 20
THE THATCHER PERIOD: 1980–90   21
    Thatcher and Atlanticism 22   Thatcher and Globalism 23
    Thatcher and Europeanism 26
BRITISH FOREIGN POLICY IN THE 1990s   28
FOREIGN POLICY LANDMARKS   29

iii

3 FRENCH FOREIGN POLICY: THE QUEST FOR RANK 32

Roy C. Macridis

BACKGROUND FACTORS 34
    Persistent Patterns 35
THE SUBSTANCE OF FOREIGN POLICY TRENDS AND PROBLEMS 35
    France and the Empire 38
THE LEGACY OF THE FOURTH REPUBLIC (1946–1958) 39
THE FIFTH REPUBLIC AND GENERAL DE GAULLE—
    WORLDWIDE ASPIRATIONS (1958–1969) 40
    The Basic Assumptions 40
THE GAULLIST YEARS 43
    End of Empire 43
THE COMMON MARKET 44
    The Soviets: The "Opening to the East" 45
BETWEEN DE GAULLE AND MITTERRAND (1969–81) 46
A SOCIALIST PRESIDENT (1981–) FRANÇOIS MITTERRAND 51
    Continuity in Style and Aspirations 52
FRANCO-SOVIET RELATIONS 55
MITTERRAND'S SECOND TERM (1988–) 55
THE EUROPEAN COMMUNITY: FGR AND "GERMANY" 59
PROSPECTS 61
FOREIGN POLICY LANDMARKS 64

4 THE FOREIGN POLICY OF THE FEDERAL REPUBLIC OF GERMANY: TRADITION AND CHANGE 68

Josef Joffe

THE FEDERAL REPUBLIC AS A SPECIAL CASE 68
THE POLITICAL STYLE: SOVEREIGNTY THROUGH INTEGRATION 73
REUNIFICATION VERSUS REALPOLITIK 75
DIPLOMACY AND DOMESTIC POLITICS 79
THE POLITICS OF DEPENDENCE 81
THE NEW OSTPOLITIK 84
    The Continuities of West German Foreign Policy 87
OUT FROM DEPENDENCE: THE HELMUT SCHMIDT ERA 88
    West Germany Ascendant 88
    Back to Basics: Afghanistan, the Euromissile Crisis, and Cold War II 90
CLOSING THE CIRCLE: FROM COLD WAR II TO REUNIFICATION 94
    A Balance Restored: The Helmut Kohl Era 94
    Mortal Rivals, Tacit Allies 97   The Collapse of the Postwar Order 98
    Beyond Bipolarity 99
FOREIGN POLICY LANDMARKS 103

5 THE FOREIGN POLICY OF THE EUROPEAN COMMUNITY: DREAM OR REALITY?   108
Christopher Hill

INSTITUTIONS AND POLICY MAKING   113
POLITICAL COOPERATION   113
THE COMMISSION   118
THE INSTRUMENTS OF EUROPEAN FOREIGN POLICY   122
   Diplomacy 122
ECONOMIC INDUCEMENTS AND PRESSURES   128
   Positive Assistance 128   The United States   130
   The Supplicants and Enlargement 131   The Delinquents and Sanctions 133
THE MISSING LINK: SECURITY AND DEFENCE   136
FOREIGN POLICY LANDMARKS   140

6 SOVIET FOREIGN POLICY   143
Vernon V. Aspaturian

THE CHANGING ROLE AND STATUS OF THE SOVIET UNION
   IN THE INTERNATIONAL SYSTEM   143
THE COLLAPSE OF THE BIPOLAR SYSTEM
   AND THE QUEST FOR A "NEW WORLD ORDER"   145
RECASTING SOVIET FOREIGN POLICY:
   THE BREZHNEV LEGACY AND THE GORBACHEV VISION   147
   Reconceptualizing Soviet Ideology and Reformulating Soviet Strategy 149
   The Changing Soviet Image of the World in the New Political Thinking 153
   Changing the Soviet Foreign Policy Agenda 157
NEW CONSTRAINTS ON SOVIET FOREIGN POLICY:
   DOMESTIC AND FOREIGN   159
   The Impact of Domestic Politics and Policies on Soviet Foreign Policy 159
   The Erosion of Central Power 163   The Emergence of Republic Foreign
   Policies 165   Soviet-American Relations 168   Arms Control and
   Reduction Issues 169   Regional Conflicts and the Third World 170
   Human Rights 172   The Soviet Union and Europe 172
   The Soviet Union and East Asia 175
FOREIGN POLICY LANDMARKS   181
EDITOR'S NOTE   185

7 THE FOREIGN POLICY OF MODERN JAPAN   186

Robert A. Scalapino

THE BACKGROUND   187
THE FORMULATION OF FOREIGN POLICY IN PREWAR JAPAN   189
JAPAN SINCE 1945: OCCUPATION AND ITS AFTERMATH   193
    The Revolutionary Era 194   Stabilization 196   The Era of Alliance 198
THE FORMULATION OF FOREIGN POLICY IN POSTWAR JAPAN   199
THE MAJOR ISSUES IN JAPANESE FOREIGN POLICY   202
THE POLITICAL DIMENSIONS OF JAPANESE FOREIGN POLICY   209
CULTURE AND FOREIGN POLICY   213
SECURITY ISSUES IN JAPANESE FOREIGN POLICY   214
IN CONCLUSION   217
FOREIGN POLICY LANDMARKS   218

8 FOREIGN POLICY OF CHINA   222

Allen S. Whiting

CONCEPTUAL FRAMEWORK   222
    Physical Factors–Real and Perceived 225   Historical Factors 230
THE PROCESS OF POLICY: THE COMMUNIST COMPONENT   233
    Ideological Content: Marxism-Leninism-Mao Zedong Thought 233
    Institutional Structure of Decision Making: The Party 240
    Institutional Structure: The Government 245
THE SUBSTANCE OF POLICY   247
    Ends and Means 247
FUTURE PROSPECTS   257
CHINESE NAME SPELLINGS   265
FOREIGN POLICY LANDMARKS   266

9 THE FOREIGN POLICY OF LATIN AMERICA   268

Riordan Roett

INTRODUCTION   268
GEOGRAPHY AND HISTORY   269
THE INDEPENDENCE PERIOD   270
LATIN AMERICA FROM MID-NINETEENTH CENTURY
    TO THE TWENTIETH CENTURY   271
THE UNITED STATES INTERVENES   271
LATIN AMERICA AND WORLD WAR II   274
FOREIGN POLICY SINCE 1959:
    UNCERTAINTY AND A SEARCH FOR NEW DIRECTIONS   279

A GROWING AUTONOMY 280
A SENSE OF DRIFT 283
AUTHORITARIAN REGIMES AND FOREIGN POLICY 284
NEW ECONOMIC REALITIES 286
THE BIG THREE OF LATIN DEBT (1989) 290
U.S. SECURITY CONCERNS 290
REGIONAL DISPUTES 293
PROBLEMS FOR THE 1990s: DRUGS AND IMMIGRATION 295
CONCLUSION 297
FOREIGN POLICY LANDMARKS 299

**10 SCANDINAVIA SECURITY, PROSPERITY,
AND SOLIDARITY AMIDST CHANGE 303**
Bengt Sundelius with Don Odom

FROM CONFLICT TO COMMUNITY 304
SECURING FIVE NATION-STATES 306

*Norway 306 Denmark 307 Iceland 308
Finland 309 Swede 312*

NEIGHBORING NUCLEAR WEAPONS
AND SOVIET INTERNAL TURBULENCE 314
SAFEGUARDING PROSPERITY 317

*Global Reach 318 Atlantic Partnership 318
Nordic Community 319 The European Base 320*

PROMOTING GLOBAL WELFARE 323
TRANSPOSING THE DOMESTIC EXPERIENCE 325
FOREIGN POLICY LANDMARKS 326

11 THE FOREIGN POLICY OF AFRICA 330
Stephen Wright

INTRODUCTION 330
COLONIALISM AND INDEPENDENCE 332
THE RESOURCES OF AFRICA 334
FOREIGN POLICY DECISION MAKING 336
FOREIGN POLICY OBJECTIVES 338
FOREIGN POLICY ARENAS 339

*Regionalism 339 North Africa 340 West Africa 342
Eastern Africa 343 Southern Africa 345*

CONTINENTALISM 346
THE FUTURE 353
FOREIGN POLICY LANDMARKS 354

12 DIMENSIONS OF THE MIDDLE EAST PROBLEM: BEFORE AND AFTER THE GULF WAR   357
Nadav Safran

INTRODUCTION 357
PART ONE: BEFORE THE GULF WAR   358
THE DOMESTIC DIMENSION 358
THE REGIONAL DIMENSION 362
THE ARAB-ISRAELI DIMENSION 366
THE GREAT POWERS DIMENSION 374
THE CONFIGURATION IN THE FALL OF 1987 384
    Eruption and Subsidence in the Arab-Israeli Arena 384
    Eruption in the Gulf Arena 393
**PART TWO: THE MIDDLE EAST PROBLEM
    AND THE GULF WAR (1987–1991): RECONFIGURATION
    OR TRANSFIGURATION?   398**
RECENT DEVELOPMENTS 398
    The Postwar Juncture 399   Gulf Security 399
FOREIGN POLICY LANDMARKS 402

13 THE UNITED STATES IN A NEW WORLD: A SHORT EPILOGUE   405
Roy C. Macridis

THE CHANGING CIRCUMSTANCES 408
    Domestic 409   Regional and Global Commitments 410

INDEX   415

CONTRIBUTING AUTHORS

Vernon V. Aspaturian is Evan Pugh Professor of Political Science and Director of the Slavic and Soviet Area Studies Center at Pennsylvania State University. He is the author of *Process and Power in Soviet Foreign Policy, The Soviet Union in the World Communist System, The Union Republics in Soviet Diplomacy*, and coauthor of *Euro-Communism Between East and West*. He has also contributed many articles to professional and scholarly journals on Soviet Politics and Foreign Policy.

Christopher Hill is Senior Lecturer in International Relations, London School of Economics and Political Science; author of *National Foreign Policies and European Political Cooperation; Cabinet Decisions on Foreign Policy: the British Experience 1938-1941*; and many articles and chapters on aspects of British foreign policy, European foreign policy cooperation and foreign policy analysis. He has been a Guest Scholar at the Woodrow Wilson International Center for Scholars, Washington DC, and a Visiting Professor at Dartmouth College, New Hampshire.

Josef Joffe was educated in the United States (Swarthmore College, Harvard University), and is foreign editor of the *Süddeutsche Zeitung*, West Germany's largest quality daily. He has taught at the University of Munich and the Johns Hopkins School of Advanced International Studies in Washington, DC. During 1990 and 1991 he held the Beton M. Kaneb Professorship of National Security Affairs at Harvard University. The author of *The Limited Partnership: Europe, the United States and the Burdens of Alliance*, his work on German diplomacy, arms control and strategy, American foreign policy, and European security have appeared in *Foreign Affairs, Foreign Policy, International Security, Survival*, and *The National Interest*, as well as in scholarly collections in the United States, Britain, and Germany.

Roy C. Macridis is Emeritus Professor of Politics at Brandeis University. He is author of *The De Gaulle Republic–Quest for Unity* (with Bernard E. Brown), *French Politics in Transition–The Years After De Gaulle; Contemporary Political Ideologies–Movements and Regimes*, among many other publications and articles.

Don Odom is an Editor at the Stockholm International Peace Research Institute (SIPRI) and a faculty member of The Swedish Program at the University of Stockholm. He is the author of *Swedish Foreign Policy Behavior: An Event Data Analysis*.

Riordan Roett is Professor and Director of the Latin American Studies Program at The Johns Hopkins School of Advanced International Studies in Washington, D.C. He is the author of *Brazil: Politics in a Patrimonial Society*. He and Wolf Grabendorff coedited and coauthored *The United States, Latin America and Western Europe: A New Atlantic Triangle*. Previous books include *The Foreign Aid in the Brazilian Northeast* and *Brazil in the Seventies*.

Nadav Safran is Murray A. Albertson Professor of Middle East Studies at Harvard. His previous books include *Egypt in Search of Political Community; The United States and Israel; From War to War: The Arab-Israeli Confrontation 1948-1967; Israel, The Embattled Ally; Saudi Arabia, The Ceaseless Quest for Security*.

Robert A. Scalapino is Emeritus Robson Research Professor of Government, Director of the Institute of East Asian Studies, and Editor of *Asian Survey* at the University of California, Berkeley. In addition to numerous writings, he is also the author of *Democracy and the Party Movement in Pre-War Japan, Parties and Politics in Postwar Japan, The Japanese Communist Movement*, and editor of *The Foreign Policy of Modern Japan*.

Bengt Sundelius is Associate Professor of Political Science and Director of the International Graduate School at the University of Stockholm. He is the author of *Managing Transnationalism in Northern Europe*, coauthor of *Internationalization and Foreign Policy Management*, and editor of *Foreign Policies of Northern Europe, The Neutral Democracies and the New Cold War*, and *The Committed Neutral: Sweden's Foreign Policy*.

Brian P. White is currently Principal Lecturer in International Relations at the Staffordshire Polytechnic University, England. He has also taught at the University of East Anglia where he was a Visiting Fellow. He holds a Master's Degree from the University of Lancaster and a Doctorate from the University of Leicester. He has research interests and has published in the fields of foreign policy theory and British foreign and defense policy. He is the author of Britain, *Detente and Changing East-West Relations* . He edited (with Michael Smith and Steve Smith) and contributed to *British Foreign Policy: Tradition, Change and Transformation* and edited (with Mike Clarke) and contributed to *Understanding Foreign Policy: The Foreign Policy Systems Approach*.

Allen S. Whiting is Professor of Politcal Science and Director, Center for East Asian Studies, University of Arizona. He served as Director, Office of Research and Analysis, Department of State (1962-1966) and Deputy Consul General, Hong Kong (1966-1968). He is author of *Soviet Policies Toward China: 1917-1924; Sinkiang: Pawn or Pivot?* (coauthor); *China Crosses the Yalu; The Chinese Calculus of Deterrence; China's Future* (coauthor); *Siberian Development and East Asia;* and *China Eyes Japan*.

Stephen Wright is an Associate Professor of Political Science at Northern Arizona University. He is the coeditor of *Africa in World Politics: Changing Perspectives* and *West African Regional Cooperation and Development*, and has contributed a number of articles on Africa to scholarly journals and volumes.

PREFACE

Many changes have occurred in the last forty years since the first edition of this book came out, and we assess them in this new edition. Yet despite these changes, notably the growth of powerful international forces—military, economic, and cultural (the latter in the rapid growth of global communications)—the individual states that comprise our political universe continue to play a dominant role. They remain the major actors. The two blocs that dominated the world and confronted each other—the Warsaw Pact and the Atlantic Alliance—are yielding to their individual parts, while European Community is still striving to define itself as a political entity. The states remain the primary actors also in the regions we discuss—Africa, Latin America, Scandinavia. They have managed to keep under control powerful ideological religious forces in the Middle East and act independently of them, as the Gulf War showed. We continue, therfore, to use the same format in stressing the foreign policy of individual states even when we cluster them into regional wholes.

Every essay has been updated to account for developments through the end of 1990 and to include a discussion of future prospects. We have included a new essay on Africa—a continent that comprises fifty-two states—ignored for so long but deserving consideration. With the two Germanys having become one, we raise critical questions about the future foreign policy course that a united Germany is likely to follow. With Japan's growing ecenomic strength, if not outright supremacy, the obvious question is whether it will be translated into national and military power. And there is, last of all, the haunting question about the future of the Soviet Union itself and the impact the forces unleashed by *perestroika* will have upon its foreign policy.

We have, regretfully, omitted the chapter on U.S. foreign policy for two mutually reinforcing reasons. First, one essay can hardly do justice to the new burdens and challenges it faces, and second, there have been, as we note in our conclusion, some recent publications that provide the analysis and discussion students can use.

As in all previous editions, I wish to thank again all contributors—new and old. Special thanks goes to our reviewers who commented on the previous edition and made many useful suggestions. My thanks goes also to Karen

Horton, the political science editor at Prentice Hall for her encouragement and support, and to Edie Riker and Joanne Riker for their excellent work in supervising the production of this edition.

Roy C. Macridis
Waltham, MA

–1–

INTRODUCTORY REMARKS

Roy C. Macridis

In this revised volume we continue to emphasize the interaction among states and their overall impact on such matters as the distribution of power in our world, defense, economic cooperation, conflict, and of course regional and collective security. The study of international relations continues, after all, to be the study of the interaction and of the patterns of interaction among states on a world-wide and regional basis. The fact that internal changes in individual states have been quite dramatic since 1989 made it even more difficult (and perhaps less important) to study in detail, as we did in previous editions, the mechanics of foreign policy-making. It is the substance and the secular patterns that count more, especially in a period of change and particularly for Eastern European states, a united Germany, and the Soviet Union. We have insisted, therefore, on patterns and have attempted to provide yardsticks for the evaluation of foreign policy.

We continue of course to discuss for each and every country the elements or ingredients of foreign policy. To wit:

A. *The relatively permanent material elements*
   1. Geography
   2. Natural Resources
      a. Minerals
      b. Food production
      c. Energy and power

B. *Less permanent material elements*
1. Industrial establishment
2. Military establishment
3. Changes in industrial and military capacity
C. *The human elements: quantitative and qualitative*
1. Quantitative—population
2. Qualitative
a. Policy makers and leaders
b. The role of ideology
c. The role of information

Nor do we ignore the processes of policy making and we continue to discuss for each country the governmental agencies responsible for foreign policy-making (executives, legislatures, and specialized agencies) and also the nongovernmental agencies: political parties, interest groups, the media, and public opinion and the changes that have taken place. But we stress substance and patterns—new and emerging—and continue to provide for tentative evaluations.

PATTERNS OF FOREIGN POLICY

A "pattern" implies the existence of goals to be realized and the mechanisms and practices through which such goals are realized. Above all, the term connotes the existence of intellectual equipment—something like a filter mechanism or lens—through which policymakers look at the outside world, sift information that comes in, and take steps that relate to the goals of the nation-state. A military coup in Ethiopia; uncertainty about the future regime in Yugoslavia; invasion of northern Cyprus by the Turks—these are events that mean different things to different nations and their policymakers. They are events that are viewed in terms of the goals of their respective nation-states. As a result reactions to them will differ from one state to another.

Objectively speaking no nation-state can expect to realize fully all its goals all the time. There are irreducible goals that are associated with clear-cut patterns of action and reaction. They generally involve the minimum requirements of security and defense as defined by the policymakers and the nation's political elite. Not much compromise is possible. The Soviets' reaction to an effort on the part of Estonia to join NATO is obvious. They will use force rather than allow it. The reaction of the U.S.A. to the installation of Soviet missiles on Cuban territory is equally certain. The harder and clearer the definition of minimum and irreducible goals and the means of action to bring them about, the higher the level of predictability in international relations and, as a result, the stability of the international system. In contrast, the situation in the Middle East is highly volatile because of the lack of clear-cut goals and of anticipated forms of action on the part of the various protagonists. Another illustration was the war in Korea in 1951 that may have originated in the inadvertent remarks made earlier by Secretary of State Dean

Acheson according to which South Korea was not within the perimeter of U.S. defense.

There are, however, goals that call for adjustment and compromise. They are what a nation-state considers desirable but not indispensable. They do not directly involve matters of security and survival but rather the expansion or consolidation of power. Such goals may be graded on a scale of priorities beginning with what is of particular importance and ending with those that can be dispensed with under pressure. For instance, a former secretary of defense in France, an ardent Gaullist, defined the goals of France to be the security of Europe, the avoidance of "certain dominations" in the Mediterranean, in Africa, and in "certain parts of the world where our flag flies." Obviously this implied a ranking of interests and goals in which Europe, North Africa, French-speaking Africa, and "certain parts" of the world would be ranked in that order.

How are patterns shaped? There is one and only one answer: by history. And by this we mean the existence over a long period of time of analogous, if not identical, reactions to analogous, if not identical, stimuli. It is only then that a "pattern" becomes firmly crystallized. It involves a goal shared widely by the elites, and it is associated with an equally accepted set of actions to bring it about. In the discussion of the individual foreign policies of the countries we cover, we identify basic patterns and indicate the force they have acquired over a given period of time.

As technological, economic, strategic, and political changes occur, and the international environment becomes transformed, two major dangers are ever-present. We have already mentioned one: the political elite may remain blind to these changes and follow patterns that were valid under different conditions in the past. The elites become ensnared in the stereotypes of the past and assume that the *same* goals are to be implemented by the *same* actions. The second danger is equally ever-present. Elites—and not only in democracies—may divide sharply on goals and means. A division may lead either to inaction or to sudden changes that create an element of unpredictability and instability.

There is a need for careful analysis of the existing patterns, their scope, their intensity, the conditions under which they change, and the liabilities— both for the nation-state and the international community—that result from prolonged rigidities and from divisions among the elites.

EVALUATION OF FOREIGN POLICY

As the student goes through the analysis of the foreign policy-making of individual countries, he or she unavoidably is concerned with evaluating them. Have the policymakers made a "good" or a "bad" decision? Has the foreign policy pursued by a given country been "successful" or "unsuccessful"? In terms of what criteria and what canons shall we judge and render a verdict?

The intense debate that went on over U.S. policy in Vietnam, just as in France over Indochina and Algeria, clearly demonstrates that clear-cut and objective tools for analysis and judgment are not always available.

To begin with, there is the perennial problem of "good" and "bad"—that is, of normative criteria and goals. Such goals generally indicate the overall commitment of a society to a way of life, and naturally influence policy-making and foreign policy as well. American isolationism was based squarely on normative considerations—primarily the belief that the American way of life was distinct and superior to those of the European countries, and that any involvement in their affairs and any involvement on their part in the affairs of the American continent would "contaminate" and perhaps corrupt the American democracy. By the same token, many French political leaders and intellectuals believed that the French colonies were a major vehicle for the dissemination of the French culture and the French language through which the "natives" would be assimilated to a higher and better way of life.

The student generally is inclined to be very sympathetic to foreign policy analysis in terms of basic ethical criteria. This is not, however, an easy job—nor is it analytically satisfactory. The first difficulty is that of agreeing on ethics. For those who consider an ethical principle more important than human life, outright destruction in its name is preferable to peace; for those who consider communism a danger far outweighing the well-being of any given generation, war and sacrifice is above that of welfare and well-being; for those who consider democracy and an open society more valuable than one man's life, again, war and destruction may be inevitable to preserve what is so highly valued. In other words, it is not always easy to find people agreeing on the highest normative goal. In a pluralistic universe, then, judgment and evaluation in terms of ethical considerations is hazardous and highly unpredictable. We prefer and we suggest here a more instrumental approach to the evaluation of foreign policy. It is based on the assumption that, at least for the time being, nation-states are here to stay and that their foreign policy must be evaluated in terms of the success and failure to implement the goals they pursue. In the international community each and every state is allotted some power which alone, or in combination with others, allows it to keep its autonomy and way of life or, conversely, prevents its destruction by others. The international community has been in this sense a world of power relations differing in degree rather than in kind from domestic politics.

An analysis based upon power must also take into consideration that it is not an end in itself. It is an instrument for preserving a national community and its way of life. Its use, therefore, must always be subjected to this test: Does it preserve the national community? Does it enhance its security and well-being? Is its use consistent with the basic interests of the national community? The analysis we suggest, therefore, involves a number of steps *before* we confront the thorny ethical question of what is "right" and "wrong." We propose simply to suggest a set of instrumental criteria in terms of which "success" or "failure," or at least a discriminating bill of particulars, can be determined.

The steps we try to follow are the following:

1. We must first provide a clear description of the predicament—what exactly was the predicament or, rather, how was the predicament perceived. In other words, we must determine why a certain situation was or is considered by policymakers to be a predicament.
2. The next step, related to the first, is to make an effort to assess the flow of information and intelligence that goes into the formation of the perception of the policymakers: Is there only one source? Which one? Are there many sources? Do they provide the same facts and figures, or do they differ? If they differ, how are differences resolved in accepting one set of information flows and rejecting another?
3. This leads us to our third required piece of information: Which governmental units are most responsible for coping with the predicament? And if it falls (at least technically) within the jurisdiction of more than one, what types of intergovernmental and interunit arrangements exist to allow for a concerted action?
4. At this stage, assuming that the nature and perception of the predicament, the information sources, and the particular governmental units and procedures are known, we need to have a clear statement and description of the action resulting from the decision actually made—for example an ambassador was recalled; economic aid was offered; an official was bribed; the marines were dispatched.
5. A knowledge of the action taken (or contemplated) must be coupled, at least when analyzing democratic foreign policy-making, with the possession of an unambiguous declaration of the anticipated consequences of the action or decision. The simpler and the smaller the number of consequences anticipated, the easier the evaluation. The greater the number and the more complex the goal, the more difficult the assessment—unless one is able to peel off the rhetoric that often accompanies a decision from its substance, or unless we can establish a set of priorities for goals ranging from the imperative ones through the desirable ones down to the least-expected but simply hoped-for. Such priority assessments are not always easy to make, for the time dimension within which policies are implemented constantly forces reconsideration and reshuffling of priorities.

Only after the preceding steps have been carefully followed can the analyst survey the actual consequences that flowed from the policies made and arrive at a very quiet, and always highly qualified, verdict.

Our frame of analysis, in other words, is instrumental, relating means to ends and linking the two by study of decision-making procedures and intermediate steps. It is based on a power theory of international politics in which the ultimate analysis of "success" and "failure" can be measured in terms of the plusses and minusses in the increments of power and influence for a given nation.

To summarize: Foreign-policy evaluation involves assessment of the goals of a given country; analysis of the various predicaments that seem to endanger these goals; an examination of the instrumentalities (policies) pursued to alleviate the predicaments; a careful examination of the manner in which such policies were formulated, with regard to both the predicament involved and the manner in which the policy was to be implemented; an account of the major governmental organs responsible for the implementation of a policy; a careful examination of the availability of alternate means and instrumentalities (were they considered? were they rejected after being considered, and if so, why?); and finally, an assessment—that is, did the policy as formulated and implemented bring about the desired goals?

BASIC REFERENCES

Aron, Raymond. *Peace and War: A Theory of International Relations.* Garden City, N.Y.: Doubleday, 1966.

Axelrod, Robert. *The Structure of Decision: The Cognitive Maps of Political Elites.* Princeton, N.J.: Princeton University Press, 1976.

Boulding, Kenneth. *Conflict and Defense.* New York: Harper & Row, 1961.

Brzezinski, Zbigniew. *The Grand Failure. The Birth and Death of Communism in the 20th Century.* New York, N.Y.: Charles Scribner, 1989.

Gilpin, Robert. *War and Change in World Politics.* Cambridge: Cambridge University Press, 1981.

Jarvis, Robert. *Perceptions and Misperceptions in International Politics.* Princeton, N.J.: Princeton University Press, 1976.

Keohane, Robert. *Power and Interdependence: World Politics in Transition.* Boston: Little, Brown, 1977.

———. *After Hegemony. Cooperation and Discord in the World Political Economy.* Princeton, N.J.: Princeton University Press, 1984.

Kissinger, Henry, ed. *Problems of National Strategy.* New York: Praeger, 1965.

Morgenthau, Hans J. *Politics Among Nations,* 4th Ed. New York: Knopf, 1967.

Rosenau, James N. ed. *International Politics and Foreign Policy.* Glencoe, Ill.: Free Press, 1964.

Spero, Joan. *The Politics of International Economic Relations,* 4th Ed. New York: St. Martin's Press, 1990.

Stoessinger, John. *Why Nations Go to War,* 3d Ed. New York: St. Martin's Press, 1981.

Ullman, Richard H., and Raymond Tanter. *Theory and Policy in International Relations.* Princeton, N.J.: Princeton University Press, 1972.

Waltz, Kenneth N. *Theory of International Politics.* Reading, Mass.: Addison-Wesley, 1978.

———. *Man, the State and War.* Columbia University Press, N.Y. 1989.

World Factbook 1989. Washington, D.C.: The Central Intelligence Agency.

—2—

BRITISH FOREIGN POLICY

TRADITION AND CHANGE

Brian P. White

There is a very powerful conventional wisdom about Britain that suggests that the history of British foreign policy since the Second World War, if not from the turn of the century, is essentially a rather sad story of decline—a "descent from power" to take the title from Northedge's influential textbook—and of failure to adapt policy objectives to the "realities" of a transformed international environment.[1] British policymakers, it is said, have been so wedded to assumptions that date from Britain's imperial past that they have simply gone on peddling illusions about an appropriate role for Britain in the postwar world. As former U.S. Secretary of State Dean Acheson commented rather scornfully in December 1962, "Great Britain has lost an empire and has not yet found a role. The attempt to play a separate power role—that is a role apart from Europe—based on a 'special relationship' with the United States—on being the head of a 'Commonwealth' which has no unity, or strength—this role is about played out."[2]

Though Britain's first application to join the European Economic Community had already been submitted and, indeed, was on the point of being rejected when Acheson made this speech, even the eventual entry of Britain

[1] Frederick, S. Northedge, *Descent From Power: British Foreign Policy 1945–73* (London: Allen & Unwin, 1974).

[2] *Keesing's Contemporary Archives,* Vol. 14 (Bristol: Keesing's Publications Ltd, 1963–64), p. 19181.

into the Community in 1973 did not signal the end of Britain's global pretensions or herald the beginnings of a more appropriate regional role—along the
lines of Acheson's prescription. Not only was Britain a "reluctant European" in
terms of adopting a minimalist, Gaullist approach to European integration, but
British leaders continued to be attracted by the lure of an extra-European role
and dazzled by the idea of special links with Washington. Even the Thatcher
governments in the 1980s, which promised to administer a sharp dose of realism
to foreign policy as to other areas of British government, did not represent a
sharp break with the past. They may have improved the economic substruc-
ture—though even this is hotly debated—but only managed in retrospect, the
conventionally wise would suggest, to reinforce the traditional aspects of British
policy, a continuing if not increasing ambivalence toward Western Europe and
a close coordination of British policy with Washington in particular.[3] Following
the surprising resignation of Mrs. Thatcher in November 1990, real choices
about the future orientation of British foreign policy—in particular the need to
resolve what may be called the "Atlantic" versus "Europe" debate—still need to
be made in the context of genuinely revolutionary changes in the contemporary
international environment.

As in all conventional wisdoms, the snapshot picture of postwar British
foreign policy that it produces has elements of accuracy and some merit in
explanatory terms. "Decline," "failure," "illusion" are all part of the story as,
indeed, are "missed opportunities" and "wrong turns." But this sort of account
fails to take note of the extent to which policy has changed over time, or at
least has been adapted in the light of changes in both the domestic and the
external environment. By focusing on the decline of British power in rather
narrow material terms, it also tends to underplay the impact of British policy
and, within certain constraints, the influence that British governments have
been able to bring to bear on the behavior of other international actors.

Nevertheless, the picture is sufficiently compelling to begin this analysis
by identifying what might be called the traditional bases of British foreign
policy and the objectives of policy as they were articulated in the immediate
postwar period. To start the story rather further back, the classic statement of
traditional objectives is contained in the famous 1907 Crowe Memorandum,
written by a then relatively junior Foreign Office official, Eyre Crowe. The
orientation of British policy in broad terms becomes apparent in the first
sentence of that memorandum. "The general character of England's foreign
policy," asserts Crowe, "is determined by the immutable conditions of her
geographical situation on the ocean flank of Europe, as an island state with
vast overseas colonies and dependencies, whose existence as an independent
community is inseparably bound up with the possession of sea power."[4]

---

[3] On the economic debate, compare Christopher Tugendhat and William Wallace, *Options for
British Foreign Policy in the 1990s* (New York: Routledge, 1988) pp. 35–39; Tessa Blackstone,
"Leaning inwards, looking outwards," *International Affairs* 65(2), 1989, pp. 305–7; Malcolm
Rutherford "A lucky country," *The World Today* 45(1), January, 1989, pp. 15–16.

[4] See G.P. Gooch and H.W.V. Temperley, eds. *British Documents on the Origins of the War 1898–1914*

This sentence immediately locates Britain in geopolitical terms and establishes the global reach of British interests. Clearly, this is not a country like the United States, which, safely insulated by geography, had some choice historically about whether or not to be involved in international relations. Nor, for that matter, is it a country which could afford to adopt a moralistic approach to the world around them. Whether they liked it or not, British statesmen and diplomats were "locked into" an international system, and there were substantial "national interests" to defend. As Crowe recognised, Britain was very much a "have" power—whether that was conceived in terms of security, influence or wealth—and the perceived object of external relations was quite simply to hold onto it. In other words, British policymakers saw themselves as conservative defenders of the status quo long before they had the benefit of a Morgenthau to develop the theory of satisfied and revisionist powers to tell them what they were doing and why they were doing it.

More specifically, the object of foreign policy was to stabilise European politics. As historical experience had shown, continental Europe was the major source of threats to British security, the point from which attempts to invade Britain were most likely to be launched. The favored method of stabilising European politics was to maintain whenever possible a balance of power on the European continent by a system of flexible alliances. Thus Europe was always important in the calculations of British policymakers, but there was an important sense in which balance of power politics in Europe was a means to an end, a way of providing the necessary security for the pursuit of a global, imperial role. This role in the context of the possession of a worldwide empire was regarded, not surprisingly, as the most important role. These two roles—the global and the more limited European role—were joined around the turn of this century by growing perceptions of what came to be known after the Second World War as a "special relationship" between Britain and the United States who came to be seen rather grandly, in the words of Boardman and Groom, as the "joint moulders of Western destinies."[5]

It was these traditional arenas of British policy that became, in Winston Churchill's famous image, the three interlocking "circles" in which Britain's primary overseas interests were seen to lie. In a famous speech to the Conservative Party Conference in 1948, Churchill metaphorically described these "three circles" of activity and located Britain unashamedly at the "point of conjunction," at the hub, in effect, of world politics.[6] Three important assumptions were built into what has arguably been the most pervasive representation of an appropriate role for Britain in the postwar world. First, it depicts Britain not as a regional power but emphatically as a global power with global interests to defend. Second, it raises pragmatism and flexibility

(London, HMSO, 1926–38) iii, pp. 415–18.

[5] Robert Boardman and A.J.R. Groom, eds. *The Management of Britain's External Relations* (New York: Macmillan, 1973), p. 1.

[6] The relevant sections of this speech are quoted in Avi Shlaim, "Britain's quest for a world role," *International Relations,* May 1975, pp. 840–41.

almost to a guiding principle. The object of foreign policy, Churchill implies at least, was to exploit Britain's position by continuing to play a leading role within all three sets of relationships but not becoming identified with or committed to any one "circle" at the expense of the other two. This idea of retaining diplomatic flexibility was later referred to by Northedge as "the policy of the free hand appropriate to an imperial power."[7] Finally, Churchill's notion that the British "have the opportunity of joining them (the three circles) all together" suggests a sort of freewheeling "bridge building" role for Britain, which has been a powerful self-image throughout the postwar period.

This notion of Britain as bridge builder—what Lord Strang called the "conciliatory quality" in British diplomacy—is interesting and worth pursuing a little further to establish the traditional context of British policy.[8] This characteristic has its roots in the leading role that Britain played in the classic European school of diplomacy where conciliation was the important norm of diplomacy. But it also reflected traditional assumptions related more specifically to the maintenance of Britain's global interests. It had long been assumed, certainly since the middle of the nineteenth century, that the preservation of peace was central to the protection of global politico-economic interests. It was this premise that Crowe appeared to have in mind when he talked rather mistily in his Memorandum about the need for British policy to be "so directed as to harmonise with the general desires and ideals common to all mankind." It was certainly what Harold Nicolson had in mind when he argued in his famous work on British diplomacy that British policymakers have traditionally had a "civilian" or a "commercial" as opposed to what he called a "warrior" conception of diplomacy.[9]

Unlike the other major European states, Britain had an empire of genuinely global dimensions that provided special reasons for pursuing a conciliatory foreign policy. As the so-called workshop of the world in the nineteenth century, Britain was at the center of a global system of trade and finance. The new liberal orthodoxy argued that this position of preeminence could best be maintained and, indeed, exploited by pursuing a policy of free trade. This policy had important commercial advantages, but it also made the British economy highly vulnerable to any disruption of trade, and to war in particular. Hence, to the extent that global economic and commercial interests required a policy of free trade, that policy in turn required the preservation of peace by conciliatory diplomacy. As Britain's economic position relative to other states began, nevertheless, to decline in the second half of the nineteenth century, the preservation of peace became even more vital.[10]

---

[7] F.S. Northedge, op. cit., p. 73.

[8] See Lord Strang, *Britain in World Affairs* (Westport, Connecticut: Greenwood Press, 1961) p. 359.

[9] Harold Nicolson, *Diplomacy* (London: Thornton Butterworth, 1939), pp. 52–54.

[10] Paul Kennedy, *The Realities behind Diplomacy: Background Influences on British External Policy 1865–1980* (London: Fontana, 1981). The arguments outlined here are developed in the first chapter of this book.

If this serves as a brief characterisation of the historical context and the traditional perspectives that British leaders brought to bear on policy issues after the Second World War, Churchill's "three circles" notion provides a convenient framework here for a general analysis of British policy in the postwar period. Specifically, it serves to highlight the most important substantive areas of policy for analytical purposes, and it will enable us to make some judgments about the extent of continuity and the degree of change or adaptation in postwar British policy. Partly though not wholly for the sake of convenience, the period is divided into three: from the late 1940s to the early 1960s; from the early 1960s to the late 1970s; and the 1980s, with some additional comments addressed to the post-Thatcher era. With respect to each period, the analytical focus is provided by an attempt to assess the relative priorities attached by policymakers to what will be called "globalism," "Atlanticism," and "Europeanism."

GLOBAL INFLUENCE AND THE LIMITS OF POWER 1945-60

With the benefit of hindsight, it is clear that in the period up to the early 1960s, British policymakers attempted to play a significant role in all three "circles" of activity, but it is equally clear that their priorities were directed toward the global and the Atlantic "circles" rather than toward Europe. The Suez crisis in 1956 undoubtedly questioned traditional assumptions about Britain as a global power, but it was less important perhaps as a "turning point" in postwar foreign policy than many commentators would suggest.

Globalism

From an immediate postwar perspective, it is not surprising that policymakers should have assumed that Britain would continue to play a leading role in constructing the new postwar order. However ravaged the British economy was as a result of the war, all the trappings of being a "great power" remained ostensibly intact. As a member of the victorious alliance against Hitler, Britain was regarded as being one of the "Big Three." A certain kudos, moreover, still accrued to the people who had "stood alone" in the darkest days of 1940. Britain had also played a leading role in the setting up of the United Nations Organisation and was a permanent member of the Security Council. Last but not least, British military power still stretched throughout the world. It may well be that, as Ovendale puts it, "Britain's position at the conference tables of world diplomacy—obscured the reality of Britain's diminished power," but this was not accepted by policymakers after the war in the sense of requiring a radical reassessment of policy objectives.[11] The decisions of 1946–47 to develop an atomic bomb capability, for example,

[11] R. Ovendale, ed. *The Foreign Policy of the British Labour Governments 1945–51* (Leicester: Leicester University Press, 1984), p. 3.

were fundamentally shaped by the simple but continuing assumption that Britain, as a great power with global interests, should possess the very latest and most potent weapon system.[12]

Where a radical reassessment might have been foreshadowed was with respect to the relationship between the 1947 decision to grant independence to the Indian subcontinent and the process of decolonisation. But, as Sanders argues, until the Suez débacle administered a great psychological shock to a range of traditional assumptions, "retrenchment" aimed at preventing any further erosion of influence rather than "withdrawal" best characterises the British approach to the empire.[13] Indeed, the fact that India, Pakistan, and Ceylon all chose to remain within the British Commonwealth boosted hopes at this time that this unique, multiracial organisation might serve as an alternative vehicle for the maintenance of British influence at the global level.

With respect to the emerging bipolar structure of postwar international relations, Britain did play a leading role in establishing the structures and the institutions that effectively severed West from East. Britain's contribution to the "first" Cold War, thanks to recent historical scholarship, has now been confirmed.[14] What is less noted by scholars is the important role that Britain played in setting up the process of East-West diplomacy that was later to be called detente. In the decade after 1953, culminating in the signing of the Partial Test Ban Treaty, so persistent and eventually fruitful were British efforts to build bridges between East and West on a range of issues that it is appropriate to regard Britain as an early catalyst of detente.[15] What is significant about the British approach to detente in this period is the extent to which it illustrates both the flexibility of policymakers and the conciliatory quality in British diplomacy. Having helped to create a confrontationary structure between East and West, a pragmatic rather than an ideological approach dictated a policy that also sought accommodation with the East, lest confrontation lead to conflict and war. The impact of British policy in this context also highlights the limitations of the "descent from power" analysis. With hindsight again, it is clear that policymakers adapted rather skillfully to Britain's evident loss of material power during this period by using "symbols of power" such as membership of a still-exclusive nuclear club and less tangible sources of influence such as diplomatic skills, a worldwide network of contacts, and even claims to moral authority. One of the most important of these sources of influence was the relationship with Washington.

[12]See, for example, Alan Bullock, *Ernest Bevin: Foreign Secretary 1945–51* (New York: Oxford University Press, 1985), pp. 185–89, 245–46.

[13]David Sanders, *Losing an Empire, Finding a Role: British Foreign Policy Since 1945* (London: Macmillan, 1990), p. 74ff.

[14]See, for example, R. Ovendale, ed. *The English-Speaking Alliance: Britain, the United States, the Dominions and the Cold War 1945–51* (London: Allen & Unwin, 1985); Anne Deighton, ed. *Britain and the First Cold War* (London: Macmillan, 1990).

[15]See Brian White, *Britain, Detente and Changing Patterns of East-West Relations,* (London/New York: Routledge, 1991).

Atlanticism

In an important sense, the relationship with the United States during this period was the key to relationships with the two other "circles" of activity. Not only was influence in Washington central to Britain's ability to influence East-West relations, but this relationship also defined the limits of Britain's interest in relations with Western Europe. Memories of the Second World War were, of course, still fresh in the minds of British policymakers during this period, and a principal lesson learned from that war was the importance of the relationship with the United States. To the extent that the United States had "saved" Britain, it was crucially necessary to postwar British security to retain that relationship at the centre of policy. Growing perceptions of a major Soviet threat after 1946 only served to underline this imperative. Thus, for Foreign Secretary Ernest Bevin as much as for Churchill before him, the need to create an effective transatlantic partnership, with Britain acting as an "arch" between the United States and Western Europe, was crucial.

The fear that the United States would revert to "isolationism," with respect to Western Europe at least, required some determined British diplomacy. Most evidently with respect to military security, Bevin successfully developed a strategy from 1947 to 1949 designed to persuade the Americans to join an "entangling alliance" with the countries of Western Europe. Central to this strategy was demonstrating to the Americans and to a skeptical American Congress in particular that the West Europeans were prepared to stand on their own feet and to organise themselves for collective security. Hence, the signing of the Brussels Treaty with France and the Benelux countries in March 1948—in effect a NATO in embryo—was a crucial stage in this process.[16] Bevin was also a key player in organising the West European response to the Marshall Plan through the creation of what became the Organisation for European Economic Cooperation in 1948.

Successful though the British contribution was to the creation of an "Atlantic community" in the late 1940s, there were significant costs attached to this role. Fears in the context of the Korean War that the United States' commitment to European security was less than solid persuaded the Attlee government to undertake a massive rearmament programme in 1950 that the British economy could scarcely afford. Similar fears once it became clear that the French Parliament would not ratify a European Defence Community agreement in 1953–54 saw the Churchill government commit a permanent British military presence to the European continent. Both moves contributed to an overcommitment to defence spending and an overextension of military forces which, given the underlying weakness of the British economy, were to create serious problems for succeeding governments. Finally, a fundamental commitment to Atlanticism necessitated an essentially ambivalent approach

[16]Richard A. Best Jr., *"Co-operation with Like-Minded Peoples"* in *British Influences on American Security Policy 1945–49* (New York: Greenwood Press, 1986).

to Western Europe at a time when important moves toward European integration were taking place.

Europeanism

At the end of a major speech to the House of Commons in May 1953, Churchill commented that the British are "with but not of Europe." This convenient summary of a distinctive British approach to Western Europe is useful to an understanding of British policy throughout the postwar period. In the period immediately after the Second World War, there was a keen and continuing interest in intergovernmental cooperation with Western Europe, particularly in the defence sphere, as we have seen. The problem was that in seeking essentially to construct a transatlantic network of relationships between Western Europe and the United States, the impression was created on more than one occasion that Britain might be interested in a relationship with Western Europe that went beyond intergovernmental cooperation. In September 1946, Churchill talked in a speech in Zurich about constructing a "United States of Europe." In January 1948, Bevin made some rather vague proposals in the House of Commons for a "Western Union" and Eden, in the early 1950s, made encouraging noises about the possibility of Britain joining the European Defence Community. But, in the end, Britain chose to remain aloof from the European integration movement at a critical time.

An explanation for this takes us back into some familiar themes but also introduces new ideas. First, Britain was unwilling to forge closer links with Western Europe because a close identification with the continent was not consistent with the prevailing conception of Britain as a global power, and, moreover, policymakers feared that it would damage relations with the Empire and Commonwealth. Second, the ambitious plans for economic integration initially outlined in the 1950 Schuman Plan offended the pragmatic British approach to policymaking. Not only were the British almost instinctively suspicious of large conceptions and grand schemes, but the feeling at the time was that these schemes simply would not work anyway. Finally, Britain had a different recent historical experience from the other six who eventually formed the European Economic Community. Unlike these countries who had either been defeated or invaded in the Second World War and who, therefore, had some reason to question the efficacy of the nation-state, the British experience served to reinforce a basic faith in the state as the basic unit of political organisation. Thus, they were unwilling to contemplate the ceding of sovereignty to supranational institutions like the European Coal and Steel Community in 1951–52 and missed an important opportunity to join what became the European Economic Community in 1956–57.[17]

---

[17]For an excellent account of this story of missed opportunities, see Michael Charlton, *The Price of Victory* (London: BBC Publications, 1983).

The Suez Crisis as a Turning Point?

There is some debate in the literature about the extent to which the Suez crisis in October/November 1956 changed the direction of British foreign policy—away from a preoccupation with globalism and Atlanticism and towards Europe.[18] The crisis followed the decision by Egyptian President Nasser to nationalise the Suez Canal, an act that was seen by the Eden Government as a fundamental threat to British interests in the Middle East. A plan was hatched with the French and the Israelis whereby a prearranged Israeli invasion of Egypt would provide a pretext for an Anglo-French invasion ostensibly to separate the combatants and to protect the integrity of the Suez Canal. The latter invasion, however, was brought to a premature halt by a run on sterling. The United States government made it clear that it would only be prepared to support the pound if Anglo-French forces were immediately withdrawn. The question is, did this ignominious episode trigger a reevaluation of British foreign policy; did it, in short, serve as a "turning point?" Well, it certainly raised a number of questions about the traditional assumptions that underpinned British policy.

What sort of a world power was it who could not defend a perceived threat to its national interests by a traditional piece of "gunboat diplomacy?" What sort of a "special relationship" did Britain have with the United States if one partner could be so humiliated by the other? Could the British ever trust the Americans again? Indeed, could they ever again act independently on the world stage without at least the tacit support of the United States? What effect did the rather sordid collusion with France and Israel have on Britain's much vaunted moral authority and, in particular, its influence in the Third World? In the longer term, Suez did appear to have a significant impact, though there was no formal reassessment of British foreign policy objectives at the time. With hindsight, it did help to trigger a second wave of decolonisation to the extent that it appeared to encourage indigenous nationalist pressures within the Empire. Macmillan's famous "wind of change" speech in 1960 was a clear indication that Britain now accepted the inevitability of change with respect to the Empire. Suez also appeared to set the scene for a reorientation of British policy towards Europe. After all, only five years after Suez, the Macmillan government completed a *volte face* on Europe by applying for membership of the EEC.

What is striking, however, given the undoubted shock of Suez is how little things changed—at least in the short term. Unlike the French, for example, who drew the opposite conclusion from Suez, Britain endeavored to repair relations with Washington as soon as possible and with some success. Under Macmillan, the British government also continued to seek a leading role in influencing the direction of East-West relations. Macmillan's visit to Moscow in 1959 and his tireless diplomacy to set up the four-power summit meeting

[18]For a useful introduction to the Suez crisis, see David Carlton, *Britain and the Suez Crisis* (New York: Blackwell, 1989).

in Paris in 1960 were not the actions of a government that had foresworn opportunities to play a significant global role. Interestingly, the development of a British hydrogen bomb appears to have been connected both to Atlanticism and globalism to the extent that this capability was intended to buy further political influence in Washington and, paradoxically, to enable Britain to play a leading role in nuclear arms control negotiations.[19] With respect to Europe, Britain not only remained apparently uninterested in the negotiations that eventually produced the Treaty of Rome in 1957—though the important negotiations had been completed before Suez—but Britain was instrumental in setting up the rival European Free Trade Association in a vain attempt to convert the EEC into an intergovernmental free trade pact without supranational powers. With hindsight, Suez appears to have contributed to a process of adaptation to change after 1956, rather than being a turning point per se. Nevertheless, there were a number of changes in Britain's external environment that were contributing towards a gradual reorientation of policy towards Europe.

TOWARDS EUROPE? 1960–80

With respect to our three circles theme, there was a surprising degree of continuity during this second period given the indications that deepening economic problems should have raised fundamental questions about the viability of continuing to pursue all three circles of activity. Nevertheless, there were problems within both the global and the Atlantic "circles" that saw attempts, particularly with respect to the global circle, to scale down Britain's interests and commitments. There was further evidence of adaptation during this period with what amounted to a progressive "Europeanisation" of Britain's external relations. In terms of attitudes, however, an ambivalent approach towards Western Europe suggests the continuing impact of traditional modes of thinking.

Globalism

By the early 1960s, policymakers recognised that Britain no longer possessed the military and economic capability to sustain what remained of its Empire. It was also recognised that in the longer term a rapid withdrawal would be less painful than a long drawn-out retreat. Thus, a "second wave" of decolonisation in Africa and the Caribbean followed, and by 1966 the process was effectively complete. Meanwhile, however, it was becoming increasingly apparent to observers, if not to British governments, that the Commonwealth would be no substitute for the Empire in terms of providing an alternative vehicle for maintaining a global role. "Although the Commonwealth survived as a formal institution" after Suez, Sanders suggests, "it lost whatever

---

[19]This was certainly the view of the prime minister, see Harold Macmillan, *Riding the Storm 1956–59* (London: Macmillan, 1971).

coherence it had possessed as an economic and diplomatic bloc." Indeed, "during the 1960s the Commonwealth increasingly provided little more than a forum in which ex-colonial states could express their disapproval of the British government's domestic and foreign policies and at the same time seek to secure special concessions from Britain's overseas aid budget."[20] The bruising affair of Rhodesia in the mid-1960s resulting from what was seen by the black members of the Commonwealth as Britain's inadequate response to Ian Smith's Unilateral Declaration of Independence on behalf of the white minority was undoubtedly a turning point here.

In spite of completing the process of decolonisation, however, Britain still retained much of the global network of bases that it had developed to protect the Empire. In the context of decolonisation and Britain's worsening economic problems, however, it is worth looking at why British bases East of Suez were retained for so long. As Philip Darby argues, the granting of independence to the Indian subcontinent in 1947 should have occasioned a full-scale review of Britain's overseas defence commitments nearly twenty years before it occurred.[21] Once again, we meet up with some traditional themes here in explaining this apparent time lag.

First, strategic planning of the sort that would have been involved in scaling down the British presence ran counter to the pragmatic British approach. On most issues, the natural British tendency was to maintain the broad lines of policy until it became no longer possible to do so, as indeed became apparent with respect to the Empire itself in the late 1950s. Second, the very process of decolonisation, it might be argued, provided an argument for retaining a global military presence. While it became increasingly difficult to provide a strategic rationale for British bases East of Suez in terms of imperial interests, reducing this presence would be a clear signal to the international community that Britain was renouncing its claims to global status. Third, a rather different strategic rationale was to hand in the shape of international communism. To the extent that this threat was conceived in global terms, the British network of bases in areas in which the United States had no traditional ties provided useful links in the deterrent chain around the Soviet Union and its allies. The fact that the Americans were keen for these bases to be retained made them a useful political asset for Britain in terms of maintaining close Anglo-American relations.[22] By the mid-1960s, however, it was the costs rather than the benefits of the East of Suez policy that began to exercise the Wilson government. In a characteristic series of incremental decisions between 1966 and 1968, the government announced its intention to withdraw its forces from East of Suez by 1971. Ultimately, it was the impact of economic decline combined with the recurrent sterling crises that plagued the

---

[20] David Sanders, *op. cit.*, p. 103.

[21] Philip Darby, *British Defence Policy East of Suez 1947–68* (New York: Oxford University Press, 1973).

[22] On American pressure in this context, see Clive Ponting, *Breach of Promise–Labour in Power 1964–70* (London: Hamish Hamilton, 1989).

Wilson governments—rather than any "rational" calculations about commitments and resources over the longer term—that made the defense burden East of Suez unsustainable in political terms.

Other dimensions of Britain's efforts to play a significant global role also became problematic during this period. As noted in an earlier section, Britain's influential mediation role in East-West relations persisted into the 1960s—with Britain playing a particularly significant role in the negotiations that eventually produced the Partial Test Ban Treaty in 1963. Indications that it would be difficult to sustain this role, however, predate this treaty. Commentators have pinpointed the spectacular failure of the 1960 four-power summit conference in Paris—which Macmillan had worked so hard to promote—as a turning point in terms of British influence in the East-West arena. The Paris failure, Avi Shlaim comments, was a "brutal blow to Britain's international pretensions."[23] The Camp David summit between Eisenhower and Khrushchev in September 1959 might, however, be a better candidate to the extent that this meeting effectively legitimised, from an American perspective at least, the idea of bilateral meetings between the superpowers at heads of government level. Whatever the precise change point, it is certainly the case that the British found it increasingly difficult to play a distinctive role in the process of East-West detente after the Cuban missile crisis, if not in East-West relations as a whole. In part at least, this was because of a downturn in Anglo-American relations after 1963, to which we now turn.

Atlanticism

From the perspective of the early 1960s, the Anglo-American "special relationship" looked in pretty good shape. The dark days of Suez seemed long past, once the much longer friendship between Eisenhower and Macmillan had successfully steered the relationship back to health. More surprisingly perhaps, the relationship between Macmillan and Eisenhower's successor Kennedy was, if anything, even closer. Admittedly, there was a major crisis over the cancellation of the American Skybolt missile that Britain was due to purchase, but this had been resolved by Kennedy's agreement at Nassau in December 1962 to sell Britain the very latest in delivery system technology—the Polaris missile—on very generous terms. Given that the President was strongly advised not to perpetuate British illusions by agreeing to Macmillan's request for Polaris, this seemed to underline the special nature of the relationship. Later indications, moreover, that Kennedy had consulted with Macmillan throughout the Cuban missile crisis provided further evidence.

Less than three years later, however, the relationship was beginning to look distinctly "normal," and the precipitating issue was Vietnam. In the wake of the decisions by the Johnson Administration to escalate that conflict, urgent requests for support were communicated across the Atlantic. The refusal of the Wilson government to provide either material assistance or, more impor-

[23] Avi Shlaim, *op. cit.*, p. 843.

tantly to Washington, overt diplomatic support led to a sharp deterioration in relations. An equal, if not more important, blow to Anglo-American relations in the longer term, however, was the British withdrawal from East of Suez. The fact that Britain was planning to reduce its global military presence and concentrate its defence efforts primarily in Western Europe simply made Britain less useful to the United States in its efforts to contain the Soviet Union. Withdrawal itself was bad enough from an American perspective, but the timing—coinciding as it did with the Vietnam conflict—heightened its impact on Anglo-American relations. An essentially similar pattern of relations in the 1970s—close even cordial on many issues but certainly not special—was established by the Heath government. Edward Heath himself made it clear at the outset that his main priority was to establish Britain's credentials as a "good European." He was not prepared to put this endeavour at risk by appearing to covet special links with Washington.

But if Anglo-American relations per se were rather pendulous from the mid-1960s through the end of the 1970s, it is important to note that *Atlanticism* remained a dominant orientation of British policy. This can be illustrated by the very active British diplomacy in a NATO context in the second half of the 1960s. First, Britain played an important role in limiting the damage done to the alliance by the French decision to withdraw from the integrated military command structure in 1966. There was an evident lack of leadership within the alliance at this critical time until the British stepped into the breach, and, with some quiet but decisive diplomacy, helped to formulate a common response that effectively managed the crisis.[24] A concern with the cohesion of the alliance was also reflected in the leading role played by Britain in the establishment from 1968 onward of a distinct European defence identity within NATO based on the so-called Eurogroup.

Initiated by Defence Secretary Denis Healey as a forum for ministerial discussion, the Eurogroup spawned a number of subgroups in the early 1970s, largely under the auspices of Healey's successor Lord Carrington and his counterpart in Bonn, Helmut Schmidt, which dealt with practical areas of cooperation. Britain also played a leading role in the creation of the Independent European Programme Group in 1976. This forum, which, significantly, included the French was designed to generate greater European defence cooperation and to facilitate a genuine "two-way street" in defence technology with the United States.[25] These activities within NATO did provide valuable opportunities for British governments to demonstrate their European credentials, and they did constitute part of a growing "Europeanisation" of British foreign and defence policy. They were evaluated in London, however, primarily in terms of their contribution to transatlantic security.

[24] See M.M. Harrison, *The Reluctant Ally: France and Atlantic Security* (Baltimore: Johns Hopkins University Press, 1981), pp. 145–47; P. Gore-Booth, *With Great Truth and Respect* (London: Constable, 1974), pp. 340–43.

[25] D.C.R. Heyhoe, "The alliance in Europe: part 6. The European programme group," *Adelphi Papers* no. 129 (London: International Institute for Strategic Studies, 1966/67).

There was little or no interest in creating an alternative European security structure.

Europeanism

It is undoubtedly the case, however, that the general attractions of the European circle increased substantially during this period, partly because of the sort of problems associated with the other two circles that we have noted. It is important to stress though that Europe was never seen as an *alternative* to the other two circles. Membership of the European Community, in particular, was seen as adding to the totality of political influence that Britain could exercise in the world. Once again, there was no *fundamental* change in the basic elements of what might be called the British world view. Certainly, there were definite limits to how "European" as opposed to "Atlanticist" or "global" British governments were prepared to be. Thus, while there were clear moves towards Europe during this period, the influence of the three circles approach was still evident.

The particular lure of Western Europe, however, lay in the economic field. As evidence mounted in the late 1950s of Britain's poor economic performance compared to its neighbours in the EEC, British scepticism about the latter notwithstanding, the attractions of being a member of a much larger market began to grow. This point needs to be set alongside the important fact that from the mid-1950s onwards Britain's trade profile began to change dramatically with the focus of that trade shifting away from the Empire/Commonwealth and towards Europe.[26] If these economic/commercial arguments for membership of the EEC were not in themselves convincing, they were reinforced by political arguments. The growing problems with the Commonwealth through the 1960s have been noted earlier. If the Commonwealth was of declining utility to Britain in both economic and political terms, there was much less reason to allow it to stand in the way of closer links with Europe. Significantly, pursuing those links also received the blessing of the Kennedy Administration, which wanted to encourage a closer British association with Western Europe—as American governments had to a greater or lesser extent since the 1940s. Finally, the prospect of joining the Community had been made more palatable for the British by the return to power of De Gaulle in France. His view of the Community as essentially an intergovernmental association of sovereign states rather than an institutional mechanism for integration were very similar to more traditional British views about European cooperation.

If the arguments for joining the EEC had became convincing, if never overwhelming, by the beginning of this period, the process of joining held up proceedings for a decade. It was to take two applications as well as, ironically, the political demise of President De Gaulle before the relevant treaties were signed in January 1972. The problem, certainly as far as De Gaulle was

[26]For further discussion and relevant data, see David Sanders, *op. cit.,* pp. 143–56.

concerned, was that he remained unconvinced—with some reason—that Britain had become sufficiently European in orientation to be prepared to give up its special links with Washington. Whether or not it was a convenient excuse, the Polaris deal at Nassau was used to justify a French veto of the first British application to join the EEC.

Even after Britain joined the Community, successive governments of both political persuasions managed to give the impression that they were less than committed to their new European role. This was partly a result of specific issues such as the terms of entry—which the British at one stage seemed to want continually to renegotiate—the recurrent question of Britain's contribution to the Community budget, and, of course, Harold Wilson's gesture to the left wing of the Labour Party, the Referendum in 1975. More damaging, perhaps, was the continuing evidence of three circles thinking that made Britain a rather awkward partner with a distinctively different perspective on Community matters.[27] To some extent, this more assertive stance can be explained in terms of Britain's late entry and the need to "take on" the established Franco-German alliance in a Community context. A consistently Gaullist approach, moreover, was never going to please the more federalist Community members. To the extent, however, that British attitudes contributed to the development of what became known as "Eurosclerosis" in the late 1970s—indicating that the process of economic integration had stagnated—this provided an unfortunate context when the Thatcher government came to power in 1979, headed by a prime minister of decidedly Gaullist views.

THE THATCHER PERIOD 1980–90

As several commentators have noted, there was a contradiction at the heart of the admixture of liberalism and conservatism that became known as "Thatcherism." In domestic policy, it stood for minimising state power, for enabling individual initiative to blossom freed from the strangulating hold of state regulation. In foreign policy. however, it stood for a "strong" rather than a "weak" state, for a determination to reassert national interests after years of declining influence abroad.[28] The notion of regeneration, however, at both an individual and a national level gave the impression that the Thatcher era would be marked by fundamental change in foreign as well as domestic policy terms. On reflection, change there certainly was in style, mood, and strength of leadership, but in terms of substantive foreign policy issues, it is difficult not to be impressed by elements of continuity rather than change through this period. With respect to our three circles theme, there was a determined reassertion of Atlanticism, an important phase of residual globalism and a

[27] See Stephen George, *An Awkward Partner: Britain in the European Community* (New York: Oxford University Press, 1990).
[28] See, for example, William Wallace and Helen Wallace, "Strong state or weak state in foreign policy? The contradictions of conservative liberalism 1979–87," *Public Administration* Vol. 68, Spring 1990, pp. 83–101.

growing hostility towards Western Europe or at least towards the European Community that was to contribute significantly to the downfall of the prime minister in 1990.

Thatcher and Atlanticism

It has been said that when Margaret Thatcher came to power in 1979 she had a profound ignorance of foreign affairs. "Her principal contribution," Hugo Young suggests, "was a world view of powerful simplicity—determined, above all, by anticommunism."[29] In the context of a downturn in East-West relations at the beginning of the 1980s, all her instincts told her that a "resolute approach" abroad was an appropriate complement to the "right approach" at home. Thus it was necessary to increase defence spending and move closer to the Americans, who were seen as providing the ultimate security guarantee. During her first year in office, decisions to purchase the Trident missile system from the United States, to support the NATO decision to increase defense spending by three per cent per annum and to endorse the "dual track" approach to the deployment of Cruise and Pershing 2 missiles contributed to an "image of strength" as far as foreign and defence policy was concerned.[30]

Underpinned by the close personal and ideological relationship between Mrs. Thatcher and President Reagan—after he came into office in 1981—and apparently evidenced by the extensive assistance afforded to Britain during the 1982 Falklands conflict, the special nature of the Anglo-American relationship received greater emphasis in London than it had for twenty years. After the Falklands, however, the continuing assumption of special links with Washington began to appear increasingly anachronistic. The notion that the relationship was characterised by dependence rather than "specialness" was highlighted by what appeared to observers as an excessive willingness to underwrite American policy in 1985–86. A series of decisions, including following the United States out of UNESCO, being the first NATO ally to agree to participate in SDI research programmes, sanctioning the takeover of Westland Helicopters by an American-led consortium, and allowing the United States to stage the April 1986 attack on Libya from bases in Britain produced unflattering references in the British press to the Prime Minister as "Little Lady Echo" or "Reagan's poodle."

An even more important problem for the Anglo-American relationship in the second half of the 1980s was the extent to which it rested essentially on the personal relationship between the two leaders. This began to concern the British as President Reagan approached the end of his second term. President Bush's first visit to Europe in June 1989 confirmed the worst British fears. While Bush offered reassurances in London that "from our side of the Atlantic,

[29] Hugo Young, *One of Us* (London: Pan), p. 169.
[30] Michael Clarke, "The Soviet Union and Western Europe," in Peter Byrd, ed. *British Foreign Policy Under Thatcher* (New York: St. Martin's Press, 1988), p. 62.

this relationship is strong and will continue to be so," the fact that he felt compelled to offer such reassurances both privately and to the press only served to draw attention to the concern on the other side of the Atlantic that British influence in Washington was indeed on the wane.[31] This seemed to be confirmed when the British government received only the most cursory advance notification of the first Bush-Gorbachev summit in Malta. Indeed, in the wake of the dramatic changes in Europe in 1989–90, the Bush Administration went to some lengths, while trying not to offend Mrs. Thatcher, to avoid encouraging any lingering illusions about special transatlantic links and to press for Britain to play a full role in the shaping of the new Europe. In the context of those changes in Europe, it soon became apparent that it would be difficult for the British to sustain the idea that their relationship with Washington was more important than, say, the United States' relationship with the West Germans, though we must return to this point in the context of the 1990–91 Gulf crisis.

Thatcher and Globalism

If Mrs. Thatcher remained an instinctive Atlanticist throughout her eleven years in office, she was also committed to restoring Britain to a position of international influence and respect. What remained of the Empire obviously provided little scope for the pursuit of this objective, though, thanks to the skillful diplomacy of the Foreign Secretary Lord Carrington, Britain managed to end the long-running problem with Rhodesia by engineering an agreement at the Lancaster House Conference that brought about formal independence and majority rule in what became Zimbabwe in 1980. An unexpected opportunity for an impressive display of national resolve, however, came with the Argentinian invasion of the Falkland Islands in April 1982. The repossession of these islands by military force over the following three months did much to confirm the international reputation of Mrs. Thatcher as a tough leader who would not flinch from doing whatever was necessary to defend Britain's national interests—as she defined them—and incidentally helped the prime minister to win a second electoral victory in June 1983.[32]

The Falklands conflict, however, was an aberration rather than an indication that the Thatcher government was trying to stem the tide of imperial retreat. This was clearly indicated by the almost immediate attempts to negotiate a settlement with China over the future of Hong Kong, another residual piece of Empire. By December 1984 an agreement had been signed that provided for a British withdrawal by 1997, after which, with certain rather optimistic safeguards, Hong Kong would revert to Chinese control. Similarly, there were few if any illusions left about the Commonwealth by the 1980s.

---

[31] Quoted in *The Guardian*, London, 2 June 1989.

[32] For an excellent introduction to the Falklands issue and to the extensive literature this issue generated, see Lawrence Freedman, *Britain and the Falklands War* (New York: Basil Blackwell, 1988).

Commonwealth Conferences during these years tended to be dominated by the issue of economic sanctions on South Africa, with Britain often in a minority of one opposed to such action. Mrs. Thatcher usually contrived to be both abrasive and indifferent to Commonwealth opinion on these occasions, patronisingly so at the infamous Nassau Conference in October 1985.

Where Britain was able to exercise some significant influence at the global level was in the field of East-West relations, particularly in the second Thatcher term from 1983 to 1987.[33] After 1979, the prime minister's strident anticommunism had certainly made a contribution to the hostile atmosphere in East-West relations, but her contribution was essentially a reaction to an already worsening state of relations. The Thatcher government—and the prime minister in particular—was ideologically in tune with the second Cold War, but Britain was in no sense the initiator, still less an architect of Western policy in the way that the Attlee government had been with respect to the first Cold War in the late 1940s.

After the 1983 election, and following a major review of policy, the Thatcher government launched its version of *Ostpolitik*. A sustained and remarkably successful attempt to improve the climate of East-West relations lasted throughout the second Thatcher term. Given the uncompromising principles that had underpinned policy in her first term, this change of policy appeared to represent something of a *volte face*. What had happened to persuade the "Iron Lady" to modify her views or at least to curb the aggressive anti-Communist rhetoric? The most obvious explanation is to suggest that the prime minister, like her Conservative predecessors Churchill and Macmillan, spotted an opportunity in 1983 to gain some personal kudos and national prestige from attempting to initiate a more conciliatory period in East-West relations. The Falklands success followed by a landslide electoral victory produced a buoyant, confident prime minister who appeared keen to establish in her second term a claim to be regarded as an international stateswoman of the first rank. An influential East-West role—not for the first time—fitted the bill perfectly. The evident determination in Washington to continue a policy of confrontation with the Soviet Union and the growing concern in Western Europe about the negative consequences of an *impasse* in East-West relations were the important international components of a situation that presented the opportunity for a more flexible approach.

To be set against an explanation in terms of what might be called "pragmatic opportunism," is evidence in this context of another strand of traditional thinking—Strang's "conciliatory quality." There are indications that the prime minister came under considerable pressure in the weeks before and immediately after the election to adopt a more conciliatory approach to the East. This pressure came largely from the Foreign and Commonwealth Office and their ministerial representatives, past as well as present. Lord Carrington, for example, who had felt it necessary to resign as Foreign Secretary following

---

[33]This section is adapted from Brian White, *op. cit.*, chapter 7.

the Argentinian invasion of the Falklands, made an important speech in May 1983 in which he not only criticised what he called "megaphone diplomacy" but also a "crude, one-dimensional moralism" in dealings with the East. In a barely coded critique of the "Iron Lady" posture of the prime minister, Carrington called for a return to a more balanced East-West policy—a "sweet and sour" approach as he called it—with the emphasis now on the "sweet," stressing the importance of "our own tradition—the peaceful resolution of potential conflict through energetic and forceful dialogue."[34]

Whatever stimulated this new emphasis on East-West relations, the second Thatcher government did make a significant contribution to the development of a less confrontational and a more constructive relationship between the superpowers, and, moreover, helped to open up contacts with Eastern Europe. As an influential third party who at that time enjoyed excellent relations with Washington and rapidly improving relations with the Soviet Union and various members of the Soviet bloc, Britain was in a good position to play an influential role. Particularly important was the personal (special?) relationship between Mrs. Thatcher, President Reagan and Mr. Gorbachev, which enabled the prime minister to play, if not a mediatory role, at least an important communications role between the superpowers and their respective leaders. As Hugo Young puts it, "Mrs. Thatcher, politically on Reagan's wavelength, and intellectually on Gorbachev's, had some of the qualities required to interpret one to the other."[35] After the resolution of the thorny issue of Britain's contribution to the European Community budget in 1984, Mrs. Thatcher could also lay claim to a European leadership role in her dealings with the superpowers. This was most evident perhaps during her visit to Moscow in 1987 when, having made a point of consulting with both Chancellor Kohl and President Mitterand in advance, she let it be known that she was representing European interests. As the superpowers moved inexorably towards an intermediate range nuclear force (INF) agreement, those interests included growing European fears about any further "denuclearisation" of Europe.

After the signing of the INF Treaty in December 1987, however, British influence began to wane again. It soon became clear that the sources of British influence were being eroded—a trend that had been evident from the 1960s. While direct superpower relations were becoming more and more institutionalised in the late 1980s, Britain's bilateral relations with each of them became more difficult and certainly less special. As changes in Europe took on a distinctly revolutionary look by the end of the decade, Mrs. Thatcher also began to appear more and more as an unreconstructed cold warrior, preoccupied with security politics, worried about the prospect of German unity, and either unwilling or unable to adapt to the changing mood of East-West relations. Finally, as a result of highly publicised differences over the future of

---

[34]Lord Carrington, "The 1983 Alistair Buchan memorial lecture," *Survival* 25:4, 1983, pp. 151–52.
[35]Hugo Young, *op. cit.,* p. 394.

the European Community—differences that spilled over into the East-West arena—Britain's relations with her West European partners also entered a particularly difficult stage. It is to relations within the European circle during the 1980s that we finally turn.

Thatcher and Europeanism

The early years of the Thatcher period saw a continued preoccupation with the issue of Britain's contribution to the Community budget. Five years of often acrimonious negotiations about both the size and the equity of the British contribution—"our" or even "my money" as Mrs. Thatcher insisted on calling it—soured relations between Britain and her Community partners throughout the first Thatcher government. The focus on this issue, however, and on the combative political style of the prime minister (a problem that was to have far more serious implications later on) tended to obscure the extent to which Britain was gradually becoming a more mainstream player in Community affairs—moving, in David Allen's phrase, "from the periphery of the Community towards the middle ground."[36] This could be seen in the role Britain was playing in helping to develop the European Political Cooperation (EPC) machinery. Britain was responsible in 1980, for example, for developing the Troika system of linking three successive presidencies together to achieve continuity in EPC.

After the resolution of the budget issue in 1984, Britain played a more high-profile role in advocating the completion of the internal market and playing a leading role in the negotiations that produced the Single European Act (SEA) in 1986. Admittedly, the single market was an objective that was consistent with Thatcherite free market ideology, but, nevertheless, it was a clear indication that Britain could work constructively within a Community framework and, indeed, help to set the Community's agenda. It had also become clear by the mid-1980s how far the main lines of British policy on specific issues had come to resemble those pursued collectively by West Europeans. On occasions—with respect to the Siberian gas pipeline issue in 1981–82, for example—this even saw Britain taking up a position in opposition to the United States.

Questions about the future direction of the Community in terms of the integration agenda, however, had reached centre stage again by the time that Mrs. Thatcher had won her third successive election in 1987. Having ratified the Single European Act, the British government, like its partners, was now committed not just to harmonising its foreign policy but also to working towards political and economic union. The prime minister's response to this prospect came in a speech delivered in Bruges in September 1988—a speech that was to have a major impact both domestically and in the Community. In this speech, Mrs. Thatcher took great care to establish her commitment to Europe as a continent—a Europe that was both "open" and "free" in political

[36] David Allen, quoted in Peter Byrd, ed. *op. cit.,* p. 52.

and economic terms as she later put it.[37] The prime minister could and did claim that her government had done much through its *Ostpolitik* to contribute to the process of political change in Central and Eastern Europe. The thrust of her speech, however, was an unprecedented attack on the European Community. In a sentence often quoted thereafter, Mrs. Thatcher not only attacked the Brussels bureaucracy but integration theology as a whole from a characteristic Thatcherite perspective. "We have not successfully rolled back the frontiers of the state in Britain, only to see them reimposed at a European level, with a European super-state exercising a new dominance from Brussels."[38]

Certainly the anti-Community prejudices of the prime minister were given full vent in this speech. As a committed Atlanticist, Mrs. Thatcher was predisposed to measure European cooperation in every sphere in terms of its contribution to the solidarity of transatlantic relations rather than in terms of meeting a series of integration objectives. In domestic political terms, her acceptance of the loss of a number of senior ministers from 1986 onwards over European or Europe-related issues was testimony to the strength of her Atlanticist convictions. Unfortunately for her, the resignation at the beginning of November 1990 of the last of these ministers, Foreign Secretary Sir Geoffrey Howe, triggered the domestic political crisis that led to her own resignation. Howe's dramatic resignation speech in the House of Commons focused on the two issues that caused her downfall—her increasingly presidential style of leadership and her anti-Community prejudices. Reading between the lines of Howe's speech, it is clear that the Foreign Secretary and other senior ministers had looked on helplessly but with growing concern for some months as Community leaders ceased to argue with an increasingly strident Mrs. Thatcher and had chosen—from the December 1989 European summit in Strasbourg onwards—simply to isolate her.

There was an important sense, however, in which the prime minister's use of the powerful symbolism of sovereignty and national independence to support a "so far and no further" approach to European integration was an indication that she had not lost her populist instincts. Though it has been apparent, certainly since the end of the 1970s, that Britain is, to all intents and purposes, a West European state, the British people and their leaders were remarkably resistant to accepting this reality. Writing at the end of the 1980s, Tugendhat and Wallace bemoaned the fact that:

> the European connection has not become a matter for the heart as well as the head. The European Community still has little appeal for most British citizens, or for many of their political leaders, even though they accept it as a necessary framework for British interests. The Community is seen as a forum for hard bargaining in defence of national interests, not as a part of Britain's international persona.[39]

[37] Margaret Thatcher, "My vision of Europe: open and free." *Financial Times*, 19 Nov., 1990, p. 17.
[38] Quoted in Hugo Young, *op. cit.,* p. 552.
[39] Christopher Tugendhat and William Wallace, *op. cit.,* p. 26.

The fact is, as this chapter has tried to show, the British reluctance to embrace a European "persona" has more deep-seated historical, political, and, even, cultural roots that predate both the 1980s and Mrs. Thatcher's prejudices. This is important to bear in mind as we come finally to consider the foreign policy problems that confront the post-Thatcher leadership in Britain.

BRITISH FOREIGN POLICY IN THE 1990s

For the first few months after the resignation of Mrs. Thatcher on November 29, 1990, the foreign policy agenda in Britain, as in many other countries, was dominated by the crisis and the war in the Gulf. In an important sense, this served as a diversion from confronting the central problems posed by the Thatcher demise. These problems relate not only to working out an appropriate relationship with Britain's European partners and with the United States in the 1990s, but also, in the wake of dramatic changes in the postwar structure of international relations—the so-called end of the Cold War—establishing the direction of Britain and, indeed, Britain's international identity for the foreseeable future.

British policy under the new Major administration with respect to the Gulf issue, not surprisingly perhaps, followed the lines established by Mrs. Thatcher. The former prime minister was in the United States at the time of the Iraqi invasion of Kuwait in August 1990, and there was speculation at the time that she helped to persuade President Bush to take a tough line in response. As the British role in the Gulf crisis developed, however, it took on more and more the appearance of an ill-fitting, perhaps, but nevertheless comfortable old suit. Once the Gulf crisis turned into a military confrontation all the traditional images came flooding back: Britain again playing a significant global role upholding international law by military force; Britain acting again as the closest and most loyal ally of the United States; British leaders berating the "Europeans" again for allegedly contributing inadequately to the coalition efforts to liberate Kuwait; British leaders using the Gulf example to pour scorn once more on the possibility of European political and economic union.

With the ending of the Gulf War, however, attention turned back to the issues dramatically highlighted by Mrs. Thatcher's resignation. One central question was whether the Major government would adopt a new approach to the European Community to avoid the isolation that had been a feature of the former prime minister's last months of tenure. Early indications did not allow any firm conclusions to be drawn. There was certainly a change of style, though this was to be expected. Contacts at Community meetings and elsewhere were cordial, and there were clear indications that the new government was seeking to build bridges with Community partners. There was a determined attempt, for example, to develop a good working relationship with the Germans after a series of frosty exchanges during the Gulf crisis.[40] It was not immediately

[40]See *The Economist*, 23 February 1991, p. 59.

clear, however, whether the substance of British European policy would undergo a significant change.

The dilemma for British policymakers in the post-Thatcher period is not only that the pace of change in all areas of interest is so rapid, but that change in one area cuts across all the others. When issues could be compartmentalised—economic issues dealt with in an EC context and security issues in a NATO context, for example—institutional arrangements roughly matched a traditional conception of Britain's role as a sort of "manager" of transatlantic relations. The ending of the Cold War, however, has speeded up the process of institutional change and is forcing British policymakers to confront some uncomfortable choices, such as whether or not to support the Franco-German plan to integrate the Western European Union—broadly the European wing of NATO—into the European Community by 1996. This development would cut right across the Atlantic/European institutional distinction that the British have sought so hard to preserve.

At the heart of all this in terms of the theme of this chapter is the increasing pressure on British policymakers to choose between the Atlantic and the European circles as a base from which to wield influence. Clearly, a compartmentalised three circles tradition—or even its contemporary two circles variant—is not a very helpful guide to the flexible, creative thinking that needs to be done about the future orientation of British foreign policy. As Christopher Hill comments, "the three circles concept implies that Britain can engage in some kind of eternal juggling act, with no need to choose priorities between the groupings."[41] The danger is that short-term pragmatism and slow adaptation to change may mean that Britain misses important opportunities through the 1990s to exert influence both within and beyond Europe at a critical time.

FOREIGN POLICY LANDMARKS

March 1946	Winston Churchill speech at Fulton, Missouri warns of Soviet "Iron Curtain" descending across Europe
January 1947	Attlee Government takes the decision to develop an atom bomb
1947	Indian subcontinent granted independence
March 1948	Brussels Treaty signed with France and the Benelux countries
October 1948	Churchill's "Three Circles" speech to the Conservative Party Conference
April 1949	Signing of North Atlantic Treaty
December 1950	Attlee Government announces massive rearmament program in the context of the Korean War
October 1952	First British atom bomb successfully tested
Sept.–Oct. 1954	Churchill Government agrees to commit permanent military force (BAOR) to continental Europe for the indefinite future

[41]Christopher Hill, "The historical background" in Michael Smith, Steve Smith and Brian White, eds. *British Foreign Policy: Tradition, Change and Transformation* (Boston: Unwin Hyman, 1988), p. 44.

Oct.–Nov. 1956	Anglo-French invasion of Suez and subsequent withdrawal
January 1960	Britain contributes to the creation of the European Free Trade Association (EFTA)
February 1960	Macmillan's "Wind of Change" speech to the South African Parliament in Cape Town
May 1960	Abortive four-power summit in Paris
August 1961	First British application to join the European Economic Community (EEC)
December 1962	Macmillan persuades the Kennedy Administration at Nassau to sell the Polaris missile to Britain following the cancellation of the Skybolt missile program
August 1963	Signing of the Partial Test Ban Treaty in Moscow
November 1965	Unilateral Declaration of Independence announced by Ian Smith on behalf of the white minority government in Rhodesia
July 1967	Announcement that Britain will withdraw all its military forces from East of Suez—specifically from Singapore, Malaysia and the Gulf—by 1971. Decision confirmed in the 1968 Defence Review
January 1973	Britain joins the European Economic Community
October 1979	Election of the first Thatcher government
April 1980	Independence of Zimbabwe (formerly Rhodesia) following the Lancaster House Conference
July 1980	Decision to purchase Trident missile from the United States
April–June 1982	Argentinian invasion of the Falkland Islands is followed by a war with Argentina to recapture the Islands
June 1983	Election of the second Thatcher government
February 1984	A British *Ostpolitik* begins with Mrs. Thatcher's visit to Hungary
May 1984	European Community summit at Fontainebleu resolves issue of Britain's contribution to the Community budget
April 1986	U.S. attack on Libya staged from bases in Britain
1986–7	Britain signs and ratifies the Single European Act (SEA)
March 1987	Mrs. Thatcher visits the Soviet Union
June 1987	Election of the third Thatcher government
September 1988	Mrs. Thatcher sets out her vision of Europe in a speech in Bruges
April 1989	Second Gorbachev visit to Britain followed by expulsion of alleged Soviet spies
October 1990	Britain joins the Exchange Rate Mechanism (ERM) of the European Monetary System (EMS)
November 1990	Resignation of Mrs. Thatcher. John Major replaces her as prime minister

SELECTED BIBLIOGRAPHY

Barber. James, *Who Makes British Foreign Policy?* Milton Keynes: Open University Press, 1976.

Byrd. Peter, ed. *British Foreign Policy Under Thatcher.* New York: St. Martin's Press, 1988.

Deighton. Anne, ed., *Britain and the First Cold War.* London: Macmillan, 1990.

Frankel. Joseph, *British Foreign Policy, 1945–73.* New York: Oxford University Press, 1975.

Freedman. Lawrence, *Britain and the Falklands War.* New York: Blackwell, 1988.

George. Stephen, *An Awkward Partner: Britain in the European Community.* New York: Oxford University Press, 1990.

Kennedy. Paul, *The Realities Behind Diplomacy: Background influences on British External Policy 1865–1980*. (London: Fontana, 1981).

Louis, William, R. and Hedley Bull, eds. *The Special Relationship: Anglo-American Relations since 1945*. Oxford: Clarendon Press, 1986.

Northedge. Frederick, S. *Descent from Power: British Foreign Policy 1945–73*. London: Allen & Unwin, 1974.

Sanders. David, *Losing an Empire, Finding a Role*. London: Macmillan, 1990.

Smith, Michael, Steve Smith, and Brian White, eds. *British Foreign Policy: Tradition, Change and Transformation*. Boston: Unwin Hyman, 1988.

Tugendhat, Christopher and William Wallace. *Options for British Foreign Policy in the 1990s*. New York: Routledge, 1988.

Wallace. William, *The Foreign Policy Process in Britain*. London: Allen & Unwin, 1977.

White. Brian, P. *Britain, Detente and Changing East-West Relations*. London/New York: Routledge, 1991.

Young. Hugo, *One of Us: A Biography of Margaret Thatcher*, revised edition. London: Pan Books, 1990.

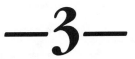

—3—

FRENCH FOREIGN POLICY

THE QUEST FOR RANK

Roy C. Macridis

France is the only middle-rank power that has undertaken a search to attain world rank. One of the foremost world powers until 1940, it refused to be drawn, as a subordinate, into the Atlantic Alliance, dominated by the U.S.A., and it sought independence within and outside of the Alliance. Unlike West Germany, which acquiesced to American tutelage for a long time; unlike England, which clung desperately to a "special relationship" with the U.S.A. that only underwrote its declining power; and unlike Japan, which accepted American protection in return for the American market for its products—France aspired to a restoration of its commanding position in Europe and elsewhere. How does a middle-rank power, confronted for so long by the Soviet Union and the United States and perhaps the growing power of China and Japan, strive for independent status and world rank?

The available means are limited, but the guidelines to be followed are quite simple. First, an increase of one's own power basis. This can be achieved through rapid industrial and economic modernization, the increase of population, and the development of modern weapons; a power basis can also be strengthened through regional alliances that provide additional weight and resources. Second, a middle-rank power, in a world of two superpowers, should avoid an entangling and integrative alliance with either of the two—for such an alliance will inevitably subordinate it to the superpower with which the alliance is made. The looser an alliance is, the more leeway and freedom it gives to a middle-rank power. Third, a middle-rank power should exert itself to prevent the development of close collaboration between the two superpowers—such a collaboration may amount to a "condominium" of the world by the two superpowers, overshadowing all other nation-states. (In fact, one of the reasons why integrative alliances with one or the other of the two superpowers is to be avoided is precisely to give to a middle-rank power the necessary freedom to maneuver against the realization of such a condominium.) But a middle-rank power should also try to prevent any direct confrontation between the two superpowers, for invariably such a confrontation will force it to take sides and, by so doing, forfeit its freedom of action. A middle-rank power must strive constantly for a détente between the two superpowers but in such a way that détente is never translated into an entente. What if one superpower weakens—as it appears to be the case with the Soviet Union? The answer is implicit in the logic of our argument. Everything possible will be done to avoid being controlled or becoming subordinated to the other—in this case the United States. In fact for a middle-rank power, a world with two superpowers is better than a world with one!

The policy of France since World War II can be easily understood in terms of the basic paradigm just outlined. As we shall see, France remained suspicious of both the Soviets and the Americans. It opposed all along, and continues to do so, any hegemony of the one or the other over any region of the world, and it deplored the division of Europe into two blocs. It gave support sometimes to the United States and sometimes to the Soviet Union—depending upon how its leaders estimated the balance of forces in the world and the relative strength and the intentions of the two superpowers. It attempted to strengthen the base of its power through economic modernization and rapid industrial development; and its population increased by almost 20 percent in the period since World War II. Its position and role within the European Common Market also created a regional base that could be used for political purposes, as did its influence and control in Africa. Finally the development of an independent nuclear force, planned before de Gaulle came to power in 1958, gave France a nuclear deterrent and, according to some of its strategists, genuine independence that ultimately made its withdrawal from the integrated military command of the Atlantic Alliance possible.

We shall examine in this chapter the background factors that have shaped France's foreign policy—its geographic position, its economic and social development, its ideology and culture, its persistent pursuit of national interests in the past, and its foreign policy objectives, as they were reformulated in the years of the Fourth Republic (1946–1958) and, more particularly, as they have been restated in the years of the Fifth Republic under de Gaulle and under his successors—Georges Pompidou (1969–1974), Valéry Giscard d'-Estaing (1974–1981), and François Mitterrand since 1981.

BACKGROUND FACTORS

The dilemma facing France at the end of World War II may be stated in rather simple terms: France, one of the great powers in the world, found its position drastically weakened. But the aspirations of greatness and rank have persisted. These aspirations were expressed succinctly by the architect of France's post-World War II policy, General Charles de Gaulle. "I intended," he wrote in his Memoirs, referring to the period immediately after the defeat of Germany,

> to assure France primacy in Western Europe by preventing the rise of a new Reich that might again threaten her safety; to cooperate with the East and West and, if need be, contract the necessary alliances on one side or another without ever accepting any kind of dependency; to transform the French Union into a free association in order to avoid the as yet unspecified dangers of upheaval; to persuade the states along the Rhine, the Alps and the Pyrenees to form a political, economic and strategic bloc; to establish this organization as one of the three world powers and, should it become necessary, as the arbiter between the Soviet and the Anglo-Saxon camps.[1]

This was an ambitious scheme, and, as he admitted, the means available to his country "were poor indeed." But it was a goal widely shared by the majority of the French elites.

In 1944, after the liberation of Paris and the establishment of a provisional government on French territory under General de Gaulle, France and her overseas possessions were in a state of dependency. Drained of manpower, with her economy seriously undermined after four years of occupation, facing urgent problems of social and economic reconstruction at home and powerful centrifugal forces in the empire, the power and even the political will to fashion the instruments that would lead to an independent course of action were lacking. France was dependent upon Britain and, primarily of course, upon the United States. In terms of Walter Lippmann's axiom that commitments in foreign policy must be commensurate with strength, it was very clear that there were few commitments that France could undertake and carry out successfully without Anglo-American support. France's liberty of action, therefore, was limited. Her aspiration to remain a top-rank power seemed to be at variance with her capabilities.

Thus the dilemma confronting France's post-World War II governments and political elites was either to accept the situation as it developed after World War II or to continue to seek "greatness" and "rank" without the physical, military, and economic resources to implement it. It called for difficult political decisions and choices; it demanded the rapid reconsideration of some of the traditional French foreign policy patterns; and, above all, it required a meaningful debate among political leaders and elites about alternatives and choices.

Neither the political system under the Fourth Republic nor the political parties and the press managed to provide for such a debate. There was no "great debate" to redefine the French position and status in the world.

[1] *War Memoirs,* Vol. 3, *Salvation* (New York: Simon & Schuster, 1960), p. 204.

Strangely enough, it was only after the return to power of General de Gaulle in 1958 and the establishment of the Fifth Republic that foreign policy themes began to be stated with enough clarity to invite debate, to elicit support, or to provoke criticism.

Persistent Patterns A number of patterns underlie France's foreign policy. In the nineteenth century they reflected France's strength, but they slowly crystallized into dogmas and myths that were ultimately separated from twentieth-century reality. It is, nonetheless, in terms of such myths that France's foreign policy was shaped—immediately after World War II—rather than in terms of the new factors that developed partly as a result of the war and partly as the result of a number of social, economic, and ideological forces that stirred the world. These myths continue to play an important role today.

The basic objectives of foreign policy remained (*a*) the continuation of France's imperial position, and (*b*) continental strength. The first meant the maintenance of the far-flung empire with all the financial difficulties and obligations it entailed. Maintenance of the empire was conceived as a part of France's mission and as a continuous challenge to French culture and influence. The resurrection of France as a continental power was also an automatic reflex; no political leader doubted it. The end of World War II with the defeat of Germany was, in a sense, France's revenge for the German occupation. Victory, it was thought, simply reestablished the prewar balance. To implement France's continental position, the same alliances with the West and with the East were contemplated—all of them directed against a Germany that lay prostrate and divided. The fact that the Soviet Union had gained a foothold in the heart of Europe did not alter the traditional French reflexes; Germany was the enemy of France. A weak Germany and a Franco-Russian alliance remained the conditions for French security. When General de Gaulle visited Moscow and signed the Franco-Russian treaty in December 1944, he was preserving French security in the best tradition of the nineteenth century.

THE SUBSTANCE OF FOREIGN POLICY: TRENDS AND PROBLEMS

France has followed four basic foreign policy objectives ever since the eighteenth century. The first is the policy of *natural frontiers* in Europe; the second was and is the policy of what might be called *European status quo* or *balance of power* in Europe; the third remains the preservation of its empire, in one form or another; and the fourth is the preservation of world power status.

The policy of status quo in Europe was based upon two assumptions:

1. No single power should gain preponderant strength in Europe.
2. France would become the protector of these small states throughout Europe and play the role of arbitrator and maintain its position of supremacy in Europe.

The immediate reaction of France after liberation in December 1944, was to attempt to reestablish its traditional position of security in Europe and of independence as a world power. From 1944 until mid-1947, a policy was followed that for all practical purposes was similar to that of 1919. France proposed the following:

1. The dismemberment of Germany and prolonged occupation of the country.
2. Heavy reparations and tight control of German industrial output.
3. The reestablishment of French control in the area west of the Rhine by the detachment of these territories from Germany.
4. A prolonged occupation, if not annexation, of the Saar.
5. The independence of the small nations of Europe.
6. An alliance with the Soviet Union directed against a threat to French security from Germany.
7. An alliance with Great Britain.

Under the first government of General de Gaulle (1944–1946) this policy was pursued with great tenacity. After the liberation, a Treaty of Mutual Assistance was signed with the Soviet Union. The two countries agreed to take "all the necessary measures in order to eliminate any new menace coming from Germany and to take the initiative to make any new effort of aggression on her part impossible" (Article 3).

In fact, until the beginning of 1947, every effort was made by France to gain the support of *either* the Soviet Union *or* the United States (along with Great Britain) in the implementation of its German policy. Neither of the two allies, however, responded favorably, since they both hoped to see, ultimately, an economically and politically unified Germany *on their side,* something that would have meant the end of French aspirations for European security and leadership. When Soviet Foreign Minister Molotov declared himself, in July 1946, in favor of a politically unified Germany, a French scholar wrote, "There was reason for France, which could count on the support of her ally in the East *against* the Anglo-Americans, to be disappointed."[2]

The Cold War and the Development of Western Alliances. The Cold War, whose origin can be traced to Yalta and Potsdam, erupted in the beginning of 1947. Conferences in Moscow and London had failed to produce any kind of agreement. The lines were being drawn, and the division of Germany into two zones—Soviet and British-American—became a certainty. The conflict implied the strengthening of a West German Republic—the Federal Republic of Germany—supported by the United States.

France managed to maintain control over the Saar, but failed in all its other claims. After June 1947, the whole of Western Europe and Great Britain received massive American aid to develop their economies. In 1948 the Brussels Pact brought together the Benelux countries, France, and Great Britain. It provided for a permanent consultative council and negotiations to promote economic development of the countries concerned, and included a

[2] In *Année politique,* 1946, p. 400.

military clause calling for common action against a German attack or aggression and to cope with a situation that constituted a menace to peace, no matter where it occurred or from where it came. In 1949 the creation of a large military umbrella was logically called for. Not only the Brussels signatories, but also most of the Western countries, including ultimately Greece and Turkey, participated. The United States became a permanent part of this alliance that still continues as the North Atlantic Treaty Organization (NATO). Article 5 stipulates that an attack against any one of the signatories, either in Europe or in North America, would be considered an attack against all, without providing, however, for *automatic* military assistance among the signatories. It further provides (in Article 9) for a permanent deliberative organization and the establishment of a common military command. The Federal Republic of Germany was originally excluded from NATO.

These developments determined France's position. France became a member of NATO, under the overall leadership and military direction of the United States. Such an alliance underwrote French security and, in general terms, the integrity of the empire. The exclusion of Germany continued to give France a strategic position in Western Europe, as well as the semblance, if not the reality, of national power and independence.

But the question of Germany's future had been only postponed. A military Western alliance without Germany hardly represented a solution of the problems of military defense. Furthermore, as the struggle between the East and the West not only continued but was intensified with the Berlin Blockade, with the takeover of Czechoslovakia by the Soviets, and with the Korean War, the prize of Germany became more important for the two major opponents. For the United States, the rearmament of the Federal Republic of Germany seemed the logical step in the construction of a strong defensive line against a potential Soviet attack.

The European Defense Community and Its Alternatives. It was, strangely enough, the French who came forth with the answer: the creation of a West European army, the European Defense Community (EDC), involving a genuine integration of national forces and a unified—and, if possible, a supranational—command. The United States endorsed this policy as an alternative to the rearming of West Germany within NATO.

No sooner had the European Defense Community (EDC) been announced and formulated, however, than it provoked a storm of protest in France. The political parties came out actively either for or against it. Extreme right-wing and extreme left-wing parties joined hands against the treaty, which was defended by a sharply divided center. To French public opinion, the most controversial part of the treaty was the envisaged German rearmament. A majority of the members of the National Assembly considered German rearmament, even within the EDC, a direct challenge to French sovereignty, clearly spelling the end of France's aspirations to remain a leading European nation.

Since there was no genuine majority for or against the treaty[3] it was on a procedural motion that, in August 1954, the EDC was rejected by the French National Assembly. The rejection climaxed four years of equivocation. It was only in December 1954, that the National Assembly, six months after defeating the EDC for fear of German rearmament, allowed Germany to become a member of NATO and eventually to rearm herself within the framework of the NATO alliance.

France and the Empire

The French Empire extended over every continent of the world. Its administration was a vestige of the Napoleonic conceptions of a highly centralized bureaucratic system—an administration in which Paris, through the colonial officials, made the ultimate decisions and legislated for the whole empire. Its cementing ideology was that of "assimilation"—the notion that ultimately every inhabitant would become a French citizen and be represented in the French Parliament—a notion at marked variance with the Anglo-Saxon conception, according to which political and cultural evolution of the colonial peoples would ultimately bring about political autonomy and self-government.

In 1944 the basic charter of colonial policy had been drafted at the Brazzaville Conference. There it was decided that "the purpose of the civilizing work accomplished by France in the colonies excludes any idea of autonomy, any possibility of an evolution outside of the French Empire. The establishment, even in the remote future, of "self-government" in the colonies must not be considered."[4]

In almost every case, the French insisted upon the maintenance of French sovereignty. In 1945 France refused to withdraw its army from Syria and Lebanon. Within a year it had to give in. In 1947 it refused to enter into negotiations with Ho Chi-minh and engaged in a war that lasted until 1954. But the Vietnam War brought other problems to a head. In Algeria, Tunis, and Morocco, the independence movements were gaining strength. These movements, however, envisaged continued cooperation with France. In every case, the French political leaders and representatives and the various military leaders in command of the French troops reiterated the philosophy of the French vocation. Time after time, the strategic interests of France were evoked. Time after time, the representatives of the French government and army intervened. By 1956, both Morocco and Tunisia became independent. The refusal to grant self-government left only one alternative: independence. The situation was similar in Algeria, where there was a very strong movement in favor of self-government after the liberation of France in 1944.

[3] The division of the political system in the French Parliament and in the various coalition cabinets reflected very closely the division of public opinion: in July 1954, 36 percent of those asked were "for" or "rather for" the EDC. Thirty-one percent were "against" or "rather against," and 33 percent did not answer.

[4] *Année politique*, 1947–45.

THE LEGACY OF THE FOURTH REPUBLIC (1946–1958)

Speaking on October 28, 1966, General de Gaulle, now back in office as president of the Fifth Republic, stated with remarkable succinctness the objectives of French foreign policy in terms that applied to the Fourth Republic (1946–1958) as well:

> In the world as it is, people sometimes feign surprise over the so-called changes and detours of France's action. And there are even those who have spoken of contradictions or Machiavellism. Well, I believe that while the circumstances are changing around us, in truth there is nothing more constant than France's policy. For this policy, throughout the extremely varied vicissitudes of our times and our world—this policy's essential goal is that France be and remain an independent nation.[5]

Despite the divisions of the political system under the Fourth Republic and the fact that they often spilled over into the area of foreign policy, there was continuity in the pursuit of basic objectives of foreign policy. What has been called *la politique du grandeur* ("the policy of greatness"), according to which France's vocation is that of a world power and therefore a partner in the development of world strategy, or—under propitious conditions—an independent force, was ever present.

The Empire: The Foundation of a New Policy. It was only in the last two years of the Fourth Republic, between 1956 and 1958, that France's leadership decided to accept the irresistible trend of colonial emancipation rather than attempt to oppose it. In 1956, the French parliament began consideration of new legislation to put an end to the theory and practice of assimilation. A loi-cadre ("framework law") empowered the government to give considerable autonomy to the African republics and Madagascar. They became semi-independent republics, with their own parliaments and responsible executives. France retained jurisdiction over important areas of policy making such as defense, foreign policy, trade, and education. But the first path toward gradual political emancipation had been made, and it proved to be irreversible.

A New Economic Policy. There was a clear perception among most of the political leaders of the Fourth Republic that France could not recover its prewar position without drastic economic effort. A rapid modernization of the French economy and a gradual movement toward increasing European cooperation were required. A strong France in a well-integrated western European economy could become even stronger. Therefore, the Fourth Republic, after many equivocations, moved after 1956 in the direction of the European Economic Community (EEC) providing for liberalization of trade, lowering, and ultimately eliminating tariffs, and providing for free movement of capital and labor among West Germany, Italy, France, and the Benelux

[5] Charles de Gaulle, *Discours et Messages,* Vol. 5 (Paris: Plon, 1970), p. 97.

countries. The treaty formalizing the EEC ("Common Market") was signed in Rome in 1956 and put into effect on January 1, 1959.

THE FIFTH REPUBLIC AND GENERAL DE GAULLE— WORLDWIDE ASPIRATIONS (1958–1969)

Whatever the background factors, it was the military uprising of May 13, 1958, in Algeria that brought the Fourth Republic to an end. It was to General de Gaulle that most of the political groups and leaders turned. He was returned to office and granted by the legislature the powers to prepare a new constitution and submit it to a referendum.

The Basic Assumptions

De Gaulle's basic assumptions—what we may call his overall philosophy— begin and end with the notion that there is one social force—the "reality of the nation" (*le fait national*)—that overshadows all others. No other force or forces—ideological, social, or economic—have succeeded in undermining the nation-state as the focal point of the ultimate loyalty of man.

From the postulate of national reality a number of inferences flow. They do not always have the logical consistency that an academician would desire; but consistency is not a necessary ingredient of statecraft. Situations change so fast in our world that the only consistency lies in the ability to adjust.[6] Yet the inferences that follow from the postulate on national reality constitute guides to action and must be spelled out.

The Reality of the Nation and the Means of Achieving Independence. The reality of the nation requires power in order fully to manifest itself. Surveying the world situation before the Allied victory in Europe, de Gaulle could not restrain his bitterness: "How dull is the sword of France at the time when the Allies are about to launch the assault of Europe." Although not the only one, the basic ingredient of power is the military. In the ruins of France after the liberation, de Gaulle set himself to recreate the French army.[7]

But there are other important factors in the equation of power. De Gaulle recognized many and used them all: alliances, diplomacy and skill in negotiations, cultural relations, spiritual influence, economic resources, and population.

A strong ingredient of power—indeed, the only valid expression of a nation—is the state and its political organization. To play the proper role, France needed a strong state. In this state, one man, the president of the republic, should make foreign policy on behalf of the nation—the "real France"—incarnating the national interests over and above the welter of particular interests and ideological factions.

---

[6] Almost always, for instance, de Gaulle, speaking on international issues, inserted the phrase "given the present conditions in the world," or "in the actual state of developments," or "things being as they are."

[7] *War Memoirs.* Vol. 2, *Unity* (New York: Simon & Schuster, 1959), p. 245.

A third ingredient of power that de Gaulle evoked very frequently led him to follow policies to which he had seemed firmly opposed. This is what he called the imperative of the *grand ensembles* ("great wholes"). Nations must establish cooperative "wholes" that provide the structural bases and the resources for the economic development and defense of each one and of all. This is not contrary to his emphasis upon national uniqueness, nor did it lead him to the espousal of projects of military integration. The building of large "wholes" creates something that is more than an alliance and less than a federation. It is a close association and a cooperation between nation states which, by pooling some of their resources, find the strength to sustain a common purpose.

The Idea of Balance. De Gaulle's emphasis upon the reality of the national phenomenon and its concomitant accessories—power, both military and political—led him to a theory of international relations that is often referred to as "realist." International relations comprise an arena of conflict in which every participant nation-state attempts to increase its strength at the expense of the other. Every political leadership, no matter what ideology inspires it, acts in terms of national consideration. *If so, it is only power that can check power—and the only possible international world is one in which an equilibrium of powers is reached.* This led de Gaulle to follow conclusions that directly shaped his actions and have influenced his successors.

The balance that emerged after World War II was unnatural, precarious, and unwise—unnatural, because it involved a polarization of the world and the creation of political satellites, which is inconsistent with the secular realities and interests of nations; precarious because both the big and small nations were continuously on the brink of war; unwise, because it gave to the two of the least qualified nation-states (the United States and the Soviet Union) full liberty to act and to decide their fate and with it the fate of others.

Both the American and Soviet efforts were expressions of national power, in one form or another. If they were allowed free sway, the two might enter upon armed conflict. If they found a temporary accommodation, it would be in order to establish a joint hegemony over the world. *Either eventuality would be to the detriment of the other nation-states* including, of course, France and Europe as a whole. This could be avoided only by creating a balance of power consistent with the growing realities of the world, in which the economic and political development of Europe was called upon to play a growing role.

General de Gaulle's conception of a balance was a permanent trait of his thinking and action. It took a number of forms. In the third volume of his Memoirs, de Gaulle pointed out that the only way to keep the Soviet Union out of the heart of Europe was to dismember Germany. Thus the threat of a new Germany would be eliminated, and the fears of the Soviet Union and the Eastern European nations alleviated. Moreover, a treaty with the Soviet Union, directed against the revival of German power, would free France to pursue her other world obligations. It was the failure of Yalta to revive the pre-World War II arrangements in Europe that also accounted for the bitter denunciations against the settlement. Although France received a number of compensations, perhaps far beyond what the French leadership had a right to expect in terms of her real power at the time, Yalta became slowly identified with a betrayal of Europe and France by the Anglo-Saxons.

De Gaulle made an open offer to Churchill in November 1944, to combine forces so that the two countries with their far-flung empires would be able to act independently of the Soviets and the Americans.

A third scheme involved an alliance with the Soviet Union, directed against German recovery and guaranteeing the status quo of Europe. Speculating before his trip to the Soviet Union in December 1944, only a few weeks after he had made his offer to Churchill, de Gaulle wrote wistfully, "Perhaps it might be possible to renew in some manner the Franco-Russian solidarity, which even if misunderstood and betrayed in the past, was nonetheless compatible with the nature of things *both with regard to the German danger and the Anglo-Saxon efforts to assert their hegemony.*"[8]

A fourth and perhaps more persistent effort to recreate a balance was the revival of Europe as a "third force." What "Europe" meant to de Gaulle, exactly, is a difficult matter. Sometimes Russia is considered a part and sometimes it is not, although emphasis is often put on the European destiny of Russia. Sometimes it is Western Europe and sometimes the whole of Europe. Sometimes "Europe" implies a dismembered Germany, sometimes a divided Germany, and sometimes a Franco-German rapprochement without qualifications. Two things are certain: "Europe," whatever it is, is distinct from the "Anglo-Saxon powers." It is also separate from Soviet Russia, without, however, always denying the European position of Russia and hence its participation.

Thus, in the name of balance, de Gaulle envisaged in the course of less than twenty years the following alliances: (*a*) with the British, in order to create an independent bloc vis-á-vis the Soviets and the Americans; (*b*) with the Soviet Union, in order to maintain French supremacy in Europe vis-á-vis Germany; (*c*) with all against the revival of a unified, militarized, and strong Germany; and (*d*) with West Germany and the other Western European states, in order to create an independent bloc—a third force in Europe that might reestablish a new worldwide balance of power.

THE GAULLIST YEARS

We shall discuss the Gaullist period of the Fifth Republic (1958–1969) with regard to (*a*) the Constitution of the Fifth Republic, (*b*) colonial and economic policy, (*c*) NATO, (*d*) Europe and the Common Market, (*e*) the atom bomb, and (*f*) relations with the Soviet Union.

---

[8] Ibid., p. 54, italics supplied.

The Constitution of the Fifth Republic. As we noted, one of the serious difficulties throughout the Fourth Republic was the lack of strong executive leadership to formulate and implement policy and to translate overall foreign policy goals and aspirations into effective decisions. The Constitution of the Fifth Republic elaborated by de Gaulle and his associates in the summer of 1958 gives to the President sweeping powers. The president of the republic "shall be the guarantor of the national independence, of the integrity of the territory, and of the respect...of treaties" (Article 5). He "shall negotiate and ratify treaties" and "he shall be informed of all negotiations leading to the conclusion of an international agreement" (Article 52). All major treaties, however, must be "ratified by law" (Article 53). The president of the republic is "the head of the Armed Forces" and "presides over...the Committees of National Defense" (Article 15).

End of Empire. In 1958, General de Gaulle pledged to all overseas territories a new political arrangement—the French Community—and, if they wished it, their independence. All of the territories, with the exception of Guinea, entered the French Community. In the course of 1959-60, the community was abandoned. Speaking in Dakar, Senegal, in December 1959, de Gaulle promised to grant "international sovereignty"—that is, complete independence—to all of France's African territories. All the African republics have become independent, and all of them have become members of the United Nations as independent, individual states with the freedom to vote as they please in the United Nations General Assembly and to participate in its organs and specialized commissions.

Thus France, under de Gaulle, put an end to colonialism. In doing so, it improved its position in Africa, where it was assured of a reservoir of good will. Large subsidies to the African republics and Madagascar continue, and technical and military assistance programs have increased. Thus, politically and economically, the road was paved for better relations.

Algeria. It was not until July 3, 1962, after a series of zigzags and equivocations (which we need not dwell on here) that Algeria was finally granted full independence. The leaders of the rebellion were released from jail. Between 1962 and 1965, almost 1 million European French citizens and a sizeable number of Algerians who had fought in the French army or in territorial units were resettled in the metropolis with substantial financial aid from the state.

NATO: Participation; Reform; Withdrawal. Immediately after his return to power, de Gaulle asserted that it was not the purpose of France to limit its foreign policy "within the confines of NATO." On September 23, 1958, he addressed a memorandum to NATO's Secretary-General Paul-Henri Spaak, to Prime Minister Macmillan, and to President Eisenhower. The memorandum contained a diagnosis of the problems facing NATO and a statement of French policy. He proposed the establishment within NATO of a "directorate" of three—England, France, and the United States—with responsibility for elaboration of a common military and political strategy for the whole of the planet, for the creation of allied commands for all theaters of operation, for joint deliberations about strategy, and for joint decision on the use of atomic weapons. "The European states of the continent," he stated on April 11, 1961, "...must know exactly with which weapons and under what conditions their overseas allies would join them in battle."[9] NATO should accordingly revise its organization to meet joint non-European problems. There was also a threat in the memorandum: France would reconsider its NATO policy in the light of the response of England and the United States.

Although ostensibly addressing problems related to NATO, de Gaulle was actually attempting to place France on a level to which no other continental European power in NATO could aspire. NATO was to remain a broad organization, according to his proposal, but with three of its members—France, England, and the United States (the Federal Republic of Germany was excluded)—jointly in charge of global strategy. The three great powers were to be in charge, at the NATO level, of the Atlantic Alliance problems, and jointly in charge of planetary strategy. De Gaulle remained adamant. When his suggestions were rejected, France withdrew its Mediterranean fleet from NATO command; refused to integrate its air defense with NATO; and prevented the building of launching sites and the stockpiling of atomic warheads over which it could have no control. But this stand was to bring France in conflict with the Federal Republic of Germany that wished to see a strong NATO alliance continue.

De Gaulle's revisionist policy with regard to NATO was an explicit reformulation of France's full-fledged independence to act as a world power. In three separate memorandums—on March 11, March 29, and April 22, 1966—the French government communicated its decision to withdraw its forces from NATO by July 1, 1966, and demanded the withdrawal, by April 1, 1967, of all United States armed forces and military personnel and of all NATO instrumentalities from the French soil.

The Common Market   On January 1, 1959, France implemented, in full, the European Common Market treaty provisions for the reduction of customs duties and the liberalization of trade. De Gaulle's acceptance of the Common Market was motivated in part by economic reasons and in part by considerations favoring the development of a European "whole." The crucial reason, however, was political. This became abundantly clear after 1960. The Common Market suggested the possibility that a larger European "whole" could be placed under the leadership of France, armed with atomic weapons that were denied to Germany by virtue of the Paris accords. Britain's participation was highly desirable, provided Britain was willing to abandon the intimate Atlantic connections that underwrote the dominance of the United States, and also

---

[9] News conference, April 11, 1961, in *Speeches and Press Conferences,* No. 162, pp. 7–8.

provided that Britain brought into a European pool—under some form of Franco-British control—her nuclear weapons and know-how. Britain's nuclear power was to be its dowry in the contemplated marriage with the Common Market.[10] When it became clear that England was unwilling to cut her "special" ties with the United States, de Gaulle decided to refuse entry to England. In his press conference of January 14, 1963, de Gaulle, alleging economic and cultural reasons, rejected England's entry. The heart of the matter, however, was political and strategic. England, de Gaulle feared, would remain under the domination of the United States, and her entry into the Common Market would thus reinforce America's influence.

With England at least temporarily out of the picture, de Gaulle turned to the Federal Republic of Germany. A Franco-German alliance providing for frequent consultations and possibly for the elaboration of common policy on military, foreign, cultural, and economic questions, would provide the hard core for consolidating Western Europe and, given France's military superiority, safeguard French leadership at the same time. In January 1963, a Franco-German treaty, embodying the principle of consultations on matters of defense, foreign policy, and cultural affairs, was signed. However, the very logic of the treaty raised serious questions. It was again based on the assumption that West Germany would accept French, rather than American, leadership and protection. But in the light of its military and economic ties with the United States, and especially in the light of the overwhelming superiority of the United States in these areas, it was unlikely that any German political leader would acquiesce to this. It was only de Gaulle that seemed to believe that Western Europe could do without the United States, and it was only France that pressed for a European solution of the European problems at the very time when Europe's defense continued to lie across the Atlantic.

The Soviets: The "Opening to the East"   As we have noted, de Gaulle never accepted the arrangements made at Yalta. Yet it was quite obvious that, as long as the Soviet threat continued and Soviet power was countered by American power, the division of Europe along the lines laid down at Yalta was inevitable. With the emergence of the Sino-Soviet split, the growing preoccupation of the Soviets with many internal problems, and last, with the emerging aspirations of many Eastern European nations for independence, the time appeared propitious to reopen the Yalta settlement. This necessitated, first, a reconsideration of the problem of German reunification and, second, the assumption by Western Europe of a relative degree of independence vis-á-vis the United States. For as long as NATO remained what it was, and as long as there was direct Soviet-American confrontation in the heart of Europe, there would be no relaxation of Soviet controls in Eastern Europe.

---

[10]France tested the first atomic device on February 3, 1960.

De Gaulle's emphasis upon a "European Europe," his often-repeated statements about a Europe stretching from the Urals to the shores of the Atlantic, were designed to suggest such a relaxation. Its implementation proved to be a much harder problem. One way was to achieve a genuine Franco-German entente within the context of the Common Market, and then to begin a dialogue with the Soviet Union. This proved difficult because of the unwillingness of the Germans to substitute French protection for American, and because of the legitimate doubts of American policymakers about the advisability of such a course of action. De Gaulle then made repeated overtures in the direction of the Eastern European satellites. Cultural and economic ties were stressed; visits were exchanged, a number of leaders of Eastern Europen countries visiting Paris; and France refused to consider any arrangement that would give the Germans a say about nuclear arms. Thus, under de Gaulle, France was returning increasingly to the pre-World War II arrangements—in which an understanding with the Soviet Union was indispensable to the maintenance of peace in Europe, and in which Germany (preferably divided) would reenter the concert of European powers, but without nuclear weapons. The Atlantic Alliance was considered necessary, but not its integrative military arrangements. The French army was reorganized in a manner that emphasized the primacy of the nuclear weapon—with improved delivery capabilities and the development of some four nuclear submarines with missiles. France stood alone, free to deploy the weapon "against anybody," as General Ailleret announced in 1967. The "opening to the East" was calculated not only to establish better relations with the Soviet Union and make American military presence less imperative, but also to convince the Soviet Union to relinquish its hold over Eastern Europe. The Soviet invasion of Czechoslovakia in the summer of 1968 was only an indication of how illusory the Gaullist hopes were.

BETWEEN DE GAULLE AND MITTERRAND (1969–81)

After de Gaulle resigned in April 1969 two Gaullists succeeded him in the presidency—Pompidou (1969–74) and Giscard d'Estaing (1974–81). When Pompidou came into office the Gaullist aspirations had not materialized. On the contrary, it seemed that the basic Gaullist design, to create an independent Europe under French leadership and protection to undermine the Soviet and American positions in Eastern and Western Europe, respectively, had failed. Even the remarkable industrial growth in France and her strong economic position in the world declined dramatically in 1968 in the wake of two months of revolutionary uprisings that left the economy crippled.

As a candidate for the presidency, Pompidou ran as a European, and it was widely rumored that he favored not only stronger European ties but also the inclusion of Great Britain in the Common Market. Only *in* Western Europe and *with* Western Europe, that is, the Common Market, could France again become a center of power. But what kind of Europe was it to be? And what would be the relations between such a Europe and the United States, the Soviet Union, and the rest of the world?

Pompidou's policies and objectives are clearly evidenced in the proceedings of three major European summit conferences—in Hague in 1969: in Paris in 1972; and in Copenhagen in 1973—aimed at enlarging and completing the European community. But when the Common Market partners urged the strengthening of the political integrative institution by giving more powers to the Commission and to the European Assembly, Pompidou demurred. He was willing to allow for the rapid exploration of means to "develop in depth" the Common Market in the direction of a monetary union, the establishment of a common patents office, and harmonizing taxation, but he opposed any form of political integration. Throughout his presidency this remained the dominant position of the French.

The Referendum of April 23, 1972. In January 1972 the four candidate members of England, Denmark, Ireland, and Norway were admitted into the Common Market in a treaty that had to be ratified in one form or another by the Common Market countries and also by the new member states. "Having assumed personally the responsibility for this," stated Pompidou in his press conference, "first in Hague, then in my meeting with Prime Minister Heath [in the summer of 1971] and having authorized the signature of the Treaty. I consider it both my duty and in accordance with democratic principles to ask the French people, who have elected me...to express themselves directly on this European policy."[11] The referendum was to be held on April 23, 1972, and was to be followed by a new European Summit meeting of all the members of the Community—including the new ones. The results were disappointing for the president. For every hundred registered voters only 37 voted "Yes"; 17 voted "No," and the rest abstained.

The summit meeting of the nine European countries (Norway decided not to join the Common Market), represented by their top political leaders, took place October 19–20, 1972 to consecrate the entry of England, Denmark, and Ireland into the European Economic Community, but also to face up to some new and urgent monetary problems and to consider the reform of its institutional structures.

The Nine (England, France, West Germany, Italy, Belgium, Holland, Luxembourg, Denmark, and Ireland) constituted a formidable economic, trading, industrial, financial, and, potentially, military bloc. Little progress had been made, however, in the establishment of an institutional arrangement that stops short of a genuine federation but is something more than a loose confederation.

A declaration was adopted stressing the following:

[11] *Année Politique,* 1972, p. 216.

1. The understanding that all bilateral arrangements made by the nine should take into greater consideration the common positions agreed by them.
2. The chiefs of state should meet more frequently.
3. The specific character of the European entity should be respected.
4. The institutions of the community must function fully, and rapid decisions must be made.
5. The relations among the Commission, the Council of Ministers, and the European Parliament should be improved in order to expedite decisions and to reinforce the budgetary control powers of the latter.

It was not, however, before 1986 that some of these propositions began to be institutionalized.

French Defense Strategy. It was France's concept of defense and her strategy within the Atlantic Alliance that created serious problems. French strategists attempted to develop a theory that reconciled France's place in the Alliance with her independent nuclear force. Their arguments ran as follows: Supposing there is an aggression from the East—then the Alliance becomes operative and the NATO and French forces together engage the aggressor on the basis of the existing bilateral arrangements—presumably somewhere in Europe. If, however, during these forward operations it becomes clear to the French leaders that the aggressor is *aiming* at France's territory, that his *intent* is indeed to occupy France, or destroy it, or seriously imperil its vital interest, then France will be free to act alone, by using its nuclear forces. This point, the so-called *critical threshold of aggressiveness,* is to be determined by the French leaders. In other words, all cooperative arrangements that may exist between France and the Alliance are set aside in favor of French unilateral action the very moment the French leaders decide that the critical threshold of aggressiveness *for France* has been reached.

The French position remained contrary to the inherent logic of the Atlantic Alliance. Why should allies agree to engage their forces in common against an aggressor while leaving one of them free to jeopardize the whole in the name of its own vital interests? Why should West Germany, for instance, act as France's first line of defense unless there is a common strategy that protects both France and the German forces and German interests? Why should the allies go along in a common effort that threatens the existence of their own forces by putting them at the mercy of one of them?

Relations with the Soviet Union. Pompidou continued to follow the guidelines laid down by de Gaulle in France's relations with the U.S.S.R. Frequent consultations between the leaders of the two states were held; however, economic arrangements were negotiated representing only a modest increase in the trade between the two countries. With the occupation of Czechoslovakia by the Russian troops in the summer of 1968, however, the last efforts on the part of France to provide an "opening to the East," based upon a withdrawal of Soviet political and military control there, had failed.

Giscard d'Estaing (1974–81). Like Pompidou, Giscard d'Estaing ran in the presidential election of May 1974 as a "European." But unlike Pompidou, he seemed inclined to follow a different approach to the realization of the reconstruction of Europe. First and foremost he appeared to return to de Gaulle's realization that it is only through a firm consolidation of the relationship between France and West Germany that a European vocation can be kept alive and prosperous. The first political leader to visit him in June 1974 was his former fellow minister of finance, Chancellor Helmut Schmidt of West Germany, and he returned the visit within a few weeks. The new minister of foreign affairs, a former French ambassador to West Germany, was appointed because of the great importance the new president attributed to Franco-German relations.

In the declaration of the NATO countries in Ottawa and subsequently in Brussels in the summer of 1974 the "identity" of Europe was recognized and so was its freedom to act and negotiate with others without any binding obligation to prior consultations with its Atlantic partners, notably the United States. But such consultations were deemed to be "necessary" and "highly desirable." Thus the declaration on "European independence" sought by the Gaullists in the past and especially by Pompidou's foreign minister gave way to an assertion of an "identity" of Europe, in the context of the realities of the Atlantic Alliance.

Similarly, in matters of defense and the disagreements between France and virtually every other member of the Atlantic Alliance every effort was made to reconcile them. There was no question of a European independent defense, as the French insisted, but of a "distinct" defense. There was a recognition of the contribution of the European (that is, French and British) nuclear deterrents to the common Atlantic defense. The general chief of staff, General François Maurin, continued to argue in favor of a French national nuclear striking force, but he conceded that it was the duty of France to foresee all possibilities, and if it were to engage in battle "in the framework of the Alliance," to determine and define in advance the procedures in terms of which France would engage its forces. Consultations for this purpose were to be undertaken with the appropriate NATO organs.

The Summit of Paris. The most important landmark in the progress of closer cooperation among the Nine was the summit meeting of the heads of the nine governments held in Paris, December 9–10, 1974. It was decided to regularize the convening of such meetings with the participation of the foreign ministers at least three times a year and to establish an "administrative secretariat" (the term *political secretariat* was dropped) to provide minimal liaison services. More important, it was agreed to bring into these deliberations the Executive Commission of the Common Market and to coordinate diplomatic action in "all areas of international affairs which affect the interests of the Community" so that the Nine could speak through their periodically designated president with one voice. The French president stated that he would live up to the timetable to establish such a "European Union" by 1980!

Africa. Giscard d'Estaing consolidated the Gaullist legacy in French-speaking Africa. He granted independence to Djibouti, the last French possession in the continent. The islands of the Comores also became independent. But at the same time he institutionalized the economic, military, cultural, and political relations between France and the former colonies. Special military accords allow for the stationing of French troops—in Djibouti, Senegal, Gabon, Centre-Afrique, and elsewhere; they have intervened frequently to support friends and punish foes and to preempt political turmoil and revolution. Special cultural and economic aid programs tie the former colonial leaders to France; economic aid either directly by France or through the Common Market provides the needed supports to many of these African regimes and leaders. Yet at the same time Giscard d'Estaing insisted on the genuine participation of the African statesmen in the elaboration of policies, visited them repeatedly during his presidency, establishing personal contacts with most of them and convinced them, apparently, of his firm respect for the principle of self-determination and of their sovereign status. His motto remained "Africa for the Africans." France's role, he claimed, was only to help its realization. Not only incidentally did France maintain a privileged position in the procurement of raw materials and through military oversight. Yet for the French president, Africa was also a demonstration of his major thesis regarding U.S. and Soviet confrontations. If France were allowed to play an influential role in military, political, and economic terms in certain regions of the world, Soviet-American confrontations would be averted and the Cold War deferred or avoided. The logic of this position was that France, especially if supported by a united Europe, could act as a buffer between the Soviets and the Americans. It is a logic that promotes French power and independence.

In the last analysis, the role Giscard d'Estaing wanted France to play was essentially similar to that desired by de Gaulle. He wished to reassert French independence within the European context, often interpreting détente in a manner that was to elicit Soviet approval; he felt, however, that a cooperative stance with the U.S.A. and the Atlantic Alliance was necessary not only to secure American support but also to reinforce his position vis-á-vis the Soviet Union. He assumed that the development of a European entity would be more acceptable to the Soviets than a Europe dominated by the Atlantic superpower and that, therefore, his Europeanism would be the better appreciated by the Soviet Union and beyond—by the Third World and in the Middle East. If his conciliatory gestures to the Soviets were calculated to maintain the climate of détente, none had any influence or provided for any restraint on Soviet policy moves—especially in Poland, Afghanistan, or some of the countries of the Third World, including Ethiopia, Mozambique, and Angola. Under Giscard d'-Estaing, the discrepancy between ambition and power continued to be the most spectacular trait of French policy and strategy. His conciliatory and cooperative tactics, however, both vis-á-vis the U.S.A. and the Soviet Union, made the discrepancy less apparent than was the case with General de Gaulle.

A SOCIALIST PRESIDENT (1981–   )
FRANÇOIS MITTERRAND

On May 10, 1981 François Mitterrand, who had headed the Socialist party for ten years, was elected president of the republic. His election was followed by the dissolution of the National Assembly and legislative elections in which the Socialist party won an absolute majority of 270 seats out of 492. Their allies—the Communists—with whom there was cooperation at the elections—saw their strength dwindle to a mere 16.5 percent of the national vote and to only 45 legislative seats. But the president ultimately invited them to participate in the new Socialist cabinet—where they were given four posts. It was a clear left-wing victory with the Socialists in full control of the government.

Two major questions regarding foreign policy were raised immediately after the election. The one regarded the constitution—would foreign policy and defense continue to be a presidential prerogative? The second regarded substance—what major changes were to be expected in the overall direction of the French foreign policy? Would it follow the Gaullist basic guidelines—independence but within the Atlantic Alliance; cooperation in the Common Market but without any overhaul of the European institutions in the direction of supranationality and an increase in the powers of the European Parliament; continuing close Franco-German ties as the basis of a European regional system; and maintenance of the French position (including military presence) in Africa, as opposed to retrenchment? Nationalism—political and cultural— were the dominant themes of the Gaullists. Would Mitterrand in the name of internationalism, which socialism embodied, stress international and regional cooperation and even integration? Finally, the Gaullists had appeared as the champions of independence and freedom—from Quebec to Central America and from the Middle East to Vietnam. Would the Socialists continue to champion it even among their many client states in Africa, and even more importantly, in their own overseas departments and territories in the Caribbean, in Reunion, and elsewhere?

The constitutional question can be easily answered. The new president, despite his previous hostility to the Gaullist constitution, assumed the full powers of the office and its prerogatives in foreign policy-making and defense. François Mitterrand continued, like his predecessors, to conduct and shape foreign policy through personal contacts (he traveled as often as his predecessors) and indirectly through his personal advisers. His first minister of foreign affairs (the title was changed to *minister of external affairs*), Claude Cheysson, gave the best account of the role of the president and, incidentally, of his own role: "With regard to foreign policy there is one policy....It is defined by the president of the republic and the government." The major guidelines come from the presidency, as in the past. They are implemented through the minister of external affairs in cooperation with the minister of foreign trade, the minister of defense, and the minister of cooperation (in substance in charge of the relations between France and the Third World countries and in particular the former African colonies of France).

The second question—have there been any substantive changes in French foreign policy?—is no more difficult to answer. Only matters of emphasis seem to distinguish the Socialist president from his predecessors.

Continuity in Style and Aspirations

As did de Gaulle, Mitterrand views France as a special country—culturally and politically—devoted to the spread of civilization and freedoms. The superiority and the uniqueness of the French culture has been emphasized by Socialists: It must be sharply distinguished from the mediocrity of all others—especially American. Unwilling and unable to stress economic or military national strength and accomplishments, the Socialist fell back upon a strident cultural nationalism now clothed in Socialist colors. Thus Mitterrand said in his inaugural address: "France...can light the path of mankind"; "For many people on this earth turn their eyes toward France....For many of them it represents hope." And not unlike de Gaulle, he opened the heart of France to all the poor and the downtrodden in Latin America in a speech in Mexico City (October 20, 1981): "To all the freedom fighters France sends a message of hope....Greetings to the humiliated, exiled, refugees....Greetings to the...persecuted, tortured and assassinated....Greetings to the brutalized clergy, to imprisoned trade-unionists, to the unemployed who sell their blood in order to live, to the Indians chased in the forests,...to the peasants without land, to the resistants without arms....To all of them France says: Courage, freedom is on the way...." Mitterrand concluded with "Long live Latin America, fraternal and sovereign!" How was France to translate the message of hope into political action, some continued to ask? And if it could, would it be extended everywhere?

The Independence of France. Indeed, Mitterrand's economic policies were at first clearly opposed to the prevailing patterns of austerity in England, West Germany, and the United States. It took more than one year before austerity measures were introduced. Secondly, in East-West trade, the French led the way in rejecting the efforts made by the U.S.A. to embargo materials produced with American patents for the construction of the gas pipeline that was to bring Soviet gas across Eastern Europe and Germany and into the Western European countries. As was the case with the Olympic games of 1980, and with the International Energy Commission in 1973, the French refused to accept American leadership and reacted negatively to its policies. The same was the case with the nomination of Communist ministers to the cabinet. It was not only a shrewd domestic move but a symbolic act of defiance against the United States, whose misgivings about the inclusion of Communists in the French cabinet had been made clear by Vice-President Bush, when he visited Paris. French independent action was also manifest in their retaliatory strike against the Druze positions in Lebanon for the attack against the French units of the peacekeeping force. It was undertaken even before the U.S.A. retaliated. But France refused to allow American planes to fly over its territory when they took off from England to attack Libya in May 1986.

Independent Defense Posture. Their atomic and nuclear weapons—the *force de frappe*, the French have insisted, should not be counted as a part of the allied nuclear force—irrespective of whether it relates to European deployment involving intermediary missiles, INF, or strategic talks involving intercontinental ballistic missiles. Their force is not integrated; it is independently targeted. It can come into play only when vital French interests are involved. Despite reconsideration in the direction of a "forward" strategy—to include the Federal Republic of Germany—French retaliatory weapons are located on the soil of France. Yet the French continue to be members of the Atlantic Alliance but not under its integrated military wing of NATO. They are *in* the Alliance and at the same time *out* of it. Their links to NATO or to individual countries of the Atlantic Alliance are determined by bilateral arrangements the French command makes with the NATO command or with bilateral arrangements between France and individual NATO members—the Federal Republic of Germany, for instance. Under the Socialist government the renovation of the French nuclear force has continued (with considerable increase in military spending), and the construction of a seventh nuclear submarine with missiles and independently targeted multiple warheards has been completed. All their supersonic planes have been virtually replaced by ground-to-ground missiles. As under de Gaulle, the French *force de frappe* under Mitterrand continues to remain the basis of French defense while increasing pressure is being put on to improve and expand their *force d'action rapide* (FAR)—conventional forces capable of rapid action and deployment anywhere.

The "Gendarme of Africa." Presidential trips to African capitals have been numerous; particular efforts continue to be made to promote trade and provide financial aid to the African countries both directly and through the Common Market; and the so-called North-South dialogue on economic development and modernization is being spearheaded by the French. This was to be expected under the Socialists, who committed themselves to France's African vocation on condition that the "neocolonialist" policies of the past be abandoned and emphasis be placed on economic assistance, social reforms, and development. Jean-Pierre Cot, the first minister of cooperation, insisted at first on the need for reform and economic aid, and so did Claude Cheysson, who had suggested the establishment of a "Marshall Plan" for the Third World countries.

But the cloud that previous presidents and governments had also known remained on the horizon—political instability and unrest, and with it, revolutionary upheavals often supported by hostile regimes in the name of anti-imperialism (both American and French imperialism!). Qaddafi, Castro, and Khomeini were ready to give them a willing hand, often to instigate violent and terrorist acts. Military aggression and revolutionary coups occurred in Tchad, Soudan, Zaire, Centrafrique, Niger—all of them within the French "preserve." They were all particularly disturbing to the established regimes in the whole region for whom continuing French support was often the condition of survival and who in most cases relied upon special military agreements with France and often the presence of French garrisons. Between 1961 and 1981 French troops had been used more than ten times in active or preventive combat. In 1961–1962 in the Cameroun; in 1964 in Gabon; in 1967 in Centrafrique to protect "Emperor" Bokassa; in 1968–1971 the French troops participated in operations against rebels supported by Libya; in 1977 the French provided logistical support and transport for Moroccan troops to protect President Mobutu in Zaire; in 1978, the French sent combat troops to Tchad—against the rebel forces; in 1978, two French companies were transported to Kolwezi in Zaire to repatriate Europeans and to stabilize the political situation; in 1979 French force supported David Decko against Emperor Bokassa, whose "imperial credentials" became increasingly tarnished—especially after the apparent murder of hundreds of children by his mercenaries; in 1980 reinforcements were sent to Tunisia. Would the Socialists confront similar predicaments in the same way or act otherwise? The answer was quickly forthcoming when in 1983 the rebel forces supported by Qaddafi of Libya began their attack, for the third time, on the government and the capital of Tchad. The government appealed to the French for help—an appeal that for many other African leaders would test the will and policies of the new Socialist president. He reacted like all his predecessors by dispatching French military forces that stemmed the advance of the rebels. He did so again in 1985 and 1986.

Without much publicity and with little rhetoric, France has maintained a military presence in her former colonies and especially in Equatorial and Western Africa. Small garrisons of highly mobile and well-equipped forces are scattered through her former colonies, capable of moving rapidly at short notice to help friends and punish enemies. There are 1,200 troops in Senegal, a contingent of 500 in Ivory Coast, another 500 in Gabon, 700 to 1,000 in the Republic Centrafique; 2,000 to 3,000 are on a quasi-permanent assignment in Southern Tchad, defending France's ally against Libyan incursions. There is, in addition, a strong contingent of 5,000 troops in Djibouti, close to the Persian Gulf. Military assistance agreements and arrangements with Madagascar, Mauritania, Congo, Zaire, the Commores and the Seychelles islands, Mali, Niger, and Guinea give France the needed instruments of control while their rapid intervention force—a highly mobile, well-equipped and trained force of some 60,000 based in France give substance to the existing agreements. Of all Western powers, France has been the only one to manage a continuing oversight over the former colonies in the African continent and beyond.

FRANCO-SOVIET RELATIONS

President Mitterrand spoke openly against the Soviet military occupation of Afghanistan. Though his foreign minister admitted that there was very little that could be done in Poland, the president condemned the dissolution of Solidarity and the imposition of martial law. In both cases we are in the realm of what may be called "declaratory" or "symbolic" foreign policy. What counted, however, was that the Socialist leaders seemed particularly concerned with Soviet aims in Western Europe and the deployment of the Soviet missiles. They spoke clearly and strongly in favor of the NATO decision of 1979 to deploy Pershings and cruise missiles in Western Germany and elsewhere. Mitterrand supported fully the attitude of the Christian Democrats *against* his fellow Socialists in West Germany, as the latter took a firm position against deployment. The Soviet menace appeared far worse to the French than the American presence, and perhaps for the first time since the Cuban missile crisis in 1962 did a president of France come so close to the American strategic concerns. In turn the French military presence in West Germany became more important than in the past, and, as we noted, the French began to consider a forward strategy that would reassure the West Germans of the French position and role in the Atlantic Alliance. In one word, under Mitterrand the French military posture became increasingly Atlanticist.

MITTERRAND'S SECOND TERM (1988-)

In the election of 1986 the Socialists lost the majority in the National Assembly and the new Prime Minister—Jacques Chirac, representing the Gaullists and Centrists—attempted to assume some of the powers of the Presidency in the exercise of foreign policy. This was the so-called period of cohabitation that lasted between March 1986 and May 1988. There was hardly any conflict, however, between the Prime Minister and the President. The foreign policy consensus was solid—and the President and the Prime Minister managed to live together. The Secretary of Foreign Affairs, appointed by the Prime Minister with the consent of the President, provided the appropriate linkage between the French Department of State—the Quai d'Orsay, the President and his immediate associates, and the Prime Minister.

Before the legislative election of 1986 the platform of Socialists, on the one side, and the two major opposition parties—the Gaullists and the Union for French Democracy—on the other, did not differ on the fundamentals of foreign policy. No foreign policy pledges divided the two political blocs that departed from the basic foreign policy objectives that we have discussed. When the new prime minister took office, there were some frictions—mostly of a symbolic character: Who represented France, for instance, in the various international conferences and who could speak authoritatively for France with other heads of state? In most cases, they were resolved by having both prime minister and the president attend such meetings, having each one separately discuss matters with other foreign leaders.

The presidential election of April 24–May 8, 1988, was an opportunity for the two major candidates, President Mitterrand for the combined Left and Prime Minister Chirac for the Center-Right, to present their points of view. It was, again, an occasion that showed the remarkable agreement between the two. They both accepted fully the Gaullist legacy—an independent France with its own nuclear deterrent, a commitment to France's independent national security policy as opposed to any integrative alliances, a commitment to pursue disarmament in Europe, and a continuing criticism of the existence of the two "blocs," as they had been fashioned at Yalta. Both candidates presented themselves, in the most unqualified fashion, as pro-European, putting all emphasis on the need to prepare France for the implementation of full economic integration, scheduled to come into effect by 1992. Neither of the candidates raised questions about the future of Germany, and both seemed to take the status quo and the division of Germany in two for granted. Mitterrand, at times, seemed closer to the Gaullist legacy in envisioning a "European" defense solution, but only when the Soviets had withdrawn their SS-20 missiles; otherwise, he came out as the champion for the installation of the U.S. Pershing missiles in West Germany and elsewhere. In the last analysis, they provided the only genuine security for France.

With his election and the subsequent formation of a socialist government with the tacit support of the Communists in the National Assembly, the period of cohabitation came to an end and Mitterrand assumed what he had enjoyed between 1981 and 1986—sole control and responsibility for the foreign policy of the country. In substance it was a continuation of the policy he had pursued during his year in office, which in turn, as we noted, was a continuation of the foreign policy of his predecessors in line with the Gaullist postulates. It was not until the reunification of Germany was fully realized with the national election held in the whole country on December 2, 1990, that the need for reconsideration was brought upon the French political elite forcefully. We shall discuss it presently.

The Third World and the Francophone World. In line with his previous pronouncements, Mitterrand continued to speak as the champion of the Third World. He spoke in favor of investments and credits, urged the cancellation of their foreign debts, officially decided for the French ex-colonies. He urged democratization and the respect of human rights and, in general, became the champion of a North-South dialogue. A new conference of all French-speaking countries—pays francophones—including Quebec, was instituted. Its purpose, presumably cultural, had both economic and political overtones. It was in such a meeting that the debts of many countries to France were forgiven. The French-African "summits" continued. They included all former French colonies of French equatorial and French Western Africa, the Maghreb, Egypt, Haiti, Lebanon and some others. Political, cultural, military, and economic issues were discussed, including matters of foreign aid. All in all, France continued to present itself as an honest broker between the United States and the Soviet Union—representing an alternative, urging—at least tacitly—the Third World and the African states to align themselves behind its leadership.

France continued to play the role of the "gendarme" in the former colonies in Africa through its continuing military presence and military interventions when they were deemed necessary to quell uprisings against the governments supported by France. In February 1987 they intervened in Chad, where they have maintained a force of about 1,500. French parachutists landed to "protect" the international airport at Rwanda in October 1990. In Dibouti their garrison of some 5,000 remains stationed in a critically important area, ready to play a role both in Ethiopia and the Middle East.

Special ties with Lebanon continued to be invoked to support General Aoun—until the French effort collapsed. Relationships with Arafat's PLO continued, and, in fact, PLO representation in Paris was elevated in status to approach ministerial (but not ambassadorial) rank. Israel's unwillingness to allow for a UN fact-finding mission was denounced by Mitterrand in November 1990. Intimate military and trade contacts between France and Iraq existed until August 1990, and Mitterrand's stance in favor of a dialogue and negotiations with Iraq accounted for the release of the French hostages. France, however, fell in line behind the U.N. resolutions, to force Iraq to withdraw from Kuwait but Mitterrand made it clear that he would act only under U.N. auspices.

Far and beyond in the Pacific the status of New Caledonia was temporarily settled to maintain the dominant position of France until 1999—when a referendum on independence will be held. The Polynesian islands continue to house nuclear testing installations. And Reunion (near Madagascar), Guadeloupe, and Martinique remain Departments of France.

It is this worldwide presence of France that continues to distinguish it sharply from all other members of the European Community, including even England. It is what permits France to claim interests that go beyond the European continent and therefore to entitle it to an independent foreign policy and to independent military arrangements. Under the presidency of Mitterrand, in other words, the world status of France continues to be maintained.

The Soviet Union and the United States. Mitterrand had come out strongly in favor of the U.S. position to place Pershing Missiles in West Germany and elsewhere to counter the Soviet SS-20s. A shift, however, in the Soviet position but also in the attitude of the Federal Republic of Germany and the Soviet Union accounted for the rapid change in the Franco-Soviet relations. Mitterrand, speaking in April 1988, returned to the need of an opening to the East. In his visit in Paris in October 1988, the Soviet Foreign Minister Eduard Shevardnadze had only kind words for France's appreciation of *perestroika.*

It was the prospect of German reunification, as well as the rapidly improving relationships between the U.S. and the Soviet Union that prompted France to seek closer ties with both. France did not wish to find itself playing only a marginal role. On the contrary, it wished to become a full participant and responsible for the dramatic changes in Europe. In October 1990 Gorbachev made an official visit to Paris in which a new treaty of understanding and cooperation was signed. France was to provide a loan of five billion francs and promised to support in full the commercial, scientific, and technological agreements in the process of being negotiated between the European Community and the Soviet Union and help the latter move in the direction of a market economy. Many were reminded of de Gaulle's efforts both in 1944 and in the early sixties to improve relations with the U.S.S.R. There were also efforts to reestablish previous contacts with the traditional allies of France in Eastern Europe, notably Poland and Czechoslovakia—both on a bilateral basis, but also within the framework of the European Community.

As for the relations of France with the United States there was little apparent change. Mitterrand appeared at first more Atlantic than any of his predecessors by supporting installations of Pershing missiles in West Germany and in other NATO countries but not, of course, in France. He eloquently evoked the prospect of a Europe splitting from the U.S. and rejected it outright. But all along—even with regard to the Gulf crisis—France maintained its aloofness or rather separateness. It was ultimately the Gulf War and the growing ascendancy of the United States that led France to seek closer ties in order to play a greater role in international politics and also to counter the threat that German reunification might pose.

Defense. The cornerstone of the Gaullist strategy since 1960 has been nuclear deterrence to preserve the French territory from aggression. The French nuclear weapons would not or could not be shared and would be used only when the French leadership considered that the aggressor aimed to attack directly the French territory. This remained a source of a constant Franco-German misunderstanding. Had the French offered to put the FRG under their nuclear umbrella, the situation would not have changed much of course, since the German leaders would still prefer the protection NATO gave them. But the issue remained—how was France to play an important role in the defense of Western Europe unless it were willing to abandon its purely *national* stance in terms of nuclear deterrence? And how were the leaders of the FRG to assume that France would come to their defense as long as the French missile with a range of about 150 miles were stationed in French territory? Between

1988 and 1990 neither the progress made to integrate the European Community, the efforts to revive the Western European Union—a military arrangement consisting of all members of the European Community except Greece, Ireland and Denmark—nor the continuing and deepening military cooperation linking the FRG and France, have provided an answer. With the reunification of Germany, the weakening of the Soviet Empire, and the reduction of both conventional and nuclear forces in Europe, the issue, and with it the importance of the French nuclear deterrent, may have become secondary. But what remains of importance is that France, unable or unwilling to put its nuclear force under the European structure, will find it equally difficult to proceed with integrative military arrangements. The nuclear force, contrary to the Gaullist legacy, may become less important strategically and more important politically as an impediment to genuine European unity.

In the last two years there has been relatively less emphasis on the French nuclear force. The French ICBMs remain in silos, and together with six nuclear submarines, they constitute the major nuclear deterrent. An intermediary missiles program envisages air-ground missiles, presumably to be constructed in cooperation with the British. An indication of changing times, however, has been the reduction in military spending and a curtailment (but not an abandonment) of new programs—notably in the construction of new tanks and the building of the new aircraft carrier. But there has been a corresponding increase for the strengthening of the FAR (Rapid Action Force) that gives France the means to intervene rapidly in Africa and, if need be, elsewhere. There is hardly any doubt that the Gulf War will bring forth a critical reexamination of the defense posture of the country—about nuclear deterrence and the need to continue building nuclear capabilities, as well as the continuation of the draft—since all French forces in the Gulf came from voluntary units and, notably, the Foreign Legion. The reevaluation is even more critical in light of the need to strengthen the rapid intervention military forces, so that the country can face up to conventional wars wherever they occur.

THE EUROPEAN COMMUNITY: FGR AND "GERMANY"

After being elected President for the second time, Mitterrand pursued, at a more even accelerated tempo, the construction of the European Community, and after 1988 began to clearly outline the prospects of "political union" in terms of a "federation" or a "confederation" or some kind of a "European home"—they all revived some of the Gaullist themes. The construction of Europe was pursued at least at two interrelated levels. First, at the European level—through European summits, the Council of Ministers and the Commission. Second, through the deepening of the Franco-German cooperation, that became increasingly the cornerstone of European unity and cooperation—politically, economically and even militarily. At this level, however, we must distinguish between efforts made *before* and *after* the reunification of Germany in 1990.

In the context of the decisions made between 1985 to 1987 to establish a true economically integrated territory for all twelve members, Mitterrand and the President of the Commission, Jacques Delors, proceeded with the outmost dispatch to prepare its full implementation by January 1, 1993 (we discuss some of the steps taken in Chapter 5.) Multiple Community summits gave guidelines to the Commission to issue directives for its implementation. From the summit of Brussels in June 1987 to the latest one held in Rome in October 1990, the progress in the direction of European integration has surprised many observers. To the incremental changes made over a period of some thirty years a strong political will was added, and even if it came from many sources, French leadership and perseverance was unmistakable. New measures to finance the Community and guarantee its resources until 1993 were formulated; the liberalization of movements of capital among its members decreed; a European audio-visual program (Eureka) was established; institutional changes providing for some increase in the powers of the European Commission and the European Parliament were introduced; a "social European charter" providing for minimal welfare measures for all members was formulated but not as yet legislated; the stages for a Monetary Union were prepared; a qualified majority voting in the Council of Ministers began to be truly implemented. By the end of 1990 the prospects of a political union—a confederal or federal—of a United States of Europe that involves major redrafting of the Rome Treaty—were clearly spelled out. It should be noted, on the other hand, that Mitterrand's emphasis on European political union began to undermine the overall consensus on foreign policy. The RPR (the Gaullists) began to criticize sharply the idea of a European federation. Instead its leadership returned to the ideas of General de Gaulle about a "Europe of states" that would include all European states, including the ones in Eastern Europe and in which each state would maintain its full sovereignty. The right-wing National Front and the Communists to the Extreme Left continued also to criticize the idea of a federal Europe.

The strengthening of the Franco-German ties went hand in hand with reforms in the European Community. The biannual Franco-German meetings, provided in the Treaty of 1963, have been continued. They began to involve not only heads of state, Prime Ministers and Ministers, but also civil servants. At the military level, the first joint military Franco-German maneuvers took place in 1987; in 1988 a Franco-German Brigade was formed and a Franco-German Council of Defense and Security was established. The council has met periodically. In September 1989 joint Franco-German military maneuvers took place in France, and in 1989 decisions were made for the joint construction of a combat helicopter and a reconnaissance plane. These agreements and the deepening Franco-German cooperation strengthened both the FRG and France individually; they strengthened them both within the Atlantic Alliance and strengthened the Alliance itself, even though France was not part of its integrated military component—NATO. At the economic and cultural levels, cooperation and agreement were also the rule. Both Chancellor Helmut Kohl and President Mitterrand agreed fully in December 1989 on the need for a European monetary union. Both agreed on a political union. A cultural joint committee was established in 1988 to accelerate and strengthen cultural contacts between the two countries and disseminate information about each.

It is German reunification that appeared at first to create problems in Franco-German cooperation. The ten-point speech given by Kohl on German unification in November 1989 (to be accomplished gradually) took the French by surprise especially since Kohl did not consult with France in advance; Mitterrand's precipitous trip to Kiev early in December to confer with Gorbachev before the latter visited Bonn to, in effect, give his blessings to German unification, surprised in turn the German leader. At the Franco-German meeting of November 1989, Mitterrand asked Kohl, bluntly, to take sides and to approve immediately the project plan for a European monetary union. Kohl assured everybody by agreeing that the "German problems cannot be solved except under a "European roof." While Mitterrand announced in February 1990, that "the reunification of Germany does not scare me," both he and his Foreign Minister demanded that Germany recognize the Oder-Neisse border that separates it from Poland as it was fixed after World War II and reconfirmed by the Helsinki Accords. The German leader took no pleasure in receiving such injunctions. [See also Chapter 4.]

Many of these disagreements, however, seem to have been ironed out at the meeting between Kohl and Mitterrand in September 1990, where the two leaders agreed to move resolutely in the direction of building a European confederation, in which "all states of our continent will cooperate on a footing of equality"; to strengthen the development of a common policy towards the East; and to move rapidly to establish a monetary union for the EEC members. Even more relevant, however, were pledges taken to continue military cooperation by maintaining and enlarging the Franco-German brigade. Finally, the all-German election in December 1990, in which Chancellor Kohl's forces won, was favorably received by the French, as he has repeatedly and categorically stressed his attachment to the European Community, to Europe, and the Atlantic Alliance. It is conceivable that a Franco-German cooperation at all levels will continue to become not only the driving force for European unity but also its major pillar—as de Gaulle had envisaged.

PROSPECTS

Aside from the irritations and verbal disagreements between the French and Germans from the time the Berlin Wall came down in December 1989 to the meeting of the four victorious powers (France, England, the United States and the Soviet Union) to ratify political union on October 1, 1990, there are some serious and fundamental problems. The French leadership will have to come to terms with them if European unity is to be realized. There are defense problems, economic problems, diplomatic and foreign policy questions, as they relate especially to Eastern Europe, the U.S. and the U.S.S.R., and of course basic institutional questions about the construction of the European Community and ultimately of a "European home."

Among the French political elite (even when public opinion seemed to favor unification), the realization that a united Germany—with over 75 million people and economic and financial resources far superior to those of France—was again to emerge in Europe aroused anxiety and fear. The Hitler-dominated past and German militarism have been evoked, looming even more frighteningly if U.S. and Soviet troops leave the German territory. So was the traditional vocation of Germany to trade and invest in the East. The financial burdens the Federal Republic was assuming in order to reconstruct the economy of East Germany were also viewed as detrimental to the prospects of economic development in the European Community. Quite a few, on the other hand, with remarkable lack of consistency, pointed out that a united Germany would dominate the Common Market and ultimately replace the French as its guiding force. To be sure, France was a nuclear power, it remained one of the five permanent members of the Security Council, and retained solid positions in Africa. But suddenly what the French had pleaded for since the days of de Gaulle—for the disappearance of the "two blocs" in Europe and for putting, in effect, an end to the accursed Yalta, seemed less threatening than the reemergence of a powerful and united Germany! Retrospectively, the benefits France had managed to derive by claiming to be in neither of the two blocs, while being protected by one, appeared far greater. Germany's repeated assertions of its commitment to the European Community, of its peaceful intentions, its solemn pledge to respect the existing frontiers with Poland, its acceptance of the nonproliferation treaty and its commitment not to manufacture nuclear weapons were, of course, well-received. But uncertainties persist.

Uncertainties are manifested in a number of ways that underline the Gaullist legacy—the constant quest for rank. In matters of defense the French have revived the Western Union—now consisting of France, Germany, Great Britain, the Benelux countries, Spain, Italy, and Portugal. Overshadowed by NATO since its early inception it may be used as a European "pillar" of the Atlantic Alliance and ultimately as a European defense and military arrangement, independent of the United States. Thus, the French hope to maintain and strengthen their position and indeed play again a ponderant role in Europe. The dimuniton of Soviet power on the other hand and the assumption of a dominant wold position by the USA before and after the Gulf War provoked also the old Gaullist reflexes. After many hesitations France joined the military forces fighting against Iraq and at the conclusion of the War Mitterrand gave on March 3, 1991 a memorable address. He extolled the victory and the role and rank of France; pointed out that the alliance with the USA was both necessary and welcome and suggested that the Security Council of the United Nations be represented by heads of states to resolve problems in the Middle East and, perhaps, beyond. It was most notable that he did *not* mention Europe or the European Community, let alone Germany which is not a member of the UN Security council. The speech was reminiscent of General De Gaulle memorandum of Sept 1958 asking that France become a member of a tripartite arrangement—with Great Britain and the USA—to decide matters of global strategy. It differed only in that France was now asking to participate on equal footing with China and the Soviet Union as well!

Many uncertainties face French policymakers at the end of 1990 as they try to define their role in a new "European home" and live in it side by side on equal terms with a unified Germany. For new European political, economic, and defense arrangements to emerge, many options must be thoroughly examined. The first is that of a European defense. Given, however, the situation today in the Soviet bloc, the demise of the Warsaw Pact, the continuing, even if progressively reduced, American forces and the strength of a German conventional force the term "defense" is anachronistic. Against whom is Europe (what Europe?) to defend itself? The proper term, and relatedly the new challenge, is for at least the twelve European powers (particularly, of course, the French, the Germans, and the British) to develop an integrated military arrangement so that they can act in common with or without their allies to cope both with intra-European conflicts and some extra-European ones—notably the Middle East and Africa.[12] With England and France providing nuclear weapons (how relevant they are is a matter of speculation) and the rest (notably Germany) providing solid conventional forces, a common military organization will command both weight and respect. With proper political arrangements, a common "defense" strategy can be developed. If England and France were to pool their nuclear weapons with the others, such a European force might even replace the U.S. presence in Europe that the French have so often decried. But will the French lead the way? Will they agree to share their nuclear force with the others—notably Germany—in a common political and military European organization?

Relatedly, there is the problem of a common European foreign policy. Will the French be willing to redefine their interests in a truly European context? And as President Mitterrand faces the last years of his presidency, the question of whether the European Community—let alone the "European home"—will become one or will remain divided may be squarely a matter that depends very much on his course of action. What will be needed is to reconsider the Gaullist legacy. National independence, an independent nuclear and military posture, avoidance of integrative alliance and the pretense of playing a leading and guiding role in Europe, or for that matter, the world, are not compatible with the strength of France or the new European order

---

[12]During the Gulf crisis NATO air forces were sent to Turkey—"at Turkey's request." No *joint* military steps, on the other hand, were taken by the European Community or the Western European Union.

that appears to be emerging. With the collapse of the two blocs in Europe, France will have to move either in the direction of a full "renationalization" of defense and foreign policy—that will ultimately undermine the economic and political arrangements of the European Community—or ponder the urgent needs of full-fledged integration and act accordingly.

FOREIGN POLICY LANDMARKS

June–Dec. 1944	Liberation of France
December 1944	Franco-Soviet Pact
1945	Potsdam Conference (France does not participate); France becomes one of the four powers "occupying" Germany; France becomes a permanent member of the Security Council of the United Nations
January 1946	de Gaulle resigns
1947	Hostilities begin in Vietnam with occupation of Hanoi by French Army. Dunkirk Pact (between England and France)
January 1947	Institutions of French Fourth Republic put in place
June 1947	Marshall Plan announced
1948	Western European Union formed; Organization of European Economic Cooperation (OEEC) formed
1949	Atlantic Alliance and NATO—France becomes a member
1951	Pleven proposes formation of European Defense Community; Coal and Steel European Community formed
1954	European Defense Community is defeated in the French Parliament; Federal Republic of Germany becomes member of NATO; end of hostilities in Vietnam and withdrawal of French forces; beginning of insurrection in Algeria
1956	Morocco granted independence; French African colonies are granted internal autonomy; French-British forces land in Egypt
1957	Treaty of Rome instituting the European Common Market signed; Tunisia granted independence
1958	De Gaulle returns to establish Fifth Republic European Common Market comes into effect
September 21, 1958	De Gaulle Memorandum asking for the establishment of a tripartite directory with United States and England to direct and plan global strategy
1960	Explosion of the first and the second French atomic bombs in the Sahara
1961	Rebellion of four French generals in Algeria against the Fifth Republic
1962	Algeria is granted independence; African French colonies are granted full independence
1964	France recognizes Communist China
1965	France withdraws from the integrated military wing of the Atlantic Alliance (NATO)
1966	Official trip of General de Gaulle to the Soviet Union

1968	Invasion of Czechoslovakia by Soviet Army puts de Gaulle's hopes for an "opening to the East" to an end
April 1, 1969	De Gaulle resigns; Pompidou elected President
1970	Death of General de Gaulle
1973	England, Ireland, and Denmark join the Common Market
1974	Giscard d'Estaing becomes President
1981	Election of President Mitterrand
1983	Speech by Mitterrand in the German Bundestag in favor of installation of American missiles in Western European countries; France intervenes militarily in Tchad
1984	Mitterrand visits the United States
1985	Renewed French military intervention in Tchad against Libyan-backed forces; Gorbachev visits France
1986	Legislative election produces victory of Conservatives with Jacques Chirac becoming prime minister
1987	Efforts to revive Western European Union; speech by Prime Minister Chirac stating France's commitment to the Federal Republic of Germany: "There cannot be a battle of Germany and a battle of France"
1988	Celebrations of the twenty-fifth anniversary of the Franco-German Treaty
April–May 1988	Presidential election in which Mitterrand is reelected with 54 percent of the votes
June 1988	New legislative elections—failure to provide a majority; the Communists have 27 deputies, the Socialists 277, the Center-Right parties 273—total number of seats 577
December 1988	Franco-African Summit at Casablanca
January 1989	P.L.O. Mission in Paris upgraded
April 1989	53d Franco-German meeting and also first meeting of the Franco-German Council of Security and Defense
May 1989	At the third Franco-African summit held at Dakar, Mitterand cancels the debts to France by some thirty-five countries
August 1989	The aircraft carrier Foch steams to the shores of Lebanon
October 1989	Mitterrand announces a four billion francs loan to Poland
November 1989	Mitterrand announces that he "is not afraid of German reunification if it comes about peacefully and democratically"
December 1989	Bush-Mitterrand meeting at St. Maarten
December 5, 1989	Mitterrand goes to Kiev to confer with Gorbachev on the prospects of German reunification
January 1990	Meeting between Chancellor Kohl and Mitterrand and agreement on the "idea" of a European confederation
February 1990	General understanding and agreement between Mitterrand and Kohl on Germany reunification
March 9, 1990	In a meeting with President Jaruslewski, Mitterrand declares the Oder-Neisse line (the border between Germany and Poland) inviolable

April 19, 1990	Kohl and Mitterrand repeat the need to take rapid steps for the construction of a European Union
May 1990	In a visit to London, Mitterrand stresses the need to reinforce Franco-British cooperation in matters of defense
June 22, 1990	Mitterrand and Kohl in a joint press conference stress the need of economic aid to the Soviet Union
September 17–18, 1990	In the 56th Franco-German summit both Mitterrand and Kohl again stress the need of close cooperation between France and a reunified Germany
October 5, 1990	French parachutists land in Rwanda
November 9, 1990	Mitterrand tells American Secretary of State James Baker that the French forces in Saudi Arabia will be used for the "strict application of the United Nations resolutions on Iraq"
December 8, 1990	President Mitterrand decides to double the number of French soldiers in the Gulf War. As of the end of the year, French ground forces were estimated at a little over 10,000.
January 1991	With the beginning of military operations after January 15, 1991, the French Secretary of Defense, Jean-Pierre Chevènement, who opposed French participation, submitted his resignation, and the French forces were brought under the overall command of the commander of the U.S. forces.
March 3, 1991	Mitterrand proclaims "victory."

SELECTED BIBLIOGRAPHY

Basic Sources

Année Politique Annual survey of political and economic events and developments. Presses Universitaires de France, Paris.

de Gaulle, Charles. *Discours et Messages*. This is a detailed compilation of the utterances of the General between 1940 and April 28, 1969–the day he resigned. (In five volumes; with comments and notes by François Goguel.) Paris: Plon, 1970–72.

———. *Memoirs of Hope: Renewal and Endeavor*. New York: Simon & Schuster, 1971. They cover the first four years of de Gaulle in office after he returned to power on June 1, 1958. Their completion was interrupted by the General's death on Nov. 9, 1970.

———. *War Memoirs*, Vol. I. *The Call to Honour*. New York: Viking Press, 1955. Vol. 2, *Unity*. New York: Simon & Schuster, 1959. Vol. 3. *Salvation*. New York: Simon & Schuster, 1960.

Books

Ailleret, Charles. *L'Aventure Atomique Francaise*. paris: Grasset, 1968.

Aldrich, R., Connell, J. (eds.). *France in World Politics*. London: Routledge & Kegan Paul, 1985.

Aron, Raymond. *The Great Debate: Theories of Nuclear Strategy*, trans. by Ernst Pawel. New York: Doubleday, 1965.

Buchan, Alastair. *Europe's Future, Europe's Choices: Models of Western Europe in the 1970's*. New York Columbia University Press, 1969.

Cerny, Philip. *The Politics of Grandeur: Ideological Aspects of de Gaulle's Foreign Policy*. Cambridge, England: Cambridge University Press, 1980.

Charlot, Jean. *Les Francais et de Gaulle*. Paris: Plon, 1971.

Cohen, Sammy. *La Monarchie Nucleaire*. Paris: Hachette, 1988.

Couve de Murville, Maurice. *Une Politique Etrangère*. Paris, Plon, 1971.

David, D. *La Politique de Défense de la France: Textes et Documents.* Paris: FEDN, 1989.

de la Gorse, Andre-Mari. *de Gaulle entre Deux Mondes.* Paris: Fayard, 1964.

de la Serre, F., Leruez, J., Wallace, H. (eds.). *Les Politiques étrangères de la France et de la Grande-Breta;amgne depuis 1945.* Paris-Manchester: 1990.

Deutsch, Karl W., Lewis Edinger, Roy Macridis, and Richard Merritt. *Elite Attitudes and Western Europe.* New York: Scribner, 1966.

Frears, J.R. *France in the Giscard Presidency.* London and Boston: Allen & Unwin, 1981.

Grosser, Alfred. *La Politique Extèrieure de la 4ième République.* Paris: Librairie Armand Colin, 1963.

———. *Affaires Extèrieures.* Paris: Flammarion, réed, 1989.

———. *La Politique de la France 1944–1984.* Paris: Flammarion, 1984. See also his excellent article "Sommes-nous Une Grande Puissance?" ("Are We a Great Power?") in *L'Expansion,* Octobre–Novembre 1985.

———. *French Foreign Policy under de Gaulle.* Boston: Little, Brown, 1965.

Harrison, Michael M. *The Reluctant Ally: France and Atlantic Security.* Baltimore: Johns Hopkins University Press, 1981.

Hoffman, Stanley, et al. *In Search of France.* Cambridge, Mass.: Harvard University Press, 1964.

———. *Decline or Renewal: French Politics since the 1930s.* New York: Viking Press, 1974. Particularly chaps. 10, 11, and 12.

Institute of International Studies. *La Politique Etrangère de la France 1936–1986.* Paris: Documentation Francaise, 1987.

Jouve, Edmond. *Le Général de Gaulle et la Construction de l'Europe, 1940–66.* 2 vols. Paris: Librairie Generale de Droit et de Jurisprudence, 1967.

July, Serge. *Les Annés Mitterrand.* Paris: Grasset, 1986.

Kaiser, K., and Lellouche, P. *Le Couple Franco-allemand et la Défense de l'Europe.* Paris: IFRI, 1986.

Kohl, Wilfred. *French Nuclear Diplomacy.* Princeton, N.J.: Princeton University Press, 1971.

Kolodziej, Edward A. *French International Policy under de Gaulle and Pompidou.* Ithaca, N.Y.: Cornell University Press, 1974.

Kulski, W.W. *de Gaulle and the World System.* Syracuse. N.Y.: Syracuse University Press, 1967.

Macridis, Roy C. *de Gaulle–Implacable Ally.* New York: Harper & Row, 1966.

———. *French Politics in Transition: The years after de Gaulle.* Cambridge, Mass.: Winthrop, 1975.

Mitterrand, Francois. *La Politique Etrangère de la France.* Paris: Flammarion, 1986. Contains the major speeches and addresses on foreign policy by the President.

Morse, Edward L. *Foreign Policy and Introdependence in Gaullist France.* Princeton, N.J.: Princeton University Press, 1973.

Newhouse, John. *de Gaulle and the Anglo-Saxon.* New York: Viking Press, 1970.

Pierre, Andrew J. *The Global Politics of Arms Sales.* Princeton, N.J.: Princeton University Press, 1982.

Robin, Gabriel. *La Diplomatie de Mitterrand ou le Triomphe des apparences,* de la Bievre. Paris, 1986.

Ruehl, Lothar. *La Politique Militaire de la Ve République.* Paris: Presses de la Fondation Nationale des Sciences Politiques, 1976.

Spencer, M., and Connell, A.W.J. *New Caledonia.* University of Queensland Press, 1988.

Williams, Philip. *French Politicians and Elections, 1951–1969.* Cambridge, England: Cambridge University Press, 1970.

Willis, Roy. *France, Germany and the New Europe, 1945–1967.* New York: Oxford University Press, 1968.

THE
FOREIGN POLICY
OF THE FEDERAL
REPUBLIC OF GERMANY
TRADITION AND CHANGE

Josef Joffe

THE FEDERAL REPUBLIC AS A SPECIAL CASE

The study of comparative foreign policy requires yardsticks by which we compare and contrast in order to distinguish the unique from the general. By virtue of its size, population and resource base, the Federal Republic of Germany (FRG) falls into the elusive category of "middle powers" such as Britain, France or Italy. Yet if we look more closely at the peculiar origins and handicaps of the Federal Republic, we detect conspicuous distinctions suggesting a special case.

To begin with, the very existence of the FRG represents something of a historical fluke. In 1945, when the four victorious powers[1] assumed "supreme authority"[2] over its affairs, Germany had virtually ceased to exist as a political entity. Given the hatreds unleashed by the Third Reich, an indefinite period of punishment and subjection appeared as Germany's most likely fate. Yet in the wake of victory, as is the case so often in history, the alliance between East and West disintegrated. A new dominant conflict, the Cold War, superseded the old one, delivering an inconceivable windfall gain to Germany. A "Super-

---

[1] The United States, the U.S.S.R., Britain, and France.

[2] Beate Ruhm von Oppen, ed., *Documents on Germany under Occupation, 1945–1955* (London: Oxford University Press, 1955), p. 30. This is a useful collection of documents covering the first postwar decade.

Versailles" did not materialize. Instead, in 1949, Germany suddenly found itself doubly reincarnated on either side of the Elbe River, the East-West dividing line.

Thus, the very establishment of the FRG (as of its "counter-state," the German Democratic Republic [GDR]) was not an act of choice, but the result of Allied fiat. The Federal Republic was an offspring of bipolarity, conceived and nurtured by the strategic imperatives of the West. While the FRG was bound to profit from the transformation of the dominant conflict, it was also its prostrate captive and, by dint of partition, its starkest symbol.

For a good part of its existence, the Federal Republic has been subjected to a unique degree of dependence and external constraints. Founded in 1949, it continued to lack sovereignty, the most essential attribute of a state, until 1955—with the United States, Britain, and France retaining "supreme authority" under the Occupation Statute. After sovereignty was granted in 1955, the three Western powers reserved important prerogatives, notably those pertaining to Berlin and "Germany as a whole." But even on the German side, there was the deliberate refusal of complete statehood. Apart from the amputation of its Eastern territories (in favor of Poland and the Soviet Union), the nation was split into two political units. Accordingly, the officially proclaimed role of the FRG was that of a *Provisorium*, a "transitional polity," which would liquidate itself on the day reunification came.[3]

Dependence imposed itself in many guises. First, there was a unique "birth defect." Deprived of full sovereignty, armed forces, and moral credibility, West German diplomacy was initially reduced to empty-handed bargaining. The main objective was not the pursuit of the traditional goals of statecraft but the right to be a legitimate player in the first place. This predicament was aptly expressed by the first Federal Chancellor, Konrad Adenauer (1949–1963) in his first Policy Statement before the *Bundestag* (parliament): "For the German people there is no other way of attaining freedom and equality of rights than...in concert with the Allies. There is only one path to freedom...: to extend our liberties and prerogatives step by step, and in harmony with the Allied High Commission."[4]

Second, instead of domestic structures shaping the FRG's foreign policy, the foreign policy of others in large part came to determine societal orientations and political institutions. On the level of society, the widespread reaction against National Socialism and then Soviet-style Communism provided a fertile soil for the seeds planted by the American occupation: de-nazification, democracy, liberalism, free-market economics. While the constitution—the Basic Law—was not imposed on the Germans (as it was on the Japanese), it did follow the guidelines laid down by the military government. Even if direct

[3] There was no constitution but only a "Basic Law" that was enacted for a "transitional period" only. Its preamble explicitly enjoined the German people to achieve reunification. When that happened on October 3, 1990, however, the FRG did not abolish itself. Instead, the GDR was absorbed in the guise of five new Federal States. With minor modifications, the Basic Law now provides the constitution for the entire country.

[4] *Verhandlungen des Deutschen Bundestages* (the official record of parliamentary proceedings), September 20, 1949, p. 29.

interference was limited, it was no accident that societies and institutions in both Germanys came to resemble those of the victors. Stalin's famous dictum was visibly vindicated: "This war is not as in the past. Whoever occupies a territory also imposes on it his own social system...as far as his army can reach. It cannot be otherwise."[5]

Third, instead of its own foreign policy affecting the Federal Republic's international milieu, the bipolar structure of the postwar world defined West German policy and interest. For an occupied and then semisovereign country, the overriding goal was the slow, patient escape from subjection—and that route inexorably led West. A shattered economy, cut off from its traditional markets in the East, had to be rebuilt in the framework of Atlantic free trade and economic integration. And as Stalin imposed ideological uniformity on Eastern Europe while making his unsuccessful bid for West Berlin (held by the three Western powers) in the blockade of 1948–49, military security became a paramount concern. And that, too, could only be had in the West. As result, Bonn became the most loyal member of NATO, tending to subordinate other interests to the demands of preparedness and alliance cohesion.

These reflexes were reinforced by an ancient trauma of German foreign policy—the "nightmare of coalitions,"[6] as Bismarck, the German chancellor from 1871 to 1890, called it. Though the Cold War had shattered the alliance of the victors, the fear of renewed Four-Power solidarity remained an enduring anxiety, leading Bonn's diplomacy into an ever-closer embrace of the West. Finally, the amputation of the Eastern territories and partition mortgaged the FRG with a powerful legacy of revisionism. Although reunification was deliberately postponed to another and better day, it remained the official *raison d'être* of the FRG. But the refusal to accept the postwar status quo embroiled the FRG in a permanent conflict with the Soviet Union that could only be sustained by the closest possible ties to the West.

The point can be made in a more general manner. A classic question of foreign policy analysis is this: What is most important—the actor or the stage, domestic sources, or the international system? In the special German case, the evidence weighs heavily in favor of "system dominance." How could this presumption be tested? An obvious test is to look at the structure of the international system, how it changed over time, and then at German foreign policy: Does the actor's script change in response to a rearranged stage? History reveals an impressive "fit"—and more than mere correlation. Throughout the past forty-odd years, the milieu changed first; the appropriate response on the inside came later.

---

[5] As quoted by Milovan Djilas, *Conversations with Stalin* (New York: Harcourt Brace Jovanovich, 1962), p. 114.

[6] The original "nightmare of coalitions," to which Bismarck and most later German statesmen kept referring over and over, materialized during the Seven Years War (1756–1763), when Frederick the Great, the King of Prussia, found himself encircled by an all-European coalition.

Tight bipolarity and the Cold War dovetailed nicely with a foreign policy that was almost exclusively Western-oriented and a domestic consensus that was highly anti-Communist. From 1949 to 1969, all chancellors of the Federal Republic were Christian Democrats, leaders who favored an Atlantic and West European orientation. Conversely, the Social Democrats (SPD), who opposed rearmament and NATO, were regularly beaten at the polls and ultimately forced to accept the pro-Western choice of the Conservatives. Toward the end of the 1960s, bipolarity became muted along with the Cold War, and so both German foreign policy and domestic politics changed pari passu. In 1969, a Social Democratic Chancellor, Willy Brandt, was elected for the first time; simultaneously, the FRG launched its New Ostpolitik, which sought to bury the country's separate conflict with the East by all but ratifying the postwar status quo.

The external cues, however, came first. Because the FRG's key allies embarked on détente, Bonn followed, and then only after protracted resistance on the part of the Christian Democrats (in opposition from 1969 to 1982). In the 1980s, when the Cold War flared up again, the reverse process occurred. The Social Democratic chancellor Helmut Schmidt tried to preserve détente with the Soviets in spite of renewed superpower confrontations during the Reagan era. It is no accident, however, that the hardening of the external setting once more brought about a change in both policy and tenure. In charge of the federal government throughout the détente-minded 1970s, the SPD's fortunes declined as the Cold War resumed. Helmut Schmidt was ousted in 1982. In the following year, Helmut Kohl, the Christian Democrat who had campaigned on a pro-NATO platform, emerged triumphant from the 1983 national election, to be reconfirmed in 1987.

It should not come as a surprise that a country that is the very product of bipolarity should also be so uniquely beholden to its forces. But this is not the end of the story; there is a poignant dialectical twist. Precisely because the stage mattered so much, it defined an enduring imperative for the actor: to use all available influence in order to position the props for the sake of maximum maneuverability. Precisely because West Germany was so constrained, the system became the main target of necessity. If, to paraphrase Sigmund Freud, the system is destiny, then destiny can only be shaped by manipulating—and ultimately changing—the givens so as to improve one's lot.

On the deepest level, this is the story of postwar German policy. Concretely, the game throughout was to escape from dependence, which is but another name for "system dominance." Initially, the problem was sheer subjection, and so the object of the game was community building—the pursuit of a West European system that would replace imposed fetters with communal, hence egalitarian, constraints. Economic integration within the European Communities was the first road to freedom.

The Cold War spelled endemic insecurity, and so Bonn became an avid contributor to the Western alliance—on the premise that the FRG, as its most exposed member, would reap the largest profits from close military integration. Yet no matter how cold the Cold War, there was still the "nightmare of Potsdam",[7] the obsessive fear that West and East would once more try to dictate Germany's fate at Germany's expense. Hence, grand strategy was once more targeted on the "system," and the object was to keep the flanks from joining against the middle in a sweeping peace settlement that might neutralize and disarm Germany. The antidote to "Potsdam" was an intimate junior partnership with the United States that would limit American options and grant a hefty measure of borrowed influence to Bonn.

In the 1970s, means changed, but not the underlying strategy. With rehabilitation and security achieved, the profits of bipolarity began to pale and the costs began to loom ever larger. How, then, to lower the price? The answer was the New *Ostpolitik*, launched in 1969, which sought to mute Soviet hostility by granting to Moscow and its allies what they had demanded ever since: the recognition of the political and territorial status quo in Europe. In so doing, the Federal Republic did more than just adapt to the overall détente trend. On a more fundamental level, the FRG actually managed to *change* the system in its favor. How so? It was the refusal to accept the verdict of World War II that had embroiled Bonn in a permanent—and separate conflict—with the East. To withstand Soviet pressures, the FRG had to seek refuge in an ever-closer relationship with the West—and to pay "rent" for that shelter in the coinage of subordination. By satisfying Moscow and by normalizing relations with the East, Bonn simultaneously diminished its dependence on the West—thus gaining a much larger margin of maneuvering than ever before.

In the 1980s the separate conflict changed into something resembling a special relationship with the East. The underlying premise was that only stable cooperation would diminish the need for borrowed security and enhance Bonn's access to Eastern Europe. And so yesterday's Cold Warrior moved to the vanguard of détente, East-West trade, and arms control. Indeed, when the Cold War resumed in the wake of the Soviet invasion of Afghanistan in 1979, Bonn was eager to keep from refreezing what the New *Ostpolitik* had so painstakingly unthawed. That purpose forced the FRG into a complicated balancing act, a classic dilemma since the days of Bismarck. On the one hand, the FRG could not alienate the United States, the security lender of the last resort. On the other, Bonn could not return to the old posture of confrontation that would have recemented the partition of Germany and Europe.

The basic rule throughout was to keep the "system" open and permissive: to thwart the wrong kind of deal between East and West in the 1950s and 1960s, to relieve dependence on the West by opening up to the East in the 1970s, to prevent the retightening of bipolarity in Europe during the second Cold War of the 1980s. While the means changed, the basic objective of grand strategy remained the same: the quest for a European constellation that would maximize German options in the face of so many handicaps. Security and

---

[7] In Potsdam, a suburb of Berlin, the U.S., the U.S.S.R., and Britain convened after the end of World War II to decide jointly on the future of vanquished Germany.

community could only be had in the West; reunification could only be had from the East. On October 3, 1990, 45 years after defeat and dismemberment, the ultimate prize was finally delivered. Germany was reunified, and the postwar era was over.

THE POLITICAL STYLE: SOVEREIGNTY THROUGH INTEGRATION

After its establishment in 1949, the FRG, above all, had to acquire the wherewithals for a foreign policy—legitimacy and influence. For this purpose, Konrad Adenauer, the "Founding Father," followed three basic principles. First, France needed reassurance against the reemergence against the "German peril." Second, the West had to be persuaded to reverse Lenin's classic precept that "Trust is good, control is better." Accordingly, Adenauer's entire diplomacy was devoted to transmuting the constraints imposed unilaterally by the victors into mutual controls shared voluntarily by all. Third, the best way to achieve both objectives was political and economic integration that would supersede the ancient logic of power politics with the new logic of community and mutual gain.

Hence, Adenauer became a compulsive joiner, correctly calculating that voluntary compliance would make Allied imposition less likely, while membership in *any* international organization would bestow not only the trappings of equality, but also the real chance to influence events. It is impossible to understand the success story of European integration without taking into account West Germany's postwar condition. For the FRG, integration was a low-cost, high-payoff policy. Since the Occupying Powers retained supreme authority, West Germany's integrationist virtues carried their own tangible rewards. For the Federal Republic, integration merely involved trading non-existing, potential rights for actual sovereignty. Since integration was predicated on the equal subjection to common rules, self-abnegation became the condition of self-assertion.[8]

If the West insisted on reparations and international controls on the iron and coal industries of the Ruhr Valley, Adenauer complied but also proposed that the FRG *join* the International Ruhr Authority. When France moved to detach the iron-rich Saarland from West Germany, Adenauer immediately countered with a call for complete Franco-German union.[9] In other words, the

---

[8] As such, Adenauer's strategy was exactly the reverse of the early Europeanists such as Jean Monnet, one of the Founding Fathers of the European Community. The "Functionalists" saw integration as an irresistible solvent of national sovereignty because each step in any one area would force nations to integrate more and more sectors. Adenauer, however, reversed the logic by using each concession of the FRG as a lever for lifting the restraints on German sovereignty.

[9] That bold gamble even worked by forcing the French to respond with a unity proposal of their own. This was the "Schuman Plan" for the integration of Western Europe's coal and steel industries, which blossomed into the European Coal and Steel Community (ECSC), the forerunner of the Common Market. With French control instincts satisfied, Adenauer managed to persuade Paris to postpone autonomy for the Saarland. A few years later, France agreed to a referendum. When the population rejected autonomy, the area became a *Land* (federal state) of the Federal Republic in 1957.

unique quality of Adenauer's style was his persistent attempt to transcend the normal diplomatic process, which begins with haggling and ends by splitting the difference. Instead, he always tried to dwarf a particular clash of interests by enlarging the framework for its solution.

It is doubtful, however, whether the first Chancellor would have succeeded in transforming the stakes so quickly without a sudden flare-up of the Cold War: North Korea's attack on the South in the summer of 1950. "I began to understand," Adenauer was to reminisce many years later, "that in our days influence required power. Without power, one cannot conduct policy. Without power, our words will not be heeded."[10] Acting on Machiavelli's dictum that strong armies make for reliable allies, Adenauer had floated a trial balloon on German rearmament just a few months after the FRG was founded, proposing that "Germany should contribute to the defense of Europe in a European army under the command of a European headquarter."[11] In spite of angry protests at home and abroad, he kept fishing for an Allied invitation to rearm.

The North Korean attack was the turning point. It dramatized, if only by false analogy, the strategic logic inherent in the founding of NATO and the Federal Republic. By the fall of 1950, the American decision to rearm Germany finally delivered the vehicle on which the FRG could coast toward sovereignty. Furthermore, it enlarged a stubborn Franco-German contest over the extent of German sovereignty into a three-way game in which the United States switched from reluctant referee to tacit ally. This was the beginning of a "special relationship" between Bonn and Washington that would eventually bestow a large measure of derivative power on the Federal Republic.

At first, France responded with an ambitious project to supranationalize the very hard core of sovereignty (i.e., defense) in a European Defense Community, calculating that this would either postpone or defang German rearmament. At the same time, the French could never make up their mind what was more important: the containment of the Soviet Union or the control of Germany. Thus, on August 30, 1954, the French National Assembly repudiated the entire settlement. The grandest design of European unity was sacrificed to the sturdier ideal of national sovereignty. Yet the United States and Britain were now firmly committed to German rearmament. France was finally swayed by a host of new contractual constraints against the resurgence of the German threat. In 1955, the Occupation Regime was terminated. With its sovereignty restored, the Federal Republic was directly admitted into NATO. Ten years after total defeat, Adenauer had succeeded in purchasing

---

[10] As quoted by Dieter Schröder in *Süddeutsche Zeitung,* January 7, 1960, p. 3.

[11] Interview with John Leacacos, *Cleveland Plain Dealer,* December 4, 1949. There is a rich literature on the story of West German rearmament. On the German side, the best is Arnulf Baring's *Außenpolitik in Adenauer's Kanzlerdemokratie* (Munich: Oldenbourg, 1967). For treatments in English, see Laurence W. Martin's classic study "The American Decision to Rearm Germany," in Harold Stein, ed., *American Civil-Military Decisions* (Birmingham, Ala.: The University of Alabama Press, 1963). Also Robert McGeehan, *The German Rearmament Question: American Diplomacy and European Defense After World War II* (Urbana, Ill.: University of Illinois Press, 1971).

respectability and security for one half of the country—but at the price of partition. After 1955, the Soviets gave up on the idea of a unified and neutral Germany, proceeding instead to consolidate the GDR into a full-fledged state and Warsaw Pact ally.

REUNIFICATION VERSUS REALPOLITIK

In 1966, three years after his retirement as Chancellor and one year before his death, Adenauer was asked: "Let us assume...that a reunified and neutral Germany had been possible. Would you have wanted it?" The former chancellor's answer was curt and emphatic: "No, never."[12] This two-word reply contains the most concise explanation for the course of West German foreign policy in his thirteen-year tenure.

Why did Adenauer place a higher value on community with the West— although reunification, rhetorically at least, remained the supreme aspiration? An answer must resist two facile theories that assume either too much idealism or excessive cynicism. According to one, Adenauer played down reunification because he thought that Europe was more important than the nation-state. According to the other, the Catholic Rhinelander treacherously wrote off East Germany as presumptive stronghold of the Social Democracy and Protestantism, hence as a threat to his own tenure.

His reasoning probably contained traces of both elements. Adenauer's "Rhenocentrism" as been a source of endless speculation. As mayor of Cologne in the 1920s, he had an ambiguous record of separatism in favor of a Rhenish Republic economically linked to Belgium and France and politically tied to a German federation.[13] To Adenauer, the Cologne Cathedral somehow symbolized the spiritual fount and political center of an ancient European civilization, and the "Asian steppes"[14] began in Magdeburg just across the inter-German divide, Berlin being a "heathen city."[15] Similarly, Prussia represented the very nemesis of Germany, while the Social Democrats, whose electoral strength used to be concentrated in Protestant East Germany, were the latter-day political descendants of the power-hungry Prussian *Junker* class (the land-holding nobility).

Yet no foreign policy can ever be reduced to the ideology or psychology of its author. Since the problem was more complex than reunification, the explanation is also more complicated. After the war, Germany was the "prize, the pivot and the problem of European politics."[16] Accordingly, there was no

---

[12] In an interview with the historian Golo Mann on April 18, 1966. Golo Mann, *Zwölf Versuche über die Geschichtsschreibung* (Frankfurt: S. Fischer, 1973), p. 136.

[13] For the record, see the account by Karl D. Erdmann, *Adenauer in der Rheinlandpolitik nach dem Ersten Weltkrieg* (Stuttgart: Klett, 1966).

[14] Interview with Hans-Peter Schwarz, as quoted in his *Vom Reich zur Bundesrepublik* (Berlin: Luchterhand, 1966), p. 433.

[15] As quoted in *Gazette de Lausanne*, July 15, 1947; see also *Hannoversche Neue Presse*, July 16, 1947 and Schwarz, *op. cit.*, pp. 432–33.

[16] Pierre Hassner, "Europe West of the Elbe," in Robert S. Jordan, ed., *Europe and the Superpowers* (Boston: Allyn and Bacon, 1974), p. 103.

way either side would voluntarily let go of *its* German half. Politically, bipolarity in Europe was strictly a zero-sum game; whichever superpower succeeded in incorporating all of Germany on its side would have scored an enormous, unacceptable gain against the other. Militarily, though, nuclear weapons had turned the Cold War into a non-zero-sum game with an incalculable negative pay-off for both. In the face of total devastation, the use of force was out of the question.

There was one logical alternative: a reunified and neutral Germany. Yet Germany was not Austria (also occupied), which was neutralized in 1955. For good reasons, the West was not interested. A neutralized Germany would have bottled up Western defenses behind the Rhine, while giving to the Soviets all the strategic and psychological advantages of proximity. More generally, neutrality raised all the uncertainties of the ancient "German problem," meaning that Germany always was either too strong or too weak. Before unification in 1871, the problem had been Germany's weakness, its inability to stave off domination by others. After 1871, Germany was too strong to be held in check by its neighbors, yet not strong enough to acquire lasting primacy.

Given Germany's critical size in the heart of Europe, neutralization would have rolled both problems into one. If the country were neutral and *disarmed,* who would keep Germany disarmed and others from dominating it? If Germany were neutral and *armed,* who would keep the country neutral and from dominating the rest of Europe?[17] By contrast, bipolarity and partition had defused all of these risks in an order that was as novel as it was stable.

The Cold War alliance system protected Germany not only from others, but also from itself. Contrary to the Bismarck Empire, postwar Germany did not have to labor under the double burden of projecting the main threat to Europe's stability *and* managing that order from a solitary position at the center. Unlike the Weimar Republic, it did not have to (and could not) play East against West as condition of self-assertion. With *two* Germanys countervailing each other in opposing blocs, German strength was both neutralized and harnessed. At the same time, the two Germanys were not left alone, but remained anchored in alliances that provided them with a shelter and a role.

Yet what about German interests? Why did Adenauer refuse to go for a reunified, but neutral Germany—something Moscow would dangle before the West until 1955?[18] In the first place, the Federal Republic hardly had any other choice than to cast its lot with the West. West Germany's peculiar condition dictated not only the style, but also the direction of its diplomacy. Sovereignty could only be attained from the West, and security meant security against the East. A traditional *Schaukelpolitik* (policy of balance and maneuver) ran the

---

[17] With two lost wars behind them, even German leaders had come to understand Germany's ancient dilemma. For an articulation of this reasoning, see Heinrich von Brentano's address to the Bundestag on February 27, 1955. *Verhandlungen des Deutschen Bundestages,* February 27, 1955, p. 3883.

[18] See especially Stalin's notorious offer of March 1952 and the ensuing exchange of diplomatic notes in Council on Foreign Relations, ed., *Documents on American Foreign Relations, 1952* (New York: Harper & Row, 1953), pp. 248 ff.

high risk of alienating the West or, worse, reactivating a collusive Four Power policy. As Adenauer put it at the time: "One false step, and we would lose the trust of the Western powers. One false step, and we would be the victim of a bargain between East and West."[19] If there was anything worse than partition, it was precisely the kind of neutralization offered by the Soviet Union to stave off West Germany's incorporation into the Western alliance. Neutrality, Adenauer proclaimed over and over again, was "an unrealistic position....We had to join one or the other side if we wanted to avoid being crushed by both."[20]

In other words, the real problem of West German policy transcended the clash between integration and reunification. The real crux was protection against yet another "nightmare of coalitions," the obsession of German diplomacy since Frederick the Great. This priority was stressed by Adenauer in a remarkable statement in 1953. It bears citing at length because it captures the article of faith (or fear) on which his diplomacy was based. If Bismarck's obsession had been the "nightmare of coalitions," Adenauer's horror vision was Potsdam:

> It is no coincidence that the Soviets keep referring to this agreement over and over again. To them it represents an eternal Morgenthau Plan imposed by the Four Powers....Potsdam signifies nothing but: Let us strike a bargain at Germany's expense....Bismarck spoke about this nightmare of coalitions....I have my own nightmare: Its name is Potsdam. The danger of a collusive great power policy at Germany's peril has existed since 1945, and it has continued to exist even after the Federal Republic was established. The foreign policy of the Federal Government has always been aimed at escaping from this danger zone. For Germany must not fall between the grindstones. If it does, it will be lost."[21]

How, then, did Adenauer propose to escape from the "grindstones?" The answer was contained in a grand bargain with the West which, while it ratified an unprecedented policy of dependence and self-denial on the part of Bonn, sharply delimited the freedom of action of the West. Known as the *Deutschlandvertrag* ("Treaty on Germany"), that bargain was akin to Washington's Farewell Address—in the sense that it guided diplomacy for almost a generation.[22] For its part, the FRG accepted a host of constraints and obligations as price of sovereignty and admission to NATO. First, Bonn accepted that the Western allies would retain crucial powers relating to "Berlin and Germany as a whole." Second, the FRG promised to raise 500,000 troops and to integrate them *wholly* into NATO (which no other member has done).

[19] Konrad Adenauer, *Erinnerungen,* Vol. II (Stuttgart: Deutsche Verlags-Anstalt, 1966), p. 88.

[20] Adenauer, *Erinnerungen,* Vol. I, p. 96.

[21] In a radio interview with Ernst Friedländer on June 11, 1953. Presse- und Informationsabteilung der Bundesregierung, *Mitteilungen an die Presse,* No 561/53, pp. 3–4. (The Morgenthau Plan, abandoned by Roosevelt in 1944, had foreseen the dismemberment and deindustrialization of Germany.

[22] The settlement was concluded in 1952 and amended in 1954, after France had vetoed the original compact. For the documents, which are crucial for the understanding of subsequent policy for the next twenty years, see Council on Foreign Relations, ed., *Documents on American Foreign Relations, 1952* and the volume for 1954 (New York: Harper & Row, 1953 and 1955). For a succinct analysis of the terms, see Charles E. Planck, *The Changing Status of German Reunification in Western Diplomacy, 1955–1966* (Baltimore: Johns Hopkins Press, 1967), pp. 6–10.

Third, the FRG renounced the right to manufacture nuclear, biological, and chemical weapons. Fourth, Bonn undertook to refrain from any action "inconsistent with the strictly defensive character of NATO" and "never to have recourse to force to achieve the reunification."[23]

But in exchange, the Western powers delivered a three-fold pledge that limited *their* options by precluding the wrong kind of settlement with the Soviet Union. First, they would regard the Federal Republic as the only legitimate "representative of the German people in international affairs." By implication that precluded Western recognition of the GDR. Second, they asserted that the "final determination" of borders had to await a *freely* negotiated settlement. This was a critical pledge because it assured the FRG against an *imposed* peace treaty, which was Adenauer's enduring nightmare. Third, the Western powers promised to work for a reunified Germany "enjoying a liberal democratic constitution like that of the Federal Republic and integrated within the European Community." This was, theoretically, the "efficient" part of the bargain. If the first two pledges were to hold open an unacceptable status quo, the third bound the West to *transform* it. In short, the West refused to concede the finality of the status quo, thus keeping alive the hope for reunification, while granting to Adenauer what he cherished most: a contractual pledge not to go for a collusive settlement with the Soviet Union.

The function of this bargain was two-fold. Diplomatically, it had put the government of a vanquished nation, if not into the driver's seat, into the brakeman's caboose. Adenauer had gained an immensely valuable prize by rearranging the diplomatic stage in such a manner as to block any postwar settlement at the expense of Germany. Never have losers scored so well in such a short time after total defeat. But domestically, the payoff was no less impressive. On the home front, Adenauer was forever hounded by a Social Democratic opposition that kept hammering home the contradiction between integration and reunification. Yet now the Chancellor could deflate the best arguments of the Social Democrats by waving his bargain with the West in their faces. The settlement was no obstacle to reunification, but indeed a vital precondition as it bound the West to undo partition. "I assure you," he told the nation, that "this treaty is the first step toward reunification."[24] How so? Rhetorically, the gap between aspiration and reality was spanned by the dominant myth of the 1950s, the "policy of strength," echoing the idea of "roll-back" then touted by Washington as the proper approach to the Soviet Union.

"Only the sufficient strength of the West," Adenauer proclaimed, "will create a real basis for peaceful negotiations. Their objective is to liberate

[23] Lest there remain any doubt, these good-conduct pledges were reinforced by an Allied declaration that was certainly directed against the Federal Republic, the heir of the Third Reich. If any member government used force for nondefensive purposes, it would forfeit its "right to any guarantee and any military assistance," and the Western allies would then "act...with a view to taking other measures which may be appropriate." *Documents on American Foreign Relations, 1954,* p. 115–17.

[24] As quoted in *Frankfurter Allgemeine Zeitung,* May 27, 1952.

peacefully not only the Soviet Zone but also all of enslaved Europe east of the Iron Curtain."[25] The "policy of strength" provided Adenauer with a vital myth that would obfuscate his choice and flummox the opposition. When *would* the West be strong enough to achieve reunification? Only time would tell. In the meantime, however, Adenauer's domestic base was stabilized, and the moment of truth had receded into a dim future. What mattered was that the promise was kept alive, in spite of the hardening of partition. And so, revisionism was put on ice, assuring the world at large and neutralizing an opposition that, throughout the 1950s, would unsuccessfully try to gain power at the polls by accusing the Conservatives of national betrayal.

DIPLOMACY AND DOMESTIC POLITICS

At this point, a closer look at the domestic bases of West German foreign policy is in order. As was previously pointed out on page 70, the foreign policy of others (the "system") tended to determine domestic sources rather than the other way round. And in the past, especially after World War I, that influence was hardly benign. In many ways, the Federal Republic found itself in the same situation as the Weimar Republic. Both were tenuous democratic experiments, and both had to live with imposed restraints. Similarly, the built-in revisionism of both[26] was at odds with international realities. The Weimar precedent was hardly encouraging. As the rise of Hitler had shown, national grievances, especially when coupled with economic misery, could become the breeding ground for ultra-nationalist revolt and dictatorship.

Yet Bonn was not Weimar, and it is perhaps Adenauer's greatest achievement that he managed to turn potential disaster into social stability and democracy. The most crucial difference between Weimar and Bonn was economics. Unlike its forebear, the FRG could *enjoy* the economic consequences of peace. In the 1920s, security for France spelled reparations and indefinite economic controls on Germany. In the 1950s, however, security for the United States spelled speedy recovery and sustained prosperity for West Germany. Instead of a staggering reparations burden, there were massive infusions of American capital. Instead of "beggar-thy-neighbor" policies and competitive devaluations, there was free movement of goods and capital, encouraged and enforced by the United States.

Partition and amputation had robbed West Germany, the Reich's industrial heartland, of its traditional markets. But with the help of an American-sponsored free trade system, markets lost in the East were opened up in the West. That plus West European integration provided outlets and competitive pressures, feeding a long-term export-led boom. Moreover, partition provided

---

[25] In a broadcast interview, as reproduced by Presse- und Informationsamt der Bundesregierung, *Bulletin,* No. 27, March 16, 1952, p. 262.

[26] The Weimar Republic had lost territory in the East, most importantly the so-called Polish Corridor that separated East Prussia from the Reich. Post-1945 Germany was not only divided but also had to cede even larger territories to Poland and the U.S.S.R.

a blessing in disguise. About nine million people came from the territories incorporated by Poland, Czechoslovakia, and the Soviet Union. Until 1961, when East Germany was sealed off with concrete and barbed wire, about three million—the young and the highly trained—came from the GDR. Apart from fueling a sustained expansion, the millions of refugees exerted downward pressure on wage levels. The sheer numbers of the population transfer surely explained the astounding discipline of West German labor unions, modest wage increases, a high investment rate, the competitiveness of West German exports; hence the stuff from which the "economic miracle" was made.

With sustained growth, the political institutions of the Federal Republic could draw legitimacy from an ever-expanding economic base. In contrast to Weimar, democracy was *not* associated with economic catastrophe. Unlike Weimar leaders, Adenauer thus succeeded in divorcing revisionism from economic grievances. Although long forgotten (or precisely because it is), the deliberate integration of the Eastern refugees was an act of enormous foresight. The contrast to the Palestinian refugees is instructive: These were just as deliberately interned by Arab regimes in camps around Israel to keep revisionism alive. With their economic problems rapidly divorced from their political complaints, the refugees never formed that reserve army of the frustrated and alienated that was mobilized against the Weimar Republic. Economic cooptation soon paid off politically. The refugee party (BHE) gained seats in the Bundestag only once—in 1953—and then it was absorbed by the larger parties.

Nationalism, the less clamorous brother of revisionism, was similarly defanged. After World War I, Germany was spared the trauma of total defeat and occupation, and surrender—transfigured by the notorious "stab-in-the-back" legend—soon gave way to rampant nationalism. By contrast, the apocalyptic collapse of the Third Reich had left a profound revulsion against ultranationalism. And whatever energy was still left could be safely enveloped in the transnational ersatz nationalism of Europeanism and anticommunism. Transcending national boundaries, these were the right ideologies at the right time, delivering rich domestic payoffs. In the first place, they dovetailed perfectly with the dominant conflict and the choices of West German policy. And so, diplomatic necessity went hand in hand with prevailing domestic values—a rare condition in the life of nations. Second, the "European Father-land" served as a safe and constructive outlet for affective needs. Aggressive impulses, on the other hand, could be channeled into a communal ideology of anticommunism. For the first time, Germany did not stand alone; its "nationalism" was embedded in Europe and in the West. Enveloped in a larger community, Adenauer could reap the benefits of a unifying "us-against-them" credo without having to pay the price of actual conflict, as did German leaders before and after World War I.

Third, the Cold War was an invaluable asset in the contest for domestic power. Given the Soviet threat and the Communist blueprint implemented in

East Germany, socialism was quickly discredited while West German nation-building proceeded under liberal-capitalist auspices, tempered by the welfare-minded "social market economy." In terms of domestic politics, the result was twenty years of uninterrupted Christian-Democratic tenure (1949–1969). Anticommunism delivered a potent electoral weapon against the Social Democratic opposition. It did not matter that the SPD was staunchly anti-Communist. Yet its residual Marxism, preserved throughout the 1950s, allowed the Christian Democrats to discredit the SPD as a party of crypto-Communism and ultimately national treason. Here, too, the system proved to be destiny—in the sense that it skewed the domestic power balance for almost a generation.

THE POLITICS OF DEPENDENCE

It was just argued that the FRG had to *manipulate* its milieu precisely because it was so beholden to its forces. And with the grand bargain struck in 1952–54, the Federal Republic had acquired a certain veto power over the course of East-West relations in Europe. Given the terms of the *Deutschlandvertrag*, there were a number of things Bonn's Western partners could *not* do: recognize the GDR, consecrate the new borders, and negotiate a European settlement with Moscow at the expense of Germany. Any such deal would have to be flanked by progress on reunification "in peace and freedom," which, decoded, meant: a united Germany on the Western side. This approach, known as *Politik des Junktims* ("policy of linkage") was the linchpin of Bonn's diplomacy all the way into the late 1960s.

Of course, the Soviet Union would not accept such a deal (which would have shifted the balance of power dramatically), and so the various quadripartite conferences of the 1950s ended in predictable stalemate. But if we distinguish between the proclaimed purpose and the actual function of policy, the *Junktim* turns out to be a powerful device in the annals of German diplomacy. Since Soviet proposals were all designed to freeze the status quo and to reassert Four-Power supervision over Germany, stalemate was always better than any conceivable Soviet offer. As long as Bonn succeeded in persuading its allies that its own quarrel with the Soviet Union was but part and parcel of the overall East-West conflict, that resolution of the latter required progress on reunification, the Federal Republic could block any return to "Potsdam."

Obviously, the FRG's veto power was derivative. It was power on lease, predicated on the West's willingness to subordinate its quest for a *modus vivendi* with the East to West German interests. Paradoxically, the completion of the twin-alliance system in 1955 marked the zenith of West German influence. The West had obtained what it cherished most: the addition of the West German asset on the side of NATO. In response, the Soviet Union went for a second-best solution: the consolidation of the GDR. And Bonn was now stuck with an abiding anxiety. Though it was now a bulwark for the West, it could at any time become a stumbling block toward accommodation with the East.

The crisis was not long in coming, and its trigger was the shifting nuclear balance. In 1953, the Soviet Union acquired the hydrogen bomb, in 1956 it launched its first intercontinental ballistic missile, and soon the notorious "missile gap" was born. In response, the United States decided to deploy medium-range missiles and tactical nuclear weapons in Europe. And with NATO about to go nuclear, the FRG was faced with yet another fateful choice, akin to the one between integration and unity.

After a brief effort to resist the nuclear tide[27], the Federal Republic decided to acquire a nuclear armory of sorts, that is, nuclear delivery vehicles and tactical warheads under American control. Britain and France were developing their national deterrents, and for Bonn to have no say in the nuclear strategy of the Alliance was seen as a retrograde fallback to an earlier role of voiceless dependence. The Soviet Union had minced no words in warning the FRG against a nuclear choice. Thereafter, events unfolded with brutal force. In its attempt to escape from inferiority, the FRG soon found itself entangled in even greater dependence on the West as a result of the "Berlin Ultimatum" flung down by Soviet General-Secretary Nikita Khrushchev in the winter of 1958.[28]

It was a brilliant opening move toward a "movable status quo,"[29] and the locale was well-chosen. Khrushchev knew full well that the West could not concede West Berlin, the prime locus and symbol of Western resistance in the Cold War. So the Allies would have to offer compensation elsewhere—by rescinding West Germany's nuclear armament, recognizing the GDR and/or agreeing to a pan-European security system which, as Adenauer claimed, would reduce the FRG to a "second-rate state."[30]

It did not take too much arm twisting before the West began to cringe and offer concessions on European security and the de facto recognition of the GDR in order to shore up its position in Berlin. As a result, the Federal Republic was confronted with an insidious problem. Like any client state, the FRG drew its derivative strength from an intimate association with its patron powers, above all, the United States. The weak become strong if they can persuade their protectors that their interests are alike. A threat to the client then becomes an obligation for the patron. Until the Berlin Crisis exposed the heterogeneity of interests between the West and the FRG, Bonn could extract

[27] Adenauer was afraid that the "New Look," the attempt to substitute nuclear firepower for conventional force, would lead to a withdrawal of American troops from Europe.

[28] The Soviet message of November 27, 1958, called on the West to recognize the abnormality of its presence in West Berlin. If after six months West Berlin was not turned into a demilitarized Free City, Moscow would turn the access roads over to the GDR and eventually negotiate a separate peace treaty with East Germany. Thereafter, the West would have to negotiate with (and hence recognize) the GDR but face the military might of the Warsaw Pact if it resorted to force. Furthermore, both German states ought to withdraw from their respective alliances and become largely demilitarized.

[29] Herbert Dinerstein, *Fifty Years of Soviet Foreign Policy* (Baltimore: Johns Hopkins Press, 1968), p. 34.

[30] On the Berlin Crisis, see Philip Windsor, *City on Leave* (London: Chatto and Windus, 1963); Jean Smith, *The Defense of Berlin* (Baltimore: Johns Hopkins Press, 1963); and Jack M. Schick, *The Berlin Crisis, 1958–1962* (Philadelphia: University of Pennsylvania Press, 1971).

leverage from impotence by identifying its own separate conflict with the East as an inextricable part of the bipolar contest round the world.

The Berlin Crisis was a watershed because it cut through the "indivisibility of conflict"[31] that underlay Bonn's borrowed clout. From then on, the Allies began to draw an increasingly rigid distinction between Bonn's and their own quarrels with the U.S.S.R. While demonstrating resistance to Soviet pressures with a defense build-up and the reinforcement of the U.S. garrison in Berlin, the new Kennedy administration was obsessed with quite a different problem: mutual nuclear devastation. "This had changed all the answers and all the questions."[32] And so, Kennedy placed maximum emphasis on superpower negotiation. Regardless of Germany or other political quarrels, the military milieu had to be stabilized through arms control. While Alliance cohesion was important, German national aspirations could no longer act as the touchstone of the East-West relationship.

"The reunification of Germany seemed to him an unrealistic negotiating objective."[33] Instead, American policy now came to obey the following premise:

> Germany has been divided for sixteen years and will continue to stay divided. The Soviet Union is running an unnecessary risk in trying to change this from an accepted fact into a legal state. Let the Soviet Union keep Germany divided on its present basis and not try to persuade us to associate ourselves legally with that division and thus weaken our ties to West Germany and their ties to Western Europe.[34]

The Berlin Crisis marked a definite break in West German foreign policy. The climax of the Crisis—the erection of the Berlin Wall in August 1961, which sealed the division of Germany in concrete—shattered the vital myth of reunification. As Willy Brandt, the mayor of West Berlin who would become Chancellor in 1969, put it: "After twelve years, we must recognize our aspirations as illusions....Today there is no discernible price of reunification except the renunciation of freedom."[35] The immediate price was paid by Adenauer, which once more underlines the impact of the system on society. In the September election the CDU/CSU lost its absolute majority, while the Social Democrats, picked up almost five points. In 1963, Adenauer was forced to hand over power to his economics minister Ludwig Erhard. Most importantly, the Crisis toppled the key pillar of German diplomacy. If the West was ready to pursue détente regardless of German preconditions, then the FRG either had to go along or go it alone. If the latter raised the specter of isolation, the former required a fundamental change of policy. It required accepting

[31] Richard Löwenthal, *Vom kalten Krieg zur Ostpolitik* (Stuttgart: Seewald, 1974), p. 57.

[32] John F. Kennedy, as quoted by Theodore C. Sorensen, *Kennedy* (New York: Bantam Books, 1966), p. 577.

[33] Arthur Schlesinger, *A Thousand Days* (Greenwich, Conn: Fawcett Crest, 1967), p. 371.

[34] Kennedy in a conversation with Finnish President Kekkonen in October 1961, as quoted in Schlesinger, *Ibid.*, p. 371.

[35] Address to the Bundestag, December 6, 1961, in Willy Brandt, *Der Wille zum Frieden* (Hamburg: Hoffmann & Campe, 1971), p. 68.

the consequences of World War II, which the Soviets exacted as the price of accommodation.[36]

THE NEW *OSTPOLITIK*

By the end of the 1960s, twenty years of West German diplomacy had come to a dead halt. In the years following Adenauer's resignation (1963), a halfhearted policy of rapprochement with the East was launched by the Christian Democratic Chancellors Ludwig Erhard (1963–1966) and Kurt-Georg Kiesinger, who ruled in tandem with the SPD (1966–1969). The policy of the Grand Coalition was flexible on tactics, but unyielding on the basics: no ratification of postwar boundaries, no recognition of the GDR.[37] The answer of the Soviets was *nyet*, and the separate conflict with the East even intensified. In the past, Bonn had been able to sustain that conflict with borrowed power. Yet even after the Warsaw Pact invasion of Czechoslovakia in 1968, the West continued to bypass the German problem on the road to détente, thus calling in the power loan to Bonn.

To oppose the Soviet Union on the shoulders of the strong was one thing; to do so without their support was impossible. By the end of the 1960s, the American agenda had changed completely. The Nixon administration (1969–1974) was about to embark on the most determined détente push ever, trying to weaken Soviet support for North Vietnam by holding out a "stable structure of peace" to the U.S.S.R. The main vehicle was the strategic arms limitation treaty (SALT), negotiated from 1969 to 1972, which bestowed the badge of "nuclear parity" on the Soviet Union. Robbed of its derivative strength and facing the full brunt of Soviet hostility, the Federal Republic sooner or later would have to follow suit. And follow it did, thus paying tribute to the systemic imperatives of German diplomacy once more. Or as Herbert Wehner, the Social Democratic Minister of All-German Affairs during the Grand Coalition, put it: "Up to now, we have lived beyond our means—as if we had been a victor power by adoption."[38]

A thorough overhaul, however, had to await domestic change. That moment arose on September 28, 1969, when a twenty-year cycle of German electoral politics came to an end. On September 28, 1969, Willy Brandt's left-of-center Social Democrats and their smaller allies, the Liberals (FDP) emerged as the victors of the national election; for the first time in West German history, the Christian Democrats were in the opposition. The campaign had been heavily dominated by foreign policy, with the SPD presenting itself as the party of long-overdue rapprochement with the East. As result, the

---

[36] For the first halting steps, the *Ostpolitik* of the Grand Coalition (made up of Christian Democrats and Social Democrats) from 1966 to 1969, see the author's chapter in the previous (1989) edition of *Foreign Policy in World Politics*, pp. 93–99.

[37] For an analysis, see this chapter in the previous edition of *Foreign Policy in World Politics* (1989), pp. 93–99.

[38] As quoted in *Die Welt*, February 20, 1967.

outcome of the September 28 election suggested a popular mandate for unshouldering the sterile, if not counterproductive diplomacy of the past.

The new Brandt government quickly began to signal its resolution to do what all previous Bonn governments had sought to resist: to accept the postwar status quo for what it was. Reunification would no longer act as the stumbling block of détente. Instead, the new policy boiled down to the refusal to shelve reunification once and for all. (Hence Bonn withheld de jure recognition from the GDR until reunification in 1990.) Accordingly, Willy Brandt did not even mention the word "reunification" in his inaugural address. Dispensing with the FRG's claim to "sole representation" of Germany as a whole, he spoke of "two German states in one nation." While a joint nationhood precluded formal recognition, Brandt offered "contractually regulated cooperation" to the GDR.[39] Having served notice that it was ready to unlink and quarantine the German issue, Bonn signed the Non-Proliferation Treaty (NPT) in November 1969. This was a signal as well as a turning point, since West German access to nuclear weapons had been a prime focus of the Soviet-German quarrel since 1957.

The stage was now set for an incredibly complex diplomatic exercise that amounted to a virtual settlement of World War II. Only a formal peace conference was missing. Resolution unfolded in a crisscrossing pattern of multilateral and bilateral negotiations. The vehicles of reconciliation were renunciation-of-force treaties (based on the affirmation of the territorial status quo) with Moscow and Warsaw, the "Basic Treaty" with East Berlin (regulating coexistence without formal recognition), and a quadripartite agreement on Berlin (ensuring access and the ties between the FRG and West Berlin).

It was no surprise that the prime obstacle proved to be the GDR. Like the FRG in the 1960s, the GDR mounted an all-out effort to retain its role as "guardian at the gate" between the blocs. Both had gained their identity and derivative power from their forward-position in the Cold War. Monopolizing the national heritage, each Germany had drawn its own legitimacy from denying it to the other. Both had been able to harness their alliance to a hard-line policy against the other side by cultivating intimate links with their bloc leader. However, as with the United States in the 1960s, the Soviet Union was now no longer willing to defer to the claims of its junior partner. Indeed, Ulbricht's quiet ouster in May 1971 (no doubt with Soviet prodding) evoked comparison with the fate of Adenauer, whose political decline began in earnest in the aftermath of the Berlin Wall and America's turn toward superpower détente.

Moscow's prime aim was a West German treaty and an all-European conference that would finally ratify the territorial redistribution wrought by World War II. In its quest to escape from inferiority, the GDR had more

---

[39]Bundesministerium für innerdeutsche Beziehunge, *Texte zur Deutschlandpolitik*, Vol. IV (Bonn: Vorwärts-Duck, 1970), pp. 11–13, 38–39.

demanding objectives. It sought not only long-denied diplomatic recognition by the West but also a changing status for West Berlin, a Western enclave whose mere existence posed a permanent challenge to the sovereignty of the GDR. But in West Berlin, where their wartime rights were at stake, the interests of the three Western powers were still the same as the FRG's. A deal could not come at the expense of Western positions in the former capital of the *Reich*. With that leverage in hand, the Brandt government could outflank its hostile brother in the East by tying the Eastern treaties to a satisfactory Berlin settlement.

And so Berlin became the touchstone of the entire détente mosaic. Washington, London, and Paris began to define the traditional flashpoint of crisis as the key test of Soviet intentions, and therefore they predicated the convocation of a European security conference and the recognition of the GDR—both at the top of the East German and the Soviet agenda—on a Berlin agreement. After years of recalcitrance, Bonn's Eastern policy was now reintegrated into the larger framework of Western diplomacy. This was one of Brandt's greatest achievements. On the one hand, the Berlin link strengthened Bonn's hand in the East. Failure in Berlin would threaten the entire détente edifice, and hence the Soviet Union was forced to rein in its obstreperous East German ally. On the other hand, the Berlin link helped to relieve American anxieties about the haphazard pace of German Ostpolitik. Since the three Western powers were in charge of a Berlin agreement, and since a bilateral deal between Bonn and Moscow had to await a breakthrough on Berlin, the West had acquired a handle on German-Soviet relationship that had awakened a good deal of suspicion.

The Berlin Agreement was signed on September 3, 1971. For the first time since the war, the Soviet Union pledged to ensure "unimpeded access" to Berlin. While reaffirming that West Berlin was not a "constituent part" of the FRG, the agreement did concede the crucial point that the ties between both could be "maintained and developed."[40] The Eastern Treaties (with Poland and the U.S.S.R.) were ratified on May 17, 1972. On June 3, the Berlin Agreement entered into force. Having narrowly escaped from a no-confidence vote in Parliament, Willy Brandt called for an out-of-turn election in November 1972. It was again heavily dominated by Ostpolitik. Its outcome, a comfortable majority for the Brandt coalition, suggested that the quasi ratification of the status quo abroad had been accompanied by the transformation of the ideological consensus at home. Thereafter, the de facto recognition of the GDR was formalized in the Basic Treaty between both German states concluded on December 21, 1972. The fine distinction between de facto and de jure was drawn by the fact that both states would maintain "permanent missions" rather than embassies in each other's capital.

---

[40]For the German and English texts of the Agreement, see *Europa-Archiv*, no. 19, 1971, pp. D443–53.

The Continuities of West German Foreign Policy

Having surmounted the tortuous obstacle course of negotiation and ratification, Brandt's *Ostpolitik* spelled something of a diplomatic revolution. Yet in spite of stark differences between the Founding Father, Konrad Adenauer, and his Social Democratic heir, both phases were linked by profound continuities that reflected enduring givens of West German diplomacy.

First and foremost, Adenauer had sought to escape from subjection and isolation. Given the tightening strictures of bipolarity, the long-term partition of Germany was the price of security and sovereignty for its Western half. Adenauer's "disingenuity" may have been the mark of true statesmanship. By proclaiming that integration would lead to reunification, he anchored the young republic in a sturdy community that softened the blow of partition and underwrote democratic evolution. For once in the course of German history, the "international system" acted as a benign influence on domestic politics. In the Weimar Republic, the political center was crushed by the ruins of the economy and the resentment of the outside world. For the Federal Republic, on the other hand, community with the West, which offered a shelter as well as a legitimate outlet, undercut the political extremes and smoothed the way for a flourishing, centrist democracy. So when the moment of truth dawned many years later, West German society reacted with remarkable political maturity to the loss of illusion.

In the 1970s, Willy Brandt actually reenacted Adenauer's strategy. Domestically, Brandt's *Ostpolitik* forged a new consensus by carefully dismantling the "vital myth" of revisionism; diplomatically, it reintegrated the FRG into the détente trend of Western diplomacy. Both Adenauer and Brandt sought to defuse German revisionism, and both were haunted by the perils of Germany's vulnerable position in the European center. During the ratification debates on the Eastern Treaties Brandt again evoked the ancient nightmare of German diplomacy in defense of his *Ostpolitik:* "An anti-German coalition has been Bismarck's as well as Adenauer's nightmare. We, too, are faced with this problem, and we should make sure that our own policy does not turn this problem into a burden."[41]

Brandt thus heeded one of the oldest lessons of German diplomacy: don't go it alone. ("Try to be in a threesome" in the five-power world of Europe, Bismarck had put it.) Britain, an insular power tied to the United States, could always seek safety in "splendid isolation." France could afford a policy of "splendid aggravation" precisely because France remained safely ensconced behind American forces in West Germany. And both nations had acquired the ultimate insurance of a national nuclear deterrent. For the Federal Republic, the avoidance of isolation virtually amounts to an unwritten law. If Adenauer had integrated the FRG into the Western community, Brandt's *Ostpolitik*

[41] *Verhandlungen des Deutschen Bundestages,* May 17, 1972, p. 10897. Compare this with Adenauer's statement on June 11, 1953; see p. 84 and note 26.

returned Bonn's policy to the mainstream of Western diplomacy. Indeed, in the very process of resolving the separate conflict with the East, the treaties with the Soviet Union and Poland explicitly affirmed previous "bilateral and multilateral" agreements, i.e., those on NATO and the EEC.

Still, *Ostpolitik* was a crucial departure that would doubly reshape West Germany"s future role. First, the diplomatic revolution between 1969 and 1972 reduced the Federal Republic's unique dependence on the West. Second, it restored a long-suppressed return to diplomacy. The result was an enduring tension between the FRG's Western obligations and Eastern mission. Indeed, yesterday's separate conflict with the East would soon gestate into a special relationship, if not a separate peace. It was based on an ironclad premise: Reassociation of the two Germanys would have to supplant the impossible goal of reunification. Reassociation, meaning ever-increasing human, economic, and political ties, in turn, required reassurance—for the GDR, the East Europeans, and the Soviet Union. Hence, foreign policy came to obey a virtually permanent détente imperative.

OUT FROM DEPENDENCE: THE HELMUT SCHMIDT ERA

West Germany Ascendant

"At best you can stand on one leg, but you can't walk on it."[42] With these words, the Social Democrat's floor leader, Herbert Wehner, tersely described the momentous changes wrought by *Ostpolitik*. The acquisition of a "second leg," ending the artificial truncation of diplomacy after a quarter-century of self-denial, would not only allow for mobility in the East but also relieve pressure on Bonn's "Western leg." The counterpart of Bonn's separate conflict with the East was excruciating dependence on, and deference to, the West.

Hence, the Federal Republic had diligently paid for American troops stationed in Germany. Concessions on the European Community's agricultural policy were heavily conditioned by the need for French diplomatic support against the East. With Helmut Schmidt arrived a new era.[43] "Our margin of diplomatic maneuver," the Chancellor told the Bundestag in 1975, "has been enlarged enormously." First of all, the Eastern treaties "have largely...liberated our country from its role as a client...Second, *Ostpolitik* and the Berlin Agreement have greatly reduced the numerous reasons why we had...to seek, and beg for, continuous reassurance."[44] Third, there was growing

---

[42]Herbert Wehner, Parliamentary Leader of the Social Democrats, before the Bundestag, November 6, 1974. *Texte zur Deutschlandpolitik,* Series II, Vol. 2 (Bonn: Bundesministerium für innerdeutsche Beziehungen, 1976), p. 295.

[43]Willy Brandt had resigned from office in May 1974 when one of his close collaborators, Wilhelm Guillaume, was exposed as an East German spy planted in the Chancellor's office. With their majority intact, the Social Democrats and Liberals elected the SPD Defense Minister Helmut Schmidt as Chancellor.

[44]Address to the Bundestag, July 25, 1975. *Bulletin,* July 29, 1975.

economic clout. Thus, it was the "great success...of Germany's...economic policy" that had "increased our weight."[45]

Economic strength was doubly significant. Not only did it bespeak wealth and worldly success; it was also the most valuable currency of power in an international system that had apparently shifted from "high politics" to "low politics" in the wake of the 1973 oil crisis.[46] With the Cold War waning, the ancient East-West conflict seemed to have given way to a new contest between North and South. In this world, according to Helmut Schmidt, the key issue was no longer military security but the "struggle for the world product."[47] And in this game, the FRG was a "player whose counsel is being asked and whose voice is being heard."[48] By the end of 1975, the *Sunday Times* celebrated Helmut Schmidt as the "first West European leader of genuine world status since Charles de Gaulle."[49] Four years later, *Time* magazine devoted a cover story to Helmut Schmidt and his country: "West Germany has finally come of age as a Continental power [and] Schmidt has shouldered his way into the front row of international leaders."[50]

Hardly in office, the new Chancellor served notice on the European Community (EC) that the FRG would not longer act as the Common Market's trustiest "Euro-payer." Bonn forced the EC Commission to cut its proposed 1975 budget by 20 percent, and the Chancellor personally blocked a five percent rise of the Community's agricultural prices. That move was a jejune way of marking a historic transition. Exactly ten years earlier, France and the FRG had squared off over the Community's grain prices, but within days Chancellor Erhard had caved in because he could not afford to lose French support against Moscow. *Ostpolitik* had reduced such leverage to naught. Or as Schmidt's Finance Minister Hans Apel put it, "Germany's past is no longer a building block of European integration."[51]

The distance Bonn had traveled could be measured best in terms of its sustained revolt against the United States. In June 1975, Schmidt informed Washington that he would not sign a new "offset agreement" to pay for U.S. troops in Europe. Also in June 1975, West Germany and Brazil concluded the largest nuclear transaction in history. The four billion dollar deal encompassed the entire fuel cycle from enrichment to reprocessing, the two roads to a nuclear weapon. Jimmy Carter, an avid antiproliferationist who became President in 1977, saw this as a nasty blow to his fondest aspirations, and so he

---

[45] "Wir sind ein erstklassiger Partner," interview with *Der Spiegel,* January 1, 1975.

[46] The Organization of Petroleum-Exporting Countries (OPEC) used the 1973 Yom Kippur War as an occasion to quadruple oil prices. That acted as a gigantic tax on the rest of the world, shifting income to the OPEC states and pushing the Western world into inflationary recession. In Western Europe, the FRG weathered the oil crisis better than most.

[47] Helmut Schmidt in "The Struggle for the World Product," *Foreign Affairs,* April 1974.

[48] Declaration before the Bundestag, as reprinted in *Vorwärts,* April 15, 1976.

[49] Godfrey Hodgson, "The Professional: A Profile of Helmut Schmidt," *Sunday Times* supplement, November 16, 1975.

[50] "Leading from Strength," *Time* (European Edition), June 11, 1979.

[51] As quoted in "Wer reich ist, muss zahlen," *Der Spiegel,* September 30, 1974.

demanded that Bonn withhold the critical equipment or place it under multinational control. But "the Germans stood firm, and all [we] received was their assurance that they would observe existing safeguards."[52]

Here, too, history offered a lesson in the shifting fortunes of power. Fourteen years earlier the United States and the Federal Republic had engaged in a similar clash over East-West trade. The stake was the delivery of large diameter steel pipes to the Soviet Union. As in the Brazil case, the United States intervened in force only after the contract had been signed and sealed. Yet whereas the Schmidt government insisted on the sanctity of contracts and won, Konrad Adenauer had caved in. In March 1963, he imposed an embargo, defying for the sake of harmony with Washington the steel industry and even his own party. Nor did Jimmy Carter succeed in pushing Bonn to assume the role of "locomotive" in the world economy. Instead, Jimmy Carter received endless lectures on sound economic management. According to Schmidt, American policy was "irresponsible." The Americans had "neither accepted nor even understood their leadership role in the international economy." It was "unbelievable that the strongest economic power in the world has a balance-of-payments deficit at its current high level."[53]

Back to Basics: Afghanistan, the Euromissile Crisis, and Cold War II

Schmidt's assertiveness rested on three factors. First, as the chancellor put it: "*Ostpolitik...*gave us a much greater freedom of action."[54] Second, détente had profoundly changed the political climate in Europe; the quest for military security was losing its hold. Third, with military force apparently devalued, economic power was pushing to the fore, and here, the Federal Republic looked like a virtual superpower.

Yet this halcyon state was not to last. Two trends conspired to undo the détente of the 1970s, to trigger Cold War II, circa 1979–87, and to transform the benign setting of German foreign policy. Cold War II began in earnest in 1979 when the Soviet Union marched into Afghanistan. For the Carter administration, heretofore dedicated to "world order" politics and nuclear disarmament, the invasion was tantamount to a call to arms. Jimmy Carter let the SALT II Treaty go unratified, imposed a grain embargo on the Soviet Union, and initiated rearmament. Ronald Reagan picked up where Carter had left off, summoning the allies to oppose the "evil empire" around the world.

The second trend unfolded closer to home. Regardless of détente, the Soviet Union had continued to arm across the board in the 1970s. In Europe, the star player was the SS-20 missile, incapable of reaching the United States but threatening all of Western Europe. The triple-warhead SS-20 entered

[52]Zbigniew Brzezinski, *Power and Principle* (New York: Farrar Straus Giroux, 1983), p. 131.
[53]Address before an economics conference in Hamburg, April 28, 1978, as quoted in reports of the *New York Times*, April 29, 1978, the *Süddeutsche Zeitung*, April 29, 1978, and *Die Welt* ("Das sagte Helmut Schmidt zum deutsch-amerikanischen Verhältnis"), May 24, 1978.
[54]In an interview with the *Economist*, September 29, 1979, p. 47.

deployment around 1976, and in the fall of 1977, Helmut Schmidt was the first to raise the alarm. These missiles posed a separate threat to Europe, and they were potent "instruments of pressure."[55] Worse, superpower arms control not only ignored the tilting "Eurostrategic" balance but also left Moscow free to intimidate Western Europe with weapons unconstrained by SALT II. In Schmidt's words, "Strategic arms limitations confined to the United States and the Soviet Union will inevitably impair the security of [Western Europe]...if we do not succeed in removing the disparities of military power in Europe parallel to the SALT negotiations." The German chancellor preferred to solve the problem by arms control, but if not, "the Alliance...must be ready to make available the means to support its present strategy."[56] Decoded, this meant that NATO might have to counterdeploy similar missiles if negotiations failed.

Cold War II was the beginning of the worst and longest freeze in East-West and German-Soviet relations since the Berlin Crisis from 1958 to 1962. The ten-year contest offered a dramatic lesson in "system dominance." Suddenly, the great stakes were no longer economic but strategic, reminding a middle power like the FRG of its continuing security dependence. Imposing fearful diplomatic choices on Bonn, Cold War II also triggered a nasty battle at home that polarized West German society and ultimately toppled the Schmidt government.

Initially, the Soviet Union even refused to negotiate, pretending that "an approximate balance" existed even as it was deploying about fifty new SS-20 missiles per year. In December 1979, NATO responded with the "Brussels Decision," also known as the "two-track" approach. The Alliance offered to negotiate for four years; failing an agreement, NATO would deploy 464 American cruise missiles in Britain, Belgium, Holland, Italy, and West Germany and 108 Pershing II ballistic missiles in the Federal Republic alone.

Helmut Schmidt was now caught in a double squeeze. Cold War II threatened to refreeze what *Ostpolitik* had so painstakingly unthawed. Renewed confrontation would increase dependence on the West and diminish access to the East, prompting defense minister Hans Apel to note "how limited the margin of movement of lesser alliance members becomes when superpower tensions increase. On the one hand, *Ostpolitik* could "not proceed against or around the Soviet Union."[57] On the other, Schmidt could not afford to alienate the United States, the FRG's key protector.

The squeeze abroad was compounded by mounting pressure at home. By 1981, the clamor of a burgeoning peace movement filled the streets and squares of West German cities. Hundreds of thousands beleaguered Bonn in 1981 and 1982. For the activists, the deployment of U.S. Pershing II and cruise

---

[55]This was a recurrent leitmotiv, see for instance his "A Policy of Reliable Partnership," *Foreign Affairs*, Spring 1981, p. 747.

[56]"The 1977 Alastair Buchan Memorial Lecture," October 28, 1977, reprinted in *Survival*, January–February 1978, p. 3–4.

[57]Address before the Bundestag, May 11, 1978; *Vezhjandlungen des Deutschen Bundestages*, May 11, 1978.

missiles would turn Germany into a "shooting gallery of the superpowers." The domestic debate was shot through with nationalist and anti-American codewords, and for many in the outside world, especially in France, it looked as if West Germany was about to succumb to pacifist neutralism.

Though the noise was great (and amplified by key segments of the West German media), the numbers were simply too small. At no point in the "Battle of the Euromissiles" was the peace movement even remotely strong enough to turn antinuclear moods into antinuclear majorities. The data of public opinion consistently told the same story.[58] Antinuclearism remained a minority quest; as in the first battle against nuclear weapons in the late 1950s, the issue was simply not salient enough to overturn traditional voter loyalties. To illustrate: In the fall of 1981 West Germans were asked to assess NATO's "two-track" approach (negotiate first, but deploy if necessary). About four out of ten approved, and about 20 percent were opposed. The most striking figures emerged from the rest of the sample: Exactly 40 percent admitted that they "did not know" or "did not care." The next 15 months witnessed the grand flowering of the peace movement. Prominent figures of moral and political authority (such as former Chancellor Brandt) added their voices to the growing chorus of protest. In 1983, the West Germans were asked the same question about the two-track approach, and the responses were virtually identical, signaling astounding voter immunity to the passions of the self-selected few.[59] In other words, neither militant nationwide agitation nor Soviet pressure had changed the attitudes of the electorate.

The real problem lay elsewhere—in Helmut Schmidt's Social Democratic Party (SPD). As the Chancellor embarked on his tightrope act between Washington and Moscow, the balance of power in the SPD tilted inexorably to the left, which was more interested in gaining control of the party than in keeping control of the government. Nuclear weapons, depicted as harbingers of collective victimization, offered a perfect vehicle for wresting power from the middle-of-the-roader Helmut Schmidt, who once said of himself: "The people [at large] would have been glad to see me belong to no party."[60]

For Schmidt, there was only one way out of this double squeeze. At a minimum, he had to protect West Germany's détente with the Soviet Union. Returning to Bismarck, he stressed his nineteenth-century predecessor's key idea: to "keep both countries, the great, powerful Soviet Union and the Federal Republic of Germany permanently attached to the process of peace."[61] Yet Schmidt had to do so without incurring the charge of disloyalty to the United States. So Bonn joined the Olympic boycott against Moscow but refused to impose economic sanctions. Then Schmidt took another page out of Bismarck's book by putting himself forward as "honest interpreter of Western

[58]For an analysis, see Josef Joffe, "Peace and Populism: Why the European Anti-Nuclear Movement Failed," *International Security,* Spring 1987.

[59]For the data, see *ibid,* p. 10–11.

[60]As quoted in "Schmidt plaudert aus dem Nähkästchen," *Bild-Zeitung,* May 5, 1984.

[61]Address to the Special General Assembly of the UN, May 25, 1978; *Bulletin,* May 30, 1978.

policy." (Bismarck, in 1878, had tried to play the "honest broker" between Britain and Russia.) "We have an important role to play" in preserving the dialogue between the superpowers."[62] The test came in 1980 when the Chancellor traveled to Moscow to snatch the most vital pieces of détente from the jaws of the rattled giants. If Soviet leader Leonid Bhrezhnev would halt the SS-20 deployment in favor of arms control, relations would return to calmer waters. Just as important, West Germany would be spared the necessity of counterdeployment, and that would undercut the anti-Schmidt *fronde* within his own party.

But the Federal Republic was not the Bismarck Empire. While an economic giant, the FRG was a political dwarf when it came to playing in the superpower arena. As a nation that depended on American protection and the good will of the Soviet Union, the FRG was badly positioned to exact moderation from either. Thus Moscow refused to negotiate while continuing to add to its SS-20 arsenal, assuming, perhaps, that the West German peace movement would carry the day.

It was Helmut Schmidt's personal tragedy that he desperately clung to an equipoise while the times demanded choice, that he tried to play the mediator long after his own country—the pillar and prize of Europe's postwar order—had turned into the foremost stake of the Soviet-American battle. That task became even more improbable when Bonn's trustiest Continental ally, France, changed course in 1981. Worried that France's glacis to the East would yield to Soviet pressures and blandishments, the new French President François Mitterand came to act as Ronald Reagan's most stolid ally. "Soviet SS-20 missiles...are destroying the equilibrium in Europe," he told the Germans one month after his election. "I cannot accept this, and I admit that we must arm to restore the balance."[63]

Unable to budge the Soviet Union, the FRG could not afford to defy its two most important allies, the U.S. and France, simultaneously. The European system, so promising at the beginning of Schmidt's rule, had now hardened into all-but-implacable restraint. And so, nine months before his fall from power, Helmut Schmidt returned to first principles: "Let nobody make a mistake. We Germans are not wanderers between the worlds [of the East and the West]. Our allies can rely on us, and we can rely on them."[64]

Technically, Schmidt fell on October 1, 1982, because his Liberal (FDP) coalition partners abandoned him in the heat of budgetary battle. In a larger sense, however, he was the victim of external forces that he could no longer control. Nor was this a unique outcome in the annals of the Bonn Republic. With one exception, all of Schmidt's predecessors had stumbled not at the polls but in the midst of their tenure, and they were pushed by events intruding

[62] In a speech to the Federation of German Newspaper Publishers, November 10, 1981, as quoted in *Süddeutsche Zeitung,* November 11, 1981.

[63] In an interview with the German mass circulation magazine *Stern,* July 9, 1981, p. 83.

[64] Before the Bundestag on January 14, 1982; *Bulletin,* January 15, 1982.

from without: Adenauer by the Berlin Wall, Erhard by Lyndon Johnson's insistence on the punctual disbursement of "tribute" that went by the name of "offset payments" for American troops, and Brandt by an East German spy lodged in the heart of his Chancellor's Office.

In Schmidt's case the fateful link between the system and society came in the guise of nuclear weapons, the very symbol of bipolarity and West German sovereignty denied.[65] Schmidt could have easily weathered the antinuclear revolt in the streets, but not in his own party. By early 1982, the Chancellor was battling for his political life. At the Munich party congress in April he could only avoid a final test of strength by yielding to the Left on economic policy in exchange for a temporary cease-fire on the missiles. The global economic tide, meanwhile, had also turned against the Chancellor. Worldwide recession, set off by the second oil price explosion in 1979, had finally reached hit the FRG, too; in 1982, unemployment reached 7.5 percent. When the SPD Left called for a massive increase of deficit spending, Schmidt recalled, "I simply had the stamina no longer to fight yet another battle against my comrades."[66] And so he allowed the Party to overwhelm his government's tight fiscal policy which, in turn, offered to the deployment-minded Free Democrats the final reason or pretext for abandoning the coalition. Joining forces with the Christian Democrats, the FDP helped to elect the CDU's Helmut Kohl as Chancellor on October 13, 1982.

The final humiliation came on November 22, 1983, when a huge majority of the SPD's deputies voted to reject the impending deployment of Cruise and Pershing II missiles *against* Schmidt's pleas. They did so in the presence of the former Chancellor as he vented his frustration by sailing paper airplanes into the debating chamber of the Bundestag.

CLOSING THE CIRCLE: FROM COLD WAR II TO REUNIFICATION

A Balance Restored: The Helmut Kohl Era

The Conservative-Liberal coalition, led by Chancellor Helmut Kohl (CDU) and Foreign Minister Hans-Dietrich Genscher (FDP), called for elections in early 1983 to have the electorate certify the new marriage. Free of Helmut Schmidt, the Social Democrats fought the campaign largely on foreign policy and defense issues. Their key slogan was "In the German Interest," a codeword calculated to mobilize neo-nationalist (if not anti-American) and pacifist sentiments. The choice was clearer than in most democratic elections. While the SPD, if victorious, would seek to derail the deployment of cruise and Pershing II missiles, the coalition parties (CDU/CSU and FDP) made no bones about their determination to deploy, absent an arms control agreement.

---

[65] In the grand bargain with the West, by which the FRG regained sovereignty in 1954, Bonn had to forswear the right to an independent nuclear deterrent.

[66] In a conversation with the author, Hamburg, March 3, 1985.

On March 6, 1983, Kohl and Genscher were returned to power with an impressive margin (53.4 percent), while the Social Democrats emerged with their worst showing since 1961 (37 percent). This outcome was hardly surprising, conforming to long-established patterns of democratic voting behavior. Only in very exceptional times do foreign and defense policy dominate the average voter's choice. In the Federal Republic, four issues had emerged as the decisive ones prior to the 1983 election: unemployment, social security, inflation, and the national debt. Conversely, foreign policy had sunk to the bottom of the agenda.[67] In other words, nuclear missiles were simply not "salient" enough to make for a winning issue—as in Britain where the strongly antinuclear Labour Party did worse in 1983 than at any time since 1918.

On November 22, 1983, the Bundestag confirmed the Government's pro-missile choice; on the next day, the first Pershing II and cruise missile components arrived in West Germany. In the moment of truth, then, the Federal Republic chose deterrence over détente and alliance obligations over Ostpolitik. The new Christian Democratic Chancellor, Helmut Kohl, had presumably learned a lesson from his predecessor's diplomatic failure. Yes, Schmidt's premise had been correct: The FRG could only flourish in a permissive East-West climate. But his attempt to "Germanize" East-West relations during Cold War II—to mute superpower confrontation or at least to keep it from engulfing Central Europe—overtaxed German power. As Bonn, emulating Bismarck, had tried to act as a bridge and a brace between East and West, the FRG actually became the premier stake of renewed superpower rivalry. Though acted out on the chessboard of strategy, with Euromissiles as the pawns, the real issue was, as in Cold War I, the balance of power in Europe. And that issue has always boiled down to the age-old question: Who controls Germany? At that point Ostpolitik began to collide mercilessly with Westpolitik, raising the great question of détente: How much dissolution in the West for how much evolution (and access) in the East?

Conscious of Schmidt's failure and of the costs his "honest interpreter" role had exacted in the West, the Kohl coalition presented more modest answers than its predecessor. "In my view," Helmut Kohl said, "it is a hoary illusion to believe that the relationship between...the GDR and the Federal Republic of Germany can really improve while the global political climate remains at subzero temperatures." And then the Chancellor cited an old peasant's saying: "A big stream carries the smaller river along with it." By which he meant to say: For Ostpolitik to flourish, the larger setting has to be favorable.[68]

The most comprehensive statement on Kohl's *Ostpolitik* was a speech by the cabinet-rank Director of the Chancellor's Office, Wolfgang Schäuble. On the one hand there were several changes in emphasis in comparison to the

---

[67]See "Polit-Barometer," an opinion analysis broadcast by Second German Television (ZDF), December 7, 1983.

[68]Interview with Süddeutscher Rundfunk (South German Radio), December 18, 1984, as cited from mimeographed record of the Bundespresse- und Informationsamt, December 19, 1984, no. II/1218–5.

Schmidt era. There was the stress on the "opposition of freedom and bondage" that separates the two German states. "The profound clash of values between East and West is not a matter of compromise." There was also a more sober assessment of West Germany's strength and the explicit recognition of the indispensable Western connection: "Any estrangement from the Atlantic Alliance would render the Federal Republic incapable of conducting a *Deutschlandpolitik* and *Ostpolitik* deserving of the name."[69]

At the same time, Kohl's confidante did stress the legacy bequeathed by Willy Brandt and Helmut Schmidt. "The effects of partition for [our] people" must be "rendered more tolerable." The emphasis on the value conflict between East and West must not "provoke the GDR." There has to be "dialogue and cooperation." Finally, he paid homage to principles that could have been Brandt's or Schmidt's: "Overcoming the partition of Germany means to overcome the partition of Europe." In other words, détente and cooperation with the East were as critical as ever. Finally, homage was due to Soviet sensitivities and interests. Bonn knew only too well that "a *Deutschlandpolitik* that would try to circumvent Moscow could not succeed."[70]

Moscow, however, was determined to punish the Federal Republic for the deployment of Pershing II and cruise missiles that had allowed the United States to carry the day in the great test of strength of the early 1980s. To demonstrate that the Soviet Union held the key to Bonn's relationship with the East, the Kremlin vetoed the eagerly awaited first trip to West Germany by East German leader Erich Honecker, scheduled for the fall of 1984. After his accession in 1985, Soviet General-Secretary Mikhail Gorbachev demonstratively left out Bonn as he traveled to Britain and France and met three times with the American President (1985, 1986, 1987). Only in 1988 did a lower-level emissary—Soviet Foreign Minister Shevardnadze—visit Bonn, and then only after the larger relationship between the two superpowers had been sorted out.

Cold War II began to wane when Soviet leader Gorbachev met with Ronald Reagan at the Geneva Summit of 1985. Détente II was formally declared during the Washington Summit of December 1987, when the U.S. and the U.S.S.R. concluded a treaty eliminating intermediate-range nuclear forces (INF) in the range of 500 to 5000 kilometers worldwide. SS-20, Pershing II, and cruise missiles had been at the heart of the superpower contest in the 1980s. Hence, the Washington Treaty signaled the crucial permissive condition of Central European détente: a modicum of agreement between the two great powers. But as in decades past, the change in the major conflict relationship forced West Germany once more to adapt to trends beyond its control. In the face of the coming INF Treaty, Bonn had launched a determined rear-guard action to keep its own 72 Pershing I missiles (with a range of 700 kilometers

[69] In German usage, *Deutschlandpolitik* refers to FRG-GDR relations, while *Ostpolitik* designates the policy toward Eastern Europe and the Soviet Union.

[70] "Die deutsche Frage im europäischen Rahmen," address before the Swedish Institute for International Relations, May 15, 1986, as published in *Europa-Archiv*, Vol. 41 (June 1986).

and with American warheads) out of the grasp of the superpowers. When the Soviet Union all but predicated the INF accord on the removal of the German Pershings, the Kohl government had to yield. It did so on August 26, 1987, when Kohl let go of the missiles, claiming: "I merely want to help the American President toward a successful conclusion of the Geneva [INF] negotiations."[71]

Mortal Rivals, Tacit Allies

As general East-West détente began to blossom again, the two German states came to enjoy a larger scope for their own *Mitteleuropa* détente. Indeed, an amazing transformation of the inter-German relationship had become manifest. Once hostile brothers who used to play a vanguard role in each other's containment, the two mortal enemies had virtually become tacit allies. Symbolized by the pomp and circumstances of Erich Honecker's week-long visit to the Federal Republic in the fall of 1987, that tacit partnership was born in the early 1980s. As Cold War II threatened to engulf Central Europe, both Helmut Schmidt and Erich Honecker began to talk about *Verantwortungsgemeinschaft* ("community of responsibility") which was but another word for a separate, intra-German détente that must flourish independently from the ups and downs of the superpower relationship.

For West Germany, it was the very impossibility of reunification that animated the tacit partnership. The prize was progressive reassociation in a relationship where the inter-German border might be no more forbidding than the Austrian one. That purpose required the relentless reassurance of the GDR regime, on the premise that reassurance would engender liberalization. To sweeten the risk, Bonn threw in vast economic incentives, delivering technology and billions of cash subsidies. But why would the GDR, a totalitarian regime, suffer the risks of interaction? One reason was the Wall, which had eliminated the threat of depopulation while bringing about an apparent convergence between totalitarian controls and popular consent. Second, the GDR had belatedly learned the lessons absorbed by Bonn a long time ago: East-West antagonism does not enhance the freedom of states on the battlelines of bipolarity.

So at the height of Cold War II, the Honecker government, once the most hardline regime in the East, suddenly discovered the virtues of arms control and détente. Disarmament might diminish not only the American presence in the FRG but also the burden of 400,000 Soviet soldiers stationed in the GDR. If there are fewer nuclear weapons in West Germany, why have so many Soviet missiles in East Germany? By the mid-1980s East Berlin had turned into an avid supporter of a chemical weapons ban and of a nuclear-free zone along the Elbe River because that would not only diminish the GDR's wartime risk but also undercut Soviet arguments for keeping the bulk of its

---

[71] As quoted in "Kohl erklärt Bereitschaft zum Verzicht auf die Pershing-1-A-Raketen," *Süddeutsche Zeitung,* August 27, 1987.

Warsaw Pact forces in East Germany. Moreover, the more secure détente, the larger the diplomatic freedom of Moscow's client states.

The Collapse of the Postwar Order

The supreme historical irony was that the bell for the GDR was beginning to toll just as both German states had accepted each other's permanence and legitimacy. Seemingly ultra-stable, Europe's political tectonics began to shift in 1989, and within a year the architecture of partition had all but collapsed. Soviet expansionism in the 1940s had triggered the competitive response of the United States, spawning NATO and cementing the partition of Germany and Europe. Conversely, the retraction of Soviet power, launched by Mikhail Gorbachev in the late 1980s, overturned the Cold War system in a matter of months.

Presumably, Gorbachev lost his East European empire in a fit of absentmindedness. Presumably, his purpose was not to relinquish, but to reform Moscow's Communist bastion between the rivers Bug and Elbe. But once he withdrew his support from the old guard in Prague, Sofia, East Berlin and Budapest, he reaped a revolution which revealed the enormous, irreducible weakness of the regimes installed by Stalin in the late 1940s. In the fall of 1989, Communist regimes in Eastern Europe fell in quick succession while hundreds of thousands gathered in the cities of the GDR—at first to demand democracy, and then unity. (The key slogan of the demonstrators in Leipzig changed from "We are the people" to "We are *one* people").

Regimes everywhere in Eastern Europe simply evaporated. On October 18, 1989, Erich Honecker was ousted by his own comrades, who were still hoping to hold on to power with marginal changes in personalities and policies. (Honecker was briefly replaced by his hand-picked "crown prince" Egon Krenz, and then by the mayor of Dresden, Hans Modrow.) Curiously enough, reform-plus-continuity was also the implicit assumption of the Kohl Government which, on November 28, enunciated a Ten-Point Plan that was still predicated on the *persistence* of two German states. Accordingly, the Plan merely foresaw a "contractual community" between both states that would eventually gestate into a confederation. Yet, in the meantime, the postwar order in Germany had literally collapsed, and appropriately enough in the very place—in Berlin— which had served as prime focus and symbol of the Cold War. The Wall was breached on November 9 by jubilant Berliners, and that was the beginning of the end of the GDR.

With the constraints of the postwar system crumbling into dust, diplomacy was shunted aside and society took over. Tens of thousands were crossing the line into West Germany, threatening to turn the GDR into a hollow shell. Governmental authority simply dissolved, and the GDR economy was grinding to a halt. Ironically, reunification was now *forced* on a Federal Republic that had dispensed with the dream a long time ago. Bonn was pushed into the curious position of a "White Knight" called upon to execute the "friendly takeover" of a state on the verge of bankruptcy.

But before the deal could be closed, external stockholders had to be satisfied. The United States was the first to read the handwriting on the wall. Eager to assure a European future with a democratic Western Germany, the Bush Administration took the lead in smoothing the diplomatic transition. Skillfully running interference for Bonn, the U.S. succeeded in blocking a host of Soviet designs which ranged from Germany's dual membership in NATO and the Warsaw Pact to unification outside of NATO. Why Moscow finally dispensed with a 40 year policy which had fought unity within the Western alliance with all means short of war, must await the judgment of history.[72] Presumably, Mikhail Gorbachev had simply come to the conclusion that the Soviet Union could no longer sustain the duel, that good relations with the West were more profitable than holding on to a moribund empire.

It helped that Bonn was willing to pay a hefty price. First, the FRG consented to reduce the armed strength of united Germany by 40 percent, to an armed forces total of 370,000 (down from 495,000 in the FRG and 140,000 in the GDR). Second, Germany reaffirmed the commitment made by the FRG in 1954 not to acquire nuclear weapons. Third, neither NATO forces nor NATO nuclear weapons would be deployed in Eastern Germany. Fourth, united Germany formally renounced all territorial claims against Poland and Soviet Russia. Fifth, Germany agreed to sweeten the Soviet withdrawal (to be completed by 1994) with 12 billion deutschemarks ($8 billion). Finally, there was the bilateral treaty agreed upon by Gorbachev and Kohl in a meeting in Stavropol (July 16, 1990) that formalized a future of cooperation, regular contacts, and joint crisis management. Article Three echoed Bismarck's vaunted "Reinsurance Treaty" of 1887: "If one of the two states should become the target of aggression, then the other side will give the aggressor no military aid or other support." Formally united on October 3, 1990, Germany—though in and of the West—was now once more tied to the Soviet Union in a special relationship.[73]

Beyond Bipolarity

This chapter has argued that the system is destiny: In the special case of Germany, we must above all look at the stage to explain the behavior of the actor. Yet the retraction of Soviet power, unleashing the East European revolution of 1989 and unblocking the road to reunification, has demolished most props of the postwar era. Complete withdrawal, especially if paralleled by Soviet democratization, will hardly leave the remaining elements unchanged. At the threshold of the 1990s, to be sure, both the American presence in Europe and the Atlantic Alliance were still intact—and the European Community was poised to achieve a truly common market by 1993. But even

---

[72] For a contemporary analysis, see Hannes Adomeit, "Gorbachev and German Reunification: Revision of Thinking, Realignment of Power," *Problems of Communism*, July–August 1990.

[73] For a helpful account of the events in 1989 and 1990, see Karl Kaiser, "Germany's Reunification," *Foreign Affairs: America and the World, 1990/91* (Vol. 70, No. 1).

if Western institutions have outlived their Eastern counterparts (Warsaw Pact and Comecon), it is worth remembering that no coalition has long persisted in the aftermath of victory.

Enemies are each other's best organizers, and if the Cold War is truly dead, then the remaining structures of bipolarity will lose their rationale. Whence two logical conclusions follow: The European state system will become more fluid, and German foreign policy will become more indeterminate. As the country in the middle was liberated from its postwar constraints, the contending demands on its foreign policy increased. America remains the security lender of the last resort, but the Soviet Union, the strongest military power on the Continent, has acquired new claims on Germany. France and Britain are close friends, but they are also rivals for influence and prestige. Within the European Community, Germany must balance the quest for ever closer integration against Eastern Europe's search for inclusion. Forty years of membership in the Western communities have instilled the habits of multi-lateralism and self-containment, but after the costly reconstruction of the former GDR, Germany is bound to re-emerge as the strongest "civilian" power of Europe. Will Germany be content to continue in the role of a "super-Switzerland," or will economic power engender greater ambitions?[74]

In the past, German power poisoned both German and European history. But in the 1990s, three critical ingredients of conflict are missing. Germany is neither authoritarian nor totalitarian, but a solid liberal democracy. Second, the volcanoes of European nationalism seem to be extinct; yesterday's engines of war have fallen silent. Third, the entire game seems to have changed: It is welfare, not warfare, exports rather than expansion, that animate most European states.

The new Germany hardly bears any comparison with its three successors: the Third Reich, the Weimar Republic, and the Wilhelmine Empire. In the Second Reich, founded by "blood and iron" in 1871, democracy was sacrificed to the imperatives of national power, and nationalism, the heady cry of "us against them", was proffered as a substitute for liberty and real equality. In the Weimar Republic (1919–1933) democracy was born in the moment of national humiliation, weakened by the punitive peace of Versailles, and laid low by hyperinflation and the Great Depression. All of this provided a perfect breeding ground for an ultra-nationalist revolt in the guise of Hitler's Nazi party. And in the "Reich of the Thousand Years," democracy was simply torn to shreds by the most "perfect" totalitarian regime the world has ever seen.

Yet when democracy was imported into Germany for the second time (after 1945), the soil and climate conditions were far more benign than ever before. In contrast to the post-World War I period, the tender shoots of democracy were nourished by relentless economic growth and protected by an alliance system that delivered guaranteed security. Together with NATO,

---

[74]For an answer that opts for continuity, see the author's "One-and-a-half Cheers for German Reunification," *Commentary*, June 1990.

the European Community provided West Germany with a legitimate outlet for its resurgent energies. If in the past, Germany had stood alone, now it was part of various international communities which instilled and rewarded the habits of multilateralism. The parties of the extremes—on the left and on the right—vanished one by one, leaving in place a sluggishly centrist party system within which tenure alternated between the center-right and the center-left.

When crisis hit—be it recession and the student revolt in the 1960s or "oil shocks" and terrorism in the 1970s—the structures held and absorbed the blows. Interestingly enough, the addition of the former GDR barely made a dent in long established voting patterns. During the first all-German election (December 2, 1990), voters in Eastern Germany more or less cast their ballots in the same way as their brethren in the West, previously having established virtual clones of the traditional West German parties in the five new *Länder*. Today, at any rate, Germany is not just a democracy in name, but in substance— and in some respects, a more liberal polity than either France or Britain.

Internally then, the new Germany is lightyears removed from its previous incarnations. What about its future foreign policy? To begin with, the habits of community—profitable beyond belief in the postwar past—will not rapidly be unlearned. The message can be put more forcefully: For the first time since the founding of the Bismarckian Reich, the rules of the international game *favor* Germany. To seek status, it need not clamor a "place in the sun." Unity was accomplished not by "blood and iron," but with the consent of *all* the great powers. Influence need not be sought with the rattling of swords; it is accumulated on the basis of economic clout and performance. And though, for instance, many Europeans resent the fact that European currency parities are determined *de facto* by the *Bundesbank* in Frankfurt, that is still a different, far more benign game than was previously acted out with armies on the march. In such a game, accounts are settled in the balance-of-payments ledgers, not on the field of battle. Though rivalry persists, the competition is inherently peaceful and encased by cooperation.

Unleashed from the fetters of the postwar order, will Germany try to change the rules of the game—perhaps go for nuclear weapons and push for the revision of its Eastern frontiers? Cataclysmic breaks with previous behavior can never be ruled out, but in the German case they are hardly likely. Why overturn a game that has benefited the Germans above all? In that case, the country would reap precisely those countervailing coalitions, uniting East and West, that proved Germany's undoing in two world wars. Moreover, the tortuous process of *real* reunification, above all the economic reconstruction of Eastern Germany, presumably will absorb German energies for a long time to come. According to a 1991 estimate of the International Monetary Fund, the rebuilding of the East will exact $1 trillion for the next decade. Indeed, as the Second Gulf War (1990/91) suggested, not German aggressiveness but German abstentionism may be the problem—the country's deeply rooted resistance to the use of force far from its borders.

On the other hand, it is the Long Peace, the longest in the history of Europe, that has eclipsed traditional power politics. And that peace has rested not just on democracy and economic growth, but on an American security guarantee and a military stalemate which may not outlive the peculiar historical circumstances that gave rise to them. German reunification was made possible by the very transformation of the postwar order, i.e., the retraction of Russian power, that will hardly leave the traditional pillars of stability in place. The Warsaw Pact formally liquidated itself on April 1, 1991. NATO, by contrast, emerged from the Cold War alive and well. Yet if history offers any lesson, it is this: alliances do not live long past the point of victory.

Alliances require both a threat and a foe, and once Soviet troops have left Central Europe, the Atlantic Alliance will face but a pale copy of the real thing. Will the United States continue to extend its security guarantee, and will the Europeans be content to live with its burden, i.e., U.S. nuclear weapons and troops on their soil? And if these props go, how will nations adapt to the vanishing parameters of security? There are two opposite answers.

First, the habits of cooperation are now so deeply rooted in Europe that they will survive the passing of bipolarity. Indeed, the forward march of integration will finally breach the last ramparts of sovereignty, harnessing the nations of Europe in a true defense community that could dispense with the Great Atlantic Protector and hold the balance against the Soviet Union on its own. In this scenario, the old order will give way to a more perfect union which removes the traditional sources of conflict by transcending the nation-state.

Yet the opposite is also plausible. Take away bipolarity (which spared the Europeans the necessity of developing autonomous defenses), and defense will be re-nationalized. That does not imply the return to 1914 or 1939. But if defense *were* renationalized, such a trend would not leave the other sectors of integration untouched. Once nations have to worry about assuring their own security, they will seek to strengthen autonomy across the board. In such a setting, community would no longer provide the dominant purpose, and nations like Germany would have to recalculate their foreign policies. No longer ensconced under an American nuclear umbrella, Germany would have to look elsewhere for protection. As was argued above, an independent deterrent will carry too high a political price tag for a long time to come. But in order to re-establish equilibrium, nations do not necessarily have to add to their supply of military security; another option is to reduce their demand for it by propitiating their most likely enemy. Concretely, Germany could revert back to an earlier tradition of maneuver and balance, re-creating a special relationship with Russia that would relieve dependence on, and deference to, the West. In this case, the magnificent record of European integration would be soured by revived security concerns and mutual suspicion.

Which will it be—community or re-nationalization? In the German case, the argument of this chapter has been that the system is destiny. With the passing of the bipolar order, which dictated so many responses of German foreign policy, only one conclusion is for certain: The game of nations in Europe is bound to change, and Germany's range of choices will be enlarged. How much change and how much choice? That depends, once more, on the larger setting of European foreign policy—on the outcome of the "Second Russian Revolution" and the course of American policy in Europe.

FOREIGN POLICY LANDMARKS

May 8, 1945	Capitulation of the Third Reich
May 23, 1949	Proclamation of the Basic Law (Constitution)
September 7, 1949	Founding of the Federal Republic of Germany (FRG); First Chancellor: Konrad Adenauer (CDU), who rules until 1963
May 5, 1955	The Federal Republic regains sovereignty and joins NATO
1957	The FRG decides to acquire dual-purpose nuclear delivery vehicles with warheads under U.S. control
November 27, 1958	The Soviet Union delivers the so-called Berlin Ultimatum
August 13, 1961	The Berlin Wall is built
October 1962	The Cuban Missile Crisis
January 22, 1963	France and the Federal Republic conclude the Treaty on Friendship and Cooperation
November 16, 1963	Ludwig Erhard (CDU) replaces Konrad Adenauer as Chancellor
May 12, 1965	The Federal Republic establishes diplomatic relations with Israel; in response many Arab states sever their diplomatic ties with the FRG
December 1, 1966	Grand Coalition of CDU, CSU, and SPD with Kurt Georg Kiesinger as Chancellor and Willy Brandt (SPD) as Foreign Minister
April 19, 1967	Adenauer dies
October 21, 1969	Coalition of SPD and FDP with Willy Brandt as Chancellor and Walter Scheel (FDP) as Foreign Minister
November 28, 1969	FRG signs the Non-Proliferation Treaty
March 19, 1970	First official encounter between FRG and GDR occurs when Willy Brandt meets with East German Prime Minister Willy Stopf in Erfurt, East Germany
August 12, 1970	FRG concludes treaty on normalization of relations with the Soviet Union followed by similar treaty with Poland and with Czechoslovakia; these treaties are collectively known as "Eastern Treaties"
December 21, 1972	FRG and GDR conclude the "Basic Treaty"
April 16, 1974	Helmut Schmidt (SPD) replaces Willy Brandt as Chancellor
December 1979	Soviet Union invades Afghanistan
December 12, 1979	NATO announces the so-called Brussels Decision, which provides for the deployment of 572 Pershing II and cruise missiles beginning in 1983 if arms control negotiations with the Soviet Union do not remove the Soviet SS-20 missile threat
October 10, 1981	250,000 demonstrators assemble in Bonn to protest against the missile deployment

October 1, 1982	Helmut Kohl (CDU) replaces Helmut Schmidt as Chancellor as result of no-confidence vote in the Bundestag
March 6, 1983	National election confirms Helmut Kohl in power
November 23, 1983	First Pershing II missile components arrive in the Federal Republic; in response the Soviet Union ruptures the Geneva nuclear arms talks
March 12, 1985	The United States and the Soviet Union resume nuclear arms control negotiations in Geneva
May 5, 1985	President Reagan visits German military cemetery in Bitburg. Intended as gesture of reconciliation forty years after the capitulation of the Third Reich, the ceremony was widely condemned in the United States because of the presence of Waffen-SS graves. (The Waffen-SS was the military arm of the Nazi SS which played a key role in the annihilation of European Jewry.)
October 8, 1985	Richard von Weizsäcker becomes the first president of the Federal Republic of Germany to visit Israel
November 19, 1985	First Reagan-Gorbachev summit meets in Geneva
May 16, 1986	During their national congress in Hannover, the Greens resolve to pull the FRG out of NATO
October 12, 1986	Second Reagan-Gorbachev summit held in Reykjavik, Iceland.
January 25, 1987	National elections confirm Helmut Kohl's CDU/CSU-FDP government in power; the Christian Democrats lose 4.5 percentage points while Hans-Dietrich Genscher's FDP picks up an additional 2.1 percent of the vote
June 14, 1987	Hans-Jochen Vogel replaces Willy Brandt as chairman of the SPD
August 26, 1987	Chancellor Kohl declares his readiness to scrap the FRG's seventy-two Pershing Ia missiles (with U.S. nuclear warheads) if the United States and the Soviet Union agree on the worldwide elimination of INF (intermediate-range nuclear forces, that is, Pershing II's, ground-launched cruise missiles, SS-4's, SS-20's, SS-12/22's and SS-23's)
December 8, 1987	The United States and the Soviet Union, during the third Reagan-Gorbachev summit in Washington, sign treaty on the worldwide elimination of INF
January 22, 1988	On the twenty-fifth anniversary of the Franco-German Treaty of Cooperation, the FRG and France announce the formation of a joint brigade and a joint Defense Council
September 1989	Flight of 50,000 GDR citizens to the FRG via Hungary after Hungary opens the "Iron Curtain"
October 9, 1989	100,000 East Germans demonstrate in Leipzig; the army does not intervene, allegedly on Russian order
October 18, 1989	East German General-Secretary Erich Honecker is ousted and replaced by Egon Krenz
November 9, 1989	Opening of the Berlin Wall
November 28, 1989	West German chancellor Helmut Kohl announces his "Ten-Point Program" for a confederation of the two Germanys

May 5, 1990	The foreign ministers of the U.S., the U.S.S.R., Britain, France, the FRG and the GDR launch the "2 + 4 Talks" on German reunification, concluded on September 12
July 1, 1990	Economic and Monetary Union concluded between FRG and GDR
October 1, 1990	Four-Power rights in Germany are suspended
October 3, 1990	The GDR disappears, Germany is reunified
December 2, 1990	First all-German elections; Helmut Kohl is reconfirmed
March 4, 1991	Soviet parliament ratifies the 2 + 4 Agreement about the restoration of complete sovereignty to united Germany.
April 1, 1991	Dissolution of the Warsaw Pact

SELECTED BIBLIOGRAPHY

Primary Sources and Documents

Auswärtiges Amt, ed. *Die Auswärtige Politik der Bundesrepublik Deutschland.* Cologne: Verlag Wissenschaft und Politik, 1972.

Bundesministerium für innerdeutsche beziehungen, ed. *Texte zur Deutschlandpolitik* (a series of volumes containing documents and speeches on intra-German relations published in loose succession since 1969).

Bundesminister der verteidigung, *Weissbuch* (a posture statement by the Defense Minister, published in irregular intervals in English and German. The latest was issued in 1983.)

Deutscher Bundestag. *Verhandlungen des Deutschen Bundestages* (record of parliamentary proceedings).

Embree, George D., ed. *The Soviet Union and the German Question, 1958–1961.* The Hague: Nijhoff, 1963.

Oppen, Beate Ruhm Von, ed. *Documents on Germany Under Occupation, 1945–1955.* London: Oxford University Press, 1955.

Presse- und Informationsamt der Bundesregierung. *Bulletin* (a regular compilation of important speeches, documents, press conferences, etc., in a German and an English edition).

Books and Articles

Adenauer, Konrad. *Memoirs, 1945–1953.* Chicago: Regnery, 1966.

Ardagh, John. *Germany and the Germans: An Anatomy of Society Today.* New York: Harper & Row, 1987.

Bark, Dennis L. and David R. Gress, *A History of Germany,* 2 vols. (Oxford: Basil Blackwell, 1989).

Barnett, Richard J. *The Alliance.* New York: Simon and Schuster, 1983.

Birnbaum, Karl E. *East and West Germany: A Modus Vivendi.* Lexington, Mass.: Heath Lexington Books, 1973.

Blechman, Barry, and Cathleen Fischer. *The Silent Partner: West Germany and Arms Control.* Cambridge: Ballinger, 1988.

Brandt, Willy. *A Peace Policy for Europe.* New York: Holt, Rinehart & Winston, 1969.

Bulmer, Simon and William Paterson. *The Federal Republic of Germany and the European Community.* London: Allen and Unwin, 1987.

Childs, David. *From Schumacher to Brandt: The Story of German Socialism, 1945–1965.* Oxford: Pergamon Press, 1966.

Craig, Gordon. *From Bismarck to Adenauer: Aspects of German Statecraft.* New York: Harper & Row, 1965.

Deutsch, Karl W., and Lewis J. Edinger. *Germany Rejoins the Powers: A study of Mass Opinion, Interest Groups and Elites in Contemporary German Foreign Policy.* Stanford: Stanford University Press, 1959.

Edinger, Lewis J. *Kurt Schumacher: A Study in Personality and Political Behavior.* Stanford: Stanford University Press, 1965.
Feld, Werner. *West Germany and the European Community.* New York: Praeger, 1981.
Frey, Eric G. *Division and Detente: The Germanies And Their Alliances.* New York: Praeger, 1987.
Gatzke, Hans W. *Germany and the United States: A Special Relationship?* Cambridge: Harvard University Press, 1980.
Genscher, Hans-Dietrich. *Deutsche Aussenpolitik.* Stuttgart: Bonn Aktuell, 1981.
Gimbel, John. *The American Occupation of Germany: 1945-1949.* Stanford: Stanford University Press, 1968.
Goldman, Guido. *The German Political System.* New York: Random House, 1974.
Griffith, William E. *The Ostpolitik of the Federal Republic of Germany.* Cambridge: MIT Press, 1978.
Grosser, Alfred. *The Western Alliance.* New York: Seabury Press, 1980.
Hanrieder, Wolfram. *The Stable Crisis: Two Decades of German Foreign Policy.* New York: Harper and Row, 1970.
———, ed. *Helmut Schmidt: Perspectives on Politics.* Boulder: Westview Press, 1982 (a useful collection of speeches and interviews).
———, *Germany, America, Europe: Forty Years of German Foreign Policy.* New Haven: Yale University Press, 1989.
Joffe, Josef. "Germany and the Atlantic Alliance: The Politics of Dependence, 1961-1968," in William Cromwell et al., *Political Problems of Atlantic Partnership.* Bruges: College of Europe, 1969.
———. "European-American Relations: The Enduring Crisis," *Foreign Affairs,* Spring 1981.
———. "German Defense Policy: Novel Solutions and Enduring Dilemmas," in Gregory Flynn et al., *The International Fabric of Western Security.* Montclair: Allenheld, Osmun, 1981.
———. "Squaring Many Circles: German Defense Policy Between Deterrence, Detente and Alliance" in Gordon Craig et al., eds. *The Federal Republic of Germany and the United States: Political, Social and Economic Relations.* Boulder: Westview Press, 1984.
———. *The Limited Partnership: Europe, the United States and the Burdens of Alliance.* Cambridge, Mass.: Ballinger, 1987.
———. "The Tacit Alliance: West German Policy Toward Eastern Europe," in Lincoln Gordon, ed., *Eroding Empire: Western Relations With Eastern Europe.* Washington, D.C.: Brookings Institution, 1987.
———. The Revisionists: Germany and Russia in a Post-Bipolar World," in Michael T. Clark and Simon Serfaty, eds., *New Thinking and Old Realities.* Washington: Seven Locks Press, 1991.
———. "The End of the Postwar Order and the Future of European Security," in Richard Perle, ed., *Defense and Security: The United States Faces a United Europe.* Washington: American Enterprise Institute Press, 1991.
Kaiser, Karl. *German Foreign Policy in Transition.* London: Oxford University Press, 1968.
———. "Germany's Reunification," *Foreign Affairs: America and the World, 1990-1991.*
Kissinger, Henry A. *The Troubled Partnership.* New York: McGraw-Hill, 1965.
Blechman, Barry, and Cathleen Fischer. *The Silent Partner: West Germany and Arms Control.* Cambridge: Ballinger, 1988.
Marsh, David. *The Germans: The Pivotal Nation.* New York: St. Martin's Press, 1990.
McAdams, James. *East Germany and Detente.* Cambridge: Cambridge University Press, 1985.
Merkl, Peter H. *The Origins of the West German Republic.* New York: Oxford.
———. *German Foreign Policies, West and East.* Santa Barbara, Calif.: Clio Press, 1974.
Morgan, Roger. *The United States and West Germany, 1945-1973: A Study in Alliance Politics.* London: Oxford University Press, 1974.
Nerlich, Uwe and James A. Thomson. *The Soviet Problem in American-German Relations.* New York: Crane Russak, 1985.
Noelle-Neumann, Elizabeth, ed. *The Germans: Public Opinion Polls, 1967-1980.* Westport, Conn.: Greenwood Press, 1981.
Richardson, James L. *Germany and the Atlantic Alliance: The Interaction of Strategy and Politics.* Cambridge: Harvard University Press, 1966.

Rosolowsky, Diane. *West Germany's Foreign Policy: The Impact of the Social Democrats and the Greens.* New York: Greenwood Press, 1987.

Schick, Jack M. *The Berlin Crisis, 1958–1962.* Philadelphia: University of Pennsylvania Press, 1972.

Schmidt, Helmut. *Men and Powers.* New York: Random House, 1989. This is the quasi-memoirs of the former chancellor.

Simonian, Haig. *The Privileged Partnership: Franco-German Relations in the European Community, 1969–1984.* Oxford: Clarendon, 1985.

Stern, Fritz. *Dreams and Delusions: The Drama of German History.* New York: Alfred A. Knopf, 1987.

—5—

THE FOREIGN POLICY OF THE EUROPEAN COMMUNITY

DREAM OR REALITY?

*Christopher Hill**

Over the last four decades the European Community[1] has made itself into a new kind of actor in international relations. From apparently parochial beginnings, as a device to prevent the iron and steel industries of the Ruhr from ever again providing the motor force for German militarism, the Community has become the world's largest trading unit, the most significant provider of development aid, and the source of wide-ranging diplomatic initiatives that attract a host of other states keen to be associated with European positions. Its common policies on agriculture and the regulation of civilian nuclear power act as benchmarks for all interested third parties. The European Monetary System acts as an important stabilising zone in the international financial system, and the Community is generally recognised as the crucial element in the process now underway to fashion a new European order to replace that symbolised by Yalta and the Berlin Wall. In short, the Community seems to

---

* In writing this chapter I have found the essays written in the sixth and seventh editions by Françoise de la Serre, immensely useful.

[1] The term "European Community" is now in common use, although some feel that it still bestows more unity and dignity on the institution than is yet deserved. The correct title, strictly speaking, is "the European Communities," as there are three: the European Coal and Steel Community (ECSC, 1951) the European Atomic Energy Community (EURATOM, 1957), and the European Economic Community (EEC, 1957). The institutions of the three were merged in 1967, but the umbrella term is still rare in official documents.

have become as powerful as any other actor in the world system, with the exception of the two superpowers, and now that the Soviet Union is in crisis we may have to revise even that judgment.

Matters are not, however, quite as straightforward as this description leads us to suppose. The European Community is not a single state, but a collection of twelve separate states that have joined together for certain purposes, to which ends they have made limited sacrifices of sovereignty. Its processes of integration have certainly deepened steadily over the years, just as membership has doubled[2], but the Community still does not have many of the attributes of statehood; and in the area of foreign policy it lacks both the crucial dimensions of supranationality and a defence policy. It may be that historians who look back on these years will see in them the origins of the European superpower that emerged in the twenty-first century. Alternatively these years may be seen as a time in which an improved version of the nineteenth-century Concert of Europe was born, bringing states together in close patterns of cooperation, but leaving their national identities and ultimate political rights intact. Either scenario may still triumph; neither is inevitable. But in the 1990s the pressing need is to understand the existing structure of the Community's external relations, and to analyse how it came into being. For apart from a very small group of diplomatic practitioners and specialist commentators, few Europeans (let alone those on the outside looking in) have a clear conception of the multiple layers and contradictions that go to make up what is often called "European foreign policy." The consequent misunderstandings and false expectations can sometimes have serious political and economic consequences.

In order to understand the reality of the European Community's role in the world, it is important to bear in mind the political context in which the question of a European foreign policy is discussed, as well as the differing levels of European actions. The political context is central because the issue of what European foreign policy is and might become provokes intense partisan debate between two powerful groups. The first wishes to see the Community progress rapidly into a fully cohesive body capable of expressing its needs at the international level through the full range of instruments available to states, and with the same degree of internal cohesion as, say, a successful federal state is able to achieve. This group has historically had its doubts about whether a common foreign policy should be attempted until internal integration has first been achieved, and indeed remembers all too well that it was de Gaulle, the champion of national sovereignty, who first proposed (in the Fouchet plans of 1961–62) a system for foreign policy cooperation, precisely as a way of deflecting enthusiasm for European cooperation into channels which the states would be able to control. However, since the Tindemans Report of 1975,

---

[2] The original member-states of the Communities were Belgium, France, the Federal Republic of Germany, Italy, Luxembourg, and the Netherlands. They were joined in 1973 by Britain, Denmark, and Ireland (Norway was forced to give up the offer of entry after a referendum of its people), in 1981 by Greece, and in 1986 by Portugal and Spain.

the enthusiasts for integration have come to see that foreign policy cooperation can be harnessed to the original economic common policies to boost the
Community's image and sense of dynamism. The Single European Act put the
seal of legitimacy on this approach by bringing the classical foreign policy side
of Europe's activities (known as European Political Cooperation, or EPC,
extant as a voluntary system since 1970) under the legal umbrella of the treaties
that underpin the Communities.

The opponents of this view argue that the member-states of the Community need not, and in any case probably cannot, go much further than the
coordination of distinctive national foreign policies that is the hallmark of the
present system. They argue from a variety of different political standpoints,
namely that the Community should not ape superpower behaviour, that
domestic pressures exert too much of a centrifugal pull, that defence is the
preserve of NATO, and that a single foreign policy would be in itself a major
step towards the truly federal system that many still shy away from.

Thus the question of a common European foreign policy is very much a
live political issue inside the Community—and indeed between the Community
and outsiders, particularly the United States. Much of the public commentary
on the subject, and not a little of the academic analysis, is consequently a
contribution to political debate, more than reflection considered in tranquillity.
Nonetheless, with the evidence of thirty years of Community activities in the
international system, it is now possible at least to trace the action-channels (in
Graham Allison's phrase) through which the complexities of European external
relations are managed and to assess the extent to which an embryonic foreign
policy is already in place. To this end we will begin by discussing the historical
evolution of the Community's role in the world, move on to a description of
the relevant institutions and policy processes, and then concentrate on an
analysis of the effectiveness of the Community's various instruments in relations
with other members of the international system. Throughout, the discussion
revolves around the three levels at which European foreign policies are expressed: the continued existence of national foreign policies, whether made in
Paris and London, Dublin or The Hague; the sophisticated system for harmonising these national policies (that is, European Political Cooperation), which often
produces a single Community voice on such questions as the Arab-Israeli
dispute; and the external economic relations of the Communities, handled by
the Commission and deriving from commitments set down in the treaties. This
last involves commercial negotiations, development policy and other matters
not traditionally supposed to be part of "foreign policy."

THE HISTORICAL BACKGROUND

The European Communities were the product of great international issues,
just as they have come increasingly to shape them. The idea of an organisation
in which elements of national sovereignty would be relinquished was born out
of the tragedies of two world wars in fifty years having flared up from the

embers of the Franco-German conflict. The Coal and Steel Community, its founders thought, would bind the region of Western Europe together and "lay the first concrete foundations of the European federation which is indispensable to the maintenance of peace."[3] Equally, when the Treaty of Rome opened up much wider areas of cooperation it was inevitable that the Six (as they then were) would soon have a significant collective impact on the rest of the international system.

The very fact of the progress of European integration and its likely boost to the prosperity and influence of its members soon unnerved Britain, for instance. In 1959 the British government led the way in setting up the European Free Trade Area (EFTA) as an alternative to the EEC, but the organisation lacked not only a customs union or any source of political dynamism, but also the weight that would have come from having another major state as a member. This soon led London to apply to the EEC itself in 1961. Another twelve years were to elapse before this change in attitude bore fruit, by which time other countries had also come into the EEC's orbit. Denmark, Ireland, and Norway all decided that they could not afford to be excluded were Britain to join the Communities. This first round of enlargement demonstrated how the inside and outside faces of European cooperation were linked, Janus-like, for it at once made the "Common Market" (as it was then usually known) a more powerful bloc in the eyes of third parties and affected the process of internal integration (not always for the good).

The superpowers were also quick to notice the Communities' emergence and potential for affecting their respective positions. The Soviet Union, in line with Lenin's condemnation in 1915 of the idea of a United States of Europe, issued a strong warning in 1957 against the signing of the Treaty of Rome, which they took to inaugurate another hostile western bloc. Thereafter, apart from the occasional flash of recognition that something genuinely new might be happening in international politics, the Soviets settled down into the view that the EC was the economic arm of NATO—until Mikhail Gorbachev awoke his country from its long sleep in 1985.

The United States' position was more complex. Washington supported European integration from the outset and soon came to encourage the enlargement of the EEC to include Britain and the smaller states in its slipstream. The Americans saw the advantages of a system which at last promised to set limits on old-style European nationalisms, while at the same time unleashing rapid economic growth through its freeing up of internal trade. They also constructed the western version of the Soviet Union's hostile image by increasingly seeing the Communities as the foundations of a European "pillar" in the western alliance. In particular President Kennedy proposed in 1962 "a grand design" in which an Atlantic partnership would join

---

[3] These are the last lines of the draft for the French Declaration of May 9, 1950, which launched the Coal and Steel Community, a draft prepared by Jean Monnet and his colleagues.

together the two great regions of capitalist enterprise for political as well as economic purposes.

On the other hand, it did not take long before the United States became aware that a European bloc represented a set of competing as well as complementary interests to its own. In 1963 a "poultry war" broke out as a result of the new Common Agricultural Policy's protectionist barriers against U.S. chicken imports, which damaged many American farmers and led to retaliation across a range of unrelated products. This was to be the first of many such clashes, as European commercial power began to take on a practical meaning for those excluded from the free trade club. The Dillon Round of multilateral trade negotiations (1960–62) and the Kennedy Round (1964–67) demonstrated that the EEC's common commercial policy was no mere internal device. It meant that the Six could maintain solidarity in international organisations such as the GATT (the General Agreement on Tariffs and Trade), as often as not in order to better strengthen their hand against the United States. The Americans had the new realities of international relations brought further home to them by the EEC's conclusion of special agreements with France's ex-colonies (the Yaoundé Conventions of 1963 and 1969) and with Greece and Turkey (1962 and 1963), for whom eventual accession was envisaged. All this looked suspiciously like the beginnings of a European sphere of influence, economic style.

If the arrival of the EEC largely made its external mark in terms of economic policy, politics was not far behind. There was, of course, no mechanism at this stage for the formulation of common foreign policy positions, even though the European Political Community proposal of 1952 and the Fouchet plans of ten years later had both sketched out how one might work. As yet few members of the world's diplomatic community even thought in terms of what "Europe's" view might be on the major problems confronting them. France under de Gaulle was taking an increasingly critical line on American foreign policy in a way that foreshadowed later arguments between Washington and the Community as a whole, while it was evident that European opinion was increasingly dismayed by the Vietnam War. Despite the French President's lead, however, it was clear that he was not speaking for Europe. Nothing that resembled a collective position on the war or the many developments in superpower relations that so directly affected the region in fact developed during the 1960s. Such things had to await the departure of de Gaulle and the (not wholly coincidental) arrival of the EPC soon afterwards, and it is thus only over the last two decades that anything resembling a "European foreign policy" can be said to have existed. From 1950 to 1970 the process of European integration certainly came to affect more and more states outside the original Six, but it was not accompanied by any overarching political intelligence to give it meaning and strength. Since then, however, considerable progress has been made, and the 1980s, in particular, have witnessed an ever-closer drawing together of the various strands of the Community's role in the world.

INSTITUTIONS AND POLICY MAKING

The location of the governing intelligence, which is what is implied in the term "foreign policy," is less certain than some outside observers assume. Political Cooperation has no central institution, other than (since 1987) a small secretariat, which helps out the rotating presidency. Conversely, the European Commission, which is a permanent institution and a focal point, is constrained by watchful member-governments from forging a general international strategy, and in any case is still restricted to certain limited areas (mostly commercial) of external relations. Yet insofar as a European foreign policy is in the process of development, it can be observed in the collective procedures and lines of policy that EPC has produced. It is impossible to imagine such a phenomenon emerging from the Commission without the prior decision of the states to move further towards political union in such a way as to give the Berlaymont a central role;[4] whereas the Twelve might just as well be capable of deciding to promote further foreign policy cooperation by setting up single embassies in third countries, or even a European Ministry of Foreign Affairs, entirely separate from the Commission and the skeletal network of Directorates in Brussels and Offices abroad that it already has in place. The Commission is currently anxious to seize the opportunity provided by the Intergovernmental Conference on Political Union to press its claims to act for Europe internationally, but President Delors and his colleagues continue to be at the mercy of such changes in the political environment as the Gulf War. In international relations it is dangerous to assume anything other than the perpetual primacy of politics.

POLITICAL COOPERATION

It is with Political Cooperation then, that any analysis of the Community's attempts to forge a coherent stance towards the outside world must begin. Over two decades EPC has grown into the world's most extensive and sophisticated system of diplomatic coordination, but its basic structure has changed surprisingly little since its foundation. In 1970 the Luxembourg (or Davignon, after its author) Report recommended that the Foreign Ministers of member-states should meet at least twice a year, so as to make the time come nearer "when Europe will be able to speak with one voice" and "to show the whole world that Europe has a political mission."[5] A "Political Committee" made up of the Directors of Political Affairs (soon to be known simply as the "Political Directors") of the various foreign ministries was to prepare ministerial meetings and to meet at least four times a year.

---

[4] The Berlaymont is the striking building in Brussels where the Commission is located.

[5] "First Report of the Foreign Ministers to the Heads of State and Government of the Member-States of the European Community of 27 October 1970," in *European Political Cooperation (EPC)*, 5th edition (Bonn; Press and Information Department of the Federal Government, 1988), pp 24–31.

This system was to be built upon and fleshed out in the years that followed, but it was not to be altered fundamentally (see Figure 5-1). By 1973 four ministerial meetings a year were permitted, and since then the actual number has crept steadily up to the point where the foreign ministers (a politically durable breed) act like members of an exclusive and often informal club, sometimes seeing each other weekly and understanding each other rather better than they may do national cabinet colleagues. This is how the "coordination reflex" (described as such in the second major document setting up EPC, the Copenhagen Report of 1973[6]) came into being, whereby the individual states naturally turn to each other for consultations in the collective forum when facing a new foreign policy problem. The political directors, who not only meet often but are in constant touch through secure communication channels, have become even more "collegial."

EPC is organized and given direction by the same device used for the Community as a whole, the six-monthly rotating presidency held by each country in turn according to an alphabetical order derived from the names of the countries in their own languages (see Figure 5-2). There have thus been more than forty presidencies since EPC was set up in 1970, with each country's turn coming round at first every three years, then every five, and by now every six, as the Community has enlarged. Each state likes to set an agenda for its

Figure 5-1 The Workings of European Political Cooperation

[6] *Ibid.* pp 34–48, "Second Report of the Foreign Ministers to the Heads of State and Government of the Member-States of the European Community of 23 July 1973."

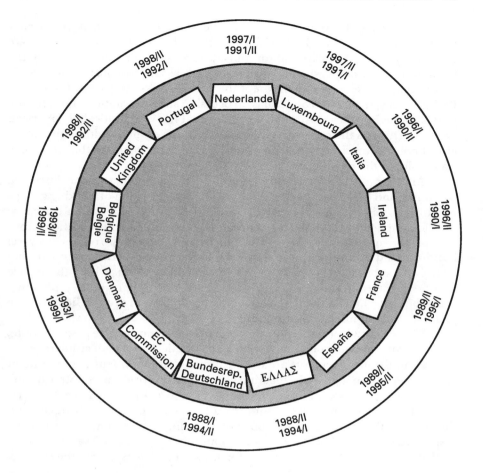

Figure 5-2   The Rotating Presidency of EPC.

This diagram of European Political Co-operation (EPC) shows the seating arrangements at the conference table. The outer ring indicates when each country holds the Presidency. The Federal Republic of Germany holds the Presidency in the first half of 1988 (it assumes the Presidency from Denmark on 1 January 1988 and hands it on to Greece on 30 June 1988). Rotation takes place anti-clockwise.

As from the first half of 1993, each pair of countries will swap positions so that every Member State holds the Presidency alternatingly in the first and second halves of a year. The original sequence will then apply again as from the first half of 1999.

Source: This is an updated version of a diagram contained in *European Polictical Cooperation (EPC)*, 5th Edition, (Bonn Press and Information Office of The Federal Republic of Germany), 1988, p 19.

term of office, and some leave a distinctive mark, like the Italian presidency of 1980, which produced the Venice Declaration on the Middle East. The presidency is the focal point for outside states wishing to deal with the Community, although when a small state such as Luxembourg is in office it may struggle to keep the attention of the superpowers away from London or Paris. Equally, the United States has on occasion shown irritation about having to talk to the Europeans through a country that has been critical of American policies. This was the case with Greece in 1983, for example, although here as elsewhere, the machinery has almost always run well whatever the size of the state holding the presidency.

Another distinctive feature of EPC that has been present since the beginning and has expanded steadily ever since is the system of working groups in which foreign ministry experts monitor key problem areas and prepare position papers for the Political Committee. A consolidated list of the various groups convened over the years would by now probably run into several hundred, and at any one time there are likely to be several dozen working actively on subjects of short- or middle-range concern. Since 1983 there have also been intermittent meetings of the heads of foreign ministry planning staffs, but here no less than at the national level, it has proved difficult for the planners to hold ministers' attention.

There are two other important parts of the administrative jigsaw to note, together with an important innovation at the political level of decision making. The administrative elements are the Group of Correspondents, consisting of able young national officials, meeting regularly to ensure the smooth running of the EPC networks, and the COREU telex network, which since 1973 has enabled Member State foreign ministries to contact each other directly and thus cut out the time-consuming business of going through embassies in their respective capitals. COREU generates about thirty separate messages a day, or 10,000 in a year, and is indispensable for any system that aspires to the capacity for flexible diplomatic response.

The important political innovation for EPC was the setting up of the European Council in 1974, in which heads of government initially met three times a year (now twice, plus exceptional meetings) to oversee the whole of Community business. Increasingly they found themselves discussing more and more foreign policy questions, with the result that the profile of EPC was raised even if its proceedings became somewhat more cumbersome, with a tendency to evade responsibility at lower levels and to push decisions up to the European Council. Its role also tended to emphasise the intergovernmental, even infor-mal, character of EPC, for until the Single European Act of 1987, neither EPC nor the heads of government summits operated under any constraint deriving from the founding treaties of the Community.

For most of its brief history EPC has been an evolutionary process, building on the solid structure laid down at the beginning, and occasionally

---

7 See discussion below.

codifying incremental changes in public declarations that are marker posts more than starting guns. Thus in the London Report of 1981 the foreign ministers agreed to "maintain" the pragmatism "which has made it possible to discuss...certain important foreign policy questions bearing on the political aspects of security," and formalized the "troika" system that was coming into being, whereby officials from the foreign ministries of the preceding and succeeding presidency countries were attached to that of the president-in-office, to ensure continuity and administrative burden sharing.[8] Equally that section of the Single European Act of 1987 that deals with foreign policy is for the most part concerned with laying down in treaty form the proceedings and obligations that were already being observed.

There has been, however, a certain amount of institutional tinkering, partly to meet demonstrable deficiencies in the machinery, and partly as a substitute for the more radical leaps forward that some states would have liked but were unable to deliver. The London Report was not all retrospective. It also allowed for the Commission to be "fully associated with Political Co-operation at all levels"—a provision that transformed the previously fitful working relationship between the two sides of the Community's international policy making.[9] Furthermore it set up a mechanism whereby any three foreign ministers can convene a meeting of the whole group (known as the "Conference of Foreign Ministers," to distinguish it formally from the same people meeting as the Council of Ministers of the Communities, and thus dealing with treaty-based matters) at 48-hours notice. This was to deal with the kind of paralysis that had been evident when the Soviets invaded Afghanistan during the Christmas holiday of 1979. Then, the departing Irish and incoming Italian presidencies had not been willing or able between them to muster an immediate European response. Similarly, the Single European Act not only gave EPC a legal base, it also set up a small Secretariat in Brussels to help the presidency and demanded that the external policies of the Community (i.e., largely economic) and Political Cooperation should actually be consistent. This, together with talk of working together to maintain "the technological and industrial conditions" necessary for the Community's security, was all new and showed unusual boldness both in looking to the future and in going beyond high-flown rhetoric to set concrete targets.[10]

[8] "Report on European Political Cooperation issued by the Foreign Ministers of the Ten on 13 October 1981" (the London Report), in *European Political Cooperation (EPC)*, pp 61–70.

[9] *Ibid.* See also Simon Nuttall, "Where the European Commission comes In," in Alfred Pijpers, Elfriede Regelsberger, and Wolfgang Wessels, eds., *European Political Cooperation in the 1980s: A Common Foreign Policy for Western Europe?* (Dordrecht: Martinus Nijhoff, 1988), pp 104–117.

[10] For the text of the Single European Act, see *European Political Cooperation (EPC)*, pp. 79–87, and the associated Ministerial Decision of 28 February 1986, pp. 87–92 which contains the procedural detail of EPC. The importance of the Act for EPC is analysed in Christopher Hill, "European Political Cooperation: Article 30 of the Single European Act," in Ami Barav, ed., *Commentary on the Single European Act* (London: Oxford University Press, forthcoming), and Renaud Dehousse and Joseph Weiler, "EPC and the Single Act; From Soft Law to Hard Law?" EUI Working Paper EPU No.90/1 (Florence: European University Institute, 1990).

THE COMMISSION

The Commission of the European Communities, that unique institution in Brussels where some 11,000 European civil servants safeguard the purposes enshrined in the founding treaties, has gradually arrived at the point where it now participates in the shaping of collective foreign policy stances (where they exist), rather than wait to be informed about them. In the past some outsiders have misguidedly assumed that the Commission is (a) just a secretariat or (b) concerned only with the internal functioning of the Community. But this was always far from the truth. The Commissioners are entrusted with both implementing common policies and proposing new ways of carrying forward the Community endeavour. Each of these tasks has an external face. To take the two main policies of the Community—the Common Agricultural Policy and the Common Commercial Policy—neither can be pursued in isolation from non-member states, with the result that all too often significant disputes break out over such issues as subsidised export competition and disguised protectionism.

The Commission is directly involved in external relations because it is empowered, under Article 113 of the Treaty of Rome, with commercial negotiations, both bilaterally and in multilateral fora like the GATT. The member-states supervise the Commission through the special "113 Committee" and restrict its freedom of manoeuvre by setting its negotiating "mandate," but they also see the advantages of not weakening the European hand through internal divisions; and the Commission has thus been able to impress third parties with its steadily increasing ability to defend European interests and pursue consistent strategies.

Commerce is not, of course, in itself foreign policy, while to some degree it has suited the Europeans to keep the various strands of their external relations and the decision-making processes attached to them in separate compartments. Nonetheless, over time it has been true that external economic relations have become inevitably politicised and that the members of the Community have come to see the advantages of the linkages that can be made between economic diplomacy and Political Cooperation. To paraphrase Henry Kissinger, economics and politics are usually "linked in reality," and to the extent that the Community's importance in the world has risen, so it has proved necessary to think more holistically about the Community's attitudes to the many other states and institutions with which they interact at different levels.

The link was tacitly there from early on, with the Commission running an expanding development policy that served political ends in terms of both French national interests (French ex-colonies got the lion's share of the Development Fund and French firms the largest portion of the contracts flowing from it[11]) and the building of a satisfactory relationship between Europe and the Third World, at a time when the growing strength of the Communities in the world was bound to attract accusations of neocolonialism.

[11]Commission Report to the Council, COM (84) 358, June 1984.

The Commission's Directorate-General VIII (DG8) dealing with development policy became a significant source of influence and ideas in its own right in the 1970s and early 1980s, particularly during Claude Cheysson's time as Commissioner. It was consequently prone to disputes with Directorate-General I (DG1), which held responsibility for general External Relations.

By 1975 the Commission had gone on to take an active part in the Conference on Security and Cooperation in Europe (the CSCE) and was an important player in the new Euro-Arab Dialogue (nominally a Political Cooperation matter). It had also been the initiator of the parallel "global Mediterranean policy" in which the Community granted preferential trade agreements to the countries of the Maghreb and Mashreq regions, and to Israel—a policy that was at least as much concerned with deflecting anti-Western sentiment away from Europe after the 1973–74 oil crisis as it was with seizing new commercial opportunities.

Throughout the 1980s the Commission has been pitched ever-nearer to the high politics of international relations, a process it has hardly discouraged. In 1983 it was the Commission rather than the member-states in EPC (or even individually) who expressed regret about the need for the U.S. invasion of Grenada, and in 1986 the Commission provoked anger in national foreign ministries by beating the presidency to the draw in condemning a South African military incursion into Botswana, Zambia, and Zimbabwe on the flimsy ground that since the front-line states had signed the Lomé Conventions it was therefore Community business.[12]

The split personality of the Community, between the states and the Commission, is sometimes reintegrated in the conduct of external relations and sometimes not. In the CSCE and Lomé, for example, the mixed policy-making style has worked effectively over decades in terms of defending European interests while allowing individual states flexibility over their national positions. On others there have been public rows over whether the Community was entitled only to one collective seat or dual state/Community representation. This was the case in the Conference on International Economic Cooperation in Paris between 1975–77, when Britain tried to insist on its own seat for the discussions over energy, while in the intermittent discussions after 1974 with the states of the Arab League (the "Euro-Arab Dialogue") there has been a certain lack of clarity as to whether the Commission or the member-states in EPC have been leading for the Community.[13]

Most of the time, however, the Commission has expanded its role in external relations because it has performed useful functions in so doing. There has been no better demonstration of the fact than the decision of the "G7"

---

[12]The attacks took place on May 19, 1986, and it took the Dutch Presidency three days to issue a statement. See *European Political Cooperation Documentation Bulletin,* "Statement on the South African Military Action of 19 May," Vol.2, No.1, (1986).

[13]See David Allen, "Political Cooperation and the Euro-Arab Dialogue," in David Allen, Reinhardt Rummel, and Wolfgang Wessels, eds. *European Political Cooperation,* (London; Butterworths, 1982), pp. 79–82.

group of major industrialised countries, at their Paris summit in July 1989, to ask the Commission to act as coordinator of the aid being provided by 24 Western countries (the "G24") for eastern Europe. This is a political as well as a technical task, and although the Commission will be watched over closely by the major states, it still has important discretionary powers and opportunities for initiatives in the implementation of the policy.

This trend towards greater involvement in foreign policy proper, accelerated by the Single Act's requirement of "consistency" between Community external relations and Political Cooperation, has produced signs of heady excitement in Jacques Delors's Commission about the prospects for a genuinely common European foreign policy. Needless to say, in the scenario envisaged the Commission would play the leading role, an embryonic foreign ministry and a Cabinet for Europe all rolled into one. There is still much politics to take place, however, before anything like this development occurs. The Commission cannot be regarded either as the present or the potential controller of Europe's foreign policy, although it has undoubtedly now moved into a position of close cooperation with the states in EPC, making the strategic management of collective external relations more possible than at any previous time.

THE VIEW FROM OUTSIDE

This is the picture from inside the Community. But it is not surprising if outsiders have sometimes failed to grasp the distinctions between the various levels of European policy and have anticipated by many years the convergence which is now happening. For just as states increasingly accepted in the 1970s the need for diplomatic relations with the EC and opened missions in Brussels, so they naturally expected the Commission to speak for the Community. The peripatetic presidency, often in the hands of the smaller states in any case, was more difficult to conceptualise as the source of European policy than were the multinational staff of the Berlaymont. This has led to certain disappointments, as for example with the Latin American states in the early 1980s, who focused their diplomatic efforts for a closer relation with Europe on the group of their ambassadors in Brussels (GRULA) only to find that the Commission was not in a position to deliver a substantive new agreement. Equally, in the late 1970s China rather naively assumed that the early development of EPC would soon flower into a fully-fledged defence system that would tie up more Soviet military resources in the West and thus relieve the pressure on Beijing.

The consequence of the inevitable realisation on closer acquaintanceship that Brussels is not the heart of a European superpower can be an excessive realist reaction, whereby power has been assumed to lie exclusively with the three or four big member-states of the Community. Yet actual experience of negotiating with the Community, particularly at the official level, has in recent years allowed the pendulum to settle down in between the two extreme positions of exaggerated expectations and disillusioned scepticism towards the

Community's influence in the world. For one thing, the coordination of the member-states diplomacy in third country capitals has become increasingly sophisticated. It is now routine for the presidency to convene meetings of designated diplomats from the other embassies—sometimes indeed of the Ambassadors themselves—to facilitate the taking of common positions. Where there is an important Community office, as in Washington, the Community's representative is likely to play a central role, and even in the 90 or so offices of lesser importance (dealing mostly with development aid questions, or information), the head of mission is nowadays more likely to be treated as a member of a European team than as an upstart functionary by most national embassies abroad. Indeed, when one of the smaller Community member-states holds the presidency there will be many countries in which the presidency does not have its own mission and therefore has to rely on the bigger states and any Community delegation working together to fill the vacuum and provide a cohesive European presence.[14]

In international organisations the EC has perhaps its highest collective profile. In the United Nations General Assembly states have become accustomed to European caucusing and expect that even if the Twelve do not vote identically, they will at least (by abstaining rather than voting against each other) avoid too many public displays of disunity.[15] The Security Council, of course, does not have a single European voice, as Britain and France show no sign of wanting to relinquish their separate seats in favour of a single European vote, and this does, at times of crisis highlight the limitations of EPC. On the other hand having two of the five permanent members within its ranks does give the Community disproportionate access to the top levels of international diplomacy, as is the case in the G7 summits made up of the United States, Japan, and Canada, together with no less than four EC states plus the President of the Commission to represent the smaller members of the Community. These summits have discussed macroeconomic policy and (since 1980) major issues of international politics as well.[16]

Thus despite the complexity of decision making and a certain confusion amongst outsiders, the Community has gradually come to seem a major actor in international affairs. Indeed it has a higher reputation and profile than its actual performance always deserves. Essentially the Community is a hybrid in international relations, neither state nor mere talking shop. It has a range of

[14]For some indication of the varying pattern of national diplomatic representations, not so different from today's, see Christopher Hill and William Wallace, "Diplomatic Trends in the European Community," *International Affairs*, Vol.55, No.1, (January 1979).

[15]By the late 1980s the Community states were voting unanimously on between 40–50 percent of the resolutions and decisions in the General Assembly (excluding resolutions adopted by consensus). This was a rise from the nadir of 30 percent soon after Greece's accession to the Community, but still well below the 60 percent levels of the mid-1970s. See Pijpers, Regelsberger, and Wessels (1988), p. 48; also *European Political Cooperation Documentation Bulletin*, sections on "U.N. Voting," from Vol.2 (1986) on.

[16]The four European states are Britain, France, Germany, and Italy. For a good overview of the G7, see Robert D. Putnam and Nicholas Bayne, *Hanging Together: the Seven-Power Summits* (London; Heinemann for the Royal Institute of International Affairs, 1984).

instruments open to it much wider than that of many states, and yet it lacks one of the defining characteristics of statehood, the ability to defend itself. At the same time the EC's capabilities are steadily growing, and their impact is being felt more keenly by other states. It is worth examining the means by which Europe exercises its power in the world more closely.

THE INSTRUMENTS OF EUROPEAN FOREIGN POLICY

Diplomacy

The Community is above all else a diplomatic actor, so much so that the label "civilian power," coined in the 1970s to capture the essence of a European foreign policy that did not aspire to the use of force, still seems as good a description as any. The Twelve represent a diplomatic bloc whose cohesion is sufficient to enable them to bring considerable influence to bear on various different kinds of international problems, inside and outside their natural geo-political spheres of Europe and the Mediterranean. This influence takes four forms.

Solidarity. Firstly, the Twelve are concerned to exploit the economy of scale available to them. That is, together they represent a more impressive coalition than would be possible if they remained entirely separate and came together only for occasional matters of common interest. Their *solidarity,* and even more their potential unity, leads outsiders to be wary, and their organisational infrastructure gives them a head start when it comes to mobilising support for positions in the U.N., CSCE, or elsewhere. The various historical experiences of the member-states gives them, *qua* group, unrivalled contacts in and understanding of almost every trouble spot on the earth's surface.

Every passing year consolidates the habit of coordination further, so that it becomes more difficult for third parties to break European unity or to lure member-states into other alignments. The individual states of the EC still at times fall out on foreign policy issues, but the differences are increasingly over matters of emphasis or timing. It is becoming rare for a member-state to identify more with non-European than with European positions, or to break radically with a view held by the majority of its partners. Foreign policy in this sense has become fundamentally less contentious than such internal EC issues as the rate of progress towards monetary union.

Initiatives. If solidarity is in itself an important achievement of EC foreign policy cooperation, it also makes possible the second form of diplomatic influence, namely the taking of *initiatives* designed to break logjams at crucial points of the international system. Of these, the best-known has been the European initiative on the Middle East. This began in 1977, was put on ice while the United States midwifed the rapprochement between Egypt and Israel, and resumed in 1979. In June of the next year the Nine (as they then were) produced in the Venice Declaration an "even-handed" policy for the

Middle East that sought to balance Israel's right to exist in conditions of security with the need to acknowledge the suffering of the Palestinian people and their "legitimate rights," particularly that to "self-determination." It promoted the idea of negotiations and the association with them of the Palestinian Liberation Organisation (P.L.O.)[17]

The Europeans followed up this Declaration, for which they had carefully prepared the ground, with an intensive round of diplomatic contacts, not least in the Middle East itself, conducted primarily by the next two presidencies (Luxembourg and the Netherlands) and by the British Foreign Secretary Lord Carrington, who had made EPC a priority ever since taking office in May 1979. For much of 1980–81 the European Initiative held centre ground in the international politics of the Middle East, until it finally had to give way before the intransigence of the newly reelected Likud government in Israel (culminating in the Israeli invasion of Lebanon in June 1982) and the consequences flowing from the assassination of Anwar Sadat in Egypt in October 1981.

At much the same time the Europeans were engaged in a second major diplomatic initiative, this time designed to resolve the problem of Afghanistan, which had been under Soviet military occupation since late December 1979, and which was rapidly becoming a focal point for the revival of the Cold War. By February 1980 the Nine were clear that they had an important interest in promoting conditions in which the U.S.S.R. would withdraw from Afghanistan, and the United States feel reassured about Soviet strategic intentions towards what President Carter's National Security Adviser Zbigniew Brzezinski had called the "arc of crisis," stretching from the Horn of Africa to the Persian Gulf.

Thus on February 19, 1980 the foreign ministers of the Nine proposed the neutralisation of Afghanistan as a means of ensuring a Soviet pullback. This concept proving too ambitious, however, on which to make immediate progress, the Europeans renewed their efforts in June 1981. This time they proposed a two-stage international conference in which the permanent members of the Security Council and relevant regional powers would first work out the arrangements whereby external interventions would become redundant, to be followed by an implementation stage involving "representatives of the Afghan people." This was a concrete and assertive proposal that the new British presidency followed up with vigour, offering Moscow the carrot of a face-saving way out from Afghanistan and waving the stick of damage to European detente if no response were forthcoming. The Soviets, however, were unmoved, and by 1984 after various perfunctory attempts to revive the initiative, it was clear that it would finally have to be abandoned.

The fact that neither of these two major initiatives produced solutions to the problems they addressed seems on the face of things to suggest that the Community is in fact a paper tiger when it comes to the sharpest international

---

[17]The Venice Declaration, together with other relevant documents and a long analysis of European policy towards the Middle East, is to be found most conveniently in Panayotis Ifestos, *European Political Cooperation: Towards a Framework of Supranational Diplomacy?* (Aldershot: Avebury, 1987).

conflicts. But this would be to employ unreasonable standards of judgment. "Solutions" are rarely to be found in international relations, particularly in the perpetual maelstrom that is the Middle East. The two superpowers have done little better. What can be said on the negative side is that this was a period in which EPC's reach exceeded its grasp—when the optimism of Lord Carrington, Gaston Thorn, and Hans-Dietrich Genscher perhaps persuaded them to place too much faith in pure negotiation, backed up by shuttle diplomacy. Certainly since 1981 when the Europeans have taken diplomatic initiatives they generally have done so with far less fanfare and with rather more modest ambitions, as in Central America or the support in the late 1980s for a conference in the Middle East. When circumstances have forced a European initiative to the forefront, as with the publicity in July 1986 over Sir Geoffrey Howe's visit to southern Africa, the gap between aspiration and performance has again been all too evident.[18]

More positively, the fact that in 1980–81 nine still rather disparate states were able to come up with major creative initiatives on some of the most challenging issues of the day, and to sustain them over years rather than months, suggests that Community foreign policy had already, ten years ago, gone beyond the stage of "procedure as a substitute for policy," in Allen's and Wallace's telling phrase.[19] Moreover in both of the initiatives we have touched upon it can be argued that the Community was, if anything, somewhat ahead of its time. It was a correct judgment that the Soviets would need to pull out of Afghanistan and that they would need help from the West in order to stand the humiliation, although it was to take another seven years of suffering and a change in regime in Moscow to bring it about. Afghanistan is still internally turbulent, but externally it is now neutralised in all but name, as the Europeans had proposed.

The Arab-Israeli dispute, of course, has proved far less mutable, but even here a dogged consistency in the European approach has brought some results, despite a good deal of abuse and scepticism from—at various times—almost every side. The United States in the late 1980s at last came around to the realisation that the Palestinian question was central to any eventual settlement in the region, and even (before the Gulf crisis of 1990) began to distance themselves from Israel. The Soviet Union, for its part, accepted the need for a proper relationship with Israel, and the gap between the views of the major outside powers on the way forward both narrowed in itself and converged around the evenhandedness that the EC had been advocating for more than a decade. This is not to claim credit for the Europeans; after all nothing

---

[18]Sir Geoffrey was attempting, at the request of the European Council, to build upon work done by the Commonwealth's "Eminent Persons Group" and to make possible the beginnings of political dialogue in the region between the Botha government, the front line states, and genuine representatives of black South Africans. See *European Political Cooperation Documentation Bulletin,* (1986), Vol.2, No.2, p. 244.

[19]William Wallace and David Allen, "Political Cooperation: Procedure as Substitute for Policy," in Helen Wallace, William Wallace, and Carole Webb, *Policy-making in the European Communities* (New York; Wiley, 1977).

substantive has yet been achieved towards an Arab-Israel settlement. But it is to suggest that the European initiative has not necessarily suffered through being essentially diplomatic in nature (the superpowers' military capacities have not proved notably effective in bringing about movement in the dispute) and that the member-states have demonstrated their ability to converge around a single policy so long as it is a genuine reflection of their collective interests. Spain and Greece, for example, known for their sympathies for the Arab cause, have both assimilated the common policy since joining the Community, despite the necessity thereby of opening diplomatic relations with Israel.

Moral Suasion. The third kind of diplomatic influence exerted by the Community and its member-states is what might be termed *moral suasion*. That is, the Europeans have sought to carve out a distinctive set of positions for themselves that represents as much a general view on how to conduct international politics as pressures for change in particular cases. This has taken place in parallel to the growing perception that European interests are diverging from those of the United States, as the Community sought in the 1970s to moderate the excesses of the Cold War and to make a virtue of their own lack of military power.

This diplomacy by example has had some effect in encouraging other blocs—such as the Association of South East Asian Nations (ASEAN) or the Caribbean Community (CARICOM)—to develop their own forms of foreign policy cooperation and in some circumstances institutional relations with the EC. The EC is now analogous to a combination of collective security and collective defence, in that it seeks on the one hand to pacify and stabilise foreign relations within the group, and on the other to maintain an effective defence of European interests in the world outside. But in this ambitious task, given the lack of the full range of instruments available to states, it has to fall back on the projection of values that are both consonant with European traditions and likely to appeal to other actors in the international system.

Foremost among these values is the notion of an heterogeneous international community in which sovereignty and nonintervention are more important norms than hegemony and sphere of influence. Despite having to tread very carefully in the Western Hemisphere and (before 1989) in Eastern Europe so as to avoid direct clashes with the superpowers, the Europeans have gradually asserted the claim that peace and security are most likely to be ensured by accepting the principle of self-determination and avoiding the temptation to view "regional" conflicts through the lens of great power competition.

The philosophy of international relations—or "communauté de vues"—that EPC has gradually worked out also involves a commitment to mediation in international disputes, a belief in dealing with the long-term causes of conflict rather than the mere symptoms, and the acceptance of global economic interdependence as the basic framework of modern international relations. This is a collection of assumptions, of course, rather than a systematic theory. It overlaps with the values institutionalised in other liberal organisations, notably the United Nations, and it is also a rather high-minded, self-regarding form of moralising, which has led the Community to condemn human rights violations wherever they come to light and to issue calls for change wherever conflict breaks out within or between states. Since the early 1980s such a stream of statements and condemnations has flowed forth from the presidencies, encouraged by Members of the European Parliament (MEPs) about events from the Philippines to Chile, Uganda to Peru, that a new journal has had to be launched to record them and a Secretariat set up in Brussels (by the Single European Act) to act as institutional memory for the system.[20]

Of course this moral suasion provokes irritation more than acceptance, and much of it remains so much hot air. But in the longer run, partly because the Community has had such success in creating its own internal zone of peace and partly because of a general disillusion with the costs of military force, it may be that the EC will begin to be influential by example. Certainly there is no shortage of external requests for the Community to provide financial assistance, political support, and special institutional relationships. Although the Twelve are still rather limited as a traditional power-centre in international relations, they are seen by many states as providing a model and an element of structure in an otherwise dangerous and chaotic world.

Bloc Diplomacy. This is why the Community has been approached over the last decade not only by other regional organisations anxious for bloc-to-bloc relations (see Table 5-1 for the scope of these relations), but also by individual states wishing to slipstream the initiatives taken by the Twelve or simply shelter under the cover provided by EPC's diplomatic community. Japan was the first of the latter, sending its Foreign Minister to wait in the corridors outside European Foreign Ministers' meetings in 1973–74 so as not to be forced into the choice of isolation or pro-Americanism during the oil crisis of that period. Since then Australia, China, India, and Norway have at different times established permanent mechanisms of dialogue, and issue-based groups such as the Contadora countries (Mexico, Venezuela, Colombia, and Panama) have sought to enlist European support for their cause—in the Contadora case, that of a settlement of the conflict in Central America. This is to say nothing of the superpowers, whose special cases we shall look at shortly.

---

[20]The journal is the *European Political Cooperation Documentation Bulletin,* dating from 1985 and produced by the European University Institute in Fiesole, and the Secretariat consists of a permanent Head, together with representatives from the Presidency, the two preceding Presidencies, and the two succeeding ones. See Pedro Sanchez da Costa Pereira, "The Use of a Secretariat" in Pijpers, Regelsberger, and Wessels, *op cit* (1988).

Table 5-1 European Community dialogues with other groups of states

Dialogue Partner	Economic Cooperation	Date Begins	Political Cooperation	Date Begins
ACP states (69)	yes	1975	yes	1988
Andean Pact	yes	1983	yes	1980
Arab League	yes	1975	yes	1974
ASEAN	yes	1980	yes	1978/80*
Contadora and	no	N/A	yes	1984
Central America	yes	1985	yes	1984
CMEA	yes	1988	no	N/A
Council of Europe	yes	1959 (1987)*	yes	1983
EFTA	yes	1984	no	N/A
Front Line states	no	N/A	yes	1986
G8	no	N/A	yes	1987
GCC	yes	1988	yes	1986
Mediterranean states	yes	1975	yes (Maghreb only)	1990
SELA	yes	1971/5*	no	N/A

*Note: Where more than one date is given, this denotes a false start in the dialogue.

Key to Table 5-1

ACP	African, Caribbean, Pacific states associated under Lomé conventions
Andean Pact	Bolivia, Colombia, Ecuador, Peru, Venezuela
Arab League	21 countries plus P.L.O. (Euro-Arab Dialogue)
ASEAN	Association of South East Asian Nations (Brunei, Indonesia, Malaysia, Singapore, Philippines, Thailand)
Central American states	Costa Rica, Guatemala, El Salvador, Nicaragua, Honduras
CMEA	Council of Mutual Economic Assistance (COMECON): U.S.S.R., Czechoslovakia, Cuba, Vietnam, Mongolia, Bulgaria, Hungary, Poland, Rumania
Contadora group	Mexico, Venezuela, Panama, Colombia
Council of Europe	(i.e., the non-EC members): Austria, Sweden, Norway, Turkey, Cyprus, Malta, Lichtenstein, Iceland, Switzerland
EFTA	Austria, Finland, Iceland, Norway, Switzerland, Sweden
Front Line states	Angola, Botswana, Mozambique, Tanzania, Zambia, Zimbabwe
G8	Contadora, plus Argentina, Brazil, Peru, Uruguay
GCC	Gulf Cooperation Council, i.e., Bahrain, Kuwait, Qatar, Oman, Saudi Arabia, United Arab Emirates
Mediterranean	Arab Maghreb Union (Algeria, Morocco, Tunisia, Libya, Mauritania), Mashreq (Egypt, Lebanon, Jordan, Syria), plus Malta, Israel, Cyprus, Turkey and Yugoslavia
SELA	Sistema Economico Latinoamericano: 26 states on the continent

Source: Adapted, by kind permission, from Elfriede Regelsberger, *The Dialogue of the EC/Twelve with other Groups of States*, Institut für Europäische Politik, Bonn, 1988, p. 22. See also Geoffrey Edwards and Elfriede Regelsberger (Eds.), *Europe's Global Links: The European Community and Inter-regional Cooperation*, London, Pinter, 1990.

ECONOMIC INDUCEMENTS AND PRESSURES

Because the European Community is the richest single group of states in the world, outsiders often see considerable advantage to themselves in being on good terms with the Community. Because the EC has no military arm, it has to rely on economic strength to back up its diplomacy. These two facts mean that much of the Community's external relations are taken up with economic negotiations: with states whose partnership the Europeans value; with supplicants whose requests they cannot afford to meet; and with delinquents whose behaviour can only be punished by the removal of economic favours. These three categories of relationship need exploring further, although it should be noted that the Europeans cannot afford to look upon economic power simply as a political resource. If they constantly tried to play "linkage politics" across the boundary between economic and politics, it would soon bring forth hostile reactions from negotiating partners and thus prove counterproductive. Moreover, the Europeans themselves have strong interests in treating economic issues on their own merits and in keeping trade free from political interference—if only because in economic relationships the Twelve usually have the whip hand. Yet events often produce convergence regardless, and neither the Community nor its interlocuteurs can always resist the temptation to give them a helping hand. There is almost always a subtle political backdrop to the Community's economic diplomacy.

Positive Assistance

Among the states that the Community goes out of its way to help, the 69 ACP states of the Lomé system are the most prominent. But here the payoff is indistinct and long-term. If this is indeed a neocolonial relationship as some critics have argued, then the benefits to the Europeans consist mostly in giving their firms a head start over rivals in the countries concerned, and in some securing of mineral supplies under the small "Minex" scheme.[21] It is true that there is also still a presumption in many of the ACP countries that the Europeans are a more acceptable partner than other developed states, and Lomé has probably helped at the margin here by consolidating the legacy of imperialism while softening the harsher memories of it. More direct political leverage is not easily available; however, as Britain discovered in the late 1970s, when it urged that aid transfers to the ACPs should be made conditional on a state's human rights record. The strength of the reaction against this attempt to cross the sacred sovereignty barrier prevented progress on this and subsequent proposals of the same type.

[21]Since 1974 the EC has run a scheme to help the ACPs stabilise their export earnings (STABEX) by transferring funds when the price of a commodity particularly crucial to a country's economy fell below a certain point. In 1979 this was extended to a short list of minerals, such as copper and tin (MINEX). Neither scheme has worked as it was intended, largely through insufficient funds. See Chris Stevens, *EEC and the Third World: A Survey* (London: Hodder & Stoughton), in association with the Overseas Development Institute and the Institute of Development Studies, yearly from 1981–87.

We have already seen how European policy in the Middle East has been grounded in a solid sense of self-interest in preventing further wars in the region and, in particular, a repetition of OPEC's oil embargo. That the strength of OPEC has slowly waned over the subsequent seventeen years is hardly the product of European foreign policy, although the Europeans have diversified their energy supplies and made some progress on conservation. The aim of the Euro-Arab Dialogue from the European side was to keep the Arabs talking and to dilute their hostility at least to one part of the western world.

To the extent that this strategy succeeded, it did so only because the EC was also willing to promote its Middle Eastern political initiative in the face of American hostility. On its own, economic diplomacy was not enough, because the EC had little to offer that oil-rich states did not already have access to through the operation of the private market and the recycling of the petrodollar surplus in Bond Street and the Faubourg St. Honoré. Yet when the Gulf Cooperation Council emerged in 1981 and from 1984 showed interest in access to the European market for its petrochemical products, the EC could not agree and tended to emphasise more the political side of the dialogue. The imminence of the 1992 Single Market, however, together with the Gulf War, will almost certainly reinforce this relationship.

The Community has been able to use economic diplomacy in other areas of the world where its "civilian power" has proved attractive. In Southeast Asia for example, the Vietnam War has left states wary of reliance on the United States, and the members of ASEAN have been keen to develop ties with the Community. Thus a relationship was initiated that has now lasted for more than ten years, based on a Cooperation Agreement. This, in fact, does little other than provide a basis for regular meetings at all levels and to foster an atmosphere of business confidence in an area of growing commercial importance. In double harness with the economic relationship, however, is a political dialogue. From the European viewpoint this has been important as a way of encouraging multipolarity and discouraging anti-Western attitudes, to which Indonesia and Malaysia (ASEAN's principal states) have both at times been prone. In its turn ASEAN has exacted a price from the EC, namely opposition to Vietnam, and the regime the latter supported in Cambodia from 1979 to 1989. The balance of power reasoning of both ASEAN and the Europeans is transparent—Vietnam was both an ally of the Soviet Union and perceived as a potential regional hegemon—but the upshot of the policy was simply more suffering for the Cambodian people.

Economic and political actions have also combined in the EC's forging of a policy towards Central America from the early 1980s on. This was a surprising development, given the sensitivity of the United States towards external involvement in what it perceives as its own backyard, but it was a sign of the Europeans' increased self-confidence, as well as the seriousness with which they looked upon a possible East-West clash in the region that they went ahead with it. The very fact of the political dialogue that EPC opened up by sending all ten foreign ministers to Costa Rica in 1984 to meet with their colleagues from the Contadora and Central American countries was an important signal to Washington that the Europeans would oppose a solution imposed by military force. But diplomacy was accompanied by economic assistance, as the EC began to accept that political activism involved responsibilities for building stability in the long term. Forty-one million ECU was hardly a Marshall Plan in reverse, but it did represent 60 percent of the total EC aid towards Latin America; and it signalled new economic and political openings for the Central American countries, who are after all not members of the ACP group.[22] The Europeans were not the decisive factor, but they certainly contributed to the eventual loosening up of the conflict in Central America, so that civil war did not degenerate into full-scale great power involvement, and political change could be envisaged that might not occur entirely at the point of a gun.

The United States

Far and away the most important state amongst those whose friendship the EC values is the United States. The relationship across the Atlantic has always been close. But by the same token it has also sometimes been uncomfortable, and there is clearly a correlation between European unease at American foreign policy and the growth spurts of the Community's own developing foreign policy system. At the economic level the United States is the Community's most important trading partner, with a 60 percent bigger share of European imports than Japan and being five times more important as a market for European goods (see Figure 5-3). It is also the most powerful potential adversary in the GATT and a major rival in third-country markets (although here sometimes outstripped by Japan).

The commercial disagreements that occurred between the two giant markets in the 1960s have continued intermittently over the last twenty-five years over such questions as steel, pasta, and aeroplane manufactures. Some observers consider that they have now reached a serious impasse over agriculture, and the United States fears the impact of 1992 on its own economy. But the record thus far is one of disputes always being resolved, of rhetorical exchanges never leading to fundamental breaches, and of economics and politics being effectively compartmentalised from each other. To be sure, the Europeans have always had at the backs of their minds the fear that the United States would lose interest in their security, and Washington (in particular, Congress) has sometimes found it necessary to remind their allies of their dependence. But ultimately the two sides have had such important common interests in the maintenance of both economic and political order as to make the resolution of disagreement their highest priority.

---

[22] Regelsberger op. cit (1988), p. 31. The 41m ECU refers to the figure for EC aid to the region in 1984. It has since risen to more than 100m ECU.

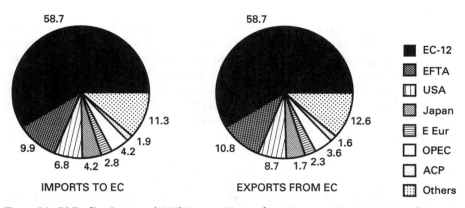

Figure 5-3 EC Trading Partners (1987) Source: Figures from *Eurostat: Basic Statistics of the Community*, 26th ed., Luxembourg, Office of Official Publicaions of the Community, 1989, pp. 33 and 267-69.

In general, the Community has been successful in the sense that it has increasingly flexed its economic muscles at American expense, without having to pay a heavy price. Trade liberalisation has thus far occurred without impinging on the Europeans' sacred cow—the CAP—and the EC has continued to offload surplus food production at subsidised rates in third-country markets. Moreover, the United States was not able to bring the Europeans into line with their own combative response to OPEC in 1973–74, and President Reagan was forced to back down in 1982 when he tried to compel European subsidiaries of American firms not to honour their contracts as part of the Siberian gas pipeline deal with the Soviet Union. In the 1970s and 1980s the United States found it difficult to stop European economic interests being pursued in the Eastern bloc (except for some limitations on strategic exports via CoCom), and a gap opened up between the U.S. view that trade only strengthened an implacable enemy and the European view that trade promoted detente.[23] The Community was not the only player in all this, but undoubtedly the Europeans have stood up for their economic interests with increasing robustness, without necessarily endangering their wider political interests in the relationship with the United States. The other two categories of states with which the EC has important economic dealings—the supplicants and the delinquents—tend to bring forth negative reactions from the Community and may, in consequence, be dealt with more briefly.

The Supplicants and Enlargement

There are, increasingly, more *demandeurs* than the Twelve can hope to satisfy, even if on general political grounds they might wish to build goodwill by doing so. This was evident as far back as 1975, when the first Lomé

[23]See Roy H. Ginsberg, "US-EC Relations," in Juliet Lodge, ed., *The European Community and the Challenge of the Future* (London: Frances Pinter, 1989). CoCom is the Coordinating Committee of western states (i.e., NATO less Iceland plus Japan), set up in 1949 to monitor and control strategic exports to the Communist bloc.

Convention (despite being formulated to cope with the impact of British entry to the Community on the EC's development policy) could find no room for the important but populous Commonwealth states of South Asia. Any serious attempt to help India, Bangladesh, and Sri Lanka would have bankrupted the European Development Fund or necessitated a radical increase in its size. Although these states have benefited subsequently as "nonassociables," the sums available have been mere tokens. The states of South America, likewise, have failed to gain any significant concessions from the Community, despite persistent efforts in the 1980s to raise their profile in Brussels. The size of their problems is too daunting (particularly since the Debt Crisis) and European interests too marginal to make a positive response very likely.

The other main supplicants are more difficult to keep at arm's length, as they tend to be both geographically proximate and interested in joining the Community. Turkey is the most delicate case, as it looks back to an Association agreement signed in 1963, and in 1987 actually made a formal application to join the Twelve. This has effectively been stalled. The Community has important interests in maintaining good relations with Turkey, which is in an important geo-strategic position and which (with its rapidly growing population) is a potentially important market and source of contracts. On the other hand, Turkey is too big, too poor, and possibly too far away to integrate easily into the EC. Thus the Community has had little option but to keep Ankara in play through political consultations (beginning in 1971, but strengthened in 1980), while seeking to deflect embarrassing requests over membership with talk of further economic cooperation and commercial privileges.

Other Mediterranean states present similar dilemmas. The newly formed Arab Maghreb Union is seeking closer ties with the Community, alarmed by the effect on its members' agricultural exports to Europe of Spanish and Portuguese accession and by the prospect of 1992. Malta and Cyprus also show signs of anxiety about being left out in the economic cold. For its part the Community fears damage to its relations with North Africa deriving from a flow of illegal migrants northwards and from the growth of Islamic fundamentalism in the western Mediterranean. But there is little that the Community can do to address these important questions, other than to make such economic concessions as are feasible and to maintain dialogue and technical cooperation. The "global" Mediterranean policy of the 1970s has to some extent raised expectations that cannot be met. In this sort of context, "economic diplomacy" means the EC trying to fend off an endless stream of requests (however understandable or even morally justified) without doing violence either to its own internal cohesion or to a pattern of regional relationships that may be brittle and potentially troublesome.

The hopes of traditional partners like the Mediterranean countries have been further set back by the collapse of the Soviet states-system in Eastern Europe, a main consequence of which has been to focus the Community's attention on the rebuilding of that region and the construction of a new political order. Poland and Hungary have received sizeable credits, and all the ex-Communist states have now signed cooperation agreements with the Community. Even the Soviet Union itself has had to turn to Brussels for money and food aid. The Community faces a major challenge, as its concern to restabilise Eastern Europe under democratic conditions could easily lead to resources being poured into a bottomless pit and to the granting of new privileged relationships that will have opportunity costs for other states equally deserving but less close at hand. When this is also analysed in relation to the negotiations going on with EFTA, and the pressure from Austria, Sweden, and possibly even Norway and Switzerland, to join the EC, we can see that the Community is now a victim of its own success. A major part of its external relations, therefore, both economic and political, is going to consist for the foreseeable future in finding a way to deal with the external pressure for enlargement, and in discriminating between the various claims of the supplicants: what to give to whom, and when?

The Delinquents and Sanctions

The "delinquents," or those states to whom the EC has wished to signal displeasure, dominated the 1980s in the way that the supplicants seem likely to dominate the 1990s. There was frequent resort to economic sanctions, partly because international relations in general went through a particularly conflictual phase and partly because the Europeans either did not wish, or did not have the capability, to resort to military force. Even before the Gulf crisis, there were four main targets of European sanctions policies—the Soviet Union, Iran, Argentina, and South Africa—that all involved major problems of implementation and consensus building. On the other hand, they enabled EPC to counter to a degree the common accusation that it cannot go beyond words into action. In the latter two cases at least the sanctions may have had some real impact on events.

In the first two cases, however, the main impact of the European resort to sanctions was on their own alliance relations with the United States. After the Soviet invasion of Afghanistan, President Carter's ban on grain exports and pressure on athletes not to attend the Moscow Olympics of 1980 brought forth a cool response from the Europeans. They agreed that the U.S.S.R. should only receive "traditional" levels of grain supply—a loose definition inviting abuse—but did not prevent the Commission from quietly increasing its sales of subsidised butter to Moscow. Moreover, most European athletes went to the Olympics. By the time Ronald Reagan cancelled the grain embargo in April 1981, the sanctions had become a shambles, and Euro-American relations had been damaged. The Europeans had shown that they would not be stampeded where they perceived detente and economic interests to be at stake.[24]

---

[24]On this and the other cases of sanctions discussed here see Christopher Hill and James Mayall, "The Sanctions Problem: International and European Perspectives" (Florence: European University Institute, 1983), pp. 13–25, EVI Working paper No. 59.

A similar outcome attended the sanctions that the United States imposed on the Soviet Union after the imposition of martial law in Poland on December 13, 1981. Angry about the lack of advance consultation, the Ten announced merely that they had "taken note" of American actions, and they eventually agreed only to impose derisory sanctions on a short list of luxury goods. The episode confirmed the Europeans in their inherent reluctance to make trade hostage to American foreign policy through the use of sanctions and brought out further the fact that the United States no longer held all the cards in the transatlantic relationship.

In the case of the sanctions imposed upon Iran because of the occupation of the American embassy, the Europeans accepted sanctions as a middle way that might pressurise Teheran while forestalling the use of force. In any event they did neither, largely because of a European failure to think through the strategy in sufficient time. When Washington requested support the Europeans dragged their feet, aware of their economic stake in Iran, and by the time they agreed to act Carter had decided to take the military option. Part of the problem was the "theological" wrangling inside the Community over the proper legal basis of sanctions (this was one case of the inconsistency the Single Act later enveighed against). Clearly the Europeans' reliance on economic strength had here turned against them, since Washington had expected a show of alliance solidarity expressed through sanctions, and the Europeans' unwillingness and inability to act quickly and firmly exacerbated tensions with their major ally over wider issues than just Iran.

In the other two main cases of sanctions in the 1980s, however, the EC's economic power was applied more deliberately and with less collateral damage. When Argentina invaded the Falkland Islands in April 1982, for example, the Ten reacted with unprecedented decision. General Galtieri was unpleasantly surprised to find himself faced with a one-month ban on imports into the Community and an open-ended ban on arms deliveries. Yet unity could not be sustained. Largely through anxieties about Britain's turn to military force, Ireland and Italy backed away from the agreed measures within two months. Yet this was not a demonstration of the limitations of economic diplomacy as such. Had Britain been content to rely upon economic sanctions plus diplomacy, it is likely that European cohesion would have lasted for a good deal longer. Even so the psychological impact of the collective condemnation, backed up by measures that hurt the imposers as well as the targets was considerable—not least on the wider world opinion whose support Britain needed.

The last case of sanctions—South Africa—is different inasmuch as it concerned the internal affairs of a single state rather than a transgression of international law. Moreover, here, just as in the case of Iran and the Soviet Union, the Europeans acted slowly and without conviction. It was not until September 1985 that the Twelve decided to tighten their implementation of the U.N. arms embargo, to stop oil exports, prohibit nuclear cooperation and discourage "cultural and scientific events." Even then the United Kingdom issued a "footnote" excepting itself from the measures. A year later unanimity had been restored for the announcement of bans on new investment and the import of iron, steel, and gold coins. But the crucial sanction on coal imports could not be agreed.[25]

Paradoxically, despite the difficulties, it can be argued that the EC's eventual ability to put collective sanctions together against South Africa and to sustain them (at least until the United Kingdom jumped the gun in announcing an end to the new investments ban in early 1990) represented an important form of pressure on the apartheid regime. Because of the internal disagreements and the economic stakes involved, the measures taken were limited and cautious. But they were not insignificant, and South Africa realised that they might yet be worse. The deliberate decision of twelve developed countries known to be sceptical about sanctions in principle was also noted by the market and may have helped to convince international companies that an apartheid-based South Africa had no future. The EC could not force Pretoria into concessions, but it could and did concentrate its mind on the inexorable trend of events.[26]

The economic instruments available to the European Community, both pressures and inducements, are a major factor in the calculations of a wide range of types of state; and it has proved impossible to resist the temptation to use economics for political purposes. Because diplomatic persuasion has obvious limits, and because the Community's wealth is so great, the demands on its resources have grown steadily. But this is not to say that the relationship between the two sides of Community external relations has been easy or that economic power has often been delivered in effective form. Legal and tactical considerations prevent economic diplomacy simply being at the disposal of high politics, and where economic power can be deployed, it is most likely to be effective in the long term and as an indirect, background factor. In particular, the punitive withdrawal of economic ties tends to be either ineffective or actually counterproductive, given the inevitability of unforeseen side effects. The carrot of economic concessions and privileged relationships appears to be more useful than the stick of sanctions, but at the same time the resources available for inducements have always been limited and are now coming under extreme cross-pressures. Does this mean, then, that the incentive exists for the Community to develop that traditional capability of state foreign policy, military power?

---

[25] "Press statement by the EPC Council of Ministers on South Africa" (Luxembourg, September 10, 1985), and "Statement by the Twelve on South Africa" (Brussels, September 16, 1986), *European Political Cooperation Documentation Bulletin,* Vol.1, No.2, pp. 45–47 and Vol.2, No.2, p 83.

[26] See Martin Holland, *The European Community and South Africa: European Political Cooperation under Strain* (London; Frances Pinter, 1988), and Sir Patrick Moberly, "The World and South Africa: A New Perspective," *The World Today,* Vol.46, No.4, (April 1990).

THE MISSING LINK: SECURITY AND DEFENCE

Since the beginnings of EPC the member-states have discussed security matters. They have not always admitted the fact, and they have sometimes not even recognised it themselves, but they have not been able to keep security and foreign policy in separate compartments. If a state's security consists in its ability to preserve from threat its core elements and interests, and foreign policy is the sum of a state's official actions towards a potentially dangerous outside world, we can see that the two concepts are inherently related. Security concerns will be at the heart of foreign policy, even if the latter also encompasses a much wider range of issues. The European Community, therefore, as it has gradually moved towards a common foreign policy, has inevitably nudged up against the question of a common security policy.

This has been an embarrassment for various reasons. First, as a neutral country, Ireland does not wish to be associated with any stances that smack of military alignment—although it can be argued that its very participation in EPC makes a nonsense of the policy of neutrality.[27] Second, the idea that the Community might move towards responsibility for its own security naturally raises questions about European commitment to NATO and seems to be subversive of western unity. Third, it seems to cast doubt on the Community's idea of itself as not aping superpower politics, but placing more emphasis on diplomacy and peaceful conflict resolution.

None of these concerns *need* prevent the discussion of security questions in EPC—it is well-known, for example, that Irish diplomats have simply been prepared to turn a deaf ear on occasion, rather than disrupt the consultations of the other eleven. And over the twenty years of EPC's existence, security questions have come increasingly onto the agenda without yet compromising either the western alliance or the Community's reputation in the Third World. This has been managed partly by a convenient but increasingly academic distinction made between *defence* (off limits) and *security* (safe ground). In practice this has meant that military hardware, armed services, and strategic planning are not EPC subjects, while confidence-building measures, military advisers, and terrorism increasingly have been. There is, of course, a large grey area in between.

From the early 1970s the European performance in the CSCE has been one of their most effective displays of sustained unity. Both the United States and the Soviet Union were surprised, in the meetings leading up to the Helsinki Accords of 1975, at how the Community was able not only to hold together but also to lead the western countries in complex discussions covering economics, politics and human rights. Unity, if not leadership, was maintained through the various review conferences in the fifteen years that followed, so that by the time the Paris Charter of November 1990 finally put an end to the Cold War and gave the CSCE a central place among the institutions of the new

[27] As argued, *inter alia*, by Trevor Salmon in *Unneutral Ireland* (Oxford: Oxford University Press, 1990).

Europe, it was clear that the Community would be a crucial source of initiatives and stability within this otherwise cumbersome framework organisation of thirty-four states.

Except in the context of the CSCE Review Conferences, security did not formally become part of the Community's brief until the London Report of 1981, which talked of continuing the "flexible and pragmatic approach that has made it possible to discuss in Political Cooperation certain important foreign policy questions bearing on the political aspects of security."[28] Thereafter attitudes loosened up rather more quickly, so that by 1986 the Single Act was referring to security cooperation as essential to the development of a European external identity and to the need not only for coordination on "the political and economic aspects of security" but also the maintenance of the "technological and industrial conditions for security."[29]

This shift occurred partly because "security" was increasingly coming to represent a more acceptable outlook than "defence," with the latter's connotations of a narrow reliance on the use of military force or its threat. Security promised a more political approach, and could be conceptualised in positive sum terms, as "common security."[30] But it also happened because of the momentum of European cooperation. As EPC provided the integrationists with renewed hope for a great leap forward, and the areas of foreign policy discussion naturally lapped towards the edges of defence, so more ambitious proposals emerged to formalise the drift of events. German-Italian ideas (the Genscher-Colombo Plan of 1981) about a possible council of defence ministers were still premature, but with widespread unease in Europe about President Reagan's foreign policy and the revival of the Cold War, it was not long before concrete progress was being made. It took the form of extra-Community cooperation, through the revival at French instigation of the Western European Union, an organisation set up to integrate West Germany into western defence arrangements in 1955 and then neglected in favour of NATO. The seven members (the EEC's original Six plus Britain) conveniently excluded the so-called troublemakers in EPC, that is Denmark, Ireland, and Greece, who were all unhappy (though for different reasons) about a higher security profile for the EC. Spain and Portugal, however, joined the WEU in 1988, less than three years after their accession to the Community.

The WEU has quietly and steadily progressed since that time, to the point where if there is to be a common security policy grafted onto EPC, it will only be feasible through the WEU. A wide range of defence concerns have been discussed in WEU, from the Strategic Defence Initiative and Intermediate Nuclear Forces to minesweeping in the Gulf—where a successful European operation took place in 1987. Care has been taken not to cause unnecessary

---

[28] *European Political Cooperation (EPC)*, p. 62.

[29] *European Political Cooperation (EPC)* p. 84 (Article 30, para. 6 of the Act).

[30] See, for example, Palme Commission, The Palme Report, *Common Security: A Programme for Disarmament* (London; Pan, 1982), and Barry Buzan, *People, States and Fear: the National Security Problem in International Relations* (Brighton; Wheatsheaf, 1983).

tensions with NATO, and in the 1990–91 Gulf crisis the WEU slipped easily and without undue publicity into providing important functions of operational coordination for European naval forces on the one hand, and political liaison with EPC on the other. By February 1991 two meetings had taken place in Paris in which WEU and EPC business and personnel had been deliberately brought into physical proximity, and it was not surprising that at about the same time Italy should be proposing that the two institutions merge by 1998, when the WEU Treaty runs out.

Europe is still a long way from possessing a common security policy, or even a consistently worked-out security side to EPC. The member-states continue to be wary of the Commission extending its powers over commercial and competition policy to arms procurement and arms imports. "Out of area" problems, such as those in the Gulf, will continue to place the EC states in agonies of indecision over how to cope with the conjunction of political and military factors. While NATO exists—and who will want to risk abolishing it?—defence questions will remain difficult to discuss. Security and national sovereignty will remain closely associated, with France and Britain unlikely to volunteer changes in their independent nuclear deterrents or status as permanent members of the U.N. Security Council.

Yet the progress is undeniable. The security dimension of European cooperation is no longer the taboo subject it was for nearly thirty years after the failure of the European Defence Community proposal in 1954. It is possible to argue that something like a European navy has been operating in the Gulf through WEU coordination of national forces. An effective antiterrorist system—the Trevi network—has been operating under the wing of EPC since 1976. The crisis consultation procedures set up after the Afghanistan fiasco have given EPC much greater flexibility in emergencies. In short, while defence may be still an obvious missing link in the way the Community presents itself to the outside world, the ever-expanding concept of security has brought the Europeans to the very edge of fundamental choices about taking responsibility for their own protection.

CONCLUSIONS

Where, then, does the European Community stand in the world, as the last decade of the millennium begins to unfold and yet another war in the Middle East puts to the test the political resources of all the major actors in the international system? A popular reaction has it that the Gulf crisis has shown up both the emptiness and the undesirability of claims on behalf of a common European foreign policy. What unity, it is asked, have the Europeans displayed under pressure? The British have stuck closely to American policy, while France has ploughed its own furrow of peace initiatives. German opinion has seemed hostile to the war, and Bonn not only pleaded constitutional restrictions on its ability to contribute troops to the allied effort, but even had to be pressurised into making a financial contribution. Other European states, like Spain and Portugal, have adopted the lowest possible profile in the hope that the problem would pass over their heads.

There is another side to this argument, however, which a longer time perspective makes clear. The European response to the Gulf crisis has only been seriously deficient if one makes either of two questionable assumptions; first, that a common foreign and security policy was already in place and being claimed by European governments; and second that the Europeans needed to make a input distinctive from that of the United States and the United Nations. But only the idealists or the sworn enemies of integration could have expected a swift and united European response to Iraq's aggression against Kuwait. Those with any knowledge of how the Community works appreciated that its "foreign policy" still coexists with national traditions and national diplomatic services, while cooperation on the operational side of security policy had only begun three years before. It would have been extraordinary if the Twelve had suddenly taken a qualitative leap forward in the midst of this crisis, to produce the genuine common foreign policy that they had only been edging towards over the previous twenty years. As it is, significant progress has in fact been made under the WEU umbrella in the Gulf, which is likely in the long run to boost rather than set back the overall process of foreign policy integration.

The second assumption, that the Europeans *should* have provided a separate policy input, only holds water if on political grounds the U.N. Coalition's handling of the crisis is thought unacceptable, and the move to war opposed. Otherwise, an insistence on a separate European line would at worst have actually endangered Coalition unity, and at best simply have been redundant. It is in fact possible to argue that certain benefits have flowed from the diversity of European views that has been displayed, as this has softened and complexified the image of the West in Arab eyes without seriously undermining the anti-Saddam strategy.

In any case, there is a deep paradox about the events that have taken place since 1989. While there has been a political furore about the apparent weaknesses of European actions in the Gulf crisis (with, typically, integrationists like Commission President Delors and some MEPs quickest to express disappointment), this parallels the attention given to the Community as the main player in the rebuilding of Europe's political and economic structures in the aftermath of the Cold War. The Community is going to be indispensable in central Europe in the next decade, for its funds and commercial expertise, but also as a diplomatic force in what might otherwise be a serious political vacuum.

This paradox is easily resolved. The truth is that much political opinion, inside and outside Europe, still has too high expectations of what the Community can do in the world. The Twelve do not yet have a fully-fledged foreign policy, let alone a defence system, and they are far more effective in some areas, particularly where politics and economics blur into each other, and in their own geographical region than in others, such as out of area military crises.

The present Intergovernmental Conferences on Monetary Union and Political Union may well take important steps forward for the Community towards a more profoundly integrated structure than the present rather patchy, evolving, system of coordination. Alternatively, they may only tinker with the institutions and succeed in making minor improvements. There is no historical ineluctability about progress towards a single European foreign and defence policy, let alone a European superpower. That possibility remains a dream or a nightmare, according to political taste. What is true, however, is that the Europeans have put in place a set of sophisticated mechanisms and wide-ranging external policies that, even twenty-five years ago, would have seemed most unlikely. This is the reality, and it is one that the other states and regions of the world are increasingly having to take into account.

FOREIGN POLICY LANDMARKS

April 18, 1951	Treaty of Paris establishes the European Coal and Steel Community; Pleven plan for a European Defence Community (EDC)
August 30, 1954	EDC proposal defeated in the French National Assembly
March 25, 1957	Treaty of Rome establishes the European Economic Community and the European Atomic Energy Community
1963	Yaoundé Convention associates seventeen African states and Madagascar with the EEC
1969	Hague Summit "agreed to instruct the Ministers for foreign Affairs to study the best way of achieving progress in the matter of political unification, within the context of enlargement"
October 27, 1970	Luxembourg Report, also known as Davignon Report, sets up political cooperation on foreign policy
1972	Paris Summit calls for "transforming...the whole complex of the relations between the Member States into a European Union"
January 1, 1973	Britain, Denmark and Ireland join the Community
July 23, 1973	Copenhagen Report further codifies EPC
1973–74	Sharp disagreements with the United States during and after Middle East war and OPEC oil embargo
1974	European Council established bringing EEC and EPC together under one roof
1974	First informal weekend meeting of Foreign Ministers held at Schloss Gymnich
1975	The first Lomé Convention between the EC and forty-six African, Caribbean, and Pacific countries
1975	Conference on security and cooperation in Europe leads to Helsinki Final Accords
1976	First Meeting of the General Committee of the Euro-Arab Dialogue
December 1979	Soviet invasion of Afghanistan—EPC very slow to react
1980	Venice Declaration of the Nine on the Middle East—even-handed between Israel and Palestinians

January 1, 1981	Greece joins the EC; German-Italian proposal, known as the "Genscher-Colombo Plan," for a "European Act" put forward
October 13, 1981	London report on EPC—creates "troika" system plus crisis-consultation mechanism; Commission to be "fully associated" with EPC "at all levels"
April 2, 1982	Argentina invades the Falkland Islands, precipitating EC sanctions
1983	Solemn declaration on European union adopted at Stuttgart
1984	European Parliament adopts draft treaty on European union
September 1984	Ten European foreign ministers fly to Costa Rica to meet with Central American and Contadora ministers
January 1, 1986	Spain and Portugal join the EC
February 28, 1986	Single European Act agreed (ratification in 1987), Title 30 of the Act formalises EPC for the first time, with a treaty obligation to consult on foreign policy, and a new secretariat on EPC, to be sited in Brussels. EPC and EC external relations to be "consistent," and member-states agree to work on "the technological and industrial conditions necessary for their security."
September 1986	Limited EC sanctions against South Africa (bans on iron, steel, and gold coin imports and on new investment in South Africa)
1988	Joint EC-COMECON Declaration
1989	Events in China in June lead to limited sanctions on part of Twelve, as signal of disapproval of repression
December 1989	Signature of EC-U.S.S.R. Cooperation Agreement
February 1990	Britain partially and unilaterally withdraws from agreed sanctions against South Africa (after consultation as SEA requires)
April 1990	Franco-German proposals for further progress towards "Political Union" revive discussions on new developments in EPC
August 1990	Iraq's invasion of Kuwait starts the Gulf crisis. WEU takes the running in coordinating European policy. As the January 15 U.N. deadline approaches, EPC efforts at mediation are overshadowed by France's national initiative.
December 1990	Intergovernmental Conference on Political Union begins in Rome. Proposals for majority voting in EPC and for the merging of EPC and WEU have been floated during the year.
January 17, 1991	Gulf War begins. European opinion soon solidifies behind the Coalition after early peace demonstrations in France, Germany, and Italy.
February 23, 1991	Allied ground offensive begins
March 2, 1991	Ceasefire after Coalition victory in expelling Iraq from Kuwait

SELECTED BIBLIOGRAPHY

Allen, David and Alfred Pijpers, eds. *European Foreign Policy-Making and The Arab-Israeli Conflict.* The Hague: Martinus Nijhoff, 1984.

Allen, David, Reinhardt Rummel, and Wolfgang Wessels, eds. *European Political Cooperation.* London: Butterworths, 1982.

Deporte, A.W. *Europe between the Super-Powers: The Enduring Balance.* New Haven: Yale University Press, 1979.

De Vree, J.K., P. Coffey, and R.H. Lauwaars. *Towards a European Foreign Policy: Legal Economic and Political Dimensions.* Dordrecht: Nijhoff, 1987.

Edwards, Geoffrey and Elfriede Regelsberger (Eds.). *Europe's Global Links: The European Community and Inter-regional Cooperation.* London: Pinter, 1990.

Galtung, Johan. *The European Community: A Superpower in the Making.* London: George Allen and Unwin, 1973.

Ginsberg, Roy. *The Foreign Policy Actions of the European Community.* Boulder, CO: Lynn Reinner, 1989.

Hill, Christopher ed. *National Foreign Policies and European Political Co-operation.* London: George Allen & Unwin, 1983.

Ifestos, Panayotis. *European Political Cooperation.* Gower, 1987.

de La Serre, Françoise. "Foreign Policy of the European Community," in Roy C. Macridis, ed., *Foreign Policy in World Politics: States and Regions,* (7th ed.). Englewood Cliffs, N.J.: Prentice Hall, 1989.

Lodge, Juliet ed. *The European Community and the Challenge of the Future.* London: Pinter, 1989.

Pijpers, Alfred *et al.,* eds. *European Political Cooperation in the 1980s: A Common Foreign Policy for Western Europe?* Dordrechet: Martinus Nijhoff, 1988.

Rummel, Reinhardt ed. *The Evolution of an International Actor: Western Europe's New Assertiveness.* Boulder, Co.: Westview, 1990.

de Schoutheete. Philippe *La Cooperation Politique Europeènne,* Brussels: Editions Labor, 1980.

Sjostedt, Gunnar. *The External Role of the European Community.* Farnborough: Saxon House, 1977.

Taylor, Paul. *The Limits of European Integration.* London: Croom Helm, 1983.

Tugendhat, Christopher. *Making Sense of Europe.* Harmondsworth: Viking, 1986.

—6—

SOVIET
FOREIGN POLICY

Vernon V. Aspaturian

THE CHANGING ROLE AND STATUS
OF THE SOVIET UNION IN THE INTERNATIONAL SYSTEM

As the world moves towards the third millenium, dramatic events and transformations have already left their imprint on the Soviet Union, Eastern Europe, the Communist universe, and indeed upon the entire international landscape. The year 1989 signalled the beginning of a process that brought about the collapse of a world socio-political system, which embraced more than one-third of the world's population and territory, whose center and nucleus was the Soviet Union. In less than two years, Communist regimes were swept from power or radically reformed in Eastern Europe, sometimes with Moscow's encouragement and always with its permission. East Germany disappeared from the map as a separate state as it was unified with West Germany in 1990, although Soviet military forces still remained on its soil. Non-Communist and anti-Communist governments were propelled into power in Poland, Czechoslovakia, and Hungary, whereas in Romania (after a bloody overthrow of the Ceausescu regime), Bulgaria and Albania, the Communist leadership reformed itself into "reformist socialists." In Yugoslavia, the two northern republics of Slovenia and Croatia emulated the example of the northern tier of Eastern Europe and established freely elected non-Communist governments, whereas the Serbian Republic instituted its own brand of "reform socialism." As a result the Yugoslav Federation is on the brink of dissolution and civil war as Slovenia first, and then Croatia proceeded to secede, and Serbia announced its determination to prevent it.

But the revolution sweeping the Communist world is more than simply the collapse of a world system. It also represents the collapse of the Soviet Union as a global power, leaving the United States once again as the only authentic global power in the world. The United States is no longer restrained or constrained by countervailing Soviet power around the globe, which means that self-regulating mechanisms and sensitivity to concerns and interests of allies and others become more imperative in shaping U.S. behavior as a global power. Soviet global power had been under attack by reformers in the Soviet Union, who blamed Moscow's inordinate power ambitions as responsible for the deformation of Soviet society, the ravaging of its economy, and its insensitivity to the interests of others, particularly its geographical neighbors and allies. At the same time, Mikhail Gorbachev is under increasing attack from conservatives for allegedly dismantling Soviet power and its status in the world unilaterally in order to win hollow kudos from the Western media. Gorbachev even had to publicly deny the charge that he was "working for somebody," i.e., for Western and American interests. But the more Gorbachev came under attack from conservative directions, the more quickly he moved to erode the power, authority, and legitimacy of the Communist Party Apparat and to shift power and authority from the Secretariat and Politburo of the Party to his new position as President of the U.S.S.R. and the new executive-administrative bodies under his direction.

As Gorbachev consolidates and concentrates more power in the center and in his person, the Soviet periphery is in the process of unraveling as its multilayered empire peels away in successive stages. The Soviet Empire consisted of three distinct but interrelated empires. First, there was the extended empire. This empire was the Soviet variant of the old European overseas colonial empires and consisted of a motley collection of Third World client states scattered across Asia, Africa, and Latin America, the most important of which were Angola, Afghanistan, Ethiopia, Yemen, and perhaps a dozen more, all characterized as "socialist-oriented" countries, i.e., Third World states governed by single-party Marxist-Leninist authoritarian regimes. Cuba and Vietnam, although labelled as "socialist countries" were also part of this extended empire. This empire has come under attack by Soviet scholars and reformers as an inordinate burden upon Soviet resources and energy. As Moscow disentangles itself from its political, ideological, economic, and military associations with most of these countries, they have been left both rudderless, without an international patron, and increasingly isolated in the international community. This is particularly true of Castro's Cuba, where serious changes in relations with Moscow and Eastern Europe are impending, which will affect the island's economy and generate internal opposition to the Castro regime, whose continued survival is doubtful.

The second empire, i.e., the *outer empire,* consisting of the Warsaw Pact states of Eastern Europe and Mongolia, has also peeled away and is now beyond Soviet control. Soviet influence on internal developments in these countries has simply evaporated. Even in East Germany, 380,000 Soviet troops stood silently and invisibly on the sidelines, as the East German Communist state voted itself out of existence in favor of merger with West Germany. The "loss" of Eastern Europe, together with East Germany, and the prospect of a unified Germany joining NATO as the Warsaw Pact began to crumble from within, has brought Gorbachev the sharpest and bitterest domestic criticism, much of it from professional military officers and the KGB, who have publicly asserted that Gorbachev's policies were endangering the security of the country.

The last and most important of the Soviet Empires is its *inner empire,* the band of non-Russian rationalities organized into national republics that form an almost continuous chain along the entire western and southern periphery of the Russian heartland. Stretching from Estonia on the Baltic to the western Chinese border in Soviet Central Asia, the entire inner empire is in varying degrees of ferment, with important segments on the verge of breaking away and others demanding greater autonomy and lessened Russian control and intrusion in their affairs.

The ferment in the *inner empire* threatens the very existence of the U.S.S.R. as a *multinational* state and throws it back upon its historic identity as a *Russian* state, which is welcomed by large sectors of the Russian population, who resented the submersion of the Russian national identity into an abstract *Soviet* identity.

The collapse of the Communist order will inevitably influence the further restructuring of the international landscape, as new power vacuums develop, alignments and realignments assume shape, and new powerful actors like Germany and Japan seek to assert a political—and perhaps even military—role commensurate with their economic, financial, and scientific-technological prowess. And, finally, in its impact on the Soviet identity, role and status in the international community will be immeasurable.

THE COLLAPSE OF THE BIPOLAR SYSTEM AND THE QUEST FOR A "NEW WORLD ORDER"

The collapse of communism in the Soviet Union and Eastern Europe in 1989–90 crushed one of the two basic pillars of the bipolar international order and plunged the world into an uncertain future insofar as the regulation and discipline of the international system is concerned. The old bipolar system had its deficiencies, but uncertainty and international anarchy were not among them. The Gulf crisis provoked by the Iraqi invasion and annexation of Kuwait in August 1990 and its threat to Saudi Arabia and other Persian Gulf states is but a precursor, or dress rehearsal, of the kinds of crisis with which the international local despots seek to settle old scores or achieve old ambitions at the expense of their neighbors. And already the Soviet role in the world has been transformed as a result.

Now, more than ever, it is becoming evident that the old bipolar system and its institutionalized expression in the form of two opposing alliance systems, NATO and the Warsaw Treaty Organization (WTO), served not only as military structures guarding each other's domain from the other, but simultaneously as conflict-containing and conflict-resolving organizations in their own regions. Each alliance was dominated by a global power, although the WTO was essentially a hegemonic, involuntary alliance system, which was tightly regulated and controlled by Moscow, whereas NATO was a voluntary alliance system, with considerable autonomy for its members. The two alliance systems served to smother and postpone conflicts among its members, and when they erupted attempted to resolve them and to subordinate these issues to the more decisive and critical overarching global ideological and political rivalry between East and West. Although not always involved directly or indirectly in the two opposing alliance systems and in the face of attempts to establish in-between associations ("neutralism," "non-alignment," etc.), inevitably all members of the international community gravitated in the direction of one pole or the other or oscillated between them. The two global powers maintained peripheral alliances with a large retinue of client states in the Third World. The bipolar system served to regulate and impose an international discipline upon the entire international community, i.e., monitored and maintained order through various means and methods by the two superpowers jointly or unilaterally, including military intervention.

Under these conditions, the international system achieved a dynamic stability, which in time became rather predictable, minimizing confrontation in the center of the system (the developed world, especially Europe) and allowed for superpower energy and frustrations to be expended at the periphery (the Third World, the remoter the better). The crumbling of the bipolar system brought with it the collapse of this world order, and the Gulf crisis has demonstrated that no real surrogate has yet emerged to replace it; the world is frantically searching for a "new world order."

The collapse of the bipolar system was set into motion by the collapse of the U.S.S.R. as a functioning global power, which took place unexpectedly and with surprising rapidity, as a result of the voluntary changes introduced in Soviet aims and behavior by the Soviet leadership, namely President Gorbachev. The conscious decision to allow Eastern Europe to go its own way, including the self-liquidation of the German Democratic Republic and its de facto annexation by West Germany could not but mean a multiple collapse of the Eastern pillars supporting the Soviet end of the bipolar system. These were:

1. the collapse of the Soviet Union as a global power
2. the collapse of the Soviet Empire in Eastern Europe and the Third World
3. the collapse of communism as an integrated and Moscow-coordinated world socio-political economic system
4. the collapse of the Soviet alliance system, including the Warsaw Treaty Organization
5. the abandonment by Moscow of a messianic, universalist and expansionist policy, i.e., the abandonment of Marxism-Leninism as a guiding force in Soviet foreign policy
6. the potential dissolution of the U.S.S.R. itself as an integrated state structure and its possible replacement by several new international actors

RECASTING SOVIET FOREIGN POLICY: THE BREZHNEV LEGACY AND THE GORBACHEV VISION

Perestroika, the principal buzzword of the Gorbachev era, is conceived as a process cutting across all aspects of Soviet life, including ideology and foreign policy. Although Gorbachev has meticulously avoided using the term "restructuring" in reference to ideology, since this could open him to charges of "revisionism," he has called for the application of *perestroika* in Soviet foreign policy.

> At present, a restructuring of the work of the Ministry of Foreign Affairs is underway and a reorganization of the structure of its central apparatus and foreign institutions is being carried out. This leadership is being renewed. This line must be pursued consistently, increasing the efficiency of the activity of the diplomatic service and *striving* to have it correspond fully to the vigorous international activity of the CPSU and the Soviet State.[1]

Gorbachev, however, has introduced another term, "new political thinking," which is nothing less than the application of *perestroika* to ideology. The specific application of *perestroika* to Soviet foreign policy involves the following components: (1) recasting the ideological parameters of Soviet foreign policy and reconceptualizing perceptions of the international system, national security, defense, military doctrine and strategy, in accordance with the "new foreign policy philosophy," essentially a subset of the "new political thinking;" (2) redirecting Soviet foreign policy goals and reordering Soviet foreign policy priorities; and (3) reorganizing the foreign policy decision-making system, involving personnel, institutions and processes.

The death of Leonid Brezhnev in November 1982, after eighteen years of leadership, ended one of the longest periods of leadership and political stability in the history of the Soviet Union and marked the end of one era and the prelude for a new potentially long period of leadership under Mikhail S. Gorbachev, who became Brezhnev's definitive successor in April 1985, after a brief two and one-half year interregnum of leadership uncertainty under Andropov and Chernenko.

---

[1] *Pravda*, January 28, 1987. Report to the Central Committee Plenum of January 27, 1987, "On Restructuring and the Party's Personnel Policy."

Brezhnev's achievements, particularly in foreign and military policy were impressive and extensive in the short run, but were questionably durable or sustainable. Soviet foreign policy is shaped by many variables, but among the most important and difficult to calculate is the Soviet perception of risks, opportunities, and costs in pursuing objectives, whatever they might be at any given time. When risk and cost perceptions have been low and opportunity perceptions were high, Soviet leaders were inclined to pursue their foreign policy goals more vigorously and exploit opportunities with greater alacrity, even at the expense of neglecting serious domestic problems. When risk and cost perceptions were high, Soviet leaders were likely to behave more cautiously and prudently, consolidating and retrenching rather than expanding their power, and to concentrate on the solution of pressing internal problems rather than risk confrontation abroad. During the decade of the seventies, as a result of the Vietnam debacle, Watergate, and general U.S. disillusionment and demoralization as a consequence, the Brezhnev leadership perceived the risks and costs of acting more vigorously in foreign policy to be low, as the United States appeared to enter a period of self-paralysis and incapacity to behave assertively in foreign policy, which was viewed by many Soviet leaders as the beginning of a long period of irreversible decline for the United States. Brezhnev decided to mortgage the immediate Soviet domestic future by investing in expanding Soviet power abroad.

It was during this period that Brezhnev's achievements manifested themselves, as the Soviet Union (1) achieved status and recognition as a global power, with global interests and presence; (2) achieved and gained recognition as the political and military equal of the United States; (3) established an extended empire of dependent and client states beyond the Soviet periphery in South and Southeast Asia, the Middle East, Africa, and the Caribbean; and (4) shifted the overall world or strategic balance of power or "correlation of forces" to immense Soviet advantage.

His accomplishments were not achieved without a serious price, for which Brezhnev, posthumously, and the Soviet society will pay very dearly.

The most serious and crippling price that the Soviet Union paid for its immense military growth and globalist ambitions was the disorientation, dislocation, and deformation of the Soviet economy, which entered into a period of stagnation and decline, threatening to leave the Soviet Union and its East European client states far behind the United States, Western Europe, and Japan as the world moved at an accelerated pace into the new era of high technology, and even threatened to undercut its military prowess in the process.

The stagnation of the Soviet economy had manifold domestic reverberations. The standard of living grew at an ominously slow pace, as both workers and managers accustomed themselves to low productivity and efficiency, and as a series of shortfalls in agricultural production created serious food problems for the country. As the non-Russian nationalities, particularly the Moslems of Central Asia, grew at a rapid pace while the Russian and Slavic population neared zero-population growth, this asymmetrical demographic growth threatened not only the integrity of the labor force, but the Soviet military as well. Furthermore, as the ethnic balance tilts in favor of the non-Slavic population, the demand and competition for relatively diminished scarce resources and wealth among the various nationalities and republics becomes sharper and more aggravated. Similar problems were generated in the Soviet Bloc as a whole, as the Stalinist socio-economic model exhausted its potential for further constructive development. These accumulated domestic problems, of course, seriously compromised the capacity of the Soviet Union to advance its globalist ambitions abroad, which became painfully evident as the decade of the eighties unfolded.

Gorbachev clearly recognized that the intersection of the Soviet Union's accumulated domestic problems and the advent of a more assertive American counterresponse would lead to a catastrophic confrontation if Moscow pursued its expansionist policies. This was boldly conceptualized by Gorbachev at the Nineteenth Communist Party conference, held in June-July, 1988.

> But, while concentrating enormous funds and attention on the military aspect of countering imperialism...we allowed ourselves to be drawn into an arms race, which could not but affect the country's socioeconomic development and its international standing....To put it more bluntly, without overturning the logic of this course, we could actually have found ourselves on the brink of a military confrontation. Hence, what was needed was not just a refinement of foreign policy, but its determined reshaping. This called for new political thinking.[2]

Gorbachev's rhetoric clearly reflected his sense of urgency, as both he and his supporters have emphasized that his reform program is the "last chance" that the Soviet Union has to recover from its economic stagnation and torpor, which threatened to undermine not only its military prowess but its cherished role and status in the international system as one of the two global powers. Gorbachev wanted passionately to preserve this part of the Brezhnev legacy; to do this required the repudiation of the remaining part of that legacy and the virtual inversion of Soviet priorities. How to downgrade the priority of the Soviet overseas empire acquired under Brezhnev while simultaneously salvaging the credibility of Soviet global power emerged as one of the most vexing conundrums of the Gorbachev regime.

Reconceptualizing Soviet Ideology and Reformulating Soviet Strategy

The exact relationship between Soviet ideology and foreign policy has been subject to great controversy, ranging from the view that it is substantially irrelevant, to the conviction that foreign policy is rigidly dictated by ideology. The precise role that ideology plays in Soviet foreign policy was also subject to periodic and episodic controversy inside the Soviet Union as well, with each

---

[2] *Documents and Materials of the 19th All-Union Conference of the CPSU* (Washington, DC: *Soviet Life*, 1988), p. 31. (Hereinafter cited as *Documents and Materials.*)

new leader or set of leaders often redefining and reshaping ideology in reference to Soviet foreign policy. The most recent domestic manifestation of this periodic controversy over the relationship between Soviet foreign policy and Soviet ideology, in its broadest dimensions, was Ligachev's challenge to the publicly stated positions of Gorbachev, Yakovlev, and Shevardnadze that Soviet foreign policy should no longer be subordinated to ideology, that the class struggle was no longer the nexus of Soviet analytical perceptions of the international scene, and that class interests would have to be subordinated to the interests of nations and mankind.[3] This had been forcefully articulated at the Nineteenth Party Conference by Gorbachev himself:

> As we analyzed the contemporary world, we realized more clearly that international relations without losing their class character, are increasingly coming to be precisely relations between nations. We noted the enhanced role in world affairs of peoples, nations, and emerging new national entities. And this implies that there is no ignoring the diversity of interests in international affairs....From the standpoint of our day—with its mounting nuclear menace, heightening of other global problems, and progressive internationalization of all the processes in a world becoming, despite its contradictions, even more integral and interdependent—we have sought a deeper understanding of the interrelationship between working class interests and those of humanity as a whole....This led to the conclusion that common human values have a priority in our age, this being the core of the new political thinking.[4]

Clearly recognizing that the subordination of Soviet foreign policy to Soviet ideology, which dictated highest priority to the class struggle in international relations, generated international conflict and tensions among states and nations, Gorbachev conceded that "stereotypes" of this character "supplied arguments to those who indulged in misrepresenting our real intentions."[5]

During the decade of the seventies, as Soviet military capabilities developed and the United States reduced its international commitments in the wake of Vietnam, Soviet ideological goals appeared to reassert themselves with greater force in Soviet foreign policy behavior. The resurgence of ideological imperatives was accompanied by the increasing prominence of Brezhnev in his capacity as Secretary General of the Party in Soviet foreign policy and foreign affairs.

As the Soviet Union expanded its global activities and reached into the remote regions of Asia, Africa, and Latin America to lend military support and assistance to friendly revolutionary movements and regimes, ideology was increasingly invoked to legitimize its behavior. The apparent reideologization of Soviet foreign policy found explicit expression in the new Brezhnev Constitution of 1977. In an entirely new and juridically unprecedented Chapter on Foreign Policy, Article 28, in effect converted ideological commitments into state obligations by defining the goals of Soviet foreign policy as follows:

[3] Speech by Ligachev at Gorky, August 5, 1988, as reported in *Sovetskaya Rossiya*, August 6, 1988.
[4] *Documents and Materials*, p. 32. *Cf.* also statements by *Shevarnadze, infra.*, pp. 38 ff.
[5] *Ibid.*

The foreign policy of the U.S.S.R. is aimed at ensuring international conditions favorable for building communism in the U.S.S.R., safeguarding the state interests of the Soviet Union, consolidating the positions of world socialism, supporting the struggle of peoples for national liberation and social progress, preventing wars of aggression, achieving universal and complete disarmament, and consistently implementing the principle of peaceful coexistence of states with a different social system.[6]

It would be reasonable to assume that the seven distinct goals of Soviet foreign policy as previously enumerated were listed in order of priority and precedence, in which case, "consolidating the positions of world socialism" (3) and "supporting the struggle...for national liberation" (4) have a conspicuously higher priority than either arms control and disarmament (6) or "peaceful coexistence of states with different social systems" (7) Gorbachev seeks no less than to reorder the priority of these foreign policy goals:

> A key factor in the new thinking is the concept of freedom of choice....In this situation the imposition of a social system, way of life, or policies from outside by any means, let alone military, are dangerous trappings of the past period....The axis of international affairs is shifting way from confrontation towards cooperation, mutual understanding, and negotiations.[7]

As his evidence of sincerity, he specifically linked the INF treaty, the improvement of Soviet-American relations, to the withdrawal of Soviet troops from Afghanistan as recognition that the improvement of Soviet-American relations and the negotiation of arms control treaties had a higher priority in his calculations than "supporting the struggle for...national liberation."

The Brezhnev constitution's Chapter on Foreign Policy thus reflected the goals and ambitions of an ideological global power, sufficiently confident and self-assured to pronounce its ideological goals in foreign policy more openly and militantly rather than leaving them only to Party pronouncements.

During the Brezhnev era, the Soviet Union pursued a variation of the original Leninist-Stalinist dual-track strategy, based upon a division and distribution of labor between the Party and state. Foreign policy was divided into two spheres or realms, the sphere of interstate relations and the sphere of international class relations. In the first sphere, the Soviet state interacted with other states more or less within the parameters of traditional diplomacy, power politics, and international law. The Ministry of Foreign Affairs (formerly the Narkomindel) was the principal executing arm of state-to-state relations, and the operating tactical (later strategic) formula was that of "peaceful coexistence" between states with differing social systems. In effect, the first sphere reflected *interstate* compatibility, conflict, consensus and cooperation, whereas the second sphere reflected inevitable *intersystem* conflict with ultimate apocalyptic consequences.

The second sphere was the domain of the Party, operating through the Comintern and foreign Communist parties, as well as assorted movements,

[6] *Constitution of the USSR* (Moscow: Novosti Press, 1977), pp. 31–32.
[7] *Documents and Materials,* pp. 34–35.

fronts, "transmission belts" and other "non-state" activities. In this sphere, the international class struggle was prosecuted, whereby the Party sought to undermine, subvert, or overthrow the capitalist system in the same states with which the Soviet Union was conducting "normal" state relations. In the second sphere, not "peaceful coexistence," but "proletarian internationalism" was the operating formula, which was translated to mean the subordination of state and national loyalty to proletarian class loyalty. Relative emphasis upon one sphere or another in the conduct of Soviet foreign policy varied with circumstances, risks and opportunities as Moscow carefully modulated and orchestrated the two arms of its foreign policy.

This two-track or two-sphere approach was institutionalized in the Brezhnev constitution, and until the advent of Gorbachev's "new political thinking," was considered sacrosanct. The first sphere, relations with the West, would be based upon détente as the contemporary expression of "peaceful coexistence." Moscow would seek to lessen international tensions through arms control arrangements and other inducements, appear to support the *political* status quo, postpone indefinitely any idea of altering the ideological or system status quo, i.e., suspend "The Class Struggle," and conduct normal relations as if the West and the socialist world existed together in a separate vacuum. The SALT agreements and related arms control arrangements and the treaties with Germany and the Helsinki Accords were the principal manifestations of Soviet foreign policy in this sphere.

Meanwhile in the second sphere, the Third World, neither detente, nor "peaceful coexistence," nor political or ideological status quos were applicable, and the Soviet Union reserved the right to pursue its policies as a state in accordance with a different set of principles and formulas: "Proletarian internationalism," support for wars and movements of "national liberation," "internationalist duties," "fraternal assistance," encouraging the creation of Marxist-Leninist "socialist oriented" regimes, and directly supplying political, economic, ideological and military assistance. The culmination of this policy was the Soviet invasion of Afghanistan, and nowhere was the overt subordination of Soviet foreign policy to ideology and the priority of class interests more clearly pronounced than on this occasion:

> The experience of the revolutionary liberation struggle of the peoples shows that at critical moments solidarity with a victorious revolution calls not only for moral support, but also for material assistance, including, under definite circumstances, military assistance....Today, when there exists a system of socialist states, it would be simply ridiculous to question the right to such assistance....To refuse to use the possibilities at the disposal of the socialist countries would signify virtually evading performance of the internationalist duty and returning the world to the times when imperialism could throttle at will any revolutionary movement. In the given instance, not to come to Afghanistan's aid would signify leaving the Afghan revolution and people prey to class enemies, to imperialism and feudal reaction.[8]

---

[8] "New World Solidarity with the Afghan Revolution," *New Times*, January 1980 (No. 3), pp. 9–10.

The United States rejected this dualistic notion of two spheres and put forth the theory of "linkage," i.e., détente was universal and not Europocentric, and any attempt on the part of the Soviet Union to pursue a dual-track policy of détente in Europe and expansion in the Third World would be resisted. Moscow, firm in its conviction that the United States was unable or unwilling to enforce a universal détente, acted as if Soviet behavior in the Third World would not impact adversely upon its relations with the United States and the West generally.

The Changing Soviet Image of the World in the New Political Thinking

Under Gorbachev, Soviet ideology in general, but in terms of its application to foreign policy in particular, is still in the middle of a major restructuring process, in which all of its functional dimensions are subject to radical review and change, perhaps more far-reaching than in previous periods. It should be emphasized, however, that the process is still in flux; what the ultimate consequence will be both in terms of restructuring and its relevance for foreign policy at this point remain unknown. As Gorbachev himself noted at the Nineteenth Party conference, "the new political thinking is not a final and consummate doctrine" and is subject to further refinement.[9] The removal of Ligachev from foreign policy and ideological responsibilities, and the retirement of both Gromyko and Dobrynin (personal symbols of the old foreign policy that had come under increasingly open and persistent criticism), soon after Ligachev's attempt to reaffirm the centrality of class conflict and class interests in foreign policy, strongly suggested that Gorbachev was well on the road to imposing his vision of international relations as that of the Soviet Party and state. Furthermore, by replacing Gromyko as the ceremonial and *de jure* head of state, Gorbachev improved his chances of transforming the Soviet executive power into a new stronger presidency with defined constitutional powers over foreign policy and defense, which he accomplished in a successive series of changes in 1990. Clearly, Gorbachev sought to disestablish the two-spheres approach to Soviet foreign policy, an approach that was characterized as contributing to the generation of international tensions, the deterioration of Soviet-American relations, and the negative image of Soviet international behavior in general. This is now openly conceded in the Soviet media and the following unusually candid critique of past Soviet behavior by a Soviet historian is not at all atypical:

> Could such a severe exacerbation of tension in Soviet-Western relations in the late seventies and early eighties have been avoided? Unquestionably so. It is our conviction that the crisis was caused chiefly by the miscalculations and incompetent approach of the Brezhnev leadership toward the resolution of foreign policy tasks. Though we were politically, militarily (via weapons, supplies and advisers), and diplomatically involved in regional conflicts, we disregarded their

[9] *Documents and Materials*, p. 31.

influence on the relaxation of tension between the U.S.S.R. and the West and on their entire system of relationships.[10]

The "new political thinking" introduces a substantially revised image of the outside world from that of the Stalinist era and the residual Stalinism of the Brezhnev period. This new image of the world can be found in its various stages of evolution in Gorbachev's speeches and statements and in the speeches of his advisers and supporters, especially people like Aleksander Yakovlev, Evgeny Primakov, Alexander Bovin, Fedor Burlatsky, and others. Its most straightforward and clearest, but somewhat preliminary and unrefined, exposition is to be found in Gorbachev's book, *Perestroika*, especially in the chapter entitled, "How We See the World of Today."[11] This chapter summarizes in simple, clear language the basic outlines of Gorbachev's image of the world, but since the book was designed primarily for external audiences, many of the harsher edges of Soviet ideology were burnished away, and the result is essentially a propagandistic variant of the Gorbachev vision.

Many of the ideas in the new political thinking may have been new to Soviet ears and eyes, but not to Western, since in many respects they simply represent ideas, concepts, and themes developed in the West, co-opted by Gorbachev and his supporters, and given a Soviet twist. Ideas such as interdependence, mutual security, concern for ecology, environmental problems, depletion of natural resources, the unity of mankind, irrationality of nuclear war, etc., have long achieved platitudinal status in the West and they are new only to the Soviet political agenda.

Only residual elements of the old two-camp image of the world are to be found in the Gorbachev outlook, just barely enough to retain a semblance of continuity in the Soviet perspective. What is extraordinarily new in the Gorbachev view, for a Soviet position, is the idea that the world constitutes a material and civilization unity, integrity, and interdependence, in spite of its contradictory, diverse, and tension-laden character, whose survival has a higher priority than the expansion of *either* of the two ideologies or social systems:

> The time is ripe for abandoning views on foreign policy which are influenced by an imperial viewpoint. Neither the Soviet Union nor the United States is able to force its will on others. It is possible to suppress, compel, bribe, break or blast, but only for a certain period. From the point of view of long-term, big-time politics, no one will be able to subordinate others....The fundamental principal or the new political outlook is very simple: nuclear war cannot be a means of achieving political, economic, ideological or any other goals....Nuclear war is senseless; it is irrational. There would be neither winners nor losers in a global nuclear conflict: world civilization would inevitably perish.[12]

[10]V. Dashichev, "The Quest for New East-West Relations," *Literaturnaya Gazeta*, May 18, 1988, p. 14. Foreign Minister Shevarnadze, in his address to the Soviet foreign policy establishment on July 25, 1988, said much the same thing, but in a more muted tone. See *Vestnik Ministerstva Inostrannykh del SSSR*, August 1988 (no. 15) pp. 27–46. A shorter version of the speech can also be found in *Pravda*, July 26, 1988.

[11]*Perestroika*, pp. 135–170.

[12]*Ibid.*, p. 138.

Aside from implicitly acknowledging an "imperial viewpoint" to past Soviet behavior, the revolutionary character of Gorbachev's views, from the standpoint of a Soviet leader, is that it explicitly repudiated for the first time the conviction that the worldwide victory of socialism is inevitable under any and all conditions. It thus implicitly subverted the scientific credentials of Marxism-Leninism, which was hitherto based upon the inescapable inevitability of the demise of capitalism and the universal triumph of socialism.

Noting that "no one can close down the world of capitalism...or the world of developed socialism," Gorbachev asserts that "the new political outlook calls for the recognition of one more simple axiom: security is indivisible."[13]

Since the new political thinking explicitly contradicts some fundamental and seminal elements of Marxism-Leninism, Gorbachev goes beyond simply stating that ideological conflict should not be reflected at the interstate level, a standard strategy often invoked by his predecessors, and demands that foreign policies should no longer be shaped by ideological differences at all.

> Ideological differences should not be transferred to the sphere of interstate relations nor should foreign policy be subordinate to them, for ideologies may be poles apart, whereas the interest of survival and prevention of war stand universal and supreme.[14]

This view represented a monumental step in the repudiation of Marxism-Leninism, for it was an explicit admission that, first, ideological differences are a source of international tension and conflict; second, that they pose a barrier to the solution of world problems, and third, that survival and prevention of war take priority over the promotion of ideological positions. Gorbachev, in effect, repudiated the class struggle, although he conceded its past validity, and its current partial and residual applicability; but clearly he recognized that reliance upon the concept of the "class struggle" as the basis of political analysis is not only a barrier to peace but may in fact promote war and destruction:

> Since time immemorial, class interests were the cornerstone of both foreign and domestic policies....Marxists...are convinced that in the final analysis the policy of any state or alliance of states is determined by the interests of prevailing sociopolitical forces. Acute clashes of these interests in the international arena have led to armed conflicts and wars throughout history....Today, this tradition is leading directly into the nuclear abyss....The backbone of the new way of thinking is the recognition of the priority of human values, or to be more precise, of humankind's survival.[15]

Furthermore, according to Gorbachev, the old Marxist-Leninist ideas concerning war and revolution, particularly the idea of war as the midwife of revolution, has become not only obsolete but dangerous and must be repudiated:

[13] *Ibid.,* p. 143.
[14] *Ibid.*
[15] *Ibid.,* p. 146.

We have taken a new look at the interdependence of war and revolution. In the past, war often served to detonate revolution....The First World War provoked...the October Revolution in our country. The Second World War evoked...revolutions in Eastern Europe and Asia, as well as a powerful anti-colonial revolution. All this served to reenforce the Marxist-Leninist logic that imperialism inevitable generates major armed confrontations, while the latter naturally creates a 'critical mass' of social discontent and a revolutionary situation in a number of countries: Hence, a forecast which was long adhered to in our country: a Third World War, if unleashed by imperialism, would lead to new social upheavals which would finish off the capitalist system for good, and this would spell global peace. But when the conditions radically changed so that the only result of nuclear war could be universal destruction, we drew a conclusion about the disappearance of the cause-and-effect relationship between war and revolution.[16]

In order to underline the profundity of the Soviet change of view on the nature of the genesis, nature and likelihood of war and revolution, and its ominous implications, Gorbachev wrote the following:

At the 27th CPSU Party Congress we clearly 'divorced' the revolution and war themes, excluding from the new edition of the Party Program the following two phases: 'Should the imperialist aggressors nevertheless venture to start a new world war, the peoples will no longer tolerate a system which drags them into devastating wars. They will sweep imperialism away and bury it.' This provision, admitting in theory, the possibility of a new world war was removed as not corresponding to the realities of the nuclear era.[17]

In other words, the earlier assurances and certitudes that even in the event of a nuclear war, the world would suffer immensely, but capitalism would perish while socialism would nevertheless survive, has been repudiated.

Gorbachev's new political thinking went a long way in the tortuous process of attempting to restructure the foundations of Soviet legitimacy, shifting it away from success in transforming the external world to success in developing Soviet society. Cheap gains in the Third World proved to be an expensive and inadequate surrogate for an exhausted and impoverished universal ideology, and a less evanescent basis for legitimacy became emergent, a legitimacy founded upon effective performance (*perestroika*), and acceptability (*glasnost-democratization*) rather than upon abstract propositions. The new political thinking also went a long way in repudiating the notion that the legitimacy of the Soviet system can only be validated by the demise of capitalism, a proposition that appears not only increasingly unattainable but also one that Gorbachev recognizes can only promise to generate further international tension and conflict between the Soviet Union and the Western world. The new political thinking thus took a big step in the direction of replacing the sequential concept of coexistence with a parallel concept, and dissipating the Soviet conviction that only the destruction of capitalism can retroactively validate the Bolshevik Revolution and legitimize the Soviet system.

[16]*Ibid.*, p. 147.
[17]*Ibid.*, p. 148.

Changing the Soviet Foreign Policy Agenda

The new political thinking played an important role in changing the Soviet foreign policy agenda and recasting domestic and external priorities across the board. In the first place, deideologization of Soviet foreign policy, the subordination of the international class struggle to "peaceful coexistence" and the "interests of mankind" signaled the renunciation of code words for Soviet expansion, ideological militancy, and support of Third World regimes and movements in accordance with ideological criteria. For the Third World, in particular, it meant that the Soviet Union will no longer employ ideology as the principal measuring stick for defining friends and enemies. Indeed, according to Shevardnadze, the new political thinking even dispensed with the concept of international "enemies."

> The 'image of the enemy' in all its dimensions impedes the restructuring of international relations on the principles of morality and civilization. Having set out to lessen confrontation, we say to capitalist countries: 'Let us be honest opponents but not enemies. If you are ready to settle our disputes peacefully, we can even be partners.'[18]

Future Soviet foreign policy, including that in the Third World, according to Shevardnadze would be shaped by "national interests" rather than ideological interests, and even traditional cost/accounting criteria would be employed to establish foreign policy priorities. Thus, the Soviet Foreign Minister, in his June 1987 address to Foreign Ministry officials stated:

> The most important thing is that the country should not incur additional expenditures in connection with...its lawful foreign political interests....We must enhance the profitability of our foreign policy and achieve a situation in which our mutual relations with other states burden our economy to the least possible extent.[19]

Not only did Shevardnadze again refer to the "economic profitability of foreign policy" in an even more important address to the Soviet foreign policy establishment a year later, but he emphatically reaffirmed the subordination of the international class struggle to peaceful coexistence, gave higher priority to "national interests" over "class interests," and confirmed the priority of domestic interests over foreign policy interests in Gorbachev's outlook:

> The principles of the new political thinking...most clearly evidences the direct dependence of a state's foreign policy on its domestic affairs. And here rising before us is that mighty range of vitally important categories brought together by the concept of 'national interests.'...National interests are a very mobile category, dynamic and constantly changing....In the light of this concept, the philosophy of peaceful coexistence, as a universal principle of international relations, takes on a different content....Quite validly, we refuse to see it in a specific form of class struggle. Coexistence...cannot be identified with the class

[18]Shevardnadze speech of July 15, 1988, as cited in Note 11.
[19]Shevardnadze speech, June 1987, as reported in *Vestnik Ministerstva Inostrannhykh del SSSR*, 1987, (no. 2), p. 31.

struggle....It is difficult to reconcile the equating of international relations to a class struggle with a recognition of the real possibility and inevitability of peaceful coexistence, as a higher universal principle, and mutually advantageous coopera- tion between states with different socio-political systems....In order to correctly assess and ensure our national interests, it is essential to recognize the trends and understand the direction in the common movement of mankind.[20]

Gorbachev's new political thinking thus completely restructured the traditional relationship among development, coexistence, and expansion in Soviet calculations. Instead of a world characterized by social systems in mortal combat, Gorbachev's new political thinking shifted to a more traditional image of a diverse world of nations with interests in both conflict and harmony, and thus capable of resolution.

The first several years of the Gorbachev regime suggests very strongly that the new leadership had opted for consolidation and retrenchment abroad and to reform and upgrade at home. Gorbachev's agenda, for the most part, was a "wish list" that aroused considerable resistance from entrenched power centers in the Soviet system and ultimately proved to be too ambitious and utopian. When one analyzes Gorbachev's agenda, first and foremost of his objectives was to retain and consolidate power. The second item on his agenda was implementing his ambitious program designed to reform, renovate, and revitalize not only the Soviet economic system, but Soviet society as a whole.

The third item on Gorbachev's agenda finally addresses foreign policy, and here, the restructuring of Soviet-American relations assumed highest priority. The achievement of the first two items on his agenda required the existence of a stable and predictable international environment, which would ensure the absence of confrontation, surprise, and diversion of effort and resources, particularly in dealing with issues that involved the United States. The Soviet Union, during its restructuring, entered a prolonged period of vulnerability as it dismantled and attempted to restructure, and Gorbachev wanted to minimize the possibility of the United States taking advantage of periods of vulnerability. Hence amicable relations with the United States were an indispensable prerequisite for the success of his domestic agenda.

It is at once evident that Soviet policy in the Third World had failed to measure up not only against the new criteria of "economic profitability," but had damaged the Soviet Union's international image, tarnished the *credenda* of socialism, and seriously impeded the improvement of relations with both China and the United States. Concern for the international image and prestige of the Soviet Union assumed a conspicuous place in the attention of Soviet statesmen and scholars. Shevardnadze, in his address of July 1988, devoted considerable emphasis to the importance the Gorbachev leadership attached to the image and international prestige of the Soviet Union. The image of the state, he said, defines "a nation's reputation as an important element in foreign policy and as a component of state interests and national security."

[20]Shevardnadze speech of July 1988, as cited in Note 11.

Furthermore, he said:

> The image of a state, or how it is perceived by the rest of the world, develops directly and primarily from the general trend of its policy, from values and ideals that the nation defends and carries out, and from the degree to which these values and ideals conform with dominant, common human ideals and standards with its own conduct....Comrades, we must not pretend that the standards and ideas of the proper or of what is termed civilized conduct in the world community do not concern us. If you wish to be accepted in it, these must be observed.[21]

The new foreign policy outlook of the Soviet Union thus required not only a reconceptualization of its basic strategy and purposes, but reliance upon a more accurate and reliable empirical picture of actual events in the world, undistorted by ideological preconceptions.

NEW CONSTRAINTS ON SOVIET FOREIGN POLICY: DOMESTIC AND FOREIGN

The Impact of Domestic Politics and Policies on Soviet Foreign Policy

Confronted with mounting domestic problems, new constraints have emerged to shape and contain Soviet foreign policy behavior and Soviet foreign policy has become a lowered priority item on the Soviet political agenda, as the country progressively descends into a morass of social, economic, ethnic, legal, and political problems, which have deprived it of any excess energy to expend upon Soviet foreign policy activity. But ironically, the higher priority assigned to domestic issues does not so much reflect Gorbachev's *perestroika* program as it does a reflection of the old axiom that the foreign policy of any country, in the first place, is shaped and determined by domestic policies and/or conditions. In the present case, it is more the domestic conditions (deteriorating) rather than policies (ineffective) that have contributed to the lower priority of Soviet foreign policy.

To be sure, Gorbachev was awarded the Nobel Peace Prize in 1990 for his immense and undoubted contributions to world peace, and given the nature of the changes in the international system his policies have wrought, it is probably the most deserved of any Nobel Peace Prize granted since the award was instituted. What policies, virtually executed by a single statesman, have left such a fundamental impact upon the configurations of the international landscape in favor of world peace?

The same accomplishments that have earned him widespread plaudits abroad are responsible for his increasing unpopularity at home and the near universal contempt with which he is held throughout his own vast country, which seems to be on the verge of decomposition.

Initially, when Gorbachev set his reforms in motion, he apparently calculated that free expression and the generation and dissemination of

[21] *Ibid.*

information about the past and proposals for the future, together with widening participation of the citizenry, free elections and new political institutions and processes, would concurrently reform and make the economy more efficient and productive. Thus all elements of his reform program would develop in tandem. Unfortunately for Gorbachev, his ambitious program soon floundered, since it was based on a gross miscalculation of the magnitude of the obstacles and an overestimation of the capacity and willingness of the country to carry out his program. In the first place, it was easier to unleash *glasnost,* expand political participation, i.e., democratization, and to change political institutions and processes than to reform the economy and render it more efficient and productive. As *glasnost* and democratization proceeded at a rapid pace, expressions of discontent and dissent appeared at the proliferation of agendas for the future that departed from Gorbachev's vision. Economic reform hardly moved beyond the dismantlement and disorientation of existing productive forces. Destablization set in and the country started to decompose.

At the same time a curious dynamic symbiosis developed between Gorbachev's foreign policy and his domestic agenda. The highest item on Gorbachev's domestic agenda was to preserve himself in power, so that he might carry out his grand vision for the country. Since such an ambitious program would have to pass through a period of dismantlement and turmoil that might render the Soviet Union vulnerable to outside forces, Gorbachev needed a calm and predictable international environment free from tensions and possible confrontation with other powers, particularly the United States. Hence, the second item on Gorbachev's agenda was to reduce tensions with the United States and the West and to improve Soviet/American and Soviet/Western relations in order to provide a congenial international environment in which to carry out his reform program free from concern about the international situation.

The improvement of Soviet relations with the West would be extremely costly in terms of Soviet imperial positions, but the trade-off was the possibility of securing assistance from the West in rebuilding the Soviet economy. As a consequence, both the United States and Western Europe hailed and supported Gorbachev's internal reform program. Moscow, in return, became more and more accommodating on a wide range of issues: arms control and reductions, often through unilateral actions either taken voluntarily or under pressure; acceptance of the inevitability of German unification and acquiescence of a united Germany's membership in NATO; continued cooperation in settling regional conflicts in Southern Africa, Ethiopia, and Vietnam; toning down support for the Arab states and the P.L.O. in their conflict with Israel; virtual abandonment of the Sandinistas in Nicaragua and the Castro regime in Cuba, which has become increasingly isolated; exercising prudence and caution in dealing with secessionist Lithuania, refraining from the use of overt force in attempting to prevent the separation of the Baltic republic; allowing larger numbers of Jews to emigrate to Israel in spite of importunings and even threats from Arab extremists.

Whereas Gorbachev's relations with the West continued to improve and his image and popularity increased abroad, these same events created increasing difficulties for him at home. This did not mean that any credible alternative to Gorbachev had appeared either to his right or to his left on the Soviet political spectrum, although criticism from both directions continued, often neutralizing one another. The Left critics, symbolized by Boris Yeltsin and the Communist reformers and liberals in the Inter-Regional Group of Deputies and Democratic Alliance, supported Gorbachev's general foreign policy line; they applauded the even more radical reforms sweeping Eastern Europe and favored Moscow's increasing integration with the West, even the demands of the Baltic states for greater autonomy and independence. They were, however, distressed at what they considered to be Gorbachev's equivocation and, perhaps even incompetence, in dealing with the economy. Although they applauded his political reforms, including the establishment of the new Soviet presidency, they were suspicious of Gorbachev's intentions and the Soviet leader's increasing tendency to reverse fields and spring surprises.

The conservatives, on the other hand, had a great deal more about which to be concerned. They were fighting a rear-guard defensive action, were generally not in sympathy with Gorbachev's unilateral concessions and retreats in foreign policy, were opposed to even the mild reforms introduced into the economy, were scandalized by what they considered to be excesses unleashed by *glasnost*, and were outraged at Gorbachev's shrinking of the Party apparat's authority, the deprivation of the Party's political monopoly and the impending dissolution of the U.S.S.R. Many openly lamented the loss of Eastern Europe and the Soviet Union's hard-earned role and status as a global power, although even the conservatives seem relatively unconcerned with Moscow's withdrawal from the Third World.

Although not necessarily aligned with the conservatives, the professional military and its spokesmen, including Minister of Defense Dmitri Yazov, were unhappy with Gorbachev's announced military reductions, withdrawals from Eastern Europe, troop reductions in East Asia, including substantial reductions in the size of the Soviet navy and the proposed abandonment of Soviet naval installations in Vietnam. Furthermore, the Soviet military viewed with considerable apprehension the loss of East Germany and the prospect of a united Germany within the NATO alliance, as Soviet positions in Eastern Europe crumbled and the Warsaw Pact alliance dissolves. Similarly, the prospect of a revived Japan and a developing China posed insuperable hypothetical problems for those who are charged with maintaining the defense and security of the Soviet Union. As various positions along the Soviet political spectrum congealed into polarized distinct right and left aggregations, the middle ground that Gorbachev has sought to claim as his own narrowed, and ultimately Gorbachev had to choose between these two major trends.

New political movements, national fronts, and proto-political parties spontaneously proliferated, ranging from chauvinistic, even neo-Nazi type Russian nationalistic movements on the right to anarchist movements on the left, with all kinds of ideological gradiations in between. Nationalist and ethnocentric parties and movements also mounted in all the republics and among the smaller nationality groups as well. These movements also found their expression in the freely elected legislative bodies at all levels—the Congress of People's Deputies and the Supreme Soviet in particular—as various parliamentary groupings and caucuses were formed, which supported or opposed Gorbachev's views from many directions, forcing their withdrawal or revision in many cases. Free elections throughout the republics and localities in 1990 further affected Gorbachev's grand vision as non-Communist and even anti-Communist governments were elected in many republics and in the major cities, including Leningrad and Moscow. In the Russian republic, Boris Yeltsin emerged as the single most important personality and withdrew from the Communist Party—thus removing himself from its discipline—and announced his own political economic reform program, which vividly departed from that of Gorbachev. Yeltsin threatened to create a new, powerful center of power, separate from that of the central government in the Russian republic, the country's largest, containing half of the Soviet Union's population and about 75% of its territory. In the Baltic states, anti-Communist governments in Estonia, Latvia, and Lithuania declared the "restoration" of their independence and intention to secede from the Soviet Union. Similar governments were elected in Georgia and Armenia, and all other republics declared some form of "sovereignty" and "independence," but not necessarily separation.

The impending fragmentation of the U.S.S.R. and Gorbachev's vacillation impelled conservative and antiseparatist forces to close ranks and exert greater pressure. These elements had the support of the Armed Forces leadership and the KGB, as well as the residual elements of the Party Apparatus; and in late 1990 they forced Gorbachev to arrest further reform, change direction, and place at the top of his agenda preserving the Union and arresting the deterioration of Soviet power and influence in the international community. At the beginning of 1991, not only has Gorbachev removed all the old Brezhnev holdovers from the leadership, but his own reformist partisans as well. Alexander Yakovlev, the philosophical architect of Gorbachev's reform program, Foreign Minister Edward Shevardnadze, the reformist minister of foreign affairs, Vadim Bakatin and all of his reformist economic advisors were shunted aside in Gorbachev's move to the right as he relied more upon the military, the KGB, and assorted conservative party figures. Virtual martial law descended upon many areas of the country as Gorbachev sanctioned the use of force in the Baltic states and increased the power and authority of the KGB and the military to combat "corruption" and "illegality."

The Erosion of Central Power

With the delegitimization of the Party and its ideological Marxism-Leninism, Gorbachev in a single stroke deprived the U.S.S.R. of its only unifying structure and its *raison d'etre*. As Gorbachev single-mindedly relocated formal authority from the Party and its central organs, the Politburo, Secretariat, and Central Committee to the new institutions of state and government, especially his own presidential office and its various extensions, much real power flowed right through the new central institutions into the capitals of the republics, especially the Russian Federation. Under Boris Yeltsin's direction, the Russian Federation has become a center of power rivalling that of Gorbachev and the Kremlin. Both are located in Moscow, the dual capital of the U.S.S.R. and RSFSR (Russian Soviet Federated Socialist Republic). Gorbachev, as President, has concentrated immense formal juridical powers in his office, more than that of the U.S. or French Presidents, and in fact has amassed more constitutional-legal authority than any leader in the entire history of the Soviet Union, even more than Stalin. At the same time his *real* power diminished with each passing day, since he possessed no administrative-executive structure to enforce or administer his decrees and pronouncements, which were frequently ignored or greeted with legal edicts of nullification issued by the Republics, which then triggered counter-edicts of nullification by Gorbachev. With the destruction of the Party apparatus, the only administrative apparatus left intact was the governmental-state structure, which was formally under the jurisdiction of the republics. The U.S.S.R. was a loose federation in theory, but a tightly centralized state in practice, because the Party apparatus directed and controlled the state apparatus, called Soviets. With the dissolution of Party Apparatus control, the Soviets were set free, and assumed a life of their own, as the center was deprived of its controlling levers. Again, this was accomplished willfully and deliberately by Gorbachev, who expected real power would flow from the Party into the new central constitutional institutions, but instead flowed right through them and into the republics. The Politburo and Secretariat have been sidelined as decision-making bodies of the Soviet political system and are now essentially Party organs, as is Gorbachev's post of General Secretary. Party directives are no longer binding on state institutions or the republics but merely suggestive. Furthermore, the disestablishment of one-Party rule relegated the Communist Party to the position of being simply another party among many, and it may suffer the devastating fate of Communist parties in Eastern Europe, where they have been crushingly rejected in multiparty competition.

Thus, who is or is not on the Politburo and Secretariat has become irrelevant to the Soviet political process, an event, which standing by itself in more normal times, would have been hailed as of monumental significance. The new Soviet presidency is the third variant of a Soviet president with which Gorbachev has been invested in less than two years. In September 1988,

Gorbachev displaced Gromyko as Chairman of the Presidium of the Supreme Soviet, essentially the position designed by Stalin many years ago and slightly upgraded by Brezhnev in 1977. It was essential a ceremonial position that gave legal weight to the political power invested in the General Secretary. A year later Gorbachev replaced this position with a new position, more powerful and authoritative, but not yet a real president—Chairman of the Supreme Soviet. Less than a year later Gorbachev created the first authentic *Prezident* of the U.S.S.R., clearly modelled on that of the United States, with some features of the French presidency thrown in. Invested with a wide range of executive powers, the new Soviet President can issue decrees with the force of law; declare emergencies and martial law in the country; introduce and veto legislation; contract treaties and agreements; send and receive ambassadors; and function generally as the chief executive, legislative and administrative officer of the Soviet Union. He is also Chief of State, Commander-in-Chief of the Armed Forces and the supervisor of the Chairman of the Council of Ministers, which, however, was responsible to the legislative bodies. With the installation of a functioning authentic multiparty system, the relationship between these two positions could become complicated as in the French system and be a source of conflict.

Gorbachev reorganized the executive power of the Presidency and created new executive enforcement agencies under his direction. He abolished his Presidential Council and upgraded the Council of Federation as a sop to the republics; he abolished the Council of Ministers and its chairmanship (which were responsible to the legislative bodies) and replaced it with a *Cabinet* of Ministers headed by a Prime Minister, both appointed by the President and directly subordinate to him, thus assuming constitutional powers greater than that of the American or French President. The Council for Defense was abolished and a National Security Council installed in its place. Additionally, new executive agencies were created, essentially a "state inspector" to monitor observance and fulfillment of central laws and degrees that the republics and localities were flouting. At the same time virtually every republic and even some lower ethnic units have asserted the sovereign right to nullify and declare central laws—even the provisions of the Union Constitution—invalid on its territory. As a consequence, a hail of nullifications and invalidations of laws and constitutions have been dispatched back and forth as the central government declares invalid the nullifications of its laws by the republics.

The former power and authority of the Politburo, Secretariat, and General Secretary have been consolidated and shifted to the new President. The powers and authority of the Party Central Committee, in the process, have now been relocated in the Supreme Soviet, whereas the authority of the Party Congress has been relocated and shifted to the Congress of Peoples Deputies. Gorbachev thus finally destroyed the system of two governments, one formal and one real, and has created a credible version of a state ruled by law rather than arbitrary Party fiat. The next step in this continuing process will be the writing of a new Gorbachev constitution in order to systematize and stabilize the bewildering constitutional changes piled on top of one another during the past five years. Even the highest Soviet authorities have difficulty in finding an up-to-date version of the constitution, since no sooner has one fundamental part of the constitution been amended than it is amended and even reamended in turn.

As President, Gorbachev retains control of the armed forces in his capacity as constitutional commander-in-chief (there are no counterparts in the republics), and the KGB now reports exclusively to the President; but unlike the armed forces, the KGB has republic counterparts, which are in many cases responding to republic authorities rather than to Moscow.

As previously noted, even the armed forces are faced with a difficult choice, since, except for the professional officer corps, the military is made up of recruits from the republics, increasingly non-Russian in character. Almost all of the republics have issued declarations, pronouncements and even laws limiting the presence of the military on their soil, demanding that recruits serve on the soil of their native republics, calling for the establishment of alternative service to the military, and urging that provisions for conscientious objector status be instituted. Interethnic strife is rampant in the military, desertions are on the increase, draft evasion has risen, and republics are lax in their enforcement of existing military obligations. Native militias have also sprung up in various parts of the country, often to prevent this or that part of a given republic from splitting off from the republic itself.

The Emergence of Republic Foreign Policies

Although Soviet foreign policy remains under Gorbachev's jurisdiction, the various declarations of sovereignty and expressions of secessionist sentiment across the land, and the near complete autonomy of a number of republics—most notably the Baltic states, the Ukraine, Moldavia, Georgia, Armenia, and Azerbaidzhan—foreign policy is increasingly becoming diffused as individual republics, beginning with the Russian republic, announced intentions of pursuing their own separate, parallel foreign policies, and are considering the establishment of separate diplomatic representation abroad. Republics are already signing a limited number of cultural, trade, and other types of agreements and treaties with one another, as well as with neighboring foreign countries.

Aside from republics recognizing and reenforcing each others' declarations of sovereignty and autonomy, they have also signed various bilateral agreements with the RSFSR and other republics on trade, culture and other matters, independent of Moscow's authority. Some republics have established low-level diplomatic exchanges with Eastern European countries and have signed cultural and trade agreements. Moldavia even entered into a trade agreement with a central African state (Burundi), even though both countries are completely landlocked.

The Ukraine, Byelorussia and the RSFSR have signed separate agreements with Poland as "sovereign" states, although Byelorussia claims territory from both Poland and Lithuania, should the latter secede. The Polish-RSFSR declaration of friendship and cooperation calls for the future exchange of diplomatic and consular officials, and both have reaffirmed the validity of the current borders between the RSFSR and Poland. The RSFSR actually would have no border with Poland were it not for the Kaliningrad province (formerly Northern East Prussia), which is territorially separated from the RSFSR by Byelorussia and Lithuania. Azerbaidzhan has also signed a number of agreements with Iran.

The Baltic states have been very active, quietly and without fanfare, seeking some sort of diplomatic recognition from abroad. Sweden and Norway, for example, supported the request of the Baltic states for separate observer status in future CSCE (Conference of Security and Cooperation in Europe) meetings, and Iceland has extended diplomatic recognition of Lithuania. Other republics in the European U.S.S.R., the Ukraine, Byelorussia, Moldavia, RSFSR, Georgia, and Armenia are all contemplating separate and parallel overtures to join various European organizations and associations. It should also be expected that some, if not all, Soviet republics may ask to be admitted to the United Nations as separate members, alongside the Ukraine and Byelorussia, but no longer simply as instruments of Moscow. Even the Yakut autonomous republic (subordinate to the RSFSR) has made a separate commercial agreement with a South Korean firm to process Yakutia's resources. And other autonomous republics within the RSFSR, like the Tatar (whose population exceeds that of five Union republics), which have unilaterally upgraded themselves to Union Republics, may seek outside recognition. Since this is all allowed under the constitution, there is little that Gorbachev can do to prevent it as Moscow enters into rivalry and competition with its own republics in dealing with the outside world, especially on matters of trade and culture. Previously, the Party *apparat* ensured that the republics' foreign policy rights, which were only symbolic, remained under wraps, but now that *apparat* is gone.

Separatist sentiment is exceedingly infectious, and not only is the U.S.S.R. in danger of decomposition, but the fifteen republics, in turn, are faced with the prospect of fragmentation as well, especially republics like the Russian, Georgian, and Azerbaidzhani, which have subrepublics within them. Of these, it is the RSFSR (that accounts for nearly 150 million people and about three-quarters of the country's territory), which faces the same prospect of decomposition as does the U.S.S.R. itself. The RSFSR is made up of more than a score of autonomous republics, autonomous regions, and national districts, depending upon the size of the ethnic group involved. Some of these ethnic groups are small in number, but their names grace large stretches of territory as national republics, regions, or districts. As the RSFSR and other Union republics have issued declarations of sovereignty, autonomy, and threats to separate, these subunits are doing the same with respect to the RSFSR. Virtually every ethnic unit in the RSFSR has issued a declaration of sovereignty or autonomy of one kind or another. Autonomous republics are unilaterally declaring themselves Union republics; autonomous regions are promoting themselves to autonomous republics, and national districts are upgrading themselves to autonomous regions. Vast areas of the RSFSR, including the Irkutsk region of Siberia and the Far East are requesting regional autonomy, although they are not ethnically distinct. Yakutia, one of the largest autonomous republics in the RSFSR, has declared that all of the natural resources on its soil—gold, diamonds, etc.—are the property of Yakutia rather than the RSFSR or the U.S.S.R.

As these assertions of autonomy are pronounced, a steady stream of ethnic Russians are leaving not only the Union republics, but the ethnic units within the RSFSR itself. All this motion is creating mass paranoia among sectors of ethnic Russians, who hitherto were the dominant nationality. Given the manner in which the multinational administrative structure was erected, an ethnic Russian administrative identity seems to be missing. Up until recently, the Russians did not have their own Communist Party or their own Academy of Sciences, since this was considered to be superfluous and inefficient. It also conveyed the impression that the U.S.S.R. was really Russia in multinational drag. But as both the U.S.S.R. and the RSFSR are faced with decomposition, no definitive ethnic Russian republic or state seems to exist. Like the U.S.S.R., the RSFSR was the sum of its parts, and when the parts come apart, no Russian republic is left, since the architects of the U.S.S.R. and the RSFSR neglected to design a "Russian republic" within the RSFSR.

CHARTING THE FUTURE DIRECTIONS OF SOVIET FOREIGN POLICIES

Given the prevailing turmoil and uncertainty governing the domestic situation in the Soviet Union, charting future directions of Soviet foreign policy has been rendered even more hazardous than ever. While the continued existence of something called the U.S.S.R. or Soviet Union is being increasingly called into question, a unified Soviet foreign policy is tenuous. Will the center hold? Will the Union survive, or will it fragment into its several component national parts or shrink in dimension as several republics depart? Even the names of the revised Union may change as several proposals, including one by Gorbachev (which he later withdrew) have already been discussed. No clear answer was provided in the all-union public referendum held in March 1991. The Baltic states and some other republics (notably Moldavia, Georgia, and Armenia) continue to fan "independence."

Nevertheless, for the moment, there is a Soviet Union, and there is a declared foreign policy by the central government, and one may gingerly examine the directions in which this declared central foreign policy is pointed with respect to a number of selected functional and geographical issues. But above all it must be reemphasized that if for the near future Gorbachev's primary goal is to remain in power and to succeed, he must first preserve the Union. But as Gorbachev abandoned and was, in turn, abandoned by his original cohort of reformers and has shifted towards the right, it should be noted that he is essentially anathema to the conservative forces upon which he is relying and remains at the helm largely because the reformers are neither sufficiently united nor powerful enough to constitutionally replace Gorbachev. The conservatives, while having more powerful levers and constituencies at their disposal, lack the credentials of legitimacy and acceptability to forcibly oust the President. Although Gorbachev is vastly unpopular among all sectors of the public, he has so sufficiently institutionalized the legitimacy of his power that it will become indeed almost impossible to remove him constitutionally, except for violating the constitution (the Soviet version of presidential impeachment, which requires a two-thirds vote in the Congress of People's Deputies).

Soviet-American Relations

Soviet-American relations will remain at the top of Gorbachev's foreign policy agenda, and the selection of Bessmertykh over the open opposition of Gorbachev's new conservative allies were an indication of his determination. The new foreign minister has spent over twenty years of his professional career in the United States, is an accomplished Americanologist, well-known and liked by important American circles. Moscow will be somewhat more difficult to deal with in light of the charge that Gorbachev has been too compliant and suppliant in his relations with the United States, and hence will probably ask for more concessions and a higher price in return to continued cooperation and support of U.S. policy, and in particular, President Bush's vision of a "new world order." Soviet military decline will be arrested, or rather attempts will be made to slow down the withdrawal of Soviet troops from Eastern Europe and East Germany, perhaps as a move to extract even greater economic and financial assistance. The new foreign minister's initial move in this direction was to question the extent to which military force should be used against Iraq, once hostilities ensued in January 1991, forcing Secretary of State Jim Baker into signing a joint statement suggesting a linkage between the Iraq withdrawal from Kuwait and an international conference to consider all conflicts and issues in the Middle East, including the Arab-Israeli dispute. No sooner was the statement issued than Washington hastened to aver that no "linkage" was suggested or implied, a clear contradiction with the literal words of the declaration. Furthermore, Soviet military figures have been openly critical of Soviet support for U.S. policy in the Gulf, and it is quite likely that Moscow will attempt to gradually distance itself from the American position and adopt, if not an opposing policy, at least a parallel, rather than supporting, position.

The Soviet-American agenda, however, has been framed more by Washington, than Moscow, with Moscow as supplicant and Washington (and Western Europe) the supplier. Gorbachev has been making important political, military, and diplomatic concessions in return for economic and financial support. This has resulted in a symbiosis that will be difficult to sunder. The Soviet-American agenda revolves around four major issues: (1) arms control and reduction; (2) settlement of regional conflicts; (3) expanding human rights in the Soviet Union, including freedom of exit, and no use of force in dealing with the Baltic republic; and (4) cooperation in settling the Persian Gulf crisis.

Arms Control and Reduction Issues

Among the casualties of the collapse of the Soviet Union as a global power and the concurrent dissolution of the bipolar system has been arms control and negotiations, not necessarily because of disagreements, but because they are becoming increasingly irrelevant. Rather than arms control negotiations driving events, developments and events worldwide and within NATO and the WTO are driving arms controls negotiations, which increasingly no longer prescribe but confirm what has already transpired spontaneously and unilaterally in the Soviet Union, the United States, and their allied states. Thus, both the draft provisions of START I and the proposed reduction in conventional forces have been overtaken by political processes in Moscow and Washington.

In fact, by the summer of 1991 agreements on conventional forces in Europe had been reached that involved sizeable reductions of NATO and Soviet forces, providing for force levels that would make it impossible for either side to attack the other, and negotiations on START seem to be progressing rapidly. There was reason to expect that an overall agreement would be reached, and in fact it was, during Bush's visit in the summer of 1991. In return there was every reason to expect that the Soviets would receive economic aid from the United States and the European states, and that consideration for such aid was given at the meeting of the industrialized nations in the middle of June that Gorbachev attended. Clearly economic considerations were overtaking both political and military ones.

It should be noted, however, that as Gorbachev's constitutional powers have increased, his de facto power has diminished considerably. Currently he seems to have plenipotentiary powers only in the areas of foreign policy and defense. These are also being eroded by challenges from the republics and by critics from the left, right, and center. Whether Gorbachev can deliver what he negotiates with the West and the United States will become increasingly dubious. And the United States must be prepared at some point to be confronted with new and perhaps multiple authorities claiming to represent the U.S.S.R. in parts or as a whole. While the direction of events is generally towards lessening the possibility of all-out confrontation, the element of uncertainty and unpredictability in the specific details and timing of events simultaneously increases. As the U.S.S.R. fragments and weakens, the predictability of its behavior diminishes.

Regional Conflicts and the Third World

The United States and the Soviet Union see eye to eye on virtually every regional conflict in the world, including that in the Persian Gulf. But, regional conflicts have assumed a life of their own, independent of the global powers. The United States and the U.S.S.R. have reached agreement on their respective roles and positions in southern Africa, East Africa, Southeast Asia, and Afghanistan, but the local protagonists have their own agendas and these do not correspond with those of the superpowers. The fighting goes on in all of these areas as pure civil wars and domestic insurrections, with only the residual involvement of the superpowers. Eritrea has virtually won its war against Addis-Ababa, but the Mengistu regime continues to resist Eritrean independence. In Angola, the Luanda regime and Jonas Savimbi have yet to mend their fences and resolve their conflict into a government of national conciliation; the civil war in Cambodia drags on, even though all of the outside powers have reached agreement, and there appears to be no end in sight for the conflict in Afghanistan.

On the other hand, now that global power rivalry is a thing of the past, Washington and Moscow are devoting less attention to these marginal conflicts and are devoting greater attention to the new dangerous Gulf crisis, and the Arab-Israeli dispute looms as a big challenge to future superpower cooperation in settling regional conflicts.

Soviet policy in the Middle East and the Third World generally continues to support the reduction of tensions and the withdrawal from positions and policies that aggravate and sustain local and regional conflicts.

The most critical impact of the policies of Moscow and the developments in Eastern Europe on the Middle East has been on the psychological, political, and military correlation of forces between Israel and the Arab world. Israel's principal enemies in the region, Syria and the P.L.O., have been deprived of their principal external patron, and they have modulated their behavior accordingly, especially the P.L.O. Furthermore, several East European countries have resumed full diplomatic relations with Israel, and the Soviet Union may soon follow. Various forms of semiofficial, unofficial and lower-level diplomatic contact between Moscow and Israel have increased, and Gorbachev has opened the way for up to a million Soviet Jews to emigrate to Israel and elsewhere. Rising anti-Semitism in Russia and elsewhere in Eastern Europe will only accelerate the exodus, and many East European countries are willing to facilitate the process. In spite of terrorist threats by various Arab organizations against Soviet and Eastern European carriers flying Soviet Jews to Israel, after being initially intimidated into canceling the agreement allowing direct flights from Moscow, Budapest and elsewhere, these countries restated their intention to allow them. Whether Arab terrorists will proceed with their threats is at this point unknown, but should such threats be carried out, it may serve to sever the remaining slender threads that link Moscow with their erstwhile Arab clients.

The impact of the Eastern European revolution on Arab fortunes was so damaging that President Hafez Assad of Syria publicly hinted that the events in Eastern Europe were the product of a Jewish plot, since Israel and the Jews, in his view, were the chief beneficiaries of the revolution! The expected flow of new Jewish emigrants, perhaps up to a million over five years, was highly welcome to many in Israel but it antagonized the Arab leaders.

There is little doubt that the Arab position vis-à-vis Israel has been considerably weakened. Syria, in particular, fears that its pipeline to modern weaponry has been shut down and whatever commercial interest that Moscow had in selling arms to Syria was no longer reenforced with a diplomatic or political interest. The P.L.O. is left stranded and hanging as Israel increasingly displays little interest in entering into negotiations. Above all, the threat that the Arab-Israeli conflict was a potential tinderbox that could set off a global U.S.-U.S.S.R. confrontation has virtually disappeared.

In other parts of the Third World, in Cambodia, Ethiopia, and the Caribbean region, Soviet policy has been a moderating influence. It certainly did little to encourage the Sandinistas to spurn free elections and their unexpected outcome. Relations with Castro are strained and will probably deteriorate even more. Like Iraq and North Korea, Cuba will increasingly become a world pariah state, out of step and tune with current global trends. In East Africa, Moscow has, de facto, withdrawn whatever political and military support for Mengistu's attempt to put down the Eritrean and Tigrean rebellions and has called upon the Ethiopian regime to negotiate with the rebels. All Soviet advisers and workers in the two regions have been withdrawn. Moscow's decision to no longer support the attempt to quash these two rebellious movements, ironically followed a policy that Castro had instituted from the very beginning of Cuba's involvement in the Ethiopian war. This move by Moscow serves to strengthen the bargaining leverage of the rebels and may encourage a settlement.

In southern Africa, the paths of Foreign Minister Shevarnadze and Secretary of State Baker crossed once again as both attended the ceremonies celebrating the independence of Namibia, a principal achievement of the first successful joint venture in the resolution of regional conflicts. Although Moscow has not yet established diplomatic relations with South Africa, President de Klerk's policies have been given wide media attention, most of it very favorable. Moscow's influence over the ANC (African National Congress) is more modest than widely assumed, but the Soviet Union has clearly come out against a violent resolution of the situation in South Africa; and Moscow appears to be more in tune with Nelson Mandela's conciliatory approach than that of the ANC party line, which is still confrontational. Moscow is still searching for a way to justify early establishment of diplomatic relations with South Africa.

Human Rights

In the area of human rights, considerable progress has been made as Moscow has permitted thousands of its citizens to leave the Soviet Union. Although the new policy has yet to be codified into law, which must be done before the United States can extend "most favored nation" treatment to Soviet imports, Washington has praised Moscow for its actions. On the Baltic front, however, the situation appears to be deteriorating, and Soviet-American relations may be affected. The United States has never recognized the incorporation of the Baltic states into the U.S.S.R., but it has simultaneously refrained from encouraging Baltic separation and warned Moscow that continued economic and financial assistance would depend on Moscow's restraint in handling Baltic's separation, especially in Lithuania, even if it defies Soviet authorities and attempts to recede. This creates a complex and vexing dilemma for Gorbachev, since the top items on his domestic and foreign policy agendas are in hostage to one another, and his survival depends both upon his ability to preserve the union and to receive massive financial and economic support for his reform program. The United States is caught in a comparable dilemma. Successful resolution of the Persian Gulf crisis requires Soviet cooperation, but increasingly Moscow threatens to link cooperation in the Gulf in return for U.S. and Western restraint in punishing Moscow for using strong action in the Baltic republics to preserve the Union. At this point, Washington appears to have little or no interest in the decomposition of the Soviet Union, because the consequences might be more turmoil and uncertainty as a mighty state loaded with nuclear weapons unravels.

The Soviet Union and Europe

Almost as high on Gorbachev's foreign policy agenda is the improvement of Soviet-West European relations and Moscow's hope to be accepted into the European house. This hope was a powerful factor in Gorbachev's decision to abandon Soviet control of Eastern Europe and allow German unification.

The eruption of the Persian Gulf crisis and the threat it poses to the developed world emphasizes the inadequacy of security arrangements and institutions, which were designed specifically to diminish conflict in Europe, to prevent and resolve conflicts outside the framework of the NATO and WTO alliances. NATO and the WTO were by definition European security organizations, and the security equilibrium that resulted from their interactions created an extended security umbrella over the entire globe because the two leaders of the two organizations were simultaneously global powers with responsibilities, interests, and obligations outside the jurisdiction of the two alliance organizations. Hence, ironically, the collapse of this system simultaneously diminished the threat of military confrontation in Europe and created the circumstances that increased the possibility of regional conflicts elsewhere, which could seriously impinge upon the interests of the center.

And while the threat of military conflict between East and West diminished, the possibility of widespread instability in the Soviet Union and Eastern Europe as a whole and internationality and domestic turmoil in individual countries in the East has increased immeasurably. Thus any future international order must have security arrangements that can deal simultaneously with the instability unleashed by the disintegration of Soviet power in Eastern Europe and extra-European regional conflicts elsewhere, at a time when Western Europe was consolidating and deepening its own integration processes, which now may be interrupted or arrested.

Of the two alliance systems, the WTO was formally dissolved as a military organization on April 1, 1991. Without it, given the disintegrative processes taking place in the U.S.S.R., the crippled condition of the Soviet military establishment, and the projected withdrawal of Soviet troops from Hungary and Czechoslovakia by the end of 1991 and the evacuation of Soviet troops from Poland and Eastern Germany somewhat later, the existing countries and any new potential states that may emerge in Eastern Europe will be bereft of any viable multilateral economic, political, or security organizations and structures.

In contrast, Western Europe appears to have a plethora of overlapping multilateral organizations, whose consolidation and integration may be seriously disturbed by the atomization processes in Eastern Europe. The only acceptable organizational tie left in Eastern Europe is their membership in the loosely organized and vaguely defined CSCE, the Conference on Security and Cooperation in Europe, consisting of thirty-four members, including Canada and the United States, but excluding Albania, the only European state not involved. Based upon the Helsinki accords of 1975, the CSCE is so amorphous that until 1990 it had neither a staff nor even a mailing address and could hardly be described as an association, much less an organization. It is, however, the closest approximation to an all-European or pan-European organization and hence has inevitably become the focus of attention as the possible vehicle for the unification of Europe as a whole.

Plans have already been set into motion to transmute the CSCE from its current state into an authentic organization; i.e., to convert a "conference" into a "council" as the first stage. At the CSCE summit held in Paris on November 19, 1990, attended by the heads of state or governments of thirty-four states, including President Bush, the first steps in this process were taken. Whereas Moscow is eager to endorse Czech President Havel's suggestion that a reconstructed CSCE be structured as a pan-European security organization to replace both NATO and WTO, the United States and other NATO members still see a separate and important role for NATO, but with a new set of purposes and functions. Whereas German Foreign Minister Genscher leans towards the Havel proposal, Poland and Hungary wish to preserve NATO while abolishing the WTO and see NATO as the initial vehicle of an expanded European security organization that will keep the U.S.

presence in Europe to function as a counterpoise to both the growing power of Germany and the declining, but still considerable, power of the U.S.S.R. Furthermore, it will serve to ensure that a unified Germany will remain a European Germany and prevent Europe from becoming a German Europe.

Thus, for the immediate present, both NATO and a reconstituted CSCE will exist together. At the Paris summit, the CSCE was institutionalized and provided with a secretariat, staff, and a headquarters. It will house a Center for Conflict Prevention and Resolution, an agency to monitor elections, and will schedule regular meetings of heads of states, governments, and foreign ministers, rather than rely upon the *ad hoc* conferences that have prevailed up to now. One of the new agencies will be located in Eastern Europe, perhaps Prague.

Gorbachev's ultimate ambition is to become a full member of the European community, or for the U.S.S.R. to emerge as an authentic fourth center of economic power, alongside the United States, Japan, and Europe, playing an intercontinental role with links to both Europe and the Pacific rim. This would be the counterpart to America's role and status as an economic interoceanic power with links to both Europe and East Asia.

Soviet fears that a united Germany might dominate the European community economically are shared by many other European countries. Moscow, however, has a more specific concern as well—that East-Central Europe, which had been a Soviet sphere of influence since the war, will now gradually become a part of a German sphere, as German economic penetration and influence fill the vacuum created by the collapse of Soviet power and presence in the region. At this stage, it may be premature to speak of the possible conversion of German economic might into political and military power, but the potential is always there, even with a loosely structured federalized Germany. Hence, many prominent Soviet scholars and experts did not take seriously Gorbachev's and Shevarnadze's declarations that a united Germany could not be a member of NATO, since according to these analysts, a so-called neutral Germany outside NATO, and with the Warsaw Pact in shambles, would, in fact, be an unfettered Germany—a "loose cannon" was one metaphor employed—that could then pursue its own independent policy free from either friendly or unfriendly restraints. These Soviet observers see a united German membership in NATO as a positive development, since the organization would exercise restraints and controls over Germany's political and military ambitions within the framework of a friendly alliance. With the United States as the head of the NATO alliance, its troops in Europe, particularly in Germany, would increasingly be perceived as a restraint on German power rather than a threat to Moscow, and NATO would be viewed more as a conflict restraining and containing mechanism than as an alliance.

With the self-dissolution of the WTO, NATO becomes the only de facto security organization in Europe and the one that may assume the contours of an all-European security organization or the basis for one within the framework of the Helsinki formula. Somewhat unexpectedly, the foreign minister of Hungary, Gyula Horn, opined that Hungary might want to join NATO, or at least, its political unit. Other East European countries have expressed similar notions. As developments continue along current lines, the role of the United States in Europe may change imperceptibly into becoming the major force that keeps rising German power and declining Soviet power from clashing, thus serving as the main factor allowing for the free and independent development of Eastern Europe, relieved of inordinate worry that either the Russians will return or Germany will be tempted to reassert what it may consider its historical role in the region. It was for this reason that Moscow failed to win support from its Warsaw Pact allies at the most recent meeting of the organization this past March 1990 in Prague, for its view that a unified Germany's membership in NATO was out of the question. Czechoslovakia and Poland seemed to actually favor a unified Germany's membership, whereas the other members refrained from endorsing the Soviet position. It was widely held that the Soviet Union would never allow a unified Germany to be integrated into NATO, but in return for a generous "bribe" amounting to about 12 billion Marks from West Germany, Gorbachev relented and probably concluded that on the whole, a united Germany inside NATO would be less dangerous than one outside the framework of any security organization.

The Soviet Union and East Asia

The abdication of Soviet domination of Eastern Europe, the imminent reunification of Germany, and the movement towards Europe 1992 could not but have their impact on the East Asian scene, since the Soviet Union will function increasingly in that region less as a global power than as a regional power. Moscow, in effect, has given up its global role in this region in return for reclaiming its geocultural identity as a Eurasian actor, with its interests more focused and concentrated rather than diffused around the globe.

As a result, the equilibrium in East Asia is about to be rearranged as well, as Moscow renounces its primarily military-naval presence in East Asia and replaces it with an ambition to become a multidimensional actor in the East Asian region by expanding its political, diplomatic, and economic connections with the other actors in the region while simultaneously renouncing its former ideological ambitions and reducing its military presence. The improvement of relations with China, the defusing of the tension along the Sino-Soviet frontier, the Soviet rapprochement with South Korea, Moscow's interest in breaking the impasse with Japan, the withdrawal from Afghanistan, cooperation in settling the regional conflicts in the Indo-Chinese peninsula, and the intense interest shown in the economic successes of Singapore, Taiwan, and Hong Kong, (and, of course, South Korea) are all indications of Gorbachev's ambition to convert the Soviet Union into a full-fledged member of the new East Asian co-prosperity sphere. These ambitions are not designed to counteract the role of the United States in the region nor to diminish the role and influence of other actors in the region, but rather as in Europe, designed to allow Moscow to participate in the immense prosperity of the two regions of which it has been a part geographically.

There is little question but that the Asian-Pacific rim as a whole, and its northeastern component in particular, where five existing and potential economic giants (the United States, U.S.S.R., Japan, China, and Korea) intersect, will emerge by the year 2000 as the second center of scientific-technological-economic power in the world. Europe will remain the first, with the U.S.S.R. and the United States increasingly a part of both rather than as separate economic centers of power as they are today. The Northern Hemisphere will gradually merge into a single circumorbital region as the first and second worlds lose their separate identities and move together, with the U.S.S.R. and the United States constituting the two bridges uniting Europe and East Asia.

The Soviet abandonment of a global role, the renunciation of its ideological pretensions, and the reduction of its military capabilities have also fundamentally altered the strategic calculus of Northeast Asia. Moscow will remain a nuclear power, but given the changing strategic context, the three nuclear powers in the region (Moscow, Beijing, and Washington) must recognize that as the economic leverage of Japan and Korea grows, the nuclear calculus may change correspondingly. Either existing nuclear capabilities must be radically reduced, or new members of the nuclear club from the rising economic powers will have to be admitted. At any rate, neither Germany nor Japan can for long be excluded from decisive participation in the regulation, reduction, and distribution of nuclear weapons.

Nevertheless, in both regions, the likelihood of conflict has been reduced dramatically, and the prospects for cooperation among the major powers of the Northern Hemisphere have never been brighter, as all major parties seek to promote their interests not at the expense of one another, but through the processes of mutually beneficial transactions. The real problems will emerge not so much the consequence of policies and intentions, but the consequences of uneven capabilities and potential. The three Communist countries in the region, in contrast to the three non-Communist actors, are economic disaster areas, and whether they can develop scientific-technological capabilities sufficient to become full partners or remain for some time as primary sources of raw materials and targets of external development is by no means clear. In addition, the Soviet Union is experiencing fundamental domestic problems of a political and ethnodemographic nature that can affect not only the sociopolitical character of the Soviet Union, but the very existence of the Soviet state in its current structure. It is by no means certain that what currently constitutes the East Asian provinces of the Soviet state will even be a part of the current state that exists. The Soviet Union may fragment into its demographic and regional parts, and eastern Siberia may become part of a diminished Soviet Union, a resurrected Russian national state, or even a separate state entity.

It is no great secret that the obstacle to improved and expanded Soviet-Japanese relations stems almost entirely from Moscow's refusal to acknowledge that Japan's claim to four small islands at the bottom of the Kurile Island chain and just north of Hokkaido has a valid basis and thus refuses to discuss their possible redisposition. It is the dispute over these four small islands that has poisoned Soviet-Japanese relations, and both countries have paid a high price for their positions, especially the U.S.S.R., although the balance in costs may shift more unfavorably towards Japan, as Moscow relies more and more upon South Korea as a surrogate economic partner in East Asia. Moscow will have to pay a price here, as well, but of a different kind, which will be considered shortly.

Gorbachev is determined to change the nature of the Soviet image and presence in East Asia. Recognizing that Moscow is perceived primarily as an unwelcome military intruder in the region with expansionist aims, it has been more or less politically and economically bottled up in its northeast corner of Siberia for the past two decades. Relations with China have been tense, with Japan, uncongenial, and with the smaller tigers virtually nonexistent. Moscow has stood impotently by as the East Asian economies have become an ever greater factor of productivity in the world market, while Russia's East Asian resources remained relatively unexploited and the development of the region in a condition of stagnation.

Gorbachev has set about to normalize relations with China—which has been accomplished to a degree—to find a breakthrough in the logjammed relations with Japan, and to contrive some mechanism for taking advantage of the eagerness of South Korea, Hong Kong, Taiwan, Singapore, and other countries to expand their economic markets beyond the United States and Canada. At the same time, relations with Vietnam have deteriorated as Moscow admitted the bad developmental advice it earlier gave to Hanoi and now advocates that the Vietnamese completely restructure their development to accord with the new wisdom blowing from Moscow. Neither the economic nor political relations between the two countries have proven productive.

Recognizing that the Soviet military presence in East Asia had become not only inordinately expensive but increasingly counterproductive, Gorbachev has, in effect, decided to arrest its military-naval competition with the United States in the region and has called for a one-third reduction in Soviet naval forces and the closing down of Soviet naval facilities in Vietnam including Cam Ranh Bay. This, in turn, reduces the military-strategic importance of the islands in question. By improving relations with the new industrializing countries of the region, Gorbachev hopes to make the Soviet Union an active partner in the Pacific rim, mainly through various types of ventures that would exploit the vast potential of eastern Siberia.

South Korea occupies a central role in Gorbachev's strategy for bringing Moscow into the Pacific Rim club as a full participant. Expanding relations with South Korea can bring direct economic benefits as it simultaneously pressures and sensitizes Japan into realizing what it might lose in the way of economic opportunities. South Korea became the opening wedge of Moscow's entry into the Pacific Rim club, as the Soviet Union concentrated on initiating and expanding its relations with Seoul. By the end of 1990, the Soviet Union and South Korea established full diplomatic relations, and the Presidents of the two countries had met together twice. Mutually beneficial economic and commercial agreements were also consummated and South Korean enterprises energetically invested in Soviet economic development. With cordial relations established by Moscow and Eastern Europe with South Korea, North Korea is becoming increasingly isolated, and the foundations are being laid, unintentionally or not, for an East Asian replay of German unification, with South Korea in a good position to replay the West German role.

The Soviet-South Korean rapprochement will ultimately seriously affect the existing economic, political, and diplomatic equilibrium in East Asia, but the military implications will be minimal, except for further reducing specific military tensions. Neither the Soviet Union nor the United States is interested in seeking affirmative strategic or military advantage in the region, but the balance of economic interests may be substantially in favor of the U.S.S.R., and possibly to the disadvantage of the United States, and Japan cannot for long stand idly by and watch South Korea and perhaps the other NICs as well capture a dominant economic foothold in the large, unfulfilled Soviet and East European market. Of course, Tokyo has already made its moves in Eastern Europe, but its greatest opportunities lie in expanded relations with Moscow.

One must also expect that Moscow will continue to explore further opportunities that Hong Kong, Taiwan, Singapore, and other states of the region offer. Trade with Taiwan is increasing steadily, and much interest is evinced in Taiwan by many prominent Soviet citizens; its image in the Soviet media has also improved. But Taiwan is a much more delicate matter than South Korea; irritating North Korea may be a luxury Moscow can afford, but annoying China over Taiwan can send Sino-Soviet relations back into a tailspin. Therefore, unless Beijing's attitude changes, Moscow will continue to deal very gingerly with Taiwan as it expands its commercial relations.

GORBACHEV AT THE CROSSROADS

Given the weakness and domestic turmoil in the U.S.S.R., Soviet foreign policy has been remarkably docile and cooperative, and the two may not be unrelated. At times, Moscow's foreign policy assumed the appearance of a wagging tail attached to an American dog, as it responded favorably to American international initiatives. As a result, both Gorbachev and Shevarnadze were charged by domestic critics with undermining the country's strength and then using the resulting impotence of Moscow as the rationale for its submissive behavior. Both have been virtually accused of treason for allowing East Europe to break away, permitting the near dissolution of the Warsaw alliance, making a gratuitous gift of the GDR to West Germany, and even deserting a former ally,

Iraq, in time of need. According to the critics, none of this was necessary and was the result of deliberate policy by Gorbachev. They have further accused the two of endangering the security of the country and putting it on the path of disintegration. At one point, rumors were widespread that the military in conjunction with hardline critics was planning to overthrow Gorbachev. Although these fears eventually died down, whether Gorbachev remains in power or not, his authority and importance has diminished considerably; and he may have already exhausted his contribution in bringing the U.S.S.R. closer to the West and promoting its ultimate, if delayed, revitalization and reconstitution as a civilized normal society.

By the end of 1990, conservative critics of Gorbachev decided to make their move and put pressure on Moscow to arrest the decline of Soviet power, especially military power. Both the progressive disintegration of the U.S.S.R., in all of its dimensions, and the broad concessions that Shevarnadze and Gorbachev made in arms control negotiations with the United States, whereby Moscow agreed to substantially reduce its conventional and strategic weapons in return for a modest reduction in American arsenals, aroused sharp domestic criticism. Aside from this, Gorbachev's *perestroika*, i.e., economic reform, not only dismantled the old economic structures without creating new replacements, but plunged the country into deeper economic decline, with widespread shortages of ordinary goods and services. As a result, the ruble became virtually worthless, and Gorbachev's attempt to reduce the amount of rubles in circulation by declaring 50 and 100 ruble notes no longer legal tender aroused widespread discontent and unpopularity.

Unfortunately for Gorbachev, however, the other two legs of his reform program, *glasnost* and democratization, were succeeding all too well and contributed immensely to the destabilization and disintegration of the country, by unleashing a wide spectrum of vocal discontent and encouraging the republics and nationalities to chart their own political and economic directions, including secession from the Union.

As a result of Shevarnadze's departure from the leadership and the sidelining of Gorbachev's original team of reformers, both Soviet domestic policy and foreign policy are likely to depart from the course set by Shevarnadze. At home, Gorbachev will attempt to preserve the Union at all costs, including at least marginal use of force; and this is bound to aggravate relations with the United States and Western Europe. As a consequence, economic and financial assistance may be withheld, which in turn may impel Moscow to lessen or withdraw its support of U.S. policies in the Middle East, arrest or postpone the withdrawal of Soviet troops from Germany, and delay indefinitely implementation of conventional and strategic arms agreements. Given the state of the situation, Moscow's measures will not be a threat to Western security but can cause considerable mischief and aggravation. Whether Gorbachev's new course simply reflects his temporary weakness and involuntary improvised association with the conservatives, or whether it reflects a determination to exercise whatever leverage he has left to better advantage in extracting more from the West is unclear as of this moment, and, in fact, both reasons may be involved.

After six years of power, Gorbachev has demonstrated his consummate ability as a political survivor. Coming to power without either a power structure or constituency of his own, he managed not only to impose a drastic program of radical change in Soviet domestic and foreign policies, but by 1991, had removed all of the members of the leadership that had selected him in April 1985 (the "Brezhnev gang"), the allies he picked up along the way (Chebrikov, Ligachev, and others), and finally, his original cohort of reformers (Yakovlev, Shevarnadze, Bakatin). In the winter of 1991 he seemed to be trying to survive by leaning on the military, KGB, and conservatives but more recently by returning to his liberal backers and cooperating with the President of the Russian Republic—Boris Yeltsin.

Along the way, Gorbachev has dismantled the old economy, weakened the old power structures, purged the bureaucracies, deprived the Communist Party of its political monopoly, dispersed and weakened the Party Apparatus and *nomenklatura,* demolished the power of the Politburo, Secretariat and Central Committee, and has called for the reorganization of the country into a new multinational union.

At the same time, Gorbachev has gone a long way in reconstructing the legitimacy of the Soviet political order by relocating the source of legitimacy from the "dictates of history" to "consent of the governed," by instituting de facto multiparty free elections in selecting officials both in the center and the localities. By establishing a constitutional-legal state, or what Gorbachev calls a "law-governed state," and changing the basis of legitimacy, Gorbachev has made it extremely difficult to remove him by a coup, since there are enough forces in other bodies and in the republics who would refuse to accept the legitimacy and credentials of such a move. For irrespective of how they may disagree with Gorbachev on policy issues, they have accepted and benefitted from his "law-governed state" and processes. Thus, unless the Congress of People's Deputy impeaches him for violating the Constitution, he is unlikely to be removed by a coup, since this would almost certainly plunge the country into civil war.

Whether the Soviet Union will survive in its current form is another question, although it is intimately intertwined with Gorbachev's fate. It is more than likely that the three Baltic republics may eventually be set free, since even the Soviet authorities concede that their incorporation was illegal, coercive, and a consequence of the secret provisions of the Nazi-Soviet Pact of 1939. From this vantage point, it appears to be a matter of proper timing under opportune circumstances and conditions for the Baltic states to achieve their independence.

Georgia and Armenia, the other two recalcitrant republics, can be managed since their threat to secede is not very credible, for they have more to gain in an association with Russia than without. They insist on being masters of their own house internally, and this is something that can be arranged. Aside from Moldavia, which is really an extension of the Romanian nation, the other republics can be persuaded to remain in a new restructured Union, along the lines of a confederation in which the republics have a wide latitude of internal autonomy, including the choice of their own political, social, and economic systems, and extensive participation in the forging of foreign and defense policy. One stumbling block is Gorbachev's apparent insistence that the future Union remain a "socialist" Union, something some Republics reject, since they may desire to establish nonsocialist systems. In summary, both the Soviet Union (in one configuration or another) and perhaps even Gorbachev may survive by muddling through the morass of domestic and foreign policy problems in which they are currently enmeshed.

FOREIGN POLICY LANDMARKS

February 9, 1946	Stalin preelection speech warning Soviet people of new war being hatched by the capitalist world
March 12, 1947	Truman Doctrine proclaimed to protect Turkey and Greece
September 1947	Cominform established to control Eastern European states; "Two-Camp" Doctrine proclaimed
June 1948	Yugoslavia expelled from Cominform and Soviet Bloc; Berlin blockaded by Soviet force
March 1949	Berlin Blockade ended
February 1950	Mao Zedong in Moscow; Sino-Soviet treaties signed subordinating China to the U.S.S.R.
October 1952	Nineteenth Communist Party Congress meets
March 5, 1953	Stalin dies; collective rule established with Malenkov as Stalin's successor
August 8, 1953	Malenkov announces "new course" emphasizing consumer goods and "peaceful coexistence"
October 1954	Khrushchev heads Soviet delegation to China; Soviet bases and economic enterprises in China given up; Mao Zedong makes territorial demands upon Moscow
February 1955	Malenkov forced to resign and replaced by Bulganin; Khrushchev emerges as top Soviet leader in his capacity as First Secretary
May 1955	Warsaw Treaty Organization (Warsaw Pact) established to counter NATO
July 1955	Khrushchev-Bulganin summit with Eisenhower in Geneva; "Spirit of Geneva" proclaimed
February 1956	Twentieth Party Congress meets. Khrushchev denounces Stalin and "inevitability of war" thesis
April 17, 1956	Cominform abolished
May–June 1956	Molotov resigns as Foreign Minister; Tito visits Moscow
November 1956	Hungarian uprising put down by Soviet invasion

March 27, 1958	Khrushchev replaces Bulganin as Premier, while retaining position as First Secretary
September 15–17, 1958	Eisenhower-Khrushchev "Camp David" summit meeting; Khrushchev tours United States
May 1960	American U-2 spy plane shot down over Soviet territory; Paris summit aborted as Eisenhower refuses Khrushchev's demand for apology over U-2 incident
June 3–4, 1961	Kennedy-Khrushchev summit meeting in Vienna; Berlin crisis revived by Khrushchev
October 1962	Cuban Missile Crisis
July 25, 1963	Limited test-ban treaty signed
October 15, 1964	Khrushchev ousted from power; Brezhnev and Kosygin succeed as First Secretary and Prime Minister respectively
March–April 1966	Twenty-third Party Congress meets; Brezhnev emerges as top man and General Secretary with restoration of Politburo
June 1967	Arab-Israeli war; Moscow breaks diplomatic relations with Israel
July 1967	Johnson-Kosygin summit meeting at Glassboro, New Jersey
August 21, 1968	Soviet invasion of Czechoslovakia; "Brezhnev Doctrine" proclaimed
May 1972	President Nixon visits Moscow; SALT I Treaty signed; detente inaugurated
June 1973	Brezhnev visits United States
June 1974	Nixon visits U.S.S.R.
November 1974	Ford-Brezhnev summit meeting at Vladivostok; Soviet-Cuban intervention in Angola
July 1975	Helsinki Agreement signed; human rights organizations spring up in U.S.S.R. and are repressed
March–April 1976	Sadat renounces Soviet-Egyptian treaty of friendship and cooperation; Soviet naval point facilities in Egypt closed down
October 1977	New Brezhnev constitution replaces 1936 Stalin constitution
June 1979	SALT II Treaty signed at Carter-Brezhnev summit meeting in Vienna
November 1982	Brezhnev dies; Andropov succeeds as General Secretary
February 1984	Andropov dies; Chernenko succeeds as General Secretary
March 10, 1985	Chernenko dies; Gorbachev succeeds as General Secretary
July 2, 1985	Shevardnadze appointed Foreign Minister; Gromyko becomes President of the U.S.S.R.
November 19–21, 1985	Reagan-Gorbachev summit meeting in Geneva
February 25, 1986	Twenty-seventh Party Congress convenes; Gorbachev consolidates position
April 1986	Chernobyl nuclear reactor explodes
October 11–12, 1986	Reagan-Gorbachev summit meeting in Reykjavik
December 1987	Reagan-Gorbachev summit meeting in Washington, D.C.; Intermediate Nuclear Forces Treaty signed, banning all intermediate range nuclear missiles worldwide; President Reagan to visit Moscow in 1988

February 1988	Gorbachev announces that Soviet troop withdrawal from Afghanistan will begin in May
May 1988	Reagan visits the Soviet Union
July 1988	19th Party Conference convenes and approves restructuring of central state institutions and creation of new powerful presidency to be occupied by Gorbachev in early 1989
November 1988	Angolan-Namibian Peace Accords signed under Soviet-American auspices
December 1988	Gorbachev announces deep military reductions before U.N. General Assembly; meets with President Bush in Washington Summit
February 1989	Last Soviet troops leave Afghanistan
May 1989	Gorbachev in Beijing mending fences with China
August 1989	Anti-Communist solidarity government installed in Poland after sweeping electoral victory
November 1989	Berlin Wall opened and demolished, after thousands of East Germans defect through Czechoslovakia
December 1989	First Gorbachev-Bush summit meeting on Malta; Gorbachev meets with Pope in Vatican
Throughout 1989–1990:	Eastern Europe: Communist regimes swept from power in Poland, Hungary, and Czechoslovakia and replaced with non-Communist governments after free, multiparty elections. "Reform Communists," renamed "Socialists" replace hard-line Communist regime in Bulgaria, Romania, and Albania. Ceausescu in Romania overthrown in bloody coup and executed; otherwise revolutions were peaceful, as U.S.S.R. stands by, permits and even encourages dissolution of its empire in Eastern Europe.
	USSR: Plagued by a deteriorating economy and interethnic conflict, U.S.S.R. threatens to fragment as Estonia, Latvia, and Lithuania announce intentions to secede and other republics issue declarations of "sovereignty" and "independence." Russian republic announces intent to conduct separate foreign policy as do other republics, parallel to that of U.S.S.R. Gorbachev disestablishes Communist Party monopoly rule, emasculates Politburo, Secretariat, and Central Communist Committee, while concentrating all Soviet executive power in his person as President of the U.S.S.R.
August 1990	Iraq invades and annexes Kuwait. Soviet Union supports U.S.-sponsored U.N. Security Council resolutions calling for unconditional withdrawal and economic sanctions
September 1990	Summit meeting between Gorbachev and Bush in Helsinki; U.S.-Soviet joint announcement calling for Iraqi unconditional withdrawal from Kuwait and call for "New World Order." Soviet Union and South Korea establish formal diplomatic relations; economic agreements signed; North Korea isolated

October 1990	Unification of West and East Germany, after four occupying powers sign treaty relinquishing control. East Germany formally withdraws from Warsaw Pact; Soviet troops to withdraw from East Germany by 1994
November 1990	Paris summit meeting of 34 Helsinki heads of state and government, including Presidents Bush and Gorbachev; wide-ranging conventional arms reduction treaty signed and strategic arms-reduction preliminary agreement made
December 1990	Shevardnadze resigns as foreign minister; blasts Gorbachev drift towards right dictatorship; Bessmertykh appointed foreign minister
January 1991	U.N. coalition forces initiate military action against Iraq with Soviet assent and approval
March 16, 1991	Referendum on the proposed Treaty of the Union
April 1, 1991	Warsaw Pact formally dissolved as military alliance
April 14–16	Gorbachev's visit to Tokyo fails to settle the Soviet-Japanese dispute on the Kuzile Islands and to secure economic aid
June 1991	With the agreement on concurrent force in Europe and rapid progress in START, U.S. and European economic aid is expected to bolster Soviet economic reforms

SELECTED BIBLIOGRAPHY

Adelman, J., and D.A. Palmieri. *The Dynamics of Soviet Foreign Policy*. New York: Harper and Row, 1989.

Aspaturian, Vernon V. *The Union Republics in Soviet Diplomacy*. Paris: Librairie Droz, 1960. *The Soviet Union in the International Communist System*. Stanford, Calif.: Hoover Institution Studies, 1966. *Process and Power in Soviet Foreign Policy*. Boston: Little Brown, 1971.

——, et al, eds. *Eurocommunism Between East and West*. Bloomington, Ind.: Indiana University Press, 1981.

——, et al. *The International Department of the CC CPSU under Dobrynin*. Washington, D.C.: Foreign Service Institute, U.S. Department of State, 1989.

Bialer, S., ed. *Stalin's Successors*. Cambridge: Cambridge University Press, 1980. *The Domestic Context of Soviet Foreign Policy*. Boulder, Colo.: Westview Press, 1981.

——. *The Soviet Paradox*. New York: Knopf, 1986.

——. and M. Mandelbaum, eds. *Gorbachev's Russia and American Foreign Policy*. Boulder, Colo.: Westview Press, 1988.

——, ed., *Inside Gorbachev's Russia*. Boulder, Colo.: Westview Press, 1989.

Brezinski, Zbigniew K. *The Soviet Bloc*, rev. ed. Cambridge, Mass.: Harvard University Press, 1971.

Colton, Timothy. *Commisars, Commanders and Civilian Authority*. Cambridge, Mass.: Harvard University Press, 1979.

Dodor, D. and L. Branson. *Gorbachev*. New York: Viking, 1990.

Garthoff, Raymond. *Detente and Confrontation*. Washington, D.C.: The Brookings Institution, 1985.

Gati, Charles. *Hungary and the Soviet Bloc*. Durham, N.C.: Duke University Press, 1986.

George, Alexander. *Managing U.S. Soviet Rivalry*. Boulder, Colo.: Westview Press, 1979.

Hilger, G., and A.C. Meyer. *The Incompatible Allies*. New York: Macmillan, 1953.

Holloway, David. *The Soviet Union and the Arms Race*. New Haven, Conn.: Yale University Press, 1983.

Horelick, Arnold, and Myron Rush. *Strategic Power and Soviet Foreign Policy*. Chicago: Chicago Press, 1983.

Keep, John, ed. *Contemporary History in the Soviet Mirror*. New York: Praeger, 1965.

Laird, R., and E. Hoffman, eds. *Soviet Foreign Policy in A Changing World*. New York: Aldine, 1986.

McGwire, Michael. *Military Objectives in Soviet Foreign Policy.* Washington, D.C.: Brookings Institutions, 1987.

Medvedev, R. *Let History Judge,* 2nd ed. New York: Columbia University Press, 1989.

Rubenstein, A.Z. *Moscow's Third World Strategy.* Princeton, N.J.: Princeton University Press, 1989.

——. *Soviet Foreign Policy Since World War II,* 4th edition. Boston, Mass.: Little, Brown and Co., 1990.

Sakwa, R. *Gorbachev and His Reforms 1985–1990.* Englewood Cliffs, N.J.: Prentice-Hall, 1991.

Schvchenko, Arkady. *Breaking with Moscow.* New York: Knopf, 1985.

Scott, H.F. and W.F. Scott. *The Armed Forces of the USSR,* 4th ed. Boulder, Colo.: Westview Press, 1989.

Smith, Hedrick. *The New Russians.* New York: Random House, 1990.

Talbot, Strobe. *Deadly Gambits.* New York: Knopf, 1984.

Ulam, Adam B. *Expansion and Coexistence,* 2nd ed. New York: Praeger, 1974.

U.S. Defense Department. *Soviet Military Power.* Washington, D.C.: U.S. Government Printing Office. See latest edition.

Valenta, Jiri and William Potter, eds. *Soviet Decision-Making for National Security.* London: Allen & Unwin, 1984.

Valenta, J. and Cibulke, F., eds. *Gorbachev's New Thinking and Third World Conflicts.* New Brunswick, N.J.: Transaction Publishers, 1990.

Zwick, Pater. *Soviet Foreign Relations.* Englewood Cliffs, N.J.: Prentice-Hall, 1990.

EDITOR'S NOTE

On August 18, 1991 an effort to unseat Gorbachev, orchestrated by the military, the K.G.B., and Communist Party cadres, failed. Designed to avert the signing of a Union Treaty that provided for a loose federation, to which nine of the 15 Republics had given their qualified acquiescence, it instead strengthened the democratic and liberal forces that rallied behind Boris Yeltsin, the President of the Russian Republic. It spurred, therefore, the movement for independence, as not only the Baltic Republics, but also Ukraine, Beylorussia, Moldavia and others affirmed or reaffirmed their intent to become independent. The saliency of the questions raised by Professor Aspaturian in his essay and the possible answers he outlines continue to provide the student with the proper guidelines to evaluate the rapidly changing position of the Soviet Union (and its foreign policy) in world politics. It is quite possible that Russia and the Russian Republic will be the key player in the future and that its position may "control" the inclinations of the individual Republics (but not the Baltic ones). If so, two key issues must be watched closely. Will the Russian Republic itself manage to avert internal ethnic conflicts and rivalries? Will it become the sole repository of nuclear arms, whose overall mass rivals only that of the United States? If the answer to both questions is yes, then, and only then, may we continue to speak of a Russian foreign and defense policy—in lieu of a Soviet one. However, if the answer to either question is no, then the future is even murkier than anyone could have anticipated.

Roy C. Macridis

—7—

THE
FOREIGN POLICY
OF
MODERN JAPAN

Robert A. Scalapino

As the twentieth century moves toward a close, Japan faces one supremely important dilemma: How are its self-contained, inward looking culture and its status as an international economic power to be reconciled? Internationalization has been an oft-repeated exhortation in Japan in recent years, but the achievement of attitudes and policies giving substance to that term has thus far proven very difficult. One central reason, to be sure, lies in the fact that a low-risk, low-cost foreign policy has paid rich dividends up to now in terms of domestic development, in addition to enabling a low level of trauma. Yet the external pressures upon this nation to play a more responsible role in the global order have rapidly mounted. In addition, increasing numbers of Japanese of their own volition have come to the conclusion that Japan cannot continue its present minimal course. This has led to a growing domestic debate over whether and how to add additional political and possibly military components to what has been essentially an economic foreign policy.

Japan's strengths in its half-century march from wartime devastation to affluence—its cohesiveness, its concentration on domestic development, and its reliance upon those aspects of its traditional culture that served the purposes of modernization—now represent obstacles to the assumption of balanced regional or global leadership. Equally important is the fact that earlier

Japanese foreign policies bequeathed a negative legacy not easily liquidated, especially in Asia. Thus, uncertainty accompanied by frustration characterizes the search within Japan for a meaningful global role, notwithstanding a growing acceptance of international responsibilities.

THE BACKGROUND

A glimpse into history will make the current scene more intelligible. Japan began its first climb to power in traditional fashion at the end of the nineteenth century. After some decades of assiduous application of Western modernization techniques, not merely in the realm of science and technology, but also in the broader economic and political spheres, it emerged as Asia's first nation comparable to the states of the West. In foreign policy also, it began to emulate Western behavior. Its major victory in 1895 over China, a giant still mired in the past, led to the opening of Japan's imperial era, with Taiwan its initial acquisition. A decade later, triumph over Russia paved the way for dominance over the Korean peninsula, and the annexation of Korea came shortly thereafter, in 1910.

Japan now had an important foothold on the continent of Asia, a fact that was to be extremely significant in shaping its foreign policy in the years ahead. Like Great Britain earlier, Japan built its empire step by step, motivated in considerable part by the perceived need to protect what it already possessed. And like Great Britain also, as an island kingdom on the peripheries of a huge land mass, Japan benefitted from cultural interaction with the continent while being protected from external invasion. The sea represented both a lane and a barrier. Thus, the Japanese remained a relatively homogeneous people who, despite many foreign adaptations, have retained a strong sense of uniqueness. At the same time, the historic dilemma over isolation versus continental involvement marked the course of Japanese foreign relations over many centuries. By the early years of the twentieth century, however, Japan had unmistakably become a continental power, a development certain to represent a major challenge to Asia's largest society, China.

From the time of the First World War, Japanese pressures upon China mounted again. The so-called 21 Demands set forth during that war would have given Japan predominant influence over Chinese economic policies and in addition, would have placed Japanese advisers in strategic positions in the political and security branches of the Chinese government. Although the demands were largely rejected, the Chinese were forced to transfer the special privileges previously held by the Germans on the Liaotung peninsula to Japan.

Meanwhile, Japanese economic interests were steadily expanding in Manchuria, centering upon the rail lines and major commercial-industrial cities. By the 1920s, the Japanese economic stake in this region was extensive, and the Japanese population there was growing yearly. Naturally, political ties had to be cultivated to protect those interests. The Manchurian warlord, Chang

Tso-lin, was to become the key figure. Although Chang was considered by many to be a Japanese instrument, his relations with Tokyo—and the Japanese Kwantung army located in the region—were complex. Chang had his own agenda.

From the very beginning of its rise to power, Japan had wrestled with the question of which nation constituted the primary threat to its interests, and correspondingly, with which nation, if any, should it seek an alliance. At the onset of the twentieth century, it defined Russia as the principal danger and found in Great Britain a useful ally. Russia's defeat in 1905 and the Anglo-Japanese alliance consummated several years earlier served to safeguard Japanese interests for several decades. At the 1921 Washington Conference, however, Japan reluctantly gave up that alliance. In its place were substituted the more general agreements among the major powers. The concept of collective agreement (not, it should be emphasized, collective security) was especially attuned to the American position. The United States wanted an end to exclusive alliances, but it was prepared to undertake only the most limited commitments, and it still wished to rely essentially upon moral suasion for policy enforcement. The great symbol of this hope and this era was the famous Kellogg-Briand Pact of 1928, outlawing war.

Consequently, the decline of Japanese liberalism in the late 1920s was complemented internationally by the absence of effective external checks or controls. The old alliances had been declared obsolete in the Pacific, but no effective international order had replaced them. As a result, Japan could successfully defy the Nine-Power Agreement and the League of Nations in the name of her national interests, with no single nation or group making an effective stand against her. Inevitably, as she challenged the status quo powers, Japan gravitated toward Germany and Italy, the dissidents of Europe. The Anti-Comintern Pact sealed an alliance of mutual interest, though not one of great intimacy.

The real decision that confronted Japan as the Pacific War approached, however, had a familiar ring. Which nation or group of nations represented the most immediate threat? Should she seek a stabilization of her northern or southern flanks? Who was to be engaged, the Soviet Union or the Western allies, and most especially, the United States? The choice was not an easy one. In the late 1930s, Japan had participated in large-scale clashes with Soviet forces in the Mongolian region, and her historic rivalry with Russia was augmented by her hatred of communism.

Unquestionably, the Western embargo imposed against Japan at the end of the 1930s helped to tilt the scales. In the final analysis, the Japanese leaders decided to count on a German victory on the steppes of Russia, and Japan turned to the south, whose resources had to be unlocked and whose Western masters had to be overthrown if the Japanese vision of the future were to be attained. Possibilities for agreement with the West to avoid this fateful step were explored, as all the moderates desired, but hopes were broken on the rock of China. Too much had been invested in blood and treasure to concede to Chiang Kai-shek, and so, infinitely more was to be invested—and all in vain.

It should be noted that Japan, both in triumph and defeat, played a powerful role in stimulating the tides of Asian nationalism that surged forth in the first half of this century. From an early point, various Japanese had contacts with diverse Asian politicians, especially in China. Sun Yat-sen, for example, had a number of Japanese friends, had organized his first significant revolutionary society in Tokyo, and had periodically called for a Sino-Japanese alignment—a Pan-Asianism supportive of China's independence and economic development. After the onset of the Sino-Japanese conflict in 1937, Japanese leaders took advantage of the rivalry between Chiang Kai-shek and Wang Ch'ing-wei to support the latter in creating a rival regime under Japanese auspices.

Ironically, however, while Japan had proclaimed a primary purpose of its China policy during this period to be the removal of the Communist threat, its actions constituted a major contribution to the victory of communism in China. For nearly a decade, the Nationalist government was separated from the bulk of the Chinese people, and in the course of the war and its immediate aftermath, it displayed increasing signs of weariness and decay. Meanwhile, using a combination of reformist and nationalist appeals, the Communists steadily widened their bases in various parts of China, taking advantage of the war and the multiple problems that it spawned.

During these years, Japan had cultivated diverse nationalist movements in South and Southeast Asia. In some cases, it had provided military training; in other cases, it had offered educational opportunities; and as defeat loomed, it gave nationalists in Indonesia, Burma and Vietnam an opportunity to seize power. This contribution, however, was virtually obliterated from Asian consciousness by the brutality of the Japanese occupation in most regions. At war's end, the image of the Japanese throughout Asia, with few exceptions, was that of militarism, arrogance, and insensitivity to other peoples. And while the humiliation of the Western powers during the early stages of the conflict provided a powerful impetus to a new order in Asia, Japan's own subsequent defeat destroyed the myth of Japanese superiority and allowed anti-Japanese sentiments full rein. Thus, the task of constructing a new relationship with Asia was certain to be difficult for postwar Japan.

THE FORMULATION OF FOREIGN POLICY IN PREWAR JAPAN

In the Tokyo trials of major war criminals that followed the Japanese surrender, the Allied prosecutors repeatedly sought the answer to one central question: Who bears the responsibility for leading Japan toward aggression and war? If they did not obtain a fully satisfactory answer, no blame should be assigned. Few questions involve greater difficulties. The problem of responsibilities for policies has taken on universal dimensions as the modern state has grown in complexity and as foreign policy has developed into the composite, uncertain product of a myriad of technicians, men rigidly compartmentalized, skilled and jealous of these skills, but almost always frustrated by the limits of their power; an indeterminate number of free-roaming generalists, yet not so free, being bound by the limits of the single mind, the requirements imposed by group decision, and the pressures—subtle or direct—of subalterns; and, finally the larger, vaguer public—alternately indifferent and excited, overwhelmed by the complexities and focusing on some vital issue, ignored and watched with anxiety, molded and breaking out of molds.

Prewar Japan was a modern state, measured against the standards of the time. On the surface, however, it appeared to be a society of great personal absolutism. In both the family and the nation, the head was invested with total power. Inferiors owed complete and unswerving obedience. There seemed no measure of egalitarianism or individualism to alleviate the rigidities of a hierarchical system which, through primogeniture and an emperor-centered mythology, found its apex in a single source. But in fact, the essence of power in Japanese society has not been that of personal absolutism. The essence of Japanese decision making has lain in its collective or group character with policy initiation from below and an extensive reliance on consensus as the primary technique. It is critical to understand that, despite all superficial signs to the contrary, the basic nature of Japanese society can only be approached by a thorough appreciation of the intricate refinements of small group interaction, the great importance of induced voluntarism, and the generally eclectic and often vague quality of final agreements.

In all likelihood, it is only because these things were true that the outward signs of rigid hierarchy and absolutism were so well-maintained into the modern era. Elaborate methods had already been developed to integrate theory and appearance with the needs of a dynamic society. Just as the system of adopted sons had long preserved the necessary flexibility in the Japanese family, so the institutions of senior councillor, adviser, and go-between had each, in its own way, facilitated the making of group decisions. That process, giving extraordinary attention to form and status, was often wearisome and prolonged, but every care had to be taken to make concessions and consensus possible, with a minimum of violence to the position and prestige of those involved. Necessarily, equals were wary of confronting each other in person until the formula for consensus seemed assured; and inferiors developed, to a fine art, all forms of subtle pressures and persuasive devices, so that successful superiors paid silent homage to these in the course of final action. For this reason, the procedure was often referred to as "bottom-up decision making."

Not all these conditions sound strange to Western ears, although the aggregate process might seem extreme. In any case, how were such basic factors in Japanese social relations translated into politics and the making of foreign policy? In theory, the Meiji Constitution of 1889 paid its highest tribute to imperial absolutism but, for successful practice, it demanded a unity or consensus of its disparate working parts. The weakest of these, the two-house Diet, its lower house elected, had at least the power to withhold its consent from basic policies. The administrative bureaucracy, culminating in such executives as the prime minister, and the members of the cabinet and the Privy Council, had a vast range of powers and had legal responsibility only to the emperor, but it could not be effective alone. The military also drew its power from the emperor and had direct access to him; in practice, moreover, this branch acquired a potent weapon in that the ministers of war and navy had to come from its ranks, which served to limit sharply the independent power of the Japanese cabinet. The military, however, could operate effectively only in conjunction with the other major branches.

There was never any serious thought of having these forces coordinated by the emperor personally, despite the awesome nature of his stipulated powers. Instead, that task was handled, for some thirty years, by a small oligarchy of Meiji restoration leaders who acted in the name of the emperor as his "chief advisers." Ultimately, this group came to be known as the *genro* or "senior councillors," an institution without a vestige of legal recognition or responsibility, but central to the process of Japanese politics. Every basic policy decision was placed before the *genro,* and their approval was a prerequisite to action. Even the daily affairs of state frequently engaged their attention. With protégés in every branch of government, and with their own accumulation of experience, these men were at once the source of integration, the court of final appeal, and the summit of power. To be sure, agreement among them was not always easy; there were deep personal and political cleavages in this, as in other Japanese groups. Timed withdrawals and temporary concessions, however, enabled a consensus to operate with a minimum of crises. Until the close of the World War I, with rare exceptions, the fountainhead of Japanese foreign policy was this group.

With the postwar era, however, basic changes in government began to emerge, paralleling those in society. The members of the *genro* became old, and their ranks were not refilled. No group came forth to undertake the integrative role. Instead, Japanese politics was marked by an increasing struggle for supremacy and control among the parties, the bureaucracy, and the military. It is interesting to note that, at the outset of this era, an attempt was made to establish a liaison council under the aegis of the prime minister for the development of a unified foreign policy. It was intended to include major party, official, and military representation, but it was never accepted by the major opposition party, and it ultimately faded away.

Without a supreme coordinator such as the *genro,* Japanese constitutionalism, in both its written and unwritten aspects, revealed serious flaws. In the hectic party era, foreign policy decisions taken in cabinet or government party circles were subject not only to legitimate attacks in the Diet, but also to extensive sabotage by the ranks of the subordinate bureaucracy, and to angry challenges by the military groups. The parties never attained more than a quasi supremacy and, as they faded, the military moved from verbal challenge to open defiance. Japanese society, in the period after 1928, was a classic example of a government divided against itself. Important segments of the military operated, both in the field and at home, in such a manner as to scorn the government. They received substantial support from within the bureaucracy, and from certain party figures as well. Every branch of government was riddled with dissension. Within the Ministry of Foreign Affairs, various cliques maneuvered for position—the militarist group, the Anglo-American group, and numerous others. For a time, consensus was impossible, and conditions close to anarchy prevailed.

Gradually, however, greater stability was achieved. Making full use of traditional procedures, top court officials surrounding the emperor involved themselves in unending conferences with representatives of all major groups; innumerable go-betweens explored the possible bases of compromise; certain voluntary withdrawals, strategic retreats, and silent acquiescences were effected. Slowly, a new basis for interaction developed, one which gave due recognition to military superiority but still was broad enough to include essential elements of the civil bureaucracy, court officials, and important pressure groups. Once again, the basic decisions were reached by consensus, but with somewhat greater cognizance of the realities of power. In this period, a new group of senior councillors, the *jushin*, was organized. Although lacking the influence of the *genro*, it was fashioned after that model, indicating the continuing search for an integrative center. That search was destined never to be completely successful. Another experiment was conducted in a liaison council, the purpose being to pool military and civilian policy with particular reference to the foreign scene. Ultimately, the imperial conference, with the emperor himself presiding over a small group of top military and administrative officials, became the final decision-making body. Indeed, it was this group that determined the Japanese surrender, the emperor personally settling this great issue. Perhaps this was the only basis left for the organic unity envisaged by the Meiji constitution.

The foregoing trends are not completely meaningful without some brief reference to other important social groups. First, however, it should be noted that the type of consensus being developed during the militarist era was abetted by an increasing control over all media of communication. One of the most literate societies in the world, Japan had national newspapers and magazines with massive circulation. After the early thirties, prominent dissent from ultranationalism became increasingly dangerous and, after the Second China Incident of 1937, all the public organs were echoing the official line.

Meanwhile, a process of accommodation had been taking place between conservative militarists and the industrial and commercial world of Japan. In the initial stages of the military revolt against liberalism and "a weak-kneed foreign policy," the strong notes of a radical, anticapitalist theme were heard;

the historic cry of "internal reform, external expansion" once again sounded forth. However, after the February 26th Incident, in 1936, when army units in Tokyo under radical command rebelled, this type of revolutionary activity was suppressed. Although some liberal business elements were regarded with suspicion, and certain onerous controls were sharply protested by entrepreneurs, still the necessary compromises were made, and all of Japanese industry rose to the war effort.

Japanese labor reacted in the same way. Its radical and liberal elements had long since been silenced, and the great masses worked with patriotic fervor. It was from the rural areas, however, that the bedrock of Japanese conservatism derived. The alliance between peasant and soldier now held more meaning than at any time since the Meiji restoration. As is so frequently the case, rural provincialism bred its own type of xenophobic nationalism. The Japanese common man played a role in the formulation of foreign policy in his own way: he posed no obstacles to expansionism, his complete loyalty was assured, and no sacrifice would be too great if it contributed to the nationalist cause.

JAPAN SINCE 1945: OCCUPATION AND ITS AFTERMATH

When Japan surrendered in August, 1945, both her leaders and her people were forced to reconcile themselves to being a vanquished nation. By the terms of the Yalta and Potsdam agreements, the Japanese empire was to be dissolved and Japan reduced in size to the approximate boundaries of the restoration era. The homeland was to be occupied for an indefinite period by foreign forces. For the first time in recorded history, Japanese sovereignty was to be superseded by foreign rule. Some of the broad objectives of this rule had already been stipulated: action was to be taken to insure that Japan never again would become a world menace or a world power. Total disarmament was to be carried out, and those responsible for past aggression were to be punished; even the fate of the emperor was unclear, although Japanese leaders sought desperately to gain assurances on this point during the surrender negotiations. Along with these essentially negative tasks, the occupation was also to encourage Japanese democratic forces and movements, so that Japan could eventually take her place in a peaceful world. Thus was inaugurated, in September 1945, a radically new era for Japan, one that might well be labeled "the era of the American Revolution."

If the contemporary processes and substance of Japanese foreign policy are to be discussed meaningfully, certain pertinent aspects of this period must be set forth. In the first place, the American occupation and its aftermath can easily be divided into three broad phases: (*a*) the early revolutionary era, when the emphasis was upon punishment and reform; (*b*) the era of reconstruction, when the stress was shifted to stabilization and economic recovery; and (*c*) the era of proffered alliance, which is continuing at present. Each of these eras, in its own way, has contributed to the current nature and issues of Japanese society.

The Revolutionary Era

The American Revolution in Japan was that of 1932, not that of 1776, although some of the spirit of the latter, as it applied to basic democratic values, was certainly present. The New Deal had new opportunities along the bombed-out Ginza and in the rice fields. But first, the old order had to be eradicated. Japanese military forces were totally disbanded in a remarkably short time; before the end of 1947, some six million Japanese troops and civilians had been returned from overseas, demobilized, and poured into the homeland. The military forces within Japan proper had also been completely dissolved. The ministries of war and navy were abolished. And, in an effort to seal these actions with the stamp of permanency, the now-famous Article 9 was written into the new Japanese Constitution:

> Aspiring sincerely to an international peace based on justice and order, the Japanese people forever renounce war as a sovereign right of the nation and the threat or use of force as means of settling international disputes.
> In order to accomplish the aim of the preceding paragraph, land, sea, and air forces, as well as other war potential, will never be maintained. The right of belligerency of the state will not be recognized.

The American vision for Japan during this period became widely associated with the phrase, "the Switzerland of the Far East," although, in this case, pacifism was added to neutralization. It was a vision that had a powerful appeal to many Japanese who lived amidst rubble, without adequate food or warmth, and with vivid memories of lost ones, fire raids, and the final holocaust of the atom bomb. There could be no question as to whether this war had paid. Moreover, the extraordinary vulnerability of the great Japanese cities had been fully demonstrated during the war's last, terrible months. For most thoughtful Japanese, the early postwar era was a period of deep reflection. Its dominant theme was trenchant criticism of past leaders and institutions. Once more, there was a Japanese surge toward new ideas and ways; MacArthur, no less than Perry, symbolized the beginning of a new order, and a war-weary people turned hopefully to *demokurashi,* without being precisely sure of its contents. These sentiments, widespread as they were, aided the revolution that was getting under way.

Among the various SCAP[1] actions, none had more long-range implications than those which affected the nature and position of Japanese pressure groups. As we have noted, for more than a decade the most powerful group in Japanese society had been the military. Suddenly it was entirely liquidated,

---

[1] SCAP is the commonly used abbreviation for "Supreme Commander of the Allied Powers." It is used to designate General MacArthur personally, and the American occupation force collectively.

and it has not yet reappeared as a significant political force. Liquidation was not merely demobilization, but also the purge that barred all professional military officers from future political activity, and the war crimes trials, after which the top military men of the nation were executed or sentenced to prison. Although certain of these actions were subsequently modified or rescinded, their total effect, combined with other circumstances, was sufficient to render militarism in Japan weak for at least fifty years, and quite possibly, well into the future.

Through the purge and other measures, SCAP ate still further into prewar conservative ranks. For the old guard it seemed like the reign of terror, although without violence or brutality. Most professional politicians of the old conservative parties had to step aside because they had belonged to some ultranationalist group or had been endorsed by the Tojo government in the elections of 1942. Conservative leadership was hastily thrust into the hands of the one group that could be cleared: the so-called Anglo-American group from within the Foreign Ministry. Kijuro Shidehara, Shigeru Yoshida, and Hisashi Ashida, all from this group, became the top conservative leaders of Japan for nearly a decade. Even the commercial and industrial world felt the shock of reform. Beset by purges, a program to break down the zaibatsu ("big combines"), and the general toll of wartime ravage and postwar inflation, most business elements sought merely to survive, as if seeking shelter during a gale.

Meanwhile, with American encouragement, the labor union movement attained a massive size; within a brief period it numbered some six million workers, whereas, in the prewar period, bona fide union membership had never exceeded one-half million. These postwar figures masked many divisions and weaknesses, but it appeared that Japanese organized labor would be a new force with which to reckon on the economic and political scene. And in the rural areas, the "American Revolution" was operating in the most forceful fashion. Under a far-reaching program of land reform, absentee landlordism was almost completely abolished, tenancy was reduced to less than ten percent of total agrarian families, and land holdings were equalized beyond the wildest imagination of prewar reformers. Basically, this program was dedicated to the creation of a huge independent yeomanry. These actions destroyed agrarian radicalism, with rural interests gradually becoming a conservative pressure group closely aligned with the soon to be created Liberal-Democratic Party.

Certain reforms cut across class lines and into the broadest categories of society. Legal attempts were made to abandon primogeniture and to emancipate women. Women were given full equality before the law, including equal rights of inheritance, divorce, and suffrage. Sweeping reforms in education were inaugurated, with the purpose of developing freer, more independent students, unshackled from the old chauvinism and submissiveness. Even that very special category of men, the subordinate government officials, were given lectures on democracy, in the hope that some of the old attitude of *kanson mimpi* ("officials honored, people despised") could be removed.

To recite these various efforts in such bald fashion may lead to the supposition that a total social revolution took place in Japan during the first years after 1945. Any such impression would be false. Conservatism, both in the form of certain dominant classes and in the form of certain traditions that operated in every class, was a sturdy force. Moreover, as might be surmised, not all SCAP experiments were successful and, by the end of 1947, in any case, the era emphasizing reform was drawing to a close. In its ripest forms, it had lasted only about two years. The conservatives definitely survived. Indeed, conservative dominance has been the hallmark of Japanese politics for the past four decades, giving Japan a degree of political stability unequalled by any other advanced industrial society during this era.

It would be equally misleading however, to underestimate the changes that took place during the Occupation, whether because of SCAP reforms or as a result of the total complex of postwar circumstances. Some of these changes should be regarded as being supported by the societal evolution derived from Japanese modernization, thus having prewar roots. Others were largely the product of foreign intervention or the new conditions prevailing as a result of military defeat. In any case, the changes that developed during this period had a direct influence on the processes and substance of Japanese foreign policy.

Stabilization

Some brief consideration should now be given to the second and third phases of the occupation and the gradual emergence, once again, of an independent Japan. The shift of emphasis in occupation policy, from punishment and reform to economic stabilization and recovery, began as early as 1947. The change was motivated by many problems. Certain earlier American premises about the postwar world now seemed unjustified. The prospects for a China that would be friendly and democratic by American definition were dim; the honeymoon with the Soviet Union was clearly over and the Cold War was beginning; the threat of communism throughout Europe and Asia, as a result of postwar chaos and economic misery, was a matter of profound concern. In Japan itself, the close relation between economic recovery and the prospects for democratic success could no longer be slighted or ignored. In addition, the expenses of occupation and relief constituted a heavy burden for the American taxpayer; at its peak, the cost ran close to a half-billion dollars a year.

The new emphasis brought many changes. Increasingly, the supreme test to which any policy could be put was: Does it advance productivity and economic stabilization? An assessment was made of the primary obstacles—war damage, inflation, the lack of raw materials, and low industrial morale. SCAP began to interest itself in Japanese productive efficiency, and moved from merely keeping Japan alive to furnishing her with raw materials and acquainting her entrepreneurs with the most advanced industrial technology. The complex problem of inflation was finally faced. Under the Dodge Nine-Point Stabilization Program, stringent reforms were put into effect. These were unpopular in many quarters, but the inflationary tide was at last turned.

Meanwhile, other disruptions to production were dealt with. The deconcentration program was relaxed and gradually abandoned.

The United States also progressively receded from its early severity on the issue of reparations. By the end of this era, the American government had accepted the thesis that the Japanese ability to repay war damages was strictly limited, that large reparations would indirectly become a responsibility of the United States, and that the heavy industry on which the Japanese future was so dependent could not be used for these purposes. Finally, SCAP took a sterner attitude toward the labor movement, amending its earlier generous legislation on unionism to give the employer, and especially the government, a stronger position.

The net effect of these actions, accompanied by certain broader trends at home and abroad, was to stimulate rapid economic recovery. Japanese society could build on an industrial revolution already well advanced, and on a legacy of technical know-how. Deflation and internal readjustments were followed by new opportunities for industrial expansion. The Korean War and the great prosperity of the free world were of major assistance. Beginning in 1950, therefore, Japan entered a period of amazing economic development. For the next twenty years, the average annual rise in gross national product was approximately ten percent, one of the most spectacular rates of growth in the world, and in the succeeding twenty years, Japanese growth continued to set the pace among advanced industrial societies.

This second phase of the occupation, which triggered the economic surge, was not without internal political reverberations. In the revolutionary era, American actions had been an anathema to the conservatives; now, the conservatives became the new allies. The Left, which had cheered SCAP policies in the early days, was filled with dismay and resentment at many actions of which it did not approve but from which it had no recourse. Japanese democracy was still under the tutelage of American military rule, and effective opposition was strictly limited by that fact. Inevitably, however, the United States and its policies became the central issue in Japanese politics, paving the way for the sharp divergencies that came into the open later. For every political group, moreover, this second era was one of reflection and reconsideration of Western values. There was an unmistakable tendency, at all levels, to emphasize synthesis and adjustment rather than uncritical acceptance of foreign concepts. The pendulum had begun to swing back.

As can be seen, the beginnings of postwar Japanese foreign policy were established in this era, albeit under American direction. These beginnings followed a course that Japanese leadership itself might well have taken and even labeled "in the national interest," had it been an independent agent. Indeed, on issues like reparations and trade, the United States was widely accused of being excessively pro-Japanese. One policy which was emphasized was that of rehabilitating Japanese heavy industry and encouraging its orientation toward the needs and markets of the external world. With American encouragement, an export-oriented strategy was developed, taking advantage of cheap energy and raw materials, the new prosperity of the advanced West, and increasing access to ex-colonial markets. As a concomitant to this policy, the United States also sought to adjust Japanese political relations with erstwhile enemies. Like a benevolent warden convinced of the successful rehabilitation of his charge, the United States pressed for Japanese reentry into the world community.

With the second phase of the occupation, there thus began an intimate and largely new relationship between Japan and the United States, a relationship founded on a rising tempo of economic, cultural, and political interaction. This relation was far from an equal one. The United States was central to virtually every aspect of Japanese life, whereas Japan was only one of many concerns and influences to Americans. In power as well, the disparities were great, whatever measure was used. Yet the new ties were increasingly meaningful to both societies.

The Era of Alliance

Within these trends lay the seeds of the third era, that of alliance proferred by the United States to Japan. By 1949, American authorities realized, on the one hand, that the occupation was reaching a point of diminishing returns, and, on the other, that continuing economic and political ties between the two countries were a mutual necessity. The explorations which led to the San Francisco Peace Treaty of 1951 involved a series of decisions that deeply influenced the new Japanese foreign policy and provoked heated political debate.

The critical issue pertained to the question of Japanese defense. Two broad alternatives seemed to exist. One was Japanese pacifism, which involved seeking universal agreements guaranteeing the sanctity of Japanese territory and backing these with pledges of protection by the United Nations, and possibly by the United States, separately. The alternative was to acknowledge the Japanese need for, and right to, military defense, and to underwrite Japanese rearmament with American power. Obviously, the choice between these two broad courses would affect and shape many other aspects of Japanese foreign policy.

The Yoshida government did not hesitate to support the second alternative, that of political, military, and economic alliance with the United States, as the only course compatible with world conditions and Japanese needs. To adopt a policy of neutralism, the conservatives argued, would make Japan dependent on the mercurial policies of the Communist world. It would provide neither security nor prosperity. They insisted that both the economic and the political interests of Japan were best served by alignment with the free world, particularly the United States.

These arguments prevailed. While making known its desire for an overall peace treaty, the Japanese government agreed to sign a treaty with the non-Communist allies alone, if necessary. The Cold War had become hot in Korea while preliminary treaty negotiations were getting under way. Because of this, and because of the wide divergence between Soviet and American views on Japan, no serious attempt was made to obtain Communist approval for the treaty draft, as the Japanese Socialists had wished. In exchange for their willingness to sign a separate treaty, the conservatives were given a treaty considered generous by all, and soft by some. Reparations, and certain territorial issues (the islands to the north of Hokkaido and the Ryukyu Islands), were left open, providing Japan with some bargaining power. The treaty contained no stipulations concerning SCAP reforms. Japan was left free to make any changes desired in her internal institutions. This included the right to rearm.

Official independence for Japan finally came on April 28, 1952, the day on which the San Francisco treaty came into effect. Accompanying the main treaty was a bilateral Mutual Security Treaty with the United States providing for the continuance of American military bases in Japan until adequate defenses were prepared by the Japanese government. At least as early as 1949, the creation of a Japanese defense force was being urged in some American and Japanese circles, and Japanese rearmament was first started in the summer of 1950, shortly after the outbreak of the Korean War. The National Police Reserve was activated in August of that year with an authorized component of 75,000 men. With the coming of Japanese independence, this number was increased to 110,000, and a small Maritime Safety Force was established in May 1952. In August these were brought together under the National Safety Agency. Two years later, on July 1, 1954, the name was changed to the Defense Agency, and the armed forces were brought directly under the office of the prime minister, who was authorized to add a small Air Self-Defense Force. The slow build-up of Japanese defense forces continued. By the end of 1955, there were about 200,000 men in the total defense force.

THE FORMULATION OF FOREIGN POLICY IN POSTWAR JAPAN

In recent times, scholars and journalists have debated the nature of the contemporary Japanese state. Where is the locus of power, or indeed, is there a locus of power? One thesis has been that one must view this society as Japan Incorporated, with an interlocking directorate composed of the bureaucracy, big business, and the politicians holding power and managing the society on the basis of a consensus on what serves Japan's (and their) interests. The planning and control of both domestic and foreign policies has rested with them. Within this directorate, moreover, the bureaucracy has been preeminent, and thus the Japanese system has had a high degree of authoritarianism notwithstanding the existence of a full array of democratic institutions and political rights. In sum, the bureaucratic state posing various obstacles to an effective transmission of electorate wishes or needs via the political process coexists with, and predominates over, the democratic system envisaged by the 1947 Constitution.

Another thesis, while accepting some of the premises of this view, argues that rather than being highly coordinated and sharply focused, decision making in Japan is a process whereby no one takes responsibility because there is no clear leadership. Within each part of the governing coalition as well as between them, numerous cleavages over policy and turf exist. Moreover, since decisions in the final analysis are the result of a messy and inconclusive process of compromise with procrastination and fuzziness essential elements in the operation, no single individual or part of the system feels responsible for the final product.

Each of these interpretations has some validity, and if properly modified and combined, can provide valuable insights into the construction of Japanese foreign as well as domestic policies, and the problems attending them. Unquestionably, the locus of power—and the foundations of conservative rule in Japan—have rested primarily upon the forces noted previously, with the addition of agrarian elements. Yet this does not fully explain why the conservatives have managed to garner a significant percentage of the urban labor vote. The fact is that for various reasons, a majority of the Japanese electorate has been satisfied with the policies of the conservatives, or at least not sufficiently dissatisfied to turn to the opposition.

The latter statement warrants further comment. Conservative dominance in Japan has been sustained not merely by a combination of policies, a coalition of powerful interest groups, political institutions including the electoral system and cultural sanction, but also by the continuing weaknesses of the opposition. Never able to achieve power and confronted with policies that satisfied a sizable number of the Japanese voters, the Japan Socialist Party, the leading opposition party, has been stunted in its development. Until recently, the chief symbols of the JSP main stream were Marxism and pacifism. The Socialists had acquired little of the flexibility of their counterparts in Western Europe, a flexibility that might have made them more attractive to the voters.

In the past few years, however, there have been signs of change. Socialist leaders have been making efforts to move to a less ideological, more pragmatic set of policies, including foreign policies. The passing from the scene of many of the old dogmatists and the restructuring of the Japanese labor movement have assisted in this process. How far, and in precisely what direction the JSP will evolve is one of the important variables that will influence future Japanese politics. Despite the various scandals besetting it, and the present specter of weak leadership, the Liberal Democratic Party does not appear to be in imminent danger of losing power. However, its future will be determined by the success and popularity of its policies. Recent elections have shown that it is vulnerable when it attempts to move against public opinion.

In point of fact, coalition politics has already become a part of the Japanese political scene, with the House of Councillors, the upper house of the Diet, not controlled by the LDP. In this process, moreover, the centrist opposition parties, the Democratic Socialists and the *Komeito*, are becoming participants in decision making, especially in the foreign policy arena.

The question of whether there is any locus of power in Japan also requires careful analysis. It is abundantly clear that in Japan, as in most states, jurisdictional rivalry is very strong within the bureaucracy. Virtually all observers would account the Finance Ministry as the most powerful branch of officialdom, and together with the Ministry of International Trade and Industry (MITI), a critical actor in foreign policy making. Indeed, the Ministry of Foreign Affairs has generally been regarded as less powerful than the former two ministries.

Moreover, there can be no doubt that bureaucratic divisions, as well as official assertions of authority, have frequently led to serious problems, including stalemates, procrastination, and challenges to party authority. However, any idea that the LDP has abdicated policy making to the bureaucracy is contrary to the truth. Within the party, a central policy-making body has long been established, and certain party leaders, including the prime minister, have taken an active hand—from the bureaucratic standpoint, on occasion, too active a hand—in fashioning Japanese foreign policies. Once again, as is typical of democratic societies, an effort to reconcile differences of opinion among key figures must be made, and this can lead to delays or inaction. In the final analysis, however, the prime minister must take responsibility for key policy decisions. In this sense, there is a person or institution that is held accountable.

Generally speaking, the LDP tenure in power has benefitted greatly in the past from its factional or federated structure, enabling a change of leadership without a change of party. Thus, when a leader has spent his political capital, he resigns, and a replacement not encumbered with unpopular decisions is presented to the public. Whether this system will remain intact is now in some doubt. An older generation of politicians is departing from the scene, including almost all of the old factional leaders, and it is presently unclear as to whether they will be replaced by younger men heading key factions and slated by gentlemen's agreement or inside bargaining to take their turn at the helm of state.

Irrespective of the nature of the LDP evolution, it is clear that Japanese politics is undergoing change, with a general movement toward greater complexity—and potentially, greater instability. While still very powerful, the bureaucracy is gradually losing ground to the private sector, especially in the realm of economic policies. Japanese business, while far from united on all matters, is increasingly assertive; and the process of internationalization is abetting this trend, since business is being brought under other political jurisdictions, beyond the control of Tokyo. MITI, for example, can garner data, provide counsel, and seek to shape the broad direction of future Japanese growth, but its ability to command or coerce has lessened and will continue to lessen.

Equally important, new interest groups—ranging from environmental groups to spokespeople for the underprivileged and ethnic minorities—have entered the political scene. More importantly, public opinion has become a factor of rising significance. With polls constantly being taken, the consciousness of how the Japanese public is reacting to diverse policies and problems is regularly set before the government. The evidence is strong that Japanese politicians of whatever stripe are increasingly alert to public opinion and to constituent interests. In addition the media, and especially the press, have become more assertive, and since the Recruit Scandal investigatory journalism has risen in importance. Although still not precisely in the American mold, the adversarial position of the Japanese media vis-à-vis the government, long existent in certain quarters, has become more prominent.

To sum up, the process of formulating, executing, and defending Japanese foreign policy today remains in the hands of a conservative elite, but an elite harboring various internal differences. The formal and informal institutional processes have been altered in recent decades without having wholly lost their traditional character. A decision-making process, still bottom-up in essence, is complex and lengthy. Both the origins of a given policy and the degree of consensus achieved in the course of its adoption are frequently cloaked in obscurity. Yet since it is based upon some degree of consensus, once reached, a decision is usually difficult to alter. Limited flexibility often produces friction between Japan and other nations, with tough retaliatory measures forthcoming when it is assumed that no other approach will work. The widespread concept that "You have to treat the Japanese tough," stems from these conditions.

Japan remains a strongly bureaucratic state, but as has been noted, an evolution is underway, its speed and scope still to be determined. Rising challenges from various parts of the private sector are being felt, and the politically elected officials are increasingly sensitive to public opinion as well as to key interest groups. In these senses, the forces operating upon Japanese foreign policy are more complex than in the past. Hence, in the future, consensus may be more difficult to obtain, and once obtained, to maintain.

THE MAJOR ISSUES IN JAPANESE FOREIGN POLICY

In the past, economic considerations so dominated Japan's relations with other nations that some observers labelled that nation "an economic animal," or referred to it as an economic giant, a political pygmy. Even now, Japanese power is largely unidimensional. Yet its extraordinary economic strength, together with the evolution of international relations, has forced the Japanese government to consider the question of an expansion of Japan's role in the world with greater intensity than at any time in the past. As yet, no clear answers have been reached, but the issue is constantly before leaders and public alike. Hence, it will continue to be discussed and debated throughout the country.

Let us begin by setting forth the status of the Japanese economy and its relationship both to the Pacific-Asian region and to the larger world. After a phenomenal growth during the three decades that followed 1950, Japan continued to achieve remarkable economic advances in the 1980s. Between 1983 and 1989, GNP rose from $1,181 billion to $2,555 billion, with a growth averaging between 4.5% and 5.5%, the slightly weaker years of 1983 and 1986 excepted. Per capita GNP in 1989 reached $22,800. This record outdistanced all other advanced industrial nations.

Meanwhile, inflation was contained at around 2% per annum, lower in the 1986–88 period. Unemployment in 1989 stood at 2.3%. Japanese foreign trade in 1989 totalled $484 billion, and the current account balance in 1989 stood at $56.98 billion, lower than in the previous three years, but more than sufficient to keep Japan the world's largest creditor nation.

It is important to disaggregate the trade figures. Some 34% of all Japanese exports went to the United States in 1989, with the United States accounting for 19% of Japanese imports. By a great measure, the United States was Japan's premier market, and Japan was the second best customer of the United States, next to Canada. Exports to ASEAN totalled 6%; to Korea, 6%; and to China, 5%. Imports from Korea, however, represented 27% of Japan's total imports, and those from Taiwan exceeded 29%, reflecting both increased Japanese purchases of lower-scale electronic products and other consumer goods from these states and the importation of components for Japanese manufactures.

The expansion of Japanese trade has been accompanied by the rapid internationalization of Japanese industry, with investment flowing to all parts of the world, but particularly to the United States and East Asia. By late 1990, Japanese direct investment in the United States totalled nearly $76 billion, almost 50% of that nation's entire foreign investment. Southeast Asia also became an investment target after the mid-1980s. In 1988 alone, $3 billion in Japanese investment poured into Thailand, a promising growth site. Indonesia and Malaysia soon joined the favored places for investment. As the 1980s closed, some Japanese investors looked to Europe with increasing interest. In these various investments, two factors played primary roles: avoidance of protectionism and reduced costs of production, especially in the labor-intensive industries.

Meanwhile, a new economic order in the Pacific-Asian region has been emerging. In broad terms, the flying geese analogy, a metaphor suggested by Japanese economists, prevails. The lead goose, Japan, pioneered in an export-oriented strategy, while protecting its domestic markets through neo-mercantilist measures, a course others were soon to follow. After the mid-1980s, stimulated by the sharp appreciation of the yen and rising labor costs, Japanese entrepreneurs began to shift the manufacturing base of most labor-intensive industries to other Asian countries, initially to the NIEs (Newly Industrial Economies). Quickly, a horizontal division of labor emerged, a given product being the result of multiple processes dispersed geographically. As noted, the NIEs, following behind Japan, moved rapidly to a greater emphasis upon export orientation, with the key markets being the United States and Japan.

At this point, Japan's growth increasingly depended upon domestic demand; hence, its export surplus slowly declined. As NIE labor costs increased and their currencies appreciated, these countries began to move in the same direction as had Japan at an earlier point: direct external investment and domestic demand-led growth. Labor intensive industries were increasingly shifted to the ASEAN four (Thailand, Indonesia, Malaysia, and the Philippines). The shift from an emphasis upon foreign borrowing to foreign investment, and the greater integration into regional economy represented a major developmental advance for the ASEAN four, and they, too, began to climb up the technological ladder. Taken together, these developments— which have occurred within the space of a few decades—have resulted in the creation of an increasingly borderless economy, with economic ties jumping over political boundaries and outrunning efforts of national governments to police them.

As both the leader in this process and the strongest economic power within the new structure, Japan faces both unprecedented opportunities and complex problems. Since the United States remains the cornerstone of Japanese foreign policy in every respect, and especially in economic terms, it is appropriate to explore first the implications of Japanese (and American) economic policies and the new economic order for Japan-U.S. relations.

However much one may decry a focus on a single bilateral trade relationship, the fact is that the persistent huge trade imbalances between Japan and the United States in recent years have created a major political problem. The deficit has stubbornly remained at approximately $50 billion per annum in the last several years, out of a total trade of some $137 billion. Predictions for 1990 suggest that the deficit will be somewhat lower, but still above $40 billion.

The process of U.S.-Japan negotiations over trade issues has been lengthy and painful. In broad terms, they commenced with efforts to reduce Japanese tariffs, moved on to issues of informal barriers, and are now in a phase of discussions on "structural impediments," the so-called SII (Structural Impediments Initiative) negotiations. In these meetings, each side, in effect, outlines those obstacles to improved bilateral economic relations posed by the policies and practices of the other party. The United States asserts that the low level of Japan's manufactured imports in comparison with other industrial nations

(3% in 1989) points to continuing protectionism, despite the reduction of formal barriers; it objects strongly to the embargo on rice importation; it points to differential pricing at home and abroad; it presents evidence of collusive bidding by Japanese enterprises as a means of excluding foreign firms that are highly competitive. In addition, it urges a greater emphasis by the Japanese government on domestic programs, including expanded public works; major tax and other reforms aimed at tackling the problem of exorbitantly high land prices, thus enabling the Japanese public to increase consumption; and the greater sharing of technology in key fields.

The Japanese government points to the mismanagement of the American economy at the macro level, urging a reduction of the budget deficit. It signals the importance of improving the savings ratio, in altering practices in the private sector so as to place more emphasis upon long-term development rather than short-term profits, and more rapidly improving quality control, along with other measures that would make American industry more competitive.

If the SII talks have accomplished nothing else, they have highlighted the concerns of the two global giants (together controlling 40% of the world's GNP) with each other at this point in time. As nationalism has arisen on both sides, the atmosphere has repeatedly become tense, with explosions threatened. Americans from various sectors have accused Japan of being an economic predator, using unfair methods to exclude or limit competitors in trade and investment while moving massively on the American scene, forcing land prices up in certain areas and invading such sensitive areas as security-related high technology and the entertainment industry. Protectionist sentiment has grown, exemplified by various Congressional actions, and successive American administrations have employed coercive means, such as the so-called Super-301 legislation to take or threaten retaliatory action when violations of fair trade practices are evidenced.

On their side, the Japanese—both officials and others—charge that in addition to U.S. governmental mismanagement of the economy, the American private sector has grown lazy, refusing to undertake the necessary changes to remain competitive in a rapidly changing world. They also feel that the American public is indulgent, preferring to live for today rather than to save for tomorrow. Under these conditions, when the American position deteriorates, it is argued, Japan is made the scapegoat, with an element of racism involved.

When one steps back from the polemics, it is clear that there is sufficient blame to be allocated in ample amount to both sides. In a broader sense, two dynamic nations, coming from different traditions, employing different economic strategies, and at different stages of development have become highly interdependent, in some respects, virtually integrated, in a remarkably short period of time. It would be miraculous if serious problems had not ensued. Yet the very intensity and scope of the relationship dictates that measures be taken by both parties to ameliorate the friction, and in the process, benefit their own society. Admittedly, this course has been made more difficult because of the multiple domestic pressures upon each government and the arduous task of finding ways to carry a majority of the citizenry in support of policies that do not always have short-run payoffs or benefit all segments of the society. This is but one aspect of a much more fundamental issue, namely, the governability of democratic societies in this revolutionary age.

Meanwhile, when Japan looks beyond its economic problems with the United States, it faces crucial economic decisions at both the regional and global levels. After considerable external pressure, Japan boosted its ODA (Overseas Development Assistance) to $8.96 billion in 1989, making it the largest aid donor in the world. Of this assistance, 62.5% went to Asian countries, signalling the fact that Japan's concerns have been strongly linked with the Pacific-Asian region. However, aid has also flowed to various parts of the so-called Third World outside Asia, some of it humanitarian in character, some of it related to strategic purposes. In fashioning a doctrine of "comprehensive security" first in 1978, Japanese policy makers indicated clearly that Japan's principal contribution to regional and global security should be in the economic and technological fields.

Despite steady increases in ODA, however, Japan still ranks low among advanced industrial nations in ratio of ODA to national GNP, burden of aid to the individual citizen (approximately $70 compared to nearly $200 in the Western industrial states), and ratio of grants to total ODA. Moreover, since 38% of the Japanese ODA projects in 1989 involved procurement from Japanese companies, many outside observers saw the program as yet another means of securing Japanese economic advantage abroad.

Unquestionably, however, an ever-larger number of late developing societies are counting upon Japanese support, including almost all of the old Leninist societies that are now undertaking or contemplating significant reforms in an effort to fit into the market-oriented international economy. Moreover, this is one form of international activity that continues to enjoy wide support from the Japanese people. In a 1989 poll, only 8% of the respondents wanted to see ODA cut.

Will this support hold? There have long been complaints that the lack of coordination among Japanese agencies controlling ODA and a paucity of trained personnel were hampering the efficiency of the program. More recently, questions have been raised as whether aid was not being wasted in certain settings, and whether the emphasis should not be redirected to such activities as education, medical care, and population planning. But beyond these matters, it seems likely that the average Japanese citizen will sooner or later raise the same questions brought up in the United States, where foreign aid has garnered less and less popular support. Although Japan's per capita income appears very high when expressed in dollar terms, its purchasing power measured in terms of a "market basket" of essential commodities is only 60% of that in the United States. More startling, sewerage systems cover a bare 40% of Japanese residents. Housing is prohibitively expensive, with a modest apartment in central Tokyo costing nearly 17 times the average annual income of a white collar salaried individual. It would not be surprising if the average voter in Japan began to question the increased flow of governmental funds to various needy applicants abroad.

Nevertheless, Japanese foreign policy is strongly oriented toward using economic instruments on behalf of perceived national interests, defined in their broadest terms as helping to promote regional and global stability. In this connection, Japan has been supportive of regional initiatives, such as the Pacific Economic Cooperation Conference (PECC) and the Asia-Pacific Economic Cooperation (APEC) meetings. At the same time, Japanese leaders have sought to maintain a low profile in the promotion of such projects, lest suspicions mount that Japan is seeking leadership of an Asian bloc.

Increasingly, moreover, Japan has contributed more in funds and personnel to such international agencies as the International Monetary Fund, the World Bank and the Asia Development Bank. At the same time, it has properly demanded a greater voice in the operations of these bodies, sometimes in the face of American resistance.

In its impersonal dimensions, Japan's economic internationalization process is truly impressive and virtually certain to continue. Reflective of the statement at the opening of this essay, however, the human factor in the various types of Japanese economic intercourse abroad remains relatively weak. There is still a strong element of aloofness and exclusiveness in Japanese economic operations in foreign countries, reflective of cultural traits deeply imbedded in Japanese society, including the mode of business operations at home and a product also of language problems, limited international experience, and even concerns about being embarrassed. Thus, while a new generation of internationalists is slowly emerging, this trend is well behind the massive infusion of Japanese goods and capital abroad. Hence, the political impact of the Japanese presence is fraught with greater negative potentials, especially in the West—but not only there—as sentiments in Korea, China, and Southeast Asia make clear.

Meanwhile, as Japanese officials and economic leaders scan the international horizon, two concerns are frequently voiced. The first relates to the possibility of regional protectionism on the part of the European Community and the newly formed North American free trade consortium. As noted, Japanese leaders see little prospect of a tightly knit Pacific-Asian economic community at this point, despite the various collective efforts at consultation taking place. Like others, moreover, they are uncertain about the future of the GATT (General Agreement on Tariffs and Trade). In addition, although European leaders aver that they have no intention of creating a Fortress Europe, some of their recent actions leave room for legitimate doubt, and generally speaking, they have been harsher in their economic treatment of Japan than has the United States.

It is conceivable, moreover, that fortified by an agreement with Canada, and with Mexico possibly added to the free trade zone, the United States might also draw a protectionist curtain around itself, especially if economic grievances against Japan and the NIEs accumulate and remain unresolved. A second concern is closely related to the first one. What if the United States were to have a sustained economic crisis? The fact is that Japanese involvement in the American economy is so extensive today that it is both in a position to exercise very considerable influence on American economic policies and by the same token, destined to be a hostage to trends in the American economy. Japan has been purchasing one-fourth or more of the bonds at certain Treasury auctions. If Japanese investors were to lose confidence in the U.S. economy and withdraw their funds, this could have enormous repercussions. But the losses suffered by those investors would be huge. Thus, Japan's stake in sound U.S. economic policies and practices can scarcely be exaggerated.

Given the multiple uncertainties that exist in the international and domestic scene at present, it would be foolish to advance a single future scenario. One can sketch an optimistic picture involving the continued strength of the Japanese economy; needed corrections bolstering the American economy; the containment, then amelioration, of U.S.-Japan economic friction amid the progressive integration of the two economies; and the gradual reduction of barriers to trade and services on the part of all of the advanced industrial societies, as well as their cooperation in assisting the less developed nations.

A negative scenario, however, is also not difficult to draw. It would involve a global economic crisis spearheaded by a U.S. depression; prolonged instability in the Middle East affecting oil prices and availability; heightened protectionism either within specific industrial states or regional blocs and a refusal to share technology; and the breakdown of cooperation with respect to North-South issues.

Naturally, there are "in-between" scenarios, and in all likelihood, some mix of positive and negative factors will unfold. Majority opinion projects a strong Japanese economic performance in the years immediately ahead. It is acknowledged, however, that the population will age rapidly, requiring further changes in the industrial structure, the degree of internationalization, and the extension of social services at home. A minority argues that Japan's economic peak will soon pass, with leadership going to the regional economic blocs now in the process of formation.

It seems likely, however, that whatever the course of events, the need for capital by the developing world, including the badly tattered Leninist states, will be enormous in the immediate future, straining the capacity of even a highly prosperous Japan and a resurgent European Community. In this setting, Japan will certainly be a key player in the regional and global scene, having to make economic choices about policies and programs that will impact heavily upon the future of many nations.

THE POLITICAL DIMENSIONS
OF JAPANESE FOREIGN POLICY

Increasingly, Japanese policy makers have come to realize that however important, ODA and other forms of economic interaction, in isolation, will not suffice to enhance Japan's image as a responsible member of the global community and a nation prepared to play its role in building a new international order. Checkbook diplomacy, as it is sometimes derisively labelled, is burdened with the suspicion on the part of others that at best, it is the easy way out, since it avoids participating in the crucial aspects of challenging aggression and supporting peace-keeping, and at worst, it is an additional means of advancing Japan's economic interests.

Thus, in the past decade, Japan has been seeking to find a political role suited to its capacities and compatible with the views of its citizenry. Naturally, its overtures have been largely toward the Third World, and more particularly, with reference to East Asia. At an earlier point, Tokyo made a brief, abortive attempt to serve as middleman in the Iraq-Iran war. There followed various activities with respect to the Cambodian conflict, including an acceptance of Thai Prime Minister Chatichai's suggestion that Tokyo host a meeting of the four Khmer factions in an effort to cut through the Cambodian impasse. While the meeting was less than successful, it took place, and throughout the recent period, Japan has indicated that it would be willing to play some role in peace-keeping apart from economic assistance if and when that conflict comes to an end.

The stormy debate over participation in the Gulf crisis that took place in the fall of 1990 indicates both how significant and how divisive the issue of involvement in regional crises can become. In retrospect, it seems clear that the Kaifu government made a major mistake in involving the Self-Defense Forces in a proposed team to go to the Middle East, even though they were to be enjoined against combat activities and were to be only lightly armed. Constitutional issues relating to Article 9 were quickly raised by opponents, and public opinion polls showed that some two-thirds of the Japanese public were opposed to the proposal as first set forth. The government retreated in disarray and worked on a new plan in conjunction with the two centrist parties.

Naturally, the issue of American pressure was prominently discussed, but irrespective of this fact, the far-reaching debate over the legally permissible and desirable role of Japan in the event of a regional crisis has opened a new chapter in Japanese foreign policy that has by no means been completed. Those dissatisfied with the status quo, it might be noted, argue that until Japan is prepared to take certain risks with the lives of its own citizens in the cause of peace, it will not be credible with others.

Yet another political action on Japan's part followed the Tiananmen killings of June 3–4, 1989. The Tokyo government joined in condemnation of the Beijing government's actions and agreed to the imposition of an economic embargo covering loans. Yet Japan does not place a high premium upon human rights as a criterion for foreign policy decisions. Privately, many Japanese policy makers feel that it is both unrealistic and ethnocentric to seek to impose Western-derived standards on societies coming from a different cultural background and facing radically different conditions. Moreover, they argue that the real route to political change in such societies is to abet the developmental process and ensure to the extent possible that such societies are opened up to the world. In this, it should be emphasized, Japan's policies do not differ greatly from those of most other Asian nations. Taiwanese trade and investment with the PRC remained virtually unaffected by the 1989 events, continuing to expand rapidly. ASEAN relations were also relatively unaffected, and indeed, both Indonesia and Singapore established diplomatic relations with the PRC in the course of 1990. Despite its reservations, however, the Japanese government abided by the sanctions, both in the case of the PRC and Vietnam, while the private sector made economic decisions, when permissible, based upon hard economic criteria.

In its political relations, Japan, like other nations, has a steeply graded table of priorities. At the top is the relationship with the United States. While the growth of Japanese nationalism has engendered some increase in resentment of American pressure and calls for greater independence in the economic, political, and even security realms, such positions still represent a distinct minority, both at official and public levels, as recent polls indicate. Shintaro Ishihara, the widely publicized Japanese nationalist politician-writer, does not speak for a large number of his fellow citizens. In point of fact, anti-Japanese sentiment in the United States has grown much more rapidly, especially when questions relating to trustworthiness are asked. Even the Japan Socialist Party spokesmen now recognize the importance of ties with the United States, although they prefer to emphasize its nonmilitary aspects.

The next set of concerns for Japan relate to Northeast Asia and its near neighbors. Here, political factors are closely interwoven with economic considerations. The two large socialist states, both undergoing sweeping changes with their outcomes as yet undetermined, are watched with special concern. Enmity with Russia has dominated the twentieth century, insofar as Japan has been concerned. A new relationship may be at hand, but the factors that will decide this remain too numerous and unclear to make prediction wise. Certainly, relations with Russia, whatever may be the future shape and internal system of the U.S.S.R., will continue to bulk large in Japan's concern. Russia is a nation whose economic potential, if liberated, is a very considerable one, whose military capacities remain great—and close at hand—and whose political future, whether relatively stable or chaotic, will affect Japan along with other Soviet neighbors. Whatever the course of events, however, it seems most unlikely that given past history and current potentialities, Japanese-Russian relations can be close and trusting in the near future.

Japan's hopes for China are considerably greater, notwithstanding the many problems that beset that society. Most Japanese specialists, as well as policy makers, believe that China will muddle through, and in the course of the next century, emerge as a quasi-modern society, albeit, one that has developed in an highly uneven fashion, with extensive regional differences. Moreover, they see Japan as playing a critical role in China's evolution, serving as a principal engine advancing the economic modernization process.

Here too, however, there is an element of ambivalence. On the one hand, Japan does not want a weak, chaotic China, remembering the history of the early twentieth century. Thus, its policy makers argue against isolating the PRC or placing too heavy an emphasis upon its political transgressions, as previously noted. On the other hand, there are a number of Japanese who already worry about a China that develops too rapidly, and with its "Central Kingdom" mentality intact, elects at some future point to use military power to assert its claim to being Asia's true major state, current denials of a desire to play the role of hegemonist notwithstanding.

In China, a similar ambivalence exists. Chinese leaders recognize the importance of Japan to the PRC modernization program, and they seek to cultivate that nation, both its officials and its private sector, in the process, separating it in some degree from the major Western states. At the same time, anti-Japanese sentiment is deeply planted, both in higher political circles and at the grass roots, a product of past history and a widening cultural gap. Thus, the danger of recurrent Japanese militarism is frequently stressed, and angry responses are given to those Japanese who assert that the historical record has been distorted against their nation. Even in the economic realm, Chinese resentment against the Japanese unwillingness to transfer technology generously is manifest. In sum, the Japanese-Chinese relationship is likely to be an important, but somewhat fragile one, with elements of cooperation and competition or suspicion coexisting. Certainly, the concept of Pan Asianism,in its old form at least, seems passé.

The Korean peninsula also continues to represent a series of thorny issues for Japan combining opportunities and risks. Relations were normalized with South Korea in 1965, and as has been indicated, Japan's economic relations with the ROK have become an increasingly vital element in the economies of both nations. Various problems have emerged, reflective of the same type of issues that exist in U.S.-Japan relations (for example, Japanese charges of Korean dumping), but it is virtually certain that the economic ties between these two nations will remain substantial and important. In the political realm, however, the atmosphere is correct but cool. Deep prejudices exist on both sides, exacerbated by the presence of some 700,000 ethnic Korean residents in Japan, a population divided politically and with those of alien status subject to certain rules, including fingerprinting, that rile the political waters.

Meanwhile, after decades of noncontact at the official level, North Korea and Japan are in the process of negotiating over diplomatic recognition. The initiative here was taken by Pyongyang, its leaders traumatized by German reunification, the events in Romania, and above all, Soviet policies, including its establishment of diplomatic relations with the South. These negotiations have not yet run their course, but it seems likely that diplomatic recognition will eventuate at some point. However, already, Tokyo has incurred the unhappiness of the South, with Seoul fearing that Japanese economic reparations to the North will weaken their own bargaining power in the North-South talks and bolster a badly sagging DPRK economy.

Given all events, past and present, Japan will have to use extraordinary skill in advancing its policies toward the two Koreas if it is to avoid recurrent clashes, but the chances for peace on the Korean peninsula and for an opening of the North now seem better than at any time since the Korean War. Korean unification does not appear likely in the near term, and there is the further question in many Japanese minds as to whether unification would be in Japan's interests. Would a single Korean nation—strongly nationalistic, probably anti-Japanese, and according to some pessimists, possibly armed with nuclear weapons—be in Japan's interests?

Taiwan also represents a legacy of the past in which Japan has a strong interest, and one that is not merely economic. Like all other nations having diplomatic relations with the PRC, Japan accepts in principle the position that there is only one China and that Taiwan is a part of China. But Taiwan has been independent for more than forty years, and in terms of its political structure, it has moved away from the PRC recently, while coming closer in economic and cultural relations. There are no current indications that China-Taiwan unification is close at hand, and for some time, Japan has pursued a de facto one China-one Taiwan policy, including consultations between certain politicians of Japan and Taiwan. While Japan is most unlikely to allow this issue to become a source of cleavage with the PRC, neither is it likely to abandon its present policies unless great pressure is applied.

In the larger world of Pacific-Asia, as noted earlier, Japan is supportive of a variety of regional and sub-regional organizational efforts without wishing to appear to be the spearhead behind them. Its low-posture position, however, is gradually undergoing some change. Increasingly, Japan is taking positions, many of them nominally economic, that have strong political overtones, as well as offering its services in peace-keeping activities.

Japan's political ties with Western and Eastern Europe remain exceedingly limited, largely defined in economic terms. Assistance to various countries of Eastern Europe is advertised as both humanitarian in nature and a contribution to the growth of democracy—but it remains relatively limited in scale. Through its position in the Group of 7 as well as other agencies, Japan is party to political as well as economic discussions, but there is no evidence that it has taken a leadership role, except to request a reconsideration of the sanctions on China, and for the most part, this was done privately and with the United States.

Coupled with its request for a greater voice in international economic organizations, however, Japan has begun to raise the question informally of permanent membership on the Security Council of the United Nations. A number of Japanese—as well as many foreign observers—believe that with economics playing such a vital role in international relations at present, and with Japan one of the world's two global economic powers, it is an anomaly to have it unrepresented at the U.N. summit. The complications of this matter, of course, are recognized, since other nations have some claim to similar treatment—but this is an issue that will not go away.

In sum, Japan is groping its way toward an expanded regional and global role, one having political as well as economic components. In this quest, it is presently handicapped not only by virtue of the lack of a strong institutional position on the international stage, but by the uncertainties within Japan, including within the public, as to what political role it can and should play. It is certain, however, that the efforts in this direction will continue and be expanded, and when some degree of success has been achieved in one of its ventures, that will provide added stimulus to the quest for an enlarged role. It is most likely, however, that that role will generally be played within bilateral and multilateral contexts, not as a solo performance.

CULTURE AND FOREIGN POLICY

Social scientists may argue about the role of culture in economic and political systems, but few would deny that Japan's ability to select from its cultural traditions those qualities best suited for its modernization goals played a major part in its successful evolution. Yet today, in Japan as elsewhere, a cosmopolitan culture is emerging, especially among the younger generations, reflected in dress, music, and almost all aspects of life style. In comparative terms, to be sure, Japanese culture is still strongly influenced by its past, but the socio-economic revolution through which it is passing will inevitably result in ever-greater cultural changes in the years ahead. In this sense, the internationalization of Japan—still a very incomplete development—will be forwarded, however the results may be judged from a normative standpoint.

In recent years, a growing number of Japanese, encouraged by the purchasing power of the yen, have travelled abroad as sightseeing tourists. The number visiting the United States and its possessions, for example, now exceeds one million annually, and large numbers also go to various parts of Asia and Europe. Although most Japanese travel in groups, the opportunity to see in person diverse nations undoubtedly has had a considerable impact. Japanese television also carries the world into every Japanese home, and given the high literacy of the Japanese people, information is garnered through a number of other sources.

At the same time, as has been indicated, the introverted, relatively closed nature of Japanese small group associations continues to make itself felt in cultural relations. It is combined, moreover, with serious language handicaps and a higher educational system that has encouraged inbreeding. Consequently, the cultural network that Japan has built with foreign countries is both more formal and less comprehensive than is true of most other nations of comparable status. This can be seen even in Japan's most important relationship, that with the United States. In 1986, slightly over 13,000 Japanese students were studying in the United States (a mere 881 American students were studying in Japan). In that same year, a total of only 17,924 Japanese students were studying abroad, and the total number of foreign students in Japan was less than 13,000. Japanese foundations and new programs are in the process of expanding cultural and educational programs, but there is still a very great distance to go.

SECURITY ISSUES IN JAPANESE FOREIGN POLICY

It remains to examine one of the most volatile aspects of Japan's foreign policy at present, namely, its security policies. As has been indicated, the United States established the initial perimeters of Japanese security policy, and in doing so, created remarkably generous—some would say idealistic—terms of support. Indeed, it might be argued that the greatest gift the United States provided Japan after 1945 was neither democracy nor economic assistance, but the American willingness to take over the costs and risks of Japanese security, enabling that nation to devote its resources and energies to economic growth.

In the course of time conditions have changed, both within the two countries immediately concerned and in the world. Japan, now among the more affluent nations, has increased its security expenditures. The annual rate of growth in the defense budget has averaged between 4.5% and 6% in recent years, and using the NATO calculations, Japan now expends the third large amount in the world on defense, next to the United States and the U.S.S.R. On the other hand, those expenditures amount to only around 1% of the Japanese national budget, despite the removal of the so-called 1% barrier during the Nakasone era.

More importantly, the SDF as it is structured is heavily defensive in nature, in accordance with the prevailing interpretation of the constitution that it is legal only for purposes of defending the nation. In 1990, the armed forces totalled less than 250,000, of which 156,200 were in the army, 46,400 in the navy, and 12,000 in the air force. Their equipment was very modern and included tanks, armored vehicles, field artillery, and antitank helicopters for the ground forces; destroyers, submarines, and a range of patrol and short-range fighter aircraft for the navy; and some 337 additional highly modern aircraft for the air force.

The SDF, however, does not include long-range missiles, heavy bombers, or major capital ships of the type that would be required for overseas offensive action. In essence, this is a force tailored to the defense of the home islands for a temporary period of time, until help can arrive. It is only partially equipped to undertake the sea and air surveillance up to 1,000 nautical miles and 200 miles respectively to the south and east to which Japan has committed itself.

In addition, Japan currently assumes approximately 40% of the maintenance costs of American forces stationed in Japan, and that figure is scheduled to rise by 10% or more in the near future. Amending a policy banning the export of military weapons or technology, Japan agreed in January 1983 to export dual-use technology to the United States, and despite the ugly controversy over the FSX fighter plane where economic and security considerations were clearly intertwined, that pledge still holds.

In general, cooperation between the United States and Japan in the security field has never been closer. On security matters, Washington and Tokyo consult closely, joint defense studies have been undertaken, and joint military training and exercises take place. The FSX controversy and other developments, however, now make it clear that economic and security matters cannot be separated, raising new complications. A certain number of Americans, including members of Congress, have insisted that Japan should spend more on defense, extend its surveillance and related security activities in Asia; and a very few Americans have even argued that the Japanese should consider constitutional revision. Threats have been made in some quarters to remove U.S. forces from Japan and downgrade or abrogate the Mutual Security Treaty unless burden sharing is rapidly advanced. And while the latter voices are a distinct minority, concern in the United States about the high costs of the current Pacific-Asian defense program has already resulted in pledges of a 10% cut in personnel in the next several years, with the distinct possibility of more significant reductions.

It is in this context that discussions about security have recently unfolded in Japan. Broadly speaking, three groups can be discerned. The first group can be labelled Gaullists. Described in general terms, their position is that U.S. credibility is declining, and in any case, the era when it was necessary for Japan to be a security dependent of the United States is over. Japan should move to establish itself as an independent power with its own agenda for Asia and the world, they assert. This requires changes in the 1947 constitution, and Japanese public opinion should be prepared for that necessity, in their opinion. New threats, some of them emanating from Northeast Asia, will replace old ones, even if the U.S.S.R. ceases to be a major power. Japan must be prepared.

The Gaullists, while vocal, are still a small minority. To be sure, they have succeeded in worrying a number of Japanese and a larger group of other Asians. They have also placed certain issues on the public agenda that have long been taboo in Japanese political discussion. The likelihood that theirs will become Japanese policy, however, is very remote, unless the United States shifts rapidly to isolationism and the regional climate becomes extremely troubled.

A second group can be labelled the Minimalists. This group includes pacifists and ex-pacifists, as well as a variety of other individuals who see no reason to take greater risks and fear that a close military connection with the United States could lead Japan into trouble. Central to its membership remains the Japan Socialist Party, and yet the JSP has moved in the recent past from a strictly pacifist position to a more equivocal stance. In its most recent pronouncements, the party abandoned its support of unarmed neutrality, and even decided that in the event of a coalition government under its aegis, it would support the continuance of the Mutual Security Treaty and SDF. Earlier, in a statement that set a record for ambiguity, it pronounced the SDF "unconstitutional but legal."

JSP leaders have recently talked of reducing the military aspects of the relationship with the United States while expanding its economic and cultural dimensions. Many Minimalists remain emotionally committed to a broader collective security structure that would encompass Northeast Asia and substitute for the MST, but most have gradually accepted the fact that the time for such a course has not yet arrived. Hence, they have come to accept the SDF providing its function is strictly limited, namely, strictly for homeland defense only. Despite significant modifications in their position, the Minimalists also remain a distinct minority within the Japanese body politic. Again, depending upon developments, including their own flexibility, they might grow in numbers, especially if the costs of international risk taking appeared to be very high for Japan. And almost certainly, if U.S. credibility as an ally were to precipitously decline, the Minimalists would rise to do battle with the Gaullists in a struggle that would shake Japan to its roots.

A third group can be labelled the Alliance-Supporters, and they continue to represent the mainstream in Japan, although they divide into various sub-groups, and recent events have created heightened tensions both within their ranks and with rival groups. This group continues to insist on the need for a close U.S.-Japan security relationship, both for the sake of Japan's national interest and that of the rest of Asia. Privately, they acknowledge that an independent, armed Japan would evoke major opposition throughout the region and might create the impetus for greater militarization elsewhere. They do not regard Asia's security issues as having been resolved, seeing new threats likely to emerge and a collective security system unfeasible at this point. Nor are they sanguine about any other bilateral security relationship that could substitute for that with the United States.

They acknowledge that Japan must do more within the bilateral security structure, although their various sub-groups are not in agreement as to precisely what more should be done. Some come close to the Gaullists in insisting that it is legitimate for Japan to involve the SDF in collective defense, not being bound by artificial geographic limitations. If 70% of Japan's oil comes from the Middle East, certain Alliance-Supporters argue, is its security not intimately and directly involved in events there? Others are much more cautious, asserting that the Japanese people are not prepared to accept an enhanced military role, and any such effort would also arouse antagonism everywhere. Therefore, Japan should accept increased costs for U.S. defense upkeep, send Japanese Peace Corps, now in existence, to various regions, and in the aftermath of conflict play a role in peace-keeping operations via civilian teams.

In one sense, the old divisions with respect to security policies have become blurred in Japan, with elements from each of the previously mentioned groups shifting somewhat in their positions as new conditions have emerged. In another sense, there has been a moderate but perceptible trend toward a more independent, assertive stance, although that has not yet reflected itself fully in governmental policy. The fundamental questions being raised are what will be the coming shape of Japan's position in Asia and the world in a period when the configuration of power is changing, and how is the patron-client relationship established between the United States and Japan shortly after World War II being fundamentally altered?

IN CONCLUSION

It is not surprising that Japanese foreign policy is undergoing changes, some of them subtle and incremental, others substantial and relatively rapid. The old dilemmas remain, in some respects even heightened. But the world around Japan, including its nearest neighbors, is in the midst of the greatest upheaval in this century and possibly in recorded history. Japan's closest ally and erstwhile patron, the United States, while currently the only global power, can no longer play the role of security guarantor for its allies in the earlier manner. It must demand greater burden sharing and reciprocity. And within Japan itself, the cumulative effects of the enormous economic revolution of the past four decades—good and bad—are having an increasing social and political effect.

The uneasiness involved in Japan's rising debate over its global role is understandable. No matter what the answers, some questions are painful. When most other nations are seeking to cut back on the costs and risks of a high-posture foreign policy, why should Japan move in an opposite direction? At a time when the great Eurasian heartland is weakening, from whence comes the threat? And who, especially in Asia, would trust a high-posture, militarily powerful Japan? On the other hand, what nation has a greater stake in a stable, orderly world than Japan, and hence, a greater responsibility for punishing aggressors who seek to disrupt the global order? Can one say that a pacifist Japan, eschewing balance of power politics, would not tempt others, including neighbors, to assert their supremacy? And is Japan to be permanently condemned to have less than full sovereignty in matters pertaining to its own security, being always subordinate to some other power?

With these and similar questions the Japanese government and people will wrestle in the months and years ahead. Their responses will be shaped in considerable measure by the actions—and inactions—of others, but internal developments will also play a significant role. Few possibilities can be totally ruled out. The present trend, however, is toward a more assertive Japan, yet a Japan that continues to place a lower priority on military answers to the world's problems than the economic approaches that have served it well in the past, meanwhile raising its political voice on a greater number of occasions, usually in concert with others.

FOREIGN POLICY LANDMARKS

September 8, 1945	General MacArthur accepts the surrender of Japan on the battleship Missouri
November 3, 1946	Promulgation of the new Japanese Constitution, to go into effect six months later
April 28, 1952	Effective date of the treaties of peace and security restoring Japan's independence and alliance with the United States
July 1, 1954	Transformation of the National Safety Force to the present Self-Defense Force
November 1955	The merger of the Liberal and Democratic parties to form the Liberal Democratic Party
October 19, 1956	Joint Soviet-Japan Declaration reestablishing diplomatic relations
May–June, 1960	Strikes and demonstrations protesting the revised United States-Japan Security Treaty
December 8, 1965	The establishment of diplomatic relations between Japan and the Republic of Korea
September 29, 1972	Japan-People's Republic of China joint statement inaugurating diplomatic relations
September 1980	Establishment of the Pacific Economic Cooperation Conference
1981	The pledge by the Japanese government to develop capabilities to conduct defense surveillance up to 1,000 nautical miles south and east of Japan and several hundred miles by air
1981	The ground forces of Japan begin joint exercises with U.S. military forces
January 1985	The launching of Market-Oriented, Sector-Specific (MOSS) talks aimed at resolving United States-Japan trade problems
January 1985	U.S.S.R. Foreign Minister Edward Shevardnadze visits Tokyo
April 1986	The submission of the Maekawa Report to Prime Minister Nakasone
July 1986	A historic victory for the Liberal Democratic Party in national Diet elections
April 17, 1987	United States imposition of penalties on Japan in connection with the semiconductor dispute
1987	The Defense Agency budget exceeds 1% by 0.004%

December 1987	U.S. dollar reaches low point of 121 yen to 1 dollar
December 1987	Announcement of a new ASEAN-Japan Development Fund
January 7, 1989	The death of Emperor Hirohito
1989	U.S.-Japan disputes over the so-called Super-301 sanctions and the FS-X jet fighter production
1990	The opening of Structural Impediment Initiative discussions with the United States
Fall 1990	Japan leads movement to lift economic sanctions on the PRC
January 1991	Japan-DPRK negotiations on normalization of relations open
April 14–16, 1991	Gorbachev's visit to Japan fails to settle the dispute on the Kurile Islands (held by the Soviets since the end of World War II) and to arrange for economic aid to the U.S.S.R.

SELECTED BIBLIOGRAPHY

Although English-language materials are still far too limited, the last fifteen years have seen an increasing number of worthy articles, monographs, and general studies, many of which deal in some fashion with Japanese foreign policy.

To start with the historical background of Japanese international relations, one might mention the older work of R.H. Akagi, *Japan's Foreign Relations, 1542–1936* (Argus, 1936); but the historical writings of Sir George Sansom provide an excellent introduction to this subject as well as to other facets of traditional Japan: *Japan–A Short Cultural History,* rev. ed. (Englewood Cliffs, N.J.: Prentice-Hall, 1962); *A History of Japan to 1334* (Stanford, Calif.: Stanford University Press 1958), *A History of Japan, 1334–1615* (Stanford, Calif.: Stanford University Press, 1960), and *The Western World and Japan* (New York: Knopf, 1950). See also Herschel Webb, *The Japanese Imperial Institution in the Tokugawa Period* (New York: Columbia University Press, 1968).

For the modern period, a few general works include materials on Japanese foreign policy. One might select W. G. Beasley, *The Modern History of Japan,* 2d ed. (London: Weidenfeld and Nicolson, 1973); Hugh Borton, *Japan's Modern Century* (New York: Ronald Press, 1955); and Richard Storry, *A History of Modern Japan,* rev. ed. (London: Penguin, 1982) as works of this type.

Perhaps no single English source is as valuable as the voluminous *War Crimes Trial Documents,* running into thousands of pages, which were translated for the famous Tokyo trials. These also can be obtained; a complete set exists, for instance, at the University of California, Berkeley library.

Among existing Western memoirs, special mention should be made of J. C. Grew, *Ten Years in Japan* (New York: Simon & Schuster, 1944), and Sir R. Craigie, *Behind the Japanese Mask* (London: Hutchinson, 1946). From the Japanese side, see Mamoru Shigemitsu, *Japan and Her Destiny* (New York: Dutton, 1958).

We have a general account of this wartime period in F. C. Jones, *Japan's New Order in East Asia: Its Rise and Fall, 1937–1945* (London: Oxford University Press, 1954).

Various aspects of the postwar period are covered in certain general books: Ardath Burks, *Japan: Profile of a Postindustrial Power* (Boulder, Colo.: Westview Press, 1983); Tadashi Fukutake, *Japanese Society Today* (Tokyo: Tokyo University Press, 1982); Frank Gibney, *Japan: The Fragile Superpower,* rev. ed. (New York: Meridian Books, 1982); Nobutaka Ike, *A Theory of Japanese Democracy* (Boulder, Colo.: Westview Press, 1978); Rei Shiratori, ed., *Japan in the 1980s* (Tokyo: Kodansha, 1983); Edwin O. Reischauer, *The Japanese,* rev. ed. (Cambridge, Mass.: Belknap Press, 1983); J. A. A. Stockwin, *Japan: Divided Politics in a Growth Economy* (New York: Norton, 1975); Robert E. Ward, ed., *Political Development in Modern Japan* (Princeton, N.J.: Princeton University Press, 1968); and Joji Watanuki, *Politics in Postwar Japanese Society* (Tokyo: University of Tokyo Press, 1977). See also *Parties and Politics in*

Contemporary Japan by Robert A. Scalapino and Junnosuke Masumi (Berkeley, Calif.: University of California Press, 1962).

Recent works revealing aspects of Japanese society that provide one type of insight into Japanese attitudes and policies in international affairs include Robert Christopher, *The Japanese Mind: The Goliath Explained* (New York: Simon and Schuster, 1983); Tadashi Fukutake, *The Japanese Social Structure: Its Evolution in the Modern Century* (trans. by Ronald Dore) (Tokyo: Tokyo University Press, 1982); Takeshi Ishida, *Japanese Society* (New York: Random House, 1971); Robert J. Lifton, et al., *Six Lives, Six Deaths: Portraits from Modern Japan* (New Haven, Conn.: Yale University Press, 1979); and Ezra F. Vogel, *Modern Japanese Organization and Decision Making* (Berkeley, Calif.: University of California Press, 1975).

A few general studies of Japanese foreign policy exist in English. See Michael Blaker, *Japanese International Negotiating Style* (New York: Columbia University Press, 1977); Donald C. Hellmann, *Japan and East Asia: The New International Order* (New York: Praeger, 1972); Frank Langdon, *Japan's Foreign Policy* (Berkeley, Calif.: University of California Press, 1973); and Robert A. Scalapino, ed., *The Foreign Policy of Modern Japan* (Berkeley, Calif.: University of California Press, 1977).

For studies emphasizing the economic aspects of Japanese foreign policy, see James Abegglen and George Stalk, Jr., *Kaisha, The Japanese Corporation* (New York: Basic Books, 1985); Robert E. Cole, *Work, Mobility and Participation: A Comparative Study of American and Japanese Industry* (Berkeley, Calif.: University of California Press, 1979); I. M. Destler and Hideo Sato, eds. *Coping with U.S.-Japanese Conflicts* (Lexington, Mass.: Lexington Books, 1982); Leon Hollerman, ed., *Japan and the United States: Economic and Political Adversaries* (Boulder, Colo.: Westview Press, 1980); Chalmers A. Johnson, *MITI and the Japanese Miracle: The Growth of Industrial Policy, 1925–1975* (Stanford, Calif.: Stanford University Press, 1982); and *Japan's Public Policy Companies* (Washington, D.C.: American Enterprise Institute, 1978); Hiroshi Mannari and Harumi Befu, *The Challenge of Japan's Internationalization and Culture* (Tokyo: Kwansei Gakuin University and Kodansha International, 1983); Yasusuke Murakami and Yutaka Kosai, eds., *Japan in the Global Community* (Tokyo: University of Tokyo Press, 1986); Daniel I. Okimoto, *Japan's Economy: Coping with Change in the International Environment* (Boulder, Colo.: Westview Press, 1982); Hugh Patrick and Henry Rosovsky, eds., *Asia's New Giant* (Washington, D.C.: Brookings Institution, 1976); Fred H. Sanderson, *Japan's Food Prospects and Policies* (Washington, D.C.: Brookings Institution, 1978); and Jimmy W. Wheeler, Merit E. Janow, and Thomas Pepper, *Japanese Industrial Development Policies in the 1980s* (Croton-on-Hudson, N.Y.: Hudson Institute, 1982).

For works concentrating primarily upon security issues, see Claude A. Buss, *National Security Interests in the Pacific Basin* (Stanford, Calif.: Hoover Institution, 1985); Reinhard Drifte, *Arms Production in Japan* (Boulder, Colo.: Westview Press, 1986); Ryukichi Imai and Henry S. Rowen, *Nuclear Energy and Nuclear Proliferation: Japanese and American Views*, Boulder, Colo.: Westview Press, 1977); Young W. Kihl and Lawrence Grinter, eds., *Asian-Pacific Security: Emerging Challenges and Responses* (Boulder, Colo.: Lynne Rienner, 1986); Hisahiko Okazaki, *A Japanese View of Detente* (Lexington, Mass.: D.C. Heath, 1974); Masashi Nishihara, "Prospects for Japan's Defense Strength and International Security Role," in Douglas Stuart, ed., *Security within the Pacific Rim* (Gower Publishing Company, 1987); Yukio Satoh, *The Evolution of Japanese Security Policy* (London: Adelphi Papers, No. 178, International Institute for Strategic Studies, 1982); Robert A. Scalapino, Seizaburo Sato, and Jusuf Wanandi, eds., *Internal and External Security Issues in Asia* (Berkeley, Calif.: Institute of East Asian Studies, University of California, 1986); Richard Sneider, *U.S.-Japanese Security Relations* (New York: East Asian Institute, Columbia University, 1982); Richard H. Solomon and Masataka Kosaka, eds., *The Soviet Far East Military Buildup* (Dover, Mass.: Auburn House, 1986); *U.S.-Japan Relations in the 1980s: Towards Burden Sharing* (Cambridge, Mass.: Cambridge Center for International Affairs, Harvard University Press, 1982); Martin E. Weinstein, *Japan's Postwar Defense Policy, 1947–1968* (New York: Columbia University Press, 1970); Martin E. Weinstein, ed., *Northeast Asian Security After Vietnam* (Champaign, Ill.: University of Illinois Press, 1982); and the yearly reports entitled *Defense of Japan* issued by the Japan

Defense Agency, as well as the yearly surveys entitled *Asian Security* published by the Research Institute for Peace and Security, Tokyo.

Naturally, the American reader will tend to have a special interest in American-Japanese relations. A substantial number of books have been written on this subject. Among the older works, those of Payson J. Treat are well known: *Japan and the United States,* rev. ed. (Stanford, Calif.: Stanford University Press, 1928), and *Diplomatic Relations between the United States and Japan,* 3 vols. (Stanford, Calif.: Stanford University Press, 1932, 1938). See also Foster Rhea Dulles, *Forty Years of American-Japanese Relations* (New York: Appleton-Century-Crofts, 1937).

A broad cultural account is to be found in T. Dennett, *Americans in Eastern Asia* (New York: Macmillan, 1922). More recently, such an approach has been effectively used by Robert Schwantes in his *Japanese and Americans: A Century of Cultural Relations* (New York: Harper & Row, 1955).

For recent American-Japanese relations in addition to works cited, see *Challenges and Opportunities in U.S.-Japan Relations,* a report of the U.S.-Japan Advisory Commission, Washington, D.C., 1984; Ellen L. Frost, *For Richer, For Poorer: The New U.S.-Japan Relationship* (New York: Council on Foreign Relations, 1987); Institute of East Asian Studies, *Japanese Challenge and the American Response: A Symposium* (Berkeley, Calif.: Institute of East Asian Studies, University of California, 1982); Chae-Jin Lee and Hideo Sato, *U.S. Policy Toward Japan and Korea: A Changing Influence Relationship* (New York: Praeger, 1982); Hugh T. Patrick and Ryuichiro Tachi, *Japan and the United States Today* (Montpelier, Vt.: Capital City Press, 1986); Edwin O. Reischauer, *The United States and Japan,* rev. ed. (Cambridge, Mass.: Harvard University Press, 1976); Gaston J. Sigur and Young C. Kim, eds., *Japanese and U.S. Policy in Asia* (New York: Praeger, 1982); *The United States and Japan in 1986: Can the Partnership Work?* (School of Advanced International Studies, Johns Hopkins University, Washington, D.C., 1986) and Robert Scalapino, ed., *The Foreign Policy of Modern Japan* (Univ. of California Press, Berkeley, Calif., 1977).

Official publications from the U.S. State Department, such as the series *Foreign Relations of the United States and Japan,* contain useful major documents. See also various congressional hearings, both those of the Senate Committee on Foreign Relations and the Subcommittee on Asian and Pacific Affairs, House Foreign Affairs Committee.

No serious study of Japanese foreign policy should be undertaken, of course, without reference to the periodical literature. Among the English-language journals, those carrying articles of significance at rather regular intervals include *Contemporary Japan, Japan Quarterly* (formerly *Far Eastern Quarterly*), *Foreign Affairs, Pacific Affairs,* and *Asian Survey.*

Among the books published most recently note the following:

Frost, Ellen L. *For Richer, for Poorer: The New U.S.-Japan Relationship.* New York: Council on Foreign Relations, 1987.

Okita, Saburo. *Approaching the 21st Century: Japan's Role.* Tokyo: The Japan Times, 1990.

——, *Japan in the World Economy of the 1980's.* Tokyo: University of Tokyo Press, 1989.

Orr, Robert M., Jr. *The Emergence of Japan's Foreign Aid Power.* New York: Columbia University Press, 1990.

Romberg, Alan D. and Tadashi Yamamoto, eds. *Same Bed, Different Dreams–America and Japan Societies in Transition.* New York: Council on Foreign Relations, 1990.

Whiting, Allen S. *China Eyes Japan.* Berkeley: University of California Press, 1989.

—8—

FOREIGN POLICY
OF
CHINA

Allen S. Whiting

CONCEPTUAL FRAMEWORK

China is the world's oldest continuous civilization but our analysis of Chinese foreign policy must be largely inferential. Little primary research in Chinese archival materials has been completed to provide us with an evidential base for understanding the perceptual framework, the organizational interaction, and the political determinants which combine to make foreign policy. Too few detailed case studies exist of specific interactive situations involving the People's Republic of China (PRC) to lay a foundation for systematic generalization about behavior. Even the conventional historical record provides relatively little help. Although its political systems date back more than 2,000 years, China is a relative newcomer to contemporary foreign relations. For centuries, its relations with the outside world remained tributary in nature. No concept of sovereignty or equality interfered with domination by the Middle Kingdom over dependencies such as Tibet and Mongolia, or vassal states such as Korea and Annam.

Nomenclature Note: Most Chinese names are rendered in the new transliteration system, *pinyin*, adopted by the State Council of the People's Republic of China in 1978. This phonetic spelling differs from a previously widely used transliteration system, Wade-Giles, some examples of which are contrasted with *pinyin* on page 265. Source citations in footnotes remain in the Wade-Giles to facilitate locating them in a standard card catalog.

The collapse of the Manchu empire and the birth, in 1912, of the Republic of China failed to produce a united nation entering the world community on equal terms. Foreign governments continued to post their own troops and police in enclaves of extraterritoriality, enjoying foreign law and privilege on Chinese soil. Civil war rent China apart during the decade 1918–28, as a northern government at Beijing, dominated by shifting military factions, vied for power with a southern government at Canton, headed by Sun Yat-sen and his Guomindang cohorts. Officially, Beijing enjoyed recognition as the legal voice of China until its final defeat by the Nationalist (Guomindang) army in 1928. Its actual power, however, extended through only a small section of the country. During the turbulent 1920's, most of South China, Tibet, Xinjiang, Mongolia, and the northeast (Manchuria) lay beyond control of the capital. No sooner was the new government of Chiang Kai-shek established at Najiing in 1928, however, than Soviet troops fought to protect Soviet interests in Manchuria against the local warlord. In 1931 Japan overran this rich industrial area to create the puppet state of Manchukuo. Then, at the opposite end of China, Soviet authorities gave military and economic assistance to the local governor of Xinjiang, concluding formal agreements without reference to Nanjing and informally extending influence over its policy and army. Warlord autonomy, Japanese invasion, and growing Chinese Communist dissidence combined to deprive Chiang of control over more than a dozen provinces throughout most of the period 1931–45. Meanwhile, each of these uncontrolled areas enjoyed varying degrees of independence in its relations with foreign powers.

In fact, not until 1949 and establishment of the People's Republic of China did the world's most populous nation achieve sufficient sovereignty and unity throughout its vast domain to enjoy a monopoly of full control over foreign relations in the central government. This provides a natural starting point for our analysis. Unlike its immediate predecessor, however, the People's Republic was not formally admitted to "the family of nations" for many years, lacking diplomatic recognition from most countries outside the Soviet bloc, and denied participation in the United Nations until the 1970s. Thus, on the one hand, we have historical evidence of foreign policy conducted by a somewhat fictitious central government, ruling largely in name only from 1911 to 1928, followed by a highly fragmented regime from 1928 to 1949. This approximates forty years of seemingly "normal" international relations for a weak and divided China, formally allied with the victorious powers in two world wars and a member of the League of Nations. On the other hand, our principle object of interest, the PRC, had more than two decades of semi-isolation from much of the international system, including the United Nations and such traditional great powers as the United States and Japan.

Finally the People's Republic itself offers two distinct phases of policy, both in process and in substance. The first, from 1949 to 1976, is dominated by the personality of Mao Zedong as the founding father and ideological godhead of "New China." His premier and chief foreign affairs figure, Zhou Enlai, was China's preeminent statesman throughout this period. Both men died in 1976. Their successors, initially dominated by Deng Xiaoping, totally transformed domestic and foreign policy, inter alia, involving China in the world economy to an unprecedented degree. Their abandonment of Mao's ideological rhetoric, if not its tenets, poured new wine into old bottles. The record of Mao's domestic rule has already been rewritten by his successors to preclude a return to his catastrophic final years of the so-called Cultural Revolution. It may be that various aspects of his foreign policy will also be denounced as contrary to China's interests. In the meantime, however, we must base our analysis mainly on the evidence available, which preponderantly comes from the pre-1980s, while drawing attention to the changes that have since occurred and the factors that may give them some degree of permanence.

These historical anomalies obviate the standard approach of focusing on the nation-state as actor. Despite appearances, foreign governments were not dealing with a highly stable and continuous regime prior to 1949. To be sure, the entity "China" was an obvious empirical referent for whatever group assumed authority at whatever point in the society. Treaties were negotiated, commerce carried out (albeit through foreign-controlled customs until the 1930s), and wars fought in the name of China. However, our inquiry will concern itself primarily with the perceptions and behavior of Chinese elites, particularly the Communists, which have tried to manage China's foreign relations over the past century. It is their values and views, rather than the inheritance of tradition or the bureaucratic inertia of continuing organizational entities within government that have shaped the ends, means, and style of Chinese foreign policy.

Our general conceptual framework begins with the physical environment, both real and perceived, into which these elites moved as international actors. In addition to actual size and geography, policy is shaped by perceptions of spatial relationships. Borders may be seen as secure or threatened, as inviolate or penetrable, as indisputable or contentious and negotiable. Space may be conceived as providing isolation or inviting attack. Size may be held an asset of strength or a liability for defense. Perceptions, in turn, are in part a function of received experience, of history as it is transmitted within a culture or political system. Received experience provides "lessons" from the past whose "truth" may be reinforced through the "real experience" of the present. Just as there are objective inputs of wars and diplomacy, as in the physical attributes of geography, to shape perception and behavior, so too there is the subjective element of anticipation, which may create a "self-fulfilling prophecy" effect whereby expected hostility from an outside power is prepared for in such a way as to cause or increase hostility. Alternatively, "selective perception" focuses only on evidence of behavior which conforms with expectation and dismisses that which does not fit anticipation. These inputs of geography, history, and psychology combine to constitute what we shall call the *Chinese components* of foreign policy.

In addition, we must consider ideology or the *Communist component* of policy. Ideology is not unique to elites and cultures which articulate it in the highly formalized and conscious manner of communist systems, but its explicitness and omnipresence in their political communications make it even more of a determinant than in less ideologically structured systems. From Marx to Mao, a corpus of literature provides definitions of goals and prescriptions of means that shape the view of the world from Beijing.

These basic factors in the Chinese and Communist components do not explain everything. They will be differentially affected by specific organizational roles and responsibilities such as defense, trade, diplomacy, and revolutionary activity abroad. Moreover, they will have an idiosyncratic impact upon policy as filtered through the different "operational codes" of such individuals as Mao Zedong and Deng Xiaoping. The sum of these internal interactions constitutes the decision-making process, but this in turn must interact externally for the dynamic of international relations to be complete. Foreign policy does not operate in a vacuum, nor is it the exclusive initiative of one country, least of all China over the past century. Unfortunately, however, in the absence of any concrete data on the effect of organization and personality in Chinese foreign policy, we must remain content with a larger, looser inferential framework that deals primarily with the factors we have subsumed under the Chinese and Communist components. Moreover, in the space at our disposal we cannot hope to do justice to interaction analysis except for selective illustrative purposes. Within these limits, nevertheless, we can appreciate the goals of recent Chinese foreign policy and assess the means available and likely to be adopted by present and future elites in pursuit of these goals.

Physical Factors—Real and Perceived

We cannot look at any map of the world, regardless of its projection, and not be awed by the proportion encompassed by China. So extensive is its reach from north to south and from east to west as to conjure up images of supracontinental domination "overshadowing" Southeast Asia and India while "menacing" the Soviet Far East and Japan. Coupled with emphasis on China's population of over 1 billion, "expansionism" seems the perceived threat confronting China's neighbors.

These images receive reinforcement from Chinese official statements. Although the days of the Chinese empire are long past, modern Chinese leaders continue to pay obeisance to the memory of vanished glory in their delineation of China's territorial goals. Chiang Kai-shek, borrowing Adolf Hitler's concept of *Lebensraum* ("living space"), laid claim to past holdings on the basis of population pressure as well as of historical possession:

In regard to the living space essential for the nation's existence, the territory of the Chinese state is determined by the requirements for national survival and by the limits of Chinese cultural bonds. Thus, in the territory of China a hundred years ago [that is, circa 1840], comprising more than ten million square kilometers, there was not a single district that was not essential to the survival of the Chinese nation, and none that was not permeated by our culture. The breaking up of this territory meant the undermining of the nation's security as well as the decline of the nation's culture. Thus, the people as a whole must regard this as a national humiliation, and not until all lost territories have been recovered can we relax our efforts to wipe out this humiliation and save ourselves from destruction.[1]

Nor do Communist leaders remain indifferent to China's past holdings, although they temper their immediate claims according to time and place. Thus, Mao Zedong staked out his future realm in an interview more than fifty years ago:

It is the immediate task of China to regain all our lost territories....We do not, however, include Korea, formerly a Chinese colony, but when we have reestablished the independence of the lost territories of China, and if the Koreans wish to break away from the chains of Japanese imperialism, we will extend them our enthusiastic help in their struggle for independence. The same thing applies for Formosa....The Outer Mongolian republic will automatically become a part of the Chinese federation, at their own will. The Mohammedan and Tibetan peoples, likewise, will form autonomous republics attached to the Chinese federation.[2]

True to his word, at least in part, Mao, despite Indian protests, sent the People's Liberation Army (PLA) into Tibet after the establishment of the People's Republic of China in 1949. His implicit definition of Korea as within China's sphere of interest received implementation when Chinese armies hurled back United Nations troops from the Yalu River to the 38th parallel during 1950–51. Xinjiang which is presumably the region referred to by Mao as "the Mohammedan people" (because of its predominantly Moslem population), became an autonomous region in 1955 after considerable pacification by the PLA garrison. Only Taiwan ("Formosa"), the Nationalist refuge, and Outer Mongolia, recognized as independent by the Treaty of Friendship and Alliance concluded between the Nationalist government and Moscow in 1945 and adhered to in this particular by Beijing, remained beyond Mao's control.

Similarly, both Nationalist and Communist maps place China's borders far down in the South China Sea, off the shores of Borneo. Both could agree with statements in the official Nationalist handbook:

Both the southernmost and westernmost borders remain to be defined. The Pamirs in the west constitute a contested area among China, the USSR, and Afghanistan. The sovereignty of the Tuansha Islands [Coral Islands] in the south is sought by China, the Republic of the Philippines, and Indo-China.[3]

---

[1] Chiang Kai-shek, *China's Destiny* (New York: Roy Publishers, 1947), p. 34.
[2] Quoted in Edgar Snow, *Red Star over China* (New York: Random House, 1944), p. 96. Interviews with Mao Zedong in 1936.

At least some of these are more than mere verbal aspirations. In the past two decades Chinese Communist troops have fought over disputed border areas. The movement of Beijing's forces into Indian-claimed check-points along the Himalayas following the Tibetan revolt of 1959 triggered small clashes with Indian border guards that year. Subsequent Indian efforts in 1962 to recoup claimed land, long unoccupied until the advent of Chinese road building and patrols in 1958–61, ignited a smoldering confrontation which finally exploded that fall in a massive Chinese offensive at both ends of the 1,500-mile frontier. While larger strategic considerations than the border itself underlay the Chinese attack, the tenacity with which Beijing bargained—and finally fought—with New Delhi over marginal land of little economic or political value illustrates the persistence of "lost territories" in shaping perceptions and goals of foreign policy.

An even more dramatic example of this phenomenon came in March 1969, when Chinese border troops fought Soviet armored units over unoccupied islands in the Ussuri River along China's northeast frontier. These incidents, while far smaller in scope and briefer than the 1962 war with India, had far more threatening implications for China's security, since they involved the much more powerful Soviet military capabilities, potentially including nuclear weapons. Again, as with India, more was perceived to be at stake than the islands themselves. Nonetheless, the role the border played throughout 1969, both here and in Xinjiang, reminded the world that Chinese sensibilities and sensitivities can hearken back to times past to a degree unique among the major powers on the world scene today.

Does this necessarily mean that irredentism—the drive to recover "lost territories"—literally impels Chinese leaders to restore control over thousands of square miles ruled by Russia and the Soviet Union for a century or more?

The border problem is both less and more than the question of "lost territory" per se. It is less so in terms of the amount of land actually at issue as compared with that carried on maps and tables as the maximal extent of past Chinese rule. The problem involves more than the land, however, insofar as it involves the principles of politics, both domestic and foreign, which impinge on the posture adopted by Chinese leaders vis-à-vis questions of "unequal treaties" and "lost territory." One such principle is the traditional Chinese definition of a government possessing the "Mandate of Heaven" as capable of defending the frontiers against barbarian incursions while maintaining the peace against domestic insurrection. Thus, so remote and undesirable an area as Outer Mongolia became the subject of political controversy in 1912, when young Nationalists agitated against Beijing's concessions to Mongolian demands for autonomy under Russian protection, using the issue as a political weapon against the regime of Yuan Shikai. In 1950 Chinese Nationalist

[3] *China Handbook, 1955–56* (Taipei, Taiwan, 1955), p. 15. Although this was modified in later editions, continued Nationalist claims to the Paracel Islands 150 miles south of Hainan were forcefully implemented by the PLA in January 1974 when its navy ousted South Vietnamese units from the area.

propagandists sought to embarrass the new Communist regime in Beijing in a similar manner. They charged it with "selling out" Chinese soil to the Soviet Union by accepting Mongolian independence despite alleged Soviet violations of the 1945 agreements. In these agreements, Chiang Kai-shek had promised to abide by a "plebiscite" there, knowing it would confirm the area's self-proclaimed independence under Soviet domination but hoping thereby to woo Stalin away from supporting the Chinese Communists. Seen in this perspective Mongolia is primarily a political issue to be exploited in domestic or foreign politics according to expediency, not a compulsive constraint on Chinese policy.

Individual leaders may not believe in the importance of a particular border section or the literal necessity of recovering "lost territory," but the manipulative use of such an issue in internal politics may constrain their position, thereby posing foreign policy goals which exacerbate relations abroad. Two instances illustrate the complexity of this problem. Mongolia would seem strategically irretrievable without Soviet acquiescence. Yet authoritative Japanese and Soviet sources attributed statements to Mao that seemed to reflect a lingering aspiration to replace Soviet influence there, including an official Soviet claim that Mao raised the issue with Nikita Khrushchev as early as 1954. Were these statements merely an effort to press Soviet influence back, or also to advance Chinese influence? Was it Mao's personal *idée fixe* or a shared objective within the elite? While Beijing's propaganda publicly lamented Moscow's alleged transformation of the Mongolian People's Republic into a "colony" in 1969–70, Soviet radio broadcasts accused Beijing of harboring "chauvinist" ambitions over this vast land of desert and steppe, inhabited by a million or so nomads and herdsmen. Logic may strengthen one or another explanation, but evidence is lacking to provide any definitive answer.

A second instance concerns Taiwan. Since the founding of the PRC in 1949, its leadership has ritualistically and repeatedly sworn to "recover China's province, Taiwan." Yet after imposition of the U.S. Seventh Fleet in the Taiwan Strait in 1950 and the Mutual Assistance Treaty concluded between Taipei and Washington in 1954, no serious effort from the mainland sought to recover Taiwan by force or subversion. Is this an issue of genuine irredentism which inevitably must result in reunion with the mainland by one means or another? Is it a political matter linked to the continuing presence on Taiwan of a defeated civil-war enemy, the Chinese Nationalists, who still lay claim to representation of and rule over all China? Is it a whipping-boy for attacking "U.S. imperialism," and if so, are the implications primarily for mobilizing unity? Or is there a changing mixture of motivations, varying according to the changing perceptions and priorities of the leadership in Beijing?

Suggesting these various instrumental uses of the question is not to deny objective factors which, from the perspective of those responsible for Chinese security, make China's size a defensive liability and China's borders a vulnerable point of contention. First, vague territorial claims, Chinese or otherwise, based on concepts of suzerainty and tributary relations or on disputed treaties, are an inadequate basis for determining international boundaries. Chinese Communists and Nationalists alike agree that the use of force against Tibetan leaders, whether in 1950 or 1959, is an internal affair, and does not constitute legal "aggression." Even New Delhi acquiesced, albeit reluctantly, in the earlier instance. But where runs the legal boundary resultant from a line drawn on an inadequate map by a British official before World War I and never surveyed, much less formally ratified by the government in Beijing?

Second, even where such boundaries are fixed with rough approximation, precise definition is impeded by the absence of natural lines of demarcation. Except for the coast and the Amur-Yalu river complex in the northeast, none of China's frontiers can be readily identified topographically. Instead, they twist tortuously through jungle, mountain, and desert, according to the temporary dictates of local need and the relative power available to interested parties. The absence of natural demarcation is paralleled by an absence of natural barriers against migration or invasion, complicating the responsibilities facing the central government responsible for its citizens' welfare and defense.

Thus, the ability in 1959 of 80,000 Tibetan refugees to flee through Himalayan passes, in some cases claimed and ostensibly guarded by Indian patrols, raised the possibility of these refugees returning with foreign arms and training to carry on subversion and sabotage, if not actual guerrilla war. Indeed, precisely such clandestine activities followed the exodus, described by foreign participants and correspondents from bases in the sub-Himalayan area. Again, in 1962, the flight of up to 80,000 Uygur, Kazakh, and Kirghiz refugees across the Xinjiang border to ethnically related areas in adjacent Soviet central Asia raised Chinese fears of their eventual return as instruments of Soviet subversion in a province long known for anti-Chinese revolts among its predominantly Turki-speaking Moslem peoples. Small wonder that under these circumstances the Indian and Soviet borders appear so sensitive to decision makers in Beijing.

Few lines of communication traverse the great distances from China's traditional power centers to its remote border provinces, whereas these provinces lie relatively close to rival centers of power. Not until well after establishment of the PRC did a railroad link Mongolia with northern China, although it was circled on the north by the Trans-Siberian Railroad. Only rough roads linked Tibet with China proper until the late 1950s, while Lhasa lay within striking distance of determined troops, traders, and travelers approaching from the Indian subcontinent, as evidenced by British expeditions at the turn of the century. Nor did Beijing push a railroad into Xinjiang until the mid-1950s, despite its strategic and economic importance proximate to the highly developed transportation network across the Soviet border. Even today, land communications to most points along China's southern and western boundaries are scarce and subject to the hazards of interruption by recurring natural phenomena as well as to interdiction by potential dissidents. This combination of arduous terrain and traditionally hostile non-Chinese local populaces mocks the image of size and strength projected by simple unidimensional maps of China.

China's traditional attraction for invaders was food and wealth, luring from the interior nomadic groups against whom the Great Wall was originally designed. Modern invaders came after markets (Great Britain), raw materials (Japan), or imperial prestige (Germany). Regardless of the size and distance of the predatory power, during the nineteenth and twentieth centuries China grappled with problems of defense against external pressure to a degree unique among the countries under survey in this volume. Virtually no point along the 12,600 miles of its perimeter has been safe from one or another of these pressures during the last three hundred years. At the turn of the century, many wondered whether China would become the "sick man of Asia," to be carved up by other countries as was the "sick man of Europe," the Ottoman empire.

These physical factors have combined with the behavior of other powers to make defense a major preoccupation of Chinese foreign policy elites, be they Manchu, Nationalist, or Communist. We have dwelt at length on the border problem because it looms large in the foreign policy perspective of Beijing—not because of Communist "expansionism" or "paranoia," but rather as an outgrowth of China's remembered past. Thus, thousands of PLA troops, ostensibly engaged in roadbuilding, occupied two northern provinces of Laos adjacent to China from 1962 into the 1970s. This was not only in response to an agreement with the Royal Laotian government, but to secure a buffer against possible penetration of China by American CIA-trained Meo hillsmen or by former Chinese Nationalist soldiers living in exile in nearby Thailand. Nor can we understand recurring tensions in the Taiwan Strait around the offshore islands of Jinmen and Mazu in 1954–55, 1958, and 1962 without an appreciation of the recurring raids against the mainland launched from these islands by Chinese Nationalist teams trained and backed by the United States. Indeed, China's only major military actions—in Korea (1950) and on its borders with India (1962) and the U.S.S.R. (1969)—in the first two decades of the PRC came about in large part because of anxiety over the potential penetration by hostile powers over vulnerable borders, at times when internal tensions, economic and political, heightened fears of invasion and subversion.

Historical Factors

China's defensive attitudes intermittently explode into xenophobia. The subjective evaluation of events during the past century convinced Chinese Nationalist and Communist alike that many, if not all, of China's ills came from contact with the "foreign devil," now castigated as "Western imperialism." Two hundred years ago, Li Shiyao, viceroy of Guangdong and Guangxi, memorialized the throne on regulations for the control of foreigners, warning:

It is my most humble opinion that when uncultured barbarians, who live far beyond the borders of China, come to our country to trade, they should establish no contact with the population, except for business purposes.[4]

Chiang Kai-shek blamed the chaotic years of interregnum following the collapse of the Manchu dynasty on "secret activities of the imperialists,...the chief cause of civil wars among the warlords."[5] Indeed, he attributed the empire's disintegration to the so-called unequal treaties which "completely destroyed our nationhood, and our sense of honor and shame was lost....The traditional structure of the family, the village, and the community was disrupted. The virtue of mutual help was replaced by competition and jealousy. Public planning was neglected and no one took an interest in public affairs."[6]

This simplistic explanation errs in attributing cause and effect where coincidence is the phenomenon. Western pressures hastened the collapse of the empire and its Confucian traditions, but they came after the process of disintegration had begun. The ability of Japanese society to respond to the combined impact of feudal decline and Western influence by adapting the old content to new forms demonstrates the distortion of history in Chiang's analysis.

However, it is not the facts of history that condition political behavior, but the way in which people view those facts. Hence, the similarity of an early Communist analysis to those preceding it is highly suggestive of xenophobia as a recurring component of Chinese policy:

[The imperialists] will not only send their running-dogs to bore inside China to carry out disruptive work and to cause trouble. They will not only use the Chiang Kai-shek bandit remnants to blockade our coastal ports, but they will send their totally hopeless adventurist elements and troops to raid and to cause trouble along our borders. They seek by every means and at all times to restore their position in China. They use every means to plot the destruction of China's independence, freedom, and territorial integrity and to restore their private interests in China. We must exercise the highest vigilance....They cannot possibly be true friends of the Chinese people. They are the deadly enemies of the Chinese people's liberation movement.[7]

Thus, the Chinese Communist devil-theory of imperialism coincided with the popular mythology that evil is inherent in foreign contacts and produced suspicion and hostility at various levels. The popular mythology derives from experiencing the rape and pillage by Western troops during the nineteenth century.

Injustice was also encountered at higher levels of diplomatic relations. Chinese experience in the international arena gave good reason for bitter resentment at being cast in the role of "a melon to be carved up by the powers."

[4] Quoted in Hu Sheng, *Imperialism and Chinese Politics* (Peking, 1981), p. 4.
[5] Chiang Kai-shek, *China's Destiny*, p. 78.
[6] Ibid., pp. 79, 88.
[7] K'o Pa-nien, "Hsin min chu chu yi te wai chiao tse" [The foreign policy of the new people's democracy] *Hsüeh Hsi* [Study] 1, no. 2 (October 1949): 13–15.

Throughout the nineteenth century, gunboat diplomacy forced China to abdicate her customary rights of sovereignty without reciprocal privileges. Extraterritorial law, economic concessions, and the stationing of foreign troops in Chinese cities were sanctified by treaty but won by force. Punitive expeditions, in 1860 and 1900, delivered the supreme insult of foreign military occupation of the venerated capital of Beijing.

The twentieth century brought little relief. Japan fought Russia on Chinese soil for control of the rich provinces of Manchuria. China's own allies in World War I swept aside her protests at Versailles, and awarded to Japan concessions in China held by defeated Germany. During World War II, the Yalta Conference of 1945 rewarded the Soviet Union with important military, economic, and political privileges in China, all without consultation with Chiang Kai-shek. Although President Roosevelt reminded Premier Stalin that those inducements for Soviet entry into the war against Japan would have to be affirmed by Chiang, Allied pressure left China no alternative but capitulation.

In sum, China was the object of international relations but seldom the agent. Acted on by others, she was unable to act in her own right. Long the primary power in Asia, she has been cut deeply, during the past century, by an induced feeling of inferiority. Her fear of Japan followed a defeat caused by material inferiority. Her resentment against the West followed a capitulation caused by military inferiority and a humiliation caused by sensed political and ideological inferiority. Beijing's assertive stand on Hong Kong and Taiwan strikes a responsive chord among wide sectors of the populace. At long last, a determined elite has managed to restore China's place in the sun.

To be sure, irredentist claims to lost territories, denunciation of unequal treaties, and the playing off of power against power are all standard techniques of foreign policy. The difference in their use by the Chinese lies in the psychological convictions behind these techniques. Among Western states, the exploitation of grievances is an accepted stratagem among assumed equals who are struggling for limited gains and for the coveted position "first among equals." Between China and the rest of the world, however, the bitter remembrance of things past heightens the assertive aspects of foreign policy.

The Communist emphasis on imperialist aggression fitted into the objective and subjective factors conditioning Chinese views of world politics. The resulting xenophobia ultimately worked even to the Soviet Union's disadvantage. Whereas originally it was exploited by Soviet leaders against the West, eventually it exploded again over such real and sensed grievances as Soviet looting in Manchuria after World War II, the resentment against dependence on Soviet economic assistance, and suspected Soviet subversion in Xinjiang. In the decade 1949–59, official affirmations of the "monolithic unity of Sino-Soviet friendship" sought to repress the hostility with which many Chinese viewed the Sino-Soviet alliance. When Mao challenged Khrushchev for primacy in the Communist world, however, such protestations of friendship disappeared in a wave of anti-Soviet invective which probably won enthusiastic support among the majority of the populace always ready to believe the worst of any foreigner in his dealing with China.

THE PROCESS OF POLICY: THE COMMUNIST COMPONENT

Ideological Content:
Marxism-Leninism-Mao Zedong Thought

In addition to those aspects of continuity in policy which we ascribe to the Chinese component, there are differences in degree and substance that stem from the dedication of the present Chinese leaders to communism. As Mao declared in 1945, "From the very beginning, our party has based itself on the theories of Marxism-Leninism, because Marxism-Leninism is the crystallization of the most correct and most revolutionary scientific thought of the world proletariat."[8] More than forty years later, the constitution of the PRC adopted at the fifth National People's Congress on December 4, 1982, committed its preamble to "the guidance of Marxism-Leninism and Mao Zedong Thought."

Ideological commitment is not unique to Communists. General protestations of fidelity to Christianity, international law, and human rights appear throughout statements of Western political figures. Rarely do these protestations enable us to determine the ends and means of these leaders, especially in foreign policy. Marxism-Leninism, however, carries with it a construct of goals and ways of seeking those goals that imparts form to ideology and institutions to a degree unknown in the non-Communist world.

At the same time it is not a static ideology bound up in a few volumes and rigidly adhered to over time. Instead it has been reinterpreted and revised according to the dictates of a changing world by successive leaders in the Soviet Union, China, and elsewhere. This evolution has been no less dramatic between the regimes of Mao and Deng Xiaoping in China than it was between the regimes of Stalin and Khrushchev in Russia; in both countries the evolution of communism cautioned against a mechanistic citation of texts from one era to analyze and forecast Communist policy in another era.

For example, the foremost component of classical Marxism was its goal of world communism as a necessary and inevitable successor to capitalism, to be realized through world revolution and a final war. The postponement of this goal under Lenin and Stalin resulted from a realistic assessment of Soviet weakness and capitalistic strength, but its ultimate achievement through class struggle and international conflict remained an unquestioned assumption.

Then in 1956 Nikita Khrushchev declared that peaceful coexistence and the noninevitability of war between communism and capitalism followed from the emergence of nuclear weapons which threatened the destruction of mankind. Mao railed at this, terming it "revisionism" and declaring that the

---

[8] Mao Zedong, "On Coalition Government," *Selected Works of Mao Zedong* (Beijing: Foreign Languages Press, 1965), vol. III, p. 314.

final war would result in world communism. He argued that just as World War I had given birth to the Soviet Union and World War II to the People's Republic of China, so on the ashes of a nuclear conflict a still "higher" civilization would arise.

Mao based his analysis on the Marxist premise that conflict is omnipresent in human relations, whether between classes or between nations, in the most serious cases leading to war. Mao also followed Lenin's analysis of imperialism as "the highest form of capitalism" wherein conflict among the imperialist powers would accompany capitalist efforts to eliminate communism. In 1940 he reformulated the classic Chinese dictum of "using barbarian against barbarian" in Marxist-Leninist terms, "Our tactical principle remains one of exploiting the contradictions among...[the imperialists] in order to win over the majority, oppose the minority, and crush the enemies separately."[9] This article was reissued in 1971 to explain Mao's sudden switch from decades of attacking "U.S. imperialism" to welcoming President Richard Nixon for Sino-American détente. In his words, the Soviet Union had become "the major enemy" and the United States the "secondary enemy," thereby justifying a united front with the latter against the former.

Mao's postulates were reinforced by the attitudes and actions of the non-Communist world. In part this resulted from Chinese Communist statements and behavior that resulted in self-fulfilling prophecy. Various incidents involving American officials and property in 1948–49 complicated efforts by those in Washington who wanted to prepare the way for recognition of Mao's regime once it displaced that of Chiang Kai-shek.

Then in June 1949, Mao declared, "All Chinese without exception must lean either to the side of imperialism or to the side of socialism. Sitting on the fence will not do....Internationally, we belong to the aide of the anti-imperialist front headed by the Soviet Union, and so we can turn only to this side for genuine and friendly help, not to the side of the imperialist front."[10] Implementation of this principle followed on February 14, 1950, with the Treaty of Friendship, Alliance, and Mutual Aid between the PRC and the U.S.S.R. Mao and Stalin agreed that "in the event of one of the Contracting Parties being attacked by Japan or any state allied with her and thus being involved in a state of war, the other Contracting Party shall immediately render military and other assistance by all means at its disposal."

Mao's "lean to one side" policy aroused an image abroad of a monolithic Communist bloc spanning the Eurasian land mass under control of the Kremlin and threatening all nations on its periphery with subversion, revolution, and possibly aggression. The monolithic image was wrong as became evident when Sino-Soviet friction eventually led to open differences in 1959–60. However perceptions condition policy. The result was heightened

[9] "On Policy" (December 25, 1940), as translated in *Selected Works of Mao Zedong* (Bombay, 1954), vol. III, p. 218.
[10] "On the People's Democratic Dictatorship," Ibid., vol. IV, pp. 415–17.

American opposition to the new Chinese regime, thereby "proving" Mao's assumptions of implacable capitalist hostility to be "correct."

The interaction of antagonistic ideological predispositions and perceptions exploded in the first major Sino-American conflict when China intervened in the Korean War, inflicting a humiliating defeat on United States–United Nations forces in November–December 1950. This ended all prospects of normal relations between Beijing and Washington for twenty-one years. The United States thereupon enforced a total embargo on trade with China. It implemented this embargo worldwide for strategic goods and items with American-licensed components. Washington overtly shielded Chiang's regime on Taiwan from Communist attack, forestalling an end to the civil war by creating an island redoubt through massive economic and military aid. Covertly it helped Chiang's agents conduct raids for espionage and sabotage on the mainland, especially in Tibet. Equally frustrating from Beijing's standpoint, the United States blocked it from taking China's seat in the United Nations until 1971.

Mao's "lean to one side" policy, both in its public definition and its political implementation, contributed to a total confrontation between China and the United States at the very start and through the 1950s. His posture went well beyond the traditional policy of playing off one country against another, demonstrating the importance of the Communist component of Chinese foreign policy.

But not all aspects of that component were immutably chiseled on the Great Wall forever more. Mao's insistence on the inevitability of war between capitalism and communism disappeared with his death in 1976. Shortly thereafter Deng Xiaoping declared that war could be "postponed" indefinitely as the "forces for peace" struggled against the "hegemonic competition of the superpowers." Thus Deng brought China's position more or less into line with that of Khrushchev twenty-five years earlier. This major modification of Mao's stance paralleled Khrushchev's change of Stalin's orthodoxy, albeit within the continued commitment to Marxism-Leninism as a universal scientific truth.

So far, we have been discussing aspects of policy that stem from the Communist component as developed in Marxism-Leninism. Assumptions of conflict, antagonism against capitalism, and promoting revolution were all compatible with the ideological concepts dominant in the Soviet Union, at least until the death of Stalin in 1953. Within this framework, however, divergent strategies emerged with the rise of the Chinese Communist party (CCP). As early as 1946, Liu Shaoqi told an American correspondent, "Mao Zedong has created a Chinese or Asiatic form of Marxism. His great accomplishment has been to change Marxism from its European to its Asiatic form. He is the first who has succeeded in doing so.[11] At that time, the principal Chinese innovation appeared to be Mao's building a Communist party on a peasant guerrilla army

---

[11] Quoted in Anna Louise Strong, *Dawn Out of China* (Bombay: People's Publishing House, 1948), p. 29.

based in the countryside, as opposed to the classical Marxist method of a workers' movement which seizes power in the cities. Beneath this question of strategy, of course, lay the deeper question of historical "stages" whereby Marx posited socialism as "naturally" emerging out of advanced capitalism, in contrast with Mao's effort to move directly from China's "semifeudal" state into socialism.

Subsequent to winning power, however, new ideological differences pitted Mao's vision of the "good society" against that manifest in the Soviet Union. At issue was nothing less than the fundamental goals of revolution, not merely as manifested in the century-old slogans of Marx and Engels, but in the present practices and future values of the new society. Mao's primary aim in carrying out a revolution in China was to transform the society's ethos from a hierarchical, elitist, authoritarian culture to an egalitarian, mass-oriented, and eventually mass-directed culture. For him, this domestic revolution conditioned other goals, such as modernization of the economy and building up national military power.

This appreciation of Mao's goals did not emerge fully until his Cultural Revolution of 1966–68. In retrospect, however, it provides a clue to the intensity with which Mao waged his attack against "revisionism" as early as 1958, initially masked as "Yugoslav" revisionism and later revealed explicitly as "Soviet" when the polemic became public in the 1960s.

The important linkage between internal Soviet policy and Chinese foreign policy lay in Mao's recognition that national boundaries and governmental relations provide an inadequate frame of reference for understanding important levels of transnational interaction. Just as the missionaries and businessmen of the nineteenth century provided alternative models for emulation in China and transmitted values antithetical to the Confucian ethic, so the Soviet Union threatened to shape the new Chinese society in its own image. Such Soviet "leadership" was a compulsive dictate of Stalin's era, whereby emulation of all things Russian seemed mandatory for "membership in the socialist camp," meaning Soviet military and economic support. Even after death removed Stalin's personal tyranny, Soviet methods and motivational values dominated allied regimes through the continuing ascendance of the Soviet model, transmitted by translated texts and articles, technical assistance teams, training in Soviet institutes and research centers, and varying degrees of integration and standardization of technical systems, especially military.

The Sino-Soviet alliance promised to keep China permanently dependent—psychologically if not in fact—on the Soviet Union, since Beijing could hardly hope ever to "catch up" with Moscow's technical and material superiority, especially given China's tremendous imbalance between an enormous, largely untrained population and scarce resources of capital and food. Ideologically, the alliance confronted Mao with a model that stressed material incentives and unequal rewards of power and status for political authority and acquired skill. These values, national interest conflicts apart, threatened his twin goals of developing a China "standing on its own feet" and eliminating the hierarchical Confucian culture.

Thus, in addition to specific foreign policy conflicts which raised Sino-Soviet tensions in 1958–59, the ideological conflict eroded the alliance because Mao was willing to risk the loss of Soviet military and economic support in order to shield China from Soviet "revisionism." Another ideological dimension, dominant in the polemic at the time, concerned the strategy and tactics best suited for advancing world revolution. Each side tended to caricature the other in this debate, the Chinese accusing the Soviets of "abandoning" the revolution to "peaceful coexistence with imperialism" while sacrificing local Communists through insistence on the "parliamentary path to power," which could only end in frustration or suppression. The Soviets responded by claiming Mao to be a "nuclear madman" who would risk World War III to advance Chinese "chauvinistic, expansionistic" interests while he sacrificed local Communists to bloody "people's wars" which might escalate to global proportions.

Accordingly, China's foreign policy carried a far more militant, strident tone of support for "people's wars" than did that of the Soviet Union. Mao's dictum held that "power grows out of the barrel of a gun" and that "armed struggle in the countryside" is the most reliable path to power. Moreover, his confrontation with Moscow compelled Beijing to champion Communist causes throughout the world. Most important, however, was the root involvement of Mao's domestic ideological concerns which fueled his struggle with Khrushchev, thereby splitting the "socialist camp" and ultimately the "world revolutionary movement."

Mao's concerns were not without foundation. For instance, the transformation of China's military establishment from a backward army developed in guerrilla warfare against the Japanese into a modern, multiservice force moving toward a nuclear capability resulted wholly from Soviet assistance, both material and human. In Mao's eyes, however, the army was not merely for passive defense and exclusively military in function, but as in the guerrilla years of World War II, it was intimately associated with civilian political and economic activities, serving both as a model of selfless behavior and as a direct participant in mass campaigns of flood control, reforestation, and agriculture. For him it was no coincidence that opposition to his "Great Leap Forward" experiment of 1958–59 with its mass communes and "backyard furnaces" was spearheaded by top PLA officials whose position paralleled that of Moscow. While Soviet criticism of the communes was accompanied by the cancellation of promised assistance in developing China's atomic weapons, PLA leaders attacked Mao's experiment as endangering the economy. To be sure, their argument was shared by civilian officials. But to the extent it appeared to reflect Soviet priorities of technical efficiency and technological leadership, as well as self-defined (rather than Mao-defined) roles and relationships between the military and civilian systems, the interplay between Khrushchev's "revisionism" and domestic Chinese developments fueled Mao's determination to push the Sino-Soviet dispute.

What of the external ideological goals of world revolution? How did they weigh in the scales of priority for Beijing? Despite their salience in the Sino-Soviet dispute, the goals of revolution were of lower priority than other ends of foreign policy, such as national security and international prestige. Mao excluded serious support for such foreign ventures, neither affording them success nor saving them from failure by significant contributions of Chinese assistance. In part, this was ideologically determined by the concept that "revolution is not for export" but must be indigenous to a country's problems and won by that country's revolutionary leadership. However, this was not the only constraint which limited Chinese material help to communist parties abroad. An amalgam of prudence and Sinocentrism reduced Beijing's contribution to considerably less than might be inferred from its polemic with Moscow or from its propagandistic pledges of "support" to various insurgencies.

In light of this, the role of ideology in positing goals which require verbal, if not full, commitment should not be overlooked in understanding the factors which condition choice in Beijing. However tempting might seem the gains of disavowing world revolution for purposes of improving diplomatic, economic, or military relations the leadership can move only so far in this direction without betraying its own sense of obligation as ritualistically reiterated.

We have drawn extensively on Mao's statements and actions despite his death in 1976 and the subsequent denunciation of his domestic policies, beginning with the "Great Leap Forward" and culminating in the Cultural Revolution. Three factors justify our focus. First, Mao's strictures on foreign policy prevailed from 1949 to 1977. They shaped the thinking and writing of several generations whose perceptions of world affairs are heavily influenced thereby. Second, they have not been criticized since his death to the same degree or in the same detail as his domestic policies. While many changes have occurred in Chinese foreign policy, few have explicitly repudiated Mao's precepts.

Third and most important, no theoretical formulations have emerged from the post-Mao leadership to provide an alternative framework for foreign policy. The *Selected Works of Deng Xiaoping* constitute the most authoritative assemblage of policy statements but contain little on foreign affairs. Published speeches by officials touch on current foreign policy issues in passing but basically concentrate on domestic economic and political problems. While these problems may impact on foreign policy, they do not affect the ideological framework in any direct way.

It is true that the relevance of ideology has markedly lessened, if it has not been specifically altered. By 1980 the Soviet Union was no longer vilified as "revisionist" but instead was condemned as "hegemonist." This shifted the basis of Beijing's attack from Moscow's domestic political system to its external power projection. Similarly China's professed identification with the Third

World emphasized a common interest in confronting the two superpowers and in economic development obstructed by the North-South inequity. Meanwhile Beijing muted its support for Communist insurgents abroad and "national liberation struggles" except where they faced suppression by "superpower hegemonists," the United States and the U.S.S.R.

As the Marxist-Maoist aspects of ideology faded in both domestic and foreign policy the Chinese component reasserted itself in the latter domain during the early 1980s. An assertive nationalism keynoted Beijing's handling of such matters as the recovery of Taiwan and Hong Kong, pithily summarized in Deng's declaration, "No foreign country can expect China to be its vassal or expect it to swallow any bitter fruit detrimental to its own interests.[12] Hu Yaobang, then Chinese Communist Party General Secretary, likewise warned, "The Chinese people will never again allow themselves to be humiliated as they were before."[13]

In October 1983, the Propaganda Department of the Communist Party of China (CPC) issued a "study outline" on "The Practice of Communism and Education in Communist Ideology" which explained the need to promote patriotism as a means of winning support for communism. The article frankly admitted thirty-four years after the founding of the PRC that the formal theories of Marxism-Leninism and the application of Mao Zedong Thought had failed to win the majority of Chinese. It thereby linked domestic mobilization with mass attitudes on foreign affairs:

> We should fully realize that those staunch Communists who have dedicated themselves to the highest ideal of communism for life are in the minority, while patriots, including Communists and those who uphold socialism, are in the overwhelming majority....We must proceed from education in patriotism, whip up the people's patriotic fervor, and raise the level of their patriotic awareness. At the same time, we must link this kind of fervor with their specific practice in building socialism, and gradually help them raise their consciousness for communism."[14]

The "Study Outline" explicitly rejected the extreme isolationist policy of "self-reliance" advocated during the Cultural Revolution, arguing that "China needs to understand the world while the world needs to understand China," and citing Deng's speech to the Twelfth National CPC Congress: "Both in our revolution and construction, we should also learn from foreign countries and draw on their experience." However, while "opening China to the outside world," the outline warned, "we are influenced by the international environment and the various trends of thought at home." An echo of Li Shiyao's and Chiang Kai-shek's xenophobic strictures could be detected in the extended injunction against "bourgeois influence" through foreign penetration:

[12] *Beijing Review,* September 6, 1982, p. 5.

[13] Ibid., September 13, 1982, p. 33.

[14] "The Practice of Communism and Education in Communist Ideology (Study Outline)," by CPC Central Committee Propaganda Department, Shanghai *Jiefang Ribao,* in Foreign Broadcast Information Service (FBIS), China, October 21, 1983, p. K41.

Since the implementation of the policy of opening to the outside world, decadent ideas and lifestyle of foreign bourgeoisie have again surged into our country. More and more people are going abroad and are being exposed to the capitalist world of sensual pleasures; cases of people worshipping foreign things, fawning on foreigners, acting in an obsequious manner and bringing shame on their country and themselves have occurred time and again. There are many serious criminal offenses in the economic, political, ideological and cultural fields and in social life. This is a concentrated manifestation of the corrosive influence of the decadent ideas of the exploiting classes at home and abroad.[15]

Instead of quoting Mao's "lean to one side" with "no third road" speech, the study outline drew the same theme from Lenin:

Lenin said: "The question *can only be this*—either the bourgeois ideological system or the socialist ideological system. There is nothing in between (because mankind has not created any 'third kind' of ideological system....) Therefore, any looking down on and *departure from* the socialist ideological system signifies a strengthening of the bourgeois ideological system."[16]

In sum, the Chinese and Communist components of policy converge in reinforcing a basic suspicion of the outside world which is historically rooted in the experience of all regimes, whether imperial, Nationalist, or Communist, in world affairs. Underlying this experience, moreover, is the fundamentally felt need to fashion a sociocultural ethos that is distinctively Chinese, traditionally superior to and contemporarily distinct from the values and behavior of foreign societies. Mao's assertion of such an achievement for "New China" raised Chinese self-esteem while it rankled Moscow. Unfortunately his manic miscalculations not only undid much of what had initially been achieved but worse, embarassed China before the entire world.

This, in turn, posed new problems for the post-Mao leadership in addition to those inherited from "a century of shame and humiliation." The "study outline" represented one approach to the problem, calling on "the spirit to integrate patriotism with internationalism" while warning against the poison allegedly inherent in "foreign bourgeois" ways. Communist acceptance of the dialectic with omnipresent contradictions theoretically justifies the tension manifest in such formulations. However, their practical implications complicate foreign relations, particularly in their day-to-day implementation at the interpersonal as well as the intergovernmental level. This tension is likely to persist, given its historical, cultural, and psychological roots, reinforced through its ideological reiteration.

Institutional Structure of Decision Making: The Party

We have focused primarily on aggregate concepts such as "China" and "the Chinese," and on individual personalities such as Mao Zedong and Deng Xiaoping. Moving from these extreme opposite levels of analysis to the intermediate ground of governmental decision making is essential if we are to

[15]Ibid., p. K44.
[16]Ibid., p. K43, emphasis in original.

project a model of behavior compatible with other large bureaucracies. Rarely, if ever, does foreign policy result from an abstract concept of a monolithic "national interest," and never is it the product of a reified nation-state, in this case "China," behaving as an individual. Only under unique circumstances is policy the dictate of a single official acting wholly on his own initiative. Instead, specific interests and responsibilities shape the perceptions, information intake, and policy output of organized groups inside and outside the government. It is their complex interaction that defines policy in specific situations.

Unfortunately these commonplace observations cannot be confirmed for the Chinese policy process for much of the recent past because we lack solid evidence on which to accept, modify, or reject them. A few illuminating glimpses into bureaucratic relationships emerged in the turmoil and polemics of the Cultural Revolution. Personal interviews elicit responses that purportedly describe the policy process at one point or another. But in the absence of documentation, we must acknowledge that our knowledge is fragmentary and speculative at best for the first forty years of the PRC.

The available evidence, however, suggests that contrary to the normal bureaucratic model, major foreign policy decisions during the Maoist era were made by the Chairman personally. Informed colleagues later claimed that Mao often acted without consulting any relevant departments but simply ordered them to act. The role of Zhou Enlai as his close colleague and implementer of foreign policy is impossible to determine without further evidence. But at least in the bombardment of offshore islands in 1958 Mao personally assumed responsibility in admitting that he miscalculated the American response which stymied the attack. Finally there is little doubt that Mao determined China's probe for and response to the Nixon-Kissinger interest in détente against the known inclination of his Cultural Revolution cohorts.

This personalization of policy did not wholly end with Mao's death. Deng Xiaoping's visible behavior and the perception of lesser figures during his direction of post-Mao politics suggested that while he did not dictate decisions to the same degree, he dominated them at key moments. Support for this analysis came when Deng personally claimed credit for the 1984 Sino-British agreement on Hong Kong with the formula of "one country, two systems," and the designation of fourteen coastal cities as special foreign investment sites the same year.

At that time, Professor A. Doak Barnett won a unique series of interviews with top officials in Beijing, providing the best description to date of the foreign policy process.[17] While such information is essentially a snapshot of the moment as seen through a particular set of lenses, a view of China's foreign policy emerged as the post-Mao regime became increasingly immersed in the international economic and political network. The resultant picture challenges

[17]A. Doak Barnett, *The Making of Foreign Policy in China: Structure and Process* (Boulder, Colo.: Westview Press, 1985). The following section draws largely from this work.

the conventional concentration on the party and state constitutions for discerning institutional responsibility. Instead Barnett's account accords with the traditional Chinese pattern of personalized politics, wherein informal groups and factions or cliques prevail over formalized channels of authority.

Thus instead of major decisions being made by the CCP Politburo, or its smaller surrogate, the Standing Committee, Barnett's sources attributed them to close interaction between the CCP Secretariat and the State Council, led by the then heads of these bodies, Hu Yaobang and Zhao Ziyang. Implicitly these two men, together with Deng as the most powerful elder statesman, formed a decision-making nucleus which expanded to include other Standing Committee members on an *ad hoc* basis as the politics of the situation required. Formal meetings of the Standing Committee and the Politburo were not regularly convened, although they could be called by the Secretariat and individual Standing Committee members respectively. Whether these gatherings ever overrode decisions advanced by the Deng-Hu-Zhao triumvirate or merely debated and modestly modified them could not be ascertained. However in the case study of special economic zones examined by Barnett, the Politburo seemed to ratify the plan already designed by the triumvirate.

On the one hand, this process significantly enlarged foreign policy participation from that of Mao Zedong's ascendancy, assuming that Hu and Zhao were free to differ with Deng's views and to propose policy on their own. On the other hand, it sharply reduced the number and nature of participants from that posited in the party rules. This point was persuasively justified by Zhao, who noted that "most of the members of the Politburo are aged." At that time their average age was seventy-four, whereas the Secretariat and State Council averaged eight years less.

The Thirteenth Congress of the CCP, meeting in October 1987, retained only ten Politburo members, adding seven new ones, with an overall average age of sixty-five. Deng Xiaoping's resignation forced the hand of his older colleagues, thereby ending an historic era of party leadership. Reducing the membership from twenty to seventeen further streamlined the Politburo as a decision-making group. These developments enhanced the likelihood that Zhao's account of the policy process in 1984 will not apply in the future.

Significant changes in the CCP constitution were instituted that further aimed at regularizing the powers of the Politburo and its Standing Committee, in contrast to the earlier role of the Secretariat and the informal triumvirate led by Deng. At that time, Zhao told Barnett, "all organizations concerned with foreign affairs participate in the Foreign Affairs Small Group" under the Secretariat. Chaired by the then PRC president, it included the premier, first vice-premier, the state councillor for foreign policy coordination, the foreign minister, and the minister of foreign economic relations and trade. Meeting more or less weekly, the Foreign Affairs Small Group had its own research staff, supplemented by invited specialists from other foreign affairs institutes in Beijing.

Under the new party rules however, the locus of authority shifted. Whereas previously "The Secretariat attends to the day-to-day work of the Central Committee under the direction of the Political Bureau and its Standing Committee," now "The Secretariat is the working office" of the Politbureau and its Standing Committee. Instead of being elected by the Central Committee, the Secretariat is nominated by the Standing Committee and approved by the Central Committee. These carefully worded changes reflect the move toward greater institutionalization of the political process as Deng prepared to leave the scene altogether. The party spokesman described the constitutional changes more bluntly, "From now on decision-making involved in day-to-day affairs will fall into the realm of the Standing Committee of the Political Bureau and such decisions by the Standing Committee will be based on the decisions of the Political Bureau itself."

Consensus and collective decision making are necessary to accommodate competing bureaucracies. Complex foreign policy issues involve a process of investigation, argumentation, and negotiation before a final decision. A pioneer study of China's entry into the International Monetary Fund and the World Bank traces this process in detail.[18] Yet this does not exclude the possibility of one or more top officials exercising inordinate influence or arbitrarily adopting a posture that preempts collegial participation. A long-standing tradition in Chinese and Communist politics of one individual exercising preeminent authority argues against a collectivity of equals making decisions in all instances. As Deng neared the end of his life, Chinese as well as foreigners focused on who would succeed him and with what authority, projecting factional struggles as likely to dominate formal arrangements. Thus, although the dominant mode of foreign policy decision making resembles that of other large state systems, the role of a few key individuals cannot be excluded in advance.

Basically, however, the process involves two sets of organizations, party and government. This raises a critical question, namely the relative weight of the party versus the governmental bureaucracy. This question has plagued Communist systems from the start. Lenin envisioned the party's role as that of a pilot charting a ship's course through the channel, while the captain steers the vessel's actual movement. The pilot never touches the wheel. However, repeated efforts in the Soviet Union and China to lessen political party interference with professional management of the system failed to resolve the issue. The result is excessive political involvement in practical matters to the detriment of expertise and efficiency.

This dilemma is rooted in official doctrine. The "General Programme" or preamble to the 1982 party constitution asserts that "the party...must see to it that the legislative, judicial and administrative organs of the state and the economic, cultural and people's organizations work actively and with initiative,

---

[18]Harold K. Jacobson and Michel Oksenberg, *China and the Keystone International Economic Organizations* (draft, 1987).

independently, responsibly, and in harmony." Article 3 obligates individual members to "execute the party's decisions perseveringly, accept any job and fulfil actively any task assigned to them by the party, [and] conscientiously observe party discipline and the laws of the state." Article 10 spells out the hierarchy of authority which submits each member to rule from above, culminating in the Central Committee, in practice meaning the Politburo.

However as part of Deng's political reform program, a key provision enveloping government in the party network was revised at the thirteenth CCP Congress. Article 46 had stipulated that "A leading party members' group shall be formed in the leading body of a central or local state organ....The main tasks of such a group are: to see to it that the party's principles and policies are implemented, to unite with the nonparty cadres and masses in fulfilling the tasks assigned by the party and the state, and to guide the work of the party organization of the unit." This group "must accept the leadership of the party committee that approves its establishment." Article 48 added, "the Central Committee of the party shall determine specifically the functions, powers, and tasks of the leading party members' groups in those government departments which need to exercise highly centralized and unified leadership over subordinate units; it shall also determine whether such groups should be replaced by party committees."

The new Article 46 deleted all reference to "central or local state organ," instead limiting the party group to "the elected leading body of a central or local people's congress, mass organization, or other non-party organization." Further Article 48 was reduced to the Central Committee determining whether "a party committee should be set up" in government departments, such action not being mandatory.

These changes won specific attention in Zhao Ziyang's address to the Congress. Attacking "the lack of distinction between the functions of the Party and those of the government and the substitution of the Party for the government," Zhao declared, "The key to reforming the political structure is the separation of Party and government."[19] The problem of dual authority had been exacerbated by the fact that after Mao's death the party was predominantly composed of old revolutionary veterans and young Cultural Revolution recruits. Neither group had the education or experience required to cope with economic modernization. Yet such modernization was imperative if China were to achieve self-reliance in national security and raise its standard of living.

Whether this reform can actually be accomplished, given the vested interest of party secretaries in maintaining their power and privileges, remains to be seen. Zhao acknowledged that the reforms "should gradually become institutionalized." The official spokesman for the party congress specifically noted that "the question of political restructuring is a very complicated one...it

---

[19]Zhao Ziyang, "Advance Along the Road of Socialism With Chinese Characteristics," Report to 13th National Congress of the Chinese Communist Party, October 25, 1987 in *Beijing Review,* November 9–15, 1987, p.38.

will be a gradual abolition of the leading party's groups in the central organs as well as in the ministries and commissions of the State Council." Another question concerns retired senior party officials who are elevated to the Central Advisory Committee, presumably with prestige but without power. They are loathe to disengage completely from politics. They seek to influence policy through long-established networks and personal intervention. For these reasons, until there is convincing evidence to the contrary, it is safe to assume that the main locus of decision making in foreign as well as domestic policy will be in the CCP Standing Committee and Politburo.

Institutional Structure: The Government

In China, as in all large complex organizations, rarely does one decision determine everything that follows. Decisions are usually incremental in nature and implementation is always organizational in practice. This is a particularly important aspect of foreign policy where success or failure often depends on perceptions abroad which, in turn, are based on what is said and done by individuals and organizations far removed from the initial decision makers. Thus whatever weight may be given to individuals or party organs in initiating policy, a critical role remains for governmental bodies in day to day operations.

Seen in this perspective, the cabinet or State Council is a logical point of departure, comprising the premier, vice-premiers, state councillors, and more than forty heads of ministries and commissions. Barnett's informants described a much smaller group of fifteen key officials as actually supervising governmental operations, meeting twice a week under the premier's chairmanship. In addition to officials responsible for general foreign policy management, this "inner cabinet" includes those in charge of economic policy abroad, national defense, and organizations involved in or affected by China's growing participation in the world community. In other words it is the nexus of PRC foreign policy management.

However within this fifteen person nexus, a subgroup of three further centralized the coordination of foreign policy and the consideration of policy problems. According to Zhao Ziyang, then premier, the ministers for foreign affairs and foreign trade, together with an experienced state councillor "meet frequently" to discuss foreign affairs and communicate among themselves. When there are problems they cannot solve, they raise them with the State Council.[20] Barnett noted the omission of the defense minister in contrast with the usual practice in Washington. Zhao's comment illustrates the degree to which policy responsibility can devolve to a small, highly personalized group without formal authorization or public visibility.

Yet it would be wrong to exaggerate the degree of control and coordination in China's vast bureaucracy that extends throughout provincial and municipal offices that deal with foreign business, tourism, and journalism.

[20] Barnett, *The Making of Foreign Policy in China*, p. 67.

Multiple and conflicting interests coexist in time and may be acted on simultaneously without central direction from the capital.

It is natural to fix on the Ministry of Foreign Affairs together with the Ministry of Foreign Economic Relations and Trade as central in foreign policy, while it is seldom realized that the latter is by far the larger entity. But a broader vision must encompass those organizations whose information inputs and policy outputs directly or indirectly relate to China's foreign relations. Some, such as the Ministry of Defense, are highly visible and resemble their counterparts abroad in function and operation, although foreign military sales remain secret in scope and content. Others, such as those involved with intelligence or support for "national liberation struggles," are completely covert. Still others, such as the Ministry of Finance and the People's Bank, have primary domestic responsibilities that are affected by how China manages its external economic relations, and therefore they are engaged in foreign policy discussions.

For example, the aforementioned study of China's entry into the World Bank found the following institutions involved, in addition to the more obvious ones already named: the Chinese Academy of Social Science, the Ministry of Education, the State Economic Commission, the State Education Commission, the State Planning Commission, the State Statistical Bureau, and the Shanghai Institute of International Economic Management.[21] To envisage that entry as simply following a single decision made at the top would caricature the long, complex, and elaborate process of winning agreement to its implementation so as to satisfy both China and the World Bank.

China's extensive people-to-people bureaucracy also plays an important part in shaping the PRC image abroad, in introducing foreign techniques and concepts at home, and in forging links that supplement standard diplomatic channels. The Ministry of Culture, the State Scientific and Technological Commission, the Chinese People's Institute of Foreign Affairs, and the Chinese People's Association for Friendship with Foreign Countries are active in this regard. Indeed, as Barnett notes, the latter two organizations "are headed by senior retired diplomats and staffed in large part by personnel from the Foreign Ministry and other government foreign affairs organizations." Research institutes also play a role through their hosting of foreign scholars and their visits to foreign "think tanks," *inter alia* promoting image and policy while eliciting information to be incorporated in their policy research studies. Primary in this regard are the Institute of International Studies directly under the Foreign Ministry, the Institute of Contemporary International Relations, and the Beijing Institute for International Strategic Studies.

Just as China's participation in the global community is still evolving, so too are its governmental policy processes in flux. Beijing's exclusion from most international organizations down to 1971 was made worse by the Cultural Revolution's self-imposed isolation, which suppressed institutions, as well as individuals that had previously had experience with foreign affairs. Not until

---

[21]Jacobson and Oksenberg, op cit.

Deng's ascendancy and his proclamation of the "open door" doctrine in December 1978 did the PRC begin a rapid expansion of political involvement and economic interdependence with the global system.

The brief span of a decade hardly suffices to establish an entire bureaucratic system for managing relations between a developing society of more than a billion people and a vast international network that itself is undergoing rapid transformation, especially in the economic realm. As a final point, the People's Republic existed under a uniquely dominant Mao Zedong from 1949 to 1976 and an ascendant Deng Xiaoping thereafter, each having distinctly different political styles and power. Therefore decision making at the top as well as the bureaucratic structure and process below will inevitably evolve well beyond presently perceptible patterns. This requires continuing research and analysis to test past propositions and new hypotheses, remembering that China has maintained the oldest continuous civilization by adapting to change forced on it by internal as well as external circumstances. Nevertheless, its bureaucracy has survived through the millenia as a highly complex system, whether the regime was imperial, republican, or Communist. It is likely to remain a major conditioning force on policy, both domestic and foreign.

THE SUBSTANCE OF POLICY

Ends and Means

The People's Republic has radically changed its foreign policy rhetoric at home and abroad over the past forty years. Mao's world revolutionary fervor of the 1950s, carried to an extreme in the 1960s, stands in complete contrast with Deng's global integrative and interdependent stance in the 1980s. It is impossible to exaggerate the difference in tone and substance as between Beijing's pronouncements of 1949–54 or 1966–68 and 1985–87.

Yet contradictory rhetoric notwithstanding, a fundamental continuity characterized the ends of policy, not only during the relatively short history of the PRC but going back to its republican and imperial predecessors. Security from foreign attack was traditionally a primary concern and, as our earlier analysis showed, a preoccupation through the first half of this century. This preoccupation did not end with Mao, and it concerned Deng until the early 1980s. Meeting domestic needs sufficient to avoid rebellion was also a constant regime worry as a growing population pressed against scarce resources of food, shelter, and employment. This problem also plagued Qing, Nationalist, and Communist policymakers alike.

Mao acknowledged these practical priorities, although he mismanaged them and at times neglected them for ideological postulates of self-reliance and his own vision of communism. He recognized the linkage between external prestige and internal strength measured in economic rather than military terms. In 1961, at the depth of a prolonged economic crisis worsened by the sudden withdrawal of Soviet technical assistance, Mao declared, "Nations which are big or rich despise nations which are small or poor....At present, China still finds itself in a position of being despised. There is a reason people despise us. It is because we have not progressed enough. So big a country and we have so little steel and so many illiterates. But it is good if people despise us because it forces us to strive harder and forces us to advance."[22]

Mao's remarks reflect a national sensitivity to China's inferior position of power and status after a millenium of superiority vis-à-vis the world as it existed in Chinese perceptions and experience, at least in Asia. This historical heritage of former greatness and contemporary weakness affects both the ends and means of foreign policy alternatives implicit in current approaches to Chinese nationalism. Professor Michel Oksenberg differentiates four such variants.[23] The most extreme is "strident, xenophobic, and isolationist...seeks to eradicate foreign influence." Advanced by the Boxers in 1900 and Red Guards in the Cultural Revolution, this approach has the least support at present. A second variant is "self-pitying, self-righteous, and aggrieved...blames China's ills on the transgressions of the outside world." Although similar to nationalism in other developing countries, its strength derives from a sense of China's past grandeur juxtaposed against its recent "century of shame and humiliation." Oksenberg describes the resulting ambivalent attitude as one of "scorn and admiration, resentment and appreciation" toward the outside world. A third "militant, rigid, assertive, and occasionally muscular nationalism" characterized Mao's assault on Khrushchev and Deng's attempt to "teach Vietnam a lesson." More recently this approach accepts "a limited and cautious involvement in world affairs to terminate vulnerabilities and humiliations." How it will be manifested once China acquires sufficient military strength to pursue its unsettled territorial claims on land and at sea remains to be seen.

Oksenberg finds the fourth variant dominant since the mid-1980s, namely, "a patient and moderate nationalism rooted in confidence that China can regain its former greatness through economic growth, based on the import of foreign technology and ideas." But it partakes of the third variant in being "a determined and resolute nationalism...deeply committed to the preservation of national independence, the reunification of China (including Hong Kong, Macao, Taiwan, and disputed islands in the South and East China Seas) and the attainment of national wealth and power." His list could also have included disputed borders with the Soviet Union, India, and Vietnam.

This categorization captures the continuing linkage between domestic and foreign policy. Economic development as an internal goal links with the twin external goals of national security and self-defined territorial integrity. The categorization also reveals domestic differences over how to attain these

[22]"Notes on the Soviet Union Textbook 'Political Economy,' " *Mao Zedong Sixiang Wansui,* 1969, p. 392.
[23]Michel Oksenberg, "China's Confident Nationalism," *Foreign Affairs,* vol. 65, no. 3, (1987).

goals. Neither the linkage nor the goals are uniquely Chinese. However, during most of Mao's rule the degree to which they were misperceived abroad and the way in which they were pursued at home set China apart from other major powers.

Therefore, Deng Xiaoping moved to reorder and clarify goals in foreign perception and domestic priority. On the one hand, he articulated nationalism in blunt terms as we noted earlier, vowing that China will not "swallow any bitter fruit detrimental to its own interests." On the other hand, he insisted that China "must open to the outside world" in order to progress toward modernization. Deng also translated these general concepts into medium and long-term goals for the 1990s and beyond. For the next decade he targeted the doubling of gross national product (GNP) per capita, the unification of the PRC with Hong Kong and possibly Taiwan, and the striving to "combat hegemonism and safeguard world peace." He further declared that Hong Kong's existing socioeconomic system would last "fifty years more" while the peaceful unification of Taiwan might take a hundred years.

Of the three goals, Deng repeatedly made economic growth and modernization top priority. Meanwhile "safeguarding peace" was a means as well as an end. Only by achieving a peaceful international environment could China concentrate scarce human and capital resources on the civilian economy, postponing the acquisition of modern weapons until they could be produced at home rather than purchased abroad. Thus national security no longer outranked other objectives.

More specifically, by changing the Soviet relationship from confrontation to détente, Deng could reduce the PLA by a million men and defer indefinitely the wholesale upgrading of conventional weaponry. Similarly postponing the long-sought unification with Taiwan would safeguard relations with the United States and Japan as major sources of capital, technology, and markets. In short, domestic priorities determined foreign policy insofar as it was susceptible to Chinese management.

Opposition to Deng's "open door" policy came from some of the nationalistic variants mentioned by Oksenberg, but Deng met them head on. In an assertive speech he rebuked the isolationist xenophobes on the record of their predecessors, "Any country that closes its door to the outside world cannot achieve progress. We underwent this bitter experience and so did our forefathers....China closed the country to international intercourse for more than three centuries from the middle of the Ming Dynasty to the Opium War, or for nearly two centuries from emperors Kangxi and Qianlong. Hence the country became impoverished, backward, and ignorant."[24] His last reference also implicitly rebutted the aggrieved nationalists who blamed all of China's ills on the foreign powers.

---

[24]Deng Xiaoping to Third Plenary Session of Central Advisory Commission, October 22, 1984, *Renmin Ribao,* January 1, 1985.

Speaking to the party's Central Advisory Committee, Deng reassured his more ideological veteran colleagues, "Some of our comrades are afraid that evil practices may be introduced into the country...of seeing capitalism suddenly looming up after having worked all their lives for socialism and communism...[but] nothing will be affected. It may bring some negative factors. But it will not be difficult to overcome such factors if we are aware of them."[25]

Such reassurance seemed challenged in December 1986 when student demonstrations demanding freedom and democracy broke out in Shanghai and other cities. The resulting counterattack against "bourgeois liberalization" linked domestic dissent with foreign influences, in the process toppling Hu Yaobang as General Secretary of the CCP, one of Deng's two chosen successors. However Deng responded shrewdly. On the one hand he expelled a few prominent liberals from the party and cracked down on student demonstrations with the threat of force. On the other hand he steadfastly insisted that the open door would never be closed, regardless of the "flies and mosquitoes" that might come in.

Actually the door opened outward as well as inward. By 1990 more than 40,000 Chinese were studying in the United States with thousands more in Europe and Japan. Beginning in 1979, dozens of Chinese delegations toured the world to observe military and civilian installations, factories, and training centers. Hundreds of specialists accepted invitations to attend international conferences and workshops or to give individual lectures at research centers. Reciprocally foreign experts, especially overseas Chinese, poured into the country to offer information and advice, conduct joint research, and assess problems. Almost every subject from archeology to zoology became the province of joint study between Chinese and foreigners at home and abroad. Several hundred thousand foreign books and journals replenished the vacant libraries left desolate by the Cultural Revolution and provided starter sets for new research centers. The massive translation of scientific materials expanded their potential use pending adequate training in foreign languages.

Information alone was not enough. China needed advanced technology and the capital to acquire it. In 1980 Beijing moved to join the major international financial organizations: the International Monetary Fund, the International Bank for Reconstruction and Development—better known as the World Bank—and its affiliated agencies, the International Development Association and the International Finance Corporation. Previously these agencies had been attacked as exploitive instruments of capitalist control over Third World economies. Beijing had also protested Taiwan's occupying the China seat in them, at the same time championing PRC "self-reliance." As another deterrent to joining these institutions they required opening the economy to detailed examination and statistical reporting. Such practices ran counter to the Communist proclivity for secrecy and the Chinese sensitivity over revealing weakness.

[25] Ibid.

However in the eyes of Deng and his modernizing cohorts the potential gain clearly outweighed the costs. After forcing Taiwan out, they came in, quietly abandoning the Maoist strictures on alleged North-South confrontation and calls for a New Economic Order. Instead they maneuvered to strengthen China's position over that of India so as to maximize their opportunity to influence decisions and win loans. By 1990 World Bank approved loans to China approximated $9.1 billion.

In addition to money, the World Bank provided invaluable planning assistance through its comprehensive surveys of the Chinese economy, the first, as of 1981, issued in three closely written volumes and the second, as of 1984, in six volumes. The Bank also did feasibility studies of more than four dozen projects financed by its loans, focusing on agriculture, energy, education, public health, transportation, and science.[26] Thus the World Bank impact went well beyond the provision of funds, in effect transforming the decision-making as well as the productive processes. For example, "China in the Year 2000" is no longer a rhetorical reference for political exhortation, but a systematic research effort modeled on similar studies abroad and undertaken in cooperation with the World Bank. Centered in the State Council's Technical Economics Research Center, its responsibilities include feasibility studies of major construction projects, studying the long-term comprehensive and strategic development of the economy, and assessing major economic policies already under way.

This close interaction between China and the World Bank is only one instance whereby post-Mao policy links domestic development with foreign policy. With foreign trade in excess of $90 billion by 1990, Japan's share of Chinese foreign trade ranked first with more than a fifth of the total. Japan also occupied first place in China's foreign borrowing with $9 billion in low-interest loans committed since 1979. Acceptance of Japan, a former enemy, as the principal source of trade, technology, and credit came hard after a half century of aggression, annexation, and invasion. Reversing the traditional roles of teacher and student further exacerbated the situation for the older generation in particular.

To overcome this deep-seated antipathy, in 1983 Beijing joined with Tokyo in sponsoring the Commission for Sino-Japanese Friendship in the Twenty-first Century. Its promotion by the highest officials on both sides contrasted with the militant anti-Japanese imagery propagated by the Chinese media down to 1971 and briefly revived during a dispute over Japanese textbook revisions in 1982. Nevertheless resistance to such "friendship" prompted anti-Japanese student demonstrations on September 17, 1985, the anniversary of the Japanese seizure of Manchuria in 1931. The protests were an immediate reaction to the fortieth anniversary of Japan's surrender in World War II and its provocative commemoration in Tokyo. However student

---

[26]In addition to Jacobson and Oksenberg, op. cit., this section draws on an unpublished paper by Samuel S. Kim kindly made available to the author.

slogans also attacked "the second invasion" and "Japan's economic invasion." Yet despite this domestic opposition, PRC officials persisted in promoting the Japanese tie, explicitly justifying it as necessary for economic modernization.

In similar fashion Sino-American relations have been driven in part by domestic economic goals, thereby relegating the Taiwan issue to the background. Détente between Beijing and Washington began for security goals in 1969–71 amid Chinese apprehension over a tripling of Soviet military forces across the border in 1965–70, with actual clashes in 1969. The security aspect reopened in 1979 when China attacked Vietnam, allied with the Soviet Union, in a three-week long limited war.

While the security question did not wholly disappear, its significance lessened in the 1980s as Beijing became more confident of Moscow's intentions and problems elsewhere. Meanwhile the economic potential in Sino-American relationships loomed steadily larger as Washington loosened controls on technology transfer, particularly as regards technology with dual-use potential for military as well as civilian use. A $500 million avionics package for jet fighters to acquire all-weather capability won congressional approval, as did the sale of nuclear power generation technology, should Beijing want to purchase these goods. A sizeable investment in off-shore oil exploration failed to bring American corporations much profit or China much oil. Yet the continuation of oil exploration held out hope of an eventual strike that could ease China's domestic oil needs and perhaps earn additional foreign exchange from Asian neighbors, first and foremost Japan.

Under these circumstances, Deng's decision to stop pressing the United States to halt arms sales to Taiwan in 1982 and, instead, to accept an ambiguously worded commitment to decrease them over time made economic sense. Likewise Beijing protested in words, but not actions, after a unanimous congressional resolution condemned the Chinese suppression of Tibetan demonstrations in 1987. This once again reflected the primacy of domestic economics in foreign policy.

Last but not least in this brief review of major relationships affected by domestic priorities is Beijing's response to Moscow's repeated bids for détente, beginning in 1981 and accelerating after 1986. We have already cited the security aspect whereby downgrading the threat of Soviet attack, both real and perceived, permitted the reduction of PLA forces and the concomitant drop in the defense share of the budget, officially stated as 10 percent in 1985 as against 15 percent in 1983. In addition, the economic modernization program enjoys relatively small but worthwhile gains through improved relations between China and the Soviet bloc. Upgrading Soviet and East European equipment of the 1950s can be more economical and feasible than replacing it wholesale with machinery from other countries. Soviet equipment is also easier to pay for on a barter basis since this does not require drawing down foreign exchange reserves. Finally cross-border trade can be important locally for the northeast and far west of China where there is a limited complementarity between the two economies. While total trade remains far below that of Japan and the United States, its tenfold growth in ten years to $3 billion by 1990 makes sense to Beijing as well as Moscow.

This partly explains why Deng muted Mao's strident anti-Soviet polemics, particularly with respect to Moscow's domestic policies. To be sure, it became difficult to attack Soviet policies as "revisionist" when China's economic experiments soon surpassed them by abandoning much collective enterprise for limited private and family initiatives in the rural and urban economies. But equally important was the reintroduction of Soviet participation in economic development, where such participation might be more relevant for China's technological level than the highly advanced ways and means of Japan, the United States, and Western Europe.

Unlike Japan and the United States, however, the Soviet Union won no real respite from Chinese pressure on major foreign issues in dispute between the two countries. Beijing persisted in its support for the guerrillas fighting Soviet occupation forces in Afghanistan; and it opposed Vietnamese forces in Cambodia or Kampuchea that were backed by Moscow. It demanded a Soviet withdrawal from both situations and mobilized others to support this demand. The provision of arms in both instances, especially for the Khmer Rouge forces operating out of Thailand, showed that Beijing is willing to back its words with deeds, improved bilateral relations with Moscow notwithstanding.

Beijing's repeated declaration of an "independent" policy with no "strategic alignment or alliance" with either superpower was manifest in its public denunciation of American policy in Central America, South Africa, and the Middle East. However, nowhere did Chinese actions substantively intervene against American interests, although arms sales to Iran became contentious in 1987. Chinese denials ducked the issue, as had previously occurred with respect to the question of China's assisting Pakistan in the clandestine development of nuclear weapons. But neither case approximated the indirect confrontation with Moscow in Afghanistan and Indochina.

A less important but symbolically more sensitive instance of economics superceding politics came with the 1984 Sino-British agreement on Hong Kong's reversion to Chinese control in 1997. The year 1997 ends Britain's ninety-nine year lease to the New Territories, adjoining the original Hong Kong territory ceded "in perpetuity" after the Opium War. Both concessions resulted from "unequal treaties." Yet Beijing permitted their termination to be settled through prolonged and intensive negotiation with London. The foregone conclusion was garbed in legalistic language bereft of anti-imperialist rhetoric. Much remained to be clarified concerning the actual manner in which Hong Kong would eventually be administered, but the basic agreement pledged continuation of its existing economic system.

As with our other cases, political considerations played a part in policy. The principle of "one country, two systems" anticipated a positive response from Taiwan, where Hong Kong might provide an attractive example for negotiating union with the mainland. Specific reference to this objective by Deng and his associates failed to bring Taiwan to the table, at least in the short run. Nevertheless Beijing hoped over time to make Hong Kong a positive precedent for Taipei.

In the interim, economic incentives dictated a soft, compromising stance on the British crown colony. Hong Kong provides between one fourth and one third of China's foreign exchange earnings. This comes through a combination of direct sales to Hong Kong, transshipment through the world's second largest port, Chinese investment in Hong Kong, and overseas Chinese remittances transmitted through its facilities. Reciprocally Hong Kong investment in China soared with the opening of Shenzhen, the first special economic zone, literally on its border. Neighboring Guangdong province and its capital of Guangzhou (Canton) likewise profited through burgeoning trade and investment from the colony. In fact, Hong Kong capital and capitalists sparked local modernization to the extent that some observers wondered, only partly in jest, whether it was a question of Hong Kong "taking over China" rather than the reverse.

Moving more broadly, China's virtual abandonment of revolutionary rhetoric and activity in Southeast Asia clearly stems from Deng's desire to improve relations with ASEAN, the Association of Southeast Asian Nations. Initially he aimed at isolating Vietnam and obstructing its occupation of Kampuchea. Then economic objectives became important as Beijing wooed investors and sought markets. Both goals required a muting of support for indigenous Communists, most of whom had enjoyed Beijing's help in insurgency at some point in the past three decades.

Little remains of Mao's once touted "three worlds" approach to global economic relations. Instead of belaboring North-South problems to be solved exclusively by the northern tier of industrial states, China has hosted South-South conferences which emphasize mutual help among the southern tier developing economies. In practical terms this often means self-help. Beijing's representatives in the World Bank and its affiliates work within existing norms for their own interests, not those of other developing countries in particular. This pattern is expected to hold when the PRC enters GATT (General Agreement on Trade and Tariffs), having made application for membership in 1986, although several years of negotiation are anticipated to work out the details.

Thus the 1970s cry for a New Economic Order disappeared from Chinese statements in the 1980s. Instead Beijing promoted themes of peace, disarmament, and development in its presentations to international bodies where its participation grew rapidly under Deng's aegis. From 1977 to 1989 PRC membership in nongovernmental organizations (NGOs) jumped from 71 to 677, while it still remained apart from the two major Third World groups, the Non-Aligned Movement and OPEC.[27] China joined considerably fewer Inter-

[27]Kim, op. cit.

national Governmental Organizations (IGOs) during this time, moving from 21 memberships in IGOs to 37. Professor Samuel S. Kim speculates that hesitancy in the latter category stems in part from limited diplomatic personnel, with priority going to the United Nations and its specialized agencies. Therefore he foresees a gradual growth to roughly 50 IGO memberships in the next decade.

Parallel with its expanded organizational participation was the PRC adherence to multilateral treaties. From 1949 to 1970 it signed a total of six, adding another sixteen before Mao's death. But between 1977 and 1985 Beijing joined ninety-one multilateral agreements.[28] Still another indicator of China's reentry into the world community as a normal member came with high-level visits abroad, reciprocating a steady flow of government leaders to China. Mao only left the country twice, both times to visit Moscow. Liu Shaoqi, head of state from 1958 to 1967, made brief tours of Southeast Asia in addition to visiting the U.S.S.R. Otherwise only Zhou Enlai as premier, and sometimes as foreign minister, travelled extensively to Eastern Europe, Africa, and Asia.

Within a few years of Mao's death, however, Deng made unprecedented trips to Western Europe, Japan, and the United States. Premiers Hua Guofeng and Zhao Ziyang expanded on Zhou Enlai's itinerary, including Western Europe and Australasia. In 1985 President Li Xiannian visited Washington, the highest Chinese official in history to do so, having been preceded by presidents Nixon, Ford, and Reagan going to Beijing.

Hu Yaobang as CCP General Secretary also travelled widely before his ouster in 1987. Gone was the so-called Mao jacket and the support for radical splinter groups in Europe and elsewhere as "true Marxist-Leninists" confronted Moscow's orthodox adherents. China's worldwide offensive against "revisionism and social imperialism" had reduced its state cohorts to Albania and North Korea and its party contacts to nonentities. This policy ended with Mao's death. Ironically the first state leader to view Mao's body in the newly erected mausoleum in Tienanmen Square was Yugoslavia's Brosip Tito, Mao's initial revisionist target of twenty years earlier. By the late 1980s the CCP had not only restored relations with virtually all its major counterparts, excepting the Soviet party, but had broadened relations with socialist and left-wing parties in many countries.

As might be expected, the last and least important means of policy in the past decade has been the use of force. Except for the three week limited invasion of Vietnam in February-March 1979, the PLA has remained behind China's borders since Mao's death. Prior to that its use in defensively motivated actions had engaged United States-United Nations forces in Korea (1950–53), Indian border troops in the Himalayas (1962), U.S. aircraft over North Vietnam (1965–68), and Soviet border units along the Amur-Ussuri river complex and the Xinjiang border (1969). The PLA also seized the Xisha (Paracel) Islands from South Vietnam forces in 1974. Pursuing the civil war it

[28]Ibid.

engaged Chinese Nationalist air and sea units in the Taiwan Strait throughout the 1950s and 1960s, with concentrated attacks on offshore islands in 1954–55 and 1958, having had limited success with only the first attack.

Beijing's perception of threat was clearly much higher during Mao's regime than subsequently, in part because its sense of vulnerability was much greater. To a considerable extent, however, miscalculation by China's opponents, most notably Washington and New Delhi, aroused this threat perception. Learning on both sides, albeit costly, ushered in a more stable and peaceful situation wholly apart from Deng's determination to minimize military expenditures by reducing tensions on all fronts. Thus in the spring of 1987 mutual accusations of military buildup by Beijing and New Delhi raised tensions in the disputed border area, but no fighting occurred. Similarly minor incidents on the Sino-Soviet border were also contained to private diplomatic exchanges. Only the Vietnam border continued to flare up periodically, with each side accusing the other of initiating mortar and artillery bombardments and occasional ground action up to battalion level.

During this decade of general military stand down and claimed reductions in defense spending, China has nevertheless continued to improve its nuclear capability. The growing inventory of missiles includes medium-range (660 miles), intermediate range (1,400–1,900 miles), extended intermediate-range (2,880–3,330 miles), and intercontinentalrange (7,800 miles). In 1983 China tested its first ballistic missile submarine, firing an extended inter-mediate-range weapon. The airborne delivery of fission and fusion weapons is made possible by approximately a hundred bombers with a radius of up to 1,800 miles, although they are very vulnerable to Soviet defenses.

All but the intercontinental missiles were liquid-fuelled as of the mid-1980s, virtually precluding a surprise attack because of the lengthy firing process. This made credible China's vow never to launch a first strike. However they served as a potential second strike deterrent to the extent that dispersal, hardening, and concealment or camouflage preclude their total destruction by an enemy. The most likely threat being Soviet, this second strike capability becomes meaningful when targetted against any of the three major Far East Soviet cities: Irkutsk, Khabarovsk, and Vladivostok. The first two sit astride the Trans-Siberian railroad, just across the border. Their destruction would cut Moscow's main communications route to its Pacific bases of which Vladivostok is the primary one, equally vulnerable to missile attack.

These considerations may have contributed to Chinese confidence that Moscow would not start a war once the crisis of 1969–70 ebbed, in addition to the Sino-American détente with hints from Washington that it would not remain passive in a Sino-Soviet conflict. However such confidence could not be absolute, thereby justifying Beijing's continued research and development of nuclear weapons, most recently including MIRV (multiple independent targeted reentry vehicle) warheads.

FUTURE PROSPECTS

This profile of foreign policy ends and means is likely to remain valid for the 1990s, but it is subject to whatever short-term effect Deng Xiaoping's death may have on leadership cohesion. Uncertainty on this score stems from the convulsive events of spring 1989. At that time a growing schism between reformers and conservatives came to a head over how to cope with massive student demonstrations demanding political liberalization. During nearly two months of mounting public opposition the leadership refused to compromise with the demonstrators, despite their winning widespread support from the urban populace. Finally the geriatric party veterans, ostensibly retired, ordered the PLA to disperse the thousands of students who had camped in Tiananmen Square for weeks. On June 3–4 ill-trained troops with tanks and armored personnel carriers rampaged through the streets of Beijing, killing hundreds of unarmed civilians and injuring thousands.

Thanks to foreign television coverage, a worldwide audience witnessed this worst challenge to Chinese Communist rule since its founding. In mid-May hundreds of reporters had gathered in Beijing for the Sino-Soviet summit meeting between President Mikhail Gorbachev and his Chinese counterparts. This provided an unprecedented window on the moving spectacle of millions massed on behalf of the students followed by shocking scenes of death and destruction. Anger abroad triggered harsh public condemnation from virtually all the advanced industrial powers, a somewhat softer reproach being voiced by Japan.

China's foreign relations rapidly deteriorated. The Bush Administration won support from the European Community and Japan for various sanctions, including the suspension of new loan consideration by the World Bank, prohibition of high level official exchnages, a halt to further military sales and tightened limits on dual-purpose technology transfer, and the extension of visas for Chinese students already resident in these countries. China responded by sharply attacking the Voice of America for having allegedly caused trouble in the first place and accused the West in general and the United States, in particular, with "interference in China's internal affairs" through the sanctions. According to Deng and others, a plot to overthrow Communist rule by "peaceful evolution" utilized "bourgeois influences" to foment the "counter-revolutionary rebellion."

Although the leadership insisted the "open door" would not be shut against the outside world, an intensive propaganda campaign evoked a sense of besieged nationalism bordering on xenophobia. Its virulent attack against American policy cited all the negative instances of hostility from 1949 to 1989, omitting all the positive instances of cooperation from 1972 to 1988. This selective history recalled earlier years when China's ills were wholly blamed on foreign influences, whether under Qing, Nationalist, or Communist rule.

In the following months Congressional resolutions attacking the regime on human rights kept the issue alive. However the Bush Administration, contrary to its public posture, nonetheless secretly sent high officials to Beijing in an effort to keep relations on an even keel. Martial law eventually ended in the Chinese capital and the most celebrated dissident, Fang Lizhi, and his wife were allowed to leave the American embassy where they had taken refuge after the massacre. Washington, in turn, renewed the most favored nation agreement for one year, granting essential Chinese trade privileges. The worst had passed, but Sino-American relations remained at the lowest level in many years. Following the American lead, Japan suspended implementation of a $5.6 billion loan announced in 1988 but reopened this window in late 1990.

Thus forty years after its founding the PRC found itself somewhat of a pariah in an important sector of the international community, although its Third World relations remained unimpaired. A fundamental clash of values and differing concepts of sovereign rights versus human rights opened a gulf between Beijing and major world capitals. Despite defiant assertions of being in the right and being unaffected by economic sanctions, the leadership was forced to recognize the growing economic cost of its political isolation. In 1989 tourism fell 23 percent, with foreign exchange earnings thereby down 20 percent. Foreign investment commitments were down 30 percent from their expected level. No loans came from the Asian Development Bank, and only a few from the World Bank "for basic human needs." Commercial lending rates accordingly rose to 1 percentage point above the London Interbank Offered Rate (LIBOR), whereas before June 1989 it had been below LIBOR.

Finally in the latter half of 1990 Chinese diplomacy successfully reversed the downward trend by supporting the U.N. Security Council resolutions condemning Iraq's invasion of Kuwait and imposing a total economic embargo against Baghdad. This compromised China's long-standing opposition to "superpower interference in Third World affairs," the U.S. deployment of more than 200,000 troops, ships, and planes to the Gulf region notwithstanding. Beijing also succeeded in restoring relations with Indonesia, broken since 1965, and winning diplomatic recognition from Singapore and Saudia Arabia. By 1991 much of the lost ground had been recovered, but China's prestige abroad remained in the shadow of Tiananmen.

Yet inside China tension increased between the defenders of interdependence for economic modernization and the advocates of self-reliance to preserve a Chinese sense of identity. Eventually interdependence seems certain to prevail over self-reliance. Too many vested interests have accumulated during the ten years of "open door" policy for a dozen or so party elders to turn back the clock. These interests extend across geographic regions and functional ministries, encompassing important military as well as civilian sectors. The several million foreign tourists and the myriad of foreign media messages that penetrated China since Mao's death opened the population to the world, precluding any lasting return to his Cultural Revolution isolationism.

In the meantime, however, Deng's power was badly eroded through the ouster of Hu Yaobang in 1987 and of Zhao Ziyang in 1989, each having been his choice to succeed him as head of the party and the government, respectively. Deng's death seems certain to unleash a power struggle more serious than that which followed Mao's death in 1976. No prominent figure appears to possess the political clout that enabled Deng to restore confidence after the Cultural Revolution chaos. Moreover the regime lacks legitimacy in the urban sector, because it ordered the PLA to fire on the people, although it retains allegiance in the countryside where peasants have prospered under the reforms. Finally, the collapse of Communist rule in East Europe and its gradual disintegration in the Soviet Union, together with the loss of credibility for Marxism-Leninism-Mao Zedong Thought, confronts Deng's successors with an ideological crisis. Without clearly defined and nationally accepted values of right and wrong, a society of 1.13 billion inhabitants, many leading a marginal economic existence, cannot maintain law and order.

Under these circumstances, it is impossible to predict with confidence exactly the course of China's foreign relations during the balance of this century. Much will depend on how the succession struggle evolves and how the regime copes with the possible return of public dissidence. 1989 revealed the extent to which domestic developments are intimately linked with the external world, as well as how the external world reacts to domestic developments in China. This two-sided process has an internal dynamic that cannot be controlled by the leadership, even though it can influence it for better or for worse.

In any event, certain foreign policy issues will face the regime, regardless of its domestic performance. Annexing Taiwan has been on Beijing's agenda since 1949, although its priority has changed as has the means for acquiring it. In the 1950s millions of Chinese vowed its "liberation" in mass rallies, while leadership statements ritualistically committed the regime to this goal. By the 1980s the goal had become "reunification" through "peaceful means as a fundamental policy." Beijing refused to foreswear the use of force as its sovereign right but in deference to American policy, reiterated by every administration, it virtually abandoned any reference to this option.

The PRC made credible its peaceful policy, drawing down the military forces opposite Taiwan and opening the coastal area to foreign investment and tourism. Deng elaborated on his "one country, two systems" concept in interviews which declared that Taiwan would be even more autonomous than Hong Kong because it could keep its own armed forces and acquire weapons abroad "so long as they do not threaten the mainland." Deng pledged "not to send a single official" to the island, asking only that Taipei abandon its flag and nomenclature so as to acknowledge its subordinate status as a province in the People's Republic.

Pending negotiations Beijing proposed that trade, travel, family reunion, and mail across the Taiwan Strait be initiated. It invited Taiwan to participate in international conferences, organizations, and sporting events under the name, "China, Taiwan" or "China, Taipei," depending on the circumstances. For its part the Taiwan regime formally refused to sanction any direct mainland contact, but during the 1980s it closed an eye to trade via Hong Kong that was estimated near $3 billion in 1989. It also took no action against travel via third countries, which rose steadily, totaling 300,000 by mainland estimates. Most visible and dramatic, however, was its participation in the 1984 Los Angeles Olympics as "China, Taiwan" with neither its own flag or anthem.

In 1987 Taiwan formalized some of these developments without, however, agreeing to any negotiations. It lifted all restrictions on travel to Hong Kong, thereby opening the gate for onward movement to the mainland. It then moved to permit certain categories of mainland travel associated with family reunion. It also legitimized the publication of mainland scholarly works, provided that they were not political and were reprinted in standard Chinese characters instead of the simplified script of the PRC.

Internally the Taiwan regime introduced major reforms. It lifted martial law, retaining most of the necessary power through emergency legislation, but assuring civilian trials. It permitted opposition parties to contest Kuomintang candidates. It permitted political demonstrations without police interference. It loosened restrictions on the press. Long-held political prisoners received amnesty. The public responded with alacrity, proliferating demonstrations on a wide range of subjects and supporting opposition rallies against the ruling group.

Beijing proved ambivalent on these developments. Increased contact with the mainland was applauded as strengthening ties toward eventual unification. But increased political freedom on the island was attacked when it hinted at Taiwan independence under the opposition party's call for self-determination. President Chiang Ching-kuo died in January 1988. He was the last in the symbolic lineage of Sun Yat-sen and Chiang Kai-shek. No one appeared to combine his commitment to Taiwan's identification as the legitimate China with his political clout as a local leader.

Chiang was succeeded by Lee Teng-Kui, a Taiwanese, as both head of the Nationalist party and of the government. In addition, the cabinet and the party's key standing committee were replaced with Taiwanese, the majority in both organs, as against those of mainlander origin. This raises one key variable in China's future policy: Will Taiwan come under a leadership that declares its independence, and if so, how will Beijing respond? Deng repeatedly warned that this would necessitate the use of force. He did not spell out how force might be applied. Logically it might begin with a closure of Taiwan's ports through proclamation and perhaps blockade, thereby cutting the island's lifeline to economic prosperity, which is dependent on exports. This action would risk economic sanctions against the PRC from the United States and perhaps Japan as well. Yet political passions aroused by decades of commitment to territorial unification could override practical economic considerations.

Admittedly this is a highly unlikely scenario. Taiwan is recognized by less than two dozen states, none major, under the rubric of the Republic of China. As an independent Taiwan it could not hope to gain international legitimation in the United Nations or through diplomatic recognition, least of all from the United States. Fear of provoking PRC reaction will deter either development. Nor can Taiwan count on American military protection should the PRC react to independence with force or the threat thereof. Presumably these calculations will compel Chiang Ching-kuo's successors to stop short of that final step while continuing to maneuver so as to remain separate of mainland control. However, human behavior is not wholly predictable. The possibility remains of Taiwan being forced to the top of Beijing's agenda through developments over which it has no control, with far-reaching implications for China's relations throughout East Asia and particularly with the United States.

The alternative prospect of Taiwan negotiating mainland union is only slightly more likely, at least so long as it enjoys its present prosperity that remains far above mainland living standards, and perceives PRC politics as both unstable and stultifying when compared with the island's ambience. These are all variables subject to change. In particular, the international economic environment can turn sour for Taiwan. Monetary disarray and protectionism could shrink its export markets, whereas the mainland offers an alternative outlet with abundant natural resources to meet Taiwan's needs. These practical considerations might coincide with the continued erosion of emphasis on Marxist-Leninist ideology and the limited liberalization of mainland life, particularly in intellectual and media activities.

Yet possible as these changes are in theory, in actuality they seem far removed from realization in combination, although they may occur separately. As of 1990 Taiwan's foreign exchange reserves were among the largest in the world, approximating $75 billion, with a steady trade surplus, in contrast with the mainland's nagging trade deficit. PRC living standards and the quality of life approximated that on Taiwan of the 1960s for urban areas and the 1950s in much of the countryside. Finally, Beijing's brutal suppression of Tibetan demonstrations and its thirty-year dispute with the Dalai Lama in exile underscored the limits of autonomy that Taiwan might face once union with the mainland was achieved.

Beijing's constant reminder to Washington that "Taiwan is a major obstacle in our relationship" need not be actionable in itself, as more than a decade of reiteration demonstrates. The subject is not foremost in public consciousness, judging from extended travel and conversations at various levels. The majority of mainland family ties with Taiwan are in the coastal provinces of Zhejiang and Fujian. Thus the leadership does not face the prospect of spontaneous demonstrations on this issue as it experienced in the case of Japan in 1985. This situation, together with the aforementioned economic risks in using force, argues against the PRC initiating action on its own.

Yet should the status quo continue to frustrate a future Beijing regime with an internal component challenging the leadership's inaction, testing Taiwan through increased pressure cannot be ruled out. This issue combines the most sensitive nationalistic questions of territorial integrity and national sovereignty, explicitly challenged by Taiwan's declaring itself to be the legitimate China. Moreover American arms sales there and congressional actions place Washington in an intervening role, perceived in Beijing as responsible for Taiwan's refusal to negotiate. The resulting combination of frustrated nationalism and foreign intervention touches deep-seated sensitivities in Chinese memory and politics. A weak or divided leadership invites exploitation of such sensitivities by opportunistic or genuinely committed opponents. The possibility of such circumstances cautions against assuming that the present calculus of costs and benefits will prevail forever in Beijing with respect to the Taiwan problem.

Other territorial issues also exist although with much less potential volatility. Beijing's claims in the South China Sea are symbolically represented on its maps by markings delimiting the entire area as within PRC sovereignty. We have already noted how Beijing made good its claim to the northern islands in 1974 by seizing the Xishas or Paracels from South Vietnam before it fell to Hanoi's forces in 1975. In 1987 Beijing conducted military exercises in the South China Sea for the first time, flexing its newly acquired air and sea capabilities and evoking a warning protest from Hanoi. In March 1988 Beijing responded by forcefully reasserting its right to the southern islands, the Nansha or the Spratleys. In a separate action, the PRC had previously pressed Malaysia to negotiate disputed ownership over a minor area, conceding it to Kuala Lumpuor after having established the principle of a Chinese claim.

Unlike Taiwan, there is no clear and irrefutable basis for Beijing's position on its territorial claims, which are argued on various contentious grounds of archeological finds, historical presence, maps, and past statements by itself or its present opponents. Instead a final resolution on each claim will depend on the balance of power in each particular case at such time as Beijing chooses to bring the issue to a head. That power need not be exclusively military. Should offshore oil be discovered in the immediate vicinity, the need to acquire foreign investment and technology for its exploitation could persuade Beijing to compromise its position through peaceful negotiations. Force or the threat thereof would probably cause Western firms, mainly American, to withdraw their effort, which has persisted despite years of uneconomic discoveries, mainly of natural gas. However the Vietnamese aspect adds a political motivation that might prevail in the absence of significant oil reserves being proven. Beijing's confrontation with Hanoi partakes of emotional feelings which, as with Taiwan, can be exploited in domestic politics or, alternatively, may drive confrontation to conflict. As with Taiwan, third party considerations are likely to inhibit Beijing's actions but do not necessarily preclude them.

China's other main offshore claim extends to the coast of Korea and to the Japanese held Senkaku Islands or Daiyutai. The claim also includes the continental shelf extending from the mainland to a depth of 250 meters under the Yellow and East China Seas. PRC protests in the early 1970s warned the Republic of Korea and Japan against joint exploration of areas in their vicinity for offshore oil, and minor incidents have arisen in subsequent years involving foreign survey vessels elsewhere.

More pointedly, in 1978 more than a hundred Chinese fishing boats circled the Senkakus with signs claiming they belonged to the PRC. This proved embarrassing to Tokyo, which was in the final stage of negotiating a treaty of peace and friendship with Beijing. When Deng Xiaoping visited the capital of Japan that fall to celebrate signature of the treaty, he ducked a press question on the dispute by saying it might be better settled by future generations. The issue thereupon disappeared from public view but remained a potentially contentious issue.

In 1990 these miniscule uninhabited islands once again threatened to disrupt Sino-Japanese relations. When a right-wing nationalistic Japanese group asked that a beacon it had built on one of the islands function as an official maritime signal, the news triggered demonstrations in Taiwan and Hong Kong. Beijing reacted more moderately, denying students permission to demonstrate lest the opportunity be seized to attack the regime as well as Japan. A moderately worded official protest, together with the reactions elsewhere, prompted Tokyo to block the lighthouse request, and both sides moved to dispense with the matter diplomatically.

The issue coincided with Kaifu's abortive effort to offer Japanese troops for noncombat support roles in the multinational effort against Iraq. Opposition in Japan, China, and elsewhere attacked this proposal as a violation of the Japanese antiwar constitution and as proof of rising militarism. Kaifu abandoned the project, but only after it had aroused political passions throughout Asia. This context provided an echo chamber for the otherwise incidental islands controversy, illustrating the precariousness of Sino-Japanese relations, given the historical heritage and the extant territorial controversy.

Beijing could adopt a general principle of international law that holds that where a continental shelf adjoins neighboring countries, the boundary delineating ownership can be drawn along the median line dividing the shelf. Alternatively it could insist on total ownership, which would also be in conformance with international law. Its inaction thus far most probably results from the failure of any major oil reserves to be discovered and the desire for a peaceful environment, particularly where economic relations with Japan are paramount.

As in our other instances, these problems are not foreseen as actionable in the near future, nor are they likely to become serious in this century, all other things being equal. Much depends on the success, both real and perceived, of economic modernization as a justification for the open door to foreign trade, investment, and credits. Success can justify tacit or explicit compromises with communist ideology in general, and with Japan and the United States in particular. Yet economic modernization is a long process, in the course of which major economic and political problems will inevitably confront the regime. Many of these had already surfaced in the mid-1980s, such as bureaucratic obstructionism, corruption, and mismanagement, together with inflation, bottlenecks in infrastructure and energy, and growing inequities of income and living standards. Protectionism by the United States against the PRC was threatened by congressional bills, albeit vetoed or argued down by President Reagan. Japan's rising yen burdened the payment of imports and repayment of loans. Meanwhile the global monetary and trading environment remained uncertain in the face of a soaring American debt and a falling American dollar, with no effective solution in sight.

China is no longer an isolated or autarkic economy avowing "self-reliance." Circumstances abroad and the International Montary Fund forced devaluation of the currency by 15 percent in 1986, and further devaluation followed later. A Chinese official calculated that exports constituted 12 percent of national income in 1986, compared with only 5.6 percent in 1978.[29] Interdependence is real and growing, thus far to Beijing's benefit, but not necessarily so in the future.

Fortunately China's membership in key international economic organizations provides it with advance warning, detailed information, and participation in addressing many of these problems. Once it joins GATT, the PRC will have a major voice on trade issues. Its economists are well trained in modeling and statistical methods, and the rapidly expanding use of computers adds another strength to their analysis. Objectively the PRC is well positioned to confront these problems as they arise.

Subjectively, however, the situation may be less easily handled. Because of China's exclusion from world councils until 1971 and the Cultural Revolution closure of all universities, a wide generation gap exists between senior officials who were trained abroad prior to 1949 and very junior cadres recently returning from study overseas. Middle-age people of forty to fifty years of age lack the necessary background to understand the outside world, especially its economic ramifications. Nor does their bureaucratic security, inherent in socialism, induce them to catch up on what they missed in earlier years. This poses a potential management crisis in the foreseeable future.

Economic mismanagement and miscalculation are inevitable in all systems. They are especially likely to occur in a society as vast as that of China, where socialist planning and control combines with experiments in decentralized and private initiative among a populace that often responds excessively to governmental stimuli, yet lacks experience in running its own business.

---

[29]Jacobson and Oksenberg, op. cit., citing Liu Guoguang in an address at the University of Michigan, September 15, 1987.

This combination of external and internal factors could coalesce negatively to slow economic growth and frustrate expectations. The response could be a severe and sudden change of posture, if not of policy. In 1985–86 Beijing peremptorily suspended or cancelled contracts with Japanese and other manufacturers and traders when it discovered that decentralized access to foreign exchange had contributed to a fall in reserves from $17 billion to $11 billion in one year. This action paralleled the earlier PRC cancellation of huge contracts for the Baoshan steel plant in 1979–80. Both cases illustrated a willingness to act unilaterally without regard for foreign reaction.

Such behavior has not been typical, but its very occurrence suggests its possible repetition. Much will depend on the stability and orientation of leadership as well as on how the international environment, both political and economic, impacts on China and is perceived there. The People's Republic is clearly in transition as it moves out of the Maoist heritage and beyond Deng's reformist regime. Foreign policy is always subject to domestic developments in addition to developments abroad. A challenge therefore faces Beijing and other capitals as the world's largest population engages the global community so as to increase its security and raise its standard of living, while defining its rightful role in world affairs.

CHINESE NAME SPELLINGS

WADE-GILES		PINYIN
	PERSONS	
Chou En-lai		Zhou Enlai
Li Shis-yao		Li Shiyao
Liu Shao-ch'i		Liu Shaoqi
Mao Tse-tung		Mao Zedong
Teng Hsiao-p'ing		Deng Xiaoping
Yuan Shis-k'ai		Yuan Shikai
	PLACES	
Kwangsi		Guangxi
Kwangtung		Guangdong
Matsu		Mazu
Nanking		Nanjing
Quemoy		Jinmen
	OTHER	
Ch'ing (dynasty)		Qing
Uighur (people)		Uygur

FOREIGN POLICY LANDMARKS

October 1949	People's Republic of China established
February 1950	Sino-Soviet Treaty of Alliance signed
June 1950	North Korea invades South Korea United States intervenes
October 1950	China intervenes in Korean war, drives U.N.-U.S. forces from North Korea
July 1953	Korean War ends
July 1954	Geneva Conference ends Indochina War
September 1954	PRC bombards offshore islands of Nationalist China
December 1954	United States-Republic of China Mutual Security Treaty
April 1955	Bandung Conference; PRC proposes ambassadorial talks with United States
November 1957	Mao Zedong to Moscow, wins nuclear weapons aid
September 1958	PRC bombards offshore islands of Nationalist China
March 1959	Tibetan revolt
September 1959	Border guards clash on Sino-Indian frontier
June 1960	Soviet advisers leave China, aid stops
October 1962	Sino-Indian War
October 1964	First Chinese atomic bomb exploded
September 1965	PRC ground forces enter North Vietnam
August 1966	Cultural Revolution begins
August 1968	Violent phase of Cultural Revolution ends
March 1969	Sino-Soviet border clashes begin on Ussuri River
September 1969	Zhou-Kosygin meet in Beijing; clashes end
July 1971	Henry Kissinger secretly visits Beijing
October 1971	PRC takes U.N. seat
February 1972	President Nixon visits PRC, Shanghai Communiqué
September 1976	Mao Zedong dies
December 1978	President Carter recognizes PRC, ends treaty with Republic of China
February 1979	PRC invades Vietnam, withdraws in three weeks
September 1984	PRC signs treaty with United Kingdom on transfer of Hong Kong in 1997
May 1989	Soviet President Mikhail Gorbachev visits PRC, first Sino-Soviet summit in thirty years
June 1989	Tiananmen Square democracy demonstrations trigger Beijing Massacre; PRC suffers widespread condemnation and sanctions

SELECTED BIBLIOGRAPHY

Books

Barnett, A. Doak. *The Making of Foreign Policy in China.* Boulder, Colo.: Westview Press, 1985.

Camilleri, Joseph. *Chinese Foreign Policy.* Seattle, Wash.: University of Washington Press, 1980.

Clubb, O. Edmund. *China and Russia: The "Great Game."* New York: Columbia University Press, 1971.

Fairbank, John King, ed. *The Chinese World Order: Traditional China's Foreign Relations.* Cambridge, Mass.: Harvard University Press, 1968.

Harding, Harry, ed. *China's Foreign Relations in the 1980s.* New Haven, Conn.: Yale University Press, 1984.

Harris, Lillian. *China's Foreign Policy Toward the Third World.* New York: Praeger, 1986.

Ho, Samuel P.S., and Ralph W. Huenemann. *China's Open Door Policy: The Quest for Technology and Capital.* Vancouver, B.C.: University of British Columbia Press, 1984.

Jacobson, Harold K., and Michel Oksenberg. *China's Participation in the IMF, the World Bank, and GATT.* Ann Arbor, Mich.: University of Michigan Press, 1990.

Kim, Samuel S., ed. *China and the World: Foreign Policy in the Post-Mao Era,* 2d ed. Boulder, Colo.: Westview Press, 1989.

Liao, Kuang-sheng. *Antiforeignism and Modernization in China, 1860–1980.* New York: St. Martin's Press, 1986.

Lieberthal, Kenneth, and Michel Oksenberg. *Policy Making in China: Leaders, Structures, and Processes.* Princeton, N.J.: Princeton University Press, 1988.

Muller, David G., Jr. *China as a Maritime Power.* Boulder, Colo.: Westview Press, 1983.

Quested, R.K.I. *Sino-Russian Relations.* Winchester, Mass.: Allen & Unwin, 1984.

Samuels, Marwyn S. *Contest for the South China Sea.* New York: Methuen, 1982.

Van Ness, Peter. *Revolution and Chinese Foreign Policy.* Berkeley, Calif.: University of California Press, 1970.

Vertzberger, Yaacov. *China's Southwestern Strategy: Encirclement and Counterencirclement.* New York: Praeger, 1985.

Whiting, Allen S. *The Chinese Calculus of Deterrence: India and Indochina.* Ann Arbor, Mich.: University of Michigan Press, 1975.

——. *China Crosses the Yalu: The Decision to Enter the Korean War.* Stanford, Calif.: Stanford University Press, 1968.

——. *China Eyes Japan.* Berkeley, Calif.: University of California Press, 1989.

Periodicals

Asian Survey (Berkeley, Calif.).
China Business Review (Washington, D.C.).
China Quarterly (London).
Far Eastern Economic Review (Hong Kong).
Foreign Affairs (New York).
Journal of Asian Studies (Ann Arbor, Mich.), with annual bibliography.
Journal of Northeast Asian Studies (Washington, D.C.).
Pacific Affairs (Vancouver, B.C.).
Beijing Review (Beijing).
Problems of Communism (Washington, D.C.).

—9—

THE
FOREIGN POLICY
OF
LATIN AMERICA

*Riordan Roett**

INTRODUCTION

The legacy of colonial rule and the growing regional hegemony of the United States dominated the foreign policies of Latin American states after independence.[1] Struggling on the world scene to break their old patterns of economic and political bondage, they also had to confront the overarching ambitions of the United States. The twin themes of seeking greater global influence while struggling for autonomy from the United States provide the leitmotifs of any study of contemporary Latin American foreign policy.

Latin America was the first of the "third worlds" to achieve independence, long before much of Africa, Asia, and the Middle East, but the area's insertion into the international system has been erratic. Geographic location, political and social instability, and economic dependence on the industrial

---

* I am indebted to Mr. Thomas Schierholz for research and editorial assistance in preparing this essay.

[1] For the purposes of this chapter, I am defining "Latin America" to include all the states of the Western Hemisphere except Canada and the United States, including those, such as Guyana and Grenada, that are not "Latin."

world precluded any hope of common foreign policy goals.[2] Indeed, while a shared history and common languages and cultural traditions appear to "homogenize" the states of the region, the reality has been nearly two centuries of conflict and competition.

What is "Latin American" about the region's foreign policy? United by a common desire for economic and social development, all of Latin America wants to retain its national sovereignty and independence. Yet from country to country, the variations in geographic size, demography, wealth, development level, and politics are enormous.[3] These national differences clearly influence Latin American foreign policies. As examples of political variation, contrast the English-speaking Caribbean, which achieved independence quite recently and proudly maintains British parliamentary traditions, with neighboring states such as Haiti, which has known little but dictatorship, or the Dominican Republic, which has only recently consolidated democratic processes. Only a minority of Latin American states have any hope of achieving regional power, by virtue of their size, location, resources and level of development. Among the natural "leaders" of the region are Argentina and Brazil, traditional rivals on the Atlantic coast, and Chile and Peru, geopolitically prominent on the Pacific. Mexico has long dominated Central America.

GEOGRAPHY AND HISTORY

Geography must be combined with history to understand the contextual variables that shape the foreign policy of Latin American states. As the era of discoveries accelerated in the late fifteenth century, the rival claims of Spain and Portugal were partially resolved by a papal decision in 1494. The Treaty of Tordesillas divided the New World unequally between the two powers and gave Spain the major share of the Western Hemisphere. Portuguese-Brazilian expansion in the intervening years led to claims that doubled the earlier grants.

Conflicts in the Americas often reflected European wars and dynastic rivalries. Spanish and Portuguese sovereignty was challenged by the French and the English, who eventually settled North America and much of the Caribbean. By the end of the eighteenth century, after its 1763 defeat by England and the rebellion of Haiti, the French presence in the New World was limited to the Eastern Caribbean and French Guyana on the continent. The independence movements that erupted in Spain's empire drew their strength

[2] In 1988, Latin America was 65 percent more populous than North America (414 million as compared with 272 million). The average annual rate of population growth between 1980 and 1990 was 2.1 percent, lower than that of sub-Saharan Africa (3.2 percent) and South Asia (2.3 percent) but higher than that of East Asia (1.5 percent). The GNP per capita figure for Latin America and the Caribbean is low ($1,840 in 1988), but much higher than for sub-Saharan Africa ($330) and South and East Asia ($320 and $540, respectively).

[3] For example, while Paraguay had a population of just over 4 million in 1989, Brazil had 147 million and Mexico nearly 87 million the same year. Average annual population growth (1980–89) in Honduras was 3.5 percent but just 0.6 percent in Uruguay during the same period. Venezuela's population is 79.2 percent urban, while only 34.5 percent of Guatemala's people live in cities. Per capita incomes range from $353 in Haiti to $1,935 in Mexico and $3,399 in Venezuela (1988).

in part from traditional European competition and from the French and North American revolutionary movements.

THE INDEPENDENCE PERIOD

Napoleon's invasion of the Iberian peninsula (Portugal in 1807 and Spain in 1808) was the fuse that ignited the Latin American powder keg. Although the Portuguese royal family evaded the French soldiers and fled to Brazil in British ships, the Spanish monarch did not escape. Without the legitimizing rule of the Spanish king to define political life, Spain's New World Empire began a long and painful process of disintegration. Argentina and Paraguay quickly pressed their independence. Brazil moved relatively smoothly to independence in 1822 (after the King returned to Portugal) and quickly achieved recognition from both the United States and the European powers.

The struggle for independence led to a series of bloody civil wars.[4] After Napoleon's defeat, the restored French monarchy supported Spain's efforts to regain its New World empire. England refused to help the revolutionaries, contenting itself with a preferred commercial role in Brazilian trade. The Liberal Revolution in Spain (1820) assisted the independence movements, particularly in Mexico and Peru but, in 1823, France sent an army into Spain to suppress the constitutional regime. Under the threat of renewed Spanish efforts to reassert its rule in Latin America, British foreign secretary George Canning sought U.S. support for his policy of restraining any new initiatives to restore the ancien régime. Knowing that the British would use their military power to keep Spain and France out, the United States decided it could gain more advantage by acting unilaterally. President James Monroe enunciated the new doctrine in his December 1823 message to Congress:

> ...that the American continents, by the free and independent conditions which they have assumed and maintain, are henceforth not to be considered as subjects for future colonization by any European powers....We owe it, therefore, to candor and to the amicable relations existing between the United States and those powers to declare that we should consider any attempt on their parts to extend their system to any portion of this hemisphere as dangerous to our peace and safety.[5]

By the late 1820s the European powers had accepted the new status quo in Latin America, and the United States had successfully asserted its diplomatic pretension regarding Western Hemisphere independence. All that was left of Spain's empire was the island of Cuba.

---

[4] See John Lynch, *The Spanish-American Revolutions, 1808–1826* (New York: Norton, 1973).
[5] A copy of the full message appears in Ruhl J. Bartlett, ed., *The Record of American Diplomacy* (New York: Knopf, 1964), pp. 181–83.

LATIN AMERICA FROM MID-NINETEENTH CENTURY TO THE TWENTIETH CENTURY

After 1850, with republican forms of government under attack by local oligarchies and caudillos, the Europeans tried one last time to return. Spain unsuccessfully pressed to reincorporate the Dominican Republic into its empire, and a bloody civil war with Cuban nationalists erupted from 1868 to 1878. Napoleon III sent Austrian Archduke Maximilian to Mexico to occupy a nonexistent throne; the emperor was executed in 1867. Spain occupied a part of Peru from 1863–69, alleging financial claims.

In Central America and the Caribbean the United States and Britain competed for trade, markets, steamboat lines, and the right to construct a canal across the Isthmus of Panama. The rivalries over the Isthmus did not end until an independent state of Panama was carved out of Colombia in 1903 and construction of an American canal began.

As the United States moved toward Great Power status at the end of the nineteenth century, concern about its primacy in the hemisphere increased, as did willingness to press its claim. In 1895, President Grover Cleveland invoked the Monroe Doctrine in a border dispute between Great Britain and Venezuela over British Guiana (today, Guyana). British reluctance to seek a political solution through negotiation irritated the United States. The British yielded, and the dispute was settled by international arbitration. Implicitly, England had accepted the U.S. assertion of the Monroe Doctrine. The incident heralded the opening of a period of direct American involvement in the affairs of Latin America.

THE UNITED STATES INTERVENES

The American century opened with a series of resounding successes for those who had heard the call of empire. Cuba was independent from Spain, but the 1901 Platt Amendment (in effect until 1934), which permitted the United States to intervene in its internal affairs, made it little more than an American colony. The Venezuelan crisis of 1902–03, which ended any European pretensions to influence in the affairs of the hemisphere, occasioned Theodore Roosevelt to assert a "Roosevelt Corollary" to the Monroe Doctrine:

> ...chronic wrongdoing, or an impotence which results in a general loosening of the ties of civilized society, may in America, as elsewhere, ultimately require intervention by some civilized nation, and in the Western Hemisphere the adherence of the United States to the Monroe Doctrine may force the United States, however reluctantly...to the exercise of an international power.[6]

The United States thus took responsibility for forcing Latin American states to respect their international obligations, clearly establishing its suzerainty in the hemisphere.

---

[6] Quoted in Harold Eugene Davis, John Finan, and F. Taylor Peck, *Latin American Diplomatic History: An Introduction* (Baton Rouge, La. and London: Louisiana State University Press, 1977), p. 154.

Use of the "Big Stick" policy became the rule, not the exception. The Dominican Republic, Haiti, Nicaragua, and other Central American and Caribbean states were hosts to U.S. troops, customhouse inspectors, and other representatives of the American empire overseas. Between 1898 and 1933 there were only three years in which U.S. troops were not stationed in one or more countries.[7]

To further its economic interests, the United States formulated the concept of Pan-Americanism. Initiated by Secretary of State James G. Blaine in 1889, the short-run purpose was to foster harmonious political relations between the United States and the Southern Hemisphere; the long-range goal was to increase investment and trade between North and South America.

The Bureau of the American Republics was the first building block in the intricate Inter-American System that has emerged over the last century. The 1889 meeting in Washington led to a series of conferences of American states, often utilized by the United States either to justify its policies or seek Latin American endorsement for actions already taken. "Progressive Pan-Americanism," which made its appearance in the early 1900s, "aimed at expanding trade, building investment opportunities, and tapping sources of agricultural and mineral raw materials in Latin America" while appealing to Latin leaders who desired economic progress and who accepted both "the need for the participation of foreign interests and capital" and the secondary status that progressive pan-American policies implied.[8]

By World War I, American investment in Latin America began to grow. From 1914 to 1919, the value of U.S. investments in the region increased by 50 percent; between 1919 and 1929, it doubled. The United States was rapidly overtaking Britain as the largest investor in the region and emerged from World War II the leader.

LATIN AMERICA AND THE INTERNATIONAL SYSTEM

The early decades of the twentieth century were filled with irony for Latin America. The slow emergence of Pan-Americanism responded to the century-old wish for cooperation and collaborative action that grew out of the idealism of Simón Bolívar in the 1820s. But as the major states of the region appeared increasingly able and willing to pursue that ideal, U.S. imperial interests—political and economic—stood in the way. The new century brought opportunities for multilateral cooperation with European states that were previously not available. Only Mexico participated in the First Hague Conference (1899); a number of states attended the second, in 1907. The Latin American states used the meetings mainly to urge adoption of the Drago Doctrine: to limit the use of force in the collection of damage claims and contract debts. The Calvo principle was an extension of that doctrine, suggested by the Argentine foreign

[7] Dana G. Munro provides an overview of this period in *The United States and the Caribbean Republics, 1921–1933* (Princeton, N.J.: Princeton University Press, 1974).

[8] Robert Neal Seidel, *Progressive Pan Americanism: Development and United States Policy Toward South America, 1906–1931* (Ithaca, N.Y.: Cornell University, Latin American Studies Program Dissertation Series, January, 1973), No. 45, p. 2.

minister in 1902. But the essential Latin American demands went unheeded. U.S. intervention continued, and national differences were sufficiently strong to prevent any form of unified political action.

If Latin America needed a reminder of U.S. will to intervene, it occurred in 1914. A dispute with the United States during Mexico's revolution led President Woodrow Wilson to send troops to occupy the port of Veracruz. As a result of the bombardment and occupation, the government of General Victoriano Huerta fell, and others viewed favorably by Wilson took power in Mexico City. The revolution that ended in 1917 was later enshrined in the Institutional Revolutionary Party (PRI) and gave the Mexican government a legitimacy possessed by few others in the hemisphere. Revolutionary legitimacy also meant a staunch defense of Mexican national interests, which led to diplomatic and political confrontations with the United States that continue today.

Latin America was ambivalent about World War I. Of the principal states, only Brazil declared war. The major Spanish-American countries—Argentina, Chile, Colombia, Venezuela, and Mexico—remained neutral. Following the war, Latin American states were formally drawn into the League of Nations, but they contributed little.

The 1930s were a decade of change and conflict in the Western Hemisphere. For the first time in the century, a full-scale war erupted on the continent. The Chaco War (1932–35) pitted landlocked Bolivia against a similarly landlocked Paraguay over possession of the desert region called the "Chaco Boreal." After losing its Pacific coastline, Bolivia turned its attention to its longstanding border dispute with Paraguay—the Chaco River system provided an outlet to the Atlantic Ocean. Weak efforts by neighbors and the League of Nations failed to stop the fighting, which went in Paraguay's favor. But in May 1935 a mediating group of regional powers laboriously negotiated a cease-fire and, finally, a peace treaty in July 1938.

U.S.-Mexican relations deteriorated during the 1930s. With the 1934 election of President Lázaro Cárdenas, a wave of nationalist development swept the country. Agrarian reforms affected large numbers of American landowners. Moving quickly to "Mexicanize" the country's economy, Cardenas nationalized the railways in 1937 and all foreign-owned oil properties the following year, promising indemnification "in due course." Quick-witted diplomatic action by the Roosevelt administration led to a negotiated settlement and became a hallmark of his Good Neighbor Policy.

THE GOOD NEIGHBOR

The Hoover administration (1929–33) began to repudiate the American habit of intervention with a series of steps that, amplified by the Roosevelt administration (1933–45), became the "Good Neighbor Policy."[9] The new approach made

[9] Irwin F. Gelman succinctly summarizes this period in *Good Neighbor Diplomacy: United States Policies in Latin America, 1933–1945* (Baltimore, Md. and London: The Johns Hopkins University Press, 1979).

Washington's prestige soar to heights not seen since it recognized Latin American independence. After a successful preinaugural Latin American tour, President Herbert Hoover began removing U.S. troops from Central America and the Caribbean while his Secretary of State, Henry Stimson, effectively disavowed the Roosevelt Corollary with his 1929 Clark Memorandum on the Monroe Doctrine.

President Franklin Roosevelt went further, making nonintervention a pillar of U.S. foreign policy, while satisfying a number of longstanding Latin American political goals. In 1934, Washington ended its military occupation of Haiti and restored Cuba's sovereignty by abrogating the Platt Amendment. In 1936, the United States and Panama agreed to abolish the virtual protectorate in force since 1903. Nonintervention, noninterference, and an economically stimulating tariff deal were reaffirmed at the 1936 Inter-American conference in Buenos Aires. By 1940, after tolerating a wave of expropriations of U.S. interests, Washington had convinced the region that its respect for Latin American sovereignty was genuine.

LATIN AMERICA AND WORLD WAR II

The Good Neighbor Policy was the high point of U.S.-Latin American relations in this century, but it soon fell prey to the U.S. ideological and security imperatives of World War II and the Cold War. Through the 1920s, the United States assumed the Monroe Doctrine and the Roosevelt Corollary were binding on all other states. U.S. strategists continued to emphasize American interests, to the point of preparing contingency plans for potential destabilization in the hemisphere.[10] Hampered by isolationism at home, the United States did not begin multilateral planning with its neighbors until 1939, but by then the Fascist menace had scared the United States into allocating scarce resources to its traditional European allies.

By the late 1930s, sympathy for the Axis cause was widespread in Argentina, Brazil, Chile, Paraguay, and Bolivia, and U.S. strategists focused on Nazi penetration of the hemisphere. After Germany invaded Poland in September 1939, the isolationist logjam was broken when it seemed that the United States would soon be at war. Hemispheric foreign ministers meeting in Panama the same month agreed to establish a 300-mile "security zone" around the continent, although this meant the U.S. Navy would do the patrolling, given the state of Latin American naval forces. The 1938 "Declaration of Lima" had already approved inter-American consultation whenever a foreign power threatened the peace, security, or territorial integrity of an American republic.

At the beginning the war in Europe appeared to be going against Britain and its allies, and many, including the U.S. chiefs of staff, believed that the Western Hemisphere would become the next target of Axis aggression. The

[10]John Child, *Unequal Alliance: The Inter-American Military System, 1938–1978* (Boulder, Colo.: Westview Press, 1980), pp. 12–14.

foreign ministers reconvened in Havana in July 1940 to approve a clear statement of collective defense. Although foreign ministers met for a third time in Rio in January 1942 to create the Inter-American Defense Board (IADFB), it never performed more than a purely symbolic role. Brazil soon emerged as the strongest supporter of the U.S. war effort. In exchange for development aid and arms, the Brazilians provided vital bases and sent an expeditionary force to Italy in 1944. Aside from Brazil, only Mexico actively supported the United States, by sending 300 troops to the Far East in 1945.

The 1942 Rio meeting was the last of its kind during the war. Global strategies for maintaining peace in the postwar world increasingly appealed to the United States; Latin American preferences for regional cooperation received little attention in Washington. Amid preparations to found the United Nations, the United States finally bowed to pressures for an Inter-American meeting but effectively excluded Argentina by insisting that only active participants in the war effort attend. Convening in Mexico City early in 1945, the meeting drafted plans for a comprehensive charter for the Inter-American System, to be considered at Bogotá the following year.

The one notable accomplishment of the Mexico City meeting was the Act of Chapultepec, which for the first time in the history of Inter-American agreements sanctioned the use of armed force (but only until the end of the war). The signatories declared they would consider an attack against any state in the hemisphere as aggression against them all and approved using armed force in retaliation.

As the United States wrestled with the issue of regional versus global organization, Latin American states were becoming preoccupied with their economic future. The war had broken their traditional commercial and trade ties with Europe and ruined the European economies. With its usual economic and financial linkages gone, Latin America looked to the United States for support in postwar economic planning, but the United States offered little solace.

The Latin American states were correct if they assumed that the rapidly deteriorating relationship between the United States and the Soviet Union would determine their political and economic fate. As the war ended, the Cold War began. The recovery of Japan and Western Europe and the containment of Eastern Europe and the Soviet Union were the uppermost of Washington's priorities.

THE POST-WORLD WAR ERA

The San Francisco Conference met from April to June 1945 to draft a charter for a United Nations that would maintain "international peace and security." The Latin American states had to go along with Washington's global approach to protect their concern for regional cooperation. Six of the seven Latin American states that had not yet declared war on the Axis did so by March 1, 1945, guaranteeing their right to attend, but Argentina, which missed the deadline by declaring war on March 27, needed Soviet approval. The Soviets obliged, but only after Washington agreed to allow White Russia and the Ukraine to participate as independent states in the United Nations.

The struggle for a compromise that emphasized globalism but protected regional interests was resolved by Dr. Alberto Lleras Camargo of Colombia and Senator Arthur Vandenberg of the United States in Article 51 of the U.N. Charter, which upheld "the inherent right of individual or collective self-defense if an armed attack occurs against a member of the United Nations, until the Security Council has taken the measures necessary to maintain international peace and security." The right to regional action was preserved without limiting the Security Council's ability to intervene in a crisis.

With the United Nations launched, hemispheric issues returned to center stage. Although the 1945 Chapultepec conference had mandated another meeting to prepare a permanent collective security agreement, deteriorating relations between Argentina and the United States after the rise to power of General Juan D. Perón in late 1945 made it impossible to reach a consensus on the appropriate next step. As maneuvering continued, Washington's attitude toward regionalism grew more positive. Confronted by a recalcitrant Soviet Union in the Security Council, able and willing to use its veto, regional approaches to peacekeeping became increasingly attractive. Meanwhile, encouraged by the lavish amounts of U.S. aid for Western Europe and Asia, the Latin states had started to insist on U.S. economic support. Old suspicions about U.S. goals in the hemisphere reemerged, not only in Argentina, but also in Mexico and other states.

By the time the Rio Conference got under way in August 1947, the United States wanted a strong treaty reflecting the polarization of world politics that would allow it to get on with higher global priorities, having guaranteed the security of its backyard. With the Latin delegations demanding a regional Marshall Plan, Secretary of State George C. Marshall, who headed the U.S. delegation, stalled by getting nonmilitary issues postponed until the forthcoming conference in Bogotá.

The delegates finally concluded the Rio Treaty, a collective security arrangement that amplified Chapultepec accords and created a permanent military alliance among the states of the hemisphere. While the United States viewed the document primarily as an instrument it could use to thwart Soviet ambitions in the hemisphere, the Latin signatories saw it as having much broader application. But the treaty established neither a military command nor any planning mechanism and did not mention how the new collective security agreement would be enforced. Again, this issue was postponed for Bogotá, which was to be the last effort at creative institution building in the postwar era.

As the United States and Latin America prepared to meet in the Andean capital in March 1948 for the Ninth International Conference of American States, demands for U.S. economic and financial help in reducing Latin reliance on single crops and raw material exports emerged with greater frequency. In the Latin view, the United States had gotten what it wanted at Rio and now they wanted help from Washington to help them build local industries and increase their standards of living. Latin wishes for reciprocity on the scale they desired were to go unfulfilled. Led by Argentina and Mexico, the March 1948 meeting in the Andean capital was often bitter and recriminatory.[11] In the postwar world the private sector would be left to resolve the economic and social needs of the hemisphere, and direct, private investment by U.S. financial institutions became the predominant source of foreign capital.

The U.S. desire for an Inter-American Defense Council was thwarted by the Latin American delegations, which could agree only to create an Advisory Defense Committee, subordinate to the Rio Treaty, which has never met. The meeting also ratified the Inter-American Defense Board as a continuing agency but gave it no authority or power.

The conference then went on to approve its most lasting achievement, the Charter of the Organization of American States (OAS), which created a regional body to complement the work of the U.N., and concluded the ill-fated Treaty on Pacific Settlement (known as the Pact of Bogotá) for the resolution of intrahemispheric disputes. Only nine Latin states ratified it; the United States did not.

During the 1950s, Latin America's foreign policies were closely tied to the United States. Beginning in January 1952, the United States concluded a series of bilateral military agreements with individual Latin American states in support of hemispheric defense. The states agreed to stockpile U.S. military equipment as a strategic defensive reserve and to cooperate with the United States in limiting trade with countries that threatened the security of the continent.[12] As the decade progressed, Washington's Military Assistance Program expanded to encompass U.S. military missions in eighteen countries with up to 800 military personnel, training of Latin American soldiers in U.S. military schools, a virtual U.S. monopoly on arms sales, and the creation of a unified regional command for Latin America in the Panama Canal Zone.

Mexico emerged as a determined dissenter from many U.S. foreign policy goals in the Americas during the 1950s, particularly on the issues of nonintervention and U.S. support for military regimes. Argentina, under the dynamic nationalist leadership of General Perón, continued its independent

---

[11] As if to underscore the growing consciousness for social justice in Latin America, the preparatory stages of the Bogota conference were interrupted on April 9, 1948, by the assassination of Jorge Eliezer Gaitan, the charismatic leader of Colombia's Liberal party who had made explicit populist appeals to the poor. Gaitan's outraged supporters blamed his murder on the ruling conservatives and invaded the Capitol within hours of Gaitan's death looking for Laureano Gomez, the conservative party leader. As foreign minister, Gomez was presiding over the conference, which luckily was in midday recess when the mob arrived. The riots that swept Colombia after Gaitan's murder caused an estimated $500 million in material damages and claimed 1,500 lives. See J. Lloyd Mecham, *The United States and Inter-American Security, 1889–1960* (Austin, Tex.: University of Texas Press, 1961), pp. 300–317, for an account of the Bogota conference and the Bogotazo.

[12] Ibid., Chap. 4.

foreign policy, attempting to forge links with other actors in the international system and unsuccessfully seeking to limit U.S. freedom of action in the hemisphere. Neither Mexico nor Argentina possessed the resources to fully develop an autonomous position in world affairs. Internal instability and fiscal mismanagement quickly vitiated the Perón regime, which fell in 1955. Mexico's more aggressive foreign policy masked a civilian-authoritarian state that permitted little domestic dissent. Foreign policy served to co-opt dissident Mexican political groups frustrated in their efforts to modify domestic policy. The foreign policies of other major actors—Brazil, Chile, Peru, Colombia, and Venezuela—generally supported U.S. policy during the decade. Traditional border rivalries and territorial claims were quiescent. Elite groups continued to dominate the foreign policy process. Low levels of literacy and a concern with social and economic survival among the mass population left governments with little inclination to devote much time to foreign policy.

The most dramatic assertion of U.S. predominance in the region came with the CIA-sponsored overthrow of the government of President Jacobo Arbenz Guzmán of Guatemala in 1954. Elected president in 1951, Arbenz moved to implement a program of wide social and economic reform that threatened established foreign economic interests as well as those of the local elites. Concerned about the perceived Communist threat in Guatemala, the Eisenhower administration used the Tenth Inter-American Conference in Caracas in March 1954 to force through a resolution condemning Communist influence in the Americas. Guatemala voted against the resolution; only Mexico and Argentina abstained, while the other states of the OAS voted in favor. Using an arms shipment to Guatemala from the Soviet bloc as a pretext, U.S.-backed exiles led by Colonel Carlos Castillo Armas invaded Guatemala in June 1954. Guatemala's futile efforts to seek support from either the OAS or the U.N. were frustrated and ended abruptly when the Arbenz regime fell.

Only at the end of the 1950s could Latin American leaders reassert economic and social development as important priorities. In 1958, the overthrow of dictators in Colombia and Venezuela and the election of a constitutional president in Argentina after three years of military rule opened a period known as the "twilight of the tyrants." Brazil's President Juscelino Kubitschek proposed in 1958 that the United States help organize a hemisphere-wide program of economic development that he termed "Operation Pan-America." The Eisenhower administration politely turned down the idea, but President John F. Kennedy remembered it a few years later when he proposed the Alliance for Progress. Further pressure for a change in U.S. policy came from Vice President Richard M. Nixon's ill-fated trip to Latin America in 1958 and the subsequent overthrow of the Cuban dictator, Fulgencio Batista, on January 1, 1959, by Fidel Castro.

Responding to Kubitschek's initiative, Latin American foreign ministers who had gathered informally in Washington pushed for the creation of an inter-American financial institution for economic development and a committee to recommend additional measures for economic cooperation among the states of the hemisphere. This "Committee of 21," as it was later known, succeeded in founding the Inter-American Development Bank with U.S. support at the end of 1959. An "Eisenhower Plan" of $500 million in development aid was proposed to the Committee of 21 in 1960 and endorsed in the Act of Bogotá by the states of the region. With John Kennedy's inauguration in 1961, the Alliance for Progress, announced in March at the White House, became the bridging mechanism for new efforts to seek social and economic change in the hemisphere. It was multilateralized with the enactment of the Charter of Punta del Este in August 1961 by the American ministers of economic affairs, meeting in Uruguay. The charter signaled an important watershed in U.S.-Latin American relations, promising "to enlist the full energies of the peoples and governments of the American republics in a great cooperative effort to accelerate the economic and social development" of the continent, to maximize levels of wellbeing, "with equal opportunities for all, in democratic societies adapted to their needs and desires."[13]

FOREIGN POLICY SINCE 1959: UNCERTAINTY AND A SEARCH FOR NEW DIRECTIONS

The Cuban Revolution of January 1, 1959, opened a new chapter in the international relations of Latin America. With hindsight, the seeds of destruction of the old order had been apparent long before Castro's entrance into Havana. Unwilling to respond to hemispheric development needs, the United States had also refused to accept political deviations, such as the Arbenz regime in Guatemala. In general, the United States was hostile to change but accepting of dictatorships, which seemed to pose no threat to its interests.

Cuba's new status as an aggressive exporter of revolution and as a potential Soviet base meant not only did the United States and its hemispheric allies face a security problem, but it also implied the decline of American hegemony and the rise of a new generation of Latin leaders seeking new solutions for old problems while trying to throw off American tutelage. But change has come slowly. Hemispheric cooperation has increased, but efforts at integration have drifted. In general, Latin American states could not insert themselves into the international system without appearing as U.S. surrogates. U.S. efforts to limit external penetration of the hemisphere started with the failed Bay of Pigs invasion of 1961 and the 1962 Cuban missile crisis and continued through the 1980s with support for anti-leftist movements in Central America—that is, forces seeking to counter Soviet and Cuban influence, particularly in Nicaragua and El Salvador. Latin America's frustrations about slow economic and social development have grown while regional peace-keeping has fizzled. A period of interstate competition and conflict has reopened as Washington's hemispheric security system loosened. Irredentist

---

[13] Quoted in G. Pope Atkins, *Latin America in the International Political System* (New York: Free Press, 1977), p. 344.

claims have reappeared as the growing potential for intrahemispheric conflict climaxed in the 1982 Falklands war.

Lurking always in the background is the region's severe financial crisis (discussed in detail below). The oil price rises of the 1970s and the external debt crisis of the early 1980s have produced slow economic growth and sharply deflationary austerity programs. Economic crisis and growing social tensions caused by debt, falling exports and shrinking economies have become preoccupations of Latin American foreign policy in recent years. Private commercial banks and the International Monetary Fund (IMF) have become important actors in the foreign policy planning of all of the states of the region.

With the blighted hopes of the 1980s a common theme, the Latin countries have turned increasingly to Third World and North-South forums to establish a "dialogue" between the North and the South. How the international system responds to the frustration, drift, and uncertainty in Latin America and the Caribbean will shape both North-South relations and the hemisphere's future role in world affairs.

A GROWING AUTONOMY

Most efforts at forming regional or subregional mechanisms for consultation, development, and governance in the hemisphere prior to 1959 crumbled before the hegemonic power of the United States. The desire for common action dates back to Simón Bolívar's attempts to unify the continent to defend its interests against all outsiders, including the United States. Weakened U.S. leadership and the emergence of increasingly assertive states such as Brazil, Venezuela, and Mexico have strengthened that drive. In addition, the smaller states have sought refuge and support in subregional groupings, hoping to find their own identity in hemispheric entities.

The Caribbean Free Trade Association (CARIFTA) decided to move toward a common market in 1973 by creating the Caribbean Community (CARICOM) and, soon after, a Caribbean Development Bank, the Caribbean Investment Corporation, and the Caribbean Food Corporation, but world recession in the 1970s reduced the area's exports and frustrated efforts at integration.[14] The recovery of the economic integration efforts of CARICOM will depend directly on the economic recovery of the developed countries.

The Latin American Free Trade Area (LAFTA), created by the 1960 Treaty of Montevideo (with Argentina, Brazil, Bolivia, Colombia, Chile, Ecuador, Mexico, Paraguay, Peru, Uruguay, and Venezuela participating), was to become a free trade association by 1973. That objective was postponed until 1980 by the Caracas Protocol of 1969. LAFTA worked relatively well in spurring intraregional trade, which increased from 7 percent of all trade in

---

[14]Intraregional exports increased from $500 million in 1980 to only $530 million in 1981. The region's total exports fell from $5.6 billion in 1980 to $5.2 billion in 1981. With falling exports and the resulting foreign exchange shortage, intra-CARICOM trade had fallen 25 percent between 1980 and 1985.

1961 to 13 percent in 1978. The degree of integration varied. In 1978, exports from Argentina, Bolivia, Chile, Paraguay, and Uruguay to LAFTA countries represented about one-quarter of total exports, while for Mexico and Venezuela (the two biggest oil exporters of the region) this proportion was less than 8 percent. The Latin American Integration Association (LAIA) replaced the 1960 vintage LAFTA in 1981. The new association aimed at promoting and regulating trade, economic complementation, and expanding markets through economic cooperation. An alternative to the free trade area envisioned in 1960, the 1981 treaty, opted for areas of regional tariff preference and granted preferential treatment to the less developed countries. However, the current economic crisis and the fall in trade have thrown the future of the plan into doubt.

Colombia, Chile, Bolivia, and Ecuador formed the Andean Group with the Cartegena Agreement in 1969.[15] Venezuela officially became a party to the agreement in 1973. The Cartegena Agreement envisioned three basic mechanisms for economic integration: trade liberalization to build up a large market (while protecting local production) and common external tariffs; industrial programming; and coordinated economic policies. After a promising start the Andean Group faltered in 1976 when Chile withdrew over a difference about a common foreign investment code. In 1980, an Andean Tribunal of Justice began to monitor, interpret, and unify legal provisions and enforce the obligations derived from the integration process, but the Andean Parliament, established in 1979, has not been ratified. An Andean Reserve Fund, created in 1978, has helped countries with balance of payments difficulties. Ongoing territorial conflicts between Ecuador and Peru have slowed the work of the pact, and Bolivia temporarily suspended its participation in 1980 for political reasons. By 1982, pressured by the world economic crisis, countries began to adopt protective short-term policies that undid their commitments to liberalization and the common external tariff. These measures and the failure to decide on the agreement's fundamental mechanisms (e.g. the Common External Tariff, Sectoral Programming, Industrial Rationalization, and Agricultural Programming) meant a significant reduction in integration activities and doubts about their viability.[16]

The Organization of American States (OAS) has proven to be the most disappointing mechanism for furthering Latin America's search for autonomy. Following its creation the organization served to justify American interventions in Guatemala in 1954 and the Dominican Republic in 1965. At times of crisis, the OAS has played a marginal role in conflict resolution in the

[15]For an analysis of Venezuelan and Colombian foreign policy, see Bruce Michael Bagley, *Regional Powers in the Caribbean Basin: Mexico, Venezuela and Colombia.* The Johns Hopkins Central American and Caribbena program, Occasional Paper No. 2, January 1983.

[16]The Andean Group received a boost in late 1990 with the approval of the Act of La Paz, an agreement under which the signatories agreed formally to harmonize macroeconomic policies—particularly exchange rate policy. The date for a free trade zone was brought forward from 1995 to January 1, 1992, adding new impetus to hopes for successful integration.

hemisphere, again illustrated during the war between Argentina and Great Britain in 1982, the U.S. invasion of Grenada in 1983, and the ongoing regional conflict in Central America. The specialized organs of the OAS have made large contributions to the social, legal, and cultural life of the hemisphere, but are they sufficient to justify its continued existence?[17]

Many states, such as Brazil, prefer to pursue bilateral relations with their neighbors and do not view the OAS multilateral approach with sympathy. Small states have not been able to use the organization to protect them from intervention by the United States or any other major state. The political goals of the OAS remain undefined, although the principles of nonintervention, respect for sovereignty, mutual security, and the peaceful settlement of disputes are highly admirable. But the OAS has neither military might to enforce its decisions nor the political legitimacy in the hemisphere to expect peaceful compliance with its directives.

Because the OAS is ineffectual, Latin American political leaders have resorted to *ad hoc* consultations to deal with the regional crises of the early 1980s. With formal institutions found wanting, personal diplomacy was in vogue. In June 1984 the eleven-nation Cartagena Consensus Group formed to respond to Latin America's mounting financial obligations to creditors in the industrial countries. The Cartagena group issued several fruitless pleas for help from the North.

The "Contadora Group," composed of Colombia, Venezuela, Panama, and Mexico, tried to mediate the conflict in Central America by finding a solution acceptable both to the United States and to the Sandinista regime in Nicaragua. A "support group" which included Argentina, Brazil, Peru, and Uruguay joined the original four in July 1985. Contadora's efforts atrophied as the Reagan administration made clear that it opposed anything less than the removal of the Sandinista regime. U.S. funding for the anti-Sandinista guerrillas, or Contras, eliminated any role for Contadora until 1987 when Costa Rican President Oscar Arias's initiative pledged the five presidents of Central America to seek a negotiated, political settlement for the region's wars.

When the eight presidents of the Contadora "process" met in Rio de Janeiro in December 1986 as the "Group of Eight," they called a summit meeting for November 1987 in Acapulco, Mexico, the first summit of Latin leaders ever held outside the U.S.-dominated OAS.

The Group of Eight issued a communiqué at the end of their talks called the "Acapulco Commitment to Peace, Development and Democracy." It dramatically recommended collective negotiations with the creditor nations in order to reduce debt service by having it reflect the real market value of the debt. In addition to strongly endorsing the Arias Plan, the summit called for the readmission of Cuba into the OAS which, the Eight stated, was due for a sweeping overhaul. Finally, the Eight proposed an economic recovery program for the Central American countries.

[17]See Tom J. Farer, ed., *The Future of the Inter-American System* (New York: Praeger, 1979).

The Group of Eight (actually seven since Panama, as a nondemocratic state was excluded in 1988 and 1989) reconvened in Punta del Este, Uruguay, in October 1988 for a three-day summit and called for a new deal on the region's $420 billion foreign debt and urgent talks with the next U.S. president. In a very pessimistic assessment, the leaders said that the "grave problems" of debt and unfavorable conditions of international trade "endanger political efforts to consolidate democracy" and have produced a "serious deterioration in the quality of life of the region's people."

At the instructions of the Group of Eight, the finance ministers of those countries convened in Rio de Janeiro in December 1988; subsequently, the group of eight presidents and their negotiators would be known as the Rio Group. The ministers drafted a set of proposals for presentation to the United States and other industrial nations on ways of reducing the region's foreign debt.

With the end of the Cold War and the new emphasis on finding solutions to debt and trade problems, plus the emphasis on regional cooperation and "summitry," we can expect a growing desire for more autonomy and increased dialogue with the industrial countries on these topics. The continuation of stable democratic governments will depend, to some degree, on success in these negotiations. Such dialogue, therefore, is critical to the ongoing definition of the region's role in world affairs.

A SENSE OF DRIFT

The Latin American states have often participated in the activities of Third World groups but have little to show for their enthusiasm. The United Nations Conference on Trade and Development (UNCTAD) appealed strongly to Latin American and Caribbean states, but yielded little in the way of substantive concessions on trade and finance from the industrialized countries. Latin Americans, notably Raul Prebisch, the former head of ECLA (Economic Commission for Latin America), directed UNCTAD until the 1970s, when the direction of UNCTAD moved to the African and Asian states. Since that time, Latin American participation has been perfunctory.

Over the years, Latin American raw material exporters have joined various producer associations, such as OPEC, without greatly affecting their market relations with the North. OPEC (the Organization of Petroleum Exporting Countries) includes Latin states, such as Venezuela, a charter member that played an important role in OPEC's early days, and Ecuador, a small producer. Mexico, not a member, cooperates with OPEC. At the moment, Latin America does not play a major role within OPEC.

Despite international linkages at the public and private levels, Latin America's efforts to achieve political and economic autonomy were adrift by the early 1980s. Latin leaders have demanded more respect from the United States and the industrialized countries, particularly in multilateral efforts to capture the attention of the North. Yet the economic crisis of the 1980s frustrated their efforts to cut their dependence on U.S. trade and private capital and interfered with plans to increase trade with the Third World.[18] Latin hopes that Western Europe might provide an alternative to the United States have proven groundless. Common Market policy has sharply limited Latin American exports to Europe, and Europe has not offered easy finance terms for the hemisphere's foreign debt. At times individual European states, such as Spain under Prime Minister Felipe González, try to identify with Latin America, but cordial state relations produce mainly rhetoric and little substance in the crucial areas of trade, aid, finance, and autonomy in Latin American-United States relations.

As world power began to shift subtly at the time of the Cuban revolution around 1960, hemispheric politics have been transformed. Among the major changes were the emergence of South American authoritarian regimes featuring autonomous development goals and more independent foreign policies; world economic conditions that led to the Latin American debt crisis of the 1980s; U.S. reassertion of its security interests in Central America and the Caribbean; and an increase in "power politics" to settle disputes. Although the United States remains the region's most powerful state, its ability and willingness to intervene outside its Central American and Caribbean "backyard" is diminishing.[19]

AUTHORITARIAN REGIMES AND FOREIGN POLICY

In response to a complex set of economic and political factors, weak civilian regimes succumbed to military rule in the 1960s and 1970s. Beginning with a coup d'état in Brazil in 1964, the Argentine government fell in 1966 (and again in 1976 after a brief three-year period that witnessed the return and death of General Juan D. Peron), as did the governments of Peru in 1968, Bolivia in 1971, and Uruguay in 1973, among others. The regimes were different from the traditional military dictatorships established in the 1940s and 1950s, and before. A number of institutional developments within the armed forces, as well as a growing sense of irresoluteness and incompetence on the part of civilian political elites, resulted in coup "coalitions" that brought together the military, the business establishment, and the agricultural landowners. The major exception was the coup in Peru, driven by a desire to introduce policies of social distribution but with a "top down" control by the armed forces. Many were driven by fears of Marxism or communism; others used such concerns as an excuse for doing away with civilian regimes and establishing a different economic model under controlled political circumstances.

The authoritarian governments all disagreed with the United States on one or more issues. The military governments in Brazil developed a Third

[18]See G. Pope Atkins, ed., *South America in the 1990s: Evolving International Relations in a New Era* (Boulder: Westview Press, 1990) for an update on the continent's international ties.
[19]See Lars Schoultz, *National Security and United States Foreign Policy toward Latin America* (Princeton, N.J.: Princeton University Press, 1987).

World orientation in their foreign policy that clearly preferred to move away from its traditional identification with Washington. The two governments parted ways on the definition of the territorial sea, Zionism, nuclear development, the Third World arms industry, and—of greatest importance—the human rights policy of President Jimmy Carter. A number of governments in the region broke decades-old military training and arms purchase agreements with the United States rather than submit to a congressionally mandated annual review of their human rights record. The military regime in Argentina that seized power in 1976—which waged a "Dirty War" against alleged subversives within its own population, introducing in the process the word *desaparecido* or disappeared person to the Latin American political lexicon—also differed with Carter over his human rights policy. When Carter sought to organize a grain embargo again the Soviet Union after the invasion of Afghanistan in 1979, the Argentines took satisfaction in rejecting the President's emissary. Argentina became one of the Soviet Union's major grain suppliers, temporarily sidelining American farmers. Both Argentina and Brazil refused to ratify the Tlatelolco treaty (1968), a regional nuclear nonproliferation pact and would not subscribe to the United Nations Treaty on the Non-Proliferation of Nuclear Weapons (NPT) that has attempted to establish a worldwide regime for stopping the diffusion of nuclear war technology.

After 1968, the Peruvian military government spent years squaring off against the United States. It refused compensation for the nationalization of the International Petroleum Company, the enterprise at the center of the corruption scandal that provoked the military takeover. The Peruvian regime also invited Soviet military advisors into the country and purchased non-U.S. military equipment in a clear break with the post-1945 tradition.

The Chilean military regime that overthrew President Salvador Allende in 1973 attempted to maintain good relations with the United States, but civil liberties and human rights activists in the United States lobbied heavily and successfully for a series of congressional sanctions. The measures were strongly supported by Carter, avoided or ignored generally during the Reagan years, and, prior to Chile's 1989 democratic transition, backed by the Bush White House.

One of the darkest episodes of U.S. foreign policy was its relationship with Panama. As a result of the Reagan administration's unflinching support for the Contras, the authoritarian government and unscrupulous activities of General Manuel Noriega were condoned and overlooked by the United States for a number of years. It was only when his drug trafficking ties became overt, and thereby his utility to the United States considerably undermined, that the Bush administration felt able to intervene militarily in December 1989, removing Noriega from power.

The late 1960s and 1970s yielded slowly and fitfully in the 1980s to diverse pressures to restore civilian government. Brazil followed a path of controlled decompression and an opening that left the armed forces and their allies in control until the very end when, in 1985, a civilian opposition coalition outsmarted them and assumed power. In Argentina it took the massive defeat of the armed forces in the war with the United Kingdom in 1982, over possession of the Malvinas or Falkland Islands, that resulted in a popular revulsion and the call for democratic elections. The Uruguayan armed forces attempted to consecrate their power through a national plebiscite in 1980 but were dramatically turned down at the polls by the citizens. An uneasy transition then took place that restored a democratic regime in 1985. Peru's economic collapse in the mid-1970s forced the military to yield power a few years later. The irony was that the very man they had overthrown in 1968, Fernando Belaunde Terry, was overwhelmingly reelected in 1980.

But as the new governments were elected, restoring civilian democratic regimes for the first time in many years, new forces were emerging in the international system over which the successor regimes had little control. The 1982 debt crisis was the most challenging, but the crisis in Central America and the growing concern over the drug trade and immigration were moving up the agenda.

NEW ECONOMIC REALITIES

Financial crisis was the essential issue in Latin America's relations with the international system in the 1980s. The 1973 and 1979 oil price rises, when combined with the worldwide recession of the early 1980s, devastated Latin America's exports. Moreover, loans for billions of "petrodollars" borrowed in the 1970s at low interest rates began to fall due in the early 1980s. Loans negotiated in recent years have been at substantially higher rates of interest and for far shorter periods of time. In some instances longer term debt obligations and short-term loans have matured at the same time. As markets closed both in the developed and the underdeveloped world, Latin American export earnings fell, and foreign exchange dried up. The situation was even worse for oil-poor countries like Brazil and Chile that had to face both rising oil bills and rising debt obligations.[20]

The origins of the Latin American debt crisis have been fully and carefully examined elsewhere. Suffice it to say that by August 1982, the deteriorating international economic environment, mismanagement, too much debt, high interest rates and a series of other factors led Mexico, a major debtor as well as an oil exporter, to declare that it could no longer service its outstanding debt. Frantic negotiations produced a series of stopgap measures. The next month, at the annual meeting of the IMF and the World Bank, held in Toronto, the largest debtor of all, Brazil, arrived expecting further financing. The Brazilian authorities were turned down, and panic resulted both in the debtor countries and among the creditor institutions.

[20]See Pedro-Pablo Kuczynski, "The Outlook for Latin American Debt," *Foreign Affairs,* 66 (1), Fall 1987.

Negotiations in 1983 and 1984 only rescheduled the payments due in those particular years, extending them over periods of seven to ten years. The commercial banks were reluctant to make new loans, but IMF lending induced the banks to grant "involuntary" loans. In addition to the rescheduling of payments, the renegotiations included the maintenance of lines of credit covering external trade and international interbank deposits, as well as the granting of "new money."

The fact that the banks made only "involuntary" loans meant the loss of the region's creditworthiness. Nevertheless, "involuntary" credits continued to *increase* the regional debt to the banks until 1987, though at a very much slower pace. Slowly, the private commercial banks were withdrawing and the debt was becoming "officialized," that is, being replaced by loans from governments and international financial institutions.

Despite the considerable increase in official credits, the reduction in bank loans since 1982 has been insufficient to compensate for interest payments. Since 1982, the region has been making average annual net transfers abroad in amounts much larger ($25 billion in 1989) than the positive transfers recorded in the preceding years, and there are no signs of improvement in this situation.

The debt crisis erupted, as previously noted, as the painful transitions away from authoritarian regimes were underway. New democratic successor regimes confronted pent-up public expectations of an easy transition to economic stability and prosperity and considerable skepticism about the legitimacy of the foreign debt. Public debate in the newly democratizing states raised new questions about the debt incurred: Who borrowed it, for what purposes, and was it linked to flight capital and corruption? Brazil declared a one-year moratorium on its debt in 1987, to little avail. There were threats by other nations that they would form debtor cartels and institute unilateral moratoria, but the clever handling of the situation by the international financial institutions, orchestrated to a great degree through the leadership of Paul Volcker, then the chairman of the U.S. Federal Reserve System, prevented a collapse of the international financial system.

In the first years of the crisis, the argument was that the problem was a short-term liquidity issue. But by the middle of the 1980s, it became clear that it was a structural problem of large dimensions. At his inauguration in July 1985, President Alan Garcia announced that he would use no more than 10 percent of his country's export earnings to service the existing debt. The Cartagena countries, an *ad hoc* group of debtor nations formed in 1984 (later subsumed by the Rio Group) actively lobbied for debt relief, and the presidents of Latin America were sending letters to the annual economic summits of the G-7 industrial countries demanding relief.

Secretary of the Treasury James Baker returned to Washington after the Garcia inauguration, convinced that a shift in strategy was required. In October

1985, the Baker Plan was introduced with the objective of increasing the flow of new bank loans to foster growth, not merely to ensure debt service. That growth also required: (1) as the first condition for receipt of new loans, adoption of macroeconomic policies and structural change by the debtor nations, (2) maintenance of the IMF's role as adjustment plan coordinator and resource provider, and (3) an increase in (rapid disbursement) structural adjustment lending by the multilateral banks. The plan encompassed fifteen countries, ten of them in Latin America.

The Baker Plan was amplified at the annual economic summit of the G-7 in Venice in June 1987 when Baker offered a "menu of options" for debt management that included a mix of debt-equity swaps, expanded trade finance, and exit bonds to allow smaller banks to avoid making new loans. But by the end of 1987, neither the original Baker Plan nor the Venice version had made any real progress in reducing the burden of debt.

Moreover, by the late 1980s, the Latin American debt burden was taking its toll on already weakened private commercial banks in the United States. Burdened with bad loans in agriculture, energy, and real estate, the banks were being forced or were voluntarily writing off part of their Latin American loan portfolios.

But despite their weakened balance sheets, the creditor banks faced still greater pressure for debt relief. The Rio Group had become more vociferous in its call for action on the debt. The European and Japanese banks proved unwilling to assist the United States in working out the Latin American debt problem; indeed, they enjoyed more secure balance sheets and operated in a far healthier macroeconomic environment. And finally Mexico, the first of the troublemakers in 1982, let it be known in 1988 that its impressive economic adjustment process was not being rewarded sufficiently and that it expected a better deal after the U.S. presidential elections in November 1988.

In March 1989, U.S. Secretary of the Treasury Nicholas Brady announced a new plan. Most of the techniques included in the Brady Plan bore a similarity to those used in the Baker Plan. The Brady Plan's novelty lay in the stimulus given to easing the external debt burden. In this sense, the plan can be said to represent a change in the official perception of the debt problem: the menu selection was switched away from increasing the debt with more loans and toward seeking the debt's reduction.

The Brady Plan provided that the IMF and the World Bank would back (with funding and repayment guaranties) debt reduction agreements entered into under the plan. Japan also undertook to provide resources for that purpose. Unlike the Baker Plan, the Brady Plan did not specify which countries would benefit from it and emphasized that any countries participating in it must show evidence of macroeconomic and structural adjustment.

Mexico, Costa Rica, and Venezuela signed Brady Plan packages. But there is much to be done. The negotiations have proved to be slow and complicated.

To speed them up, the governments of creditor nations need to facilitate debt reduction efforts by banks and bilateral official lenders by modifying banking, accounting, and tax regulations. Greater emphasis should be given to official or Paris Club debt reduction or outright forgiveness, as has happened with the poorest African countries. The United States, of course, is at a disadvantage in taking any substantive initiatives. It is the largest debtor in the world. Its deficits preclude imaginative public policy proposals that would require congressional involvement—given the historical skepticism on Capitol Hill about "bailing out" private commercial banks at the expense of the American taxpayers.

It is clear that there will need to be a Brady II at some point. Debt reduction is a necessity if growth is to be resumed in the 1990s. New foreign direct investment expects a normalization of a country's international financial relations and its creditworthiness before it invests. But that will depend on debt reduction efforts, trade opportunities and imaginative use of the international financial institutions who, too, have a larger and more imaginative role to play.

The financing of Latin America's debt is spread among the industrial countries as follows:

	Brazil	Mexico	Argentina	Chile	Peru
U.S. banks	34%	36%	60%	47%	60%
Japanese banks	16	17	15	9	11
British banks	13	9	7	10	10
French banks	7	7	6	3	12
German banks	7	7	9	6	3

As discussions continue about reducing the debt, Latin states need new loans to finance interest payments and future productive investment. By the end of 1989, Latin America accounted for $423 billion of the more than one trillion dollars loaned to the Third World. Brazil leads the continent with a staggering $115 billion, followed by Mexico with $96 billion and Argentina with $60 billion.

Latin America's future is tied to economic expansion in the industrial world, lower interest rates, new trade opportunities, and reasonable prices for its raw material exports. None of these conditions were favorable in the late 1980s. Moreover, the private commercial banks have signaled that they will lend new money to Latin America only to pay outstanding interest. Private investment has dried up, given the slowdown of the Latin American economies and the drop in internal demand. Volatility in the oil market in the 1980s benefited Brazil but devastated Mexico and Ecuador as prices plunged; with the Persian Gulf crisis of 1990–91, and price inflation, oil exporters Mexico and Ecuador gained while Brazil was hurt.

THE BIG THREE OF LATIN DEBT (1989)[21]

	Debt	Growth	Inflation
Brazil	115	2.1%	296
Mexico	96	1.2%	61
Argentina	60	-1.9%	532

The debt crisis not only has shrunk markets in Latin American and the Third World, it also has accelerated a rush of exports to the United States and has intensified competition for American exporters outside Latin America. In 1981 the United States took one-third of exports from developing countries. By 1986 the figure had risen to 60 percent. Since 1982 the United States has been the only expanding market in the industrial world. Trade surplus countries, mainly West Germany and Japan, eagerly bought Latin America's cheap commodities, but used formal and informal barriers to keep Latin American manufactured products out.

Stiff competition among Latin American exporters for access to the U.S. market has put intense pressure on the U.S. Congress to keep imports out. Congress has begun to explore alternatives to the present debt crisis and passed a trade bill at the end of 1987 that would create an international debt management agency to buy Third World debt at discounted prices. The Reagan administration opposed such policies, but growing support for them in both parties suggests congressional action is likely at some point. U.S. lawmakers are acutely aware that new policy initiatives are needed. The United States will no longer be able to absorb surplus production in the Third World if it wants to eliminate its trade deficit.

In June 1990, President Bush announced the Enterprise for the Americas Initiative, which seeks to reduce debt and stimulate trade and investment. The Plan is the first comprehensive effort by the United States to address key policy issues in the Americas since the Alliance for Progress in the 1960s. But with U.S. commitments elsewhere in the world, especially those in the Middle East following the Iraqi invasion of Kuwait in August 1990, it remains unclear whether the Enterprise will ever be realized.

U.S. SECURITY CONCERNS

Although Cuban efforts failed to implant successful revolutionary movements in the early 1960s (in countries such as Venezuela), twenty years later U.S. national security concerns about its "backyard" have reemerged. While Cuba sporadically supported guerrilla movements in Colombia, Bolivia, and elsewhere into the 1970s, Cuba's foreign policy has grown increasingly interna-

---

[21] Figures are from *Economic and Social Progress in Latin America: 1990 Report* of the Inter-American Development Bank, Washington, D.C., October, 1990. The figures for growth and inflation are average annual figures for the period 1980–89 and belie large and significant fluctuations from year to year in all countries in both growth and inflation.

tional. With Africa the principal focus, Cuban troops have supported revolutions in more than a dozen states.

Cuba became more interested in Central America after the 1979 overthrow of the Somoza dictatorship in Nicaragua. El Salvador's guerrilla war, a result of repressive military rule and harsh social conditions, provided another flash point of interest to Cuban foreign policy. The United States supported the Sandinista revolution in Nicaragua until it became increasingly Marxist and less tolerant of internal dissent. At that point Washington brought pressure on the Sandinista government to hold elections and respect fundamental democratic processes. The Nicaraguan government's response was that decades of inequity, supported in part by U.S. acceptance of Somoza, required drastic social and economic reform. Political change would follow, at an undetermined point in the future.

The Reagan administration took office in January 1981, determined to stop the spread of revolutionary doctrine in Central America and the Caribbean. The new administration accused the Soviet Union of using surrogates (Cuba and Nicaragua) to support the Marxist guerrillas in El Salvador and to destabilize Honduras, Costa Rica, and Guatemala. By 1982 the United States was providing massive military assistance to the Honduran government to bolster its ability to resist the perceived Marxist threat and to provide a launching point for thousands of irregular anti-Sandinista troops, supported by the Central Intelligence Agency. A perceived Marxist threat in the Caribbean led to the U.S. invasion of Grenada in late 1983, purportedly at the request of the English-speaking states of the Eastern Caribbean.[22]

Rapid militarization in Central America and Marxist governments in the Caribbean caused the countries of the region to become increasingly concerned about the continuing impact of armed conflicts. When the OAS and the U.N. did not respond effectively, the Contadora Group (discussed earlier) took the initiative.

Although the United States acknowledged the usefulness of Contadora, it seemed to prefer bilateral diplomatic and military policies in Central America and the Caribbean rather than yield to regional or multilateral approaches that it saw as benefitting Nicaragua more than itself. With regional actors willing to assume greater responsibility for peace, the "Contadora process" offered a hemispheric strategy to deal with Marxist states and created new negotiating space between Latin America and the United States. Without firm U.S. support, however, the peace process cannot succeed.

Suddenly, in August 1987, two events redefined the debate about regional peace in Central America. Seeking to gain the diplomatic initiative, the Reagan administration announced a bipartisan peace proposal that was backed by the Speaker of the House of Representatives, Jim Wright of Texas. The Wright-Reagan plan called for a regional cease-fire within 60 days, a timetable that was

---

[22]See the collection of essays about the crisis in the hemisphere, "Hemispheric Crisis: Issues and Options," in *Foreign Policy,* 52, Fall 1983.

to end on September 30 when $100 million in Contra aid expired. If Nicaragua failed to comply with the plan, the administration would be in a strong position to ask Congress for new funding for the Nicaraguan "freedom fighters."

A few days later the presidents of Honduras, Nicaragua, El Salvador, Guatemala, and Costa Rica, meeting in Guatemala City, startled the Reagan administration by signing an historic regional peace agreement calling for cease-fires in the area's conflicts and democratic reforms that would require Nicaragua to open its internal political process. The August agreement followed an earlier effort by Costa Rican President Oscar Arias Sánchez to have the political leaders of the region assume greater responsibility for resolving the crisis. For that reason, and because of the critical role he played in Guatemala, the agreement is usually called the "Arias Plan."

The agreement had appeal, offering amnesties for government opponents in each of the five countries, cease-fires in the region's wars, democratizing reforms, a halt to military aid for insurgents, and renunciation by each country of the use of its territory for armed struggle against any of the others. These measures were to take effect simultaneously within 90 days of the August 7, 1987, signing. Key to the plan's success would be the creation of "commissions of national reconciliation" in each country to oversee, in a verifiable manner, "an authentic democratic, pluralistic and participative process" to safeguard human rights and national sovereignty.

Specifically, the agreement was designed to establish complete freedom of the press, political rights for the opposition, and free and regular elections at the municipal, legislative, and presidential levels under international supervision. Aid for "repatriation" or relocation of combatants and for their "reintegration into normal life" would be allowed.

Public and political support for the Arias agreement was overwhelming. Speaker Wright quickly backed away from the bipartisan plan and endorsed the Guatemala agreement. Implementation moved ahead with surprising speed, and President Arias visited Washington in September 1987 to drum up support for the regional peace effort. However, in a speech to the OAS in October, President Reagan reiterated his backing of the insurgent Nicaraguan Contras. While praising the Arias initiative, Reagan termed it "insufficient" for U.S. security concerns, stating that "Soviet-bloc and Cuban forces must leave" the region.

On October 13 the Norwegian Nobel Committee announced that President Arias had won the 1987 Nobel Peace Prize. Arias was the fourth Latin American to win the prize in its 86-year history. But in late 1987 his peace plan had stalled. An initial cease-fire in El Salvador and discussions between the guerrillas and the Duarte government collapsed after two Salvadoran human rights activists were murdered. Discussions between Guatemalan guerrillas and the government drifted, while the mediation efforts of Cardinal Miguel Obando y Bravo, the Archbishop of Managua, appeared doomed without more flexibility from the two protagonists.

The key issue in moving the Arias Plan ahead was progress in the Nicaragua and El Salvador conflicts, both of which resisted efforts to call a cease-fire and move forward on the Arias Plan agenda. The Arias initiative ran up against two immovable ideological forces, the Sandinistas and the Reagan administration. By the beginning of 1988, further progress seemed tied either to an agreement at the superpower summit or to U.S. presidential elections later in the year.

With the inauguration of President George Bush in January 1989, there was an immediate change in the U.S. administration's attitude toward Central America. In March Secretary of State James Baker negotiated a political agreement with the Democratic leadership of the U.S. Congress on El Salvador and on Nicaragua. The White House agreed to cease support for the Contras in exchange for a bipartisan endorsement of open and free elections in Nicaragua. Those took place in early 1990, and Mrs. Violetta Chamorro defeated Sandinista president Daniel Ortega. In El Salvador, the two parties agreed to seek a third party settlement to the civil war in that country. The United Nations was introduced as the mediator, and discussions were held intermittently in 1989–90 seeking a political solution to the oldest civil war in the hemisphere.

The renewed U.S. sensitivity during the Reagan years to threats to its security by outside states reminds many observers of the Roosevelt Corollary. The concern in the U.S. government and the response in Latin America clearly indicate that the past is not forgotten. The Latin states understand the need for appropriate foreign policies that will restore peace to the region, while providing adequate safeguards for U.S. security interests and respect for the sovereignty of all the region's states.

With the end of the Cold War and the withdrawal of Soviet economic and military sponsorship of regimes in Cuba and Nicaragua, U.S. security concerns are less easily provoked, however. Indeed, with the Soviet retreat from the hemisphere, even the three-decade long polemic challenge waged by Castro's Cuba appears to be faltering, though by the end of 1990 the guerrilla king had yet to concede the ailing health of communism.

REGIONAL DISPUTES

With the gradual diminution of the U.S. presence in Latin America and the increasingly aggressive foreign policies of many states in the 1970s, smoldering disputes burst into flame. While the Inter-American security system more or less controlled the arms supply to Latin America, territorial disputes were conditioned by Washington's largess, which was never sufficient to instigate full-scale war. New arms purchases from other states, including Latin American manufacturers, depended on favorable trade balances. Eager to demonstrate their ability to defend national sovereignty, military establishments sought to settle old scores.

The dispute between Argentina and Chile over small islands in the Beagle Channel dates from 1881. Chile has occupied and governed the islands since the end of the last century. In 1977, after a series of incidents, an arbitration award went to Chile. Argentina refused to accept the award and opened negotiations with Chile that were inconclusive. By 1978 the countries had deployed troops and naval forces and were at the brink of war. At the last minute the dispute was referred to papal mediation, which finally ended in a permanent settlement in November 1984. Under the agreement, the disputed islands go to Chile in return for limits on Chilean maritime rights in the area.

Antarctica presents a potential area for conflict. Both Argentina and Chile have established claims there, and Brazil is thinking about pursuing one. As scarce natural resources exert pressure on Third World development, the 1961 treaty that postpones the issue of sovereignty over the continent, which is thought to be rich in oil, natural gas, and minerals, now appears threatened. Other potential territorial disputes in the hemisphere include the Ecuadorean-Peruvian claims to disputed land in the Amazon that led to an outbreak of hostilities in 1981; conflict among Bolivia, Chile, and Peru over Bolivia's desire for an outlet to the sea, lost in the nineteenth century War of the Pacific; Venezuela's claim to two-thirds of the state of Guyana; Guatemala and Mexico's dispute over the state of Belize in Central America; Colombia and Venezuela's dispute over the Gulf of Venezuela, thought to be rich in petroleum; and, notably, the dispute between Great Britain and Argentina about the sovereignty of the Falkland or Malvinas Islands in the South Atlantic.

The 1982 war between Great Britain and Argentina shows how precarious foreign policy issues are in Latin America. The Argentine claim to sovereignty is a longstanding one, as is British occupation of the islands. In early 1982 an aggressive military government in Argentina, seeking to bolster its waning popularity, decided to strike. Negotiations with the British had collapsed. Argentina may have expected at least tacit U.S. support because of Argentina's backing of U.S. policy in Central America. Reacting too late to warlike signals from Buenos Aires, the Reagan administration tried to warn Argentina of the repercussions of armed action. In response to the Argentine invasion, the government of Prime Minister Margaret Thatcher dispatched a thirty-five-ship force to retake the islands. After Secretary of State Alexander Haig's "shuttle diplomacy" failed, the United States supported the British position. Argentina got support from its fellow Latin American states at the OAS. Peace efforts by a variety of intermediaries failed.

The Malvinas war did have one lasting result—the collapse of the military regime in Argentina led to the restoration of democracy and the democratic election of President Raúl Alfonsín at the end of 1983. The war showed that armed conflict is one of the few issues that can arouse public interest in Latin America, and military governments that lose them will retain little legitimacy. Yet the mismanagement of the war, more than its loss, motivated Argentines to repudiate the armed forces and seek a return to democracy.

During the years of the Reagan administration, more than at any time in the previous fifty years, the potential for regional conflict was high in the hemisphere. The continuing guerrilla war in El Salvador and the action of U.S.-armed Contra forces along the Honduran-Nicaraguan border and within Nicaraguan territory confirmed that observation. The U.S.-armed invasion of Grenada, supported politically and tactically by the states of the English Caribbean, strongly indicated the willingness of states in the area to resort to force. The sporadic armed conflicts between Ecuador and Peru, and the potential threat of war between Chile and Argentina, as well as the devastating war over the Falkland/Malvinas islands, made plain the volatility of foreign policy disputes in the Americas.

Ranging from the reassertion of U.S. security interests in its "backyard" to irredentist claims on the continent, the use of force was on the rise. Not only did the United States not have the capacity to contain conflict on the continent, it was deeply involved in the armed struggles of Central America and the Caribbean. Regional institutions were found wanting once again, unable to provide anything more than a forum for debate while, in the case of Grenada, they did not even serve that function.[23]

Following the removal of Panama's Noriega from power in December 1989, the resolution of the Nicaraguan conflict, and the quieting of revolutionary fervor in El Salvador, it appeared (by the end of 1990) that the potential for major conflict in the hemisphere had been dramatically reduced from the level of the previous decade. Still, uncertainty about the final resolution of the debt crisis and the always precarious consolidation of young democratic governments suggests that the region is not without a measure of instability. However, the problems that top the agenda of the 1990s will be more political and less military in nature.

PROBLEMS FOR THE 1990s: DRUGS AND IMMIGRATION

While this chapter has dealt primarily with state-to-state foreign relations, two policy issues of increasing importance in the Western Hemisphere need to be highlighted. The first is the traffic in drugs, and the second is the rising tide of illegal immigration to the United States, primarily from Central America and the Caribbean states.

The U.S. Congress has taken action in both areas. In 1986 it passed the "Omnibus Drug Enforcement, Education and Control Act" out of growing frustration that many nations, primarily in Latin America, were selling larger and larger quantities of drugs in the United States. The new law automatically suspends U.S. aid to countries shipping drugs to the United States, unless the President certifies annually to Congress that the country is making significant progress in stopping the flow. The law allows Congress to override the

---

[23] For a thoughtful consideration of these issues, see "Governance in the Western Hemisphere," (published by the Aspen Institute for Humanistic Studies, 1982).

certification process. The United States has no tougher automatic foreign sanctions law on the books.

Congressional concern has focused primarily on Mexico, but Colombia, Peru, Bolivia, and other countries are increasingly in the spotlight. A State Department report, issued in late 1986, stated that Mexico's production of marijuana had risen by more than 25 percent that year, while the acreage planted in poppies used to make heroin had grown by one-third in the same time period. Mexico is the largest single-country source of heroin and marijuana to the U.S. market. The U.S. government also believes that 30 percent of all cocaine entering the United States passes through Mexico. A group of drug traffickers in Colombia, known as the "Medellin Cartel" (named for the Colombian city in which they operate), sells cocaine by the ton and controls 80 percent of the U.S. market, earning as much as $6 billion a year.

Under increasing pressure by the United States to control production and shipment, Latin governments argue that with Americans clearly willing to spend large amounts on drugs, demand is as much an issue as supply. They also claim they lack the resources to find and close down the drug dealers, who often are linked to powerful political forces and operate in remote areas of the interior out of effective control by the capital city. Recognizing such difficulties, the Bush administration announced a plan in 1989 to station a U.S. aircraft carrier off the coast of Colombia in an effort to stem the flow of drug exports. Following protest from the Colombians over questions of sovereignty, the United States scuttled the plan. At a meeting of the presidents of Colombia, Peru, and Bolivia in Cartagena, Colombia, in February of 1990, with U.S. President George Bush, the heads of state made general commitments to undertake more cooperative police and military action against the drug traffickers.

Following several years of antigovernment bombings and political assassinations, the Colombian government in 1990 offered a limited amnesty to drug traffickers who would turn themselves in. Several important Medellin operatives took up the offer, but there remains widespread skepticism that the amnesty can provide any permanent victory over the drug machine as long as the commerce remains financially lucrative.

There is plenty of blame for the drug traffic to go around. Americans consume drugs in huge quantities, yet the United States has shown itself unwilling to punish its own consumers. Still, Latin American supply routes have grown dramatically since the 1970s. Moreover, with their enormous economic influence, drug lords operate with impunity in most Latin American societies. Drug money often represents a significant segment of the "informal economy." The drug question will not disappear. It promises to grow in importance and will challenge the combined ingenuity of both Latin and North American political leaders to find a comprehensive, hemispheric response. As of the February 1990 Cartagena meeting, such a response had yet to be formulated.

The U.S. Congress, after years of discussion and debate, also passed a comprehensive immigration law in 1986. The major provisions of the law include an amnesty program for illegal aliens who have resided in the United States continuously since January 1, 1982, and civil and criminal penalties for employers who hire illegal aliens in the future. Alien farm workers who can prove they worked in U.S. agriculture for 90 days in the year that ended May 1, 1986, also got amnesty.

Congress was goaded to act because of the growing inability of the federal government to control its borders. Of the three to five million illegal aliens living in the United States, 55 percent come from Mexico alone, with other Latin countries accounting for another 22 percent. According to estimates, about one-fifth of the entire population of El Salvador lives in the United States, mostly as illegal aliens.

The 2,000-mile border with Mexico is the most attractive point of illegal entry, even for immigrants from Asia and other regions of the world. The problem is aggravated by the inability of the U.S. border patrol to control the frontier. The patrol is understaffed and overwhelmed by the sheer numbers of immigrants. The issue has become a thorny domestic political problem in many states of the United States, with accusations being made that illegal immigrants are taking jobs away from American citizens. The new legislation seeks to stop the practice of hiring illegals.

The new law has created concern in Latin America as well. A surge of immigrants back into the region will place a heavy burden on most governments. Unemployment is already very high. Social service demands will increase. And workers' remittances from the United States, sent back to families in dollars, will stop. Moreover, the law will eliminate an important escape valve. For years, unemployed young people in Latin America have been able to come to the United States to work and to establish a career. If they are forcibly kept at home, their discontent will eventually manifest itself politically and create instability in the region.

Neither the drug issue nor illegal immigration have obvious solutions. Both have domestic and foreign implications, and both have aroused heat and passion on both sides of the border. Relatively new on the agenda of U.S.-Latin American relations, these issues will not simply disappear. Indeed, most specialists believe that both will grow worse, regardless of legislation, as long as few opportunities exist at home for employment and career advancement and as long as civil war and political instability plague Central America and the Caribbean.

CONCLUSION

The basic dilemmas of formulating independent positions in foreign policy continue to frustrate the states of Latin America. An increase in U.S. security concerns in the Caribbean and Central American region highlights Latin impotence when confronted with U.S. determination and will. The Contadora group failed in its attempts to mediate a settlement in Central America. The Arias Plan initiative of five Central American presidents was held hostage by the Reagan administration. It was only with the coming of the Bush team that the Plan was freed to operate.

The profound economic crisis that affects all the states of the hemisphere has demonstrated their continued dependence on the United States and the private commercial banks who provide the lion's share of the region's loans. The Acapulco agreement signed by eight Latin American presidents in November 1987 was strong on rhetoric. But in practice, it has been the leverage and negotiating prowess of individual debtor governments that appear to be breaking the logjam in debt negotiations. Still at issue is Latin America's five years of austerity. The Latin leaders have not yet identified a set of policy instruments or amassed the political will to confront the United States and its industrial allies on the critical issues of trade, investment, debt financing, and commodity prices.

A complex web of regional and subregional hemispheric institutions appears unable to clarify goals or to overcome internal dissension, scarce resources, and deep divisions between military and democratic regimes. The hemisphere's ties with the Third World are strong but based on rhetoric, since these economically dependent areas of the globe can offer little of substance. Latin America finds itself forced closer to the United States than it ever imagined possible in the optimistic days of the 1970s when autonomy seemed increasingly possible.

A danger is that the deep economic crisis may provoke unexpected reactions in Latin America—such as debt moratoria or the replacement of democratic regimes with nationalist governments. Either event may herald a period of deep distrust between the U.S. and the region. Moratoria would directly threaten the U.S. economy and the American banking system. Nationalist regimes in Latin America might decide to take measures to protect their countries that would strike directly at U.S. economic and investment stakes in the hemisphere. Desperate states with nationalist regimes might well seek to redress irredentist territorial claims. A period of border conflict and the settling of old scores would be difficult to control, given the fragility of existing regional institutions. U.S. influence has diminished significantly, particularly on the South American continent, nor would U.S. diplomatic intervention necessarily achieve any more success than it enjoyed during the 1982 Falklands-Malvinas war in the South Atlantic.

Indeed, after the skillful negotiation of the new Panama Canal treaties in the 1970s, for example, and the very useful role played by the Andean states in 1979 in removing the Somozas from power in Nicaragua, there was every reason to believe that the U.S. sought a partnership with the hemisphere in solving regional problems. But quickly, with the election of President Reagan and the appearance of a perceived security threat, the balance changed. Not even the skillful diplomatic efforts of the Contadora states or of President Arias alone were able to settle the profound differences between the United States and Nicaragua. An earlier attempt by Mexico to find a moderate solution to the differences between the United States, Nicaragua, and Cuba had failed also.

There is now a hiatus in Latin America's search for autonomy in world affairs. Problems of subversion and possible bankruptcy have moved to the top of the hemispheric agenda for the foreseeable future. At the margin, Latin America will continue to seek degrees of autonomy. Some efforts will be successful; bolder initiatives will encounter the dilemma of debt and the ongoing, though increasingly less problematic, reality of ideology. From the perspective of U.S. foreign policy, it is essential to remember that

> ...geographic and historic factors, and the international role these dynamic countries can play, especially the "new influentials" all make a constructive relationship with them of profound consequence to the United States. That in turn requires being relevant to national concerns and situations. For the larger countries, relevance means being responsive and helpful to their central anxieties—trade, access to capital, debt management, economic and social development. For revolutionary situations it means help in fostering moderate solutions of internal conflict and "drying up the ponds."

That is the challenge the hemisphere confronts in the 1990s. The United States remains profoundly important to the states of Latin America. In turn, the region is an essential element in defining the national security interests of the United States. Interdependence is obvious; it is still unclear, however, whether initiatives such as President Bush's Enterprise for the Americas (1990) can provide the guiding spirit or dynamics needed to transform old antagonisms and perceptions into a new reality of hemispheric cooperation that is the best guarantee of Latin America's eventual emergence as a serious actor in world affairs.

FOREIGN POLICY LANDMARKS

1947   The Rio treaty (Inter-American Treaty of Reciprocal Assistance) is signed by the United States and the Latin American nations; a collective security agreement, the Rio treaty served as a model for other mutual defense pacts like NATO

1948   Founding of the Organization of American States (OAS)

1954   The CIA helps overthrow the Jacobo Arbenz regime in Guatemala, whose program of moderate social and economic reform was viewed as subversive by the Eisenhower administration

1959   Fidel Castro overthrows President Fulgencio Batista of Cuba and opens a new era in Latin American politics; Castro defies the United States and, with the backing of the Soviet Union, establishes the first Marxist state in the Western Hemisphere

1961   A CIA-sponsored invasion of Cuba at the Bay of Pigs fails to unseat Castro

1961   The Alliance for Progress is begun by the Kennedy administration as a response to the Cuban revolution

1962   The Cuban Missile Crisis is a strategic victory for the United States. The Soviet Union agrees to withdraw its missiles from Cuba in return for a U.S. pledge not to invade Cuba

1964   Onset of military-authoritarian regimes in Brazil

1965   The United States intervenes in the Dominican Republic in an attempt to prevent "another Cuba"

1966   Onset of military-authoritarian regime in Argentina

1967   The death of Che Guevara in Bolivia at the hands of the Bolivian army ends the myth of guerrilla invincibility

1968   A populist-reformist military regime is started in Peru

1973   The overthrow of Chilean President Salvador Allende unleashes a long era of brutal repression and destroys the idea of a "peaceful transition" to democratic socialism in Latin America

1973   Onset of military-authoritarian regimes in Chile and Uruguay

1976   Another military-authoritarian regime is founded in Argentina

1977   The signing of the Panama Canal Treaties marks a milestone in U.S. relations with Latin America. The United States agrees to transfer the canal to Panama by the year 2000, with administrative control to be given to Panama in 1988

1979   The Sandinista National Liberation Front forcibly overthrows the dictatorship of General Anastasio Somoza in Nicaragua

1982   The Latin American debt crisis begins as Mexico narrowly averts default

1982   The Argentina-British (Malvinas or Falklands) war in the South Atlantic results in defeat for Argentina and serves as a catalyst for the restoration of democracy in Argentina and the election of President Raul Alfonsin in 1983

1983   The first meeting of the Contadora Group, which tries to find a solution to the Central American wars independent from U.S. policy

1983   The United States invades Grenada and unseats an unpopular Marxist dictatorship

1987   The Arias Peace Plan is launched by the Costa Rican president in an effort to end the armed conflict in Central America. Arias received the Nobel Peace prize for his efforts

1987   The Acapulco Declaration of eight Latin American presidents seeks a political dialogue with the industrial countries on Latin America's pressing problems

1988   In a Chilean referendum, 54.7% vote against a new term for President Augusto Pinochet, 43% vote in favor. According to the Chilean constitution, Pinochet must call presidential and congressional elections by December 1989

1988   Panamanian strong man General Manuel Antonio Noriega is indicted by U.S. federal grand juries in Miami and Tampa on charges of violating U.S. racketeering and drug trafficking laws

1989   Presidents of five Central American countries agree to draft, within 90 days, in cooperation with U.N., a plan to close Nicaraguan Contra bases in Honduras and relocate Contras to Nicaragua or third countries. Nicaragua agrees to hold presidential, legislative, and municipal elections no later than February 25, 1990, and to allow observation by international monitors. Signatories also agree to halt aid to rebel forces in other countries and to negotiate cease-fires with rebels within their own borders

1989   Mexican President Carlos Salinas de Gortari announces Mexico and 15-member advisory committee representing 500 international creditors have reached agreement to reduce Mexico's $53 billion medium- and long-term debt in the first deal arranged under the Brady Plan, the Bush administration's effort to further the debt reduction efforts begun in 1985 with the Baker Plan

1989   U.S. forces invade Panama and oversee the swearing in of a new government; General Noriega takes refuge in the residence of the Papal Nuncio

1989   Presidential elections are held in December in Chile. Opposition Coalition for Democracy candidate Patricio Aylwin captures 55% of vote, signalling the transfer of power in 1990 to the first civilian government in Chile since 1973

1990   General Manuel Noriega surrenders to U.S. troops in Panama and is imprisoned in the United States to await trail on drug trafficking charges

1990   President George Bush announces the Enterprise for the Americas Initiative—calling it a new partnership for Trade, Investment, and Growth

1990   President Bush visits five countries in South America, the first presidential visit since 1983

1990   Elections held in Nicaragua. The Sandinista government is defeated and Mrs. Violetta Chamorro is inaugurated as president.

1990   The U.S. and Mexico announce plans to negotiate a Free Trade Agreement. Other calls for FTAs in the Americas mount as does the impetus for regional economic integration in the Southern Cone with the announcement that a Common Market composed of Argentina, Brazil, Uruguay and Paraguay will be implemented by 1994.

SELECTED BIBLIOGRAPHY

Atkins, G. Pope. *Latin America in the International Political System,* 2nd ed. rev. and updated. Boulder, Colo.: Westview Press, 1989.

Burr, Robert N. *By Reason or Force: Chile and the Balancing of Power in South America, 1830–1905.* Berkeley: University of California Press, 1967.

Davis, Harold Eugene, John J. Finan, and F. Taylor Peck. *Latin American Diplomatic History: An Introduction.* Baton Rouge, La.: Louisiana State University Press, 1977.

Fagen, Richard R., and Olga Pellicer, eds. *The Future of Central America: Policy Choices for the U.S. and Mexico.* Stanford, Calif.: Stanford University Press, 1983.

Grabendorff, Wolf, and Riordan Roett, eds. *Latin America, Western Europe and the United States: A New Atlantic Triangle.* New York: Praeger, 1984.

Hartlyn, Jonathan, and Samuel A. Morley, eds. *Latin American Political Economy.* Boulder, Colo.: Westview Press, 1986.

Kelly, Philip, and Jack Child, eds. *Geopolitics of the Southern Cone and Antarctica.* Boulder, Colo.: Lynne Rienner Publishers, 1988.

Levinson, Jerome, and Juan de Onis. *The Alliance that Lost Its Way: A Critical Report on the Alliance for Progress.* Chicago: Quadrangle Books, 1970.

Lowenthal, Abraham F. *Partners in Conflict: The United States and Latin America.* Baltimore, Md.: The Johns Hopkins University Press, 1987.

Lynch, John. *The Spanish-American Revolutions, 1808–1826.* New York: Norton, 1973.

Martz, John D., ed. *United States Policy in Latin America.* Lincoln and London: University of Nebraska Press, 1988.

Middlebrook, Kevin J., and Carlos Rico. *The United States and Latin America in the 1980s.* Pittsburgh, Pa.: University of Pittsburgh Press, 1986.

Munoz, Heraldo, and Joseph S. Tulchin, eds. *Latin American Nations in World Politics.* Boulder, Colo.: Westview Press, 1984.

Pastor, Robert A., ed. *Democracy in the Americas.* New York: Holmes and Meier, 1989.

Prizel, Ilya. *Latin America through Soviet Eyes.* Cambridge: Cambridge University Press, 1990.

Roett, Riordan, ed. *Mexico's External Relations in the 1990s.* Boulder, Colo.: Lynne Rienner Publishers, 1991.

Silvert, Kalman H., Stanley Hoffman, Riordan Roett, et al. *The Americas in a Changing World: A Report of the Commission on United States-Latin American Relations.* New York: Quadrangle/New York Times Books, 1975.

Wiarda, Howard J., and Harvey F. Kline, eds. *Latin American Politics and Development,* 3rd ed. rev. and updated. Boulder, Colo.: Westview Press, 1990.

Wood, Bryce. *The Dismantling of the Good Neighbor Policy.* Austin, Tex.: University of Texas Press, 1985.

–10–

SCANDINAVIA SECURITY, PROSPERITY, AND SOLIDARITY AMIDST CHANGE

Bengt Sundelius with Don Odom

To outside observers the Scandinavian[1] countries appear to form a distinct community of nations that share great prosperity, unusual political stability, innovative social programs, and foreign policies supportive of global order and justice. Scandinavians take great pride in these features, but they often regard them less as regional characteristics and more as distinct policies of their own native countries—Denmark, Finland, Iceland, Norway, or Sweden. Although accepting the group identity of Scandinavia, the peoples of these small nations with a total population of 22 million are mainly struck by the many differences between them.

Less than a hundred years ago, Scandinavia was a place to leave for a brighter future in the New World. Since that time, the mining, forestry, farming, and fishing communities of the North have been transformed into advanced industrial countries with all of the material comforts and accompanying social problems of the modern era. Not only have Americans of Scandinavian descent found contemporary Scandinavian life intriguing, but also students of government, social welfare, economic management, and industrial

[1] The terms Scandinavian and Nordic are used interchangeably to depict the five states examined here. Although Scandinavia is the more commonly used term in English, most natives prefer the latter term as a more encompassing characterization for the region. This is symbolized in the regional parliamentary body, the Nordic Council.

relations have discovered that the experiences of these nations are worthy of closer examination.

To students of international affairs, Scandinavia has often seemed less fascinating and less controversial than many of the trouble spots around the world. Scandinavia's distinctive mark—stability—seldom attracts much journalistic or even scholarly interest. Located on the fringe of the continent, the study of these states generally contributes little to an understanding of important economic and security developments in Europe. Being small, their role in world affairs has been overshadowed by more important actors. Still, if one prefers international order and stability over conflict and turmoil, then it may be worthwhile to examine how this region, despite its location on the border of East and West, has come to enjoy such advantages.

The fortunate circumstances, however, that have kept Scandinavia out of the limelight of world affairs for some time may be a thing of the past. Increasingly, the strategic interests of the superpowers are focused on the North Atlantic and the adjacent land areas. While the postwar problems of the European continent now seem to have been settled, the interests of the major powers may still clash in the North.

The stakes for the United States in these developments are considerable. Changing priorities have already resulted in a higher American profile in this region. Historically, the Soviet Union has long recognized its strategic interests in Scandinavia. Although the Soviet presence has been felt for many years, during the last decade it has become much more visible. In the future, Scandinavia may not only serve as an illustration of a well-balanced, low-tension area, but also as an example of how such stable patterns can erode when exposed to new pressures.

FROM CONFLICT TO COMMUNITY

It is easy to forget that Nordic relations have historically been characterized as much by conflict and rivalry as by neighborliness and cooperation. During the Middle Ages efforts to form one unified Nordic state failed at the hands of Swedish separatists and, instead, two distinct entities emerged. Denmark, Norway, and Iceland composed one unit and, at first, it dominated the region. Sweden and Finland constituted the other unit.

A traditional struggle for regional hegemony continued into the eighteenth century between Sweden and Denmark. There were numerous wars fought, alliances formed, and provinces conquered and reconquered all in a quest for supremacy. This rivalry was aggravated by the temporary power vacuum in northern and central Europe. Prussia and Russia emerged, however, and began to dominate the political scene at the expense of both Denmark and Sweden.

By the end of the Napoleonic Wars, some drastic changes in the political configuration of the Nordic region took place. The Swedish province of

Finland, seized by Russia in 1809, was turned into a semiautonomous province until Finnish independence was achieved in 1917. The intense shock over the loss of one-third of its territory profoundly affected Sweden and resulted in a coup d' état and a new constitution. As a provision of the Congress of Vienna after the Napoleonic War, Norway was ceded to Sweden in 1814 as compensation for the loss of Finland to Russia. However, Norway was never integrated as a part of Sweden, as Finland had been, but was instead attached in a union under a joint monarch. The Norwegians retained their own constitution, government, and central administration. Only in foreign policy did the Swedish government represent the Norwegians.

This Norwegian-Swedish union never penetrated from the political and constitutional level down to the economic, cultural, and social levels. Instead, the two societies developed separately during the nineteenth century. Growing cultural, social, and economic differences, increased political conflicts throughout the nineteenth century until in 1905 the union was finally dissolved.

Denmark retained only Iceland, Greenland, and the Faeroe Islands after 1814. Iceland would remain a Danish colony until a grant of autonomy in 1918 and would only achieve full independence in 1944. Although the other islands have remained under Danish sovereignty, they have been granted increased autonomy in recent years.

The period between 1800 and the end of World War II has thus been described as an era of Nordic political disintegration, as the two traditional entities in the region were split into five separate nation-states. Further, since 1814 the Nordic region has not experienced any internal military conflicts. This fact contrasts sharply with the tradition of frequent wars prior to that time. Even though the Nordic region was divided into many smaller entities, these small countries acted in unison against greater power interference. Since that time violent solutions have been avoided whenever serious conflict has arisen. For example, Norway peacefully seceded from the union with Sweden in 1905; the Swedish-Finnish dispute over the rights to the Åland Islands was settled peacefully in the League of Nations in 1921; and conflicting Norwegian and Danish claims to eastern Greenland were adjudicated by the Permanent Court of International Justice in 1933.

Great power intervention in the region was to be avoided, even if it meant making sacrifices to the neighboring countries. Slowly, these separate decisions in favor of compromise solutions evolved into a pattern of peaceful regional relations.

For example, all of the Scandinavian countries remained neutral during World War I in spite of strong sympathies with the different parties to the war. Similarly, prospects of war among Scandinavian countries are no longer entertained. Thus a 'pluralistic security community' has slowly developed, where dependable expectations of peaceful settlements of regional disputes are found. It is interesting that this condition was not reached until the region was politically divided into several states, which as individual entities were reduced to small power status.

SECURING FIVE NATION-STATES

Norway

Norway is a traditionally pro-British nation of 4 million people controlling an important coastline on the North Sea. From independence in 1905 until the German invasion in April 1940 it pursued a policy of neutrality. During World War I, the German and British navies competed for dominance in Norwegian coastal waters. Under pressure, the government generally leaned toward the British. This would later prove to be costly in the second round of the British-German Conflict. On April 9, 1940, Germany launched a daring surprise attack by sea and air to preempt British plans for mine laying. After two months of fighting, Norway was occupied for five years. The king escaped into exile in London and became the symbol of resistance.

At the end of the war, Norway for a short time returned to its traditional foreign policy orientation and attempted to perform the role of international bridge builder, which included support of the newly formed United Nations. In fact, Norway's foreign minister, Trygve Lie, became the first U.N. Secretary General. In 1948, the government faced the familiar choice of balancing its allegiances. Norway could either join the emerging Atlantic alliance, or it could stay out of the bloc confrontation through an alliance with neutral Sweden and Denmark.

Since 1945 Norway has shared a 125-mile land border with the U.S.S.R. in the far north. The government feared political pressures similar to those felt by other Soviet neighbors at that time. A firm Western defense commitment to Norway was seen as a strategic necessity as well as a logical extension of the wartime collaboration with the Allies. Since joining the Alliance, Norway has been one of the most steadfast NATO members. Today, government officials note that the widely supported Alliance commitment represents a longer tradition than the previously held position of neutrality.

From the first days of its NATO membership, Norway has attempted to balance the deterrence function of the alliance with an emphasis on its defensive purpose. For example, the government has ruled out the stationing of NATO troops on its territory or the presence of any nuclear weapons in peacetime since 1949. Denmark has also followed this policy, making Scandinavia, in effect, a region free of nuclear weapons throughout the postwar period.

This concern for "reassurance" is intended to avoid turning strategically vulnerable Norway into a more likely target area in the event of war. Norway does not want to give the appearance of serving as an offensive arrow close to the vital Soviet military complex on the Kola peninsula. Norway's military presence north of the 62d parallel is, therefore, deliberately kept very modest.

Along this border area shared by NATO and the Soviet Union, few incidents similar to those along the German border have occurred.

A policy of restraint in combination with a firm alliance commitment has solid public support in Norway. The various reassurance schemes are very important as in some ways they represent a continuation of the legacy of neutrality and bridge building. While the Left tends to emphasize this dimension more than the Right, it is an important element of the Norwegian foreign policy profile that all groups can embrace. At times, the left wing of the dominant Labor Party has demanded that the government pursue various confidence building schemes more vigorously. For example, during the early 1980s, a prior Finnish proposal for the creation of a Nordic nuclear weapons free zone reappeared with great intensity in the Norwegian debate. Also, alliance agreements to strengthen the military preparedness of NATO defenses have been controversial. Like the other Scandinavians, the Norwegians have been as concerned with avoiding involvement in conflict as with being well prepared should a crisis develop.

Denmark

During the last century, the Danish international postion has been largely shaped by its dynamic neighbor to the south—Germany. Without a natural southern frontier, this tiny territory, comprising one peninsula off the Continent together with several flat islands, is easily overrun from the south or from the sea. After losing a war to Prussia and Austria in 1864, the government embarked on a policy of neutrality and appeasement through World War II.

Although occupied during the last war, Denmark emerged relatively undamaged, and the regular government machinery remained intact. The Danish king, who stayed behind to share the burdens of his people, became a symbol of calm and patience through his daily outings on horseback through the streets of Copenhagen. The country was spared any serious fighting in 1945, but one of the Danish outer islands, Bornholm, was, in fact, liberated by the Red Army. The Russians soon withdrew from this potentially valuable holding in the western part of the Baltic Sea.

With the emerging Cold War, Denmark joined NATO after the collapse of the plans for a Scandinavian Defence Alliance. Less enthusiastic than Norway in this choice, Denmark has remained an ally, but has been seen within the alliance as less supportive than most members. The United States was anxious for Danish membership due to the strategic importance of its Arctic holding in Greenland, as well as for its control of the gateway to the Baltic Sea.

Because of the NATO alliance and the postwar division of Germany, the pressures on Denmark from the south virtually ceased. The defense of Denmark proper became the concern of a NATO command dominated by allied West Germany forces. Of course, the economic surge of the vibrant West German society remained a factor for an advanced industrial nation of only 5 million people. This is best manifested in the Danish membership in the European Community since 1973.

The term "Denmarkization" has been coined in NATO circles to depict a state that fails to live up to its alliance commitments. To a greater extent than, for example, Norway, the precarious Danish economy has set limits to the financial support for the joint defense effort. In addition, a complex domestic political situation with a popular majority favoring conservative domestic policies has in the 1980s made Denmark notorious for its "footnotes" to many NATO declarations. The impression was given abroad that the country would not take its alliance obligations very seriously. In fact, it appeared to enjoy a status of free rider within the joint defense structure.

The strategic importance of Denmark's vast Greenland territory, however, is as evident today as it was during the formative years of the alliance. NATO installations in Greenland have so far not been seriously questioned. However, the leadership of the autonomous Greenland region has during the last decade shown greater independence, and, for example, it pulled out of the European Community in 1985. It may be that in the future, the strategic pressures on Denmark will come from the north rather than from the south. In this the Danish and Norwegian governments have a joint interest in the "Nordpolitik" of the Western alliance.

Iceland

Iceland shares the cultural, social, and political traditions of Scandinavia, yet its tiny population, one-sided economic dependence upon fishing, and isolated geographic location produce some vast differences from the other Nordic nations. The central foreign policy problem for Iceland has been how to reconcile a strong sense of independence with its strategic value as a bridge between North America and Europe. Attaining nation-statehood only in 1944, the Icelanders are highly sensitive to infringements on their sovereignty and cultural identity. Proud of the heritage of the Viking Sagas and acutely aware of their isolation, they are torn between the obvious need for cooperation and their negative experience with colonial interference.

During World War II, the Allies occupied Iceland. This protection was not entirely unwelcome, as the obvious alternative was even less appealing. Since the war, the United States has maintained a military presence at Keflavik, and Iceland later joined the Atlantic Alliance. The approximately 5,000 Americans stationed in Iceland represent, within the context of a native population of only 230,000, a potential disruptive force to the nation. Because of this, the American profile is kept low and several measures have been used to shield the local inhabitants from unwanted intrusions. At the same time, the NATO base represents a major military and financial asset to a small economy. Not only does it relieve the government from any expenses for defense, but it also generates significant purchasing power to the local economy as well. The NATO facility has also served as a useful bargaining chip in securing vital economic concessions in the fishing sector.

Iceland has prevailed in three "Cod Wars" in which more powerful alliance members acceded to Icelandic demands for fishing rights within a 200-mile economic zone. In these negotiations, the small but determined state could force the terms of agreement through the implicit threat about the future of the strategically vital Keflavik base. The Icelandic government has cultivated good relations with the Soviet Union, which maintains a large diplomatic mission in Reykjavik, and the Soviet Union has been a reliable source of oil.

With the military buildup in the North Atlantic, NATO's access to Iceland, for surveillance purposes and as a support base, remains essential to its defense posture. In fact, the Norwegian policy of not permitting a permanent basing of NATO forces in peacetime may be credible only as long as the Icelanders are willing to accept an American base on their territory. Thus, Iceland simultaneously helps solve a Norwegian domestic policy dilemma, supports the deterrence function of the alliance, and contributes to NATO reassurance in the North. Obviously, the Icelandic government has managed to make the most of its strategic assets and has turned vulnerability into bargaining strength.

Finland

Finland, like Denmark, has been preoccupied with developing a mutually acceptable relationship with a neighboring Great Power. After some 600 years as part of the Swedish kingdom and 108 years as an autonomous province of Imperial Russia, Finland, a nation of about 5 million people, became independent in 1917. After independence and a brief but violent civil war, Finland adopted a stiff posture toward the new Soviet state. Centuries of border wars had left a legacy of suspicion.

It followed a pro-German line, but it fell victim to the 1939 Molotov-Ribbentrop Pact and had to fight alone against the Red Army during the Winter War of 1939-40.

Soviet ambitions to install a "people's government" in Helsinki, similar to those in the Baltic states, failed. The Finnish government at the end of World War II, however, was forced to accept major territorial losses and to pay substantial war reparations. Under the leadership of President Juho Kusti Paasikivi, Finland embarked on a new relationship with its powerful neighbor to ensure that it would never again face another conflict with the Soviet Union.

The Finnish government has throughout the postwar period strived to gain the confidence of the Soviet leadership. They have been able to draw on the respect in Moscow for effective territorial defense, as displayed in the summer of 1944 when the Finns prevented the Red Army from advancing on Helsinki as instructed by Stalin. Based on the assumption that Soviet interests in Finland are defensive and strategic, and not offensive and ideological, considerations for the legitimate security needs of a major power would not jeopardize the Finnish domestic system, based on Western democratic ideals and economic values.

This policy of good neighborliness is symbolized in the 1948 Finnish-Soviet Treaty of Friendship, Cooperation, and Mutual Assistance. In its title, it parallels several Soviet pacts with Eastern European nations at that time, but its significance has obviously been quite different. The notion of pursuing neutrality outside the power blocs draws on this agreement from the Cold War era. It has been seen less as a restriction on Finnish security policy than as an opportunity to develop an independent foreign policy profile.

Soon after the Communist take-over of Czechoslovakia in 1948, a delegation of Finnish officials arrived in Moscow for negotiations on a treaty of cooperation with the Soviet Union. The Finnish leaders were summoned to lay the foundation to a constructive future relationship with the Superpower neighbor. Soviet Foreign Minister Molotov received the delegation and quickly agreed to work from a Finnish draft to a treaty text.

Experts agree that three elements of the 1948 treaty are of particular importance. First, the contracting parties agreed to "confer with each other if it is established that the threat of an armed attack against Finland or against the U.S.S.R. through Finnish territory" is present. This wording is interpreted to mean that both governments must accept this notion of an existing threat. Secondly, Finland's first obligation is to "fight to repel the attack" and any Soviet assistance "will be subject to mutual agreement between the contracting parties." Thirdly, in the preamble to the treaty the Finnish "desire to remain outside the conflicting interests of the Great Powers" is acknowledged. This formula has been the point of departure for the Finnish quest for neutrality between East and West.

At the April 1948 signing ceremony, Stalin characterized the new agreement as a point of transition from a state of mistrust between the two states to a new spirit of mutual confidence. At regular intervals, this pillar of Finnish-Soviet relations has been renewed and over the years the agreement from the Cold War era has come to symbolize a stable relationship of mutual respect unaffected by the many turns of Soviet-American relations.

With the peaceful coexistence offensive of the mid-1950s by the post-Stalin leaders in the U.S.S.R., Finland could more vigorously pursue neutrality, as was the case with the newly declared neutral Austrian state. Fears of direct Soviet intervention in the domestic life of Finland faded after the return of the Porkkala navy base outside Helsinki in 1955. Like other Europeans neutrals, Finland has played a role in fostering more harmonious East-West relations. Its efforts seem to be appreciated in Western capitals as well in Moscow. Certainly, the détente era of the 1970s opened up new opportunities for such a role. The Finnish search for legitimacy as a democratic neutral was crowned in 1975 when—in a thirty-five nation summit meeting—the 'Helsinki Accords' laid the foundation to the now permanent Conference on Security and

Cooperation in Europe (CSCE) negotiations. Finland had by then also served on the Security Council of the United Nations. The young state had overcome the disadvantages of its geography and was recognized worldwide as a member of the community of European democracies.

Yet, Finnish relations with the Soviet Union have not been without problems. The most serious crisis occurred in 1961, when the Soviet government requested consultations in accordance with the 1948 pact. West German activities were cited as a potential threat to Finnish security. Through skillful diplomacy by President Urho Kekkonen, the matter was dropped before any consultations were held.

Among Western commentators unfamiliar with the subtleties of Finnish-Soviet relations, the concept 'Finlandization' has been coined to depict a policy of appeasement toward preponderant Soviet power. In contrast to the Finnish postwar experience, this perjorative term suggests, an image of a narrowing West European margin of political maneuver in the face of a growing Soviet military dominance. The "Finlandization" term was introduced during the détente era of the early 1970s to dramatize an underlying warning against a growing Soviet threat to Western Europe. However, the logic behind this catchword fits poorly with the postwar reality of Finland. Throughout the years Finland has enjoyed a widening realm of maneuver and independence.

It is paradoxical that the Soviet Union through time seems to have gained a considerable stake in a harmonious relationship with democratic and capitalistic Finland. The attention given to this small state by the Soviet leadership is exceptional and seems to go beyond considerations based only on bilateral relations. From the Soviet viewpoint, the Finnish solution could be offered as a model for relations with other West European states. Skeptics, then, could here clearly observe that it is possible to deal with, and benefit from, close and cooperative relations with the Soviet Union.

Thus, the Soviet leadership may have been as eager as are the Finns to find mutually acceptable solutions to bilateral problems. The position of the small nation is strengthened. Indeed, the recognition of Finnish neutrality by the Soviet Union was capped in October 1989, when President Gorbachev explicitly referred to Finland as a neutral state. A year later, the Finnish government unilaterally denounced the remaining military restrictions imposed by the 1947 peace treaty with the Soviet Union as irrelevant.

The U.S. government has always shown considerable empathy and respect for Finland. Its leaders have been well received in Washington, and U.S. officials en route to Moscow have often scheduled a stop over in Helsinki. The U.S. government seems to have appreciated the relatively low-key approach to global issues adopted in Helsinki. The U.S. and Finnish governments have not engaged in the type of diplomatic spats that at times have characterized U.S.-Swedish relations. President Ronald Reagan visited Helsinki on his way to the Moscow summit in May 1988 and the 1990 Bush-Gorbachev summit meeting on the Persian Gulf Crisis was held in the Finnish capital. The next review meeting of the CSCE process will begin in Helsinki in 1992. Among many Americans, Finnish neutrality is appreciated, while Swedish neutrality is resented.

Sweden

Over the last century, Sweden has benefited from the cushioning effects of its Scandinavian neighbors. While these states have been drawn into the pattern of conflict and cooperation in Europe, Sweden has more often remained outside such activities. A policy of splendid isolation has been combined with the perhaps better known quest for international understanding. Possessing relatively strong economic and military attributes, Sweden, a nation of 8 million people, could long afford such a stand. The superior resource base, representing almost half of the total GNP in the region, has given Sweden dominance in the Nordic arena. In a larger context, Sweden is small and defines itself as a leading small state.

After World War I, Sweden enjoyed an optimal security position. With Germany defeated, the new Soviet state weak, Finland and the three Baltic states independent, and with Denmark and Norway strengthened but friendly, Sweden did not face any serious strategic concerns. Within the immediate security environment Sweden even appeared as a major player.

A benevolent policy was adopted that included acquiescence to a League of Nations ruling granting the Swedish-speaking Åland Islands to the new Finnish state against the clear wishes of the inhabitants. Similarly, the various international disarmament schemes of the period between the World Wars found support in Sweden. In 1925 Sweden set an example for other nations by greatly reducing its own defenses. Like others, notably in the United States at the time, prominent Swedes placed great faith in the abilities of statesmen to create a stable and just world order through international law and open diplomacy.

By the mid-1930s, this happy situation was replaced by the rise of Nazi Germany, the consolidation of the Soviet regime, and the collapse of the League. Joining the other small European states, Sweden declared its departure from the collective security system and its return to the traditional defense posture; namely, armed neutrality. During the war, the government's primary objective was to keep the nation out of the conflict that caused so much suffering in the other states of Europe.

In this respect, the government was successful, but at the expense of being forced at times to interpret the obligations of neutrality in less than acceptable ways. For example, the Swedish government provided assistance to its war-torn Nordic neighbors, allowed German troop transfers across its territory, and facilitated the return of Allied airmen stranded after missions over enemy territory—all apparent deviations from a strict definition of neutrality. The other neutrals of World War II were forced to accept similar compromises as well. At the war's end, Sweden could not join in the celebrations of the Allies, but it continued to assist the victims of war. Clearly, Swedish values were served by the victory, but it is an open question whether the allied cause would have been better served through Swedish combat participation.

Like the United States, Sweden entered the postwar period from a position of strength. The industrial base was intact and the defense force was rebuilt. This set the stage for the relative economic and military weight of Sweden over the next thirty years. Sweden joined the United Nations in 1946 after some debate over the compatibility of membership with the policy of neutrality. The second U.N. Secretary General, Dag Hammarskjöld, was recruited from Sweden in 1953. In 1948, an effort was made to keep the Scandinavian region out of the Cold War through a Scandinavian Defense Alliance outside the blocs. At the time, Swedish military might was still sufficiently impressive that such a defense pact could be regarded as a meaningful choice.

When Denmark and Norway opted for membership in the Atlantic Alliance, Sweden returned to its traditional stand of splendid isolation. The resulting formula—freedom from alliances in peacetime, aiming at neutrality in the event of war—remains the cornerstone for Swedish security policy to this day. Even a different internal resource base and vastly changed international conditions for armed neutrality have not undermined the domestic support for the doctrine. In the public mind, this posture has spared the country the devastation of war since 1814 and it has become almost axiomatic.

Possibly, the Swedish postwar security choice facilitated the Finnish effort to avoid the fate of the other nations along the Soviet border. The creation of a neutral buffer in the north, guarded by an impressive air force, may have reduced tensions in an otherwise sharply divided Europe. The peacetime utility of the Swedish posture can easily be appreciated when one compares Scandinavia with the record of bloc confrontation in Central Europe. The wartime credibility of armed neutrality is more open to question because of the fast developing and unpredictable nature of modern warfare.

The comparatively modest Swedish defense force should be sufficient to deter an attack based upon the assumption that neither bloc could—in a crisis—devote most of its military resources to a marginal country. In other words, the cost of an attack would be seen as too high relative to the strategic advantages of controlling the territory. Clearly, the level of conflict preparedness of the armed forces and the ability to foresee any hostile moves are crucial to the credibility of the Swedish policy. Considerable investment has been made in a mobile air force and advanced means of intelligence collection.

During the postwar period the Swedish government has—in addition to its commitment to armed neutrality—continued to promote international understanding and cooperation. Swedish involvement in multilateral initiatives rests on the belief that security can be enhanced both by national defense and by an international milieu less conducive to conflict. A strong commitment to the United Nations, including its multinational peace-keeping forces, an active role in international development issues, and a vocal concern about superpower armaments and their involvement in local conflicts in the Third World, can be understood in these terms.

Closer to home, a major concern has been how to help transform a conflict prone Europe into a setting of greater stability. Active in the Helsinki process and in the development of confidence-building measures, together with the other European neutral and nonaligned states, Sweden in 1984–86 hosted the Stockholm Conference on Disarmament in Europe. Inspired by the work of the 1982 Palme Commission on Common Security, the government proposed the establishment in Central Europe of a corridor free of nuclear weapons. Many of the ideas for European security promoted by the Swedish government during the tense years of the 1980s suddenly became realized as the bloc based security order rapidly collapsed at the turn of the decades. The yet evolving future European security pattern, without the Warsaw pact and with a united Germany, also will introduce significant new challenges for the traditional policy line of neutral Sweden. During the 1990s more emphasis will be placed on the European setting compared to other regions and to global issues.

NEIGHBORING NUCLEAR WEAPONS
AND SOVIET INTERNAL TURBULENCE

The security interdependence of the five states of the north has been mutually recognized. The Danish and Norwegian policies of non-basing of NATO forces in peacetime are seen in Sweden and Finland as positive gestures to reduce the local Atlantic Allied presence. On the other hand, Icelandic tolerance of a large American base on their territory may facilitate the Danish and Norwegian choices. Swedish armed neutrality offers Finland a shield in the West and may strengthen her relationship of trust with the security-conscious U.S.S.R. At the same time, a strong Swedish air force provides a buffer for the defense of Norway. Finnish neutrality in combination with the Danish and Norwegian choices help cushion the Swedish pillar.

Although the security postures selected are clearly based upon calculations of national interest and considerations of domestic politics, the governments often acknowledge that their positions are interlinked and that they have been well served by this pattern. It is not as evident, however, that the benefits to European stability have been as clearly understood by the superpowers. A number of strategic developments during the 1980s, shaped by the interests of the bloc leaders, may have eroded this favorable setting for regional stability.

Developments in the North Atlantic, have placed Scandinavia at the center of naval interests. A growing Soviet fleet has operated out of the Kola base complex in close proximity to the region for some time. The Soviets understandably have developed an acute sense of security for the area surrounding the considerable forces they have amassed at this ice-free port. Although presumably not targeted at the neighboring Scandinavian nations, the nuclear weapons located there play a significant role in the broader strategic picture. Thus, the North Cape became of great interest to NATO planners and to the American Forward Maritime Strategy. This new element undermined the Norwegian policy of reassurance toward the U.S.S.R. and complicated the plans for oil and gas exploration in these waters. The defense of northern Finland and Sweden was affected as well, and resulted in an upgrading of the local forces.

In addition, the Soviet Union in 1990 moved its complete nuclear weapon underground testing program to Novaya Zemlya, an island in the Barents Sea. Both Finland and Norway have expressed reservations over this move to conduct nuclear tests near their territories. The memory of the nuclear fallout from the Chenobyl nuclear power plant disaster is still fresh in the minds of many Scandinavians.

Traditionally, the U.S. military commitment to European defense has depended on NATO control of the North Atlantic for reliable transoceanic shipment of men and supplies. The Soviet Northern fleet gradually extended the scope of its operations far out into the North Atlantic. Naturally, NATO planners viewed this development with concern and urged a greater Allied presence in these waters and coastal areas to counter the Soviet advance. The strategic posturing of both sides moved closer to Scandinavia, complicating the traditional strategy of keeping the tensions as low as possible in the area. In NATO war scenarios, the North figured prominently as a potential combat zone in a super power confrontation. For example, Soviet control of the extensive Swedish air base system could significantly strengthen Soviet ability to fight for dominance of the North Atlantic skies. According to one scenario, the defense of the long Norwegian coastline would be impossible if Norway were cut off through an advance in the Trondheim area.

Also the strategic role of the Baltic Sea changed. Traditionally, the U.S.S.R. has promoted the notion of a closed sea, where the largest maritime power could dominate the waters and shorelines. Sweden and the NATO allies have insisted on the Baltic's status as an international sea open to all states. As a result of the division of Europe in 1945, the Soviets until 1990 controlled an immense coastline stretching from the Finnish border in the east to the West German border south of Denmark and west of Sweden. Several major ports and naval shipyards were constructed by the Soviets along the Baltic coast. These installations served as major overhaul and construction facilities for the vast Soviet global fleet.

The U.S.S.R. still seems to place great emphasis upon the control of the surrounding waters or at least their denial to others. Soviet security concerns may even be intensified by continual NATO surveillance patrols in the Baltic. The offensive Soviet submarine activities along Swedish coastlines, and the increased Allied presence in the Baltic highlighted the growing irritation in the area during much of the 1980s. Since October 1981, when the famed Soviet Whiskey Class submarine equipped with nuclear weapons ran aground near a sensitive Swedish naval installation, underwater activities have been a steady source of tension between the Soviet Union and Sweden. In spite of diplomatic protests in 1981 and 1983, all indicators point toward continued intrusions. Although the inability to repel such activities may not be considered a serious national security failure, it has clearly left many questions about the credibility of Swedish armed neutrality. This issue also sparked a rather intense domestic debate over the proper response to this new type of threat. When one considers these and related developments, it is not surprising that few Swedes view the Baltic as a "sea of peace," as it is sometimes called by Soviet officials.

Innovations in weapons technology have also affected the strategic posture of Scandinavia. A NATO launching of sea-based cruise missiles across the territories of Sweden and Finland may facilitate reaching targets in the U.S.S.R. but could also create serious political dilemmas for these neutrals. Doubts about the ability or the determination of these governments to resist such territorial violations could motivate preemptive moves by the other side. The pressures on the credibility of Swedish armed neutrality may be greater today than during the earlier postwar years, when the Swedish defense force was significantly larger. Allied concern over the region's role during a crisis or war may also lead to peacetime demands that would be difficult to reconcile with the domestically popular reassurance policies of Denmark and Norway. The preferred pattern of regional confidence and stability could collapse as broader strategic interests clash in the North.

Such unwelcome developments may even be unaffected by the 1990 superpower agreement on conventional force reductions in Central Europe. In fact, one could imagine that the confrontation would simply shift arenas and increasingly focus on the maritime and air related dimensions relevant to Scandinavian security. Even with a reduction of global and of European tension levels, the strategic setting of the North could slide toward instability.

Current developments inside the neighboring and nuclear weapon-armed Soviet Union appear to move rapidly toward internal turbulence. The transformation from a command to a market economy seems to generate great material hardships on the population and the political and social structures of the U.S.S.R. are clearly under great stress. President Gorbachev even declined to receive in person his 1990 Nobel Peace Prize as his presence at home seemed of primary importance.

Along the Baltic Coast, the three republics of Estonia, Latvia, and Lithuania have embarked on roads toward greater independence from the Kremlin. Other Soviet republics have followed their examples. The Scandinavian peoples, as well as governments, have tried to support this Baltic drive toward national liberation. Frequent high level visits by their government leaders have been arranged, new cultural and educational cooperation agreements have been concluded, and commercial links have been rejuvenated. To manifest these renewed ties, in December 1990 the five Nordic foreign ministers and the foreign ministers of the three Baltic republics met in Copenhagen. The Scandinavians further promoted the request for Baltic participation, as observers, in the November 1990 Paris European Security Conference. This step of great symbolic significance was vetoed by the U.S.S.R. Of more modest significance, the three Baltic republics have been awarded access to the meetings of the Nordic Council, and been allowed to establish official information offices in Copenhagen and Stockholm—first steps toward wider international involvements.

In the Nordic capitals, observers of the Soviet Union are acutely aware of the continued Soviet strategic interest in the Baltic coastal states, as well as in the land areas adjacent to the vital Kola military base. Possibly, the Kremlin concern over the Baltic territories is of increased importance as the former facilities in Poland and East Germany no longer are available to its defense forces. While Soviet troops are withdrawing from many parts of Europe, no such movements out of the Baltic Republics have been reported. In contrast, some of the armaments leaving Central Europe, as a result of the 1990 conventional forces agreement, may replace less modern equipment in the Leningrad military district, which borders on the Nordic lands.

SAFEGUARDING PROSPERITY

During the last thirty years the "prosperous corner" of Europe has enjoyed living standards comparable to, or even exceeding, the U.S. level. Within the last century, five separate, small economies have developed rapidly and are now generating a remarkable level of affluence. The factor of economy of scale—considered so important to the growth of the U.S. economy and one of the objectives of the European Community—was not present in Scandinavia. How, then, did the Scandinavian countries compensate for their relative smallness? Traditionally, Scandinavia has sought international markets both for trade expansion and for investment opportunities. Welfare at home and competitiveness abroad have been the twin pillars of Scandinavian economic policy.

Scandinavia actively participates in international economic affairs, but refuses to merely adjust its domestic economies or its social structures to the whims of the international marketplace. The principles of Western capitalism have served only as a necessary means toward fulfillment of the social and political aspirations of governments that have been largely dominated by the moderate Left. Four levels of international economic relations have been the focus of external strategies for necessary material gains: the global reach, the Atlantic partnership, the European base, and the Nordic Community. During the postwar period, the European base has dominated and has involved the greatest controversy within the Scandinavian nations.

Global Reach

Like other Western economies, Scandinavia has also greatly benefited from the U.S.-sponsored postwar economic order. Scandinavia has supported the free trade doctrine of GATT, multilateral financial management through the IMF, and global development programs by the World Bank. Today, the governments have reaffirmed their faith in multilateral solutions in spite of increased pressures for regionalization and bilateralism. Often support is given to Third World demands for international reform to better reflect the political realities and the development needs of today. The value of these international organizations is not only viewed in economic terms, but also as stabilizing elements in a turbulent global political system.

Possessing strong industrial structures—and in the case of Sweden a worldwide network of multinationals—Scandinavia has favored the international trade liberalization of the GATT era. In the final phase of the Kennedy Round of the 1960s, Scandinavia formed a negotiation bloc comparable to the European Economic Community. In the Tokyo Round of the 1970s, these nations played less prominent roles as the larger trading blocs overshadowed them. Sweden has actively promoted the now concluding Uruguay Round and served in important mediating roles along the process. For example, during the final ministerial session in December 1990, Sweden chaired the committee for agriculture, the most critical of the many topics on the negotiation agenda for further trade liberalization.

In spite of strong competition from Japan and the newly industrializing countries (NICs), Scandinavia maintains an overall free-trade posture in the belief that new economic giants have more to offer as prospective customers than as fierce competitors. It is believed that deliberate up-market shifts both in production and in export profile can sustain the small, but specialized, Scandinavian manufacturers' competitive edge against the efforts of larger firms. Scandinavia's adherence to free trade and to economic globalism may well conceal the face of what is, indeed, a hard-nosed businessman.

Atlantic Partnership

The birth of the European Recovery Program (the Marshall Plan) and the advent of the Cold War signaled the rise of the Atlantic partnership in the foreign economic polices of the North. The Marshall Plan covered all the Nordic countries, except Finland. However, trade opportunities were restricted by the U.S. strategic embargo against the U.S.S.R.

Finland moved cautiously in matters of foreign trade throughout the 1950s and only joined the seemingly apolitical OECD in 1969. Finland has maintained a close trade relationship with the U.S.S.R. and has balanced its economic profile more evenly than the other European neutrals. After 1952, with the fulfillment of the burdensome obligations of war reparations—largely in the form of industrial output—to the U.S.S.R., Finland's eastern neighbor became a stable and profitable market for Finnish industry. The Soviets, in turn, supplied oil. Trade with the East has accounted for approximately 20 percent of Finland's annual trade volume and has helped balance the effects of Western markets upon Finland. For example, during the recession and rising oil prices of the 1970s, the Finnish economy experienced speedy growth. With the present economic turmoil in the U.S.S.R., this traditionally important trade relationship will likely suffer in the future.

Norway's Atlantic relationship is based upon a seafaring tradition. During the war years, the large Norwegian merchant fleet served the Allied cause. The shipping industry has brought valuable foreign currency earnings to a Norwegian economy usually beset by a trade deficit. The offshore gas and oil industry has offered important opportunities for Norway and its Atlantic partners. American oil companies were instrumental in the early exploration of the remote North Sea fields. Norwegian ownership and technical know-how has developed substantially since then, but Stavanger—Norway's oil capital—is still known for its American "colony."

The growth of the oil sector during the 1970s, when prices were high and demand steady, drastically changed the Norwegian economy and the financial base of the government. At last Norway could catch up with the traditionally superior economic levels of Sweden and Denmark, and a sense of vulnerability was transformed into great optimism. However, rising production costs combined with fluctuating prices has dampened the initial "oil fever" somewhat, and the government has had to reassess its ambitious spending plans. Still, it is expected that with gradual exploitation of oil, and mainly natural gas, in the northern waters, Norway can enjoy offshore income for perhaps a century to come.

The decade of the 1980s witnessed a new American determination to prevent the transfer of high-technology to the East. This sustained effort brought the Atlantic dimension back into prominence in international trade. The Nordic neutrals, especially, felt pressures to conform to the export regulations of the Alliance. In fact, several front-page stories headlining technology leakage through Sweden and Norway appeared in the world press with the result being tighter national controls. Finland maneuvered cautiously between its obvious desire for advanced technology and the equally pressing need to safeguard the credibility of its neutrality. Scandinavian industry to a large extent, found the new procedures cumbersome and trade restrictive. The technology control issue illustrated well the linkage between international economic relations and national security aspirations for small trade dependent nations.

Nordic Community

Before addressing the crucial and currently topical European dimension, an overview of the Nordic aspect of Scandinavian foreign economic policy is in order. The record of Nordic cooperation is indeed impressive in many respects. In the 1950s the foundations were laid through the actions of the Nordic Council that resulted in a common labor market, a passport union, and a social security union facilitating transborder moves. Many of the items in the current plan for further European Community integration have, in fact, already been implemented in Scandinavia.

In the economic sector, however, the results have been less noteworthy in comparison with the achievements of the European Community. The prospects for Nordic economic cooperation were discussed throughout the 1950s until these negotiations were overtaken by the establishment of the European Free-Trade Association (EFTA) in 1959. Intensive talks were held between 1968 and 1970 in an attempt to form a Nordic Economic Union (NORDEK) that would have advanced the region far beyond the accomplishments of the European Community at that time. Because Europe remained the preferred option for several of the nations involved, the plans for NORDEK collapsed at the very last moment. A series of agreements were concluded during the 1970s that have, in effect, completed many of the ostensible goals of the NORDEK package, yet outside of its economic core and ambitious institutional framework. Among others, a Nordic Council of Ministers with a permanent secretariat and budget, and a Nordic Investment Bank were established.

During the 1980s, industrial expansionism and production integration transcended the Nordic borders to give substance to the idea of a unified Nordic home market for local firms. The focus of demands shifted to the removal of remaining economic barriers and to further improvement of the infrastructure on a Nordic scale. Inspired by continental developments, plans for such a revitalization of Nordic economic cooperation have been promoted by the governments. A current concern is how the emerging European harmonization process will affect Nordic standards that often go beyond those expected on the Continent. A common goal is to protect regional achievements even while accepting the obvious need to move closer to the European arena.

The European Base

It has become apparent to the Nordic nations that prosperity cannot be maintained within the confines of the immediate region, or by links with distant continents. Although Scandinavians have often been reluctant Europeans, the European market remains the most important of their international economic interests. To a greater extent than other peoples, Scandinavians have refused to identify Europe with the European Economic Community, but have instead insisted upon a wider circle of members. The Scandinavian countries—and not only the neutrals—envision a Europe that stretches beyond the Öresund Straits and the Alps. Yet, the economic core of this landscape centers on Brussels, and Scandinavia, like the U.S.S.R., has had to come to terms with the European Community.

By 1972, the negotiations between the Community and the Scandinavian governments resulted in agreements. Denmark's EC membership was ratified in a referendum in October 1972, and it entered the Community together with Great Britain and Ireland in January 1973. Fifty-four percent of the Norwegian voters rejected membership in a September 1972 referendum. This surprising verdict resulted in a government crisis and in a renewal of negotiations for a free-trade agreement. An Icelandic trade agreement on industrial goods was held up until 1976 awaiting settlement of bilateral conflicts over fishing rights. Sweden abandoned hopes for membership or a customs union, but settled for a free-trade agreement. Finnish negotiations resulted in a free-trade agreement in June 1972. This, however, was not signed until the government concluded a parallel treaty with the Council for Mutual Economic Assistance (CMEA) in July 1973.

The choices of Finland and of Sweden to remain outside of the Community can be explained in terms of the desire to safeguard their neutrality. However, other motives also played a part, as illustrated by the Norwegian turn around. Certain outspoken segments of Scandinavian voters remained in opposition to the aspirations for European unification and feared supranational controls over local social and economic conditions. Such sentiments were voiced within the leading social democratic parties, and also served as a divisive element among the nonsocialist parties. The governments that did not seek membership were saved from intense domestic controversies such as those characterizing the Danish and Norwegian EC debates. Following the events of these dramatic years, Scandinavian relations with the Community, by and large, developed smoothly over the next decade.

The most obvious result of the agreements between the Scandinavians and the EC was the gradual establishment of a free-trade area. Norway has significantly increased its trade with Europe, and this trade now accounts for around 70 percent of Norwegian exports. The EFTA, as a whole, buys more from the Community than the United States and Japan combined. Finland has been the fastest-growing Scandinavian importer of EC goods. Over half of total Swedish trade is with the Community, although Sweden has also developed a major export market in the growing Norwegian economy and in the United States. Denmark's new relationship has involved far more than trade and has added a new dimension to most aspects of public policy. Particularly, the traditionally crucial agricultural sector has been affected by the Common Agricultural Policy. In addition, the costly regional development programs in Greenland have drawn on EC funds.

The nonmember states have also participated in many of the Community programs for scientific and technical research and development, and they have cooperated in the cultural and educational areas as well. For example, Sweden has been an active partner in the European Space Program and in the French-inspired EUREKA project. In contrast, they have remained outside the European Monetary System centered around a strong Deutsche Mark. With the exception of the Danes, the Scandinavians have joined Europe à la carte, that is, selectively. Critics often point out that they have gained most of the benefits of cooperation without incurring the obligation of membership.

The EFTA survived the departure of the United Kingdom and Denmark in 1973 when they joined the Common Market. Following the loss of Portugal in 1986, for the same reason, membership was reduced to six small and mostly neutral states located in Northern and in Central Europe. When the Single European Act was adopted in 1985 (see Chapter 5), it became apparent that the outsiders, not only in Scandinavia, would again have to assess their relationships with this evolving community numbering some 320 million people.

Following a joint EC-EFTA meeting in 1984, plans for a common European Economic Space (EES) were initiated. Negotiations intensified following a speech by EC Commission President Jacques Delors in January 1989. He then proposed a more structured partnership with joint decision-making and administrative institutions. It is expected that these negotiations will lead to the establishment of the EES by the time the Community Internal Market is in place.

Many Scandinavian industrial leaders have pressed for closer ties and for Community membership to ensure continued market access and participation in research and development efforts. In contrast, some labor leaders have viewed the standards and practices of a Community beset with high unemployment, continuous budget crises, and a more marked capitalist profile, with some suspicion. One major fear is that closer ties with the Community would lead to a pullback from some of the achievements of the past that benefited workers and consumers. With the rapidly changing European political scene since 1989, advocates of more intimate links with the economic and political pillar of the newly transformed Continent, the European Community, have gained momentum in the domestic political debates.

The question of membership has returned to the political agendas of Scandinavia. After some debate and hesitation, the Single European Act was approved in a Danish referendum, while some years earlier Greenland decided to withdraw from the Community. The other autonomous Danish province, the Faeroe Islands, never joined with the rest of the nation in 1973. Recently, the Danish Foreign Minister has publicly urged the other Scandinavians to become EC members and this way help form a Northern grouping within the Community. Leading Norwegians also feel the necessity for eventual membership, although one recalls with anxiety the political strife of the 1972 referendum.

In Sweden, one can note a steady drift toward deeper involvement with Europe. The traditional obstacle to membership, the policy of neutrality, is with a dramatically altered East-West context no longer seen as an absolute hindrance. A Swedish application for membership was filed in July 1991 to enable a full partnership by the mid-1990s. Finland has retained intimate bilateral ties with the Community but only joined the Council of Europe in

1989. So far, Finnish EC membership is awarded second priority compared to the promise of the sought after wider European Economic Space. However, with Swedish and Norwegian applications for membership in the offing, Finland would not remain far behind. To the Scandinavians outside the Community, the lessons of the last eighteen years in limbo seem clear. They may be reluctant, but Scandinavians are undoubtedly Europeans.

PROMOTING GLOBAL WELFARE

The Scandinavian countries are said to pursue highly progressive policies toward the Third World. The Nordic model of development assistance policy is generally characterized by annual aid volumes that—when measured as a proportion of GNP—are among the highest in the industrial world. A sizable portion of this aid is free from any donor country purchase requirements. The least developed nations have received special consideration and rural projects with long-term development effects have been emphasized. Humanitarian assistance to national liberation groups in southern Africa and support of so-called progressive regimes has been given. For good reasons, the Nordic image has been one of progressive, generous, and committed partners in the global development process.

Yet, a more careful examination reveals that each Nordic state has established a distinct development policy. In contrast to most prominent development aid-granting countries, the Nordic nations lack a significant colonial heritage. Their unusually high aid commitment cannot be explained by previous colonial ties or by the strategic interests of a major power. Rather, the domestic experiences of peaceful political development during the last century of significant and rapid socioeconomic change have heavily influenced current attitudes toward economic and social progress in less developed countries. The successful Nordic transformation from poor, rural societies to highly advanced, postindustrial nations has also helped to form dominant political attitudes toward global development problems. The strength and political prominence of the Scandinavian labor movement has also shaped government views on socioeconomic progress and international solidarity.

Like other Western nations, the Nordic commitment to development assistance began with the founding of the United Nations Technical Aid Program (EPTA) in 1949. By 1952, three of the Nordic countries were also involved in bilateral programs. Finland remained outside of these developments during the first half of the 1950s, but after membership in the United Nations in 1955, it became more actively involved and in 1957 entered into a limited bilateral cooperation program with India. Even Iceland, a net recipient of foreign assistance until 1976, has expanded its development assistance cooperation program over the past twenty years.

Important growth for Nordic development policies ensued during the 1960s. Official program objectives were presented, new assistance agencies were created, and the one percent of GNP target for development was introduced. Multilateral aid still figured prominently as the best channel for assistance and was, perhaps, the only feasible way to spend the quickly growing funds. Scandinavian support of the U.N. development effort is still very significant compared to most states. Together, the Scandinavian countries provide about one-fourth of the funds for the U.N. Development Program (UNDP), as well as disproportionally high sums for such other agencies as the FAO, WHO, and UNICEF. The creation of new national agencies for bilateral aid, more explicit development criteria, and greater interest in the possible economic consequences from such massive outflows of assistance have shifted domestic attention to bilateral programs.

Over time, the Nordic development assistance policies matured into a common approach that differed from the prevailing standards of the OECD countries in several respects. First, the great bulk of the assistance was given as outright grants rather than in the form of loans. The emphasis was on a few program countries selected for their potential for fulfilling certain assistance objectives. Preferences of the recipient nation formed a major part in determining the focus for bilateral aid. A substantial share of the transfer consisted of untied grants for import financing. The dominant part of all aid was, in fact, unrestricted and could be used for local needs, such as health and educational program. Both in the receiving and donor country, a clear differentiation was made between assistance and export financing.

Scandinavians have earned considerable worldwide respect for high quality development aid policies. This profile complements Scandinavian support in international forums for such Third World demands as the proposal for a New International Economic Order. The designation 'Like-Minded Countries' was coined during the 1970s to depict Scandinavia, together with Holland, as Third World partners in the effort to reform the global system through multilateral negotiations in several arenas. The international stature of these small states has grown as a result of this positive record.

Nordic development assistance policies, a traditionally protected policy area, seem to have become more integrated with the overall economic and commercial objectives of these nations. The distinction between assistance and trade is far less clear today. In Scandinavia, it is more accepted now than in the past that such global resource transfers may also bring benefits to the donor. The net cost of these impressive programs is reduced considerably through the type of measures adopted recently. In two controversial decisions, Sweden's Social Democratic Government reallocated 1 billion Swedish crowns (approximately $180 million) from the traditional development assistance targets to the fledgling democracies of Eastern Europe. It also used 300 million Swedish crowns of the general development cooperation budget to support the increasingly expensive refugee resettlement program in Sweden. Perhaps such cost-conscious development assistance innovations are necessary to uphold the famed one percent of GDP target.

TRANSPOSING THE DOMESTIC EXPERIENCE

This chapter has shown how the surrounding favorable international setting has influenced the development of postwar Scandinavian foreign relations. This element, conducive to the security, the prosperity, and the global stature of these five small states, also helps explain their diverse foreign policies. Within this external context, unique historical experiences and distinct domestic features have shaped each national foreign policy profile. For reasons of space, limited attention has been paid to the domestic influences upon foreign policy formulation. However, rapid socioeconomic transformation, the peaceful emergence of stable democracies, the growth of the active state responsible for public welfare and economic management, technological innovations, and cultural changes during the last century have profoundly affected the external relations of these societies.[2]

The approach to international affairs in many ways reflects the salient features of Scandinavian domestic life. An examination of the internal dynamics of these states, then, is essential in understanding the external objectives and the strategies selected to attain them. Clearly, Scandinavian hopes for global understanding, nonviolent solutions to security dilemmas, and adherence to principles of international law and organization are inspired by the comparatively tranquil regional developments during the last century. The quest for global solidarity parallels the ideals of the influential Scandinavian labor movement. The belief in managed market solutions to international economic problems draws upon successful experiences at home that have combined economic growth with shared affluence. The international bridge building aspirations reflect the dynamics of national consensus formation, whereby sector demands are transformed into broad coalitions composed of leading parties and interest groups.

In most states, whether large or small, the domestic experience is readily transposed upon the international arena in the belief that conditions abroad are sufficiently similar to allow for such analogies. For example, the so-called American way of life has, at times, been promoted as a model for the conduct of very complex international political and economic relations.

Scandinavian efforts to project their national experiences on the world arena have less impact on world politics than the behavior by a superpower. But, after surveying the foreign policies of these five unusually civil states, advocates of world order and justice may regret the limited attention the international community has paid to the Scandinavian foreign policy experience.

---

[2] Students wanting to pursue the domestic dimension of the Scandinavian experience are referred to the chapter on Scandinavia in Professor Macridis's companion volume, *Modern Political Systems: Europe,* 7th ed. (Englewood Cliffs, N.J.: Prentice-Hall, 1990.)

FOREIGN POLICY LANDMARKS

1948–49	Establishment of the postwar Nordic security pattern: Denmark, Iceland, Norway join NATO; Finland concludes a mutual cooperation pact with the U.S.S.R.; Sweden pursues freedom from alliances
1951	The pattern of postwar Nordic Security is completed by the U.S.–Icelandic agreement on the status of the Keflavik base
1952	The Nordic Council is established, and it is followed with conventions on a passport union, a common labor market, and a social security union. A mandate to explore the potential for a Nordic Common Market is given
1955	The Soviet Union withdraws from Finnish soil, and Finland joins the United Nations and the Nordic Council
1956	Urho Kekkonen becomes president of Finland
1959	EFTA is established and inter-Nordic trade grows significantly
1961	The Finnish-Soviet Note Crisis. Danish, Norwegian, and Swedish applications to the European Economic Community
1962	The Nordic commitments are manifested in the 1962 Helsinki Agreement on Nordic Cooperation. The national development assistance programs begin
1963	The Kekkonen plan for a Nordic nuclear weapons free zone is launched
1968	A Danish initiative for a Nordic Economic Union (NORDEK) is initiated
1969	First major oil discovery in Norway
1970	Iceland joins EFTA; NORDEK plan fails
1970–73	Relations with the EEC are adjusted; the Nordic commitments are strengthened through the establishment of a Nordic Council of Ministers, joint Secretariats, and additional Nordic conventions
1973	Denmark joins the EEC; Iceland, Norway, and Sweden conclude free trade agreements. Finland concludes an economic cooperation agreement with CMEA and a free trade agreement with the EEC
1975	A thirty-five nation summit meeting in Finland results in the Helsinki Accords on Security and Cooperation in Europe (CSCE); Norway becomes a net exporter of oil
1979	The NATO "dual track" decision on intermediate-range nuclear forces (INF) deployments is followed by a prolonged Scandinavian debate over the merits of a Nordic nuclear weapon-free zone
1981	The Kekkonen era comes to an end in Finland; the first Soviet submarine incident in Sweden—'Whiskey on the Rocks'—is followed by further territorial violations and Swedish diplomatic protests
1984–86	The Stockholm Conference on Disarmament in Europe, when a thirty-five nation agreement on confidence building measures is concluded
1985	Greenland leaves the European Economic Community
1986	Swedish Prime Minister Olof Palme is assassinated. He is succeeded by Ingvar Carlsson who visits Moscow in 1986 and Washington in 1987

The radiation contamination from the Chernobyl nuclear accident in the Soviet Union sparks increased awareness in the Nordic region concerning transnational environmental threats to security

1988   Prime Minister Nikolai Ryzhkov of the Soviet Union visits Stockholm and signs an agreement to resolve the long-standing dispute between Sweden and Soviet Union concerning economic and fishing rights in the so-called 'White Zone' in the Baltic Sea. A similar Norwegian-Soviet dispute in the Barents Sea remains unresolved

1989   Following an invitation from EC Commission President Delors, the EFTA countries begin intensified negotiations with the EC concerning the establishment of the EES. The newly developed Swedish fighter aircraft, the JAS-39 Gripen, crashes upon landing after its second flight and sparks renewed debate concerning the future of Sweden's military industrial base. President Mikhail Gorbachev visits Helsinki and officially acknowledges Finland's neutral status

1990   The Baltic Sea Environment Conference issues the "Baltic Sea Declaration," which mandates a joint comprehensive program for the decisive reduction of emissions into the Baltic Sea. The foreign ministers of Estonia, Latvia, and Lithuania meet with their Nordic counterparts in Copenhagen to discuss the establishment of 'information offices' in Copenhagen and Stockholm. The U.S.-Soviet summit meeting over the Persian Gulf crisis is held in Helsinki

SELECTED BIBLIOGRAPHY

The primary academic journal devoted to Scandinavian foreign relations is the quarterly *Cooperation and Conflict*, published since 1965. The Nordic Political Science Associations sponsor *Scandinavian Political Studies*, formerly a yearbook, but since 1978 a quarterly. Some major Scandinavian language journals are also important: *Internasjonal Politikk* is published by the Norwegian Institute of International Affairs, *Internationella Studier* by the Swedish Institute of International Affairs, and *Ulkopolitiikka* by the Finnish Institute of International Affairs. The Norwegian Institute of International Affairs publishes valuable articles and documentation in the annual *Norsk Utenrikspolitisk Årbog*. The Finnish counterpart is the *Yearbook of Finnish Foreign Policy*. The Danish Institute of International Affairs publishes the annual *Dansk Udenrigspolitisk Årbog*. The Swedish version is titled *Fred och säkerhet*. *International Studies in the Nordic Countries*, a biannual newsletter published by the Nordic Cooperation Committee for International Politics, Stockholm, is the best source to follow current research, workshops, conferences, and publications in the field.

General Overviews and Regional Relations

Andersson, Stanley. *The Nordic Council: A Study in Scandinavian Regionalism*. Seattle, Wash.: University of Washington Press, 1967.

Andrén, Nils. *Power Balance and Non-Alignment: A Perspective on Swedish Foreign Policy*. Stockholm: Almqvist & Wiksell, 1967.

Berner, Örjan. *Soviet Policies toward the Nordic Countries*. Lanham, Md.: University Press of America, 1986.

Cole, Wayne. *Norway and the United States 1905–1955*. Ames: Iowa State University Press, 1989.

Essays on Finnish Foreign Policy. Helsinki: Finnish Political Science Association, 1969.

Hakovirta, Harto. *East-West Conflict and European Neutrality.* Oxford: Oxford University Press, 1988.

Haskel, Barbara. *The Scandinavian Option: Opportunities and Opportunity Costs in Postwar Scandinavian Foreign Policies.* Oslo: Norwegian Universities Press, 1976.

Heisler, Martin, ed. "The Nordic Region: Changing Perspectives in International Relations," *The Annals of the American Academy of Political and Social Science,* Vol. 512, Newbury Park, Calif.: Sage, November 1990.

Holst, Johan Jörgen, ed. *Norwegian Foreign Policy in the 1980s.* Oslo: Norwegian Universities Press, 1985.

Holterman, Henrik. *Danish Foreign Policy: Literature in Languages other than Danish 1979–1986.* Copenhagen: Danish Institute of International Affairs, 1988.

Jakobson, Max. *Finnish Neutrality.* London: Hugh Evelyn, 1968.

——, *Finland: Myth and Reality.* Helsinki: Otava, 1987.

Karsh, Efraim. *Neutrality and Small States.* London: Routledge, 1988.

Lindgren, Raymond. *Norway-Sweden: Union, Disunion and Scandinavian Integration.* Princeton, N.J.: Princeton University Press, 1959.

Lundestad, Geir. *America, Scandinavia and the Cold War 1945–49.* New York: Columbia University Press, 1980.

Odom, Jr., Donald. *Swedish Foreign Policy Behavior: An Event Data Analysis.* Stockholm International Studies 90:2, Stockholm: International Graduate School, 1990.

Scott, Franklin. *Scandinavia.* Cambridge, Mass.: Harvard University Press, 1975.

Stenelo, Lars-Göran. *The International Critic.* Lund: Studentlitteratur, 1984.

Sundelius, Bengt. *Managing Transnationalism in Northern Europe.* Boulder, Colo.: Westview Press, 1978.

——, ed. *Foreign Policies of Northern Europe.* Boulder, Colo.: Westview Press, 1982.

——, ed. *The Committed Neutral: Sweden's Foreign Policy.* Boulder, Colo: Westview Press, 1989.

Väyrynen, Raimo. *Stability and Change in Finnish Foreign Policy.* Helsinki: Department of Political Science, University of Helsinki, 1986.

Wendt, Frantz. *Cooperation in the Nordic Countries.* Stockholm: Almqvist & Wiksell, 1981.

Security Policy

Allison, Roy. *Finland's Relations with the Soviet Union, 1944–1984.* London: Macmillan, 1985.

Bjøl, Erling. *Nordic Security,* Adelphi Papers, No. 181. London: International Institute for Strategic Studies, 1983.

Cole, Paul, and Douglas Hart, eds. *Northern Europe: Security Issues for the 1990s.* Boulder, Colo.: Westview Press, 1986.

Einhorn, Eric. *National Security and Domestic Politics in Postwar Denmark: Some Principal Issues 1945–1961.* Odense: Odense University Press, 1975.

Flynn, Gregory, ed. *NATO's Northern Allies.* London: Croom Helm, 1985.

Gröndal, Benedikt. *Iceland from Neutrality to NATO Membership.* Oslo: Norwegian Universities Press, 1971.

Lindahl, Ingemar. *The Soviet Union and the Nordic Nuclear-Weapons-Free-Zone Proposal.* London: Macmillian, 1988.

Maude, George. *The Finnish Dilemma: Neutrality in the Shadow of Power.* London: Oxford University Press, 1976.

"Nordic Security Today." Special issue of *Cooperation and Conflict,* Vol. 17, No. 4 (1982).

Nuechterlein, Donald. *Iceland, Reluctant Ally.* Westport, Conn.: Greenwood Press, 1961.

Ries, Tomas. *Cold Will: The Defense of Finland.* London: Brassey's, 1988.

Sundelius, Bengt, ed. *The Neutral Democracies and the New Cold War.* Boulder, Colo.: Westview Press, 1987.

Väyrynen, Raimo. *Conflicts in Finnish-Soviet Relations: Three Comparative Case Studies.* Tampere: Tampere University, 1972.

Vloyantes, John. *Silk Glove Hegemony; Finnish-Soviet Relations 1944–1974.* Kent, Ohio: Kent State University Press, 1975.

International Economic and Development Policy

Allen, Hilary. *Norway and Europe in the 1970s.* Oslo: Norwegian Universities Press, 1979.

Carlsnaes, Walter. *Energy Vulnerability and National Security: The Energy Crises, Domestic Policy Responses and the Logic of Swedish Neutrality.* London: Pinter, 1988.

Dohlman, Ebba. *National Welfare and Economic Interdependence: The Case of Sweden's Trade Policy.* Oxford: Oxford University Press, 1989.

Frühling, Pierre, ed. *Swedish Development Aid in Perspective.* Stockholm: Almqvist & Wiksell, 1986.

Hancock, Donald, ed. "Scandinavia and the European Community," Special issue of *Scandinavian Studies,* Vol. 46, No. 4 (1974).

Huldt, Bo. "The Nordic Countries and the New International Economic Order: Consensus and Disagreement within the Nordic Group," *Cooperation and Conflict,* Vol. 14, No. 2–3 (1979), pp. 149–57.

Miljan, Toivo. *The Reluctant Europeans: The Attitudes of the Nordic Countries Towards European Integration.* London: Hurst, 1977.

Möttölä Kari and Heikki Patomäki, eds. *Facing the Change in Europe: EFTA Countries' Integration Strategies.* Helsinki: The Finnish Institute of International Affairs, 1989.

"Nordic Aid to Underdeveloped Countries." Special issue of *Cooperation and Conflict,* Vol. 5, No. 2 (1970).

"Petroleum and International Relations: The Case of Norway." Special issue of *Cooperation and Conflict,* Vol. 27, No. 2 (1982).

Robson, Peter, ed. "The European Community, EFTA and the New Europe: Changing Dimensions of Economic Integration in Europe." Special issue of *Journal of Common Market Studies,* Vol. 28, No. 4 (1990).

Sjöstedt, Gunnar. *Sweden's Free Trade Policy: Balancing Economic Growth and Security.* Stockholm: The Swedish Institute, 1987.

Underdal, Arild. *The Politics of Fisheries Management: The Case of the Northeast Atlantic.* Oslo: Norwegian Universities Press, 1980.

The Foreign Policy Process

Burgess, Philip. *Elite Images and Foreign Policy Outcomes.* Columbus, Ohio: Ohio State University Press, 1968.

Dörfer, Ingemar. *System 37 Viggen: Arms, Technology and the Domesticization of Glory.* Oslo: Norwegian Universities Press, 1973.

Goldmann, Kjell, et al. *Democracy and Foreign Policy: The Case of Sweden.* Aldershot, England: Gower, 1986.

Hart, Thomas. *The Cognitive World of Swedish Security Elites.* Stockholm: Esselte, 1976.

Hveem, Helge. *International Relations and World Images: A Study of Norwegian Foreign Policy Elites.* Oslo: Norwegian Universities Press, 1972.

Karvonen, Lauri and Bengt Sundelius. *Internationalization and Foreign Policy Management.* Aldershot, England: Gower, 1987.

Mouritzen, Hans. *Finlandization: Towards a General Theory of Adaptive Politics.* Aldershot, England: Gower, 1988.

Örvik, Nils. *Departmental Decision Making.* Oslo: Norwegian Universities Press, 1972.

Taylor, William and Paul Cole, eds. *Nordic Defense: Comparative Decision Making.* Lexington, Mass.: Lexington Books, 1985.

–11–

THE
FOREIGN POLICY
OF
AFRICA

Stephen Wright

INTRODUCTION

The African continent has traditionally stood at the periphery of world politics and the global economy. Despite the fact that the continent accounts for almost one-third of the membership of the United Nations (fifty-two states, not including the Saharawi Arab Democratic Republic), some 600 million people, and twelve million square miles of territory, or 20 percent of the world's land mass, African states, with few exceptions, have been able to exert little sustained influence upon world events. Explanations for this are relatively straightforward. Centuries of slavery and colonialism distorted and under-mined Africa's economic development, and the continent has fared little better in the postcolonial era. Twenty-seven of the world's poorest forty countries as defined by the World Bank are African, with annual GNP per capita earnings of less than $450. Colonialism also altered territorial boundaries within the continent, producing artificial states with little domestic cohesion. Independence brought serious internal and regional strains, thereby further min-imizing aspirations of a potential world role.

Besides containing some of the poorest countries, Africa also is essential-ly the "newest" continent. In 1945, only four African states (Egypt, Ethiopia, Liberia, and South Africa) were independent and eligible for membership in the United Nations (U.N.). Formal independence rippled across the continent from North Africa in the early 1950s, to West Africa in the late 1950s and early 1960s, to East Africa in the early and mid-1960s, and then finally to Southern Africa in the 1970s and 1980s. This "newness" makes it difficult to distinguish patterns of foreign policy over time, and also results in energies being diverted to nation-building and other domestic issues, rather than being dissipated on global issues over which most African states have little or no influence.

Demographic factors also help to explain Africa's limited economic and political status on the world stage. Although accounting for approximately one-third of the world's countries, the continent accounts for less than one-tenth of the global population, a fact partly attributed to, but not wholly explained by, dramatic depopulation during the slave trade era.[1] A single country, Nigeria, contributes approximately 20 percent of the continent's population, so one can conclude that there are many small countries in the continent. In fact, twenty-five countries have populations of less than ten million. In addition to this, most countries are unable to generate sufficient economic production, and food in particular, to sustain their citizens, a problem exacerbated by rapid population growth. The U.N. estimates that virtually all African states will double their populations within the next twenty years. Relative decline in agricultural production and perverse climatic conditions in many parts of the continent deepen the challenges facing these countries.

Although Africa is geographically a single entity, it is politically and culturally heterogeneous. The normal division of the continent is provided by the Sahara desert, bringing together the Maghreb states of the predominantly Islamic north, and combining the rest to the south as Sub-Saharan or Black Africa. Africans (including Arab Africans) have themselves struggled to bridge this physical divide, notably in the Organization of African Unity (OAU), although with mixed results. Sub-Saharan Africa is by no means a homogeneous unit, however, as religious, ethnic, linguistic, and colonial factors all serve to emphasize diversity. Sub-Saharan Africa has attempted to forge unified policies and programs through the development of regional organizations such as the Economic Community of West African States (ECOWAS), the Southern African Development Coordination Conference (SADCC), and the Preferential Trade Area (PTA) for Eastern Africa. These organizations have striven to harmonize economic and, at times, foreign policies primarily within their respective regions, and have deferred to the OAU or the Group of Seventy-Seven to coordinate African policies at continental and global levels.

It is important to consider briefly the colonial and early independence eras in order to assess the impact of events in those periods on contemporary foreign policy issues.

---

[1] Walter Rodney, *How Europe Underdeveloped Africa* (London: Bogle L'Ouverture, 1972).

COLONIALISM AND INDEPENDENCE

During the European colonial era of the last 300 years or so, Africa has been a victim of its own weakness to resist external intervention. But foreign conquest of the continent should not obscure the fact that Africa has a proud cultural history: The Pharaohs of Egypt; the Sudanic civilization; the Carthaginian empire; Great Zimbabwe; the sophisticated educational and cultural metropolis of Timbuctu; the renowned cultural artifacts of the Benin Empire; all these and many others point to an illustrious past that was misunderstood and, in any case, ignored when Europeans "discovered" the "dark continent."[2] In fact, one thousand years of Islamic influence prior to European intervention had left a significant legacy, one that is most obviously seen today with half of Africa's population being Muslim.

Because of the perceived climatic and health hazards to Europeans inside the African interior, colonial trade developed around coastal margins, initially dealing in slaves and then turning to exploit other commodities through ports such as Freetown, Lagos, Luanda, and Mombasa. The Portuguese predated, but were soon displaced by, British, French, and German interests that expanded rapidly in the second half of the nineteenth century.[3] European names such as the "Gold Coast" (Ghana), the "Slave Coast," and the "Ivory Coast" indicated the exploitative nature of the colonial presence, even though missionary zeal and the belief in the "white man's burden" provided rationalizations.

Only 10 percent of the continent was under direct European control in 1870, but by the end of the century only 10 percent remained outside it.[4] This "scramble for Africa" as it is often labelled was prompted by a mix of economic and political motivations among competing European powers and was facilitated by a conference of European powers held in Berlin in 1884–85. During this conference, European leaders set out the ground rules for the partition of Africa based upon what was termed "effective occupation"—whenever a European power occupied a parcel of land it could legitimately integrate that territory into its empire. This policy, taken without any African input, proved disastrous for Africa because it led to the dissection of the continent without consideration of indigenous factors, and consequently helped to produce a postcolonial continent of unstable, artificial, and relatively meaningless state entities.

In the early twentieth century, the colonizers restructured African economies to serve European rather than African interests and integrated African markets into the global division of labor. The rapid construction of commodity export economies (cash crops and minerals) was undertaken, as

---

[2] A useful introduction is Roland Oliver and J.D. Fage, *A Short History of Africa* (Harmondsworth: Penguin, 1975).

[3] Prosser Gifford and William Roger Louis, *France and Britain in Africa: Imperial Rivalry and Colonial Rule* (New Haven: Yale University Press, 1971).

[4] See Chapters 2 and 6 in Immanuel Wallerstein, *Africa and the Modern World* (Trenton, N.J.: Africa World Press, 1986).

exemplified by groundnut, cocoa and oil palm in Nigeria; cocoa in Ghana and Cameroon; cotton in Benin and Burkina Faso; coffee in Uganda, Kenya, and Tanzania; tobacco in Zimbabwe; and ores in Liberia, Guinea, and Sierra Leone. Furthermore, large-scale plantations employing coerced African labor became widespread, and the influx of significant numbers of European settlers in Eastern and Southern Africa (and Algeria) altered sociopolitical structures with serious repercussions witnessed up to the present day.

European colonists exported their own struggles to the African continent (part of Bismarck's grand design) and eventually involved their respective empires in both world wars. After the First World War, Germany's colonies (Togo, Cameroon, Tanganyika and South-West Africa) were confiscated by Britain, France, and South Africa, a process semilegitimized by calling them League of Nations' "mandates." This war stimulated African nationalism, but it was to be the Second World War that led directly to "mass" nationalism, the call for self-determination and eventual independence. Political tactics varied, but movements in most countries challenged head-on colonial supremacy, and led initially, if briefly, to repression of African leaderships by colonial authorities. Nationalist groups also coordinated their activities at Pan-African conferences, helping to develop an embryonic continentalism to be consolidated in the OAU. In some states, such as Algeria, Kenya, and Zimbabwe (and currently South Africa), where considerable European settler populations were present, the nationalist movements had little option but to resort to violence to dislodge the colonists.

The pattern of decolonization differed considerably from empire to empire. President Charles de Gaulle of France attempted in the late 1950s to slow or freeze the decolonization process by offering the colonies equal status with France within a community arrangement. Guinea opted out of this scheme and took full independence in 1958; more than a dozen other Francophone countries followed suit in 1960. Britain, in contrast, developed a typically more pragmatic style of decolonization, granting independence whenever a country was "ready." Both France and Britain had their problems, such as with Algeria and Zimbabwe, respectively. De Gaulle's resolute action allowed Algeria to gain its independence in 1962, but British hesitancy and reluctance to act against white settlers allowed the Zimbabwean war to drag on for over a decade, and independence was only eventually finalized in 1980.

Despite occasional problems, British and French decolonization went relatively smoothly in contrast to the disasters of Belgian and Portuguese experiences. Within days of Belgium leaving the Congo in 1960, a civil war broke out that exacerbated superpower rivalries and drew in large U.N. military forces in ONUC (U.N. Operation in the Congo). The overthrow of Patrice Lumumba by right-wing forces with Western connivance incensed many African leaders and increased their resolve to exclude foreign forces from the continent in future. Equally chaotic was the Portuguese withdrawal from Mozambique and Angola (and also Guinea-Bissau) in 1975, following a long war of attrition,[5] and the subsequent intervention of South African, Cuban, Soviet, and American interests. These internal wars have still not been fully resolved.

Unfortunately for most African states, formal political independence has not equated with economic independence, because European companies and governments have maintained very strong and, at times, domineering ties with local businesses throughout the continent. Radical opposition by intellectuals, such as Cabral, Fanon, Ngugi wa Thiongo, Soyinka, and Achebe, to the perpetuation of neocolonial economic and cultural[6] domination has been ineffectual as political power continues to reside in the hands of those leaders comfortable with the maintenance of these relationships.

THE RESOURCES OF AFRICA

Resource endowments are unequally spread within the continent, and so some governments have wider policy alternatives open to them than others.[7] In terms of demographics, most countries have small populations primarily located in rural areas, and consequently relatively low economic bases. Literacy levels are rarely over 40 percent, and skilled labor is also often in short supply; life expectancy averages fifty years. Half of the continent's population is below the age of eighteen years of age; half of the continent's adult population is expected to be unemployed by the year 2000.

One-quarter of the continent's countries are landlocked, so providing infrastructural and political problems for trade routes to the outside world. Diversity in physical size is also significant, ranging from very large states such as Algeria, Angola, Chad, Mali, and Sudan, to very small states such as Burundi, Cape Verde, Djibouti, Equatorial Guinea, Gambia, Guinea Bissau, and Rwanda. Mineral deposits appear to be randomly scattered about the continent, but countries (particularly in the south) such as Botswana, Namibia, South Africa, and Zambia are well-endowed, whereas others such as Burkina Faso, Kenya, and Mali are almost completely deficient. Strategic minerals such as gold (South Africa), diamonds (Angola, Botswana, Namibia, Sierra Leone, South Africa, and Zaire), chromium (South Africa and Zimbabwe), cobalt (Zaire and Zambia), copper (Zaire and Zambia), and uranium (Niger) are found in large quantities, providing these countries potential leverage in the world economic system. Oil is also found in large quantities in Algeria, Angola, Cameroon,

---

[5] Arslan Humbaraci and Nicole Muchnik, *Portugal's African Wars* (New York: Third Press, 1974).

[6] For interesting discussions of the politicization of African literature see Ngugi wa Thiong'o, *Barrel of a Pen: Resistance to Repression in Neo-Colonial Kenya* (London: New Beacon Books, 1983); Dennis Austin, *Politics in Africa*, 2nd ed. (Hanover: University Press of New England, 1984), Chap. 6; and Christian P. Potholm, *The Theory and Practice of African Politics* (Englewood Cliffs, N.J.: Prentice-Hall, 1979), Chap. 4.

[7] Mohamed T. El-Ashry and Dorsey Burger, "Population, Resources and Famine in Sub-Saharan Africa" in Robert I. Rotberg, ed., *Africa in the 1990s and Beyond* (Algonac, Michigan: World Peace Foundation, 1988), pp. 112–138.

Congo, Gabon, Libya, and Nigeria, a very important factor in these countries' foreign policies. However, the continent as a whole is chronically dependent upon commodity exports: forty-one African states rely for 60 percent or more of their export earnings on just two commodities.

The differing climatic conditions within the continent also have an impact on national development plans. Increasing desertification and environmental degradation in the Sahelian region, for example, has reduced agriculturally productive land and undermined economic bases. When endemic internal unrest is added to natural catastrophe, such as in Burkina Faso, Chad, Ethiopia, Somalia and Sudan, it is easy to understand why these countries exert little influence beyond (and often inside) their own borders.

Industrial development remains limited in many countries, promoting dependence upon imported manufactured goods and machinery. South Africa has traditionally produced industrial output roughly equivalent to the rest of the continent combined. Within regions, the development of "subimperial" industrial centers such as Nigeria for West Africa and Kenya for East Africa has often deterred foreign investment from poorer neighboring countries, and so hampered industrial productivity there. The expansion of regional markets has been encouraged in an attempt to tackle the problem of minuscule competing national markets, but cooperative industrial strategies have been slow to develop, primarily because of political rivalry and suspicion. Indigenous military production is very limited, with only Egypt, Nigeria and South Africa having mentionable capabilities, although South Africa's is considerable, with alleged nuclear capabilities. Armed forces within the continent are generally small, except for Egypt and South Africa (and Libya), whose forces are swollen by geopolitical demands.

Independence generated considerable optimism about Africa's political and economic future, but over the last three decades much of that initial hope and enthusiasm has evaporated. Industrialization and agricultural strategies have largely failed, irrespective of the ideology pursued; productivity has not matched population growth; decreasing terms of trade combined with increasing debt repayments have left much of the continent destitute; and foreign transnational corporations (TNCs) have tended to retain control of African markets, despite widespread indigenization and nationalization policies. Africa undoubtedly faces a serious economic crisis.[8]

Africa's external debt is small compared with Latin America's. For example, the two largest debtors, Egypt and Nigeria, owe $40 billion and $30 billion respectively, and the continent's total debt stands at about $230 billion, equivalent to Brazil's and Mexico's combined. But in relation to Africa's export earnings capabilities, the debt burden is crippling. During the last decade, Africa's policy agenda in the global arena appears to have been dominated by

---

[8] Adebayo Adedeji and Timothy M. Shaw, eds., *Economic Crisis in Africa: African Perspectives on Development Problems and Potentials* (Boulder: Lynne Rienner, 1985); Stephen K. Commins, ed., *Africa's Development Challenges and the World Bank* (Boulder: Lynne Rienner, 1988).

the need to promote workable development strategies[9] and secure debt rescheduling agreements, and plans to concert action on debts have been mooted in both the OAU and the U.N.'s Economic Commission for Africa (ECA). Currently half of the continent is engaged in structural adjustment programs instigated by the World Bank and International Monetary Fund (IMF). These programs may provide long-term solutions, but in the short-term are causing intense political and socioeconomic problems. These programs are also helping to denationalize indigenous economies by requiring states to privatize industries and increase foreign investment and ownership. However, in the post-Cold War era of the 1990s, with exciting economic prospects developing in Europe, the superpowers and the European Community (EC) appear less interested in Africa, and consequently the continent stands to become further marginalized in global political and economic affairs.

FOREIGN POLICY DECISION MAKING

Little scholarly work has been undertaken to explain foreign policy decision-making processes within African states. This is because information regarding these processes is very difficult for scholars to obtain and can often be dangerous for indigenous scholars to use. Attempts to utilize ethnocentric western models have shed some light on African processes, but in recent years have not advanced our knowledge. With these points in mind, one can attempt to piece together a general picture of African foreign policy formulation.

There is a consensus among scholars that a narrow elite group is involved in strategic decision making, and that normally the head of state personally will make such decisions. Foreign policy is often conducted not for the benefit of the country per se, but rather for the benefit of the decision-making elite, especially where foreign economic policies are involved. Elite groups dominate the state apparatus, which in turn controls domestic economic structures within a corporatist framework.[10] This process is facilitated by the non-democratic structures of the overwhelming majority of African states, the general absence of what could be classed as effective "public opinion," and the strong governmental control exerted over the media. Even in states with a relatively vibrant media, such as Kenya or Nigeria, implicit (or explicit) threats are made toward the media to temper criticism, and little input into the foreign policy arena is made. It would be wrong, however, to simply typify all decision making within the "great man/leader" approach, because advisors, diplomats, business and military groups, and general bureaucratic procedures are routine-

---

[9] Robert J. Berg and Jennifer Seymour Whitaker, eds., *Strategies for African Development* (Berkeley and Los Angeles: University of California Press, 1986); World Bank, *Sub-Saharan Africa: From Crisis to Sustainable Growth* (Washington D.C.: World Bank, 1989); and UNECA, *African Alternative Framework to Structural Adjustment Programmes for Socio-Economic Recovery and Transformation* (Addis Ababa: ECA, 1989).

[10] Julius E. Nyang'oro and Timothy M. Shaw, eds., *Corporatism in Africa: Comparative Analysis and Practice* (Boulder: Westview Press, 1989).

ly involved in policy making, although the specific extent is unclear and varies by decision and country.[11]

An attempt to measure the "quality" of decision making and the personnel of government is naturally subjective and problematical and must take account of considerable national differences. Nevertheless, some general conclusions can be formulated. Partly because of the authoritarian nature of most regimes, African states possess some of the world's most experienced and long-serving leaders. Those with more than twenty years in office include Houphouët-Boigny of Côte d'Ivoire, Mobutu of Zaire, Banda of Malawi, Eyadéma of Togo, Hassan of Morocco, Qaddafi of Libya, Siad Barre of the Somali Republic (overthrown in January 1991), and Kaunda of Zambia; ten years in office is mere commonplace. Of course, experience and success are not synonymous. The scarce financial and human resources of most states limit the numbers of diplomatic personnel that can be posted around the world, and so consequently lessen the flow of accurate information on which to base foreign policy decisions. By way of contrast, authoritarianism can also bring instability, and in countries such as Burkina Faso, Chad, and Uganda, governmental tenure has been considerably shorter and less decisive, and so foreign policy patterns have been even more difficult to establish.

Another interlinked factor is that more than half of the continent is controlled by military, or quasi-military, governments. Are foreign policies of military governments in Africa inherently different from those of civilian governments? Little investigation has been undertaken to answer this specific question, but evidence suggests that just as military governments have not been any more successful at promoting economic development than civilian ones, in foreign policy matters they have not fared better or worse than their civilian counterparts. This is easier to judge in countries that have fluctuated between civilian and military governments, such as Ghana, Nigeria, or Uganda, and there is no evidence from these to suggest that one type of regime fares better in foreign policy matters than another.

A serious problem afflicting African leadership is corruption, defined here simply as the misuse of public office for private gain. Corruption is present in governments throughout the world, but in Africa it takes on ominous proportions. Concrete evidence on corruption is obviously difficult to obtain, but information does exist, for example, on the role of the "Kenyatta Royal Family" in Kenya; of the $5–10 billion skimmed from the Zairean treasury by President Mobutu since 1965; of the ability of President Felix Houphouët-Boigny in Côte d'Ivoire to build a cathedral bigger than St. Peter's from his own "personal" funds; or the looting of billions of dollars from the Nigerian treasury by successive military and civilian regimes. Such corruption has damaging effects on a country's ability to implement successfully its

[11]See Robert H. Jackson and Carl G. Rosberg, *Personal Rule in Black Africa* (Berkeley and Los Angeles: University of California Press, 1982); also Bahgat Korany, ed., *How Foreign Policy Decisions Are Made in the Third World* (Boulder: Westview Press, 1986); and Peter Calvert, *The Foreign Policy of New States* (Brighton: Wheatsheaf Books, 1986).

development programs and also skews foreign relations to liaise with countries, institutions, or businesses that will be accomplices in such activities. Western governments and financial institutions, such as the World Bank and IMF, have emphasized economic, strategic, and political relations with Africa rather than democratic and human rights during the last thirty years, and so have contributed to such corruption. In the 1990s, this pattern may be changing, and greater emphasis on probity and democracy could provide a new dimension to foreign relations between African states and their dominant Northern patrons.

FOREIGN POLICY OBJECTIVES

What have been the objectives of African foreign policies since the early 1960s, and what factors have helped to shape these objectives? Again, there are naturally differences from country to country, but a general overview of objectives can be discerned. Perhaps the most common objective of the continent as a whole has been to gain respect on the world stage and for its states to be treated as equals after centuries of inferiority witnessed in slavery and colonialism. Given the regional instability and territorial fragility of many states, with half the countries in the continent involved in border disputes since 1960, policies aimed at simply maintaining the state's existence have received high priority. To facilitate these policies, stability has been preferred to democracy.

Other significant factors have been the legacy of colonialism, the dominant Cold War tensions, the opposition to racism, and the occasional presence of foreign troops, particularly (but not exclusively) French, on the continent. These have led to rhetorical policies of nonalignment and anticolonialism in order to remain outside of Western influence, and specifically to refrain from any military commitment to the Cold War. These factors motivated the creation of an OAU Defense Commission, ostensibly to provide an African military force to solve African problems. In practice, however, this defense force has not materialized and many African states have been definitely aligned, although alignment has tended to be on economic rather than military bases. Nevertheless, foreign military presences in countries such as Angola, Ethiopia, and many Francophone countries do undermine the purported foreign policy strategy of nonalignment. African states have pursued nonalignment into the nuclear arena in calls since 1964 for a nonnuclear continent. South Africa's alleged possession of nuclear weapons has apparently broken this and has changed the policies of some countries, notably Nigeria, who now claim justification for the proliferation of nuclear weapons, even though little has been done to date to achieve this goal.

Opposition to South Africa and its apartheid political structure has been the single most important unifying foreign policy theme for the continent. At times this uniformity has been broken by calls for "dialogue" and "accommodation" by the governments of Cape Verde, Côte d'Ivoire, Gabon and Malawi (and occasionally Zaire) or by the necessity of Front-Line States, such as Botswana, Lesotho, Swaziland, and Zimbabwe to trade with South Africa. But overall, the marked opposition to racism has bound together the continent, although African diplomatic pressure has brought little visible success.

A more intriguing and complex policy agenda has been that toward Israel.[12] The Arab-African states have consistently called for the isolation of Israel, and this was most notably achieved after the 1973 Yom Kippur war, when African states were lured by the promise of OPEC petrodollars and lavish aid programs, and upset by what they perceived as the close Israeli-South African axis. This strong political partnership between African and Arab states in the 1970s also helped to form the nucleus of the Third World "voice" within the North-South "dialogue." While the formal diplomatic breach between the majority of African states and Israel has survived into the 1990s, increasing commercial, technical, and military contacts (and some diplomatic) between Israel and a host of Sub-Saharan states had developed in the late 1980s. These were prompted by the feeling that Arab finance to Africa had not matched expectations, that Israel had much to offer African states, and that Egypt and the Palestinians had themselves recognized Israel and so somewhat undermined the logic of Africa's diplomatic position.

A final policy objective to mention briefly here concerns economic "modernization" and development. Foreign economic policies have been geared to promote development priorities, whether perceived in socialistic or capitalistic terminology. Unfortunately, no great records of success spring to mind, for a variety of reasons already mentioned, and this has helped to encourage African leaders to press forcibly for a New International Economic Order (NIEO) within the U.N. and its associated agencies. Africa may have the voting numbers but lacks the muscle to bring about reforms at the international level; yet the continent's vocal stance on North-South issues is an important one and appears set to dominate the African foreign policy agenda in a postapartheid continent.

FOREIGN POLICY ARENAS

Regionalism

Given the limited resources of most African states, and the sometimes tense relations with neighboring states, foreign policy priorities are normally focused at a regional level. This focus involves political, economic, and military policies, even though trade links for most African countries remain vertically oriented toward the markets of Europe. The artificiality of state borders results in ethnic groups straddling borders, and this has made it difficult to bind peoples together in a true nation-state. Policing, demarcating, and consolidating borders have been major policy problems since the 1960s, and in regions such as the Horn of Africa, continue to pit countries against each other. The

---

[12]See Olusola Ojo, *Africa and Israel: Relations in Perspective* (Boulder: Westview Press, 1988).

OAU strongly supports the principle of acceptance of the territorial status quo as found at independence, and this has helped considerably to diminish territorial disputes.

The haphazard way in which colonialism developed in the continent has bequeathed an interesting mosaic of linguistic and cultural patterns. In West Africa, Francophone, Anglophone, and Lusophone countries are found next to each other, the former two traditionally holding mutual suspicions that have proved difficult to overcome. But even where there is a common colonial legacy, such as with French rule in North-West Africa or British rule in East Africa, this has proved insufficient to prevent tensions between neighbors.

In the early 1990s, relatively low levels of economic interchange exist between neighboring states, regional organizations notwithstanding. In West Africa, for example, after sixteen years of ECOWAS cooperation, intraregional trade remains less than 10 percent of total trade. Besides occasional residual antipathies, economic problems seriously deter greater expansion of intraregional trade. Transport connections between countries continue to be poor, as do telecommunications links; few currencies are easily convertible, and foreign exchange is always in short supply; little trade complementarity exists between countries, as many of them produce similar products; and most smaller countries try to resist the expansion of the dominant regional actors, Nigeria and Côte d'Ivoire. Similar problems exist in other regions.

Africa's grand strategy for economic development was formulated in 1980 in the Lagos Plan of Action (LPA). The LPA aims to build upon regional organizations to push for the goals of self-sufficiency and self-sustainability until a continental common market can be forged by the year 2000. This is the ultimate continental objective of economic policy but appears likely to be elusive.

In the following sections, four regional arenas are highlighted, namely North, West, Eastern, and Southern Africa. These regions are not really self-contained or unambiguous, and considerable overlap exists between them. Nevertheless, there are sufficient commonalities in their foreign policy arenas for us to justify the four regions.

North Africa

The main foreign policy focus of Arab states in North Africa has traditionally been the Middle East, (see Chapter 12). Here the aim is to consider North Africa in terms of its interrelationship with the rest of the African continent. Trade with Sub-Saharan Africa has been extensive throughout history, either by camel across the Sahara desert or along the Indian Ocean coast. Religion went hand in hand with this trade, to the extent that most West African states have considerable Muslim populations, notably Nigeria where Muslims account for roughly half of the 120 million population. Despite these many centuries of contact across the Sahara, it is interesting that only in the last decade has an all-weather Trans-Sahara road been completed, part of the Trans-Africa road system.

With the apparent uniformity of both religion and language in the North, it is somewhat surprising that the region has been less united than one would anticipate. Different colonial experiences (Spain in Western Sahara; Italy in Libya; Britain in Egypt; France in the others) helped to influence contrasting perspectives, while its war for independence radicalized Algeria vis-à-vis its more conservative neighbors. Muammar Qaddafi's sudden rise to power in 1969 provided a Libyan leader whose ideology and foreign policies (and well-armed military!) served to destabilize the region. A boundary dispute between Morocco and Algeria during the 1960s, and Morocco's claim to Mauritania (as well as Western Sahara) further soured the political atmosphere. The fact that Morocco, Algeria, Libya, and Egypt all aspired to regional leadership and a strong continental role also increased animosity and tension between them.

Morocco played a strong role in continental diplomacy immediately prior to the formation of the OAU in 1963. It was an active player (with Ghana) in the "Casablanca" group, which supported greater continental unity and flirted with the idea of a single continental government. This viewpoint was overridden by the conservative majority, to which Morocco acquiesced in becoming a founder member of the OAU. Diplomatic problems arose for Morocco in 1975 when its troops (and people in the "Green March") occupied Western Sahara following the withdrawal of Spain. Morocco found itself increasingly isolated as the whole continent became embroiled in the dispute, until in November 1985 it withdrew from the OAU following that organization's recognition of the Saharawi Arab Democratic Republic (SADR). Through today, the SADR exists only in name as Morocco continues to occupy the country, with the blessing of the U.S. government. Support for the Polisario Front (Frente Popular para la Liberación de Saguia el-Hamra y Rio de Oro) in the SADR by Algeria (and by Libya), and the presence of a government-in-exile in Tindouf in southern Algeria, soured relations between Morocco and Algeria until the late 1980s, when a larger prize, a Maghreb Union, relegated the SADR issue to the sidelines.[13]

Libya's activist foreign policy, both in terms of its forceful anti-Israeli stance and its radicalist tendencies, has led it to support dissident movements and junior officer coups across the continent. This activity has naturally angered many conservative African leaders, including Libya's neighbors, and led them to fear and distrust Libyan intentions. The country's most notable foray into Sub-Saharan Africa has been its intervention in Chad in the 1980s, partly triggered by potential oil deposits in the country. Libya's support for northern Muslim factions and the use of Libyan troops in the fighting drew a direct military response from both France and Nigeria, as well as a sharp rebuke from many other OAU members. This led to a Libyan withdrawal at

---

[13] See I. William Zartman, *Ripe for Resolution. Conflict and Intervention in Africa* (New York: Oxford University Press, 1985), Chap. 2.

the end of the 1980s, though not an end to the instability in Chad, whose government was overthrown at the end of 1990.

Prospects for North African regional harmony appear brighter in the early 1990s, following agreement on the fledgling Maghreb Union. This union aims to facilitate greater political cooperation within the region, helped by the 1984 Moroccan-Libyan Treaty of Union and a later rapprochement between Algeria and Morocco over the Western Sahara, and to increase economic linkages between members. This priority of settling their disagreements is reinforced by events across the Mediterranean, where European countries move toward closer integration. The Maghreb's orientation is increasingly northward rather than southward, and foreign policies are aimed to maximize the region's trade opportunities with the EC.

West Africa

The West African region is the largest numerically within the continent, containing about twenty countries stretching from Mauritania in the northwest down to Cameroon and Gabon in the south, and including the large, arid, landlocked states of Mali, Niger and Chad (and Burkina Faso). Climatic contrasts are sharp, ranging from areas of dense tropical forest to arid desert. Diverse cultural/linguistic/colonial legacies are also present, representing Portuguese, Spanish, British, and French influences.

In the early 1960s, the colonial legacy partly helped to distinguish policies of French- and English-speaking countries, but rivalries also existed within the language zones of purely African derivation; Côte d'Ivoire vied with Senegal for leadership of the Francophone bloc, while the radical policies of Kwame Nkrumah set Ghana at loggerheads with the more conservative Nigeria. Suspicion of Ghanaian involvement in the assassination of Togo's President Sylvanus Olympio in 1963 stirred up regional animosities, but it was the Nigerian civil war between 1967–70 that highlighted the fragility of regional cooperation. Nigeria's Francophobia, being geographically surrounded by French-speaking countries, was heightened by those countries' (and the French government's) sympathy for the Biafran secessionists.[14]

It was Nigerian determination and diplomatic acumen (and desire to expand its regional trade and political influence) that helped repair relations with neighbors in the aftermath of the civil war, and it is surprising that a sixteen-country economic community, ECOWAS, could be agreed upon as early as 1975.[15] ECOWAS planned to provide for free movement of persons and goods and to increase prosperity through greater regional economic linkages. The community has been slow to meet the goals for several reasons: residual distrust between language blocs remains a factor, especially as the Francophone grouping, the Communauté des Etats de l'Afrique de l'Ouest

---

[14] Côte d'Ivoire, Gabon, Tanzania, and Zambia were the only countries to give formal recognition to Biafra.

[15] Cameroon, the Central African Republic, Chad, and Gabon do not belong to ECOWAS.

(CEAO), continues to exist within the larger ECOWAS grouping; industrial development programs at a regional level have not been implemented; free movement of peoples has not been completely accepted, most spectacularly exemplified by Nigeria's expulsion of almost three million West African "aliens" in 1983 and 1985; the unequal relations between dominant coastal states and capitals (Dakar, Abidjan, Accra, Lomé, Lagos) and the poorer, dependent countries of the internal Sahel; and the chronic political instability of many countries with repeated military coups since 1960 in Benin (seven coups), Burkina Faso (seven coups), Ghana (five coups), and Nigeria (five coups), many attempted coups, and severe problems in political relations between personalist regimes.[16]

Nigeria has the most active foreign policy within the region, the continent, and the global stage. After independence in October 1960, Nigerian foreign policy followed a conservative, pro-Western line, influenced considerably by the perceptions of the country's Islamic leadership. The West's reluctance to be involved in the Nigerian civil war led Nigerian policy makers to turn toward the Soviet Union for assistance, so diversifying military and economic links.

It was not until the mid-1970s that Nigeria consciously exerted its influence within West Africa and the continent, a shift in policy made possible by the vast wealth generated from large oil export revenues. It was Nigeria's support for the Popular Movement for the Liberation of Angola (MPLA) faction in 1975 that helped to break the diplomatic deadlock within the OAU, and financial aid to other liberation movements in Southern Africa and neighboring governments in West Africa have given Nigeria a status unmatched in the continent. Nigeria's lead in organizing the African boycott of the 1976 Olympic Games was another example of its new activism and influence, and by the end of the 1970s, Nigeria's economic muscle was being directed at Western countries. The "oil weapon" was used, for example, in 1979 in nationalizing British Petroleum's Nigerian activities in order to pressure the British government to expedite Zimbabwean independence. The world oil glut in the early 1980s, combined with the massive squandering of Nigeria's national wealth and the increasing debt burden, decreased Nigeria's leverage and influence, and its foreign policy commitments and postures shrunk in the late 1980s.

Eastern Africa

Eastern Africa is a more difficult geographical area to define, because it overlaps with both northern and southern regions. At its heart are the three former British colonies of Kenya, Tanzania, and Uganda. They participated in the most ambitious regional organization in the continent to date—the East African Community (EAC)—for a decade until its demise in 1977. Cooperation

---

[16]Julius Emeka Okolo and Stephen Wright, eds., *West African Regional Cooperation and Development* (Boulder: Westview Press, 1990).

between these countries dated back to the 1920s, when colonial authorities attempted to rationalize their administrative control over the region. For a decade after the EAC's inception in 1967, the three countries shared common currency and banking systems, common postal services, shared railways and airline, and a common university system. Although these required extensive coordination of policy, there was less agreement on common foreign policies or economic development programs. Kenya remained essentially the model of capitalistic development, retaining very close relations with the West under both President Jomo Kenyatta and his successor, after 1978, Daniel arap Moi. Tanzania promoted the *ujamaa* socialistic alternative under its president, Julius Nyerere, and had more troubled relations with Western powers. Tanzania's relations with Uganda also deteriorated after the overthrow of Milton Obote and the accession to power of Idi Amin in 1971. The strong growth of the Kenyan economy vis-à-vis its neighbors, the failure to agree upon cooperative regional industrial strategies, and Nyerere's refusal to meet with Amin, led to bitterness and recriminations and contributed substantially to the collapse of the EAC. For a decade after this, Tanzania kept closed its borders with Kenya, and Uganda compounded its problems with civil war. This came to a head when Tanzania invaded Uganda in 1979 and secured the overthrow of Amin.

Disputed territorial boundaries, sporadic conflicts, and extracontinental involvements have plagued relations between states in the region. Kenya and the Somali Republic have engaged in sporadic conflict since 1964 over disputed border regions. Ethiopia and the Somali Republic went to war in 1973 and 1977 over the Ogaden region, and that issue remains festering in the background. A long-time alliance between Afro-Marxist Ethiopia and capitalist Kenya against perceived Somali expansionism is an intriguing example of the effects that territorial instability have on foreign policy. A French military presence in Djibouti prevents annexation by its bigger neighbors. Sudan and Ethiopia (and more recently the Somali Republic) have also been involved in long-standing civil wars, with secessionist groups struggling against the central government, and these conflicts have often spilled over into neighboring countries. Ethiopia is troubled by secessionist claims by Eritrea, as well as claims to the Ogaden by the Somali Republic. Sudan is bitterly divided between Muslim north and non-Muslim south, while political authority in general appears to have collapsed in the Somali Republic in the early 1990s in the face of dissidence from within the country.

Such instability poses serious problems for cooperation between these countries, and remains a constant theme, and thorn, of foreign relations. Despite these problems, a Preferential Trade Area (PTA) has developed linking Eastern and some Southern African states together in an attempt to improve trade between, and promote economic growth of, the members. The PTA is not as far-reaching or elaborate as the EAC and does not attempt to coordinate political policies. It is still too early to measure the success of this arrangement, but both Kenya and Zimbabwe appear to be emerging as the PTA's twin centers, and this may prove to be unsettling for other members in the future.

Southern Africa

The Southern African region is distinctive because of the dominant influence exerted on it by one country, namely the Republic of South Africa, as well as because it contains countries that fought, and waited, longest for independence—Angola and Mozambique (1975), Zimbabwe (1980), and Namibia (1990). The predominant regional foreign policy goal of South Africa has been to keep neighboring states under its influence, and conversely, these countries have tried to pursue policies that would loosen the control of South Africa. The latter task has proved to be virtually impossible to achieve, partly because most regional trade routes traditionally cross South Africa. Other routes, such as the Benguela railway, cannot be relied upon, and the Tanzania-Zambia railway, completed in 1976 with Chinese aid of $500 million, has not fully proved to be the economic lifeline originally envisaged. The result of this has been Front-Line States beating a radical and hostile diplomatic drum against South Africa, but in reality being humbled and forced to trade with the apartheid state.

South Africa's destabilization of its neighbors has been the latter's primary concern. Financial and military assistance given by South Africa to rebels in Angola and Mozambique continue to undermine governmental authority there, and it is still too early to see clearly what South Africa's intentions are with newly independent Namibia. Most countries in this region (including Zaire, which normally would be classified as Central African) are mineral rich, and so potentially can be strong economic units, but internal divisions, political instability, poor terms of trade, and the proximity to South African physical intimidation, have made them fall short of their potential.

In an attempt to develop economic ties independently of South Africa, the region established in 1980 a cooperative grouping, the Southern African Development Coordination Conference (SADCC). SADCC has succeeded in bringing together its disparate members by underplaying political issues and by concentrating purely upon economic ones, but its progress has been hampered by the omnipresence of South Africa. SADCC currently excludes the apartheid regime, but with the rapidly changing political conditions in South Africa there is a dialogue underway on closer collaboration. This is inevitable, as post-apartheid South Africa will continue to be the region's dominant economic actor, and so will have to be included in any meaningful grouping.

South Africa's foreign policy has been underpinned by strong anti-Communist, pro-Western sentiments, and these characteristics, combined with its mineral wealth and strategic location, have led to very close ties with the United States and Europe. These links have been shaken by antiapartheid pressures, sanctions, and divestment, but remain strong overall. In the early 1990s, following a significant transformation in post-Botha South Africa, it appears as though sanctions will be dropped, Western investment will increase, South African athletes will be allowed back into international sports, and South Africa will be gradually given some international respectability. These mark foreign policy successes for the de Klerk regime, and will only strengthen South Africa's (legitimate) influence in the region.

CONTINENTALISM

The Organization of African Unity (OAU) is the world's largest geographically based regional organization, containing all the countries of the continent except South Africa (and temporarily Morocco).[17] Founded in May 1963, it was the natural culmination of decades of cooperation between nationalist movements. It built on the concept of Pan-Africanism originally espoused overseas by "displaced Africans" including Marcus Garvey and W.E.B. Du Bois, and was consolidated in conferences such as the ones held in Manchester (UK) in 1945 and Accra in 1958.[18] Immediately prior to the OAU's foundation, there was lively debate as to what Pan-Africanism and African unity actually meant, whether African peoples should forge close links with other "Africans" of the diaspora, and how postindependent Africa should look. The debate essentially polarized around those states who championed a "United States of Africa" with close integrative ties across the continent (the radicals or Casablanca group), and those who favored state sovereignty and purely intergovernmental arrangements, thereby allowing individual countries to pursue independent foreign and economic policies (the moderates or Monrovia group).

The moderates were in the majority, and the OAU Charter reflects their convictions. The location of the OAU headquarters in Addis Ababa, the capital of Emperor Haile Selassie's Ethiopia, underlined the OAU's moderate credentials (although, somewhat ironically, after 1974 Ethiopia was controlled by the Afro-Marxist military regime of Mengistu Haile Mariam). The OAU attempts to coordinate fifty or so disparate national foreign policies and present some form of unified stance on African and global issues, particularly in the area of economics. The OAU operates through intergovernmental rather than supranational machinery. All important decisions are taken by the annual Assembly of Heads of State and Government meetings, and the biannual Council of Ministers meetings provide the preparatory discussions. A Commission of Mediation, Conciliation and Arbitration is also available to mediate disputes between members. The Banjul Charter on Human and People's Rights came into force in 1986 in order to protect the rights of Africa's citizens, but this is commonly ignored by the continent's authoritarian regimes.

Ideological consensus is often difficult to achieve, but has normally been reached through secret dialogue. Consensus has broken down, however, on

---

[17] Gino J. Naldi, *The Organization of African Unity: An Analysis of its Role* (London and New York: Mansell, 1989).

[18] Immanuel Geiss, *The Pan-African Movement* (New York: Africana, 1974).

several important occasions and subsequently threatened the existence of the organization. In 1975, the OAU was deadlocked over which liberation faction to recognize in Angola, and only after intense lobbying (particularly by Nigeria) did the OAU support the MPLA. In the early 1980s, the OAU heads of state meetings could not convene for several years because of strong opposition to the potential chair, Muammar Qaddafi. Similarly, the OAU was paralyzed by dissension concerning recognition of the SADR. This was eventually approved in 1984, but caused Morocco to leave the organization.

Perhaps an even more serious threat to the functioning of the OAU is that the majority of states has fallen way behind in subscription payments and so virtually paralyzed many operations. The economic problems of its members have become the main issues promoted by the OAU in attempting to present common strategies on development and debt negotiations to the outside world. An example of this is the OAU's success in calling a special session of the U.N. General Assembly in May 1986 to discuss Africa's economic predicament, and the U.N.'s adoption of a five-year Program of Action for African Economic Recovery and Development (PAAERD). In addition, the OAU works within the Group of Seventy-Seven and maintains a strong relationship with the UN's Economic Commission for Africa (also based in Addis Ababa, and in fact the first Pan-African organization following its creation in 1958). The continent's economic planning document, the Lagos Plan of Action, was heralded a great success of cooperative African policy, even though a decade later very little of the document has ever been implemented.

Much of the traditional political role of the OAU has proved inconsequential, although its firm support for the acceptance of territorial boundaries as found at independence (enshrined in the 1964 Resolution on the Intangibility of Frontiers) has undoubtedly helped to limit the number of territorial disputes between neighbors. The Liberation Committee has met regularly at its headquarters in Tanzania (the southernmost independent country at the committee's inception in the mid-1960s), but its policies have brought little change in South African policy. An OAU Defense Commission can in theory constitute an all-African defense force to intervene between disputing parties, but this has not proved popular. An OAU force was used in Chad in 1981-82, with great cost and controversy, and a force has not been constituted since. All in all, continental cooperation on foreign policy issues is difficult to expect with fifty countries involved, and the OAU must be credited with some success given the magnitude of its task. Nevertheless, on most issues individual countries are left to chart their own paths making the term "African Unity" something of a misnomer.

EURAFRICA

Throughout the continent, the most important extra-Africa relations are with the countries of Western Europe, traditionally the former colonial powers of Britain, France, and Portugal, but increasingly with Germany and other EC members.[19] This strong connection to Europe should not come as a surprise, because the colonial period bound Africa economically to Europe; and three decades or so is too short a time to alter such dominant relations, especially as few African leaders actually desire to alter the close ties with Europe. These Eurafrican (the concept conveying the natural ties between the continents) linkages appear resilient in the early 1990s, even though African states have diversified from dependence upon a single metropole to develop trade and political relations with a number of European states.

Of all the Eurafrican relationships, those between Africa's Francophone community and France remain the strongest and most constant. *Plus ça change, plus c'est la même chose.* Overcoming the debacle of Algerian independence, France has invested considerable energy and resources in maintaining its position of influence, prestige, and *grandeur* in the continent. Francophone states have been content to be partners in *la coopération* and receive French technical assistance, investment and, in particular, guarantees, both in terms of economic backing for the CFA currency (*Communauté Financière Africaine*) used widely by Francophone countries, or else in military support, with French troops stationed in many countries, including Central African Republic, Côte d'Ivoire, Djibouti, Gabon, and Senegal, but also used as interventionary forces in Chad, Western Sahara, and Zaire.[20] Even where ideological differences separate African leaderships from France, such as in Benin, Congo, and Madagascar, close economic arrangements have continued; and even Guinea decided to return to the fold after the death in 1984 of its socialist leader, Ahmed Sékou Touré, who had held office since 1958. But it is not only in *la francophonie* where France is a dominant player, because French business with governmental backing has pursued a vigorous program of expansion over the past twenty years throughout the continent. Both Nigeria and South Africa, for example, have very strong economic connections with France, and both have also been involved in military cooperative ventures. Even though French investment in the continent has been declining in the last three years, the mystical bond with Africa continues, and the continent remains central in French policy.

Britain's role in Africa is less pervasive today than France's, partly because African relations have not been given the same priority, but also because British business appears to be less competitive and interested in these markets. Britain's consistent support for the South African minority regime, particularly under former Prime Minister Margaret Thatcher, combined with Britain's reluctance to dislodge the white minority regime in Rhodesia (Zimbabwe) after the 1965 unilateral declaration of independence, also somewhat disadvantaged British diplomatic and commercial interests against French, German, and other European competitors. Britain's primary political linkages with the

[19]Amadu Sesay, ed., *Africa and Europe: From Partition to Interdependence or Dependence?* (London: Croom Helm, 1986).

[20]John Chipman, *French Power in Africa* (Oxford: Basil Blackwell, 1989).

continent are found within the Commonwealth, to which sixteen African states (all former colonies) belong. These African states have consistently used the Commonwealth to lobby Britain to modify its African policies, notably over Zimbabwe prior to its 1980 independence, as well as South Africa since the 1960s.

Relations between Africa and the EC are maintained through special agreements for the North African Arab states, and through the four successive Lomé conventions since 1975 for Sub-Saharan Africa. All these arrangements have received strong support from France. The four Lomé conventions have provided preferential access for specified African exports to the EC market, and offered compensatory mechanisms (through STABEX) to provide guaranteed markets and prices for listed commodities. The EC has supported this relationship because it facilitates political and economic objectives in keeping a considerable portion of the world within its sphere of influence. But these arrangements have also been beneficial to African states, because they provide preferential treatment and bring investment, technology, manufactured goods, food supplies, and export markets that otherwise would be difficult to maintain. Many African states have expressed concern about the impact of European integration after 1992 on these relations, especially in terms of fresh EC investment, French guarantees for the CFA franc, and the increasing lure of new markets in Eastern Europe. The Lomé IV Convention has just come into force in 1990 for a ten-year period, and so African states hope that these favorable arrangements can be continued.

SUPERPOWERS AND THE GLOBAL ARENA

The African continent has never been a true battleground of the Cold War, but rather the superpowers involved themselves in contests of strength in specific zones, notably the Horn and Southern Africa. African states rhetorically committed themselves to nonalignment in the Cold War, but few states succeeded in remaining uncommitted, at least in an economic sense. Nevertheless, it would be wrong to conclude that either superpower could "control" its allies in the continent, as African states maintained some degree of maneuverability.

It is probably true to say that neither the United States (except perhaps under Jimmy Carter's presidency) nor the Soviet Union was ever particularly interested in Africa for Africa's sake, but perceived the continent as one part of the global power game. Since many pundits claim the Cold War to have ended in 1990, this may paradoxically damage African states as the superpowers divert their attentions from the continent to more pressing issues.

The U.S.S.R. appeared to have a natural advantage over the United States in developing its ties with Africa in the early 1960s because of the expressed anticolonial, anti-Western sentiments of many African states. The U.S.S.R., however, was itself disadvantaged by its complete lack of experience in dealing within the African environment (although the United States had little experience, either), and by the fact that in the 1950s and 1960s no African state at independence had diplomatic relations with the U.S.S.R. Algeria, Congo (Brazzaville), Egypt, Ghana, Guinea, Mali, and Tanzania all attempted to provide "balance" in their relations with the superpowers by developing friendly links to the socialist bloc. In the 1970s, the growth of Afro-Marxist regimes in Angola, Ethiopia, Guinea-Bissau and Mozambique (and Zimbabwe), and the appearance of other radical regimes such as Libya, provided opportunities for the U.S.S.R. to expand its influence directly and through proxies such as Cuba, which in turn exacerbated regional confrontations against U.S. strategic interests. Soviet influence was rarely significant beyond these few countries, except in Egypt, Sudan, and the Somali Republic, but Soviet advisors were expelled from Egypt in 1972 and from the others in 1977. In some countries, such as Kenya and Zaire, factions supported greater links with the U.S.S.R., but these groups were suppressed with some vigor by the authorities (with covert support by the United States). Even in Nigeria, where Soviet assistance to the government was vital during the civil war, relations remained formal but did not substantially increase in the 1970s and 1980s.[21]

Following the dramatic internal developments within the U.S.S.R. after 1985, Soviet involvement and general interest in Africa has been steadily declining, although this trend was evident after the death of Leonid Brezhnev in 1982. President Mikhail Gorbachev has made it clear that there will be reduced Soviet aid to Africa, and the U.S.S.R. will not provide military assistance in conflict situations. The U.S.S.R., in any case, has little economic assistance that it can provide to African states, and this traditionally has been an advantage that the United States has exploited.

The United States has tended to defer to British and French interests in Africa both during and after the colonial period and has viewed the African continent (from a position of relative ignorance), primarily in strategic terms. It was not until 1958 that the U.S. government established a Bureau of African Affairs, and Jimmy Carter has been the only modern day president to ever visit Sub-Sahara Africa while in office. The United States, starting with the Kennedy administration, tried to spread its influence in the continent using economic and technical assistance, particularly through the U.S. Agency for International Development (AID) and the Peace Corps. These, of course, have political strings and connotations, but actions against U.S. personnel, such as Nigeria's expulsion of the Peace Corps in the civil war, have been rare. U.S. involvement has been more activist in regions of tension, or where countries are deemed important to the overall balance of power in the continent.[22] But it is only in Zaire during the Congo civil war (1960–65), with Cold War rivalries paramount, that U.S. direct physical involvement has been seen in any consistent force, including assistance given to Mobutu to take power; other actions

---

[21] R. Craig Nation and Mark V. Kauppi, *The Soviet Impact in Africa* (Lexington: D.C. Heath, 1984).
[22] See Robert I. Rotberg, ed., *Africa in the 1990s and Beyond: U.S. Policy Opportunities and Choices* (Algonac, Michigan: World Peace Foundation, 1988).

are covert or more discrete, except perhaps for the strike against Libya in 1986. As Ali Mazrui has shrewdly remarked, "On balance the USA has done fewer bad things in Africa than she has done in Asia and Latin America. But she has also done fewer good things in Africa than elsewhere."[23]

South Africa has maintained strong ties to the United States despite all the protests, rhetoric, human rights oratories, and apparent divestment. Similarly, Zaire has been allowed to maintain good relations with the United States because of its mineral wealth and strategic importance, and the human rights abuses and other excesses of the Mobutu regime have been overlooked. U.S. efforts in the late 1970s and 1980s to undermine the governments of Angola and Mozambique (with a little help from friends in South Africa and Zaire) have not been hidden either. Following the Iranian revolution in 1979, the U.S. government perceived the need to develop a Rapid Deployment Force (RDF) to protect U.S. vital interests in the Middle East, but allies were needed in Africa to provide landing rights for such a force. Egypt, Kenya, Morocco, Sudan, and the Somali Republic were courted by Washington and entered into RDF military agreements in exchange for financial rewards; these are the main recipients of American foreign aid in Africa.

Despite the fact that most African states have significant economic ties with the United States, there is a residual resentment against the United States for its perceived imperialistic (and clumsy) manner in which it treats Africa. The assault on Libya in 1986, for example, was widely condemned, but did not seriously affect the continent's foreign relations with the United States. Similarly, African states have been quick to condemn American carte blanche to Israel and U.S. gunboat diplomacy in the Gulf, but little beyond these rhetorical attacks develops. African foreign policy orientations are grounded in the realization that African states lack the capability to influence the United States, and that economically the continent requires U.S. support for debt rescheduling and loan agreements with the World Bank and the IMF.

Almost half the continent's countries is undergoing structural adjustment programs (SAPs) imposed upon them by the IMF, an indication of these countries' vulnerability in their foreign economic policies. The SAPs are introduced as a precondition to further external finance and impose severe domestic restructuring that usually results in tremendous societal hardship. The increasing economic deterioration being experienced by the majority of African states, combined with the growing futility of debt rescheduling, have contributed to increased calls for a New International Economic Order (NIEO), with better terms of trade for African states, greater foreign investment being sent to the continent, and increased African participation in the institutional decision making of the World Bank and the IMF. African states have coordinated their policies through UNCTAD and the Group of Seventy-Seven, but economic weakness undermines their potential to change the status

---

[23] Ali A. Mazrui, *Africa's International Relations: The Diplomacy of Dependency and Change* (London: Heinemann and Boulder: Westview Press, 1977), p. 156.

quo. African states have also played an active role within the Nonaligned Movement, particularly in the early 1970s, when conferences were held on the African continent in Lusaka (1970), Algiers (1973), and Dakar (1975).

The U.N. General Assembly has also been an important forum for promoting African foreign policy agendas, especially through related organs such as the Anti-Apartheid Committee. Given the numerical strength of the continent, accounting for almost one-third of the vote, African states have combined to push through declarations on economic rights and opposition to South Africa, even though more concrete action could have resulted from these votes. Nevertheless, African states have succeeded in removing South Africa from U.N. organizations including UNESCO, the ECA, the World Health Organization, and the Food and Agricultural Organization.

African states maintain economic and political ties with countries outside of Europe and the superpowers, as could be expected, but few relations are significant (especially given the space constraints of this chapter). Perhaps the most notable relations have been with China. In the 1960s, China's Premier, Chou En-lai, pursued an active policy in the continent to radicalize the political economies of many states, to bolster its own status in the Third World and Nonaligned Movement, and also to counter Soviet and American influence. Chou En-Lai's famous comment in the early 1964 that "Africa was ripe for revolution" perhaps underlined the original policy intent, but China's overall impact has been economically productive but politically marginal. During the 1970s and 1980s, relations between African states and China emphasized this economic cooperation and the political element diminished, partly reflective of China's own domestic reorientation and its foreign policy objectives in courting Western partners.[24]

Several countries on the Atlantic coast, notably Angola and Nigeria, have fostered strong relations with Brazil over the last decade. These ties have helped to promote South-South linkages across the South Atlantic, and have been used to try to prevent Brazilian (and other Latin American) links to South Africa. Canadian foreign aid programs are very common and popular throughout the continent, as Africans generally perceive that they receive the best aspects of North American assistance without the U.S. imperial hand. Likewise, Scandinavian linkages are strong throughout the continent, as they come heavy in aid and light in political strings. Sweden, in particular, has been very supportive of African development programs and liberation movements, especially the African National Congress in South Africa. Japan and South Korea have increased their economic contacts with many African countries, and in recent years Japanese companies have increased their presence in South Africa as American and European investors have withdrawn. In North Africa, relations with countries in the Middle East, notably Saudi Arabia, are naturally

---

[24] Alaba Ogunsanwo, *China's Policy in Africa 1958–71* (London: Cambridge University Press, 1974). See also Warren Weinstein and Thomas H. Henriksen, eds., *Soviet and Chinese Aid to African Nations* (New York: Praeger, 1980).

strong. But none of these relations come close to the predominant foreign relations between Africa and EC countries.

THE FUTURE

The near future does not appear to hold much promise for African states either individually or collectively. Most states have not pursued active foreign policy agendas outside their own regions, and there is little evidence to suggest that this pattern will change in the near future. If anything, the African continent stands to become even less influential and involved in world politics. Stagnant economies and rising debts will preoccupy the continent's political leaders and will undermine any potential for exerting influence on global events. Increasing pressure on African states to preserve the physical environment will also tend to put them on the defensive.[25]

Despite pronouncements on self-reliance and self-sustainability, Africa's future development path is far from clear, but does depend to a considerable extent on the support of forces outside the continent. Unfortunately, these appear to be increasingly disinterested and less favorably disposed to the continent. Rapid change in Europe has thrown up investment and business opportunities far more enticing to European, North American, and Japanese investors than those that most of Africa can offer. In a wider perspective, the superpowers no longer need to tussle over allies in Africa, and their strategic disinterest is already leading to lower foreign aid.

Prospective political changes may not necessarily help the continent either. The premier objective of African foreign policies, namely the end of apartheid in South Africa, may soon be reached. This would be heralded as a great political achievement for African foreign policy, but may unglue the reflex unity engendered by opposition to South Africa in the continent. The overall economic impact for the continent would also be mixed. On the positive side, the destabilization of the region would probably end, providing new opportunities in addition to savings on military expenditures. However, South Africa will become the greatest economic attraction to foreign investors, and would rapidly expand its strength economically and politically, probably to the detriment of the neighboring states.

Finally, democratization pressures are being witnessed in many African states.[26] In the past, trade and political relations were not linked to human rights by European or North American countries. This is slowly changing. Africa's relationships with overseas partners, including the World Bank and IMF, may well become conditional on domestic political reforms. Whatever

---

[25] Lloyd Timberlake, *Africa in Crisis: The Causes, the Cures of Environmental Bankruptcy* (Philadelphia: New Society, 1986).

[26] Walter O. Oyugi et al., eds., *Democratic Theory and Practice in Africa* (Portsmouth, N.J.: Heinemann and London: James Currey, 1988); also John A. Wiseman, *Democracy in Black Africa. Survival and Revival* (New York: Paragon House, 1990); and Henry Bienen, "The Politics of Trade Liberalization in Africa," *Economic Development and Cultural Change*, 38(4), July 1990, pp. 713–32.

happens, there could be instability: no change will increase external and domestic political pressures, whereas internal reforms could set off events the results of which are difficult to foresee. All in all, the prospects are not promising for Africa to strengthen its internal political and economic bases and to utilize those to become more influential in the world arena. In fact, the signs are that the continent will play an even weaker global role in the decade to come.

FOREIGN POLICY LANDMARKS

1945	Egypt, Ethiopia, Liberia and South Africa only African states to join the U.N.; Arab League formed
1948	Apartheid formally begins in South Africa following the electoral success of the National Party
1951	Libya becomes independent; mutual defense agreement signed between South Africa and the United States
1952	Kwame Nkrumah becomes Prime Minister of Gold Coast (Ghana); Mau Mau uprising begins in Kenya (until 1956); army coup in Egypt
1954	Start of the Algerian war of independence (until 1962)
1955	Many African nationalist movements attend Nonaligned Conference in Bandung; Simonstown Agreement signed between Britain and South Africa (until 1975)
1956	Morocco, Sudan, and Tunisia independent; British/French invasion of Suez
1957	Ghana independent
1958	Guinea independent; U.N. Economic Commission for Africa established
1960	Nigeria and most former French colonies become independent; Sharpeville massacre in South Africa; U.N. troops to the Congo (Zaire) (until 1964)
1961	South Africa leaves the Commonwealth and becomes a Republic
1963	Organization of African Unity (OAU) formed by thirty states; Kenya-Somali border war (until 1967)
1964	Kenya, Tanzania, and Uganda call in British troops to restore order after army mutinies
1965	Rhodesian (Zimbabwean) unilateral declaration of independence
1967	East African Community formed (until 1977); Nigerian civil war begins (until 1970)
1969	Col. Qaddafi comes to power in Libya
1973	Yom Kippur war; most African states cut diplomatic links with Israel
1974	Emperor Haile Selassie overthrown in Ethiopia
1975	First Lomé Convention signed with European Community; Angola and Mozambique independent; ECOWAS established
1976	African boycott of Olympic Games; Polisario campaign against Morocco and Mauritania begins; Soweto riots in South Africa; the Chinese-financed Tanzania to Zambia railway opened
1977	Ogaden war between Ethiopia and Somali Republic

1979   Tanzania invades Uganda and Amin is deposed
1980   Zimbabwe independent; Lagos Plan of Action signed; SADCC established
1981   PTA formally launched; OAU peacekeeping force in Chad
1982   OAU deadlocked over its failure to convene in Tripoli; OAU admits SADR as a member
1983   Nigeria expels two million West African "aliens"
1984   Morocco leaves the OAU; Union between Libya and Morocco signed (ended in 1986)
1986   U.S. strike on Libya; U.N. General Assembly extraordinary session on African economic crisis; Banjul Charter of People's and Human Rights becomes operational
1988   Angola, Cuba, and South Africa sign agreements paving way for Cuban withdrawal and Namibian independence (in 1990)
1989   President F. de Klerk in office in South Africa; apartheid structures begin to be dismantled
1990   Namibia independent; Nelson Mandela freed

SELECTED BIBLIOGRAPHY

Adedeji, Adebayo, and Timothy M. Shaw. eds. *Economic Crisis in Africa: African Perspectives on Development Problems and Potentials.* Boulder: Lynne Rienner, 1985.

Aluko, Olajide, ed. *The Foreign Policies of African States.* London: Hodder and Stoughton, 1977.

Austin, Dennis. *Politics in Africa,* 2nd ed. Hanover: University Press of New England, 1984.

Bach, Daniel C., ed. *La France et l'Afrique du Sud: Histoire, Mythes et Enjeux Contemporains.* Paris: Karthala, 1990.

Bayart, Jean-François. *La Politique Africaine de François Mitterrand.* Paris: Karthala, 1984.

Bender, Gerald J., James S. Coleman, and Richard L. Sklar, eds. *African Crisis Areas and U.S. Foreign Policy.* Berkeley and Los Angeles: University of California Press, 1985.

Berg, Robert J., and Jennifer Seymour Whitaker, eds. *Strategies for African Development.* Berkeley and Los Angeles: University of California Press, 1986.

Calvert, Peter. *The Foreign Policy of New States.* Brighton: Wheatsheaf Books, 1986.

Calvocoressi, Peter. *Independent Africa and the World.* London and New York: Longman, 1985.

Cervenka, Zdenek. *The Unfinished Quest for Unity: Africa and the OAU.* New York: Africana, 1977.

Chazan, Naomi, et al. *Politics and Society in Contemporary Africa.* Boulder: Lynne Rienner, 1988.

Chipman, John. *French Power in Africa.* Oxford: Basil Blackwell, 1989.

Clapham, Christopher, ed. *Foreign Policy Making in Developing States.* Farnborough: Saxon House, 1977.

Commins, Stephen K., ed. *Africa's Development Challenges and the World Bank.* Boulder: Lynne Rienner, 1988.

Corbett, Edward M. *The French Presence in Black Africa.* Washington, D.C.: Black Orpheus, 1972.

Gambari, Ibrahim A. *Theory and Reality in Foreign Policy Making: Nigeria after the Second Republic.* Atlantic Highlands, N.J.: Humanities Press International, 1989.

Gardiner, Robert, M.J. Anstee, and C.L. Patterson. *Africa and the World.* Addis Ababa: Oxford University Press, 1970.

Gavshon, Arthur. *Crisis in Africa. Battleground of East and West.* Boulder: Westview Press, 1984.

Geiss, Immanuel. *The Pan-African Movement.* New York: Africana, 1974.

Gutkind, Peter, and Immanuel Wallerstein, eds. *The Political Economy of Contemporary Africa.* Beverly Hills and London: Sage, 1985.

Hansen, Emmanuel, ed. *Africa: Perspectives on Peace and Development.* London: Zed, 1987.

Korany, Bahgat, ed. *How Foreign Policy Decisions Are Made in the Third World: A Comparative Analysis.* Boulder: Westview Press, 1986.

Legum, Colin, et al. *Africa in the 1980s: A Continent in Crisis.* New York: McGraw Hill, 1979.

Mazrui, Ali A. *Africa's International Relations: The Diplomacy of Dependency and Change.* London: Heinemann and Boulder: Westview Press, 1977.

——, and Hasu H. Patel. *Africa in World Affairs. The Next Thirty Years.* New York: Okpaku Publishers, 1973.

Mazzeo, Domenico, ed. *African Regional Organizations.* Cambridge: Cambridge University Press, 1984.

M'Buyinga, Elenga. *Pan-Africanism or Neo-Colonialism. The Bankruptcy of the O.A.U.* London: Zed, 1982.

McKay, Vernon. *Africa in World Politics.* New York: Harper and Row, 1963.

Naldi, Gino J. *The Organization of African Unity: An Analysis of its Role.* London and New York: Mansell, 1989.

Nation, R. Craig, and Mark V. Kauppi, eds. *The Soviet Impact in Africa.* Lexington: D.C. Heath, 1984.

Ogunsanwo, Alaba. *China's Policy in Africa 1958–71.* London: Cambridge University Press, 1974.

Ojo, Olatunde J.C.B., D.K. Orwa, and C.M.B. Utende. *African International Relations.* London: Longman, 1985.

Ojo, Olusola. *Africa and Israel: Relations in Perspective.* Boulder: Westview Press, 1988.

Onwuka, Ralph, and Timothy M. Shaw, eds. *Africa in World Politics: Into the 1990s.* London: Macmillan, 1989.

Rotberg, Robert I., ed. *Africa in the 1990s and Beyond: US Policy Opportunities and Choices.* Algonac, Michigan: World Peace Foundation, 1988.

Sesay, Amadu, ed. *Africa and Europe: From Partition to Interdependence or Dependence?* London: Croom Helm, 1986.

Shaw, Timothy M., and Olajide Aluko, eds. *The Political Economy of African Foreign Policy: Comparative Analysis.* Aldershot: Gower, 1984.

——. *Africa Projected: From Recession to Renaissance by the Year 2000?* London: Macmillan, 1985.

Stevens, Christopher. *The Soviet Union and Black Africa.* New York: Holmes and Meier, 1976.

Turok, Ben. *Africa: What Can Be Done?* London: Zed, 1987.

Wallerstein, Immanuel. *Africa and the Modern World.* Trenton N.J.: Africa World Press, 1986.

Weinstein, Warren, and Thomas H. Henriksen. *Soviet and Chinese Aid to African Nations.* New York: Praeger, 1980.

Whitaker, Jennifer Seymour, ed. *Africa and the United States: Vital Interests.* New York: New York University Press/Council on Foreign Relations, 1978.

——. *How Can Africa Survive?* New York: Council on Foreign Relations, 1988.

Wright, Stephen, and Janice N. Brownfoot, eds. *Africa in World Politics: Changing Perspectives.* London: Macmillan, 1987.

Yousuf, Hilmi S. *African-Arab Relations.* Brattleboro, VT: Asama Books, 1986.

Zartman, I. William. *International Relations in the New Africa.* Englewood Cliffs, N.J.: Prentice Hall, 1966.

——. *Ripe for Resolution. Conflict and Intervention in Africa.* New York: Oxford University Press, 1985.

–12–

DIMENSIONS
OF THE
MIDDLE EAST PROBLEM
BEFORE AND AFTER
THE GULF WAR

Nadav Safran

INTRODUCTION

The Middle East problem is often mistakenly equated with the Arab-Israeli conflict. Actually, notwithstanding the eruption of half a dozen Arab-Israeli wars in thirty-five years, that conflict is only one manifestation of a more complex problem, the roots of which go back at least two centuries to the time when the Ottoman and Persian rulers could no longer defend their empires. The essence of what was then called "the Eastern Question" was the same as that of the present Middle East problem: the weakness of the area and its importance for rival outside powers. The organization of the area has since changed, as the Ottoman and Persian empires gave way to a multitude of independent states; the meaning of "weakness" altered, as the use of military power for imperial expansion became constrained; the identity of the rival outside powers competing in the region has shifted several times; and the interests of even the latest set of rival powers have evolved over the years. Yet, the combination of the factors of regional weakness, the importance of the area, and intervention by rival outside powers has remained constant.

In the configuration it has assumed since World War II, the Middle East problem may be viewed as consisting of four distinct but interacting problems, or as a problem with four dimensions: (1) the domestic dimension, relating to internal weaknesses of the countries of the area; (2) the regional dimension, referring to problems in the relations among countries of the area apart from the Arab-Israeli conflict; (3) the Arab-Israeli conflict; and (4) the Great Powers involvement.

Each of these four dimensions has had its own particular dynamic and has also been influenced by developments in the other dimensions. Further, complicating the picture, the new issue of oil has become intertwined with each component. At various times in recent history, one or another dimension of the problem has tended to occupy the center of attention; but in all instances all four dimensions were in varying degrees relevant to understanding the problem in its totality.

The purpose of this chapter is to set out briefly, almost in outline form, a "political map" of the Middle East problem, to sketch out the particular dynamic of each component and its relationship with the other dimensions, and to conclude with a brief assessment of the configuration they have together assumed in recent months. The tangled web to be weaved may not necessarily point to a solution for the Middle East problem; but it will hopefully serve as a guide to realistic thinking about it and enhance attempts to manage it now and in the future.

In the first part, we shall give a comprehensive, even if panoramic, view of the Middle Eastern profile before the Gulf War, which erupted after the invasion of Kuwait by the Iraqi forces on August 2, 1990. In the second part, we shall discuss briefly the war itself and its aftermath as it affects the balance of forces in the Middle East and among Middle Eastern states.

PART ONE
BEFORE THE GULF WAR

THE DOMESTIC DIMENSION

While each Middle Eastern state faces its own particular domestic problems, which will be shortly discussed, all of the states of the region are experiencing the problem of transition from a traditional to a modern societal order. There are many versions of just what that problem is, specifically; from our point of view it is not important which formulation one chooses. The relevant point is that they all spell domestic instability arising from social cleavages and a lack of consensus on political structures and values. Stated bluntly, social transition is a difficult and dislocative process, accompanied by tension, conflict, and violence.

In the case of Middle Eastern societies, there are special circumstances which make the problem of transition particularly acute. First, the traditional social order of these societies (except Israel) rested on an Islamic belief system which was particularly resistant to adaptive change. In order to preserve the most absolute unity, omnipotence, and omniscience for God, Islamic doctrine eliminated the idea of causation from the universe and from history and utterly subsumed reason to revelation. There was thus no room for any notion of natural law or philosophy of history, empirical sciences or progress through human agency. Knowledge and virtue were seen as specifically defined in the divinely revealed law; conformity to that law provided the only assurance of the good society and the good man.

Second, the change that ushered in the transition period in the Middle East was not autonomously generated; it was not as in the West the result of internal processes that departed from the traditional order and pressed for its revision from within. Rather, the change that set the transition stage in motion was imposed by the rulers from above in response to military challenges from the outside.

In order to protect their realms against Western pressures, the Ottoman sultans and autonomous local leaders like Muhammad Ali in Egypt tried to emulate those features of Western society believed to be the source of its military prowess. They began by adopting Western military technology and methods of administration, and went on with economic and legal reforms which undermined without destroying the system based upon Islamic tradition, still considered valid and strong by the great bulk of its adherents. There was thus created a legitimacy gap between rulers and ruled, with no indigenously generated middle class whose interests and occupations disposed it to strive for a new world outlook, and designated it to be the agent of social transformation. The modernizing lawyers, military officers, bureaucrats, and intellectuals whom the reforms from above called forth did not form such a class. They were an extension of the state, which they sometimes took over by means of the armed forces. They carried further the process of borrowing from outside, and thus further widened the gap between the rulers and the ruled. As a result there have often arisen fundamentalist movements based on visions of a utopian Islamic polity which in fact never existed. Today's Iran is only the most recent, and most politically successful, manifestation of this phenomenon.

Third, geography and history have combined to make particularly difficult the integration of Middle Eastern societies on the basis of the nation-state principle. Throughout history, the political units of the area were organized on the basis of religion, rather than on territory or any political principle. Even the Greeks and Romans, when they controlled the area, had to adapt their customs to utilize the religious principle of organization. The reason is that the area from the Atlantic Ocean to the Persian Gulf is extremely cut up, consisting basically of a vast desert and mountainous regions interspersed with oases and strips of fertile land. All the current states in the region (with the exception of Iran, Egypt, and perhaps Tunisia) have therefore had no previous political existence in the territory they now occupy; they were largely created by Western imperialism. Consequently, during most of their political independence, their legitimacy has often been questioned by unintegrated groups within their borders, and by Arab nationalists seeking Arab political unity. (Though with the passage of time there is evidence of growing acceptance of the legitimacy of the states as they now exist.)

Finally, if one takes the region as a whole, one notices that the problem of transition is manifested in greatly varying degrees, with societies standing at widely separated positions on the continuum between tradition and modernity. This is a consequence of the geographical discontinuities of the region, which also led to different degrees of exposure of these societies to outside threats, and to their coming under the rule of different colonial powers. Thus, at one end of the continuum Egypt has been coping with the transition process for nearly two hundred years, while at the other end Saudi Arabia has been doing so for barely twenty.

These problems are common to all Middle Eastern states, save Israel. Yet each also has major specific problems which blend with the general ones and exacerbate the difficulties of achieving a stable domestic order.

Very briefly, here are the problems facing the individual countries at present and their recent internal record:

Egypt. A very poor population-to-resources ratio. Tremendous pressure of unchecked population growth and a continuing migration from the countryside to already bursting cities. An agricultural base which is contracting rather than expanding. An industrialization program choked by a bureaucratic incubus, which has not kept pace with the demands for employment.

Internal record since 1945: liberal democracy destroyed; monarchy overthrown; massive riots (three instances); coups and coup attempts (three instances); leaders assassinated (three instances).

Syria. Regionally fragmented by history and geography with resultant instability. Since 1970, ruled by a small group of military officers from the minority Alawite sect (about 15 percent of the total Syrian population). Increasing opposition from the majority Sunni Moslem community, spearheaded by the fundamentalist Muslim Brotherhood.

Internal record since 1945: liberal-democratic republic destroyed; union with Egypt and secession; popular revolts (three instances); coups and coup attempts (twenty instances?); leaders assassinated (twelve instances?).

Lebanon. Extreme sectarian fragmentation that has prevented any form of social cohesion save uneasy compromise among the autonomous groups. Recent intrusion of the Palestinian and Arab-Israeli issues into the country, fracturing the tenuous social compromise and leading to the civil war which began in 1975 and continues today.

Internal record since 1945: civil war (two instances); leaders assassinated (countless instances).

Iraq. Problem of political integration in a state which lacks any historical political tradition. Compounded by the extreme ethnic-sectarian fragmentation of the population (approximately 50 percent Shi'ite Muslims concentrated in the south; 30 percent Sunni Moslems, who now rule, in the center and northwest; and 20 percent Kurds in the northeast).

Internal record since 1945: liberal democracy destroyed; monarchy overthrown; revolts (two instances); Kurdish war (fourteen years); coups and coup attempts (a dozen instances); leaders assassinated (countless instances).

Saudi Arabia. Underpopulated state with far-flung frontiers in an environment which has been historically inhospitable to centralized rule. Strains of rapid development on a traditional social and political system. Special problems include the presence of large numbers of foreign workers, strains within the modern state structure (traditional elements versus new bureaucracy, Army versus National Guard), and the possibility of dissension in the large royal family.

Internal record since 1945: one king deposed, one assassinated; revolts (at least two instances); attempted coups (four known instances).

Libya. Vast, underpopulated, yet oil-rich state, lacking any historical political tradition or contemporary sense of national identity. Headed by a maverick leader possessed by a sense of mission (a blend of Arabism and Islam) who is prepared to use all means to advance his cause.

Internal record since 1945: Monarchy overthrown; attempted coups (several instances); leaders assassinated (countless instances).

Jordan. Typical artificial creation of Western imperialism. Poor resource-to-population ratio. Depends upon, and makes good use of, extensive Western and Saudi help. Tension between Palestinian and native Jordanian elements, potentially ignitable by outside Palestinian and other elements. Jordan neither can solve nor can avoid involvement in the Arab-Israeli conflict. Problem of control over West Bank of the Jordan River.

Internal record since 1945: king assassinated; civil war; massive riots; leaders assassinated (three instances).

Iran. Traditional empire historically governed by strong military ruler through compromise with local influentials. Shah's suppression of local elements left him to face alone an alienated population and revolution. Need to reconstruct a legitimate political order and viable economic base out of the turmoil of the revolution.

Internal record since 1945: monarch overthrown, restored, overthrown; total revolution; mass riots; revolts; assassination of leaders (countless instances).

Israel. Formerly fragmented political system becoming largely polarized along communal lines (European-origin versus oriental Jews). Sharp differences between two major parties over destiny of the country and future of occupied territories blends with communal problem. Explosive issue of relation between state and religion unresolved. Increasing economic dependence on the United States; massive inflation. Potentially troublesome Arab minority problem.

Internal record since 1948: local riots on religious or ethnic grounds (a dozen instances?); resort to anti-Arab terror by extremists.

THE REGIONAL DIMENSION

In the summer of 1982, the Middle East region was the scene of two wars, one in Lebanon involving Israel against Syria and the PLO, and the other at the head of the Persian Gulf, between Iran and Iraq. The latter war had been going on for nearly two years entirely independently of the hostilities in Lebanon and of the Arab-Israeli conflict. Moreover, with Iran's invasion of Iraq after expelling its forces from Iranian territory, the Gulf war appeared to hold potential international consequences at least as momentous as any arising out of the Arab-Israeli problem.

Yet the Gulf war is only the most recent illustration of regional conflicts apart from the Arab-Israeli issue. For much of the period since the end of foreign rule after World War II, the Middle East was raked by conflicts and strains among the Arab countries, centering on the issue of pan-Arabism. While that issue has often been intertwined with the Arab-Israeli conflict, it has had its own roots and dynamics, which have often interacted with the politics of the big powers to produce strains and crises independently of the Israeli factor. These strains and crises are illustrated by the following summary record of actions taken in the last three decades by the Arab countries under discussion in the name of pan-Arabism:

> Egypt at one time or another attempted to instigate or support revolution in Syria, Lebanon, Iraq, Jordan, Saudi Arabia, Yemen, and Libya. It deployed troops against Arab opponents in Syria, Iraq, Kuwait, the Sudan, Yemen, and Algeria. Its armed forces engaged in hostilities against the Yemeni royalists, Saudi Arabia, and Libya.
>
> Syria attempted to instigate rebellion in Iraq, Jordan, Lebanon, and North Yemen. It deployed troops against Arab opponents in all those countries, and engaged in hostilities against Jordan, the Yemeni royalists, and the leftist-PLO forces in Lebanon as well as their rightist-Christian opponents.
>
> Iraq attempted to instigate rebellion in Jordan, Syria, the Gulf emirates, Saudi Arabia, and North Yemen. It deployed forces against Jordan, Syria, and Kuwait, and used force against the latter.
>
> Jordan deployed forces against Iraq (in Kuwait), Syria, and the Yemeni republicans, and used its armed forces against the PLO and Syria.
>
> Saudi Arabia attempted to instigate rebellion and political assassination in Syria, Jordan, Egypt, North Yemen, and South Yemen. It deployed troops against Arab opponents in Jordan and Kuwait, and engaged in hostilities by proxy against the Egyptians in Yemen, and by proxy as well as directly against South Yemen.
>
> Libya attempted to instigate rebellion and political assassination in practically every Arab country, deployed forces against Egypt and Tunisia, and used proxy forces against the latter.

Pan-Arabism may be empirically described as an idea and a movement that recognize a close affinity among the Arab peoples and seek to give that affinity a meaningful political expression. In an immediate sense, the problem of pan-Arabism has been twofold. First, Arab governments and politically relevant groups have differed sharply as to the significance of that affinity and the form of the political expression into which it should be translated. Ideas on the subject have ranged all the way from conceptions which sought to achieve voluntary cooperation among sovereign states on particular shared interests to notions which viewed the Arab peoples from the Atlantic Ocean to the Persian Gulf (or rather the Arab Gulf) as constituting one nation, and sought to bring about their integral political unification.

Second, even within the framework of one conception, there have been sharp rivalries and conflicts over particular issues of policy and tactics and over leadership of the movement. In the 1940s and 1950s, for instance, when the notion of pan-Arabism as voluntary cooperation prevailed, there were clashes between state groupings centered on Cairo and Baghdad. When the more comprehensive notion of pan-Arabism gained ascendancy in the 1950s and 1960s, there were no less sharp clashes between, for example, Nasser and Qassem, Nasser and the Ba'th, the Syrian and the Iraqi Ba'th, and Qaddafi and sundry others.

From a broader perspective, however, the problem of pan-Arabism has been rooted in the balance between the real impulses that have driven it and the obstacles that have obstructed it. That balance has generated a force that was strong enough to raise aspirations beyond the level of cooperation, yet not sufficiently strong to support integral unity, giving rise to a situation wherein various parties have felt entitled to meddle in the affairs of the others in the name of Arab unity, without any of them being able to enforce such unity on the others.

The real impulses for unity have included the following:

1. The absence of a heritage of distinct political identity among all but one or two of the twenty-two countries which are members of the Arab League (the exceptions being Egypt and possibly Tunisia). This disposed the peoples of those countries to receptivity to the notion of an all-embracing Arab identity.
2. Unity of religion, and a tradition, already alluded to, of viewing religious affiliation, rather than territory or anything else, as the principle of political organization.
3. A certain degree of unity of language. Not the spoken Arabic, which is fragmented into various regional dialects, which in some instances defy intercommunication, but the classical language, whose uniformity has been preserved thanks to the Qoran and the classics, and increasingly the modern literate Arabic promoted by the media.
4. A certain sense of unity of historical experience and of aspiration. Not a concrete, specific common history, and shared particular objectives—today's Arab states and peoples have had very different histories for many centuries and there is little agreement among them on particular ideologies, the nature of the state, and the ideal social order. There is, rather, a common psychological experience of certain

major historic moments and a common psychological urge derived from them. One of these is the sense that Muhammad's mission, marking the birth of Islam among the Arabs and its rapid spread through their conquests, constituted a related set of events of cosmic importance—a *kairos*. Another is a sense of shock—a *trauma*—caused by the subjugation of the Arab and Muslim lands by infidels, contrary to the right order of things. Related to the preceding is a shared urge to heal that trauma and achieve a purgation of the emotions—a *catharsis*—by reasserting Arab-Muslim power against the infidel oppressor.

These impulses have provided a very strong but rather inchoate sense of unity, lacking both a focus on a particular, commonly desired end and a shared view of means. On the other hand, the obstacles in the way of unity, most of which have already been mentioned or alluded to, have been hard and concrete. They include the following:

1. Geographical discontinuities despite territorial contiguity, and even, in one critical instance caused by the presence of Israel, a lack of territorial contiguity between the western and eastern halves of the Arab world.
2. Different particular histories which, together with the geographical discontinuities, have led to different patterns of development in government, law, education, economic systems, social stratification, military systems, and bureaucracies.
3. Unstable governments unable to commit their constituencies to unity, compounded by the existence of substantial regional, ethnic, and sectarian minorities opposed to being swallowed by a large, inevitably Sunni Muslim Arab state.
4. The development of strong vested interests in and around existing state structures. These interests include the current regimes and groups which benefit from association with them. There has been no matching growth of countervailing groups with vested interests in unity and the ability to sustain abstract emotional-ideological commitment.

Historically, the interplay between impulses and obstacles, and the impact of events, produced a dialectical evolution in the concept of pan-Arabism. In the early 1950s, the dominant concept was voluntary cooperation. Within that framework, Egypt and Saudi Arabia tried to oppose Iraq's endeavor to join what came to be known as the Baghdad Pact and bring Jordan and Syria along. Egypt and Saudi Arabia were prompted by national or regime interests of their own, but they fought the Iraqi proposal in the name of collective Arab interests. When Iraq persisted, Nasser broke new ground in inter-Arab relations by appealing, over the heads of their governments, to the Arab publics concerned in the name of Arab solidarity. His conclusion of an arms deal with the Soviet Union as part of his campaign against the Western-sponsored Baghdad Pact put him in the Arab limelight and started a chain of events which led to his nationalization of the Suez Canal, and his political victory in the 1956 Anglo-Franco-Israeli war against him. By then he was cast in the role of an all-Arab hero, and when, in the following year, Syrian leaders, trapped in an internal political imbroglio, turned to him with a proposal for unity, he could not turn them down. The formation of the United Arab Republic in February 1958 marked the emergence of pan-Arabism as integral unity in opposition to pan-Arabism as mere voluntary cooperation.

Pan-Arabism as integral unity became the dominant concept in the next decade, even though in practice it made no further progress but, rather, suffered several setbacks, including the dissolution of the United Arab Republic in 1961. The setbacks merely led to an intensification of inter-Arab struggles as Nasser simultaneously clashed with rival Iraqi and Syrian proponents of integral unity, and escalated his struggle against opponents of the concept of unity who upheld a more limited concept of cooperation. The latter struggle manifested itself in a bitter war in Yemen between Egypt and a client republican regime on one side, and royalist and tribal forces supported by Saudi Arabia on the other. The war lasted for nearly five years and the hostilities spilled into the border areas of Saudi Arabia and threatened to engulf that country altogether. The conflict ended only when a sudden eruption of the Arab-Israeli conflict brought war, and total defeat, to Egypt and its Syrian and Jordanian allies in June 1967. That war was also a turning point in the evolution of the concept of pan-Arabism.

From 1967 to the present, the concept of pan-Arabism as cooperation regained its dominance; however, its previous clash with the concept of pan-Arabism as unity had endowed it with a new meaning. The principle of respect for sovereignty was restored, but cooperation among the sovereign entities came to be viewed more as an obligation than as a matter of discretion. Moreover, the substance of cooperation was expanded greatly from politics to economics and other spheres, and reached down from the governmental level to embrace people of all classes. This evolution began hesitantly during Nasser's remaining years, as he was caught between the desire to recover his standing as leader of Arab nationalism, and the necessity to accommodate other Arab countries and leaders in order to secure their assistance in recovering Egyptian national and other Arab territories lost in the war. It picked up after Nasser's death as Egypt and, coincidentally, Syria came under the leadership of men whose commitment to cooperation was more credible than Nasser's. The evolution reached its highest point in the 1973 war and its aftermath, as the oil-rich countries led by Saudi Arabia used the "oil weapon" to support the confrontation countries politically, and employed their vastly increased oil-derived wealth to assist them economically. Moreover, the massive expansion of development projects undertaken by the generally underpopulated oil-rich countries created employment opportunities for masses of migrant or guest workers from the poorer Arab countries. A symbiosis of interests thus emerged which, for the first time, provided the basis for enduring cooperation.

The triumph of a higher concept of cooperation subdued but did not obliterate altogether the ideal of integral unity, which Qaddafi has continued to promote and to which Syria and Iraq have paid occasional obeisance. It did not mean the end of inter-Arab conflicts as a major dimension of the Middle East problem. This was clearly demonstrated by the clashes between Sadat and Assad after the former signed the Sinai II agreement with Israel; by the proxy civil war which many Arab parties fought in Lebanon in 1975–76; by the breach between Egypt and most of the Arab countries over Egypt's 1979 peace with Israel; by the opposite positions taken by various Arab countries in connection with the Iran-Iraq war; and, most recently, by the mutual accusations in connection with the Lebanon war. The triumph of pan-Arabism as cooperation has merely removed a general, diffuse ground for inter-Arab conflict in the form of the ideal of integral unity, leaving ample room for conflict and for reconciliation on grounds of particular interests and policies.

THE ARAB-ISRAELI DIMENSION

Discussions of the Arab-Israeli conflict are replete with interpretations that attempt to explain it as a moral, psychological, legal, or political "case" abstracted from history. According to these interpretations, the conflict involves two sets of incompatible claims, attitudes, and points of view. On the Arab side, there is the prescriptive right to a land inhabited for more than a thousand years, the right of self-determination, the shock to the dignity of a once-great people seeking to make its place in the modern world, the fear of Israeli expansionism, and the plight of more than one million refugees. On the Israeli side, there is the indissoluble bond to the land that had been the cradle of the Jewish heritage, the urge of Jews barred from the nations of Europe to reconstruct a national life of their own in the land of their ancestors, their internationally recognized right to a share of Palestine, and their struggle for survival as a political entity and a culture.

This abstract approach to the Arab-Israeli conflict may be of some use in suggesting the reservoir of motives from which the parties draw. It is of little use, however, and tends in fact to mislead, in any attempt to understand the concrete unfolding of the problem. It fixes on feelings and emotions to the neglect of changing realities and facts which interact with them and greatly affect their practical implications. It assumes a single set of issues throughout the time in which the problem has existed when in fact these issues have changed and the conflict has evolved through a number of identifiable, critically different stages.

The following outline discussion will center on four such distinct stages: (1) pre-1948; (2) 1948 to 1967; (3) 1967 to 1979; and (4) 1979 to the present. The first three stages, in turn, may be seen in terms of two phases each.

1. The roots of the Arab-Israeli conflict lie in a struggle between the Jewish and Arab communities of Palestine going back some three decades prior to 1948. At issue in that struggle was the validity and meaning of the League of Nations mandate over Palestine which was given to Britain, and which incorporated an earlier promise given by the British government to the Zionist movement in the 1917 Balfour Declaration to support the creation of a Jewish "national home" in Palestine.

(a) The Arabs protested from the outset the terms of the mandate, but their resistance to it was initially weak. It manifested itself in sporadic, local outbursts of violence which the British treated as specific incidents and to which they applied specific remedies. Opposition to the mandate was in fact muted because, until the early 1930s, the threat of the projected Jewish homeland did not seem to be so imminent. Jewish settlers had established many proto-national institutions, but their numbers had grown far more slowly than the Zionist movement had hoped and the Arabs had feared. From the end of World War I through 1932, Jewish immigration averaged about 10,000 a year, bringing the total Jewish population of Palestine to 175,000 at the end of that year. The Arab population at the time was 800,000.

(b) However, Hitler's rise to power the following year and the beginning of Nazi persecution of the Jews released a flood of immigration adding up to some 200,000 in five years, which brought the total number of the Jewish population to 400,000 in 1937. This influx converted the threat of the national home into a clear and present danger and triggered Arab resistance on a national scale for the first time, in the form of a general strike launched and maintained in 1936. In 1937, the British appointed a royal commission to inquire into the entire problem of the mandate and make recommendations. Its report recognized for the first time that what was at issue was a conflict between two national communities contesting the same territory, and indicated partition as the only solution. The British government espoused the proposal after the Jews had intimated their acceptance; but the Arabs rejected partition and from 1937 to 1939 launched a wholesale campaign of sabotage and terror against the British and Jews to resist its application. In response to this violence and in order to placate the Arabs in the face of impending world war, the British tried to promote an agreed settlement at a conference in London that brought together Jewish leaders and leaders of several Arab countries. When the conference failed, the British unilaterally proclaimed their policy in the 1939 White Paper. This imposed severe restrictions on Jewish immigration and land purchases during a ten-year transition period, which would be followed by the establishment of one Palestinian state, controlled by the Arab majority, with constitutional protection for the Jewish minority.

It was now the Zionists' turn to resist. During the first years of World War II, the resistance was confined to promoting "illegal" immigration and settlement; but as the war receded from the Middle East, that resistance assumed, in addition, the form of violent rebellion. By 1947, the combination of Jewish resistance, British exhaustion, world sympathy for the Jews in the wake of the Holocaust, and American pressure led London to hand the Palestine question over to the United Nations. A U.N. Special Committee on Palestine comprising of representatives of small, disinterested countries, recommended, as the British royal commission a decade before, that Palestine be partitioned into Jewish and Arab states. Once again, the Jews accepted the recommendation and the Arabs rejected it. When the U.N. General Assembly adopted the proposal in November 1947, the Arabs resorted to force to prevent its application and the Jews responded with force for the opposite end. In the all-out intercommunal war that ensued, the Arabs initially had the upper hand, to such an extent that in March 1948, the United States proposed the shelving of partition and the imposition of a U.N. trusteeship instead. However, the tide of the war shifted shortly thereafter, and on May 15, 1948, Israel declared its independence. The same day, Egypt, Jordan, Syria, Lebanon, and Iraq marched their armies against the fledgling Jewish state.

2.(a) The improvised army of Israel won the war against the inexperienced, disunited, poorly led, and uninspired Arab armies. The result was a far-reaching modification of the U.N. partition plan. Israel ended up in control of more territory than had been allocated to it by the plan. The remainder of the territory fell under the control of Jordan (what became known as the West Bank) and Egypt (the Gaza strip). No Palestinian state emerged. Some 700,000 Palestinians fled or were expelled from the Israeli-controlled areas in the course of the fighting and became refugees. After a series of armistice agreements formally ended the war, these issues became the subject of disputes between Israel and its neighbors (as well as among those neighbors themselves). They ostensibly precluded the conclusion of peace treaties to end what had become an international, rather than an intercommunal, conflict.

The failure to resolve the issues left by the 1948 war was not so much due to their inherent intractability as it was due to the lack of any real incentive for the Arabs to make peace. In exchange for the minor border modifications and the return to Palestine of some refugees that peace would have given them, the Arab governments would have had to admit the loss of the war and close the issue of Israel's existence. This would have had severe domestic consequences (both the Egyptian and the Lebanese prime ministers were assassinated for agreeing to sign the armistice agreements). Moreover, the potentially overwhelming Arab military superiority over Israel seduced the Arab leaders into thinking that, in a few years time, they could marshal their forces and reverse the results of 1948. At the same time, those leaders quickly realized that their refusal to conclude formal peace was highly unlikely to bring upon them further military sanctions, because of the external constraints on Israeli actions provided by the U.N. and the Great Powers. With little to gain and much to lose from peace, and no fear of a resumption of war, a no-peace, no-war situation appeared to the Arab governments to be by far the best option.

The only dissenter among the Arab leaders was King Abdallah of the newly renamed Hashemite Kingdom of Jordan. Peace with Israel would confirm his West Bank gains, legitimize his position in Arab Jerusalem, and bring in vast amounts in compensation payment for the refugees. Abdallah, therefore, entered into secret negotiations with Israel which yielded the core of a Jordanian-Israeli agreement. However, the king was assassinated in 1951 by Palestinian opponents before he felt able to implement the proposed treaty.

In the years after 1948, the Arab governments emphasized to their populations the theme of "continuing conflict" with Israel, and gave it credibility by imposing a total boycott of Israel, encouraging Palestinian incursions, and barring Jews from the Holy Places in Jordanian-controlled East Jerusalem. This atmosphere of hostility lent particular significance to the 1955 Soviet-Egyptian arms deal. Israel took the Arab states at their word, and saw the arms deal as giving them the means to carry out their promise to destroy Israel. Thus Israel participated in the 1956 Suez campaign against Egypt as a preemptive move to change the strategic situation before Egypt could absorb its new arms. To most Arabs, however, 1956 confirmed their suspicions that Israel was a tool of imperialism and an aggressive state seeking to expand its borders. In the Arab-Israeli conflict, the passage of time, which sometimes heals wounds, led only to their festering.

(b) Up to 1958, while the dispute had been bitter and bloody, the issues over which it was formally contested were the residues of the 1948 war: border modifications and the Palestinian refugee problem. However, with Nasser's espousal of the movement for integral Arab unity, the conflict escalated to a "clash of destinies." Israel's existence violated the integrity of the Arab homeland and drove a wedge between its western and eastern halves; removal of that entity became a "necessity" for the realization of Arab nationalism under Egypt's leadership. Paradoxically, however, the 1958–1967 period, during which the issues at stake in the Arab-Israeli conflict assumed these fateful proportions, was also the quietest period in the history of the conflict. Not a shot was fired in anger between Egypt and Israel, and even the Syrian front remained relatively peaceful until the Jadid government came to power in 1966. In part, this was the result of Nasser's absorption with the problems presented by the union with Syria in 1958, its secession in 1961, and his involvement in the Yemen War since 1962, which diverted much of Egypt's military strength to that arena. However, this calm was also an indication of a shift in thinking from the impulsive to the strategic. Seriously seeking the destruction of Israel, Nasser sought to choose the most propitious time for a showdown and to avoid provoking Israel prematurely. But in fact, provoking Israel is what he ended up doing, in May 1967.

On May 14, 1967, Nasser, at Soviet instigation, mobilized and deployed his forces in Sinai to deter an alleged Israeli plan to invade Syria. On the 18th he asked the U.N. Secretary General to remove the U.N. forces which had held key positions in Sinai and the Gulf of Aqaba since the end of the 1956 war. On May 22 he proclaimed the Straits of Tiran closed to traffic bound to the Israeli port of Eilat, despite repeated previous warnings by Israel that such an act would be a *casus belli*. On May 29 he declared before the Egyptian National Assembly that the issue in this crisis was not the straits but the "aggression against Palestine" that took place in 1948 and the "complete rights" of the

Palestinians. By that time, Nasser had secured the agreement of Jordan to join the Egyptian-Syrian military coalition and to put its forces under the supreme Egyptian command. Other Arab countries, notably Iraq, promised to contribute forces, too, and the Arab oil-producing countries resolved to deny oil to nations that would support Israel.

All available evidence suggests that when Nasser made his first move on May 14 he had not intended to go to war. Yet two weeks later, he was practically begging for it. In that brief span of time, he had convinced himself that all the factors that he deemed necessary for a successful military operation had fallen into place. Israel appeared weaker than he had previously estimated, precisely because it did not respond vigorously to his remilitarization of the Sinai and the closing of the Straits of Tiran. The forces at his command, on the other hand, appeared much stronger as Jordan and other Arab parties rallied to his banner. The United States had toned down its initial strong reaction to the closing of the Straits, indicating that Israel might be isolated from its possible supporter. On the other hand, the Soviets, by encouraging his first moves and then supporting the blockade after the fact, had indicated to him that they either did not fear American reactions or felt capable of neutralizing them.

By the beginning of June 1967, Nasser was ready to absorb an Israeli first strike and then fight the decisive battle. He did not want to forfeit world opinion by acting as the aggressor, or draw the United States in with a blatant attack on Israel. However, the decisive battle proved to be the first strike itself, and in six days the armies of Egypt, Jordan, and Syria were defeated on all fronts.

3.(a) The 1967 war was a turning point in the Arab-Israeli conflict in several respects. First, contrary to many contemporary comments, the Arabs, though decisively defeated, were *not* rendered helpless, as the Soviets quickly rearmed them and increased their own military presence in Egypt. Nevertheless, Nasser's defeat meant the end of the movement for Arab unity under Egyptian leadership and thus resolved the "clash of destinies" in Israel's favor. Second, the capture by Israel of the Sinai, the Golan, and the West Bank injected a new element into the conflict. From 1948 to 1958, the Arab countries had clashed with Israel over the residues of the 1948 war on behalf of the Palestinians; from 1958 to 1967, their rationale for conflict was pan-Arabism. In either phase, they had nothing to gain from peace. Now, Egypt, Syria, and Jordan had something to gain: the recovery of national territories they had lost in the war. This meant that, at least in principle, a bargaining situation emerged for the first time in the Arab-Israeli conflict, and that the conflict became more akin to other international disputes.

A third consequence of the war was the resurgence of the Palestinians as actors in their own right, contesting Palestinian territory against Israel. For a while, this did not much alter the previous picture; but before long the Palestinians, organized in the PLO under new leadership, were to become a major complicating factor, obstructing the conclusion of any actual bargain between Arab states and Israel while being unable to agree among themselves on a position that would permit their being dealt a negotiating hand.

Despite the emergence of a bargaining situation in 1967, no specific deal was struck during the next six years because of lack of symmetry in the parties' assessment of their relative positions at various times. Right after the war, for instance, Israel, confident in its superior military power, was prepared to trade off all of Sinai for a peace treaty with Egypt. Nasser, however, unable to give up entirely his pan-Arab dreams, and hoping to rebuild a military option with Soviet help, did not agree to either a formal peace or a separate deal. The most he was prepared to contemplate was a "political settlement" involving return of all the territories in exchange for arrangements regarding specific issues such as navigation, demilitarization, etc. Jordan was prepared to make peace in exchange for the territory it lost in the war, but Israel was unwilling to relinquish Arab Jerusalem and bits of the West Bank. Syria was opposed to any deal with Israel—the loss of the Golan being not too burdensome immediately— and was primarily interested in preventing Egypt and Jordan from making a separate deal. In these circumstances, U.N.-sponsored efforts to promote a settlement drifted, and fighting was resumed in the form of a "war of attrition" proclaimed by Nasser in March 1969.

Nasser's strategy was to take advantage of Egypt's numerical superiority in standing forces to put pressure on Israel, while relying on Soviet warnings to deter Israel from mobilizing and launching an all-out assault across the Suez Canal. His aim was to compel Israel to yield to his terms by inflicting on it unbearable losses or by driving a wedge between it and the United States, capitalizing on the latter's concern for its interests in Saudi Arabia and other Arab countries and its desire to avoid confrontation with the Soviets. Israel, however, reacted by successfully using its air power to counter Nasser's advantage in ground forces, and, after sixteen months of grinding and costly fighting, it was Nasser who was forced to relent without attaining his objectives, and it was the Egyptian-Soviet alliance that began to crack.

Nasser died heartbroken in September 1970, one month after he had agreed to an American-mediated cease-fire. Five months later, his successor, Anwar Sadat, formally indicated to U.N. Ambassador Jarring his willingness to sign a peace agreement with Israel in exchange for the return of all of Sinai. By then, however, Israel, having just come out of a grueling war with a rebuilt Egyptian army, flatly rejected such a deal and insisted on retaining parts of Sinai for security reasons. Secretary of State Rogers, anxious about American interests in Saudi Arabia and elsewhere, and eager to follow up on his success in mediating the end of the war of attrition, tried to put pressure on Israel to negotiate on the basis of Sadat's offer; but President Nixon and National Security Adviser Kissinger held him back. In September 1970, the latter two had engineered with Israel a concerted operation that had saved Jordan from a Soviet-supported Syrian intervention on the side of the PLO. The success of that operation, coming after Israel had foiled Nasser's Soviet-supported war of attrition, had convinced them that a powerful Israel was the most effective check against Soviet encroachment and the best protection for friendly Arab countries. In the absence of military or diplomatic pressure on Israel to move toward Egypt, and with Sadat unable to renounce Egyptian territory, a stalemate set in. To break that stalemate Sadat engineered the 1973 Yom Kippur War.

(b) The 1973 war did finally break the logjam. Thanks to the achievement of an "inconceivable" strategic surprise, the standing and ready forces of Egypt and Syria achieved impressive initial gains against the vastly out-numbered regular and conscript Israeli forces, and disrupted the mobilization of the reserves and the prepared battle plans. Although the Israeli forces were eventually able to reverse the tide and put themselves in a position to win decisively, the losses they suffered in the process were very heavy for Israeli sensitivities. Moreover, because of the way the war opened, it was prolonged beyond anyone's expectations, and this led to the intervention of the Soviet Union and the United States, first to resupply their respective clients through competing airlifts, and then to jointly sponsor a cease-fire order and bring about the end of the fighting before Israel could consummate the total victory that was within its reach. Another critical consequence of the way the war unfolded was that Saudi Arabia and other Arab oil producers brought the "oil weapon" into play two weeks into the war, including the imposition of a total embargo on the United States. All of this created suitable conditions for striking actual deals out of the bargaining situation that originally arose in 1967. The Arabs regained their dignity and no longer feared to negotiate as an inferior, defeated party. Israel was war-weary and less certain that strategic territory was preferable to peace as a means of national security. The United States had an immediate as well as a long-term interest in advancing peace, and had established a measure of credibility as a mediator with Egypt—by saving it from total defeat—and an enhanced credit with Israel—by airlifting supplies to it in its most difficult moment.

The process of working out specific deals proved to be slow and tortuous, and its outcome was incomplete and problematic, yet its effect on the Arab-Israeli conflict was decisive. Before the process could begin, the cease-fire had to be solidified and the entangled forces in the battlefields had to be disentangled. Secretary Kissinger took on this task, and the first Egyptian-Israeli agreement he mediated suggested to him "step-by-step" diplomacy as the way to advance toward comprehensive settlement involving all the parties. This approach produced one disengagement agreement between Israel and Egypt and another between Israel and Syria in 1974, but ominously, because of Israeli resistance, failed to produce one with Jordan concerning the West Bank. A second round in 1975 produced, with greater difficulty, and only after a crisis in American-Israeli relations, a second agreement on Sinai between Egypt and Israel, but the same could not be attempted with Syria. Because of lack of space in the Golan, Israel insisted on a comprehensive settlement or nothing, and the Syrians not only refused to make a separate peace, but strongly attacked Egypt for making a separate limited agreement with Israel. The dispute among the Arab parties became exacerbated by their getting entangled in a civil war that had broken out in Lebanon, which absorbed their attention for a whole year in 1975–76, until a new administration took over in the United States and adopted a new approach to peace.

The Carter administration began with a strong commitment to achieve a comprehensive peace involving all parties through a general peace conference in Geneva. However, the efforts to convene the conference were ultimately stymied by disagreement among the Arabs over the question of Palestinian representation at the conference. After tense and laborious negotiations, the United States and Israel—which was now led by a government, headed by Menachem Begin, with a strong ideological commitment to retain the West Bank (which it called Judea and Samaria)—had agreed to a formula which, among other points, barred "known" PLO members from participating in a Jordanian-Palestinian component of an all-Arab delegation. Egypt was prepared to go along but Syria and the PLO refused, bringing the project to a halt. In order to cut through a stalemate he could not bear, Sadat made another fateful move by undertaking his dramatic trip to Jerusalem in November 1977, starting a peace process that bypassed Geneva altogether.

In Jerusalem, Sadat, and Begin vowed that they intended to pursue a comprehensive peace, not a separate treaty between Egypt and Israel, and the United States chimed in. However, as other Arab parties boycotted the negotiations that ensued, the two inevitably gravitated toward a separate agreement. The Camp David Accords, concluded in September 1978, and the Egyptian-Israeli peace treaty, signed in March 1979, were accompanied by an agreement on a "framework" for settling the West Bank question and the "Palestinian problem in all its aspects." However, the two pacts were independent of each other legally, in substance, and in the timing of their application; and, indeed, while realization of the Egyptian-Israeli peace proceeded smoothly, the negotiations for the application of the framework to the Palestinian question treaded water and then stopped altogether.

4. The 1979 Egyptian-Israeli peace treaty marked the most important turning point in the more than thirty-year-long Arab-Israeli conflict. Not only did it break the "spell" by bringing together an Arab country and Israel for the first time, but, by removing Egypt from the ranks of the confrontation states, it fundamentally altered the military and political balance in the Arab-Israeli arena. Syria tried to compensate for the "defection" of Egypt by creating an "eastern front," and to that end attempted to conciliate the hated Iraqi regime and bring it into the coalition along with Jordan and the PLO. However, the attempt foundered and, before long, Syrian forces were confronting Jordan over alleged involvement in Syrian internal troubles, and Syria was assisting Iran in its war against Iraq. Assad also tried to draw closer to the Soviet Union

for protection, but Begin was so little impressed that he gratuitously annexed the Golan in December 1981.

More important, Begin, having given back all of Sinai in order to gain a free hand in Judea and Samaria, now proceeded to accelerate the process of creeping annexation of that area. He did not repudiate the Camp David "framework," but rather used it and the stalled autonomy negotiations as a screen in order to "establish facts" that would foreclose the determination of the "final status" of the area—such as settlements and formal absorption of Arab Jerusalem into the "single, undivided, eternal capital of Israel." Egypt, which had taken the road to peace because it believed that the Arabs collectively had no military option against Israel and because it had despaired of Soviet help, was not inclined to react in a manner that risked the treaty with Israel, especially after it had thrown in its lot entirely with the United States and been ostracized and penalized by the other Arab countries.

The latest manifestation of the changed Arab-Israeli balance was seen in the Israeli invasion of Lebanon, starting in June 1982. Partly in order to secure Israel's northern settlements against PLO shelling, partly to remove the obstacle which the PLO presented to his creeping annexation of the West Bank and limited autonomy plans, Begin ordered the Israeli army to move in on the PLO forces and, if necessary, the Syrian forces, in Lebanon. The full political consequences of that war were not fully apparent at the time of writing; but two things have stood out with striking clarity: the awesome military power displayed by Israel, and the utter military and political paralysis of the remainder of the Arab camp during the longest Arab-Israeli war since 1948.

THE GREAT POWERS DIMENSION

As has been indicated, the interplay between the weakness of the area and the involvement of rival outside powers has been at the heart of the Middle East problem (whatever the name given to it) for some two centuries. During the period, the specific geographic focus of the problem often shifted, the particular configurations of domestic and regional weakness changed, the identity of the rival outside powers and the nature of their interests altered, but the matrix that made up the problem remained constant. It always involved the extension into the Middle East arena of big-power struggles involving external interests and wider power configurations.

The importance of the Middle East to outside powers is reflected in the fact that all the principal belligerents in World War II except Japan were involved in military operations in most of the region. All the countries of North Africa, from Egypt to Morocco, were major battlefields; Iraq, Syria, Lebanon, and Iran were the scenes of substantial military campaigns; and Palestine and other countries served as important staging areas.

Right after the war, Britain briefly emerged as the chief, almost the exclusive outside power in an area stretching from Russia's southern borders to the eastern border of Tunisia, with treaties and bases in half a dozen countries and major influence in all the others. However, the burden of holding on to these positions proved to be beyond Britain's exhausted postwar resources, and in the course of the next ten years it was compelled, under the pressure of other outside powers and local nationalisms, to retreat from most of them.

Thus, in 1947, Britain passed on to the United States the responsibility for defending Greece and Turkey against ongoing Soviet pressures. In 1948 it was forced to give up the mandate over Palestine. In 1955, it gave in to Egyptian nationalist pressure and American prodding and agreed to leave its Suez Canal base. The following year Britain invaded Egypt together with France and Israel in an attempt to overthrow Nasser, who had previously nationalized the Suez Canal and engaged in subverting Britain's remaining Middle East positions; but the endeavor was frustrated by active American opposition coupled with Soviet threats. After the 1956 fiasco, Britain held on to its positions on the rim of the Arabian Peninsula and retained some influence in Iraq for two more years, while France cultivated a position in Israel which lasted a while longer. However, the reality, underscored by the 1956 fiasco, was that the United States and the Soviet Union had become the principal rival powers in the Middle East.

The specific interests of the United States and the Soviet Union in the Middle East and the policies they adopted in pursuit of them have shifted over the years as a function of the strategic balance between them globally and of developments in the area itself. In addition, since 1973 access to oil has become a major specific focus of American interest and policy, connected to but transcending the strategic rivalry with the Soviet Union. The course of American-Soviet rivalry in the Middle East and its interaction with other dimesions of the Middle East problem may be delineated in terms of the following seven stages.

1. Right after World War II, the northern tier of the Middle East was the scene of some of the first postwar encounters between the United States and its erstwhile Soviet ally. In 1946, the United States successfully exerted political pressure on the Soviets to evacuate their forces from Iran in accordance with the wartime Teheran agreement, and thus helped the Iranian government reassert its authority over the secessionist Soviet puppet regime in the Azer-baijan province. Since the end of the war, the Soviets had been putting pressure on Turkey for a favored position on the Bosphorus and Dardanelles and had been supporting communist rebels in Greece. In 1947, after the British notified the United States of their intent to end the support they had hitherto been providing to Greece and Turkey, the United States responded by proclaiming the Truman Doctrine. The doctrine not only promised aid to Greece and Turkey, but also committed the United States to resist "Communist aggression" everywhere. It was in fact a herald of the Cold War and a harbinger of the formation of NATO and the adoption of the containment strategy which came shortly thereafter.

In its initial version, containment called for buttressing weak countries and regions around the periphery of the Soviet bloc to stem Communist expansion. The Middle East heartland, with its weak regimes, regional conflicts, and nationalist agitation, appeared as a prime area in need of such measures. Accordingly, the United States joined with Britain and France in issuing the 1950 Tripartite Declaration, which sought to deter the use of force in the Arab-Israeli conflict and pledged to regulate the flow of arms to the parties so as to prevent an arms race and prepare them to take their part in collective security arrangements. The following year, the same powers invited Egypt to participate in the creation of a Middle East Defense Organization which, among other things, would take over the British bases in the Suez Canal zone and thus settle the threatening dispute between Britain and Egypt. The project failed when Egypt rejected it on nationalist grounds and because of neutralist inclinations and unwillingness to be associated with Israel.

2. The United States had gone to war in Korea as part of its containment strategy. That costly and unsatisfactory exercise undermined the value of containment even as it induced a buildup of the United States' nuclear arsenal. Starting from these factual premises, the new administration of President Eisenhower adopted the New Look strategy, which threatened nuclear "massive retaliation" against Communist encroachments anywhere, at times and places of America's own choosing.

Unlike containment, the New Look strategy did not, in itself, require any comprehensive regional association of Middle Eastern countries, or substantial indigenous military contributions. All that was needed was a few well-placed allies around the Soviet periphery who were willing to provide bases from which nuclear-armed bombers could reach various parts of the Soviet Union. Accordingly, Secretary of State John Foster Dulles came forward in 1953 with a proposal for a new alliance between the West and Middle Eastern countries of the northern tier—Turkey, Iran, and Pakistan—which had shown sensitivity to the Communist threat and willingness to cooperate with the West.

Secretary Dulles's proposal had the merit of bypassing the countries of the Middle East heartland and their regional problems. However, the British, whose presence in Iraq was under nationalist pressure, sought to solve that problem by urging the Iraqi government of friendly Prime Minister Nuri al Sai'd to join the proposed pact. Nuri not only agreed, but sought to draw other Arab countries in—Jordan, Syria, and Lebanon—as a way of serving Iraq's self-aggrandizement schemes. This aroused the apprehensions of the Saudis, ever-fearful of the Hashemite rulers of Iraq and Jordan, and the jealousy of Egypt, which considered itself the natural leader of the Arab countries and sought to use Arab solidarity to advance its own national cause against the British. In opposing Iraq's intent, the Egyptians and the Saudis accused it among other things of deserting the Arab coalition against Israel, while Iraq defended itself by arguing that its project would gain access to Western arms which would strengthen the Arabs against Israel. Thus what came to be known as the Baghdad Pact got tangled from the outset with local nationalist quarrels with Britain, pan-Arabism, inter-Arab rivalries, and the Arab-Israeli conflict. The consequences were momentous.

The Soviets had viewed with alarm the American strategy based on massive retaliation and were, naturally, most anxious to deny to the United States the bases on their periphery that were essential for it. The hostility of Nasser to the Baghdad Pact created a shared interest which led to the conclusion of a major Soviet-Egyptian arms deal in 1955. In the perspective of the multibillion dollar arms contracts of the 1970s and 1980s, the $100 million deal of 1955 appears a modest affair. However, on the scale of the time it was large enough to threaten to overturn the local balances of power. Most important, the deal broke the monopoly of the Western powers in the supply of arms to the area, which they had used to try to stabilize the Arab-Israeli conflict and lure Iraq and others into the Baghdad Pact. It also opened the way for Soviet influence in the Middle East heartland for the first time, giving them a chance to outflank and undermine the northern tier.

The United States, stunned by the move, reacted to it in a piecemeal, inconsistent manner which ultimately contributed to the destruction of British and French positions in the region and left it with the sole responsibility for the defense of the region. Secretary of State Dulles first tried to counter the new Soviet influence by promising to help Egypt build a mammoth dam at Aswan and by turning a deaf ear to Israel's pleas for American arms to counter Nasser's Soviet arms. Next, he relented partly on the question of arms to Israel by supporting Canadian and French moves to supply some from inventory assigned to NATO, and then he reacted to minor Egyptian provocations by withdrawing the Aswan dam offer. This led Nasser to retaliate by nationalizing the French- and British-owned Suez Canal Company. The British and French governments threatened forceful action to compel Nasser to yield control of the vital waterway and Secretary of State Dulles initially supported their cause. However, he subsequently subordinated the issue of recovering control over the canal to the aim of preventing his allies from resorting to force, for fear of inflaming Arab anti-Western feelings and playing into the hands of the Soviets. When Britain and France finally took matters into their own hands and, in collusion with Israel, invaded Egypt, the United States condemned its allies and took actions, ironically parallel to Soviet endeavors, which utterly frustrated their design.

3. The failure of the British-French expedition thoroughly undermined the historic role of these countries as Middle Eastern powers, enhanced tremendously Nasser's stature as leader of Arab nationalism, and greatly strengthened the position of the Soviets as his proven friends in time of need. The United States, fearing that a continuation of Nasser's Soviet-supported Arab nationalist drive could overrun the remaining Western positions in the area, sought to rally as many Middle Eastern countries as possible under the banner of the Eisenhower Doctrine, which promised American assistance to

any country requesting help to resist aggression by international communism. The practical expression of this latest, purely American attempt to organize part of the region in the Western camp was a concerted overt and covert campaign to stem and roll back the Nasserist drive. After scoring one success in Jordan, where the United States helped King Hussein overthrow his own pro-Nasser government, the campaign got bogged down in Syria and then backfired. Syria, split from within and threatened from without, threw itself into Nasser's arms and merged with Egypt to form the United Arab Republic. Next, the Arab nationalist enthusiasm generated by that union helped polarize Lebanon's delicate political system and plunged the country into civil war. Then, in July 1958, Iraqi troops which had been ordered to advance to the Syrian border turned on the regime in Baghdad, overthrew it, took the country out of the Baghdad Pact, and turned to the Soviet Union for support.

The United States reacted by sending the marines into Lebanon and the British assisted by sending paratroopers to Jordan, while the Soviets tried to convey an impression of willingness to support forcefully the Arab nationalist cause by holding major military maneuvers in the Caucasus. By the time the crisis was defused a few weeks later, the American and British interventions had managed to save Lebanon and Jordan from being swept by the Soviet-supported Nasserist tide, but Iraq had been lost to the West and had joined Egypt and Syria as a protégé of the Soviet Union. Other Arab countries had openly dissociated themselves from the Eisenhower Doctrine.

4. Hitherto, each time the Soviets had scored a gain in the Middle East heartland—after the 1955 arms deal, the 1956 war, the 1957 Syrian crisis—they had proposed a big-power conference to neutralize the Middle East. That is to say, they offered to give up their positions in the heartland in exchange for the West's giving up its positions in the northern tier. Since the latter were an essential part of the Western strategic deterrent, the United States had naturally refused. After the 1958 Iraqi revolution, the Soviets repeated their offer, but when the United States at last showed a willingness to agree, the Soviets retracted it. The change in the attitudes of the two superpowers reflected the beginning of a change in the nature of the global strategic balance between them as well as the shift that had taken place in their relative positions in the Middle East region itself.

Soviet advances in nuclear technology and delivery capability, dramatized by the launching of Sputnik, had made massive retaliation an untenable strategy as the United States itself became a potential target for a Soviet second strike. The United States, for its part, had begun to develop its own second strike capability based on ICBMs and Polaris-carrying submarines in addition to manned bombers. As a balance of terror resting on invulnerable, independent deterrents emerged, the rivalry between the superpowers took on the form of "peaceful competition." Under the influence of Mao Zedong's "rural strategy" and his view of the unindustrialized countries as the "countryside of the industrialized world," peaceful competition meant striving for positions and influence in the Third World, caught in the throes of accelerated decolonization. In that context, the Middle East region, although no longer critical to the nuclear balance, remained a prime arena for competition because of its nodal geographic position between Europe, Asia, and Africa, its oil resources, the fact that both superpowers already held some positions in it, and the opportunities that its multiple problems seemed to present to each to score against the other.

In the actual competition that unfolded in the late 1950s and early 1960s, the United States fared better than the Soviets, mainly because the latter were now the ones who got caught in the midst of feuding clients and domestic upheavals. In 1959, Nasser's Arab nationalist drive stalled as Iraq's new ruler, General Kassem, resisted it and offered his own rival plan for unity, and in 1961 it suffered a disastrous setback when Syria seceded from the United Arab Republic. Nasser's attempt to revive the drive by intervening militarily in Yemen to support a republican coup miscarried and left him in a morass from which he could not extricate himself for five years. Two almost simultaneous Ba'thist-led coups in Iraq and Syria in 1963 briefly revived the hopes of union between these countries and Egypt only to dash them and leave behind three rival centers contending for leadership of the Arab nationalist movement. The Soviets, who had started out in 1958 as the patron power of Cairo, Damascus, and Baghdad, inevitably got caught in the midst of these crosscurrents and suffered severe damage, the most serious of which being the loss of their image as the unselfish champion of Arab unity. In contrast, the United States' position during those years resting on Turkey and Iran in the northern tier, and Israel, Jordan, and Saudi Arabia in the heartland, remained secure. The first three, being non-Arab, not only were inured to the unrest of Arab nationalism, but also provided a counterpoise to the Arab nationalist countries, which helped protect Saudi Arabia and Jordan against assaults from those directions.

Having found the vehicle of Arab nationalism troublesome, the Soviets began at the end of 1964 to seek to consolidate their position by promoting cooperation among their clients in hostility toward Israel—a dangerous tack they had hitherto avoided. The occasion for their taking this approach was the completion by Israel of a project to divert the Jordan River. Initially frustrated by continuing inter-Arab disputes, the Soviets came back to the charge in 1966, after a new regime had come to power in Syria that they particularly favored because it took Communists into the government for the first time. This time they were able to mediate a mutual defense agreement between Syria and Egypt. The following year, as tension and border clashes between Syria and Israel escalated, the Soviets prodded Nasser to activate the Sinai front in order to deter Israeli action against Syria. Nasser responded, but was led by the momentum of his actions and the enthusiasm they aroused in the Arab world to raise the issue at stake again and again until he left Israel with no choice but capitulation or war. Israel chose war, and the results of its decision have dominated the configurations of the Middle East problem from that time until the eruption of the Persian Gulf in 1979.

5. In the wake of the 1967 war, the contest between the United States and the Soviet Union came to center almost entirely on the Arab-Israeli conflict. It took the form of two opposed alignments, one between the United States and Israel, the other between the Soviet Union and Egypt. The contest was complicated by the interplay of two sets of factors: first, an evolving situation in the leadership of some of the parties involved and in the global climate of American-Soviet relations and, second, the fact that the interests of each superpower and its respective client overlapped a great deal but did not entirely coincide. Thus, as events unfolded, the contest assumed the character of a double struggle: one between the two alignments, and one within each of the two alignments.

The interests of the United States were closely identified with those of Israel. Both wanted to use Israel's war gains to liquidate the Arab-Israeli conflict through comprehensive peace—Israel for obvious reasons, the United States in order to end the exploitation of the conflict by Nasser and the Soviets to its own detriment and consolidate its position in the area. The Soviets' interests, likewise, were closely linked to those of Egypt, and at one remove from Syria's. Both Nasser and the Soviets wanted to "liquidate the consequences of the war," i.e., to recover the lost territories and eliminate Israel's military predominance, without liquidating the conflict juridicially—Nasser on personal, domestic, and pan-Arab grounds, the Soviets in order to restore their position, endangered by their failure to save their clients from defeat.

On the other hand, the United States for itself was only interested in peace and was rather indifferent to terms and procedure, whereas Israel insisted on direct negotiations and certain unspecified but substantial territorial modifications. American support for Israel's specific position involved the risk of prolonging the confrontation unnecessarily and alienating friendly Arab countries in which the United States had additional and very substantial interest. The Soviet Union, for its part, while interested in the same ends as its principal client, disagreed over the means to be used in pursuit of them. Nasser (and Syria, too) had asked the Soviets to join with their forces in an all-out war to achieve their goals; however, the Soviets not only balked at the idea for fear of confrontation with the United States, but became wary lest their clients use their assistance to start a general war on their own. The Soviets feared that such a war might force on them the choice of either becoming involved, or seeing their clients suffer another, possibly final, disaster.

The struggles between and within the two alignments unfolded in three stages over the following seven years: from June 1967 to March 1969; March 1969 to August 1970; and August 1970 to October 1973.

The first stage saw the formation of the alignments and assertion of positions. As the Soviets' assistance in rearming and retraining the Arabs reached a level that threatened Israel's military supremacy, the United States committed fifty Phantom fighter-bombers to its ally in the last days of the Johnson administration.

The second stage was dominated by the war of attrition and alternating strains within the two alignments. The new Nixon administration, worried about friendly Arab countries and anxious to gain Soviet cooperation on Vietnam, engaged the Soviets in talks aimed at helping to resolve the conflict. Six months into the war of attrition, which was going well for Nasser, the talks produced agreement on an outline for a settlement based on peace in exchange for all the conquered territory. In preliminary explorations, both Egypt and Israel rejected the proposals. However, whereas the Soviets retracted their support for the proposals, the United States, worried about the effect of the continuing war on friendly Arab countries, developed and presented them publicly as its own plan, dubbed the Rogers Plan. The American-Israeli alignment was strained as the United States thus deliberately distanced itself from its client.

Starting in January 1970, Israel turned the tables on Nasser in the war of attrition through a campaign of sustained bombing of Egypt's interior. Nasser went to Moscow and asked for advanced missiles and fighter planes and Soviet personnel to man them. The Soviets, fearing to be implicated, were reluctant. However, when Nasser indicated that he might otherwise be unable to remain in power, they agreed, but extracted from him in exchange a promise to seek a political solution once the military position was restored.

In July Soviet-Egyptian missile crews were able to penetrate the combat zone and managed to bring down several Israeli aircraft. Kissinger charged the Soviets with seeking to achieve predominance in the Mediterranean and let out that the United States was out to "expel" them. Nixon announced acceleration of arms deliveries to Israel, while Secretary of State Rogers proposed a cease-fire and negotiations. Soviet-manned aircraft challenged Israeli fighters over the combat zone, and the Israelis shot down five of them. Nasser went to Moscow to urge the Soviets to continue the military pressure on Israel. The Soviets refused adamantly. Nasser went back and accepted the American cease-fire proposal in August 1970.

Insofar as the cease-fire represented the failure of the Egyptian-Soviet alignment to change the status quo by force, it was a victory for the Israeli-American alignment. The latter went on to score yet another victory at the outset of the next stage, when American-Israeli action, this time concerted jointly and deliberately, helped defeat the Soviet-supported Syrian military intervention in Jordan on the side of the PLO in September 1970. These successes paved the way for important changes in American policy. The concern to keep some distance from Israel was dropped and the Rogers Plan was quietly shelved even after President Sadat departed from his predecessor's position and agreed, in February 1971, to the idea of a formal peace in exchange for all the territories. Instead, the United States adopted the policy advocated by Kissinger which called for unequivocal political support for Israel and help to enable it maintain absolute military superiority. These steps were seen as the best means to achieve America's objectives, which were to deter war, undermine the Soviet position, press Egypt to further modify its stance to make possible fruitful negotiations, and at the same time indirectly protect friendly Arab countries.

The revised policy was brilliantly vindicated in one respect. In July 1972, Sadat expelled the Soviet advisers and military personnel from Egypt after mounting frictions between the erstwhile partners over arms supply and policy. The Soviets had refused to provide Sadat with the weapons he wanted to maintain a war option because they feared another Arab defeat and the prospect of greater involvement on their part, and because they did not want to jeopardize an incipient détente with the United States, which had taken on critical importance for them after the American opening to China. However, the break with the Soviet Union only led Egypt to revise its strategy, not its position regarding a settlement with Israel. Rather than make concessions, Sadat decided to gamble on a surprise war with a view to achieving some limited military gains and upsetting the status quo, and thus forcing negotiations under more favorable circumstances.

6. The 1973 war profoundly altered the positions and interests of the two superpowers. During the war, they both talked détente yet mounted massive resupply operations in support of their respective clients, involving themselves for the first time in an Arab-Israeli war. Next, they jointly sponsored a cease-fire to end the fighting, and then engaged in one of their most serious confrontations over the issue of enforcing the cease-fire: the Soviets threatened to send troops to Egypt to do it, and the United States called a global alert to deter them.

After the war, the two superpowers, still talking détente, jointly sponsored a project to convene a general Arab-Israeli peace conference, yet each tried to use the results of the war to undercut the other. Although the united Arab confrontation with the United States in the form of the oil embargo seemed to put the Soviets in an advantageous position, in fact the American leverage with Israel—which underlay the embargo—proved to be far more effective in causing the Arabs to turn to the United States in quest of an acceptable settlement.

While America's relationship with Israel gave it the leverage with the Arabs that enabled it to push the Soviets aside, it also placed before it a new dilemma. The Arab oil embargo had demonstrated the fallacy implicit in prewar American policy which had separated oil and Arab-Israeli questions. At the same time, the devastating effect of the embargo on Western solidarity and the rocketing of prices it caused made access to oil—uninterrupted flow at "bearable" prices—a vital goal for the United States. The dilemma was how to accommodate those requirements with the continuing American interest in Israel. Kissinger's "step-by-step" diplomacy temporized by dealing with the issue on a piecemeal basis; but after that diplomacy ran its course, the problem came back to haunt American policy in unexpected forms.

The Carter administration tried a radical solution to the problem by seeking to promote a comprehensive Arab-Israeli settlement. However, after the endeavor to get the parties to Geneva bogged down because of inter-Arab disagreements, it threw its weight fully behind Sadat's initiative and embarked on the path to peace opened by his trip to Jerusalem. That effort eventually resulted in a peace treaty between Egypt and Israel; however, that breakthrough, crucial as it was in other respects, resulted in the isolation of Egypt from the Arab world and the oil-producing countries, and an intensification rather than a resolution of the dilemma confronting the United States. A reflection of the added trouble was seen in the oil policy pursued by the Saudis after the conclusion of the peace treaty in 1979, which resulted in a doubling of the already high oil prices within a short period.

7. The signing of the Egyptian-Israeli treaty coincided with the final collapse of the Shah's regime and the triumph of Khomeini's Islamic fundamentalist revolution. This development added several new dimensions to the problem of access to oil. The most obvious, namely the control of Iranian oil by a government bitterly hostile to the United States, was the least serious in the short run because of the glut in the world oil market. A second problem was the loss of the insurance which the Shah's regime provided in the event of internal upheavals in Saudi Arabia or other Gulf countries which could threaten the flow of oil.

A third problem was the impact of Iran's revolution on the internal stability of Saudi Arabia and other oil producers, which manifested itself partly in the seizure of the Mecca Mosque by Islamic fundamentalists and the mutiny of Saudi Arabia's Shi'ite minority in Hasa in late 1979. A fourth problem was the collapse of the balance of power in the Persian Gulf region and the effect of the resultant instability on the potential flow of oil and on superpower relations. That problem manifested itself in the Soviet invasion of Afghanistan in December 1979, and even more clearly in Iraq's invasion of Iran in September 1980, starting a war that went on for eight years. The disruption of Iraqi and Iranian oil production has not caused severe problems because of the state of the oil market; but a spillover of the hostilities to other regional producers, especially Saudi Arabia, could have disastrous consequences.

The intertwining of the Gulf and Arab-Israeli arenas manifested itself in another way, rather beneficial from the point of view of the United States. Partly because of the role that the United States played in protecting the Gulf countries despite their reticence to cooperate more fully with it, the United States was not made the target of attacks, let alone sanctions, by those countries in connection with Israel's invasion of Lebanon. However, the Lebanon war created pressures on the United States to address the Palestinian problem in a basic way, which led the president to enunciate the "Reagan Plan" in

September 1982, and this ultimately placed the United States in a cross fire between its Israeli ally and Arab friends.

THE CONFIGURATION IN THE FALL OF 1987

By the fall of 1987 a major reconfiguration of the Middle East problem had taken place as the focus of the problem shifted from the Arab-Israeli to the Persian Gulf arena. The shift had been in the making for some time, but it became apparent in the course of the summer of 1987, when over one hundred Soviet, American, and West European warships converged on the Persian Gulf in response to developments in the Iran-Iraq war. And the shift was fully acknowledged in the deliberations and resolutions of the Arab Summit held at Amman in November 1987, which, for the first time in the twenty-five-year history of that institution, gave priority to the Gulf War over the Arab-Israeli conflict.

As with previous historic mutations of the Middle East problem, this reconfiguration, too, was the result of developments that took place along all the dimensions of the problem; but the main thrust for the change was provided by two processes that unfolded at the regional level: (1) the eruption and subsidence of the strategic and political upheaval that followed the conclusion of the 1979 Egyptian-Israeli peace, and (2) the suspension and then eruption of the strategic and political turmoil that had been latent in the simultaneous triumph of Iran's Islamic revolution. Cutting across both processes was the development of a persistent glut in the world oil market and its ramifications.

Eruption and Subsidence in the Arab-Israeli Arena

The conclusion of the 1979 Egyptian-Israeli peace treaty had profoundly altered the balance of power in the Arab-Israeli arena. Egypt's exit from the Arab-Israeli conflict (and the concurrent confirmation of its switch from the Soviet to the American camp) eased Israel's concern about its southern flank and left it with a vast amount of "disposable" power. This development raised two crucial questions: How would Israel use its greatly enhanced power vis à vis its remaining opponents—Syria, the PLO, and, to a lesser extent, Jordan? And how would the opponents react as they confronted an Israel made much stronger?

It turned out that Israel under the leadership of Prime Minister Begin and Defense Minister Sharon tried to use its military superiority to start a war in Lebanon in an attempt to impose on its remaining opponents a settlement to its liking. Its endeavor proved to be a costly failure and a lesson in the limitations of military power. Syria, Egypt's erstwhile ally in the 1973 war, and the foremost advocate of "steadfastness and confrontation," tried to build a new "strategic balance" in order to deter Israel, regain a war option, and be able to force negotiations from a position of strength. Its effort met with considerable success but was exhausted well short of its ultimate goal. The net result of Israel's and Syria's endeavors was the emergence of a strategic stalemate that discourages war but also provides little pressure for movement toward peace. This evolution, coupled with the eruption of the Persian Gulf arena, relegated the Arab-Israeli conflict to the sidelines of the Middle East problem.

The Lebanon War. Begin, freshly reelected for a second term in June 1981, and Sharon, recently appointed as defense minister, used Israel's disposable power to launch what everyone agreed was a "war of choice" to advance particular policy goals, in contrast to a "war of necessity," imposed or clearly made inevitable by the enemy. The goals of operation "Peace for Galilee" approved by the cabinet and proclaimed to the world were relatively modest and arguably defensive: to destroy the PLO forces in southern Lebanon and secure a forty kilometer buffer zone that would put Israel's northern settlements beyond the reach of long-range artillery. Sharon and Begin, however, had in mind far more ambitious objectives, for which they hoped to secure the necessary political support on a piecemeal basis as the campaign unfolded under their direction.

They sought to destroy the PLO presence in Lebanon altogether in a concerted action with the forces of the Christian Lebanese Front led by Bechir Gemayel, to force the Syrian army out of the country, and to establish an effective central government headed by Gemayel that would conclude a formal peace and a formal or informal alliance with Israel. Moreover, the elimination of the PLO and the weakening of Syria would make it possible, in their view, for Israel to consolidate its rule in Judea and Samaria. These achievements would allow Israel, for instance, to resume, with better chances of success, plans to establish unilaterally a regime of limited autonomy in those areas and in Gaza, which had hitherto been obstructed by PLO intimidation of Palestinians who were willing to collaborate. Sharon estimated that the military campaign would be completed in a few days, before any international intervention could galvanize, and that a reduced Israeli military presence would be required for three months thereafter to secure the establishment of the new order in Lebanon.

In fact, the Lebanon war proved to be the longest of Israel's half dozen wars, and the costliest in casualties next to the 1948 War of Independence. Moreover, despite the awesome military power deployed by Israel, the final results of the war were worse than nil. A complete analysis of the events of that venture would require a separate volume, but the highlights are as follows: The Israeli forces attacked in three more or less parallel prongs, and in the first five days the campaign proceeded auspiciously from Sharon's point of view. The western and central prongs overcame or surrounded PLO positions and advanced steadily in the general direction of Beirut. The eastern prong advanced toward the Syrian-held positions and then halted, while the central prong advanced so far on the flank of the Syrians as to place them in a position where they had either to withdraw or to fight. As they chose to fight, the Israeli air force successfully attacked Syrian SAM batteries. A battle for control of the skies developed which Israel won handily. In less than three days, starting June 9, its air force shot down nearly one hundred Syrian combat aircraft while losing none of its own. The Syrian ground forces, which in the meantime had come under attack by Israeli armor from the front and the flank, were now doomed to destruction. They were saved by a U.N. cease-fire injunction, which Israel obeyed on June 11 at the behest of the United States, who had in turn chosen to heed a mildly threatening Soviet note. Begin and Sharon may have comforted themselves with the thought that the Syrian forces were neutralized and remained hostage to Israel's power. However, although the Syrian army gave no further military trouble, its continuing presence in Lebanon was to prove quite troublesome, indeed, to Begin and Sharon's plans.

On the PLO front, too, things began to go awry after the first few days. As the Israeli army approached Beirut, the Christian Lebanese Front forces failed to march against the PLO and its allies in West Beirut as they were supposed to do, and they contented themselves with helping to close the ring around the city. Even Sharon was not prepared to risk the high casualties that would be involved in storming a vast built-up area, and consequently he and Begin had to modify their aim and tactics. Instead of the destruction of the PLO, they now sought its removal from Beirut, and they hoped to achieve that by means of a siege and intense bombardment designed to turn the Beirut people against the PLO. They assumed that the operation would not take long, but events beyond their control decreed otherwise.

U.S. Secretary of State Haig had made halfhearted attempts to restrain Israel from going to war, but once the war broke out he saw it as an opportunity to score major gains in Lebanon and advance a settlement of the Palestinian question through a Jordanian-Israeli peace. His concept on the latter question was diametrically opposed to Begin and Sharon's, but his thinking regarding Lebanon coincided almost entirely with theirs. He enunciated United States policy as seeking the withdrawal of Israel "in the context" of the removal of all foreign forces from Lebanon and, after the Israeli Army reached Beirut, had President Reagan offer the services of Special Envoy Philip Habib to mediate the withdrawal of the PLO from the city. Haig, like Begin and Sharon, saw the acceptance of Habib's mission by the Arab side as a sign that it would succeed quickly; however, before that happened, Haig became involved in a dispute over policy management within the administration which led to his resignation. George Shultz replaced him. The division in the U.S. government and the fall of "pro-Israel" Haig gave heart to the beleaguered PLO and its supporters, and it ended the prospect of a successful short siege.

Habib's negotiations dragged on inconclusively for nearly a whole month, during which public opinion in the world and in Israel itself was aroused against the continuing siege. However, in the last week of July, Begin and Sharon submitted parts of the city to savage relentless bombing and bombardment in order to force a decision, and eventually succeeded. On August 6, the PLO agreed to leave Beirut, and its evacuation was completed on August 30 under the supervision of an international peacekeeping force comprising U.S. Marines and French and British contingents.

Shortly before the evacuation of the PLO the Lebanese Parliament had elected Bechir Gemayel to be president. The two events seemed to place Begin and Sharon at last within reach of their goal for Lebanon; but that only begat new, worse troubles. On September 1, 1982, the United States, seeking to capitalize on Israel's successes, enunciated what was dubbed the Reagan Plan to settle the Palestinian question on the basis of Palestinian autonomy in the West Bank and Gaza in association with Jordan. The plan ran counter to one of the main reasons for Begin's going to war in Lebanon, and his prompt and categorical rejection of it revealed a wide rift between the United States and Israel, which was exploited by Syria and the Soviet Union. Begin had not recovered from that blow when Bechir Gemayel was killed in an explosion in his headquarters on September 14. That same night Begin authorized Sharon to send the Israeli army into West Beirut in an endeavor to gain leverage over the choice of Gemayel's successor. Sharon advanced his troops the next day, but enlisted elements of the Christian Lebanese Front to enter the large Palestinian refugee camps of Sabra and Shatila and flush out PLO fighters who, Sharon believed, had hidden among the population. The Christian Lebanese Front fighters used the occasion to avenge their "martyred" leader and massacred hundreds of innocent Palestinians regardless of sex or age.

The massacres stirred an international uproar and triggered huge demonstrations in Israel itself that demanded, and obtained, the appointment of a judicial commission to investigate possible responsibilities of Israeli officials in the tragedy. In the meantime, the United States demanded the withdrawal of Israeli forces from Beirut and sent back a contingent of U.S. Marines, subsequently joined by other elements of the International Peacekeeping Force, to take over. More important, the United States now sought to distance itself from Israel even further and took direct charge of pursuing its goals in Lebanon, starting with successful lobbying to elect Amin Gemayel to succeed his brother Bechir over other candidates favored by Israel. That only added to the friction between the American and Israeli governments and contributed to defeating the purposes of both.

The United States did not commit the military resources necessary to secure the withdrawal of the Syrian army and the suppression of the potential opposition of various Lebanese factions to Amin Gemayel's government. It needed Israel's military power to attain those ends, but it was unwilling to give Israel sufficient incentive to cooperate. Israel's government needed at least a peace agreement with Lebanon to justify its costly war, but the United States advised Gemayel to hold back because it did not want to arouse negative Arab reaction at a time when it was still seeking Arab support for the Reagan Plan (an Arab summit in September had neither rejected nor accepted the plan, but King Hussein was trying to secure support for the plan from the PLO's Arafat, under the cover of an alternative plan adopted by the summit). When the Israeli government threatened to redeploy its forces without regard to Gemayel's interests, the Americans advised him to negotiate but to drag his feet and delay.

By the spring of 1983, the attempts to salvage the Reagan Plan had finally failed and the report of the Kahan commission on Sabra and Shatila had led to the censure and punishment of several senior Israeli officers, the dismissal of Sharon from his defense post and his replacement by the suave, American-educated Moshe Arens. These developments impelled the administration to seek in earnest an Israeli-Lebanese pact that would lead to Israel's withdrawal, which in turn would meet the condition that Syria had set for its own withdrawal. In May 1983, Secretary of State Shultz personally mediated a Lebanese-Israeli agreement that was, in his view, sufficiently short of peace to protect Gemayel's government and anticipate Syrian objections, but was close enough to peace to satisfy Israel and allow it to withdraw its forces. He then took the agreement to Damascus to confirm Syria's promise to withdraw.

By that time, however, the circumstances that had induced Syria to contemplate withdrawal had changed, and President Assad accordingly relented. On the one hand, the Soviets, prompted by the direct American military involvement and eager, under a renewed leadership, to regain some of the credibility they had lost by their earlier passiveness, more than replaced Syria's losses of equipment in the war. They provided it with advanced weapons, including SAM 20 missiles, and, as an added deterrent, sent Soviet personnel to man the advanced arms they provided and train the Syrians in the use of these weapons. On the other hand, it had become apparent to Assad that the United States was unwilling to commit its own resources to support its policy, and that the rift that had developed between the United States and Israel, coupled with Israel's apparent loss of stomach for war, made it unlikely that the two would concert action to drive his army out of Lebanon by force. Consequently, Assad not only refused to withdraw, but also rejected the May 1983 agreement *in toto* and vowed to bring about its abrogation; and he began a discrete campaign to force unilateral and unconditional withdrawal of the Israelis and of the Americans as well.

Assad's calculations proved correct, and his campaign succeeded entirely within a year or so. The upheaval that had forced Sharon out had also caused Begin to lose the will to act; he lapsed into a state of despondency for several months before resigning in September 1983. Before he had quit, his government had settled on a defensive policy of shortening supply lines by partial withdrawal in the face of American entreaties not to do so, and bracing for a long stay in south Lebanon in the faint hope that the United States might find a way to overcome Syria's resistance or otherwise enforce the May 1983 agreement.

The United States, for its part, ran afoul of most Lebanese armed factions, who saw it as seeking to reimpose on them Maronite domination under the guise of a national government. They began by fighting the government's forces with Syrian assistance and incidentally hit U.S. Marine positions; after American forces retaliated, they turned against the American presence itself. Their attacks reached a tragic climax in October 1983, when a truck loaded with explosives was detonated in the heart of the U.S. Marines' compound, killing 241 servicemen—more than 17 percent of the marine contingent—in one blow. The United States responded by firing battleship guns on Syrian positions, the Syrians returned fire, the United States struck with aircraft, the Syrians shot down two of the attacking planes, and for a moment it looked as though the exchange of blows would escalate to a full war. However, when President Reagan considered that possibility, his advisers were sharply divided, and the review of the situation only set the ground for the withdrawal of the U.S. Marines and American disengagement from Lebanon the following February.

The disengagement of the United States led Gemayel to abrogate the May 1983 agreement in an endeavor to conciliate Syria. This reduced Israel's policy under Begin's successor, Yishak Shamir, to hanging on in south Lebanon in the face of increasing attacks by Syrian-supported Shi'ite militias and a mounting toll of casualties in the hope of being able eventually to trade withdrawal for practical security arrangements, without which the withdrawal would amount to a politically disastrous admission of total defeat. Shamir's problem, however, was that the Lebanese government could not enforce any security provisions; the Syrians who could enforce security provisions would not discuss a trade off; and the local Shi'ite militia was only willing to offer general assurances based on good faith in exchange for withdrawal. His struggle with the dilemma was, fortunately for him, interrupted by a successful opposition motion in the Knesset on March 22 for early elections, which were set for July 1984.

The elections resulted in an absolute tie, with neither the Labor party nor Likud party able to form a coalition. In the end, the two major parties and their allies agreed to form a government of National Unity based on a peculiar distribution of offices and a limited program that included working for a prompt withdrawal from Lebanon. The government assumed office in September, and, after vainly exploring its options for three months, decided in January 1985 on unilateral complete withdrawal with security measures in a narrow strip adjacent to Israel to be enforced by an Israel-supported local militia assisted by Israeli advisers. The evacuation was completed on June 6, 1985, on the third anniversary of the invasion.

From the perspective of Israel in the fall of 1987, the results of the Lebanon War were almost entirely negative. None of the objectives entertained by Begin and Sharon was achieved, not even the modest ones that they had used as a ploy to gain authorization for their venture. For, by 1987 the

PLO was back in Lebanon, playing once more an important, if no longer or not yet dominant, role in the kaleidoscopic power politics of the country. And the PLO was back even in the south in sufficient strength to fight the Shi'ite militia to a standstill on the turf the latter came to claim as its own. The price paid by Israel included 654 soldiers killed and 3,873 wounded, 1.5 to 5 billion dollars in war costs, and the breakdown of the precious national unity with which Israel had faced wars since its creation. One possible positive outcome is that the Israeli leaders may have learned a lesson about the unpredictability of war and the limitations of sheer military power. At any rate, the war surely consumed Israel's surplus power for some time to come and thus cancelled one of the strategic consequences of the Egyptian-Israeli peace.

Syria's Quest for "Strategic Parity." Already after the conclusion of the September 1978 Camp David accords that laid the grounds for the Egyptian-Israeli peace treaty signed in March 1979, Syria had given utmost priority to the task of rebuilding a strategic balance with Israel. For the short run, such a balance was seen as essential to deter Israel from attacking or pressing Syria; for the longer run it was seen as creating an indispensable condition for an eventual settlement of the conflict on terms favorable to Syria.

Just what those terms were was never made quite clear, but what was clear was that they had to be different from what the Camp David accords held out for Syria. At best, these would have restored the Golan to Syrian limited sovereignty in exchange for normalization of relations with Israel and for Syria's becoming another client of the United States, third or fourth in rank after Israel, Egypt, and perhaps Saudi Arabia. What Syria wanted was a settlement that would leave it free to maneuver between the superpowers and among the Arab countries for maximum autonomy and advantage; and such a settlement was possible only if it was negotiated from a position of at least equal strategic strength with the opponent, Israel.

Strategic strength, in Syria's conception, had to go beyond a capacity to deter Israel to acquiring a war option against it. Not one that would seek to destroy Israel's capacity to resist dictation—that was precluded by Israel's assumed possession of nuclear weapons—but one that could inflict on it a serious enough defeat to compel it to concede a desirable settlement. The acquisition and exercise of such an option required, in turn, an array of interrelated conditions, including Arab diplomatic and material support, vast financial resources, access to advanced weapons, and international (mainly Soviet) backing; and underlying them all, keeping Egypt isolated and preventing other Arab parties from seeking a separate settlement.

Syria's pursuit of strategic balance and its attendant conditions since 1979 was sustained through many tribulations before coming to a pause or a halt in 1987. By then Syria had definitely acquired a strong deterrent against Israeli pressure as well as against outright attack, but it had fallen short of gaining the option of initiating war. That outcome does not suffice to prompt it to force a showdown, but it may make it less reluctant than it had been to contemplate negotiations for a settlement if a move developed in that direction. Barring such a move, the situation favors a continued stalemate, which because of Assad's failing health and the pivotal role of his leadership, may not be advantageous to Syria.

Syria's quest for strategic balance went through many ups and downs but these can be reviewed in terms of three phases:

1. In 1978 Syria sought to promote an *Arab* counterbalance to Israel, hinged on a Syrian-Iraqi alliance. After a major initial success, the endeavor failed. Syria then salvaged elements of the success and incorporated them in a new endeavor, starting in 1980, that sought to achieve *Syrian* "strategic parity" with Israel.

Right after the Camp David accords, Assad reached out in desperation to his mortal foe, Saddam Hussein of Iraq, and the two concluded an agreement in principle to merge their countries. Assad also seconded Saddam Hussein in steering two Arab conferences held in Baghdad in November 1978 and in March 1979 to adopt resolutions that ostracized Egypt and committed the oil-rich countries to provide massive annual grants to support Syria, Jordan, and the PLO in their continuing confrontation with Israel. The Soviet Union expressed its support for the Baghdad resolutions.

In 1979 the Syrian-Iraqi unity talks failed. Syria felt that Iraq had tried to exploit its security vulnerability to impose itself on Syria. The two regimes reverted to their traditional mutual hostility. Furthermore, the Soviet invasion of Afghanistan at the end of that year split the Baghdad front between a Saudi-led majority that condemned the Soviet Union, and included some that contemplated strategic cooperation with the United States under the Carter Doctrine; and a minority led by Syria that sought to preserve Soviet good will and avert diversion of Arab attention away from the Arab-Israeli conflict. Finally, Iraq's invasion of Iran in 1980 renewed the problem of diversion with greater intensity, and caused Saudi Arabia to actually request the United States to provide military assistance in the form of AWACS aircraft to help protect it against possible Iranian attacks. That, to Syria, portended Saudi Arabia's slipping into a position of support for the American-sponsored peace process.

In response to these developments, Syria renounced the idea of an Arab coalition to balance Israel and decided, in mid-1980, to seek "strategic parity" by itself, encouraged by the oil-induced economic boom that Syria was enjoying. To meet the need for deterrence in the short run and better secure the arms it needed in the longer run, Syria concluded in October 1980 a Treaty of Friendship and Cooperation with the Soviet Union. As part of an effort to retain Arab financial support and prevent defections to the American-promoted peace process, Syria boycotted an Arab summit that met in Amman in November 1980 to deal with the Iran-Iraq war. Syria also deployed large forces menacingly against Jordan, ostensibly because Jordan considered joining the peace process. Its maneuvers succeeded in obtaining the assurances it desired and renewed commitment of financial support from the oil-rich countries.

2. Between mid-1980 and mid-1982 Syria's quest for parity made substantial headway while overcoming serious problems. In June 1981 it faced the danger of premature war with Israel as a result of a confrontation in Lebanon (Israel shot down Syrian helicopters fighting the Phalanges. Syria deployed SAM missiles, and Israel threatened to attack them if not removed), but Saudi and American mediation defused the crisis. Later that year Syria was able to prevent a move toward premature peace by torpedoeing the Fahd Plan advanced by Saudi Arabia, yet it managed to win specific Saudi support for its quest for parity in exchange for helping to moderate Iranian policy and actions.

The premature war and premature peace moves that were averted in 1981 came to pass in 1982, along with setbacks in all other aspects of Syria's quest for parity. We have already reviewed Israel's invasion of Lebanon, its attack on Syria's army there and the crippling of its air force, the desertion of Syria by the Soviet Union and the Arab countries, America's promotion of the Reagan peace plan and its assumption of a leading role in Lebanon and its mediation of a Lebanese-Israeli agreement. We have also discussed how Syria managed to overcome all these adversities, regain Soviet military support and Arab financial assistance, foil all settlement projects, and end up as the sole outside power in Lebanon.

3. Even before all the adversities had been overcome, Syria had resumed its quest for parity with the acquisition of vast amounts of Soviet arms. The large number of Soviet personnel manning some of the new advanced equipment contributed an element of immediate deterrence while the weapons were assimilated. By 1985 or 1986, Syria had built up a military establishment that matched or surpassed Israel's in terms of sheer numbers. There remained a large recognizable gap in the quality of the weapons commanded by the two sides, and a difficult to assess, but perhaps larger disparity in the quality of the personnel. Nevertheless Israel repeatedly demonstrated respect for Syria's capabilities by adopting more cautious responses to incidents in which Syria had a presumed or indirect involvement.

For a while, Syria's quest for parity appeared to have advanced so far as to raise the issue of asymmetry in the Syrian-Israeli balance and its destablizing potential. (Syria aimed to balance Israel by itself, whereas Israel had to balance Syria plus contributions from other potential Arab belligerents, making for constant escalation of the arms race and putting a premium on prevention.) However, by the fall of 1987 it had become apparent that Syria's quest had exhausted itself. The oil glut that started in 1982 and the decline of oil prices, especially the precipitous drop in 1986 from $32 to less than $10 per barrel, ended the period of economic prosperity and reduced the flow of remittances and grants from oil-rich countries that had sustained the military buildup. The resulting economic strain actually forced a small but instructive cutback in the military establishment in 1986–87 for the first time in over a decade.

Another significant development affecting the quest for parity was the accession in the Soviet Union of a new leadership, headed by General Secretary Gorbachev, committed to "new thinking" in domestic and foreign policy. In the Middle East, the new thinking was reflected in attempts to escape the Soviet's exclusive dependence on Syria, to diversity and modulate Soviet relations with countries of the area, including Egypt and Israel, and to seek a settlement of the Arab-Israeli conflict without resort to force.

Far more important was the development that took place in the inter-Arab arena as a result of the eruption of the Gulf crisis and the polarization of relations between Iran and its Arab neighbors. The confrontation reduced or eliminated Syria's role as a moderator of Iranian policy, on which it had cashed in, handsomely for many years. Above all, the confrontation impelled the Saudis and the Gulf countries to reach out to Egypt for help and press, successfully, in the November 1987 Amman summit for ending Egypt's ostracism. Underscoring the significance of that move was the fact that the summit's agenda and resolutions gave first priority to the conflict with Iran. They addressed the Arab-Israeli conflict secondarily, and even then the dominant note was not the usual pledges for continuing confrontation but a call for an international conference to seek a peaceful settlement. The fact that Syria, contrary to its behavior in several previous summits, went along was probably an indication of recognition, half-resigned and half-satisfied, that it had reached the limit in its quest for parity. This, coupled with Israel's retrenchment after its Lebanon misadventure, ended the period of strategic instability resulting from the Egyptian-Israeli peace.

Eruption in the Gulf Arena

Iran's Islamic revolution, like the other major revolutions of modern time, was a climactic moment in the contest of historical forces and, as such, had potential implications far transcending its place of origin for other parts of the world where these forces contend. Iran's revolution represented a triumph of Islamic revivalists, seeking to restore an idealized Islamic polity, in an historic struggle against secularizing modernizers, who have aspired to build and develop national states. It potentially appealed to the vast masses of mostly lower-class Muslims everywhere who have felt aliens in the midst of the imported cultures and political orders promoted by their modernizing rulers, and who yearned to reassert their identity and roots.

Iran's revolution inspired militant fundamentalist activity in many countries, but its full impact was held in abeyance by the inconclusive war it has fought with Iraq since 1980. In 1987, however, it became increasingly apparent that Iran was apt to prevail any moment, and that prospect precipitated new reactions by parties most likely to be affected by such a victory and the delayed consequences of the Islamic revolution. These reactions led to intervention by the superpowers, internationalization of the Gulf conflict, and polarization of relations between the Arab countries and Iran. It also set in motion a realignment of forces and a revision of priorities that completely altered the shape of the Middle East problem.

We have pointed out before that the successful encroachment of Western powers on the realms of Islam in the latter part of the eighteenth century was at the root of a crisis of orientation in the Middle East. That encroachment had generated responses among Muslim societies, which became articulated in the nineteenth century under the impetus of increasing foreign domination, into two ideological and political currents: Islamic revivalism and secularizing nationalism. In the twentieth century, the two currents evolved and bifurcated, but joined sporadically in endeavors to get rid of foreign control. By the time independence of these Arab-countries was achieved, the two currents had spawned extreme versions that were mutually hostile. Islamic revivalism, initially concerned mainly with reformulating the traditional Islamic belief system to allow greater scope for reason, had generated varieties of fundamentalist currents or movements that aspired to replace the existing political systems with Islamic polities modeled after an idealized original Islamic community-state. Nationalism, initially identified with liberalism, had taken on various authoritarian or radical populistic forms committed to forced-pace modernization.

In general, the Islamic currents had far greater appeal to the tradition-bound masses than the nationalist, and that appeal grew stronger as the chauvinistic and populistic programs pursued by the nationalist governments fell far short of their promise and only intensified the restlessness of the masses by further disrupting the familiar moulds. The nationalists, however, commanded the state's instruments of coercion, and they used them to repress any expression of fundamentalist tendencies they deemed dangerous, and to intimidate the masses and neutralize their sympathy.

Iran's Islamic revolution undermined that syndrome by demonstrating, for the first time in history, that a fundamentalist movement enjoying the support of the masses could overcome all odds and wrest state power from a seemingly omnipotent modernizing regime. This provided inspiration for acts of fundamentalist militancy such as the seizure of the Grand Mosque of Mecca, the assassination of President Sadat of Egypt, the sabotage and terror campaign mounted by the Muslim Brethren against the Syrian regime, the rise of Hizbollah in Lebanon, and so on. However, Iran's example failed to generate similar kinds of upheavals at least in part because its revolution was itself subjected to an attempted repression by radical nationalist Iraq, and because, after repelling that attempt, Iran made the overthrow of Iraq's regime a test of the validity and destiny of its Islamic revolution.[1]

When Iraq decided to invade Iran in September 1980, its rulers, as well as those of other neighboring Muslim countries, had a sense that the accession

---

[1] In a dark moment of Iran's war with Iraq, Ayatollah Khomeini said that Allah commands us to do our duty but does not assure us of success. This statement contradicts other statements of his to the effect that successes of the revolution were a sign of Allah's approval, and it suggests, at any rate, that his audience thought so.

of the fundamentalists to power in Iran presented a danger to their regimes, but they wrongly assessed what had happened in Iran. They thought that the success of the fundamentalists there was due to fortuitous circumstances, and, feeling encouraged by the ensuing disorganization of Iran's armed forces, thought they could undo it with a decisive "police action." By defeating what remained of Iran's armed forces and seizing its main ports and oil-producing region, the Iraqis and their supporters hoped to bring about the collapse or overthrow of the new regime.

The Iraqis made some gains but fell far short of their target and could not press their attack further. By the end of October 1980, they had halted and had prepared to trade the gains they had achieved for some kind of favorable settlement. Iran refused to negotiate, but as its initial counterattacks failed, as its regime got caught in domestic struggles and purges, as it became embroiled in a conflict with the United States over the seizure of American hostages, and as it lost its principal source of supply of arms and spare parts, it seemed that the war had settled into a stalemate favoring Iraq.

However, in the fall of 1981 Iran began a series of offensives that went on intermittently through the winter, and by the spring of 1982 they had routed the Iraqis and driven them out of nearly all the territory the Iraqis had captured. Iraq sued for a cease-fire and a settlement based on the *status quo ante bellum*, but Iran insisted on the removal of the "godless Ba'thist regime" of Saddam Hussein as a condition for ending the war, and threatened to invade Iraq to achieve that end. Since the Iraqi forces had been routed in the recent offensives, the Iranians, as well as others, expected an attack to succeed quickly, and give the Islamic revolution renewed momentum and irresistible appeal.

Saudi Arabia and the other Gulf countries made frantic efforts to dissuade Iran from attacking. They approached Egypt to intervene militarily on Iraq's side, and when Egypt refused, they tried to promote mediation by third parties, enlisted Syria to use its influence with Iran, and discretely elicited American warnings to Iran. The Iranians appeared, or pretended, to be swayed for a while; but, in July 1982, they attacked in force, seeking to cut off and capture the Basra region. Only the unexpectedly successful resistance of Iraq prevented a major cataclysm.

The Iranians came back again and again. Since that first attack on Iraq in the summer of 1982, they have mounted one or two major offensives every year in addition to many smaller attacks. Some of these operations scored significant successes, albeit at enormous costs in casualties, but none has achieved a breakthrough. Interested third parties and analysts reached the comforting conclusion early in the process that Iraq's superior armament would indefinitely check Iran's superior numbers, and that the war would remain stuck in an unbreakable stalemate until the death of Khomeini opened up a possibility for a political accommodation.

Iraq's leaders, however, apparently knew better. Sooner than others they realized that Iran was deliberately pursuing a grinding war of attrition in which it had a better chance of eventually prevailing because of its larger size, more favorable geostrategic position, stronger cohesiveness, superior morale, and the unquestionable authority of the Ayatollah Khomeini. Iraq's leaders could not admit this fact to their people and allies for fear of being abandoned by them, but their anxiety was reflected in the desperate actions they took to foil Iran's strategy. In 1984, for instance, Iraq resorted to chemical weapons to repel an Iranian offensive, openly sought Egypt's support for its war effort, though Iraq had taken the lead five years before in pressing for the ostracism of Egypt, and moved to restore diplomatic relations with the United States, whom it had denounced as the sworn enemy of the Arabs since 1967.

In an effort to force Iran to end the war or at least change the odds that favored Iran, Iraq used its superior air power and newly acquired Exocet missiles to start, in 1984, a campaign against ships carrying Iranian oil exports, which financed its war-making capability. Iran suffered an initial setback, but eventually devised effective shipping arrangements that enabled it to recover and maintain its rate of exports. In the meantime, Iran had also reacted by attacking the shipping of Iraq's Arab friends in the Gulf in order to compel them to press Iraq to desist from attacking Iranian shipping, and that gave Iraq a new reason to persist in its attacks. By provoking Iranian retaliation against third parties it hoped to embroil them more deeply against Iran, that is, "internationalize" the conflict and cause international intervention to end it.

Iraq's gambit seemed to have failed until, ironically, the deterioration of its situation reached a point that could not be ignored by others. Early in 1986 its forces suffered their biggest and most obvious defeat since 1982, as the Iranians broke through south of Basra, captured most of the Fao peninsula, and held it against costly massive counterattacks. In July of that year, the Iraqis suffered another defeat in the Mehran region, and in January 1987 they lost ground in the Basra front but were able to prevent the Iranians from capturing the city only at an enormous cost in casualties. These setbacks finally drove home to interested outside governments the notion that Iraq could go under, and that, in turn, put a different perspective on their view of the "tanker war" and triggered a chain reactions, that brought the Gulf war to the forefront of regional and international attention for the first time.

In January 1987, the Soviet Union, who had for a long time a keen concern about the implications of an Iranian victory for its position in Afghanistan and perhaps for its own Muslim population, condemned Iran for continuing the war and for its anti-Soviet attitude. Shortly thereafter, Kuwait, whose ships had been a prime target of Iranian retaliatory attacks, asked the United States and the Soviet Union to help protect its shipping. The United States tabled Kuwait's request, but when the Soviets agreed in May to charter five of their tankers to Kuwait, the United States followed immediately by offering to put eleven Kuwaiti tankers under American registry and to protect them. The Saudis, who had previously been careful to keep a line open to Iran and avoid too close an association with the United States, agreed to facilitate the operations of the American escort forces. The Iranians retaliated by organizing disruptive demonstrations during the pilgrimage to Mecca, which resulted in hundreds of Iranian and other pilgrims being killed and brought Saudi-Iranian relations into open confrontation. The Iranians also responded by mining the waters of the Gulf, which, in turn, brought in naval forces of several NATO countries to protect their own shipping and to help keep the Gulf waters open. Meanwhile, Iran vowed to make everyone's shipping unsafe as long as its own was made so, and Iran backed up its threat with selective attacks on unescorted ships.

While these developments unfolded in the Gulf arena itself, the powers involved engaged in efforts aimed at bringing the war to an end or to confront Iran if it insisted on its continuation. One interesting result of these endeavors was joint action by the United States and the Soviet Union to put through the U.N. Security Council a resolution enjoining a cease-fire in the war and threatening sanctions in case of noncompliance, followed by consultations between the two superpowers on a follow-up resolution that would proclaim and enforce an arms embargo against a recalcitrant Iran. Another no less intriguing result was the convening of an Arab summit in Amman in November 1987, which put the conflict with Iran at the top of its agenda and resolutions, ahead of the Arab-Israeli conflict. The resolutions condemned Iran as aggressor, proclaimed the determination of the Arabs to resist it, and called for international sanctions against it. They ended the ostracism of Egypt in an endeavor to enlist its strategic weight against Iran and authorized the restoration of diplomatic relations with Egypt, despite its peace with Israel. The resolutions also supported an international conference with the participation of all parties, including the PLO, to settle the Arab-Israeli conflict peacefully. Syria, Iran's ally, the archantagonist of Egypt, and the proponent of strategic parity, participated in the summit and went along with all the resolutions.

Thus, Iraq's strategy of bringing about the internationalization of the conflict, which did not work when it seemed to be holding Iran at bay, began to succeed when it became apparent that the tide of the war had turned against it. Although the international intervention, the polarization of relations between Iran and the Arabs, and what came to be known as the Gulf crisis seemed to have come about as a result of discrete actions by many actors in response to various specific events, the actions were conditioned by the fear of an Iranian victory and its likely consequences. That is why the actions went beyond the events that had elicited them, and began to reorder priorities and shape a tacit coalition to contain Iran's Islamic revolution. That incipient coalition included such unlikely partners as the United States and the Soviet Union, Syria as well as Iraq, Egypt and Saudi Arabia, in addition to all the Arab countries (except Libya), and even, however implicitly and remotely (through the rehabilitation of Egypt, cooperation with the United States, and downgrading of the Arab-Israeli conflict), Israel itself.

PART TWO
THE MIDDLE EAST PROBLEM
AND THE GULF WAR (1987–1991):
RECONFIGURATION OR TRANSFIGURATION?*

The period from the fall of 1987 to the spring of 1991 witnessed important events in all the regional facets of the Middle East problem, but these were overshadowed by developments in the problem's big power dimension. In the Arab-Israeli arena, the *intifadah* broke out in December 1987, triggered a spate of intense but abortive diplomatic activity in the next two years, and kept sputtering on. In the Arab-Iranian arena, the American-led international naval and air intervention, coupled with Iraqi local military successes in ground operations, finally brought the eight-year old Iran-Iraq war to an inconclusive end in August 1988. In the inter-Arab arena, Iraq's invasion of Kuwait in August 1990 set off an American-led international response that culminated in a major six-week successful war against the invaders early in 1991.

The United States played a leading role in the diplomacy that followed the *intifadah,* and an instrumental diplomatic-military role in the developments that led to the end of the Iran-Iraq war; but its response to Iraq's invasion of Kuwait was epoch-making. It represented a forceful expression of one of the implications for the Middle East of the American victory in the global Cold War. Whether the first American war against a Middle Eastern country would transfigure the Middle East problem or merely reconfigure it was still not clear in the spring of 1991.

RECENT DEVELOPMENTS

There were two crucial developments in the *structure* of the Middle East problem. The first was the end of the Cold War in American victory and the virtual elimination of the Soviet Union as a Middle East power. The parties to the regional problems can no longer play on that rivalry, and can only look to the United States, beyond the region itself, in any endeavor to advance their interests. Thus, the United States has found itself in a crucial position that involves enormous potential leverage and great potential troubles, as we shall see.

The second critical change was the apparently abortive attempt made by Saddam Hussein to preempt the prospect of American predominance by seizing regional predominance himself. ("Apparently abortive" because Saddam Hussein and his regime are still in place; as long as they are, they cannot be written off completely.) He used the enormous power that he had accumulated with the help of others in the course of fighting Iran for eight years, in order to seize the rich resources of one of those others—Kuwait—so as to maintain that power and further develop it and gain ascendancy in the region.

---

* This part is based on a synopsis of a lecture given by N. Safran in April, 1991. (Ed.)

What did Saddam Hussein actually have in mind when he rejected every chance to pull back from military confrontation with the United States? How did he expect to win? His strategy had two keys and one prerequisite. One key was to embroil Israel in the conflict and disrupt the alliance fashioned by the United States and the Arab states. The other was to withstand the expected American air attack and then engage the United States in a big land battle in which he would trade casualties at a ratio that he could afford but the United States could not tolerate. The prerequisite was to be able to hold on long enough against the initial air assault.

None of Saddam's hopes materialized. Saddam was able to strike at Israel to the very end, but not powerfully enough to force it to respond. He held on for a remarkably long period against the air assault, but the assault went on and on, and eventually broke the back of his forces. By the time the ground assault came, the "mother of all battles" turned into the mother of routs!

The Postwar Juncture

The military defeat of Saddam Hussein left the United States in the position of the sole predominant outside power in the region for the first time in history (except perhaps for a year or two at the end of World War II, when Britain had its moment).

This does not mean that the United States can *impose* a pax Americana as some have glibly argued, but that:

1. Although the turbulence and the conflicts in the region will persist for a long time, no outside power will be in a position to capitalize on them in order to undermine the U.S. position; and
2. The parties to the conflicts have every incentive to look to the United States for support in dealing with the conflicts in which they are involved. This doesn't mean they will do the United States' bidding, but they will be very reluctant to reject it and will seek to pass the burden of doing so to their opponents.

What has the United States made of its position so far?

The Bush administration began by spelling out an encouragingly sound agenda for the postwar order:

1. Providing for Gulf security
2. Promoting the Arab-Israeli peace process
3. Advancing settlement in Lebanon
4. Arms control and nonproliferation of weapons of mass destruction
5. Promoting regional economic development

Gulf Security

With regard to Gulf security, the United States and the allied Arab governments quickly agreed that long-term security should rest on a regional grouping comprising the *GCC* countries[2] plus Egypt and Syria, with a limited

---

[2] The GCC countries are Saudi Arabia, Kuwait, Bahrein, the United Arab Emirates, Qatar, and Oman.

American support (e.g., expansion of the base in Bahrein, prepositioning some equipment, a small military mission) and a substantial American naval presence.

The agreement, if it should hold, would avoid a high American profile; balance Iran but reassure her through the participation of Syria; institutionalize shared interests among key Arab countries (Saudi capital in exchange for Egyptian and Syrian military support); and structure shared interests between the United States and these countries (security for secure access to oil). The arrangement was intended, of course, also to provide for security against Iraq—to contain it and prevent it from attempting future aggression; but precisely that item revealed the flaw in the way America has pursued Gulf security, and, for that matter, its entire postwar agenda. The major points to keep in mind are:

1. The defeat of Saddam Hussein, coupled with America's administrative encouragement, triggered massive revolts by Shiites in the south and Kurds in the north.
2. The dispositions within the administration at that point were mixed. The United States wanted Saddam Hussein out of office but feared Lebanonization. This led to a confusing policy: e.g., warning Saddam Hussein not to use chemical weapons and aircraft against the rebels, but doing nothing when he used helicopters with devastating effect.
3. The Saudis, concerned about their own Shiites if Iraq's Shiites were given any right to share in power, played on America's fear of Lebanization and depicted Iraq's Shiites as potential puppets of Iran. The Administration shifted course and adopted a hands-off policy that allowed Saddam Hussein to drown the revolts in blood.
4. The Administration justified its policy on the grounds that the military mission authorized by the U.N. and Congress was accomplished, and there was no warrant to intervene in the domestic affairs of Iraq. However, the weakness of that posture soon became apparent when Turkey complained that the flood of Kurdish refugees released by Saddam Hussein's repression created a major national security problem for it. This, plus initiatives taken by Britain, France, and the European Community compelled the administration to reverse course, commit troops to seize Iraqi territory to set up safe havens for the refugees, and warn Saddam Hussein against attacking those havens.

In the meantime, independently of these developments, Saudi Arabia was unable to reach specific agreements with Egypt and Syria on the terms of their participation in the Gulf security arrangements, thus casting further doubt on the future of the American-sponsored scheme.

What the future holds depends on whether the administration formulates and pursues a coherent, comprehensive policy for the region or whether it continues to mortgage its policy to the whims of the Saudis and narrow perspectives of regional powers.

Arab-Israel Peace Promoting the Arab-Israeli peace process is crucial if the United States is to avoid being constantly pulled in opposite directions by its interests in Israel and in Arab countries. Additionally, the notions of a *regional* conference and of pursuing two parallel tracks simultaneously (Israeli-Arab and Israeli-Palestinian) are creative and promising.

But the Administration's further endeavor to gain *prior* acceptance by the Israelis of the principle of land for peace to settle the Israeli-Palestinian conflict could lead quickly to stalemate. A more promising approach is to pursue a conference without prior conditions while advancing at the same time negotiations on additional issues that could help the Arab-Israeli peace process.

Lebanon. The application of the Riyad agreement (on a constitutional redistribution of powers) endorsed by all the Lebanese factions continues to hold promise of ending Lebanon's sixteen-year tragedy. One of the threats to that prospect is the military presence that Syria and Israel maintain in the country for reasons of national security vis-à-vis each other. Now that the United States has rapport with both, and the Soviets do not obstruct and may even be enlisted to help, it can try to promote an agreement wherein the two parties would serve their national security interests by coordinated withdrawals. That kind of agreement may be facilitated if the two parties were simultaneously engaged in peace talks, and could itself help the further progress of those talks.

Arms Control This issue provides an excellent example of how to circumvent the old sterile approaches to the Arab-Israeli conflict. The Arabs are deeply concerned about Israel's nuclear monopoly in the region, while Israel even under Shamir has expressed interest in trading off its monopoly for a comprehensive arms control agreement. This basic bargaining situation provides a real opportunity for creative diplomacy. Not that arms control can be a substitute for peace, but, if successful, it can immensely facilitate the peace process. Arms control should be also pursued on the "supply side." An agreement among the suppliers to limit flow of arms would help the parties reach agreement on their side.

Unfortunately, this item was the first casualty, if not fatality, among the items in the peace process. The U.S. Secretary of Defense invoked the old argument that the United States must arm its allies to defend themselves (as if defense could not be pursued at lower overall levels), and others used the tired argument about the need for the United States to hold its own against competitors (if we don't supply arms others would, as if collective restraint-accord is out of the question).

Finally, cooperation for economic development has not been advanced at all, but at least nothing has been done to prevent it either. Here, if the United States doesn't take the lead, others are apt to do it or the parties may eventually do it on their own, and thus the United States would miss a great chance to gain and maintain the initiative.

In sum, the United States emerged from the Gulf War in a unique position to break the historic gridlock of the Middle East problem and espoused the appropriate agenda for doing so. In the actual pursuit of the agenda, however, the administration may have followed wrong trails. As of the spring of 1991 it was still possible to correct course and move forward—and the administration may yet do so.

FOREIGN POLICY LANDMARKS

1945	Formation of the Arab League
1947	U.N. resolution to partition Palestine into a Jewish state and an Arab state
1948–1949	Palestine War (Israel's War of Independence)
1955	Soviet-Egyptian arms deal, the first between the Soviet Union and a Middle Eastern country
1956	Invasion of Suez by Britain and France; Sinai War Between Israel and Egypt
1957	Eisenhower Doctrine
1958	Union between Syria and Egypt, creating the United Arab Republic (UAR)
1961	Syrian secession from the UAR
1962–1967	Yemen War with heavy Egyptian involvement
1967	Six Day War
1968–1970	The "war of attrition"
1973	October War (Yom Kippur War)
1978–1979	Camp David Accords and Egyptian-Israeli peace
1979	Soviet invasion of Afghanistan
1980	Iraqi invasion of Iran
1982	Israel invades Lebanon, pulls out in 1985
1987	Iran-Iraq war generates "Gulf crisis"
August 1988	8-year Iran-Iraq war ends. War leaves Iraq with an $80 billion debt and a long-term national security problem vis à vis Iran.
February 17, 1989	Egypt, Iraq, Jordan and North Yemen form the Arab Co-Operation Council (ACC)
March 27, 1989	Saudi Arabian King Fahd and Iraqi President Hussein sign a nonaggression agreement in Baghdad
March 31, 1989	The *Washington Post* reports from Israeli sources that Iraq is developing nuclear warhead capabilities with partial funding from Saudi Arabia
1989	Saudi King Fahd asserts that financing is only for a nuclear power plant, not for weaponry
January 17, 1990	President Bush declares that expanding trade with Iraq is a U.S. national interest.
February 15, 1990	Voice of America editorial criticizes Iraqi government's treatment of citizens; maintains that rule by force must end
February 21, 1990	U.S. State Department publishes annual report on Human Rights abuse; Iraq is heavily criticized
February 24, 1990	Hussein declares at an Arab Summit Meeting that the U.S. interests in the Middle East are inimical to Iraq's; U.S. encouragement will lead Israel to "new stupidities" in the next five years

March, 1990	Iraqi Foreign Minister Aziz and other Iraqi officials tell U.S. officials that Israel is preparing to attack Iraq
March 15, 1990	U.S. pressure on Israel to resolve the Palestinian problem causes dissolution of Israeli government. Shamir finally forms a Likud-led coalition on June 8, 1990.
April 1, 1990	Saddam Hussein announces at an Arab Summit that if Israel attacks Iraq, "...we [the Iraqis] will make fire eat half of Israel."
July 20, 1990	Kuwait places armed forces on alert in wake of Iraqi threats in connection with oil and financial dispute
July 23, 1990	United States dispatches six war ships near Kuwait
August 1, 1990	Iraq-Kuwait peace talks in Jidda break down
August 2, 1990	Iraq invades Kuwait
August 2, 1990	Security Council votes unanimously to condemn Iraqi invasion of Kuwait and demands Iraqi withdrawal (Resolution 660)
August 6, 1990	Security Council votes 13–0 with Yemen and Cuba abstaining, to impose mandatory economic sanctions on Iraq (Resolution 661)
August 6, 1990	King Fahd of Saudi Arabia requests U.S. and British protection
August 8, 1990	Egyptian President Mubarak indicates that he is willing to form an Arab force to facilitate an Iraqi withdrawal without Western intervention; Arab Summit is called
August 9, 1990	U.N. Security Council declares the annexation of Kuwait null and void (Resolution 662)
August 10, 1990	12 of the 21 Arab League members vote to send troops to Saudi Arabia
August 25, 1990	Security Council votes 13–0, with Yemen and Cuba abstaining, to allow the use of force in upholding the embargo against Iraq (Resolution 665)
September 9, 1990	United States and Soviets issue joint statement calling for unconditional Iraqi withdrawal; United States acknowledges Soviet role in future Arab-Israeli peace talks
November 8, 1990	U.S. troop build-up in the Gulf reaches 200,000. President Bush orders a troop increase to 400,000; wants to guarantee an "adequate military option."
January 12, 1991	The U.S. Congress and Senate grant President Bush the authority to go to war with Iraq in order to liberate Kuwait
January 16, 1991	United States begins air campaign against Iraq
February 25, 1991	The allies initiate the ground war
February 26, 1991	The allies enter Kuwait City
February 28, 1991	President Bush declares victory in the Persian Gulf; announces cease-fire

SELECTED BIBLIOGRAPHY

Abrahamian, Ervand. *Iran Between Two Revolutions*. Princeton, N.J.: Princeton University Press, 1982.

Ajami, Fouad. *The Arab Predicament*. New York: Cambridge University Press, 1981.

al-Khalil, Samir. *Republic of Fear*. University of California Press, 1990.

Andersen, Roy, et al. *Politics and Change in the Middle East*. Englewood Cliffs, N.J.: Prentice-Hall, 1982.

Batatu, Hanna. *The Old Social Classes and the Revolutionary Movements of Iraq*. Princeton, N.J.: Princeton University Press, 1978.

Bill, James, and Carl Leiden. *Politics in the Middle East*. Boston: Little, Brown, 1979.

Freedman, Robert O. *Soviet Policy Toward the Middle East Since 1970*. New York: Praeger, 1982.

Heikal, Mohammed. *The Road to Ramadan*. London: Collins, 1975.

——. *The Sphinx and the Commissar*. New York: Harper & Row, 1978.

Herzog, Chaim. *The Arab-Israeli Wars*. New York: Random House, 1982.

Holden, David, and Richard Johns. *The House of Saud*. New York: Holt, Rinehart & Winston, 1981.

Hourani, Albert. *Arabic Thought in the Liberal Age, 1789–1939*. New York: Cambridge University Press, 1983.

Hudson, Michael. *Arab Politics: The Search for Legitimacy*. New Haven, Conn.: Yale University Press, 1977.

Kerr, Malcom. *The Arab Cold War*. New York: Oxford University Press, 1971.

Kerr, Malcolm, and Yassin, El Sayed, eds. *Rich and Poor States in the Middle East*. Boulder, Colo.: Westview Press, 1982.

Khalidi, Walid. *Conflict and Violence in Lebanon*. Cambridge, Mass.: Center for International Affairs, Harvard University, 1979.

Lewis, Bernard. *The Emergence of Modern Turkey*. New York: Oxford University Press, 1961.

Mylroie, Laurie, and Judith Miller. *Saddam Hussein and the Crisis in the Gulf*. New York, New York Times Books, 1990.

Quandt, William. *Decade of Decisions*. Los Angeles: University of California Press, 1977.

Safran, Nadav. *Egypt in Search of Political Community*. Cambridge, Mass.: Harvard University Press, 1961.

——. *From War to War*. Indianapolis, Ind.: Pegasus, 1969.

——. *Israel: The Embattled Ally*. Cambridge, Mass.: Harvard University Press, 1978.

——. *Saudi Arabia: The Ceaseless Quest for Security*. Cambridge, Mass.: 1985.

Sifry, Micah L., and Christofer Carf, eds. *The Gulf War Reader: History, Documents, Opinions*. New York: Random House, 1991.

Stephens, Robert. *Nasser*. New York: Simon & Schuster, 1971.

Vatikiotis, P.J. *Politics and the Military in Jordan*. London: Frank Cass, 1967.

Van Dam, Nikolaos. *The Struggle for Power in Syria*. London: Croom Helm, 1979.

Waterbury John. *The Egypt of Nasser and Sadat*. Princeton, N.J.: Princeton University Press, 1983.

Yaniv, Avner. *Dilemmas of Security: Politics, Strategy, and the Israeli Experience in Lebanon*. New York: Oxford University Press, 1987.

Yergin, Daniel. *The Prize: The Epic Quest for Oil, Money, and Power*. New York: Simon and Schuster, 1991.

Yodfat, Areyh, and Yuval, Arnon-Ohana. *PLO Strategy and Tactics*. New York: St. Martin's Press, 1981.

—13—

THE
UNITED STATES
IN A
NEW WORLD
A SHORT EPILOGUE

Roy C. Macridis

In the 1990s the United States will need, for the third time in this century, to redefine its overall foreign policy goals.[1] The first time was after World War I, when it opted for what became known as "isolationism" and it refused to follow Woodrow Wilson's leadership to make the United States a member of the League of Nations, and by so doing, to assume worldwide responsibility for collective security. Between 1920 and 1940 "entangling alliances" were avoided and a policy of neutrality was pursued. The United States refused to take sides in all wars, including, notably, the Italian invasion of Ethiopia in 1936, the invasion of China by Japan, and the Spanish Civil War. No effort was made to organize a concerted opposition against Hitler's Germany or to put pressure upon Japan. Isolationism came to an end, in effect, only after World War II began. President Roosevelt came to the aid of England with a number of economic and military arrangements and provided economic and military aid to the Soviet Union after it was attacked by Germany in June 1941. When Japan attacked Pearl Harbor on December 7, 1941, and Germany declared war

---

[1] Among the many books published recently, note the following: *Peril and Promise: A Commentary on America,* John Chancellor. Harper and Row, 1990. *The Myth of America's Decline: Leading the World Economy into the 1990s,* Henry R. Nau. Oxford University Press, 1990. *Bound to Lead: The Changing Nature of American Power,* Joseph S. Nye, Jr. Basic Books, 1990. *America's Economic Resurgence: A Bold New Strategy,* Richard Rosecrance. Harper and Row, 1990, New York, NY.

against the United States, the country became a full-fledged belligerent and subsequently led the allies to victory against Germany and Japan.

The second opportunity came with the defeat of the German armies, and the capitulation of Japan by August 1945. The United States emerged as one of the two world powers (in fact it was the only world power and, retrospectively, it is clear that the strength of the Soviet Union had been grossly overestimated). Would the United States return to its isolationist posture? There was no clear debate and no election hinged on the foreign posture of the country as it had in 1920. In the years of Truman's presidency (1945–52), the President, with the massive support of Congress, formulated a new foreign policy posture that was to last for almost 40 years. First, through the Truman Doctrine, the United States came to the aid of Greece and Turkey in 1947; through the Marshall Plan, which came into effect in 1948, it provided massive economic aid to our European allies; finally, through its membership in the United Nations, the United States became a full player in world politics. But even more, in 1949 the Atlantic Alliance, brought under the military leadership of the United States most western European countries and shortly afterward, Greece and Turkey. It was the first military alliance with worldwide implications made by the United States in peace time.[2]

While it is true that the enormous economic and military weight of the country imposed upon it a new world role, the reasons that accounted for what became a worldwide commitment (implemented through a variety of military alliances and organizations, of which the Atlantic Alliance and the North Atlantic Treaty Organization were but one) were rooted in the world situation and, in many respects, were forced upon the United States. The first and foremost was the posture of the Soviet Union under Stalin (who died in 1953), but also of his successors until virtually 1985. An American-Soviet cooperation, on which Roosevelt counted until a few weeks before his death, did not materialize. On the contrary, the Yalta agreements to allow for free elections in Eastern Europe were not respected, and an aggressive and expansionist effort on the part of the Soviet Union and the spread of Communist domination in Eastern Europe and beyond in many parts of the world in the name of national independence movements began to threaten the security of the United States. The acquisition of the nuclear weapons by the Soviet Union further aggravated the situation. In the meantime the other two allies on which the United States had counted—England and China under Chang Kai-shek—proved to be of little help. England, without resources, could not play the role it was expected to play in Europe and the Middle and Near East and was unable to maintain its Empire. Chang Kai-shek and his regime collapsed and the Soviet-supported Communist regime under Mao Zedung took over. Nor did it become possible, as many American statesmen had hoped, to use the United Nations, and especially its Security Council, to maintain world order in

---

[2] It was preceded by the "Rio Pact," providing for the military security of Latin American countries under the aegis of the United States.

cooperation with England, France, the Soviet Union, and China. In its early stages the Soviet veto prevented common action. As for the Assembly, it became increasingly dominated by the Third World nations and assumed a strong ideological antiimperialist stance, generally equated with anti-Americanism. By 1952, the Soviet Union and Eastern Europe, China, Cuba, North Korea, North Vietnam on one side, and the United States and its allies on the other, confronted each other. Some fifty "nonaligned" nations were coveted by both sides.

By the beginning of the 1950s, a new foreign policy clearly emerged. It was the one suggested by George Kennan in a "long telegram" to the State Department, while he was Ambassador to the Soviet Union, and subsequently published under the signature X in *Foreign Affairs* in July 1947. It was the policy of "containment." In Kennan's own words:

> The United States has it in its power to increase enormously the strains under which Soviet policy must operate, to force upon the Kremlin a far greater degree of moderation and circumspection than it has had to observe in recent years, and in this way to promote tendencies which must eventually find their outlet in either the breakup or the gradual mellowing of Soviet power. For no mystical, Messianic movement—and particularly not that of the Kremlin—can face frustration indefinitely without eventually adjusting itself in one way or another to the logic of that state of affairs.

"Containment," as it developed, consisted of three pillars. One was military preparedness and strength (on which Kennan insisted the least) and the ability to counter any Soviet moves with adequate force in order to preempt them or stop them; secondly, economic—the sheer strength of the American economy would allow the country to develop the appropriate weapons faster and at less of an economic drain in terms of its gross national income than it was the case for the Soviet Union. An increase in the productivity and the standard of living of the United States and the allies would challenge the leaders and the peoples in the Communist bloc and undermine their faith in their own system. Finally, politically and ideologically, if democracies were able to stand up to Soviet pressures, they would become an object of emulation. The Soviet Empire—committed to expansion, unable to live up to the promises inherent in the Communist ideology to provide well-being, and compelled at the same time to subsidize their satellites and revolutionary movements in the Third World—would begin to crack.

Both the repugnance of the Americans and many of their allies for the Communist ideology and the fear of Soviet military expansion, sustained American foreign policy until well into the Reagan administration. NATO and the Warsaw Pact confronted each other over the body of a divided Germany and throughout the world Soviet-supported revolutionary movements confronted American-supported guerrilla or "counterrevolutionary movements." A divided world lived precariously at peace as the two nuclear superpowers jockeyed with each other for strategic superiority. Unable to attain it, they relied for peace upon the so-called Mutual Assured Destruction that nuclear weapons would entail. Neither allowed itself into a position of inferiority in any of the theaters of possible confrontation—especially in Europe. The fear of nuclear war had also another stabilizing factor. Both sides were loathe to allow any regional conflict to escalate into a confrontation between them— hence they were prone, by and large, to rein in their client states—Israel, Cuba, Syria, Iran, Egypt, Vietnam, South and North Korea, Turkey, Greece, Pakistan and others.

Until the late 1980s, containment remained the centerpiece of the United States policy. The country assumed global defense responsibilities, established military bases throughout the world, shaped and attempted to maintain numerous, notably regional alliances, and provided massive economic and military aid to many countries and antiguerrilla movements. Increasingly, and contrary to what Kennan had in mind, American power was projected in military terms. Democracy and economic liberalism as an ideology were also cast in terms of anti-communism. So was the commitment to human rights. Until the 1970s, the United States, in the name of containment, supported military regimes in Latin America and elsewhere. Moral and humanitarian imperatives were frequently sacrificed or bypassed. Our enemy's enemies, potential or real, became our friends.

The confrontation between the United States and the Soviet Union and with it "containment"—the guide post of our foreign policy for almost half a century—has come to an end. The reason: the weakening of Soviet power, the dismantling of the Warsaw pact and the unanticipatedly rapid reunification of Germany, followed by the gradual withdrawal of Soviet forces from Eastern Europe and Germany, and the equally inevitable, even if more gradual, withdrawal of American forces from Europe. Arms reduction agreements— both with regard to conventional forces and intermediary missiles have been made. Suddenly the opponent seems to have vanished from the ring, and the whole foreign policy edifice constructed by the United States has virtually collapsed. A new foreign policy outline spelling major guidelines (as it was Kennan's "long telegram") is needed to first spell out the rapidly changed world circumstances and second, to provide new guideposts for U.S. foreign policy.

THE CHANGING CIRCUMSTANCES

1. While the United States continues to be one of the major industrial and financial powers in the world, it is losing ground to Germany, Japan, and even to the European Community (when it manages to establish a genuine common currency and a European central bank). Its trade deficit makes it one of the major debtor nations and, notwithstanding many warnings, its growing dependence upon oil imports makes it a hostage to Middle East conflicts and vulnerable to Arab-Israel or Arab-Arab confrontations.

2. Militarily, the United States remains the foremost power, but the costs of maintaining the defense establishment are beginning, as it was the case with the Soviets, to affect adversely economic and industrial growth. There is additionally the question of how much and what kind of military strength is needed.

3. Western Europe is clearly emerging as an industrial, financial and military power that commands respect and can play on its own a decisive role in mitigating conflicts, both in the continent and also beyond—in Africa and the Middle East.

4. Japan has all the industrial and financial means to build a formidable military power and to become the foremost power in the Far East.

5. Unless ethnic conflicts lead the Soviet Union into chaos (which will pose a different set of problems), it is still an awesome military power and will continue to play a decisive role in the Asian subcontinent and claim a strong voice in Europe and the Middle East.

6. The end of the Cold War will not necessarily bring about an abatement of local and even regional wars. In fact, many were averted because each of the two superpowers feared that if they were allowed to escalate, they might lead to a confrontation between them. Now that the confrontation has ended, many smaller countries will have greater freedom to engage in the realization of their ambitions. This situation, therefore, may call for a different strategic doctrine emphasizing, for instance, a rapid deployment force and flexible conventional responses to local conflicts as they arise, rather than massive weapons of destruction and deterrence.

What is before us then is the emergence of a polycentric world with a number of roughly equal power centers even if the United States appears for the time being to be a little more equal than the others! It calls for a redefinition of U.S. foreign policy commitments and overall strategy. Three major concerns should be outlined: *domestic, regional,* and *global.*

Domestic

An indispensable ingredient of national power—to be used in terms of one's national interest independently of others or in intimate cooperation with others—is domestic economic growth and an economy that provides for an equitable distribution of goods and services to as many as possible. The foremost emphasis, therefore, should be placed on reviving U.S. economic growth, eliminating waste, providing for long-range priorities (of which the environment is increasingly one), and diverting resources allocated to non-productive activities into ones that will enhance growth and wealth. In other words, attention must be given immediately to the domestic social and economic problems that have been neglected. Urgent reforms are needed in the restructuring of industrial companies so that they plan their investments for long-range growth rather than short-term profit; renewed regulatory mechanisms may be needed to avoid crises similar to the S and L crisis;

conversely, the public sector should be reformed so as to avoid waste; above all, educational reforms are needed to provide a better trained and sophisticated labor force. Lastly, the bloated political establishment should be reformed and trimmed down. Politics in the United States has become one of the largest and most lucrative professions. It is expensive and it amounts to a wasteful allocation of resources. A bloated political structure is unable to generate leadership and set goals of achievement as it is becoming increasingly a burden on the national economy.

Finally, while economic growth will provide increased employment, higher incomes, and reduce the numbers of the poor the free market clearly is unable to provide all the services needed—affordable housing, health care, education, of drug rehabilitation and rebuilding the inner cities. Carefully coordinated governmental plans are therefore needed and should not be deferred in the name of economic liberalism and the free market.

Regional and Global Commitments

A stronger economy and a more prosperous society will have to redefine its role in the world, in the light of the changing circumstances. Clearly the first task is to seek in unison with others the worldwide commitments the United States has undertaken. This calls for:

1. Regional arrangements in areas of immediate interest and proximity to the United States—Canada and Latin America—to provide for aid and trade, as the case may be, to regulate immigration and to develop a security and conflict resolution mechanism. Unquestionably, the United States will have to play a leading role in such arrangements for the North and South American continents—especially when the latter has been neglected for so long. Similar arrangements will need to be made for the Caribbean region, with the participation of the British, French, and Canadians. With a population of well over 700 million, the continent provides both a secure and rich in resources base that can satisfy virtually all its needs while promoting increased prosperity for all.

2. Historic, ideological, and military ties link the United States with Europe. They will be maintained, but clearly the new circumstances call for equal sharing at first and for an increased assumption of leadership by the European Community as years go by. NATO may survive for a few years, but only in order to play the same role the Marshall Plan played after World War II—namely, to promote integrative military and political arrangements headed by France, England, and a unified Germany until "Europe" (allied with the United States and with close economic and political contacts with the United States) assumes progressively an independent role. The moment promised by President Roosevelt almost half a century ago will have to come soon and American soldiers will return home—hopefully directly!

3. As a world power, the United States has interests and responsibilities everywhere, but careful thought must be given as to whether it should assume them and exercise them alone. If the world is becoming polycentric, both

"decentralization" and "collectivization" of power should be undertaken either tacitly or through multilateral treaties or through the U.N. Security Council. Clearly this relates to regions such as the Middle East, the African Continent, Eastern Europe, the southern rim of Asia, including the Philippines and the so-called "European home." In each and every of the regional arrangements, the United States will have a role, but many decisions will have to be made by their constituent members.

4.   On a worldwide basis and through the United Nations, collective arrangements will have to be undertaken about arms sales, nuclear, chemical, and bacteriological weapons and the progressive reduction and, ultimately, elimination of nuclear weapons. Regarding economic and financial matters, the "seven" industrialized nations, with the possible inclusion of the Soviet Union, and perhaps China, India, and the wealthy oil-producing states, will continue to play, but in a more comprehensive way, the role they have been playing, while matters of trade will continue to be ironed out through GATT.

Decentralization and collectivization of responsibility involve both a greater cooperation, but also the continuing assumption of worldwide responsibilities and commitments by the United States. They do not lead to a retrenchment or a return to isolationism.

NEW GUIDELINES?

Fifty years after the end of World War II, a literally new world confronts the United States. It is a world in which American exceptionalism seems to have come to an end. Other countries are becoming like the United States—in terms of per capita income, industrial production, consumer tastes and habits, social mobility, the growth of mass culture, the influx of millions of immigrants, and the ever-growing appetite for greater and greater material well-being; they seem also to have accepted economic liberalism. Both the United States and all other industrialized societies face the same problems of inflation, unemployment, a growing underclass, and trade imbalances—excepting, for the time being, Japan and Germany. And while every country of the world can be targeted by U.S. nuclear weapons, so can every city in the United States. The United States is no longer "protected" by the Pacific and the Atlantic. And despite the proverbial wisdom of the framers, the American political way of life has lost whatever claims to superiority it could have made in providing stability of governance, popular participations, justice, and individual rights and political freedoms vis-à-vis other democratic societies—to which Germany and Japan have been added.

The world we now face is far less manageable than it was fifty years ago. Before 1945, four or five powers dominated it, and their interactions decided issues on which war or peace depended. On two occasions, the United States had to be dragged into war to settle its outcome in Europe and to fight for the first time a major war in Asia. The British and French Empires policed a huge area of the world and provided a ready made way to settle local conflicts. There were not more than forty "sovereign" states, but most of them were under the control or directly influenced by France, England, Russia (or the Soviet Union) and Germany, while Japan was attempting to maintain and expand its dominion over China. Today there are over 170 states, many subscribing to no regional cooperation; most of them armed with sophisticated weapons. The sales of arms to all of them, with the United States, the Soviet Union, and France accounting for the bulk of military exports, has given to most the illusion of a military option and the spread of chemical, and, perhaps, nuclear weapons new means of devastation. Under the circumstances, it is physically, economically, and militarily impossible for one power—the United States—to impose security and order. More than ever the need of collective security, through the United Nations, and internationally accepted conflict resolution mechanisms agreed upon by all members, becomes necessary. There can be no single world policeman.

From an economic standpoint, new centers of power have emerged—the European Community, Japan, Germany, the oil-producing states, soon perhaps China and India. The United States is unable (even if it continued to be willing) to be the world banker; in fact, as noted, it is in desperate need of finding one and may perhaps have found one—in Japan. Economic world policy has become multidimensional just as it is interdependent. Competition from new countries has become the rule, and survival for the United States, if it were not to share the fate of England, depends upon renewed industrial, technological, and productive effort. Such an effort calls for prudent management of national resources and careful allocation of spending, in which domestic investment and aid will have to replace foreign aid.

There is, finally, to return to American exceptionalism, the moral dimensions of foreign policy and the tendency of the American leadership and public to view matters in terms of such moral imperatives as human rights, international law, and the integrity of states and, quite frequently, in terms of democracy (equated naively with elections) and individual freedoms. These are noble objectives, but they are not unique to the United States, nor have they been practiced uniformly. The Council of Europe, for instance, excluded Greece from membership when a military junta took over power; the United States continued its relationship with the Greek junta! Moralism led also to a manichean view of good and evil, with communism invariably identified with the second. Without communism, a far more qualified approach is needed. But the point is that more nations than ever share a common belief in the moral values American foreign policy pretended to monopolize for so long. The time has come, in other words, as it is the case with military and economic matters, to pool with others our concern with moral values and implement them collectively. Undoubtedly, such a collective implementation will fall short of what the views of the United States may be, but compromises will become inevitable. Nothing, of course, can stop the United States leadership for pressing its cause until it becomes accepted.

What emerges from these remarks is a new foreign policy profile for the United States—according to which the country becomes one, albeit and for the time being the most powerful, among many centers of power—economic, financial, military and ideological. It is a profile in which accommodation and compromise is needed to shape regional centers of power, each with allotted responsibilities; a profile in which international and worldwide interests and conflicts are compromised and resolved in common by as many participants as possible. Finally, it is a profile in which cooperative arrangements ease the burden on the United States and allow it to do its best in industrial growth, technology and medicine, environmental policies, human rights and economic well-being for the disadvantaged peoples and countries. With communism gone, the enemies are poverty, the sale and spread of arms, the degradation of the environment, ignorance, the management of world resources to cope with the population explosion that ticks according to some like a nuclear bomb. If the United States were to become, in the words of President Bush, a "kinder and gentler nation" at home and abroad, it will regain its mission as the foremost world power. To paraphrase the Kennan quote, we may say that:

> The United States has in its power *to lessen* enormously the strains that afflict our world today and in so doing bring about greater cooperation among the peoples of our world.

NAME INDEX

Abdallah, King, 368-69
Abegglen, James, 220
Abrahamian, Ervand, 403
Achebe, Chinua, 334
Acheson, Dean, 2-3, 7, 8
Adedeji, Adebayo, 335n, 355
Adelman, J., 184
Adenauer, Konrad, 69, 73-80, 82, 83, 84, 85, 87, 90, 94, 103, 105
Adomeit, Hannes, 99n
Ailleret, Charles, 66
Ajami, Fouad, 403
Akagi, R.H., 219
Aldrich, R., 66
Alfonsín, Raúl, 294, 300
Ali, Muhammad, 359
al-Khalil, Samir, 403
Allen, David, 26, 119n, 124, 141
Allen, Hilary, 329
Allende, Salvador, 285, 300
Allison, Graham, 110
Allison, Roy, 328
al Sai'd, Nuri, 376
Aluko, Olajide, 355, 356
Amin, Idi, 344, 355
Andersen, Roy, 403
Andersson, Stanley, 327
Andrén, Nils, 327
Andropov, Yuri, 147, 182
Anstee, M.J., 355
Aoun, General, 57
Apel, Hans, 89, 91
Arafat, Yassir, 57, 66, 388
Arbenz Guzmán, Jacobo, 278
Ardagh, John, 105
Arens, Moshe, 388
Arias Sánchez, Oscar, 282, 292, 299, 300
Aron, Raymond, 6, 66
Ashida, Hisashi, 195
Aspaturian, Vernon V., 184
Assad, Hafez, 171, 365, 373-74, 388, 391
Atkins, G. Pope, 279n, 284n, 301

Austin, Dennis, 334n, 355
Auswärtiges, Amt, 105
Axelrod, Robert, 6
Aylwin, Patricio, 301
Aziz, T., 403

Bach, Daniel C., 355
Bagley, Bruce Michael, 281n
Bakatin, Vadim, 162, 180
Baker, James, 66, 168, 171, 287-88, 293
Banda, Hastings Kamuzu, 337
Barav, Ami, 117n
Barber, James, 30
Baring, Arnulf, 74n
Barnett, A. Doak, 241-42, 245, 246, 266
Barnett, Richard, J., 105
Bartlett, Ruhl J., 170n
Batatu, Hanna, 404
Batista, Fulgencio, 278, 299
Bayart, Jean-François, 355
Bayne, Nicholas, 121n
Beasley, W.G., 219
Befu, Harumi, 220
Begin, Menachem, 373, 374, 384, 385-87, 388, 389
Belaunde Terry, Fernando, 286
Bender, Gerald J., 355
Berg, Robert J., 335n, 355
Berner, Örjan, 327
Bessmertykh, A., 168, 184
Best, Richard A., Jr., 13n
Bevin, Ernest, 13, 14
Bialer, S., 184
Bienen, Henry, 353n
Bill, James, 404
Birnbaum, Karl E., 105
Bismarck, 70, 72, 77, 87, 92, 93, 95, 99, 333
Bjóol, Erling, 328
Blackstone, Tessa, 8n
Blaine, James G., 272

Blaker, Michael, 220
Blechman, Barry, 105
Boardman, Robert, 9n
Bokassa, "Emperor," 54
Bolívar, Simón, 272, 280
Borton, Hugh, 219
Boulding, Kenneth, 6
Bovin, Alexander, 154
Brady, Nicholas, 288
Brandt, Willy, 71, 83, 84, 85, 86, 88n, 92, 94, 96, 103, 104, 105
Branson, L., 184
Brezhnev, Leonid, 93, 147, 148-49, 150, 164, 182, 350
Brownfoot, Janice N., 356
Brzezinski, Zbigniew K., 6, 90n, 123, 184, 356
Buchan, Alastair, 66
Bull, Hedley, 31
Bullock, Alan, 12n
Bulmer, Simon, 105
Burger, Dorsey, 334n
Burgess, Philip, 329
Burks, Ardath, 219
Burlatsky, Fedor, 154
Burr, Robert N., 301
Bush, George, 22-23, 28, 53, 65, 168, 169, 173, 183, 184, 290, 293, 296, 299, 301, 402, 403, 413
Buss, Claude A., 220
Buzan, Barry, 137n
Byrd, Peter, 22n, 26n, 30

Cabral, Amílcar, 334
Calvert, Peter, 337n
Calvocoressi, Peter, 355
Camilleri, Joseph, 266
Canning, George, 270
Cárdenas, Lázaro, 273
Carf, Christofer, 404
Carlsnaes, Walter, 329
Carlsson, Ingvar, 326

Carlton, David, 15n
Carnesdale, Albert, 6
Carrington, Lord, 19, 23, 24-25, 123, 124
Carter, Jimmy, 89, 90, 123, 133, 134, 250, 266, 285, 349
Castillo Armas, Carlos, 278
Castro, Fidel, 54, 171, 279, 299
Ceausescu, Nicolae, 183
Cerny, Philip, 66
Cervenka, Zdenek, 355
Chamorro, Violetta, 293, 301
Chancellor, John, 405n
Chang Tso-lin, 187-88
Charlott, Jean, 66
Charlton, Michael, 14n
Chatichai, Prime Minister (Thailand), 209
Chazan, Naomi, 355
Chebrikov, 180
Chernenko, Konstantin U., 147, 182
Chevènement, Jean-Pierre, 66
Cheysson, Claude, 52, 54, 119
Chiang Ching-Kuo, 260, 261
Chiang Kai-shek, 189, 223, 225, 226n, 228, 231, 232, 234, 235, 239, 260, 406
Child, Jack, 302
Child, John, 274n
Childs, David, 105
Chipman, John, 348n, 355
Chirac, Jacques, 55, 56, 65
Chou En-lai, 352
Christopher, Robert, 220
Churchill, Winston, 9, 10, 11, 13, 14, 24, 29, 42
Cibulke, F., 185
Clapham, Christopher, 355
Clarke, Michael, 22n
Clavert, Peter, 355
Cleveland, Grover, 271
Clubb, O. Edmund, 266
Coffey, P., 142
Cohen, Sammy, 66
Cole, Paul, 328, 329
Cole, Robert E., 220
Cole, Wayne, 327
Coleman, James S., 355
Colton, Timothy, 184
Commins, Stephen K., 335n, 355
Connell, A.W.J., 67
Connell, J., 66
Corbett, Edward M., 355
Cot, Jean-Pierre, 54
Couve de Murville, Maurice, 66
Craig, Gordon, 105
Craigie, Sir R., 219
Crowe, Eyre, 8, 9, 10

Dalai Lama, 261
Darby, Phillip, 17

Dashichev, V., 154n
David, D., 66
Davis, Harold Eugene, 271n, 301
de Carmony, Guy, 66
Decko, David, 54
de Gaulle, Charles, 20-21, 33, 34, 35, 36, 39, 40-46, 48, 49, 50, 51, 52, 53, 58, 60, 61, 62, 63, 64, 66, 89, 109, 112, 333
Dehousse, Renaud, 117n
Deighton, Anne, 12n, 30
de Klerk, F., 171, 355
de la Gorse, Andre-Mari, 67
de la Serre, Francoise, 67, 108n, 142
Delors, Jacques, 60, 113, 120, 139, 322, 327
Deng Xiaoping, 224, 225, 233, 235, 238, 239, 240, 241, 243, 244, 247, 248, 249, 250, 251, 252, 253, 254, 255, 256, 257, 259, 263, 265
Dennett, T., 221
de Onis, Juan, 302
Deporte, A.W., 141
de Schoutheete, Philippe, 142
Destler, I.M., 220
Deutsch, Karl W., 67, 105
De Vree, J.K., 142
Dinerstein, Herbert, 82n
Djilas, Milovan, 70n
Dobrynin, 153
Dodor, D., 184
Dohlman, Ebba, 329
Dore, Ronald, 220
Dörfer, Ingemar, 329
Drifte, Reinhard, 220
Du Bois, W.E.B., 346
Dulles, Foster Rhea, 221, 376, 377
Dumas, Roland, 66

Edinger Lewis J., 67, 105, 106
Edwards, Geoffrey, 127n, 142
Einhorn, Eric, 328
Eisenhower, Dwight D., 18, 44, 181, 182, 376
El-Ashry, Mohamed T., 334n
Embree, George, D., 105
Engels, F., 236
Erdmann, Karl D., 75n
Erhard, Ludwig, 83, 84, 89, 94, 103
Eyadéma, Gnassingbe, 337

Fage, J.D., 332n
Fagen, Richard R., 301
Fahd, King, 402, 403
Fairbank, John King, 266
Fang Lizhi, 258
Fanon, F., 334
Farer, Tom J., 282n

Feld, Werner, 106
Finan, John J., 271n, 301
Fischer, Cathleen, 105
Flynn, Gregory, 328
Fontaine, André, 67
Ford, Gerald, 182, 255
Frankel, Joseph, 30
Frears, J.R., 67
Frederick, S. Northedge, 7n
Frederick the Great, 70n, 77
Freedman, Lawrence, 23n, 30
Freedman, Robert O., 404
Freud, Sigmund, 71
Frey, Eric G., 106
Friedländer, Ernst, 77n
Frost, Ellen L., 221
Fruhling, Pierre, 329
Fukutake, Tadashi, 219

Gaitan, Jorge Eliezer, 277
Galtieri, Leopoldo, 134
Galtung, Johan, 142
Gambari, Ibrahim A., 355
Garcia, Alan, 287
Gardiner, Robert, 355
Garthoff, Raymond, 184
Garvey, Marcus, 346
Gati, Charles, 184
Gatzke, Hans W., 106
Gavshon, Arthur, 355
Geiss, Immanuel, 346n, 355
Gelman, Irwin F., 273n
Gemayel, Amin, 386, 388, 389
Gemayel, Bechir, 385, 387
Genscher, Hans-Dietrich, 94, 95, 104, 106, 124, 173
George, Alexander, 184
George, Stephen, 21n, 31
Gibney, Frank, 219
Gifford, Prosser, 332n
Gilpin, Robert, 6
Gimbel, John, 106
Ginsberg, Roy H., 131n, 142
Giscard D'Estaing, Valéry, 33, 46, 49, 50-51, 65
Goldman, Guido, 106
Goldmann, Kjell, 329
Gomez, Laureano, 277
González, Felipe, 284
Gooch, G.P., 8n
Gorbachev, Mikhail, 25, 30, 58, 61, 65, 96, 98, 99, 104, 111, 144, 145, 146, 147, 149, 150, 151, 152, 153-65, 166, 167, 169, 170, 172, 174, 175, 177, 178-81, 182, 183, 184, 219, 257, 266, 311, 316, 327, 350, 393
Grabendorff, Wolf, 301
Grew, J.C., 219
Griffith, William E., 106
Grinter, Lawrence, 220
Gromyko, Andrei, 153, 164, 182

Gröndal, Benedikt, 328
Groom, A.J.R., 9n
Grosser, Alfred, 67, 106
Guevara, Che, 300
Guillaume, Wilhelm, 88n
Gutkind, Peter, 355

Habib, Philip, 386
Haig, Alexander, 294, 386
Hakovirta, Harto, 328
Hammarskjöld, Dag, 313
Hancock, Donald, 329
Hanrieder, Wolfram, 106
Hansen, Emmanuel, 355
Harding, Harry, 266
Harris, Lillian, 267
Harrison, Michael M., 19n, 67
Hart, Douglas, 328
Hart, Thomas, 329
Hartlyn, Jonathan, 302
Haskel, Barbara, 328
Hassan, King (Morocco), 337
Hassner, Pierre, 76n
Havel, V., 173
Healey, Denis, 19
Heath, Edward, 19, 47
Heikal, Mohammed, 404
Heisler, Martin, 328
Hellmann, Donald C., 220
Henriksen, Thomas H., 352n, 356
Herzog, Chaim, 404
Heyhoe, D.C.R., 19n
Hilger, G., 184
Hill, Christopher, 29, 117n, 121n, 133n, 142
Hitler, Adolf, 11, 79, 100, 225, 367, 405
Ho, Samuel P.S., 267
Ho Chi-minh, 38
Hodgson, Godfrey, 89n
Hoffman, E., 185
Hoffman, Stanley, 67, 302
Holden, David, 404
Holland, Martin, 135n
Hollerman, Leon, 220
Holloway, David, 184
Holst, Johan Jörgen, 328
Holterman, Henrik, 328
Honecker, Erich, 96, 97, 98, 104
Hoover, Herbert, 274
Horelick, Arnold, 184
Horn, Guyla, 175
Houphouët-Boigny, Felix, 337
Hourani, Albert, 404
Howe, Sir Geoffrey, 27, 124
Hua Guofeng, 255
Hudson, Michael, 404
Huenemann, Ralph W., 267
Huerta, Victoriano, 273
Huldt, Bo, 329
Humbaraci, Arslan, 334n
Hu Sheng, 231n

Hussein, King, 378, 388
Hussein, Sadam, 391, 395, 398, 399, 400, 402, 403
Hu Yaobang, 239, 242, 250, 255, 259
Hveem, Helge, 329

Ifestos, Panayotis, 123n, 142
Ike, Nobutaka, 219
Imai, Ryukichi, 220
Ishida, Takeshi, 220
Ishihara, Shintaro, 210

Jackson, Robert H., 336n
Jacobson, Harold K., 243n, 246n, 251n, 264n, 267
Jakobson, Max, 328
Janow, Merit E., 220
Jarring, U.N. Ambassador, 371
Jaruslewski, W., 65
Jarvis, Robert, 6
Joffe, Josef, 92n, 106
Johns, Richard, 404
Johnson, Chalmers A., 220
Johnson, Lyndon, 94, 182
Jones, F.C., 219
Jordan, Robert S., 76n
Jouve, Edmond, 67
Jukutake, Tadashi, 220
July, Serge, 67

Kaiser, Karl, 67, 99n, 106
Karsh, Efraim, 328
Karvonen, Lauri, 329
Kassem, Abdul Karim, 379
Kaunda, Kenneth David, 337
Kauppi, Mark V., 350n, 356
Keep, John, 184
Kekkonen, Urho, 83n, 311, 326
Kelly, Philip, 302
Kennan, George, 407, 413
Kennedy, John F., 18, 83, 111-12, 182, 278, 279
Kennedy, Paul, 10n, 31
Kenyatta, Jomo, 344
Keohane, Robert, 6
Kerr, Malcolm, 404
Khalidi, Walid, 404
Khomeini, Ayatollah, 54, 383, 394n, 395, 396
Khrushchev, Nikita, 18, 82, 181, 182, 228, 232, 233, 235, 237, 248
Kiesinger, Kurt-Georg, 84, 103
Kihl, Young W., 220
Kim, Samuel S., 251n, 254n, 255, 267
Kim, Young C., 221
Kissinger, Henry A., 6, 106, 118, 241, 266, 371, 372, 381, 382

Kline, Harvey F., 302
Kohl, Helmut, 25, 61, 65, 66, 67, 71, 94-97, 99, 104, 105
Kolodziej, Edward A., 67
K'o Pa-nien, 231n
Korany, Bahgat, 336n, 355
Kosai, Yutaka, 220
Kosaka, Masataka, 220
Kosygin, Alexei, 182, 266
Krenz, Egon, 98, 104
Kubitschek, Juscelino, 278
Kuczynski, Pedro-Pablo, 286n
Kulski, W.W., 67

Laird, R., 185
Langdon, Frank, 220
Lauwaars, R.H., 142
Leacacos, Joh, 74n
Lee, Chae-Jin, 221
Lee Teng-Kui, 260
Legum, Colin, 356
Leiden, Carl, 404
Leites, Nathan, 185
Lellouche, P., 67
Lenin, V.I., 73, 111, 233, 234, 240, 243
Leruez, J., 67
Levinson, Jerome, 302
Lewis, Bernard, 404
Liao Kuang-sheng, 267
Lie, Trygve, 306
Lieberthal, Kenneth, 167
Lifton, Robert J., 220
Ligachev, 150, 153, 180
Lindahl, Ingemar, 328
Lindgren, Raymond, 328
Lippmann, Walter, 34
Li Shiyao, 230, 239
Liu Guoguang, 264n
Liu Shaoqi, 235, 255
Li Xiannian, 255
Lleras Camargo, Alberto, 276
Lodge, Juliet, 131n, 142
Louis, William Roger, 31, 332n
Lowenthal, Abraham F., 302
Löwenthal, Richard, 83n
Lumumba, Patrice, 333
Lundestad, Geir, 328
Lynch, John, 270n, 302

McAdams, James, 106
MacArthur, 194, 218
McGeehan, Robert, 74n
McGwire, Michael, 185
Machiavelli, Niccolo, 74
McKay, Vernon, 356
Macmillan, Harold, 15, 16n, 18, 24, 30, 44
Major, John, 30
Malenkov, Georgy Maksimilianovich, 181

Malzacher, S., 67
Mandela, Nelson, 171, 355
Mann, Golo, 75n
Mannari, Hiroshi, 220
Mao Zedong, 181, 223, 224, 225, 226, 228, 232, 233-42, 244, 247, 248, 249, 253, 254, 255, 256, 258, 259, 266, 378, 406
Mariam, Mengistu Haile, 346
Marsh, David, 105
Marshall, George C., 276
Martin, Laurence W., 74n
Martz, John D., 302
Marx, Karl, 225, 236
Masumi, Junnosuke, 220
Maude, George, 328
Maurin, François, 49
Maximillian, Archduke, 271
Mayall, James, 133n
Mazrui, Ali A., 351, 356
Mazzeo, Domenico, 356
M'Buyinga, Elenga, 356
Mecham, J. Lloyd, 277
Medvedev, R., 185
Mengistu, 171
Merkl, Peter H., 106
Merritt, Richard, 67
Meyer, A.C., 184
Middlebrook, Kevin J., 302
Miljan, Toivo, 329
Mitterrand, François, 25, 33, 51-61, 62-63, 65, 66, 67, 93
Moberly, Sir Patrick, 135n
Mobutu Sese Seko (Joseph Mobutu), 54, 337, 350
Modrow, Hans, 98
Moi, Daniel arap, 344
Molotov, V.M., 36, 181, 310
Monnet, Jean, 73n, 111n
Monroe, James, 270
Morgan, Roger, 106
Morgenthau, Hans J., 6, 9
Morley, Samuel A., 302
Morse, Edward L., 67
Möttölä Kari, 329
Mouritzen, Hans, 329
Mubarak, H., 403
Muchnik, Nicole, 334n
Muller, David G., Jr., 267
Muller, Judith, 404
Munoz, Heraldo, 302
Munro, Dana G., 272n
Murakami, Yasusuke, 220
Mylroie, Laurie, 404

Nakasone, 219
Naldi, Gino J., 346n, 356
Napoleon, 270
Napoleon III, 271
Nasser, 15, 363, 364, 365, 369-70, 371-72, 375, 377, 379, 380, 381

Nation, R. Craig, 350n, 356
Nau, Henry R., 405n
Nerlich, Uwe, 106
Newhouse, John, 67
Ngatugi wa Thiongo, 334
Nicolson, Harold, 10
Nishihara, Masashi, 220
Nixon, Richard M., 182, 234, 241, 255, 266, 278, 371, 381
Nkrumah, Kwame, 342, 354
Noelle-Neumann, Elizabeth, 106
Noriega, Manuel Antonio, 285, 295, 300, 301
Northedge, F.A., 10
Northedge, Frederick S., 31
Nuechterlein, Donald, 328
Nuttall, Simon, 117n
Nyang'oro, Julius E., 336n
Nye, Joseph S., Jr., 405n
Nyerere, Julius, 344

Obando Y Bravo, Miguel, 292
Obote, Milton, 344
Odom, Donald, Jr., 328
Ogunsanwo, Alaba, 352n, 356
Ojo, Colatunde J.C.B., 356
Ojo, Olusola, 339
Okazaki, Hisahiko, 220
Okimoto, Daniel I., 220
Okita, Saburo, 221
Okolo, Julius Emeka, 343n
Oksenberg, Michel, 243n, 246n, 248, 249, 251n, 264, 267
Oliver, Roland, 332n
Olympio, Sylvanus, 342
Onwuka, Ralph, 356
Oppen, Beate Ruhm Von, 68n, 105
Orr, Robert M., Jr., 221
Ortega, Daniel, 293
Örvik, Nils, 329
Ovendale, R., 11n, 12n
Oyugi, Walter O., 353n

Paasikivi, Juho Kusti, 309
Palme, Olof, 326
Palmieri, D.A., 184
Pastor, Robert A., 302
Paterson, William, 105
Patomäki, Keikki, 329
Patrick, Hugh T., 220, 221
Patterson, C.L., 355
Peck, F. Taylor, 271n, 301
Pellicer, Olga, 301
Pepper, Thomas, 220
Perón, Juan D., 276, 277, 284
Perry, O.H., 194
Pierre, Andrew J., 67
Pijpers, Alfred, 117n, 121n, 126n, 141, 142
Pinochet, Augusto, 300

Planck, Charles E., 77n
Pleven, René, 64, 140
Pompidou, Georges, 33, 46, 47, 48, 49, 65
Ponting, Clive, 17n
Pope John Paul, 183
Potholm, Christian P., 334n
Potter, William. 185
Prebisch, Raul, 283
Primakov, Evgeny, 154
Prizel, Ilya, 302
Putnam, Robert D., 121n

Qaddafi, Muammar, 54, 337, 341, 347, 354, 363, 365
Qassem, 363
Quandt, William, 404
Quested, R.K.I., 267

Raimond, Jean-Bernard, 67
Reagan, Ronald, 22, 25, 90, 93, 96, 104, 131, 133, 137, 182, 183, 255, 264, 289, 292, 311, 386, 389
Regelsberger, Elfriede, 117n, 121n, 126n, 127n, 130n, 142
Reischauer, Edwin O., 219, 221
Richardson, James L, 106
Rico, Carlos, 302
Ries, Tomas, 328
Robin, Gabriel, 67
Robson, Peter, 329
Rodney, Walter, 331n
Roett, Riordan, 301, 302
Rogers, William Pierce, 371, 381
Romberg, Alan D., 221
Roosevelt, Franklin, 77n, 232, 274, 405, 406, 410
Roosevelt, Theodore, 271
Rosberg, Carl G., 336n
Rosecrance, Richard, 405n
Rosenau, James N., 6
Rosolowsky, Diane, 106
Rosovsky, Henry, 220
Ross, G., 67
Rotberg, Robert I., 334n, 350n, 356
Rowen, Henry S., 220
Rubenstein, A.Z., 185
Ruehl, Lothar, 67
Rummel, Reinhardt, 119n, 141, 142
Rush, Myron, 184
Rutherford, Malcolm, 8n
Ryzhkov, Nikolai, 327

Sadat, Anwar, 123, 182, 365, 371, 372, 373, 381, 382, 383, 394
Safran, Nadav, 398n, 404
Sakwa, R., 185

Salinas De Gortari, Carlos, 301
Salmon, Trevor, 136n
Samuels, Marwyn S., 267
Sanchez de Costa Pereira, Pedro, 125n
Sanders, David, 12n, 16-17, 20n, 31
Sanderson, Fred H., 220
Sansom, Sir George, 219
Sato, Hideo, 220, 221
Sato, Seizaburo, 220
Satoh, Yukio, 220
Savimbi, Jonas, 170
Scalapino, Robert A., 220, 221
Schäuble, Wolfgang, 95
Scheel, Walter, 103
Schevchenko, Arkady, 185
Schick, Jack M., 82n, 107
Schierholz, Thomas, 268
Schlesinger, Arthur, 83n
Schmidt, Helmut, 19, 49, 71, 88, 89, 90, 91, 92-94, 95, 96, 97, 103, 104, 107
Schoultz, Lars, 284n
Schröder, Dieter, 74n
Schwantes, Robert, 221
Schwartz, Hans-Peter, 75n
Scott, Franklin, 328
Scott, H.F., 185
Scott, W.F., 185
Seidel, Robert Neal, 272n
Selassie, Haile, 346, 354
Sesay, Amadu, 348n, 356
Shamir, Yishak, 389, 401
Sharon, Ariel, 384, 385-87, 388, 389
Shaw, Timothy M., 335n, 336n, 355, 356
Shevardnadze, Eduard, 58, 96, 150, 154n, 157, 158-59, 162, 171, 174, 178-79, 180, 182, 184, 218
Shidehara, Kijuro, 195
Shigemitsu, Mamoru, 219
Shiratori, Rei, 219
Shlaim, Avi, 9n, 18n
Shultz, George, 386, 388
Siad Barre, Mohammed, 337
Sifry, Micah L., 404
Sigur, Gaston J., 221
Silvert, Kalman H., 302
Simonian, Haig, 107
Sjöstedt, Gunnar, 142, 329
Sklar, Richard L, 355
Smith, Hedrick, 185
Smith, Ian, 17, 30
Smith, Jean, 82n
Smith, Michael, 29n, 31
Smith, Steve, 29n, 31
Sneider, Richard, 220
Snow, Edgar, 226n
Solomon, Richard H., 220
Somoza, Anastasio, 291, 298, 300

Soyinka, Wole, 334
Spaak, Paul-Henri, 44
Spencer, M., 67
Spero, Joan, 6
Stalin, 70, 76n, 163, 164, 181, 232, 233, 234, 235, 236, 310, 406
Stalk, George, Jr., 220
Stein, Harold, 74n
Stenelo, Lars-Göran, 328
Stephens, Robert, 404
Stern, Fritz, 107
Stevens, Christopher, 128n, 356
Stimson, Henry, 274
Stockwin, J.A.A., 219
Stoessinger, John, 6
Stopf, Willy, 103
Storry, Richard, 219
Strang, Lord, 10, 24
Strong, Anna Louise, 235n
Stuart, Douglas, 220
Sundelius, Bengt, 328, 329
Sun Yat-sen, 189, 223, 260
Tachi, Ryuichiro, 221
Talbot, Strobe, 185
Tanter, Raymond, 6
Taylor, Paul, 142
Taylor, William, 329
Temperley, H.W.V., 8n
Thatcher, Margaret, 8, 22-28, 30, 294, 348
Thomson, James A., 106
Thorn, Gaston, 124
Timberlake, Lloyd, 353n
Tito, Brosip, 255
Touré, Ahmed Sékou, 348
Treat, Payson J., 221
Truman, Harry S., 406
Tugendhat, Christopher, 8n, 27n, 31, 142
Tulchin, Joseph S., 302
Turok, Ben, 356

Ulam, Adam B., 185
Ulbricht, Walter, 85
Ullman, Richard H., 6
Underdal, Arild, 329

Valenta, Jiri, 185
Van Dam, Nikolaos, 404
Vandenberg, Arthur, 276
Van Ness, Peter, 267
Vatikiotis, P.J., 404
Väyrynen, Raimo, 328
Vertzberger, Yaacov, 267
Vloyantes, John, 328
Vogel, Ezra F., 220
Vogel, Jans-Jochen, 104
Volcker, Paul, 287
von Brentano, Heinrich, 76n
von Weizsäcker, Richard, 104

Wallace, Helen, 21n, 67, 124n
Wallace, William, 8n, 21n, 27n, 31, 121n, 124
Wallerstein, Immanuel, 332n, 355, 356
Walter, Kenneth N., 6
Wanandi, Jusuf, 220
Wang Ch'ing-wei, 189
Ward, Robert E., 219
Washington, George, 77
Watanuki, Joji, 219
Waterbury, John, 404
Webb, Carole, 124n
Webb, Herschel, 219
Wehner, Herbert, 84, 88
Weiler, Joseph, 117n
Weinstein, Martin E., 220
Weinstein, Warren, 352n, 356
Wendt, Frantz, 328
Wessels, Wolfgang, 117n, 119n, 121n, 126n, 141
Wheeler, Jimmy W., 220
Whitaker, Jennifer Seymour, 335n, 355, 356
White, Brian, 12n, 24n, 29n, 31
White, Dorothy S., 67
Whiting, Allen S., 221, 267
Wiarda, Howard J., 302
Williams, Philip, 67
Willis, Roy, 67
Wilson, Harold, 21
Wilson, Woodrow, 273, 405
Windsor, Philip, 82n
Wiseman, John A., 353n
Wood, Bryce, 302
Wright, Jim, 291
Wright, Stephen, 292, 343n, 356

Yakovlev, Aleksander, 150, 154, 162, 180
Yamamoto, Tadashi, 221
Yaniv, Avner, 404
Yassin, El Sayed, 404
Yazov, Dmitri, 161
Yeltsin, Boris, 161, 162, 163, 180
Yergin, Daniel, 404
Yodfat, Areyh, 404
Yoshida, Shigeru, 195
Young, Hugo, 22, 25, 27, 31
Yousuf, Hilmi S., 356
Yuan Shikai, 227
Yuval, Arnon-Ohana, 404

Zartman, I., William, 341n, 356
Zhao Ziyang, 242, 244, 245, 255, 259
Zhou Enlai, 224, 241, 255, 266
Zwick, Pater, 185